María Consuelo O'Brien

UNDERSTANDING CRIMINAL PROCEDURE

Joshua Dressler

Professor of Law
Wayne State University

LEGAL TEXT SERIES

1991

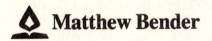 **Matthew Bender**

 Times Mirror
Books

MATTHEW BENDER & CO., INC.
EDITORIAL OFFICES
11 PENN PLAZA, NEW YORK, NY 10001-2006 (212) 967-7707
2101 WEBSTER ST., OAKLAND, CA 94612-3027 (415) 446-7100

LEGAL EDUCATION PUBLICATIONS

ADVISORY BOARD

TO DAVID B. DRESSLER

May Your Life Be as Happy

As You Have Made Mine and Your Mother's

PREFACE

Purpose of the Text. This book is designed for use by law students enrolled in a class in Criminal Procedure. It parallels the curriculum in virtually all three–unit and four–unit versions of the law school course. In schools that offer two classes on the subject, the text should benefit those taking either or both courses.

Although lawyers and judges should find the book of value, their needs, quite frankly, were not uppermost in my mind when I wrote the text. My intent was to write a book that would meet the special needs of law students. Put another way, my intention was to prepare a text that professors can (and, hopefully, will) recommend or assign to their students with confidence that it will enhance the classroom process.

I assume that most teachers want their students to think as much about the forest as they do about the trees. That is, they want students to come away from class with an understanding of the law that has developed, but also with an appreciation of the values that have shaped it. They also want their students to be sensitive to some of the broader issues in the field, relating to the use of judicial power to effectuate legal reform, to judicial craftsmanship, and, of course, to the proper role of the government *vis a vis* the individual in the investigation and prosecution of crime. This book should help students understand these topics and, thus, improve class dialogue.

The text covers the most important Supreme Court cases in the field. The Federal Rules of Criminal Procedure, federal statutes, and lower federal and state court cases, where they are apt to be pertinent to classroom discussion, are also considered. The broad overarching policy issues of criminal procedure are laid out; and some of the hottest debates — *e.g.*, the Fourth Amendment exclusionary rule, the *Miranda* decision — are considered in depth and (I believe) reasonably objectively. Where my teaching experience has indicated that a particular area of the law is unusually daunting, I have provided an overview to the subject.

Readers should find the book user–friendly. Students who want a thorough grasp of a topic may read the relevant chapter in its entirety. However, each chapter is divided into sub–sections, so that readers with more refined research needs can answer their questions efficiently. I also include citations to books and articles, both old and very new, that will be of value to readers who wish to delve more deeply into specific subjects. And, because so many of the topics interrelate, I have included many cross–referencing footnotes, so that readers can deftly move from one part of the book to another, if necessary.

Gender policy of the text. In today's system of criminal justice, women are not simply crime victims: they are also lawyers, judges, police officers, legislators and criminal suspects. To deal with this modern reality, I have generally balanced the accounts in the text: in even–numbered chapters, I use the male pronoun in discussing hypothetical and generic parties in the criminal justice system; in odd–numbered chapters, women get equal time.

I followed this procedure in my first text, UNDERSTANDING CRIMINAL LAW. At least based on the comments I received about the book, most readers liked the approach or, at worst, found it only temporarily disconcerting. (Occasionally, of course, I goofed: a stray man wound up in a chapter where he didn't belong; and, stupidly, a woman showed up as a rapist, a legal impossibility at common law. But then, who's perfect?)

Acknowledgements. Many people helped me in many ways to write this book. I name only a few of them here.

Some of my colleagues at Wayne State were remarkably generous with their time. In particular, Lee Lamborn and Joe Grano read every page of every chapter I wrote, offering written comments on every section of the treatise. I have no doubt that the book is better because of their observations and criticisms. And, because they look at many of the issues of criminal procedure through a different looking–glass than I, I am more confident than I would otherwise be that this book deals fairly with the controversial topics under consideration.

I am grateful to Darcie Brault (Class of '90), Michael Friedman ('91), Sheila MacDonald ('91), Jill Phillips ('92), and Christine Scarnecchia ('90), each of whom provided invaluable research assistance. Special thanks to Darcie, who also offered insightful editorial advice; and to Michael, who did an exhaustive study of law school curricula, to make sure that this book would meet student needs.

I must also acknowledge the outrageously expensive colleges to which my son, David, is now applying, since they inspired me to write this book as a means of delaying my impoverishment. Unfortunately, I doubt that I have succeeded in that venture.

My wife, Dottie, deserves the most heartfelt thanks. I am not exaggerating when I say that without her wisdom, patience, and love, this book would not have been written. Thank you, my love.

Huntington Woods, Michigan
    January, 1991

TABLE OF CONTENTS

Chapter 1

INTRODUCTION TO CRIMINAL PROCEDURE

§ 1   "Criminal Law" versus "Criminal Procedure"   1
§ 2   Sources of Procedural Law   2
§ 3   Stages of a Criminal Prosecution.   3
        [A] In General   3
        [B] Investigatory Stage   3
        [C] Adjudicatory Stage   4
             [1]   Issuance of a Complaint   4
             [2]   *Gerstein v. Pugh* Hearing   4
             [3]   First Appearance Before the Magistrate   5
             [4]   Preliminary Hearing.   5
             [5]   Grand Jury Proceeding   6
             [6]   Arraignment   7
             [7]   Pre–trial Motions   7
             [8]   Trial.   8
             [9]   Appeal 10
             [10] Collateral Attack: Habeas Corpus 10
§ 4   Studying Constitutional Law Cases 11
        [A] Read Concurring and Dissenting Opinions 11
        [B] Learn Case Names. 11
        [C] Count Votes 11
        [D] Learn the Views of Individual Justices 12
        [E] Be Sensitive To Supreme Court History 13

Chapter 2

OVERARCHING POLICY ISSUES IN CRIMINAL PROCEDURE

§ 5   "Due Process" versus "Crime Control" 17
        [A] Models of Criminal Justice 17
        [B] The Values of the Crime Control Model 18
        [C] The Values of the Due Process Model 19
§ 6   The Value of "Truth" In the Criminal Justice System 20
§ 7   Accusatorial versus Inquisitorial Systems of Justice 22

Chapter 3

INCORPORATION OF THE BILL OF RIGHTS

§ 8   The Issue of Incorporation 25
§ 9   Incorporation Theories 26
       [A] Total–Incorporationism 26
       [B] Fundamental–Rights Doctrine 27
       [C] Total–Incorporationism–Plus 27
       [D] Neo – Incorporationism (or Pseudo–Fundamental–
            Rights) 28
§ 10   The Incorporation Debate 28
       [A] General Comments 28
       [B] What Did the Framers Intend? 29
       [C] Textual Claims: What Does "Due Process" Mean? . . . 30
       [D] Which Doctrine is More Libertarian? 30
       [E] Which Theory Is Structurally Preferable? 30
       [F] Which Theory Has "Won"? 31

Chapter 4

GENERAL CONSTITUTIONAL LAW DOCTRINES

§ 11   Retroactivity 33
       [A] Explanation of the Issue 33
       [B] Common Law of Retroactivity 34
       [C] The *Linkletter* Doctrine 34
       [D] Abandonment of *Linkletter* 35
            [1] Cases Not Yet Final: Direct Review 35
            [2] Cases Already Final: Collateral Review 36
                 [a] General Rule 36
                 [b] Meaning of "New Rule" 37
§ 12   Waiver of Constitutional Rights 37
       [A] Definition of "Waiver": The *Zerbst* Test 37
       [B] Non–"Waiver" Relinquishment of Constitutional
            Rights 38
§ 13   Harmless Error 39
       [A] Nonconstitutional Trial Error 39
       [B] Constitutional Trial Error: The *Chapman* Rule 39
       [C] *Per Se* Prejudicial Constitutional Error 41
§ 14   Supervisory Power 41
§ 15   Prophylactic Rules 43

Chapter 5

FOURTH AMENDMENT: OVERVIEW

§ 16   Fourth Amendment: The Text 45
§ 17   Historical Purposes of the Fourth Amendment 46
§ 18   Standing to Raise Fourth Amendment Claims 46
§ 19   Exclusionary Rule 47
§ 20   "Private" Searches and Seizures 47
§ 21   Extra–Territorial Searches and Seizures 48
§ 22   Abandonment of Houses, Papers, or Effects 48
§ 23   Fourth Amendment Issue Checklist 49

Chapter 6

FOURTH AMENDMENT:
"PERSONS, HOUSES, PAPERS, AND EFFECTS"

§ 24   Significance of the Constitutional Phrase 51
§ 25   "Persons" 51
§ 26   "Houses" 52
§ 27   "Papers and Effects" 52

Chapter 7

FOURTH AMENDMENT TERMINOLOGY: "SEARCH"

§ 28   Constitutional Significance of the Term "Search" 55
§ 29   "Search": Original Pre–*Katz* Analysis 56
§ 30   "Search": The Modern *Katz v. United States* Analysis 57
       [A]   The Fall of the Trespass Doctrine 57
       [B]   In Search of a New Test 58
       [C]   "Reasonable Expectation of Privacy" Test 58
       [D]   Analysis and Critique of the New Test 60
             [1]   Do We Need a New Test? 60
             [2]   Should We Have the Subjective Prong? 60
             [3]   The Objective Prong: What *Precisely* Is It? 61
§ 31   Post–*Katz* "Search" Cases: An Overview 62
       [A]   Factors in "Search" Analysis 62
       [B]   Lurking Issues in "Search" Cases 63
§ 32   Surveillance of Conversations By "False Friends" 64
       [A]   "False Friends" versus *Katz* 64
       [B]   "False Friends" 65
       [C]   "Wired" False Friends 66

Page

§ 33   Open–Fields Doctrine 67
       [A]   Rule 67
       [B]   "Open Field" versus "Curtilage" 68
       [C]   Criticism of the Doctrine 68
§ 34   Technological Information–Gathering 69
       [A]   Pen Registers 69
       [B]   Electronic Tracking Devices 70
§ 35   Aerial Surveillance 72
       [A]   Rule 72
       [B]   Surveillance by Airplanes 72
       [C]   Surveillance by Helicopters 73
§ 36   Testing for Contraband 74
       [A]   Dog Sniffs 74
       [B]   In–the–Field Chemical Tests 75
§ 37   Inspection of Garbage 75

Chapter 8

FOURTH AMENDMENT TERMINOLOGY: "SEIZURE"

§ 38   Constitutional Significance of the Term "Seizure" 77
§ 39   "Seizure" of Property 77
       [A]   General Rule 77
       [B]   Installation of Electronic Devices On or In Property 78
§ 40   "Seizure" of Persons 79
       [A]   General Rule 79
       [B]   "Seizure" by Questioning? 80
       [C]   "Seizure" by Pursuit? 81

Chapter 9

FOURTH AMENDMENT: "PROBABLE CAUSE"

§ 41   The Constitutional Role of "Probable Cause" 83
§ 42   Probable Cause: General Principles 83
       [A]   "Probable Cause": Definition 83
       [B]   "Probable Cause": Objective versus Subjective 84
       [C]   "Probable Cause": Arrests versus Searches 84
       [D]   "Probable Cause": With or Without Warrants 84
       [E]   "Probable Cause": Search For and Seize What? 85
           [1]   "Mere Evidence" Rule 85
           [2]   Abolition of the "Mere Evidence" Rule 85

Page

§ 43   How Probable Is "Probable Cause"? 87
        [A] Governing Law 87
        [B] Reflections on the Issue. 88
§ 44   Determining "Probable Cause": Overview 90
        [A] Types of Information: In General 90
        [B] "Bald and Unilluminating" Assertions 91
        [C] Direct Information 91
        [D] Hearsay ("Informant") Information 91
§ 45   The *Aguilar* Two–Pronged Test 92
        [A] In General 92
        [B] Basis–of–Knowledge Prong 93
             [1] In General 93
             [2] "Self–Verifying Detail" 93
        [C] Veracity Prong 94
        [D] Corroboration 95
§ 46   The *Gates* "Totality of the Circumstances" Test 95
        [A] Nature of the Test 95
        [B] The Practical Effect of *Gates* 96
        [C] Criticism of *Gates* 97
             [1] Is the "Message" of *Gates* a Good One? 97
             [2] Can One Prong Logically Compensate for An-
                  other?. 97
§ 47   Balancing Competing Interests: The *Camara* Principle 98
§ 48   "Probable Cause": A Sliding Scale? 100
        [A] *Is* There a Sliding Scale? 100
        [B] *Should* There Be a Sliding Scale? 101

Chapter 10

SEARCH WARRANTS: IN GENERAL

§ 49   The Constitutional Role of the Search Warrant 103
        [A] Nature of the Constitutional Debate 103
        [B] Competing Rules and Policy 103
             [1] The "Warrant Requirement" Rule. 103
             [2] The "Reasonableness" Rule 104
             [3] Which Theory Has "Won"? 105
§ 50   The Warrant Application Process 106
§ 51   "Neutral and Detached Magistrate" 107
§ 52   "Oath or Affirmation". 108
§ 53   Search Warrant "Particularity". 109

Page

[A]   In General 109
[B]   "Place to be Searched" 109
[C]   "Persons or Things to be Seized" 110
§ 54   Execution of Search Warrants 111
[A]   Time of Execution .111
[B]   Mode of Entry 111
[C]   Search of Persons While Executing a Warrant 112
[1]   In Premises Open to the Public 112
[2]   In Private Homes 113
[D]   Detention of Persons During Searches 113

Chapter 11

ARRESTS

§ 55   Nature of an "Arrest" .115
§ 56   Common Law and Statutory Arrest Rules 115
§ 57   Arrests: Constitutional Law Overview 116
[A]   General Rules 116
[B]   How Arrest–Warrant Issues Arise 116
§ 58   Arrests in Public Places: The *Watson* No–Warrant Rule 116
§ 59   Arrests in the Home: The *Payton* Warrant–Requirement
Rule 118
§ 60   Scope of the *Payton* Rule 119
[A]   *Payton vs. Watson*: "Home" versus "Public Place" . . .119
[B]   Exigencies Justifying Warrantless Entry 119
[1]   Hot Pursuit .120
[2]   Other Exigencies 120
[C]   Entry Into a Third Person's Home 121
§ 61   Use of Unreasonable Force in Making an Arrest 122
[A]   Deadly Force 122
[B]   Non–Deadly Force 124

Chapter 12

WARRANTLESS SEARCHES: EXIGENT CIRCUMSTANCES

§ 62   Nature of the Warrant Exception 125
§ 63   Intrusion Into the Human Body 126
§ 64   External Search of the Body 126
§ 65   Entry and Search of a Home 127

Chapter 13

SEARCHES INCIDENT TO LAWFUL ARRESTS

§ 66   Chapter Overview 131
§ 67   Nature of the Search Warrant Exception: In General 131
       [A]   Rule 131
       [B]   Rationale of the Warrant Exception 131
       [C]   The Probable–Cause Requirement 132
       [D]   Seizure of Evidence During the Search 132
§ 68   Prerequisites to the Use of the Warrant Exception 132
       [A]   "Custodial" Arrest 132
       [B]   Lawfulness of the Arrest 133
       [C]   Contemporaneousness of the Search 133
           [1]   Area Within Arrestee's Immediate Control 133
           [2]   Of the Person 133
§ 69   Scope of the Warrant Exception 134
       [A]   Search of the Person 134
       [B]   Area Within the Immediate Control 135
           [1]   In General .135
           [2]   Automobiles 136
       [C]   Protective Searches for Dangerous Persons 137
§ 70   *Chimel v. California*: Setting the Rule's Contours 137
§ 71   *United States v. Robinson*: The Traffic Arrest Case 139
       [A]   Holding 139
       [B]   *Robinson* versus *Chimel* 140
§ 72   *New York v. Belton*: Bright Lines for Automobiles 140
§ 73   Bright Line Rules vs. Case–by–Case Adjudication 142
§ 74   Pretextual Police Conduct 144

Chapter 14

SEARCHES OF CARS AND CONTAINERS THEREIN

§ 75   Automobile Search–Warrant Exception: General Rules 147
       [A]   Overview 147
       [B]   Searches "At the Scene" 147
       [C]   Searches "Away From the Scene" 148
§ 76   *Carroll v. United States*: The "Mobility" Rationale 148
§ 77   *Chambers v. Maroney*: The Mobility Rationale Is Undermined 149
§ 78   From *Cady* to *Cardwell* to *Carney*: The "Privacy" Rationale 150

Page

§ 79   Special Problem: Search of Containers in Cars 153
        [A] Clarification of the Issue 153
        [B] Are There Containers "Unworthy" of Protection? 153
        [C] When Are "Worthy" Containers in Cars Protected? 154
             [1] Overview 154
             [2] Requiring A Warrant: The *Chadwick–Sanders*
                  Doctrine 155
             [3] Not Requiring a Warrant: The *Ross* Doctrine 157
             [4] Making Sense of It All: Some Examples 158

Chapter 15

THE "PLAIN VIEW" DOCTRINE

§ 80   General Principles 161
§ 81   "Plain View": Examining the Elements 162
        [A] Element 1: Lawful Vantage Point 162
        [B] Element 2: Right of Access to the Object 162
        [C] Element 3: Seizability is "Immediately Apparent" 163
§ 82   Application of the Plain–View Doctrine: *Arizona v.*
        Hicks 164
§ 83   "Inadvertent Discovery": The Plain–View Debate 166

Chapter 16

INVENTORY SEARCHES

§ 84   Automobile Inventories: General Principles 169
        [A] Rule 169
        [B] Rationale of the Rule 169
§ 85   Elements of the Warrant Exception: Specifics 171
        [A] "Routine" Nature of the Inventory 171
             [1] In General 171
             [2] Nondiscretionary Inventories 171
             [3] Discretionary Inventories 171
        [B] Administrative Nature of the Search 172
        [C] Irrelevance of the Car Owner's Wishes 173
§ 86   Scope of an Inventory Search: Specifics 173
        [A] Containers 173
        [B] Locked Portions of the Automobile 174
        [C] Inspection of Papers 174
§ 87   Arrest Inventories 174

Chapter 17

CONSENT TO SEARCH

§ 88   General Rule and Rationale 177

§ 89   The Nature of Lawful Consent: General Principles 178

      [A]   Requirement of Voluntariness 178

      [B]   Claim of Authority by the Police 178

      [C]   Police Deception 179

§ 90   Special Issue: Awareness of the Right to Refuse Consent 180

§ 91   Third–Party Consent .182

§ 92   "Apparent Authority" .183

Chapter 18

MINIMALLY INTRUSIVE SEARCHES AND SEIZURES: THE *TERRY* PRINCIPLE

§ 93   *Terry v. Ohio*: An Overview 185

§ 94   *Terry v. Ohio*: The Opinion 186

      [A]   Majority Opinion .186

      [B]   Justice Harlan's Concurring Opinion 187

§ 95   "Reasonable Suspicion" 188

      [A]   Quantum of Information 188

      [B]   Types of Information 188

          [1]   Personal Police Observation 188

          [2]   Drug–Courier Profiles 189

          [3]   Hearsay Information 190

          [4]   Information from Another Police Department 192

§ 96   Distinguishing a "*Terry* Stop" From an Arrest 192

      [A]   Extended Duration of the Detention 193

      [B]   Forcible Movement of the Suspect 193

      [C]   Existence of "Less Intrusive Means" 194

§ 97   Grounds for "*Terry* Stops" 195

      [A]   Crime Prevention versus Crime Detection 195

      [B]   Nature of the Crime 195

      [C]   Fingerprinting 195

§ 98   Weapons Searches: Of Persons 196

      [A]   Permissibility 196

      [B]   Method 197

          [1]   Pat–Down ("Frisk") 197

Page

[2] After the Pat–Down 198
§ 99   Weapons Searches: Of Automobiles 198
§ 100 Protective Sweeps of Residences 200
§ 101 *Terry*–Level Seizures of Property 201
§ 102 Suspicionless *Terry*–Level Seizures 202

Chapter 19

"SPECIAL GOVERNMENTAL NEED" (FORMERLY, "ADMINISTRATIVE") SEARCHES

§ 103 "Special Governmental Needs" Exception: In General 207
§ 104 Administrative–Code Searches 208
§ 105 Fire–Scene Inspections 210
§ 106 International Border Searches and Seizures 211
      [A] At the Border 211
      [B] Near the Border .211
§ 107 Searches of Public School Students 212
§ 108 Drug and Alcohol Testing of Public Employees 214
      [A] Overview 214
      [B] *Skinner* and *Von Raab*: Analysis 215

Chapter 20

FOURTH AMENDMENT: "STANDING"

§ 109 The Role of "Standing" in Fourth Amendment Law 219
§ 110 Rationale of the Standing Requirement 220
§ 111 Target Standing 221
§ 112 Derivative Standing 222
§ 113 Automatic Standing 222
§ 114 General Principles of Standing: Pre–*Rakas* 224
§ 115 General Principles of Standing: *Rakas v. Illinois* 224
§ 116 What Has *Rakas* Wrought?: An Analysis 227
      [A] "Standing" as a Separate Concept 227
      [B] Contesting a Search of Another Person's Home 228
      [C] Contesting a Search of Another Person's Automo-
          bile 229
          [1] When the Owner is Absent 229
          [2] When the Owner is Present 229
      [D] Contesting a Search Resulting in the Seizure of One's Own
          Property 230
      [E] Contesting a Seizure or Subsequent Search of One's Own
          Property 232

Chapter 21

FOURTH AMENDMENT: EXCLUSIONARY RULE

§ 117 Development of the Exclusionary Rule 235
    [A] *Weeks v. United States* 235
    [B] *Wolf v. Colorado* 235
    [C] *Rochin v. California* and Its Progeny 236
    [D] *Mapp v. Ohio* .237
§ 118 Rationale of the Exclusionary Rule 238
§ 119 Is the Exclusionary Rule Constitutionally Required? 239
§ 120 Exclusionary Rule: Is It a Good Idea?. 241
    [A] General Observations 241
    [B] Does the Rule Deter? 241
    [C] Is the Rule (Even If It Deters) Worth Its Cost? 243
        [1] Should This Question Even Be Asked? 243
        [2] The "Costs" .244
            [a] The Rule Protects the Wrong People 244
            [b] The Rule Promotes Public Cynicism 245
            [c] The Rule Has a Disproportionate Effect. . . .245
    [D] Are There Better Remedies? 246
§ 121 Limitations On The Scope of the Exclusionary Rule 247
    [A] Non–Criminal Proceedings 247
    [B] Criminal Proceedings 247
        [1] Non–Trial Proceedings 247
        [2] At a Criminal Trial 248
            [a] Good–Faith Exception. 248
            [b] Impeachment Exception 248
§ 122 The *Leon* "Good Faith" Exception: General Principles . . .249
    [A] Rule 249
        [1] In General 249
        [2] "Good Faith" 250
        [3] "Exceptions" to *Leon* 250
    [B] Rationale of the *Leon* Exception. 251
§ 123 Criticism of the *Leon* "Good Faith" Exception 252
§ 124 The Long–Term Implications of *Leon* 254
    [A] Warrant Cases 254
    [B] Non–Warrant Cases 255
§ 125 "Fruit of the Poisonous Tree" Doctrine 256
    [A] General Principles .256
    [B] Identifying the Nature of the Poisonous Tree 256

Page

[C] Independent–Source Doctrine 257

    [1]   General Rule 257

    [2]   Evidence Initially Discovered Lawfully 257

    [3]   Evidence Initially Discovered Unlawfully 257

    [4]   A Statement Obtained After an Unlawful Arrest 258

[D] Inevitable–Discovery Rule 259

[E] Attenuated–Connection Principle (The *Wong Sun* Rule) 260

    [1]   General Rule 260

    [2]   "Attenuation" Factors 261

        [a]   Temporal Proximity 261

        [b]   Length of the Causal Chain 261

        [c]   The Existence of an Act of Free Will 261

        [d]   Flagrancy of the Violation 261

        [e]   Nature of the Derivative Evidence 262

Chapter 22

INTERROGATION LAW: OVERVIEW

§ 126   Historical Overview 263

§ 127   Relevant Constitutional Provisions 263

    [A]   Due Process Clauses 263

    [B]   Self–Incrimination Clause 264

        [1]   Traditional "Voluntariness" Analysis 264

        [2]   *Miranda* "Voluntariness" Analysis 264

    [C]   Assistance of Counsel .264

        [1]   Sixth Amendment 264

        [2]   Fifth Amendment 265

§ 128   Interrogation Law: The Policy Debate 265

    [A]   The "Uneasy Conflict of Worthy Interests" 265

    [B]   Society's Ambivalence Toward Confessions 265

        [1]   Why the Public Favors Confessions 266

        [2]   Why the Public Disfavors Confessions 266

    [C]   Has the Law Gone Too Far To Disfavor Confessions? 266

    [D]   Questions To Think About 267

Chapter 23

COERCED ("INVOLUNTARY") CONFESSIONS

§ 129   Coerced–Confession Law: Historical Development 269
         [A]   Common Law 269
         [B]   Constitutionalization of the Common Law 270
         [C]   *McNabb–Mallory* Federal Rule. 271
§ 130   "Involuntariness": General Constitutional Rule 272
§ 131   Rationale of the "Voluntariness" Requirement. 272
§ 132   "State Action" Requirement 273
§ 133   "Voluntariness": Totality–of–the–Circumstances Test 274
         [A]   Critical Overview 274
         [B]   "Voluntariness": Factors 276
§ 134   Standing to Raise an "Involuntariness" Claim 278
§ 135   Scope of the Coerced–Confession Exclusionary Rule 278
         [A]   In General 278
         [B]   Fruit–of–the–Poisonous–Tree Doctrine 278

Chapter 24

MIRANDA v. ARIZONA

§ 136   Introductory Observations 281
§ 137   *Miranda*: Placing It In Legal Context 282
§ 138   The Road to *Miranda*: *Escobedo v. Illinois* 283
§ 139   *Miranda*: The Case 285
         [A]   The Facts 285
         [B]   The Holding 286
               [1]   General Rule 286
                     [a]   Self–Incrimination 286
                     [b]   Right to Counsel 286
               [2]   Procedural Safeguards 286
               [3]   Waiver 287
                     [a]   In General 287
                     [b]   Voluntariness of the Waiver 287
                     [c]   Intelligence of the Waiver 287
               [4]   Enforcing the Rights 287
                     [a]   Right to Silence 287
                     [b]   Right to Counsel 288
         [C]   Reasoning of the Court 288
               [1]   Custodial Interrogation As "Compulsion" 288

Page

    [2]   The Limited Importance of Confessions in Law
          Enforcement .289
    [3]   The Importance of the Adversarial System 289
§ 140   Criticisms of *Miranda* 290
  [A]   "*Miranda* Lacks Historical and Textual Support" 290
  [B]   "The Rule Is Unnecessary and Irrational" 290
  [C]   "*Miranda* is Against Confessions and In Favor of 'Fox
       Hunts' " 291
  [D]   "*Miranda* Is Injurious to Law Enforcement" 292
§ 141   *Michigan v. Tucker*: Deconstitutionalizing *Miranda* 294
§ 142   Meaning of *Miranda*: "Custody" 295
  [A]   Definition: In General 295
  [B]   Specific Issues 296
    [1]   "Custody" versus "Focus" 296
    [2]   Site of the Interrogation 296
    [3]   Nature of the Crime 296
    [4]   Duration of the Detention 297
§ 143   Meaning of *Miranda*: "Interrogation" 297
  [A]   Definition: *Rhode Island v. Innis* 297
  [B]   A Closer Look at the *Innis* Definition 298
  [C]   Supreme Court Application of the *Innis* Test 299
    [1]   *Innis* 299
    [2]   *Arizona v. Mauro* 300
    [3]   *Pennsylvania v. Muniz* 300
§ 144   Adequacy of the *Miranda* Warnings 301
§ 145   Waiver of *Miranda* Rights 302
  [A]   Burden of Proof .302
  [B]   Types of Waiver: Express versus Implied 302
  [C]   Elements of a Valid Waiver 302
    [1]   Voluntariness of the Waiver 302
    [2]   "Knowing and Intelligent" Nature of the
       Waiver 303
      [a]   In General 303
      [b]   *Moran v. Burbine* 303
  [D]   Waiver After the Suspect Asserts His Rights 305
    [1]   Assertion of the Right to Remain Silent 305
    [2]   Assertion of the Right to Consult With Coun-
       sel 305
      [a]   General Rule: *Edwards v. Arizona* 305
      [b]   Ambiguous Request 306
      [c]   Incomplete Request 306

Page

[d] Definition of "Initiation" 306
§ 146 *Miranda*: Exceptions to the Rule 307
[A] Public–Safety Exception. 307
[B] Covert Custodial Interrogation 309
[C] Routine–Booking–Questions Exception 309
§ 147 Scope of the *Miranda* Exclusionary Rule 310
[A] Impeachment Exception 310
[B] Use of Post–*Miranda* Silence at Trial 310
[C] Fruit–of–the–Poisonous–Tree Doctrine 311
[1] In General 311
[2] *Michigan v. Tucker* 311
[3] *Oregon v. Elstad* 312

Chapter 25

INTERROGATION LAW: SIXTH AMENDMENT RIGHT TO COUNSEL

§ 148 Sixth Amendment Right to Counsel: In General 313
§ 149 *Massiah v. United States* 314
[A] Historical Overview 314
[B] *Massiah*: The Facts 314
[C] The Holding 314
[D] The Rationale 315
[E] Making Sense of *Massiah*: The Role of Counsel 315
§ 150 The *Massiah* Doctrine: In General 317
§ 151 "Adversary Judicial Criminal Proceedings" 318
§ 152 "Deliberate Elicitation" 319
[A] "Deliberate Elicitation" versus "Interrogation" 319
[B] What Does "Deliberate" Mean? 320
[1] "Deliberate" as "Purposeful" 320
[2] "Deliberate" As Less Than "Purposeful" 320
[a] *United States v. Henry* 320
[b] *Maine v. Moulton* 321
[3] Summary 322
[C] What Is "Elicitation"? 322
[1] Why the Question Matters 322
[2] The Court's Answer: *Kuhlmann v. Wilson* 323
§ 153 Waiver of the Right to Counsel 323
[A] General Principles 323
[B] Relinquishment of the Right 323

Page

[C] When May a Waiver Be Secured? 325

    [1] After *D* Requests Counsel: The *Jackson* Rule 325

    [2] If *D* Does Not Request Counsel 326

       [a] Before Counsel is Appointed or Hired 326

       [b] After Counsel is Appointed or Hired 327

[D] Elements of a Valid Waiver 327

    [1] "Voluntary" 327

    [2] "Knowing and Intelligent" 327

§ 154 Standing to Raise a Sixth Amendment Claim 328

§ 155 Scope of the Sixth Amendment Exclusionary Rule 328

[A] General Observations 328

[B] Good Motive: No Exception to the Exclusionary Rule 329

[C] Different–Crime Evidence 329

[D] Use of Evidence for Impeachment Purposes 330

[E] Fruit–of–the–Poisonous–Tree Doctrine 330

§ 156 Right–to–Counsel Summary: Sixth Amendment versus *Miranda* 331

Chapter 26

**PRIVILEGE AGAINST SELF-INCRIMINATION:
GENERAL PRINCIPLES**

§ 157 Fifth Amendment Self–Incrimination Clause: Overview . . .333

§ 158 History of the Privilege Against Self–Incrimination 334

§ 159 Is the Privilege a Good Idea?: The Controversy 335

[A] In General 335

[B] The Purposes of the Privilege: The Debate 336

    [1] Compelled Self–Accusation As a Moral Wrong 336

    [2] The "Cruel Trilemma" Thesis 336

    [3] The Privilege as Part of the Adversary System . . .337

    [4] Protection of the Innocent 337

§ 160 The Fifth Amendment Privilege: Who Is Protected? 338

[A] Collective–Entity Doctrine 338

[B] Required–Records Doctrine 338

§ 161 The Privilege: At What Proceedings May It Be Asserted? . . .339

§ 162 Procedures Relating to the Invocation of the Privilege . . .340

§ 163 Elements of the Privilege: What Must Be Proved 341

[A] The Evidence Is "Testimonial or Communicative" 341

    [1] Nature of the Requirement 341

Page

    [2] Identifying "Testimony or Communications" . . .342

        [a] In General .342

        [b] Verbal Conduct 342

        [c] Non-verbal Conduct 342

    [3] A Closer Look: *Pennsylvania v. Muniz* 343

  [B] The Possibility of Incrimination Is Real 344

  [C] The Privilege–Holder is Being Compelled to Testify. 344

    [1] Nature of "Compulsion" 344

    [2] Connecting the Privilege–Holder to the Compulsion 345

§ 164 —Privilege Against Self–Incrimination: Exclusionary Rule . . .346

Chapter 27

EYEWITNESS IDENTIFICATION PROCEDURES

§ 165 Eyewitness Identification: The Problem 349

§ 166 Corporeal Identification Procedures: Right to Counsel . . .350

  [A] Rule. 350

  [B] How and Why the Rule Developed 351

    [1] *United States v. Wade* 351

    [2] *Kirby v. Illinois* 352

  [C] The Role of Counsel In the Identification Process 352

§ 167 Non–Corporeal Identification Procedures: Right to Counsel 354

§ 168 Identification Procedures: Due Process of Law 354

§ 169 Identification Procedures: Other Constitutional Issues . . .355

  [A] Fourth Amendment 355

  [B] Fifth Amendment (Self–Incrimination) 356

Chapter 28

ENTRAPMENT

§ 170 Entrapment: In General 357

§ 171 Entrapment: The Subjective Test 357

  [A] Rule. 357

  [B] Rationale of the Rule 359

  [C] Procedural Features of the Rule 359

    [1] Role of the Judge and Jury 359

    [2] Proof of Predisposition 359

    [3] Burden of Proof 360

Page

§ 172   Entrapment: The Objective Test 360

     [A]   Rule 360

     [B]   Rationale of the Rule 361

     [C]   Procedural Features of the Rule 361

§ 173   Entrapment: The Debate .362

     [A]   Overview 362

     [B]   Criticisms of the Subjective Test 362

         [1]   "The Legislative–Intent Rationale is Fiction-
al" 362

         [2]   "The Subjective Test Acquits Culpable Per-
sons" 363

         [3]   "The Subjective Test Is Unfair" 363

     [C]   Criticisms of the Objective Test 363

         [1]   "The Test Leads to Inappropriate Results" 363

         [2]   "The Test's Stated Rationales are Indefensi-
ble" 364

§ 174   Entrapment: Due Process 364

     [A]   *United States v. Russell* 364

     [B]   *Hampton v. United States* 365

Chapter 29

THE RIGHT TO COUNSEL: AT TRIAL AND ON APPEAL

§ 175   The Importance of Defense Lawyers in the Adversary
System 367

§ 176   The Right to Counsel: At Trial 367

     [A]   The Right to Employ Counsel 367

     [B]   Indigents: The Right to Appointed Counsel 368

         [1]   Overview 368

         [2]   The Road to *Gideon* 368

            [a]   *Powell v. Alabama* 368

            [b]   *Betts v. Brady* 369

         [3]   *Gideon v. Wainwright* 369

         [4]   Post–*Gideon* Law: The Misdemeanor Cases 370

            [a]   *Argersinger v. Hamlin* 370

            [b]   *Scott v. Illinois* 371

            [c]   *Baldasar v. Illinois* 372

         [5]   Summary of the Law 372

§ 177   The Right to Counsel: On Appeal 373

     [A]   Overview 373

Page

[1] Inapplicability of the Sixth Amendment 373
[2] The *Griffin* Equality Principle 373
[B] First Appeal of Right 374
[1] Recognition of the Right to Assistance of Counsel 374
[2] Special Problem: Frivolous Appeals 374
[C] Discretionary Appeals 375
§ 178 The Right of Self–Representation 377
[A] *Faretta v. California* 377
[1] Recognition of the Right 377
[2] Reflections Regarding the Right 378
[B] Procedural Issues .379
[1] Informing the Accused of the Right 379
[2] Timeliness of the Request 379
[3] Hybrid Representation 379
[4] Standby Counsel 379
[5] Legal Significance of Poor Self–Representation . . .380
[6] Legal Effect of an Erroneous Denial of the Right 380
§ 179 The Right to Representation by One's Preferred Attorney 381
[A] In General 381
[B] Special Problem: Seizing Lawyers' Fees 381
[1] The Law 381
[2] The Objection: The Value of Private Counsel 382
§ 180 Interference With The Right to Counsel 383
§ 181 Effective Assistance of Counsel: General Principles 383
[A] Nature of the Issue 383
[B] "Ineffective Assistance": The *Strickland* Test 384
[1] General Principles 384
[2] The First Prong: The Deficiency of Representation 385
[a] The Standard 385
[b] Application of the Standard: Case Law 386
[3] The Second Prong: Prejudice 387
[a] The Standard 387
[b] Application of the Standard; Case Law 387
§ 182 Effective Assistance of Counsel: Conflicts of Interest 388
[A] Nature of the Issue 388
[B] Pre–Trial Procedures to Avoid Conflicts 389
[C] Post–Trial Proof of a Conflict 389

Page

[D] Waiver of the Right to Conflict–Free Representation 390
§ 183 Effective Assistance: How Far Must Defense Counsel Go? 391

Chapter 30

PRETRIAL RELEASE OF THE DEFENDANT

§ 184 Pretrial Release: Procedural Context 393
§ 185 Pretrial Release: Interests at Stake 393
[A] The Community's Interest 393
[B] The Arrestee's Interest 394
§ 186 Pretrial Release: Eighth Amendment 395
§ 187 Pretrial Release: Statutory Law 396
[A] Pre–Reform 396
[B] Federal Bail Reform Act of 1966 396
[C] Federal Bail Reform Act of 1984 397
§ 188 Preventive Detention 398
[A] Federal Bail Reform Act of 1984 398
[B] The Policy Debate 399
[C] The Constitutional Debate: *U.S. v. Salerno* 401
[1] Substantive Due Process 401
[2] Procedural Due Process 402
[3] Eighth Amendment 402
[4] Dissenting Opinions 403

Chapter 31

PLEA BARGAINING AND GUILTY PLEAS

§ 189 Guilty Pleas: Procedural Context 405
§ 190 Guilty Pleas: Constitutional and Policy Context 405
§ 191 Plea Bargaining: General Principles 406
[A] Overview 406
[B] Types of Plea Agreements 406
[C] Federal Plea Agreement Procedures 407
§ 192 Plea Bargaining: Policy Debate 407
[A] Is Plea Bargaining Inevitable? 407
[B] Is Plea Bargaining Good in Principle? 408
[1] In Support of Plea Bargaining 408
[2] In Opposition to Plea Bargaining 409

Page

    [a] Overview 409
    [b] Sentencing Differential 409
    [c] Prosecutorial Overcharging 410
    [d] Inadequate Representation 410
    [e] Conviction of the Innocent 411
§ 193 Plea Bargaining: Judicial Participation 412
§ 194 Plea Bargaining: Broken Deals 413
§ 195 Validity of a Guilty Plea: Constitutional Principles 415
    [A] In General 415
    [B] Voluntariness of the Plea 415
    [C] Intelligent Nature of the Plea. 416
        [1] In General .416
        [2] Nature of the Charges. 416
        [3] Consequences of the Plea 416
        [4] "Bad" Legal Advice 417
    [D] Factual Basis of the Plea 418
§ 196 Obtaining a Guilty Plea: Federal Procedures 418
    [A] Ensuring Voluntariness 418
    [B] Ensuring An Intelligent Plea 418
    [C] Determining the Factual Basis 419
§ 197 Effect of a Guilty Plea on Prior Constitutional Claims . . .419
    [A] General Rule 419
    [B] Exceptions to the General Rule 420
    [C] Conditional Pleas .421
§ 198 Prosecutorial (and Judicial) Vindictiveness 422
    [A] Explanation of the Issue 422
    [B] The Original Vindictiveness Rules 422
        [1] Judicial Vindictiveness 422
        [2] Prosecutorial Vindictiveness 423
    [C] Narrowing the Vindictiveness Rules. 424
        [1] *Pearce–Blackledge* as a Rebuttable Presumption 424
        [2] Applicability of the Presumption 424
            [a] Judicial Vindictiveness 424
            [b] Prosecutorial Vindictiveness 425
        [3] Rebutting the Presumption 426
            [a] Judicial Vindictiveness 426
            [b] Prosecutorial Vindictiveness 427

Chapter 32

DOUBLE JEOPARDY

§ 199 Double Jeopardy Clause: General Principles 429

    [A] Constitutional Text 429

        [1] In General 429

        [2] "In Jeopardy" 429

        [3] "Of Life or Limb" 429

    [B] "Dual Sovereignty" Doctrine 430

    [C] Guarantees of the Double Jeopardy Clause 431

    [D] Values Underlying the Double Jeopardy Clause 432

§ 200 Reprosecution After a Mistrial 432

    [A] Overview of the Issue 432

    [B] Mistrials Over the Defendant's Objection 433

        [1] The "Manifest Necessity" Standard 433

        [2] "Manifest Necessity": The Case Law 433

            [a] The Early Cases 433

            [b] The "Radical Transformation" 434

            [c] *Illinois v. Somerville* 435

            [d] *Arizona v. Washington* 436

        [3] Making Sense of the Case Law 437

    [C] Mistrials With the Defendant's Consent 438

        [1] General Rule .438

        [2] Exception: Intent to Provoke a Mistrial Motion 438

§ 201 Reprosecution After an Acquittal 439

    [A] General Rule 439

    [B] Rationale of the Rule 441

§ 202 Reprosecution After a Dismissal 442

    [A] Nature of a "Dismissal" 442

    [B] General Rules 442

        [1] Dismissal on the Defendant's Motion 442

        [2] Dismissal Over the Defendant's Objection 443

§ 203 Reprosecution After a Conviction 443

    [A] General Rule 443

    [B] Exception to the Rule: The *Burks* Principle 444

    [C] Special Problem: Convictions With Implied Acquittals 445

        [1] Verdict Acquittal 445

Page

[2]   Sentence "Acquittal" 446
§ 204   Government Appeals of Criminal Sentences 447
§ 205   Multiple Prosecutions of the "Same Offense" 447
    [A]   Explanation of the Issue 447
    [B]   "Same Offense": The *Blockburger* Test 448
    [C]   "Same Offense": Beyond *Blockburger* 449
        [1]   *Harris v. Oklahoma* 449
        [2]   *Grady v. Corbin* 449
    [D]   Exceptions to the No–Successive–Prosecution Rule 451
§ 206   Multiple Punishment for the "Same Offense" 452
    [A]   Excessive Punishment for a Single Crime. 452
    [B]   Multiple Punishment for Different Crimes 453
§ 207   Collateral Estoppel. 453
    [A]   Nature of the Doctrine 453
    [B]   Limits on Application of the Doctrine 454
Table of Cases TC–1
Federal Rules of Criminal Procedure. FR-1
Federal Statutes FS-1
Index I-1

FREQUENTLY CITED SOURCES

The following is a list of sources frequently used in this text, and the short-hand form used to cite them in footnotes.

Amsterdam, *Perspectives on the Fourth Amendment*, 58 Minnesota Law Review 349 (1974) — "Amsterdam"

J. Dressler, Understanding Criminal Law (Matthew Bender, 1987) — "J. Dressler"

Federal Rules of Criminal Procedure — "FRCP" (followed by the rule number)

W. LaFave, Search and Seizure (West 2d ed. 1987) (4 volumes) — "W. LaFave"

Uviller, *Evidence From the Mind of the Criminal Suspect: A Reconsideration of the Current Rules of Access and Restraint*, 87 Columbia Law Review 1137 (1987) — "Uviller"

R. Van Duizend, L. Sutton, & C. Carter, The Search Warrant Process: Preconceptions, Perceptions, and Practices (National Center for State Courts 1984) — "R. Van Duizend, *et al.*"

C. Wright, Federal Practice and Procedure (West 2d ed. 1982) (4 volumes) — "C. Wright"

CHAPTER 1

INTRODUCTION TO CRIMINAL PROCEDURE

§ 1 "Criminal Law" versus "Criminal Procedure"

At one level, the relationship of criminal procedure to criminal law is straightforward: criminal procedural law, or "criminal procedure" for short, is composed of the rules that regulate the inquiry into whether a violation of a criminal law ("substantive" criminal law, to distinguish it from "procedural" criminal law) has occurred and whether the person accused of the crime committed it.

Logically, substance is anterior to procedure.[1] The substantive criminal code defines the conduct that society wishes to deter and/or condemn as morally wrong. Procedural law functions as the means by which society implements its substantive goals. Nonetheless, the relationship of procedure to substance is more complicated than this simple description might suggest.

First, some legal doctrines involve a mixture of procedure and substance. For example, the constitutional rule that the government must prove beyond a reasonable doubt "every fact necessary to constitute the crime . . . charged,"[2] is procedural in nature. However, the rule cannot intelligently be enforced unless the term "crime," a substantive criminal law concept, is defined.

Second, procedural rules can affect society's willingness to prohibit certain conduct. For example, if a rule forbids the police to entrap perpetrators of a "victimless" crime, such as fornication, successful prosecution of that offense can become so difficult that lawmakers may hesitate to prohibit the conduct.[3]

Third, procedural rules can frustrate the implementation of the community's substantive goals. For example, if the rules unduly hinder the police and prosecutors in their pursuit of law violators, some persons who deserve to be punished are apt to avoid criminal sanction, and the deterrent value of the criminal law is likely to be undermined.[4] On the other hand, if the rules are too lax, some persons suspected of crime are apt to be mistreated by the police, and innocent persons might also be unjustly convicted.

---

[1] Packer, *Two Models of the Criminal Process*, 113 U. Pa. L. Rev. 1, 3 (1964).

[2] *In re Winship*, 397 U.S. 358, 364 (1970).

[3] Packer, n. 1 *supra*, at 4.

[4] *See* Hinds, *Philadelphia Justice System Overwhelmed*, New York Times, Aug. 15, 1990, A1, col. 2 (in which a city's criminal justice system was described by the District Attorney as being "on the verge of collapse," resulting in the automatic release of certain suspects, "which has, in effect, decriminalized some kinds of crimes.").

§ 2 Sources of Procedural Law

Various layers of laws and regulations govern the conduct of the participants in the criminal justice system. First, some agencies involved in criminal investigation or prosecution have promulgated written regulations that their employees must follow. For example, some police departments have rules governing, among other matters, the use of deadly force to effectuate arrests, the techniques to be followed in conducting lineups, and the procedures to be used in inventorying the contents of automobiles taken into police custody. Although these regulations do not have the force of law, their violation may result in internal sanctions.

Second, legislatures have enacted statutes and courts have adopted written rules of criminal procedure that govern many aspects of the state and federal criminal justice systems. For example, at the federal level, Congress has enacted laws governing such matters as electronic surveillance by the police of private conversations,[5] pretrial detention of dangerous persons,[6] and the qualifications for jury service.[7] Also, Congress has granted authority to the Supreme Court to promulgate written rules to govern proceedings in the federal courts, which the Court has done in the form of the Federal Rules of Criminal Procedure.

Third, on occasion the Supreme Court has invoked its so-called "supervisory authority" over the administration of criminal justice in the federal courts to announce rules that apply throughout the federal judicial system. Similarly, some federal circuit courts have developed rules that apply to the district courts within their jurisdiction. Federal supervisory-authority rules do not apply in the state courts and are subject to revision by Congress.[8]

Fourth, various provisions of the United States Constitution, in particular those found in amendments 4, 5, 6, 8, and 14 thereto, restrict the power of the government in its relations to persons suspected of criminal activity. Particularly in the 1960s and 1970s, the United States Supreme Court interpreted these constitutional provisions broadly, *i.e.*, in a manner favorable to the rights of criminal suspects. As a result, the study of criminal procedure is largely a study of constitutional law.

Fifth, state constitutions are a source of procedural law. Increasingly, as the Supreme Court and many lower federal courts have become less sympathetic to the constitutional claims put forth on behalf of criminal defendants, a body of state constitutional jurisprudence — so-called "judicial federalism" — has developed, in which some state courts, interpreting their own constitution, have granted relief to criminal defendants that is unavailable in the federal courts.[9] This

---

[5] 18 U.S.C. §§ 2510–2521.

[6] 18 U.S.C. §§ 3141–3150.

[7] 28 U.S.C. § 1865.

[8] The concept of "supervisory authority" is discussed more fully at § 14 *infra*.

[9] *See* Collins & Skover, *The Future of Liberal Legal Scholarship*, 87 Mich. L. Rev. 189, 217 (1988). Not all state courts have the authority to interpret their constitution more broadly than the United States Constitution. *E.g.*, Calif. Const. art. II, § 8 (in which the state constitution was amended by the initiative process to provide that in criminal cases various enumerated constitutional rights of the defendant "shall be construed by the courts of this state in a manner consistent with the Constitution of the United States"); Fla. Const.

trend is significant because a state supreme court is the final arbiter of the meaning of its own constitution.[10]

§ 3   Stages of a Criminal Prosecution

[A] In General

Analytically and, often, in law school curricula, "criminal procedure" is divided into two parts, the "investigatory" and the "adjudicatory" stages. In the investigatory phase, the principal actors in the "drama" are the police and those whom they suspect of criminal activity. This is the "cops and robbers" stage of the process.

The adjudicatory phase begins when the government commits itself to bringing the suspect to trial for her alleged criminal conduct. In this stage, the focus of attention turns to the legal profession — the prosecutors, defense lawyers, and judges — who participate in the adversarial judicial system. This is the "bail–to–maybe–jail" phase of the process.

In studying criminal procedure, it is important to understand the procedural context in which the legal rules apply. What follows, therefore, is an overview of the stages of a typical criminal prosecution. Because adjudicatory procedures differ by state and depend on whether the defendant is charged with a felony or a misdemeanor, primary emphasis is on felony prosecutions in the federal system.

[B] Investigatory Stage

A criminal investigation commonly begins when an officer, on the basis of her own observations and/or those of an informant, determines that criminal conduct may be afoot or have already occurred. Because there are no formal stages of a criminal investigation, most criminal procedure classes survey the constitutional law pertaining to the most common police investigative practices.

Police officers usually search and seize persons and property in the investigatory stage. Searches and seizures occur in an almost infinite variety of ways: for example, by stopping ("seizing") a suspect on the street and frisking her ("searching") for weapons or evidence; by entering a house in order to look for a suspect or evidence of a crime; by opening containers found in an automobile stopped on the highway; and by wiretapping in order to monitor the conversations of suspects.

---

art. I, § 12 (in which the state charter was amended by initiative to provide that it "shall be construed in conformity with the 4th amendment to the United States Constitution, as interpreted by the United States Supreme Court").

[10] For discussion of judicial federalism, *see* Brennan, *State Constitutions and the Protection of Individual Rights*, 90 Harv. L. Rev. 489 (1977); Cooper, *Beyond the Federal Constitution: The Status of State Constitutional Law in Florida*, 18 Stetson L. Rev. 241 (1989); Dix, *Judicial Independence in Defining Criminal Defendants' Texas Constitutional Rights*, 68 Tex. L. Rev. 1369 (1990); Marcus, *State Constitutional Protection for Defendants in Criminal Prosecutions*, 20 Ariz. St. L.J. 151 (1988); Mosk, *State Constitutionalism: Both Liberal and Conservative*, 63 Tex. L. Rev. 1081 (1985); Special Project, *State Constitutions and Criminal Procedure: A Primer for the 21st Century*, 67 Ore. L. Rev. 689 (1988).

Generally speaking, the Fourth Amendment to the United States Constitution provides that the police may not search or seize property unless they have a search warrant, supported by probable cause, issued by a judge (or "magistrate"). However, so many exceptions to the search–warrant requirement are now recognized that warrants are the exception rather than the rule.

The police also interrogate suspects and witnesses during criminal investigations. Some interrogations occur in a police–dominated atmosphere, such as in a police station. In other cases, questioning occurs in a less coercive environment, such as in a suspect's home, in the presence of family or friends.

An interrogation may trigger various constitutional questions, including: (1) Is the suspect entitled to be represented by counsel during the questioning?; and (2) Was any ensuing confession obtained voluntarily? In particular, the Fifth Amendment privilege against compulsory self–incrimination, the due process clauses of the Fifth and Fourteenth Amendments, and the Sixth Amendment guarantee of assistance of counsel during criminal prosecutions, are potentially implicated in the interrogation process.

The police also place individuals in lineups, show witnesses photographs of suspects, take handwriting and voice exemplars, and conduct other identification procedures. The police may conduct many of these activities without prior judicial approval and without intervention by defense counsel. Nonetheless, in some cases the Sixth Amendment right–to–counsel provision applies and, in all cases, the procedures must be conducted in a constitutionally reliable manner.

Assuming that the criminal investigation results in a determination that there is probable cause to believe that the suspect committed a crime, she may be arrested. Under limited circumstances, primarily when a routine, *i.e.*, non-exigent, arrest occurs in a private home, the police must have a warrant before taking the suspect into custody.

Immediately upon arrest, the suspect is searched and taken to the police station or to a jail, where she is "booked," *i.e.*, her name is logged in an arrest book or on a computer, photographed, fingerprinted, and more fully searched. Typically, any personal belongings found in her possession at the station or jail are inventoried and placed in custody for safekeeping.

[C] Adjudicatory Stage

[1] Issuance of a Complaint

After a suspect is arrested and booked, a complaint is prepared by the police or a prosecutor and is filed with the court. A "complaint" is "a written statement of the essential facts constituting the offense charged."[11] It serves as the official charging document until either an "information" or an "indictment," each of which is discussed below, is issued.

[2] *Gerstein v. Pugh* Hearing

The police may not constitutionally arrest a person unless they have probable cause to believe that a crime has occurred and that the suspect committed it. In

---

[11] FRCP 3.

order to implement the Fourth Amendment protection against unfounded invasions of liberty, the Supreme Court has held that the determination of probable cause should be made by a neutral and detached magistrate, rather than by a police officer.[12]

When the police arrest a suspect without a warrant, a prior judicial determination of probable cause is lacking. Therefore, the Supreme Court held in *Gerstein v. Pugh*[13] that the Fourth Amendment requires that a person arrested without a warrant be provided "promptly after arrest" with "a judicial determination of probable cause as a prerequisite to extended restraint of liberty following arrest."

Because the so–called "*Gerstein* hearing" serves as the post–arrest equivalent of a pre–arrest warrant–application hearing,[14] it is permissible for the proceeding to be conducted in the defendant's absence, and for the probable–cause determination to be based on hearsay testimony. If the arrested person is allowed to be present during the hearing, she is not constitutionally entitled to representation by counsel or to the full panoply of adversarial safeguards available at trial. In many jurisdictions the hearing is conducted in the suspect's presence at her first appearance before a judicial officer, which is discussed immediately below.

[3] First Appearance Before the Magistrate

An arrested person must be taken "without unnecessary delay,"[15] usually within 24 hours except on weekends, before a judicial officer, for a hearing variously called the "initial arraignment," "arraignment on a warrant," "arraignment on a complaint," "presentment," or, simply the "first" or "initial" "appearance."

At the hearing, the arrestee receives formal notice of the charges against her, her constitutional rights in the impending prosecution are explained to her, and a date is set for a preliminary hearing. If the suspect is indigent and unrepresented by counsel, a lawyer is appointed for her at this time. If the suspect was arrested without a warrant, a probable–cause determination (a "*Gerstein* hearing") often is made at the first appearance. Finally, and perhaps most significantly, the magistrate determines at this time whether the arrestee should be set free on her own recognizance, released on bail, or detained pending further proceedings.

[4] Preliminary Hearing

In most jurisdictions, a preliminary hearing (or "preliminary examination") is held within two weeks after the arrestee's initial appearance before the magistrate, unless the defendant waives the hearing. The purpose of a preliminary hearing is to determine whether there is probable cause to believe that a criminal offense has occurred and that the arrestee committed it.[16]

---

[12] Johnson v. United States, 333 U.S. 10 (1948).

[13] 420 U.S. 103 (1975).

[14] *See* § 50 *infra.*

[15] FRCP 5(a).

[16] FRCP 5.1(a). Some states apply a stiffer test, sometimes termed the "directed verdict" or "prima facie" test. It provides that the defendant should be held for trial only if there is evidence which, if unexplained, would warrant a conviction by a jury. *E.g., Commonwealth v. Prado*, 481 Pa. 485, 393 A.2d 8 (1978).

A preliminary hearing is adversarial in nature, and runs somewhat like a trial. Because it is considered a critical stage of the prosecution, the defendant is constitutionally entitled to representation by counsel.[17] At the hearing, the prosecutor and the defendant may call witnesses on their behalf and cross–examine adverse witnesses. However, most jurisdictions permit the introduction of hearsay and of evidence obtained in an unconstitutional manner, although such evidence usually is inadmissible at trial.[18]

The significance of the preliminary hearing in the criminal process depends on whether the state is an "indictment jurisdiction" (*i.e.*, a state in which the defendant ordinarily cannot be brought to trial unless she is indicted by a grand jury) or an "information jurisdiction" (*i.e.*, a state in which an indictment by a grand jury is not required).

In information jurisdictions, once the magistrate determines that there is sufficient evidence to "bind over" the defendant for a trial, the prosecutor files an "information" with the trial court. The "information" is a document stating the charges against the defendant and the essential facts relating to them. The information replaces the complaint as the charging document.

In the alternative, if the magistrate in an information jurisdiction does not find sufficient evidence to bind over the defendant, she dismisses the complaint and discharges the defendant. If the prosecutor wishes to proceed with the dismissed case, various options are available: (1) she may file a new complaint, in which case the prosecution begins anew; (2) in some states, she may appeal the magistrate's dismissal to the trial court; and/or (3) in some circumstances, she is permitted to seek an indictment from a grand jury.

In indictment jurisdictions, the preliminary hearing functions as little more than an adversarial *Gerstein*–type hearing. The magistrate's probable–cause determination may be superseded by the actions of the grand jury. In the federal system, which is an indictment jurisdiction, the preliminary examination is not held if the defendant is indicted before the date set for the preliminary hearing.[19]

[5] Grand Jury Proceeding

In an indictment jurisdiction, a defendant may not be brought to trial for a serious offense unless she is indicted by a grand jury or waives her right to a grand jury hearing. The purpose of a grand jury is to stand "between the accuser and the accused . . . [in order] to determine whether a charge is founded upon reason or was dictated by an intimidating power or by malice and personal ill will."[20]

Because of the grand jury's historical role as the guardian of the rights of the innocent, the Fifth Amendment to the United States Constitution provides that in federal prosecutions, "[n]o person shall be held to answer for a capital, or otherwise infamous crime, unless on a[n] . . . indictment of a Grand Jury. . . ." The constitutional term "infamous crime" encompasses all felony prosecutions.

---

[17] Coleman v. Alabama, 399 U.S. 1 (1970).

[18] FRCP 5.1(a).

[19] FRCP 5(c).

[20] Wood v. Georgia, 370 U.S. 375, 390 (1962).

For various reasons, a grand jury proceeding may not in fact shield an innocent person as well as a preliminary hearing. First, the putative defendant, *i.e.*, the person targeted for possible indictment, is not allowed to be present during the grand jury proceedings, except if and when she is called as a witness. Only the grand jurors, the prosecutor, the witness, and a transcriber of the proceedings, may be present in the jury room during the proceedings.[21]

Second, witnesses, even including the putative defendant, do not have a constitutional right to the presence of counsel while they testify before the grand jury.[22] Third, because a judge is not present during the proceedings, no rules of evidence apply. An indictment is not invalid although it is based solely on inadmissible hearsay evidence[23] or unconstitutionally obtained information.[24]

In the typical grand jury proceeding, the prosecutor determines what witnesses and evidence will be presented to the jury in the investigation. Upon the conclusion of the prosecutor's presentation of the evidence in the case, the jurors deliberate privately. If a majority of them determine that sufficient evidence (usually, "probable cause") was presented by the prosecutor, the jury (through the prosecutor) issues an "indictment," a document that states the charges and the relevant facts relating to them. If the jury votes not to indict the defendant (a "no–bill"), which is uncommon, the complaint issued against the defendant is dismissed.

[6] Arraignment

If an indictment or information is filed, the defendant must be arraigned in open court. At the arraignment, at which defense counsel may be present, the defendant is provided with a copy of the indictment or information, after which she enters a plea to the offenses charged in it. She may plead "not guilty," "guilty," "*nolo contendere*,"[25] or (in some states) "not guilty by reason of insanity."

[7] Pre-Trial Motions

After arraignment, the defendant will often make various motions. In most cases, motions that are capable of resolution prior to trial may not be made for the first time at trial.

Among the defenses, objections, and requests that often are raised prior to trial are: (1) that the indictment or information is defective, such as that it fails to allege an essential element of the crime charged or that it fails to give the defendant sufficient notice of the facts relating to the charge against her; (2) that the venue of the prosecution is improper or inconvenient;[26] (3) that the indictment or information joins offenses or others defendants in an improper or prejudicial

---

[21] FRCP 6(d).

[22] In re Groban, 352 U.S. 330 (1957) (dictum); United States v. Mandujano, 425 U.S. 564 (1976) (dictum) (plurality opinion).

[23] Costello v. United States, 350 U.S. 359, *reh'g denied*, 351 U.S. 904 (1956).

[24] *See* United States v. Calandra, 414 U.S. 338 (1974).

[25] Literally, the plea means "I will not contest it [the charge]." For most purposes in a criminal proceeding, the plea is treated the same as a guilty plea.

[26] *See, e.g.*, FRCP 18, 20(a).

manner;[27] (4) that evidence in the possession of one of the parties should be disclosed to the opposing party;[28] (5) that evidence should be suppressed because it was obtained in an unconstitutional manner; and (6) that the prosecution is constitutionally barred, such as by the double jeopardy and/or speedy trial clauses of the Constitution.[29]

In some circumstances, if the defendant's motion is successful, the judge will dismiss the charges on her own or on the prosecutor's motion.[30] For example, if the prosecution is barred by the double jeopardy clause, a dismissal is obligatory. Or, if the judge grants the defendant's motion to suppress key evidence, the prosecutor might determine that a continuation of the proceedings is futile and, therefore, request a dismissal.

[8] Trial

If the defendant does not plead guilty and the charges are not dismissed, a trial is held. The Sixth Amendment entitles the defendant to a trial by jury in a criminal prosecution of any serious, i.e., non–petty, offense. Although the boundaries of the term "non–petty" have not been fully laid out, the right to a jury trial applies to any offense carrying a potential punishment in excess of six months incarceration.[31] Although trial juries usually consist of twelve persons,[32] one as small as six in number is constitutionally permitted.[33]

Under the Sixth Amendment, the jury that serves must be impartial. Although the accused is not entitled to a jury that mirrors the community as a whole, she is entitled to a jury drawn from a pool of persons constituting a fair cross–section of the community.[34] This right is violated if large, distinctive groups of persons, such as women or members of a racial group, are systematically excluded from the jury pool for reasons that are incompatible with a significant state interest.

A juror is not impartial if her state of mind in reference to any person involved in the trial or in regards to the issues involved in the case would substantially impair her performance as a juror in accordance with the law and the court's instructions.[35] In order to discover possible bias, the trial judge and/or the attorneys examine the prospective jurors ("venirepersons") regarding their attitudes and beliefs (i.e., conduct a "voir dire"). If either side believes that a venireperson is partial, that side may challenge the juror "for cause." If the judge grants the challenge, the prospective juror is excused.

---

[27] See, e.g., FRCP 8, 14.

[28] See, e.g., FRCP 16.

[29] U.S. Const. amend. V (". . . nor shall any person be subject for the same offence to be twice put in jeopardy of life or limb . . . "); U.S. Const. amend. VI ("In all criminal prosecutions, the accused shall enjoy the right to a speedy . . . trial. . . .").

[30] See, e.g., FRCP 48.

[31] Blanton v. City of North Las Vegas, 489 U.S. 538 (1989).

[32] See, e.g., FRCP 23(a).

[33] Williams v. Florida, 399 U.S. 78 (1970) (jury of six is allowed); Ballew v. Georgia, 435 U.S. 223 (1978) (jury of five is not allowed).

[34] Taylor v. Louisiana, 419 U.S. 522 (1975).

[35] See Adams v. Texas, 448 U.S. 38 (1980).

Both sides are also entitled to exercise a specified number of "peremptory" challenges, *i.e.*, challenges not based on cause.[36] The primary purpose of a peremptory challenge is to allow a party to exclude a venireperson it believes as a matter of intuition or as the result of the *voir dire* is not impartial, but whose prejudice has not been proved.

Although the tradition of peremptory challenges is said to be "venerable,"[37] "important,"[38] and even "a necessary part of trial by jury,"[39] the Supreme Court ruled in *Batson v. Kentucky*[40] that the Fourteenth Amendment equal protection clause is violated if a prosecutor exercises peremptory challenges to remove from the venire members of the defendant's race solely on account of race. Although the prosecutor is permitted to seek the exclusion of venirepersons of the same race as the defendant for reasons that might not justify a challenge for cause, she may not challenge a person on the assumption that the juror is biased in the case solely because of her race.

The defendant is constitutionally entitled to be represented by counsel at trial. An indigent is entitled to the appointment of counsel in all felony prosecutions, as well as in any misdemeanor case in she will be incarcerated if convicted.[41] At the trial, the defendant may call witnesses in her own behalf and confront and cross–examine the witnesses who testify against her.[42] The defendant is not required to testify in her own behalf, and she "must pay no court–imposed price for the exercise of [her Fifth Amendment] constitutional privilege not to testify."[43]

In most jurisdictions, the jury verdict to acquit or to convict must be unanimous.[44] However, state laws permitting non–unanimous verdicts are constitutional.[45]

---

[36] *See, e.g.,* FRCP 24(b) (in trials of non–capital crimes punishable by imprisonment for more than one year, the government is entitled to 6, and the defense to 10, peremptory challenges).

[37] Holland v. Illinois, 110 S.Ct. 803, 808, *reh'g denied*, 110 S.Ct. 1514 (1990).

[38] Batson v. Kentucky, 476 U.S. 79, 98 (1986).

[39] Swain v. Alabama, 380 U.S. 202, 219 (1965).

[40] 476 U.S. 79 (1986).

[41] Gideon v. Wainwright, 372 U.S. 335 (1963) (felony cases); Argersinger v. Hamlin, 407 U.S. 25 (1972) (misdemeanor cases).

[42] U.S. Const. amend. VI ("In all criminal prosecutions, the accused shall the enjoy the right . . . to be confronted with the witnesses against him; [and] to have compulsory process for obtaining witnesses in his favor. . . ."). *See generally* Haddad, *The Future of Confrontation Clause Developments: What Will Emerge When the Supreme Court Synthesizes the Diverse Lines in Confrontation Decisions*, 82 J. Crim. L. & Crimin. 97 (1990).

[43] Carter v. Kentucky, 450 U.S. 288, 301 (1981); *see also* Griffin v. California, 380 U.S. 609 (1965).

[44] *See, e.g.,* FRCP 31(a).

[45] Johnson v. Louisiana, 406 U.S. 356 (1972) (upholding a 9–3 guilty verdict because the vote constituted a verdict by a "substantial majority" of the jurors; *but see Burch v. Louisiana*, 441 U.S. 130 (1979) (striking down a statute permitting a verdict by a six–person jury on the basis of five votes).

[9] Appeal

If the defendant is acquitted by the jury or by the judge in a bench trial, the government is barred by the double jeopardy clause from appealing the acquittal.

If the defendant is convicted, she has no constitutional right to appeal her conviction.[46] However, all jurisdictions statutorily permit a convicted defendant (now the "appellant") to appeal. In state court systems, she may appeal the conviction to an appellate court below the state supreme court or, if there is none, directly to the state supreme court. In the federal courts, a defendant may appeal her conviction to the United States Court of Appeals for the circuit with jurisdiction over the case.

If the appellant is unsuccessful in her statutory appeal of right, she may be permitted further discretionary appeals to a higher court. For example, in a state in which an appeal of right is brought to an intermediate appellate court, the state supreme court is permitted, but usually is not required except in capital cases, to hear the defendant–appellant's second appeal. She may also petition the United States Supreme Court to consider her case. The Supreme Court also has discretion to consider a federal appellant's petition if the circuit court affirms her conviction. If her appeal is ultimately successful, she may be reprosecuted.

[10] Collateral Attack: Habeas Corpus

After a defendant's appeals are exhausted — *i.e.*, her conviction is final — she may file a petition for a writ of habeas corpus in a federal district court, if she believes that her continued incarceration is in violation of the United States Constitution or of a federal law.[47]

The purpose of a habeas petition is to convince the district court that it should compel the warden of the jail or prison holding the petitioner to bring her before the court so that it can determine whether or not she is being held against the law. Habeas corpus jurisprudence is complicated and involves many intricate rules: however, if the proper allegations are made, the district court may grant the habeas petition and conduct an evidentiary hearing regarding the federal claim.[48]

A post–conviction habeas corpus proceeding is not part of the criminal appeal process itself; rather, it is a civil action designed to overturn a presumptively valid criminal judgment. As such, it is considered a collateral attack on a criminal conviction, as distinguished from a direct criminal appeal.

---

[46] *See* McKane v. Durtson, 153 U.S. 684 (1894) (dictum); Jones v. Barnes, 463 U.S. 745 (1983) (dictum).

[47] 28 U.S.C. §§ 2241–2244, 2254–2255.

[48] *See generally* G. Hughes, The Decline of Habeas Corpus (Occasional Papers from the Center for Research in Crime and Justice, New York University School of Law, No. VIII, 1990); Hoffmann, *Retroactivity and the Great Writ: How Congress Should Respond to Teague v. Lane*, 1990 B.Y.U. L. Rev. 183; Weisberg, *A Great Writ While It Lasted*, 81 J. Crim. L. & Crimin. 9 (1990).

§ 4   Studying Constitutional Law Cases

Because the study of criminal procedure is often a study of constitutional law, especially the decisions of the United States Supreme Court, the following suggestions are offered to students inexperienced in analyzing Supreme Court constitutional cases.

[A]   Read Concurring and Dissenting Opinions

To the extent that your casebook permits, pay attention to concurring and dissenting opinions, if any, in the cases. Various reasons support this recommendation. First, the ideas expressed in the concurring or dissenting opinions of today sometimes become the majority views of tomorrow.

Second, often a concurring or dissenting opinion explains the views of the majority better than the latter's own opinion, calls attention to unresolved issues, or suggests where the logic of the majority opinion may lead. Indeed, on occasion a concurring opinion takes on a life of its own, and is cited or used by later courts in lieu of the majority opinion.

Third, as discussed in subsection [C], it is often necessary to analyze these opinions in order to determine the long–term significance of a constitutional holding.

[B]   Learn Case Names

Pay attention to the names of Supreme Court cases. Unlike cases applying common law doctrine, which often are fungible, constitutional decisions of the Supreme Court represent the final word on the issue in question.[49] These opinions have the "power to shake the assembled faithful with awful tremors of exultation and loathing."[50] Consequently, lawyers tend to talk about constitutional issues in a shorthand (*e.g.*, "Was the suspect given her *Miranda*[51] rights?"). It is helpful, therefore, to understand and speak "case–name–ese."

[C]   Count Votes

If the casebook permits, take note of the vote breakdown in important cases. For various reasons, vote counting can prove insightful, sometimes essential. First, the long–term importance of a decision may depend on the size of the majority. A 5–4 decision is not equivalent to a 9–0 ruling. A unanimous opinion often carries greater moral suasion with the public and within the legal community than one decided by the slimmest of margins. Moreover, a 5–4 precedent is a prime target for overruling (or, at least, narrowing) if one of the justices in the majority leaves the Court. For example, Supreme Court opinions in which Justice William Brennan was a member of a five–justice majority immediately became vulnerable when he resigned from the Court in 1990.

---

[49] Of course, the Court can overrule itself, or the Constitution can be amended to "repeal" an unpopular decision, but neither of these occurrences is common.

[50] Amsterdam, *The Supreme Court and the Rights of Suspects in Criminal Cases*, 45 N.Y.U. L. Rev. 785, 786 (1970).

[51] Miranda v. Arizona, 384 U.S. 436, *reh'g denied*, 385 U.S. 890 (1966).

Second, vote counting is essential in ascertaining the precedential value of some cases. For example, suppose that *D* appeals her conviction on two independent grounds: (1) that police officers conducted an unconstitutional search of her house (issue A); and (2) that the officers coerced a confession from her (issue B). Assume that if either of these claims is successful *D*'s conviction must be overturned.

Assume the following scenario: four justices vote for *D* on issue A, but express no opinion regarding issue B. One justice concurs in the judgment; in her opinion she rules against *D* on issue A, but in her favor on issue B. Four dissenters reject both of *D*'s claims. Thus, *D* gets what she wants: she wins her appeal, as five justices believe that she is entitled to a new trial, albeit for different reasons.

However, a good lawyer with a client who wishes to raise issue A on similar facts would observe that her chances of success are not good: four justices are likely to favor her client's claim regarding issue A, while five justices (the dissenters and the concurring justice) will probably oppose her. Likewise, another attorney, but one who seeks to raise issue B, can expect that at least four justices will oppose, and only one will favor, her client. The case would depend on the views of the four justices who expressed no opinion on issue B.

[D] Learn the Views of Individual Justices

Suppose that a lawyer is considering the wisdom of appealing a criminal conviction in a case in which the law is fuzzy — *i.e.*, there is no rule or precedent on point. In order to determine whether to recommend an appeal and, if so, what arguments are most apt to be persuasive, the attorney must "get into the head" of the judges on the court that will hear the case. One way to do this is to identify each justice's judicial and legal philosophy.

It is usually too simplistic (although not always [52]) to treat a judge as a "liberal" or a "conservative" (or as an "activist" or a "non-activist"), whatever those terms may mean to the user. Some judges are "liberal," for example, in matters relating to freedom of speech but are "conservative" on question of criminal justice. Even in the latter area, a particular judge might believe that the government should be given leeway in interrogating suspects, but not in relation to double jeopardy claims.

Therefore, in order to be aware of the justices' views in particular areas, lawyers — and law students — need to pay attention to the voting patterns of individual justices. Over time, an observer can develop a sense of a justice's philosophy and can more accurately predict that person's vote on specific issues.

---

[52] For example, Justice William Douglas took the "civil libertarian" position in 90 percent of the cases in which he cast a vote between 1953 and 1975. In contrast, Justice William Rehnquist took a civil libertarian position in only 19.6% of the cases decided between 1972, when he joined the Court, and 1985. *See* Segal & Spaeth, *Decisional Trends on the Warren and Burger Courts: Results from the Supreme Court Data Base Project*, 73 Judicature 103, 105–06 (1989). Justice Kennedy's voting pattern in his first two years on the Court suggests that he may be a fairly predictable opponent of the civil liberterian position. *See* Melone, *Revisiting the Freshman Effect Hypothesis: the First Two Terms of Justice Anthony Kennedy*, 74 Judicature 6 (1990).

[E] Be Sensitive to Supreme Court History

Just as individual justices have specific philosophical perspectives, the Supreme Court as a body (or, at least, a majority of its members) often possesses a group philosophy and even a group personality. It is worthwhile, therefore, to be sensitive to the place of a Supreme Court opinion in the larger historical constitutional picture.

Lawyers tend to talk in general terms about the philosophical views of the "Warren Court," the "Burger Court," and now the "Rehnquist Court," the shorthand titles for the Supreme Court, and the opinions decided by it, under the recent Chief Justices, Earl Warren (1953–1969), Warren Burger (1969–1986), and William Rehnquist (1986–Present).

Many book and articles have been written about the judicial philosophies of the Warren, Burger, and Rehnquist Courts.[53] In general, the Warren Court was an activist Court that sought to use its judicial power to develop rules favorable to the individual *vis a vis* the government. In the context of criminal procedure, the Warren Court was responsible for most of the constitutional decisions that expanded the rights of persons suspected of criminal activity. Overall, this Court adopted the so–called "due process" model of criminal justice.[54]

In contrast, the Rehnquist Court (and, somewhat less so, the Burger Court) has favored the "crime control" model of criminal procedure,[55] in the sense that it has granted legislatures and prosecutorial agencies substantial discretion in defining, investigating, and prosecuting crime. Warren Court holdings, although not often overruled, have been undercut by the adoption of narrow interpretations and new exceptions. The practical effect has been that government power has been expanded at the expense of individuals suspected of crime.

Some criminal procedure casebooks include a chart that shows the dates on which individual justices joined the Court. If your book has such a chart, look

---

[53] For discussion of the Warren Court, *see generally* Allen, *The Judicial Quest for Penal Justice: The Warren Court and the Criminal Cases*, 1975 U. Ill. L. Forum 518; Pye, *The Warren Court and Criminal Procedure*, 67 Mich. L. Rev. 249 (1968); Choper, *On the Warren Court and Judicial Review*, 17 Cath. U. L. Rev. 20 (1967).

Regarding the Burger Court and a comparison of it to the Warren Court, *see generally* The Burger Years (H. Schwartz ed., Viking Press 1987); Alschuler, *Failed Pragmatism: Reflections on the Burger Court*, 100 Harv. L. Rev. 1436 (1987); Arenella, *Rethinking the Functions of Criminal Procedure: The Warren and Burger Courts' Competing Ideologies*, 72 Geo L.J. 185 (1983); Israel, *Criminal Procedure, the Burger Court, and the Legacy of the Warren Court*, 75 Mich. L. Rev. 1319 (1977); Saltzburg, *The Flow and Ebb of Constitutional Criminal Procedure in the Warren and Burger Courts*, 69 Geo. L.J. 151 (1980); Schulhofer, *The Constitution and the Police: Individual Rights and Law Enforcement*, 66 Wash. U. L. Rev. 11 (1988); Seidman, *Factual Guilt and the Burger Court: An Examination of Continuity and Change in Criminal Procedure*, 80 Colum. L. Rev. 436 (1980); Weisberg, *Criminal Procedure Doctrine: Some Versions of the Skeptical*, 76 J. Crim. L. & Criminology 832 (1985).

Regarding the Rehnquist Court, *see generally* Bradley, *Criminal Procedure in the Rehnquist Court: Has the Rehnquisition Begun?*, 62 Ind. L.J. 273 (1987).

[54] *See* § 5[C] *infra.*

[55] *See* § 5[B] *infra.*

at it often to see where specific cases fit in. If your book does not have such a chart, and even if it does, the following brief review should be helpful.

In theory, the "Warren Court" began in 1953 when President Dwight Eisenhower appointed Earl Warren as Chief Justice. However, the civil libertarian thrust of the Court did not develop immediately, but took effect gradually as new justices were appointed.

Already on the Court in 1953, and sympathetic to the Chief Justice's views as they developed, was William Douglas, who was appointed to the Court in 1939 by President Franklin D. Roosevelt. After the Chief Justice was appointed, William Brennan (1956), a major participant in the Warren Court decisions, and Potter Stewart (1958), a less consistent advocate of defendants' rights, joined the Court.

The Warren Court reached its civil libertarian peak in the mid–1960s, after Presidents John F. Kennedy and Lyndon B. Johnson replaced outgoing members of the Court with: Arthur Goldberg (1962, by J.F.K.), who was himself replaced by Abe Fortas (1965, by L.B.J.); Byron White (1962, by J.F.K.); and Thurgood Marshall (1967, by L.B.J.). Of the replacements, only Justice White was not a strong advocate of the Warren Court values.

The shift away from the Warren Court philosophy was as gradual as its ascendancy. It began in 1969 with the election of Richard Nixon to the presidency, who campaigned for office on the promise to nominate "law and order" justices.[56] President Nixon almost immediately filled two Court vacancies: Warren Burger (1969) and Harry Blackmun (1970), who replaced Warren and Fortas respectively. He appointed two more justices later in his term: Rehnquist (1972) and Lewis Powell (1972), who replaced centrist Justice John Harlan and liberal Justice Hugo Black, respectively. President Gerald Ford appointed John Stevens (1975) to replace Justice Douglas.

In the context of criminal procedure, each of the changes in Court personnel in the 1970s resulted in a more conservative Supreme Court, although Justices Blackmun, Powell and Stevens frequently supported the legal positions taken by defendants in criminal appeals.

It was not until the 1980s that the shift away from the underlying values expressed in many Warren Court opinions became evident. During this decade, Sandra Day O'Connor (1981), Antonin Scalia (1985), and Anthony Kennedy (1988) were appointed by President Ronald Reagan, replacing Justice Stewart, Chief Justice Burger,[57] and Justice Powell, respectively. With the appointment of Justice Kennedy, the balance of power definitively tipped in favor of the crime control model of criminal justice.

In July, 1990, Justice Brennan resigned. President George Bush nominated, and the United States Senate approved, David Souter to replace him. Therefore, at the beginning of the 1990-1991 Court term, only two members of the original Warren Court (Justices Marshall and White) remained on the bench. Of the nine

---

[56] *See* L. Baker, Miranda: Crime, Law and Politics 219–324 (Atheneum 1983).

[57] Technically, Chief Justice Burger was replaced by Justice Rehnquist, who was elevated to Chief Justice. Justice Scalia filled Rehnquist's old spot.

members of the Supreme Court, all but the latter two were appointed by Republican presidents.[58]

---

[58] For a political history of the appointments to the Supreme Court, *see* H. Abraham, Justices and Presidents (Oxford 1974). For a perspective on various twentieth century justices, *see* The Supreme Court and its Justices (J. Choper, ed., Am. Bar Assoc., 1987). For a valuable statistical analysis of each Supreme Court term, including figures on voting alignments, *see* the annual study of the Supreme Court term, published in the first issue of each volume of the Harvard Law Review.

CHAPTER 2

OVERARCHING POLICY ISSUES IN CRIMINAL PROCEDURE

The law does not develop in a philosophical or policy vacuum. In order to appreciate fully criminal procedural law, it is important to be aware of some of the overarching controversies in the field. This chapter briefly notes three of the more important debates.

§ 5 "Due Process" versus "Crime Control"[1]

[A] Models of Criminal Justice

Professor Herbert Packer once identified two models of criminal procedure, with identifiable and different value systems, "that compete for priority in the operation of the criminal process."[2] He termed them the "Due Process" (DP) and "Crime Control" (CC) models of criminal justice.

Packer's analysis has been criticized and alternative models of criminal justice have been suggested by other commentators.[3] Nonetheless, his articulation of the models has influenced thought in the field.

The competing models are summarized below, but some preliminary points are important. First, as with any effort to systematize, the models are oversimplified. Second, the models represent certain typically connected values, but they should not be regarded as expressions of the views of any single individual in the real world.

Third, although Packer usually speaks of the models as if they were polar opposites, some common ground exists between them. For example, advocates of both models agree that the criminal justice process should be invoked whenever it appears that a crime has been committed and that there is a fair chance of apprehending and convicting the perpetrator. Both sides also agree that limits should be placed on the power of the government to investigate and prosecute criminal suspects, although they disagree on what the limits should be.

---

[1] *See generally* H. Packer, The Limits of the Criminal Sanction 149–246 (Stanford 1968); Arenella, *Rethinking the Functions of Criminal Procedure: The Warren and Burger Courts' Competing Ideologies*, 72 Geo. L.J. 185 (1983); Damaska, *Evidentiary Barriers to Conviction and Two Models of Criminal Procedure: A Comparative Study*, 121 U. Pa. L. Rev. 506 (1973); Griffiths, *Ideology in Criminal Procedure or A Third "Model" of the Criminal Process*, 79 Yale L. J. 359 (1970).

[2] H. Packer, n. 1 *supra*, at 153.

[3] *E.g.*, Arenella, n. 1 *supra*, at 209–228; *see generally* Griffiths, n. 1 *supra*.

Finally, both models assume the existence of an adversarial system of justice, which is itself a controversial concept discussed later in this chapter.

[B] The Values of the Crime Control Model[4]

The critical proposition on which the CC Model is founded is that repression of crime is the most important domestic goal of government. It was crime — the "law of the jungle" — that caused people to join together and promulgate laws to govern themselves.

In a society riddled with crime, an important condition of human freedom is lost.[5] Crime undermines the social order. It threatens life and stimulates unwanted and undesirable emotions, including fear. Fear of crime itself limits freedom: all persons, not only the direct victims of crime, are hesitant to walk on streets at night or even to open windows on a muggy summer evening. The criminal makes us feel this way; he diminishes our freedom; he makes social interaction more difficult.

In light of the importance of crime prevention, the advocate of the CC Model believes that the criminal justice system should promote efficient investigation, prosecution, and sentencing of law violators.

How do we make the system efficient? First, the process should be as informal as possible. This means that CC advocates prefer nonjudicial processes to formal, judicial ones. In the CC Model, police officers are permitted substantial opportunity to function free of legal impediments ("ceremonious rituals"[6]), as they search for the evidence necessary to arrest and convict criminals; the adjudicatory process (with its formality, rigid rules of evidence, and adversarial conditions) is delayed as long as possible.

Second, the CC Model favors uniformity. That is, if large numbers of cases are to be handled efficiently, criminal law procedures must be "routine" and "stereotyped." As Packer puts it, the CC Model should look like "an assembly–line conveyor belt down which moves an endless stream of cases, never stopping."[7] Cases should be taken off the belt if, but only if, the informal procedures suggest that the suspect is innocent.

Third, the CC Model presumes the guilt of criminal suspects. One must be careful in understanding this point. The CC advocate does not necessarily reject the constitutional presumption of innocence, which is based on the principle that people ought to be treated at trial as if they were innocent. The CC adherent believes, however, that society should not lose sight of the fact that most suspects are factually guilty of some crime related to that for which they are being prosecuted. By presuming the factual guilt of a suspect, the CC Model advocate expresses his confidence in the criminal justice system; the presumption helps to reinforce society's desire to promote an efficient system.

---

[4] Although the descriptions that follow in this and the next subsection are based on Packer's articulation of the two models, I have added to and subtracted from his conceptualization.

[5] *See* C. Silberman, Criminal Violence, Criminal Justice 3–20 (Random House 1978).

[6] H. Packer, n. 1 *supra*, at 159.

[7] *Id.*

[C]   The Values of the Due Process Model

The values of the DP Model can best be understood by contrasting them to the CC Model. First, the DP advocate does not discount the harm of crime or the desirability of repressing it, but he believes that the purpose of government in this context is not simply to deter crime but is to maximize human freedom. Human freedom, in turn, includes protection of individuals from undue restrictions on their liberty by government. In general, when the rights of the individual and of the community conflict, the DP advocate is more likely to favor the interests of the individual, including persons suspected of crime, than is the CC Model proponent.

Second, the advocate of the DP Model questions the reliability of informal systems of criminal justice. Whereas the CC system pictures the police officer as a skilled criminal investigator likely to ascertain the truth if obstacles are not placed in his way, the DP Model emphasizes the risk of human error in the informal, investigative process.

The DP advocate believes that the best way to increase the reliability of the process is to promote the early intervention of judges and lawyers — and, thus, of formality — in the criminal justice system. Thus, if the CC Model looks like a conveyor belt, as Packer asserts, the DP Model tends to look like an obstacle course from the police officer's perspective.

Third, while the CC Model is predicated on the assumed factual guilt of suspects, the DP system focuses on the doctrine of legal guilt. That is, a criminal suspect is not legally guilty of a crime unless and until (guilty pleas aside) the prosecutor proves the defendant's guilt beyond a reasonable doubt, in the courtroom through the adversarial process, on the basis of legally admissible evidence.

The legal presumption of innocence, like the CC Model's belief in the factual guilt of the suspect, represents a mood, a way of thinking about criminal cases: by thinking of suspects as innocent persons, DP Model advocates believe that we are more apt to appreciate the value of setting limits on government power. Moreover, the presumption of innocence increases the likelihood that innocent persons will avoid wrongful conviction, although it also increases the possibility that factually guilty persons will escape conviction.

Fourth, the models differ in their evaluation of the importance of redressing economic inequality in the criminal justice system. Adherents of the DP Model agree with the principle that "there can be no equal justice where the kind of trial a man gets depends on the amount of money he has."[8] Therefore, to the extent possible, they seek to place the indigent defendant in the same position as the more wealthy suspect. In contrast, in the efficiency–driven CC system, the indigent is given only as much help as is required to provide him with a fair opportunity to demonstrate his factual innocence, although this does not place him on an equal footing with the non–indigent.

Finally, the judiciary has a more active role to play in the DP Model than in the CC system. Judicial activism is appropriate in the DP Model because its

---

[8] Griffin v. Illinois, 351 U.S. 12, 19, *reh'g denied*, 351 U.S. 958 (1956).

advocates believe that the "central purpose of our written Constitution, and more specifically of its unique creation of a life–tenured federal judiciary, [is] to ensure that certain rights [*i.e.*, those included in the Bill of Rights] are firmly secured against possible oppression by the Federal or State Governments."[9]

Thus, all else being equal, a system modeled on DP values will be less efficient, more costly, more inclined to favor a strong judiciary *vis a vis* the legislature, more apt to protect individual liberties, less likely to convict innocent persons, and more likely to allow the guilty to go free, than one based on CC values.

§ 6 The Value of "Truth" In the Criminal Justice System[10]

How important is the "truth" in the criminal justice system? Put another way, to what extent is it appropriate for the criminal process to promote goals other than that of ensuring a factually reliable result, *i.e.*, that guilty persons are convicted and that the innocent are set free?

Many participants in the criminal justice system believe that subordination of the truth to any other value is indefensible. They believe that separating the innocent from the guilty is not a casual concern of the criminal justice system, but is its utmost goal.[11] When the truth is not discovered, or the implications of the discovery ignored, the system fails in its mission.

Advocates of this view argue that the criminal justice process should not be treated like an athletic contest in which rules are devised to ensure that each side has an equal opportunity of winning.[12] Rather, the system should want the defendant to win if, but only if, he is innocent. The claim is made that too often rules are devised that give the "fox" a chance of winning the "hunt." Such a system, they contend, "makes for good sports, but in a criminal investigation we should be seeking truth rather than entertainment."[13]

Other persons believe that the criminal justice system should not focus exclusively on the truth–finding process. First, it is worth noting that the relative importance of truth in the system depends in part on the penological goals of the community. In a system of criminal laws premised on retributive values,[14]

---

[9] Florida v. Meyers, 466 U.S. 380, 385 (1984) (Stevens, J., dissenting).

[10] *See generally* Alschuler, *The Search for Truth Continued, The Privilege Retained: A Response to Judge Frankel*, 54 U. Colo. L. Rev. 67 (1982); Brennan, *The Criminal Prosecution: Sporting Event or Quest for Truth?*, 1963 Wash. U. L.Q. 279; Frankel, *The Search for Truth: An Umpireal View*, 123 U. Pa. L. Rev. 1031 (1975); Freedman, *Judge Frankel's Search for Truth*, 123 U. Pa. L. Rev. 1060 (1975); Meese, *Promoting Truth in the Courtroom*, 40 Vand. L. Rev. 271 (1987); Pulaski, *Criminal Trials: A "Search for Truth" or Something Else?*, 16 Crim L. Bull. 41 (1980); Pye, *The Role of Counsel in the Suppression of Truth*, 1978 Duke L.J. 921.

[11] Meese, n. 10 *supra*, at 271.

[12] Pye, n. 10 *supra*, at 926.

[13] Grano, *Selling the Idea to Tell the Truth: The Professional Interrogator and Modern Confession Law*, 84 Mich. L. Rev. 662, 677 (1986).

[14] Retributivism is based on the principle that persons should be punished if, but only if, they have acted in a morally wrongful manner, and that they should be punished in proportion to the harm that they have caused and their culpability for having caused it. J. Dressler, at § 2.03[C].

reliability is critical, because punishment of innocent persons and excessive punishment of the guilty is morally wrong. But, in a utilitarian system,[15] punishment of an innocent person is not intrinsically wrong. Indeed, as one scholar bluntly put it, in the latter system, "[s]o long as the appearance is maintained that the guilty are punished and the innocent vindicated, procedures designed actually to achieve that result need never be utilized."[16]

Second, advocates of the Due Process Model of criminal justice believe that the system should include some procedural obstacles to the truth. They believe, as one English court put it, that "[t]ruth, like all other good things, may be loved unwisely — may be pursued too keenly — may cost too much."[17] From their perspective, "truth must find its place in the context of a larger concern to do justice."[18]

"Justice," in this sense, means more than that a factually reliable result is reached; it includes the principle that reliable results should be reached in a morally acceptable manner. For example, when the truth is obtained through the use of torture, it is probably preferable to allow a potentially guilty party to go free — out of respect for his human rights or in order to deter future abuses by the State — than it is to seek the truth of his possible guilt at trial.

Third, some abridgement of the truth currently is accepted in the adversary system of justice. For example, although the prosecutor is ethically obligated to promote a just outcome, not necessarily to obtain a conviction,[19] the defense attorney in an adversarial system has a duty of loyalty to his client,[20] which includes the qualified obligation on his part to retain the client's confidences,[21] even at the expense of the truth.

Therefore, the question that confronts participants in the criminal justice system, as well as students of the law, is whether (to paraphrase the English court), in the pursuit of other good things, we have pursued truth keenly enough.

---

[15] Classical utilitarianism is based on the principle that punishment is only justifiable if it prevents crime more mischievous than the punishment itself. *Id.* at § 2.03[B].

[16] Seidman, *Factual Guilt and the Burger Court: An Examination of Continuity and Change in Criminal Procedure*, 80 Colum. L. Rev. 436, 501 (1980).

[17] Pearse v. Pearse, 63 Eng. Rep. 957, 970 (1846).

[18] Law Reform Commission of Canada, Our Criminal Procedure (Report 32) 10 (1988).

[19] *See* American Bar Association, Model Code of Professional Responsibility EC 7–13 (1981).

[20] *See* American Bar Association, Model Rules of Professional Conduct, Rule 1.7 Comment (1983).

[21] *Id.* Rule 1–6(a).

§ 7 Accusatorial versus Inquisitorial Systems of Justice[22]

It is often said that "[o]urs is an accusatorial and not an inquisitorial system"[23] of criminal justice. But, is it; and perhaps more significantly, should it be accusatorial?

An accusatorial system of criminal justice is one based on the adversarial theory of trial practice, but which also encompasses certain other fundamental premises. In its pure form, the adversary system is one in which two contending parties, usually represented by attorneys, focus on legal issues and investigate the facts in order to make partisan presentations of the facts and the law to a neutral and passive arbiter. As one commentator put it, the system is "a regulated storytelling contest between champions of competing interpretive stories."[24] It is also a system that justifies "trial by combat."[25]

As a battle between partisans, rules are developed in the adversarial system to balance the power between the combatants so that there is, if you will, fair warfare. As part of that process, the government is expected to procure its evidence against the accused "by its own independent labors";[26] it must "shoulder the entire load."[27] As one scholar has explained,[28] "an accusatorial system . . . assigns great social value in keeping the state out of disputes, especially when stigma and sanction may follow." Therefore, the defendant in the accusatorial system is treated "as if he is innocent and need lend no aid to those who would convict him."

In contrast, in an inquisitorial system, the government, rather than the parties, has the primary responsibility for developing the evidence in a given case. At the trial, the judge takes an active role in securing the facts. And, perhaps most significantly for current purposes, in this system virtually all relevant sources of information are available to the judge, including evidence involuntarily obtained from the defendant.

Sloganeering aside, the American system of criminal justice is not purely accusatorial. As is developed throughout this text, the state is not required to "shoulder the entire load" to convict a suspect. For example, a suspect may be put in a lineup, fingerprinted, and have his blood extracted from his veins against his will, all of which may assist in his conviction and punishment. Similarly, even

---

[22] *See generally* J. Grano, Police Interrogation and Confessions: A Rebuttal to Misconceived Objections (Occasional Papers from the Center for Research in Crime and Justice, New York Univ. School of Law, I, 1987); Damaska, n. 1 *supra*; Goldstein, *Reflections on Two Models: Inquisitorial Themes in American Criminal Procedure*, 26 Stan. L. Rev. 1009 (1974); Goldstein & Marcus, *The Myth of Judicial Supervision in Three "Inquisitorial" Systems: France, Italy, and Germany*, 87 Yale L.J. 240 (1977); Goodpaster, *On the Theory of American Adversary Criminal Trial*, 78 J. Crim. L. & Criminology 118 (1987); Griffiths, n. 1 *supra*; Langbein & Weinreb, *Continental Criminal Procedure: "Myth" and Reality*, 87 Yale L.J. 1549 (1978).

[23] *E.g.*, Rogers v. Richmond, 365 U.S. 534, 541 (1961).

[24] Goodpaster, n. 22 *supra*, at 120.

[25] Dressler, *Trial by Combat in American Courts*, Harper's Magazine, April, 1961, at 31.

[26] Miranda v. Arizona, 384 U.S. 436, 460, *reh'g denied*, 385 U.S. 890 (1966).

[27] *Id.*

[28] Goldstein, n. 22 *supra*, at 1017–18.

after the adjudicatory phase begins, a state may require the defendant to notify the prosecutor regarding his intended trial defenses, which in turn makes it easier for the government to prepare and win its case.[29]

The critical question is whether this mixed system is desirable. To the extent that truth–production is the goal of the criminal process, it has been argued by some that a pure adversarial system is appropriate because "[t]ruth is best discovered by powerful statements on both sides of the question."[30] Only this way, it is asserted, will an arbiter avoid the tendency to judge a controversy too swiftly.

Many commentators, however, argue that the adversarial process is not conducive to a reliable verdict.[31] They would agree with the view of one respected jurist who complained that the adversary process achieves truth "only as a convenience, a byproduct, or an accidental approximation."[32] If what we want is the truth, they ask, why should the prosecutor be prevented from using reliable evidence simply because it was obtained from the defendant?

An alternative defense of the adversary system, perhaps one that is more to the point, is that it places a needed protective barrier between the potentially innocent defendant and the far more powerful state. In this context, the Supreme Court once observed:

> We have learned the lesson of history, ancient and modern, that a system of criminal law enforcement which comes to depend on the "confession" will, in the long run, be less reliable and more subject to abuses than a system which depends on extrinsic evidence independently secured through skillful investigation.[33]

However, even if the adversary system is justifiable on this ground, the question remains for consideration whether more truth–enhancing inquisitorial techniques may safely be permitted in the adversarial system.

---

[29] *See* Williams v. Florida, 399 U.S. 78 (1970).

[30] United States v. Cronic, 466 U.S. 648, 655 (1984) (*quoting* Lord Eldon in Kaufman, *Does the Judge Have a Right to Qualified Counsel?*, 61 A.B.A.J. 569, 569 (1975)).

[31] *See* Goodpaster, n. 22, *supra*, at 121–22.

[32] Frankel, n. 10, *supra*, at 1037.

[33] Escobedo v. Illinois, 378 U.S. 478, 488–89 (1962).

CHAPTER 3

INCORPORATION OF THE BILL OF RIGHTS

§ 8 The Issue of Incorporation [1]

The first eight amendments to the United States Constitution, the so–called Bill of Rights, adopted contemporaneously with the ratification of the Constitution, were designed to limit the power of the federal government in its relations to individuals.[2] They were not intended to restrict the actions of state government.

Most criminal prosecutions, however, originate in state courts. Consequently, the provisions of the Bill of Rights that pertain to criminal procedure — primarily, the fourth, fifth, sixth, and eighth amendments — have no direct effect on the majority of criminal cases that arise in this country.

The only constitutional amendment that sets limits on state action is the Fourteenth Amendment, adopted in 1868. Section 1 of that amendment limits the states in three ways:

> No State shall [1] make or enforce any law which shall abridge the privileges or immunities of citizens of the United States; [2] nor shall any State deprive any person of life, liberty, or property, without due process of law; [3] nor deny to any person within its jurisdiction the equal protection of the laws.[3]

The relationship, if any, of the Fourteenth Amendment to the provisions of the Bill of Rights is a matter of dispute. At the center of the debate, commonly called the "incorporation" debate, is the second clause of section 1, the due process clause.[4]

---

[1] *See generally* E. Meese, *Remarks Before the Meeting of the American Bar Association (July 9, 1985)*, in The Great Debate: Interpreting Our Written Constitution (Federalist Society 1986); Cord, *The Incorporation Doctrine and Procedural Due Process Under the Fourteenth Amendment: An Overview*, 1987 B.Y.U. L. Rev. 867; Crosskey, *Charles Fairman, "Legislative History," and the Constitutional Limitations on State Authority*, 22 U. Chi. L. Rev. 1 (1954); Douglas, *The Bill of Rights Is Not Enough*, 38 N.Y.U. L. Rev. 207 (1963); Fairman, *Does the Fourteenth Amendment Incorporate the Bill of Rights? The Original Understanding*, 2 Stan. L. Rev. 5 (1949); McDowell & Baer, *The Fourteenth Amendment: Should the Bill of Rights Apply to the States? The Disincorporation Debate*, 1987 Utah L. Rev. 951.

[2] Barron v. Baltimore, 32 U.S. (7 Pet.) 243 (1833).

[3] U.S. Const. amend. XIV, § 1 (numbers in brackets added).

[4] Early on, the Supreme Court rejected the argument that the Fourteenth Amendment privileges and immunities clause prohibits states from abridging the provisions of the Bill of Rights. The Court held that this clause only prevents states from abridging privileges and immunities inherent in national citizenship, which it determined that the provisions of the Bill of Rights are not. *See* Slaughter–House Cases, 83 U.S. (16 Wall.) 36 (1873).

The question at issue is this: To what extent, if at all, are the provisions of the Bill of Rights implicitly "incorporated" (or "nationalized") by the Fourteenth Amendment due process clause so as to restrict state action? Put another way, is the Fourteenth Amendment due process clause violated if an agent of the state denies a person one of the enumerated rights in the Bill of Rights? A related question is whether persons possess rights protected by the due process clause that are not enumerated in the Constitution.

The incorporation debate is important for various reasons. First, and most obvious, the extent to which individuals are protected from overreaching by state officers depends in large part on the extent to which the Fourteenth Amendment is interpreted to incorporate the Bill of Rights. At one extreme, if none of the provisions of the Bill of Rights applies to the states, a person may be subjected to, for example, unreasonable searches and seizures by local police, coercive police interrogation techniques, and reprosecution after acquittal.[5] On the other hand, if the due process clause incorporates the entirety of the Bill of Rights, the latter charter becomes a national code of criminal procedure: federal and state action would be restricted in identical ways.

Second, as the latter observation suggests, the values of federalism are at stake in the incorporation debate. The broader the scope of the Fourteenth Amendment due process clause, the less free the states are to develop their own rules of criminal procedure. Yet, uniformity among the states is said to be "inimical to traditional notions of federalism."[6]

Third, incorporationism raises questions regarding the proper role of the judiciary in the enforcement of constitutional rights. As discussed below, certain incorporation theories arguably exacerbate the risk that judges will apply their personal views of proper governmental action rather than the Constitution.

§ 9   Incorporation Theories

[A]   Total-Incorporationism

Justice Hugo Black was the judicial architect of an incorporation theory described as "total," "full," or "traditional" incorporationism.[7] This principle has never received the support of a majority of the members of the Supreme Court.

According to Black, "one of the chief objects that the provisions of the [Fourteenth] Amendment's first section, separately, and as a whole, were intended to accomplish was to make the Bill of Rights applicable to the states."[8] In other words, the Fourteenth Amendment in general, and the due process clause in particular, incorporates all of the rights included in the first eight amendments to the Constitution, no more and no less.

---

[5] However, the state constitution or a state statute might prohibit such conduct.

[6] Rummel v. Estelle, 445 U.S. 263, 282 (1980).

[7] See Adamson v. California, 332 U.S. 46, 68–123, reh'g denied, 332 U.S. 784 (1947) (Black, J. dissenting); Rochin v. California, 342 U.S. 165, 174–77 (1952) (Black, J., concurring).

[8] Adamson, 332 U.S. at 71–72.

[B] Fundamental-Rights Doctrine

In contrast to total–incorporationism is the "fundamental rights" or "ordered liberty" doctrine. Originally asserted in 1884,[9] this theory gained ascendancy in the 1930s with the influential support of Justices Cardozo[10] and Frankfurter.[11] The essence of this doctrine is that the Fourteenth Amendment "neither comprehends the specific provisions by which the founders deemed it appropriate to restrict the federal government nor is it confined to them. The Due Process Clause . . . has an independent potency. . . ."[12]

In other words, the due process clause is not a reflection of the provisions of the Bill of Rights, as total–incorporationism suggests. To fundamental–rights theorists, rights are not protected by the Fourteenth Amendment due process clause because or even if they are included in the first eight amendments, but rather if, and only if, "[t]o abolish them is . . . to violate a 'principle of justice so rooted in the traditions and consciences of our people as to be ranked as fundamental.' "[13]

Notice that, according to this doctrine, constitutional rights are not of equal importance. A right may be included in the Bill of Rights (and thus be protected against encroachment by the federal government) and yet not be deemed fundamental (and, therefore, not be protected against state overreaching). On the other hand, a right may be fundamental and yet not be included among the provisions of the Bill of Rights.

The Supreme Court has variously articulated the test by which "fundamentalness" is determined. A right is fundamental, for example, if it is "of the very essence of a scheme of ordered liberty," if a "fair and enlightened system of justice would be impossible without [it]," if it is "at the base of all our civil and political institutions," or if its denial would "offend those canons of decency and fairness which express the notions of justice of English–speaking people.[14] "

[C] Total-Incorporationism-Plus

Justices Murphy, Rutledge, and Douglas have offered the broadest interpretation of the Fourteenth Amendment. According to these jurists, the due process clause incorporates the Bill of Rights in its entirety (total–incorporationism) as well as all fundamental rights not specified in the Constitution (fundamental–rights doctrine).[15]

---

[9] See Hurtado v. California, 110 U.S. 516, 546 (1884) (Harlan, J., dissenting).

[10] See Palko v. Connecticut, 302 U.S. 319 (1937), overruled in Benton v. Maryland, 395 U.S. 784 (1969).

[11] E.g., Adamson, 332 U.S. at 59–68 (concurring opinion); Rochin, 342 U.S. at 166–74 (majority opinion).

[12] Adamson, 332 U.S. at 66 (Frankfurter, J., concurring).

[13] Palko, 302 U.S. at 325 (quoting Snyder v. Massachusetts, 291 U.S. 97, 105 (1934)).

[14] See generally the cases cited at ns. 10–11 supra.

[15] See Adamson, 332 U.S. at 123–25 (Murphy and Rutledge, JJ., dissenting); Poe v. Ullman, 367 U.S. 497, 516, reh'g denied, 368 U.S. 869 (1961) (Douglas, J., dissenting).

[D] Neo-Incorporationism (or Pseudo-Fundamental-Rights)

Neo–incorporationism includes features of both fundamental–rights theory and incorporationism without following the logic of either doctrine. It represents, as one judicial critic put it, "an uneasy and illogical compromise"[16] between the two doctrines.

Neo–incorporationists agree with fundamental–rights theorists that not all rights included in the Bill of Rights are inevitably absorbed by the Fourteenth Amendment. On the other hand, contrary to fundamental–rights theory and more in keeping with incorporationism, neo–incorporationists believe that once a right is determined to be fundamental, it is "applicable to the States with all the subtleties and refinements born of history and embodied in case experience developed in the context of federal adjudication."[17]

The latter quotation is critical to understanding why this theory conflicts with the doctrines from which it is derived. The point of fundamental–rights theory is that a right is protected by the due process clause because it is crucial to the maintenance of justice; its inclusion in the Bill of Rights is doctrinally irrelevant. Consequently, under the fundamental-rights theory, the constitutional law that has developed regarding the *federal* right is not determinative of the scope of the *state* version of the "same" right emanating from the Fourteenth Amendment.

For example, the Fourth Amendment prohibits unreasonable searches and seizures by federal officers. The Fourteenth Amendment also prohibits such conduct by state officers under the fundamental–rights theory.[18] However, according to the latter doctrine, it does not follow that the entirety of Fourth Amendment jurisprudence regarding what constitutes an "unreasonable search or seizure" is carried over to the Fourteenth Amendment.

Neo–incorporationism, however, absorbs "all of the bag and baggage"[19] of the provisions of the Bill of Rights: once a right is considered fundamental, every feature of the federal right applies to the states. That is why the doctrine of neo–incorporationism is a *pseudo*–fundamental–rights theory; in reality, although inclusion of the right in the Fourteenth Amendment is selective (only "fundamental rights" are protected by the due process clause), once it is identified as fundamental, the right mirrors the federal provision (*i.e.*, it is incorporated).

§ 10   The Incorporation Debate

[A]   General Comments

Judicial debate regarding the relationship of the Fourteenth Amendment to the Bill of Rights has focused on the comparative wisdom of total–incorporationism and fundamental–rights doctrine. Some of the debate is "interpretivist" in

---

[16] Duncan v. Louisiana, 391 U.S. 145, 172 *reh'g denied*, 392 U.S. 947 (1968) (Harlan, J., dissenting).

[17] Williams v. Florida, 399 U.S. 78, 130–31 (1970) (Harlan, J., concurring).

[18] Wolf v. Colorado, 338 U.S. 25 (1949), *overruled on other grounds* in Mapp v. Ohio, 367 U.S. 643 (1961).

[19] Duncan v. Louisiana, 391 U.S. at 213 (Fortas, J., dissenting).

nature.[20] That is, the discourse turns on concerns of textualism (*i.e.*, which theory is more consistent with the language of the Fourteenth Amendment?) and originalism (*i.e.*, which doctrine is more consistent with the original intent of the framers of the provision?).

Two other important considerations arise in the debate: libertarianism (*i.e.*, which due process theory is more protective of individual liberty?); and structuralism (*i.e.*, which theory is more consistent with concepts of federalism and separation–of–powers?). A brief review of the debate follows.

[B] What Did the Framers Intend?

Justice Black and some scholars have accumulated evidence that they believe supports their assertion that the framers of the Fourteenth Amendment intended to incorporate the entirety of the Bill of Rights.[21]

Other scholars[22] and justices of the Supreme Court have disputed this claim. For example, in 1947 Justice Frankfurter obliquely questioned the to-tal–incorporationist claim by observing that all but one ("an eccentric exception"[23]) of the Supreme Court justices who had previously considered the question had rejected total-incorporationism. Frankfurter doubted that the state legislatures that ratified the Fourteenth Amendment thought by doing so that they were agreeing to dismantle their own systems of criminal justice and replace them with the federal system.

A recent commentator has concluded that the framers' intent is "to a considerable degree . . . shrouded in the mists of history. There is simply no clear answer [to the historical question]."[24]

---

[20] "Interpretivism" is a relatively new term used to describe the not–so–new view of constitutional interpretation that judges should confine themselves to enforcing those rights that are expressed, or are clearly implicit in a constitution. The competing approach, non–interpretivism, asserts that judges should not interpret constitutions as they would examine contracts or statutes: they may look beyond the text and the intent of the authors to discover the meaning of a constitutional provision.

As this explanation suggests, the controversy between interpretivism and non–interpretivism is broader than that involving the due process clause. *See generally* J. Ely, Democracy and Distrust: A Theory of Judicial Review (Harvard 1980); M. Perry, The Constitution, the Courts and Human Rights (Yale 1987); Bork, *Neutral Principles and Some First Amendment Problems*, 47 Ind. L.J. 1 (1971); Ely, *Constitutional Interpretivism: Its Allure and Impossibility*, 53 Ind. L.J. 399 (1978) (hereafter Ely, *Constitutional Interpretivism*); Ely, *Foreword: On Discovering Fundamental Values*, 92 Harv. L. Rev. 5 (1978); Grey, *Do We Have an Unwritten Constitution?*, 27 Stan. L. Rev. 703 (1975); Perry, *Interpreting the Constitution*, 1987 B.Y.U. L. Rev. 1157; Wechsler, *Toward Neutral Principles of Constitutional Law*, 73 Harv. L. Rev. 1 (1959).

[21] Black provided a 31–page appendix to his dissent in *Adamson, supra* in support of his historical assertion; *see also* Crosskey, n. 1 *supra*.

[22] *E.g.*, Fairman, n. 1 *supra*.

[23] *Adamson*, 332 U.S. at 62.

[24] McDowell & Baer, n. 1 *supra*, at 956–57 (statement of McDowell in debate with Baer).

[C] Textual Claims: What Does "Due Process" Mean?

Opponents of incorporationism frequently point out that if the words "due process of law" are intended to incorporate the Bill of Rights, "it is a strange way of saying it."[25] If incorporationism was the Fourteenth Amendment's framers' purpose, why did they not say so directly? Why would they have used this oblique shorthand? Indeed, since the phrase "due process of law" also rests in the Fifth Amendment, why would the phrase mean one thing in the Fourteenth Amendment and another in the Fifth?[26]

Fundamental–rights adherents, however, are not out of the textual woods. "Due process of law" is also an odd way of saying "fundamental rights" or "rights implicit in the concept of ordered liberty." Indeed, in light of the fact that the due process clause has been interpreted to protect fundamental substantive rights not found in the Constitution, such as a procreative right of privacy,[27] it is hard to see how such a *substantive* right can be textually defended by language that speaks merely of providing due *process.*[28]

[D] Which Doctrine is More Libertarian?

Adherents of each theory claim that their respective approach is better equipped to protect individuals from governmental overreaching. On its face, total–incorporationism is more libertarian because, with one sweep of the wand, the entire Bill of Rights is nationalized. In contrast, the fundamental–rights doctrine is like an accordion: it can "periodically . . . expand and contract . . . to conform to the Court's conception of what at a particular time constitutes 'civilized decency' and 'fundamental liberty and justice.' "[29]

On the other hand, fundamental–rights doctrine allows for the recognition of constitutionally unenumerated rights. Thus, whereas incorporationists do not recognize a constitutional right of privacy because it is not expressed in the document, fundamental–rights theory permits such possibilities.

[E] Which Theory Is Structurally Preferable?

Incorporationism runs afoul of traditional views of federalism because it compels states to uproot their established methods for prosecuting crime and fastens upon them the federal version of due process. Under concepts of fundamental rights, states can run their criminal justice systems comparatively freely, as they must ensure only those rights that are considered to be essential to fundamental justice.

---

[25] *Adamson*, 332 U.S. at 63 (Frankfurter, J., concurring).

[26] That is, total–incorporationists believe that the Fourteenth Amendment due process clause is a shorthand for freedom of speech, freedom of religion, the right to bear arms, and so on; yet, in the Fifth Amendment the words "due process of law" could not logically have this meaning since these other rights are enumerated in the Bill of Rights.

[27] *See* Griswold v. Connecticut, 381 U.S. 479 (1965).

[28] Ely, *Constitutional Interpretivism*, n. 20 *supra*, at 419–20 ("There is simply no blinking the fact that the word that follows 'due' is 'process.' ").

[29] *Adamson*, 332 U.S. at 69 (Black, J., dissenting).

The fundamental–rights doctrine, however, is subject to criticism on separation–of–powers grounds. Incorporationists argue that one need only look at the various tests of "fundamental rights" to conclude that the latter doctrine invites judges "to roam at large in the broad expanses of policy and morals and to trespass, all too freely, on the legislative domain of the States, as well as the Federal Government."[30] The doctrine allows federal judges, unelected and serving life appointments, to behave like "dictators or philosopher kings."[31]

[F] Which Theory Has "Won"?

Precedent can be overruled, so no Fourteenth Amendment theory can gain a permanent victory in the Supreme Court. Nonetheless, various observations are possible. First, fundamental–rights doctrine has won the rhetorical war. No majority opinion of the Court has ever accepted total–incorporationism, nor does it have active support on the Court at this time.

Second, as a practical matter, and notwithstanding the first point, Justice Black's goal of incorporating the Bill of Rights has nearly been realized. In the realm of criminal procedure, all but two provisions of the Bill of Rights apply to the states, albeit via fundamental–rights analysis.[32] Also, in light of the advent of neo–incorporationism, these rights include all of the "baggage" from the federal system.

Finally, consistent with fundamental–rights doctrine, the Supreme Court has recognized rights not enumerated in the Constitution, such as a right to at least some forms of privacy. Thus, ironically, if "winners" are to be declared, they may be those few justices who favored total–incorporation–plus.

---

[30] *Id.* at 90 (Black, J., dissenting).

[31] Ely, *Constitutional Interpretivism*, n. 20 *supra*, at 445.

[32] The two rights not included are the Fifth Amendment provision that no person shall be held to answer for a serious crime except by indictment or presentment of a grand jury, *Hurtado v. California*, 110 U.S. 516 (1884), and the Eighth Amendment "no excessive bail" provision. The Supreme Court has not ruled on the fundamental–rights status of the latter provision.

CHAPTER **4**

GENERAL CONSTITUTIONAL LAW DOCTRINES

This chapter considers five constitutional law (or quasi–constitutional law) doctrines that are frequently asserted in criminal procedure litigation.

§ 11 Retroactivity[1]

[A] Explanation of the Issue

When the Supreme Court announces a new rule of constitutional law, it must ultimately determine whether the rule applies retroactively and, if so, to what extent.

For example, in 1949 the Supreme Court ruled in *Wolf v. Colorado*[2] that the Fourth Amendment exclusionary rule does not apply in state criminal trials. That is, under *Wolf,* evidence obtained by the police in violation of the constitutional prohibition on unreasonable searches and seizures was admissible in state criminal trials.

Twelve years later, the Court overruled *Wolf* in *Mapp v. Ohio.*[3] One implication of *Mapp* was obvious: the exclusionary–rule holding of the case applied prospectively. That is, evidence unconstitutionally seized by police officers *after Mapp* was handed down could no longer be introduced in state criminal trials.

But, another set of questions remained: Did *Mapp* apply retroactively and, if so, to what extent? Notice the possibilities of retroactive application. First, *Mapp* might only apply to post–*Mapp* trials involving evidence unconstitutionally seized before the *Mapp* exclusionary–rule holding was announced.

Second, the rule might apply retroactively to all criminal cases not yet final[4] when *Mapp* was announced, but to no other cases. Thus, a defendant whose trial

---

[1] *See generally* Beytagh, *Ten Years of Non–Retroactivity: A Critique and a Proposal,* 61 Va. L. Rev. 1557 (1975); Hoffman, *Retroactivity and the Great Writ: How Congress Should Respond to Teague v. Lane,* 1990 B.Y.U. L. Rev. 183; Hoffmann, *The Supreme Court's New Vision of Federal Habeas Corpus for State Prisoners,* 1989 Sup. Ct. Rev. 165 (hereafter Hoffmann, *New Vision*); Mishkin, *The High Court, The Great Writ, and the Due Process of Time and Law,* 79 Harv. L. Rev. 56 (1965); Schaefer, *Prospective Rulings: Two Perspectives,* 1982 Sup. Ct. Rev. 1; Schwartz, *Retroactivity, Reliability, and Due Process: A Reply to Professor Mishkin,* 33 U. Chi. L. Rev. 719 (1966); Weisberg, *A Great Writ While It Lasted,* 81 J. Crim. L. & Crimin. 9 (1990).

[2] 338 U.S. 25 (1949).

[3] 367 U.S. 643, *reh'g denied,* 368 U.S. 871 (1961).

[4] For purposes of retroactivity law, a conviction is "final" when the availability of direct appeals is exhausted and the time to petition for certiorari to the United States Supreme Court has elapsed or the petition to the Court has been finally denied. Linkletter v. Walker, 381 U.S. 618, 622 n.5 (1965).

was conducted *before Mapp* was decided, and thus when the evidence was "properly" (per *Wolf*) admitted, could take advantage of the new decision if it were handed down while he was appealing his conviction.

Finally, the new rule might be fully retroactive. That is, a person whose conviction was already final before *Mapp* was decided could collaterally attack his conviction in a habeas corpus proceeding on the basis that it was invalid under *Mapp*.[5]

Competing policies animate retroactivity debate. Opponents of retroactivity argue that a person only has a right to be treated in conformity with the rules in existence at the time of the disputed action. It is not unfair, therefore, to apply new rules prospectively only. Furthermore, full retroactive application of new constitutional rules impairs the desired finality of criminal judgments.

Proponents of full retroactive application of new rules respond that fundamentally like cases should be treated alike. They believe that it is unfair to deny the benefits of a new rule to people "languishing in prison who have suffered precisely the same deprivations at the hands of government that now invalidate the convictions of those fortunate enough to have run afoul of the law after, not before, the new constitutional rule was made effective."[6]

The Supreme Court has struggled with these and other policy concerns in an effort to develop a sensible jurisprudence of retroactivity. Current law is the result of a tortuous and inconsistent legal history.[7]

[B] Common Law of Retroactivity

Blackstone contended that judges in the common law era did not make law, but instead "discovered" or "declared" pre–existing law.[8] Therefore, when a court announced a legal principle in conflict with a prior judicial pronouncement on the subject, it was not declaring the previous ruling to be bad law, but rather was stating that it was not law at all. Applying Blackstone's theory to the constitutional example in subsection [A] above, *Mapp* did not announce new law; it merely stated the pre–existing law that the *Wolf* Court failed to discover.

The implication of the so-called "declaratory theory" of judicial decisionmaking was that the law announced by a court applied retroactively to all cases brought to the judiciary's attention.

[C] The *Linkletter* Doctrine

In general, the common law full–retroactivity principle applied to constitutional law until the Supreme Court's seminal decision in *Linkletter v. Walker*.[9]

In *Linkletter*, the Court considered the question of whether *Mapp* should be applied retroactively to grant relief to a habeas corpus petitioner whose conviction

---

[5] For an explanation of habeas corpus proceedings, *see* § 3[C][10] *supra*.

[6] Allen, *The Judicial Quest for Penal Justice: The Warren Court and the Criminal Cases*, 1975 U. Ill. L.F. 518, 529.

[7] Comment, *Retroactivity and the Exclusionary Rule: A Unifying Approach*, 97 Harv. L. Rev. 961, 961 (1984).

[8] *See* 1 W. Blackstone, Commentaries on the Laws of England, 69–70 (1769).

[9] 381 U.S. 618 (1965).

was final before *Wolf* was overruled. The Court rejected the common law automatic full–retroactivity rule, and replaced it with a three–factor test for determining whether, and to what extent, new constitutional rules would be applied retroactively.[10]

Predictably, *Linkletter* resulted in "incompatible rules and inconsistent principles."[11] Some new rules were applied prospectively only, other new rules (as in *Linkletter*) were applied retroactively to cases not yet final when the new law was announced, whereas still other rules received full retroactive application, *i.e.*, the new rules were applied to all cases, including those already final when they were handed down.

[D] Abandonment of *Linkletter*

[1] Cases Not Yet Final: Direct Review

Legal scholars had a "field day"[12] with the post–*Linkletter* decisions, criticizing them for their inconsistency. However, the most influential critic of the Court's retroactivity jurisprudence was one of its members, Justice John Harlan, who called on his colleagues to rethink retroactivity law.[13]

The linchpin of Harlan's analysis was that constitutionally similar cases should ordinarily be treated alike. As he put it, it is wrong for the Court to "fish[] one case from the stream of appellate review, using it as a vehicle for pronouncing new constitutional standards, and then permit[] a stream of similar cases subsequently to flow by unaffected by that new rule."[14]

In 1982, the Supreme Court shifted course, agreeing with Justice Harlan that its retroactivity law needed to be rethought, and embracing to a significant degree his criticism of its prior retroactivity jurisprudence.[15]

In 1987, in *Griffith v. Kentucky*,[16] the Court clearly broke with the past and formally abandoned *Linkletter*'s three–factor test and adopted, per Harlan's suggestion, the retroactivity principle that "a new rule . . . is to be applied retroactively to all cases, state or federal, pending on direct review or not yet final. . . ." This rule is the law today.

---

[10] The three factors were: "(a) the purpose to be served by the new standards, (b) the extent of the reliance by law enforcement authorities on the old standards, and (c) the effect on the administration of justice of a retroactive application of the new standards." Stovall v. Denno, 388 U.S. 293, 297 (1967).

[11] Desist v. United States, 394 U.S. 244, 258, *reh'g denied*, 395 U.S. 931 (1969) (Harlan, J., dissenting).

[12] Beytagh, n. 1 *supra*, at 1558.

[13] Desist v. United States, 394 U.S. at 256–69 (dissenting opinion); Mackey v. United States, 401 U.S. 667, 675–702 (1971) (separate opinion).

[14] Mackey, 401 U.S. at 679.

[15] United States v. Johnson, 457 U.S. 537 (1982).

[16] 479 U.S. 314 (1987).

[2] Cases Already Final: Collateral Review

[a] General Rule

Justice Harlan also advocated abandonment of the *Linkletter* formula in cases subject to collateral habeas corpus review. However, in light of society's interest in leaving litigation in a state of final repose, he believed that in adjudicating habeas corpus petitions, courts should ordinarily apply the law prevailing at the time the petitioner's conviction became final, *i.e.*, new rules should not apply retroactively to convictions already final.

Until 1989, the Supreme Court resisted Justice Harlan's approach to habeas corpus review. However, beginning with the plurality opinion in *Teague v. Lane*,[17] which became a majority holding in *Penry v. Lynaugh*,[18] the Supreme Court adopted Harlan's no–retroactivity principle in the context of habeas proceedings. It will no longer announce or apply new rules in cases on collateral review unless they fall within one of two exceptions.[19]

The first exception is that a new rule will be applied retroactively to a case on collateral review if it "place[s] an entire category of primary conduct beyond the reach of the criminal law, . . . [or] prohibit[s] imposition of a certain punishment for a class of defendants because of their status or offense."[20] For example, a new rule that decriminalizes possession of obscene literature in the home[21] would be applied retroactively to cases on collateral review, as would a new rule that the death penalty may not be imposed on adults convicted of rape.[22]

Second, a new rule will be applied on collateral review if it requires the observance of a "watershed rule of criminal procedure"[23] that is necessary to guarantee the fundamental fairness of the criminal proceeding, *i.e.*, a rule "without which the likelihood of an accurate conviction is seriously diminished."[24] This exception has been explained as follows:

> It is . . . not enough . . . to say that a new rule is aimed at improving the accuracy of [a] trial. More is required. A rule that qualifies under this

---

[17] 489 U.S. 288, *reh'g denied*, 109 S.Ct. 1771 (1989).

[18] 109 S.Ct. 2934 (1989).

[19] The issue of retroactivity is now treated as a "threshold question." *Teague*, 489 U.S. at 306. That is, the Supreme Court will no longer consider a case on its merits unless and until it determines that any new rule it might announce would apply to the immediate case. The practical effect of the threshold requirement, in view of the Court's no–retroactivity–in–habeas–cases principle, is that the Supreme Court will review virtually no habeas petitions from incarcerated state defendants in the future. Typically, a habeas petition will either raise uninteresting legal issues (*i.e.*, that a lower court misapplied an old rule, which is ordinarily treated as an uncertworthy matter) or will raise interesting new issues that cannot be decided in the petitioner's favor because it would require the implementation of a new rule. In the long run, this will mean that constitutional decision-making will shift to the state courts. Hoffmann, *New Vision*, n. 1 *supra*, at 187.

[20] Sawyer v. Smith, 110 S.Ct. 2822, 2831 (1990).

[21] *See* Stanley v. Georgia, 394 U.S. 557 (1964).

[22] *See* Coker v. Georgia, 433 U.S. 584 (1977).

[23] *Teague*, 489 S.Ct. at 311.

[24] *Id.* at 313.

exception must not only improve accuracy, but also "alter our understanding of the *bedrock procedural elements*" essential to the fairness of a proceeding.[25] For example, the rule that an indigent defendant is entitled to representation by counsel at trial[26] is entitled to full retroactive application.

[b]   Meaning of "New Rule"

A constitutional rule is "new," and thus will ordinarily not be applied retroactively to convictions already final, if: (1) it "breaks new ground or imposes a new obligation on the States or the Federal Government," such as when the Supreme Court expressly overrules a prior decision; or (2) "the result was not *dictated* by precedent existing at the time the defendant's conviction became final."[27]

Because the Supreme Court rarely overrules earlier decisions, the second type of "new rule" is more significant and, the Court has conceded,[28] less easy to identify. However, the Court has warned that a case announces a "new rule" even if its holding is within the "logical compass" of a previous holding or even if it is "controlled" by it, unless a lower court considering the petitioner's claim "at the time his conviction became final would have felt compelled by existing precedent"[29] to rule in his favor.

The stated purpose of this broad definition of "new rule" is to "ensure that gradual developments in the law over which reasonable jurists may disagree are not later used to upset the finality of state convictions valid when entered."[30]

§ 12   Waiver of Constitutional Rights[31]

A person may waive virtually any constitutional right during a criminal investigation or prosecution. Consequently, issues of waiver permeate criminal procedure litigation and are discussed throughout this text.

[A]   Definition of "Waiver": The *Zerbst* Test

In *Johnson v. Zerbst*,[32] the Supreme Court defined "waiver" as "an intentional relinquishment or abandonment of a known right or privilege." The Court has said that it is "unyielding in [its] insistence"[33] that the *Zerbst* doctrine be strictly

---

[25] Sawyer v. Smith, 110 S.Ct. at 2831 (*quoting Teague*, which in turn quoted Justice Harlan in Mackey v. United States, 401 U.S. at 693).

[26] Gideon v. Wainwright, 372 U.S. 335 (1963).

[27] *Teague*, 489 S.Ct. at 301.

[28] Butler v. McKellar, 110 S.Ct. 1212, 1216, *reh'g denied*, 110 S.Ct. 1941 (1990).

[29] Saffle v. Parks, 110 S.Ct. 1257, 1260, *reh'g denied*, 110 S.Ct. 1940 (1990).

[30] Sawyer v. Smith, 110 S.Ct. at 2827.

[31] *See generally* Dix, *Waiver in Criminal Procedure: A Brief for More Careful Analysis*, 55 Tex. L. Rev. 193 (1977); Rubin, *Toward a General Theory of Waiver*, 28 UCLA L. Rev. 478 (1981); Stuntz, *Waiving Rights in Criminal Procedure*, 75 Va. L. Rev. 761 (1989); Tigar, *Waiver of Constitutional Rights: Disquiet in the Citadel*, 84 Harv. L. Rev. 1 (1970); Westen, *Away From Waiver: A Rationale for the Forfeiture of Constitutional Rights in Criminal Procedure*, 75 Mich. L. Rev. 1214 (1977).

[32] 304 U.S. 458 (1938).

[33] Illinois v. Rodriguez, 110 S.Ct. 2793, 2798 (1990).

enforced when the government asserts that a defendant has relinquished a right that protects a fair criminal trial.

The *Zerbst* definition of waiver is divisible into three parts. First, the person must in fact have relinquished or abandoned the right in question.[34] Second, the relinquishment must be "voluntary in the sense that it was the product of a free and deliberate choice rather than intimidation, coercion or deception."[35] Third, the right–holder must be aware of the nature of the right and of the primary consequences of its relinquishment.[36]

Under *Zerbst*, the validity of a waiver is based on the totality of the circumstances of the particular case. However, a court is required to "indulge every reasonable presumption against waiver" of constitutional rights.

[B] Non-"Waiver" Relinquishment of Constitutional Rights

The Supreme Court does not treat every relinquishment or loss of a right as a "waiver." Therefore, the *Zerbst* rule does not apply to every case in which a person fails to invoke a constitutional protection.

For example, a person who permits the police to conduct what would otherwise be a constitutionally unreasonable search, *i.e.*, a warrantless search or a search not founded on probable cause, is not said to have "waived" his Fourth Amendment rights, but rather to have "consented" to the warrantless search. The consent, if voluntarily granted, renders the search reasonable, even if the person was unaware of his right to refuse to consent.[37]

Similarly, a defendant who requests a mistrial due to prosecutorial misconduct ordinarily may be prosecuted again for the same offense, notwithstanding the Fifth Amendment double–jeopardy prohibition, although it would be plausible to argue in such a case that the defendant was coerced by the misconduct into making the mistrial motion. According to the Supreme Court, "waiver" principles do not apply in this context; instead, the issue is whether the defendant retained primary control over the course to be followed in the case of governmental misconduct.[38]

Sometimes a right is lost as a matter of law without any regard to the right–holder's wishes or knowledge of the conditions that gave rise to the loss. For example, a defendant may lose his constitutional right to be present at his own trial if he is disruptive in the courtroom.[39] He also is precluded from raising constitutional defenses if he does not bring them to the court's attention in timely fashion.[40] Although courts do not always make the point clear, the loss of a right in such circumstances involves a "forfeiture"[41] of the right in question, or a "preclusionary penalty,"[42] rather than a "waiver."

[34] *See* Brewer v. Williams, 430 U.S. 387, *reh'g denied*, 431 U.S. 925 (1977).
[35] Moran v. Burbine, 475 U.S. 412, 421 (1986).
[36] *Id.*
[37] Schneckloth v. Bustamonte, 412 U.S. 218 (1973). *See* § 90 *infra*.
[38] United States v. Dinitz, 424 U.S. 600 (1976). *See* § 200[C][1] *infra*.
[39] Illinois v. Allen, 397 U.S. 337, *reh'g denied*, 398 U.S. 915 (1970).
[40] *E.g.*, FRCP 12(f).
[41] *See* Westen, n. 31 *supra*, at 1214–19.
[42] Dix, n. 31 *supra*, at 209.

§ 13 Harmless Error[43]

[A] Nonconstitutional Trial Error

Given human fallibility, there is rarely such a thing as an error–free trial.[44] It is unfair to the public, therefore, and wasteful of finite judicial and prosecutorial resources, to overturn convictions and conduct new trials whenever any error, no matter how trivial, occurs. Nonetheless, until the twentieth century, state and federal appellate courts usually reversed convictions automatically if they discovered an error in the trial process.

Today, a conviction will ordinarily not be overturned if a nonconstitutional trial error was "harmless." No single test of harmlessness has developed, although the federal rule, originally adopted by statute in 1919,[45] and now incorporated in the Federal Rules of Criminal Procedure,[46] is that an error is harmless if "it does not affect substantial rights."

The Supreme Court has interpreted this rule to mean that "if one cannot say, with fair assurance, after pondering all that happened . . . that the judgment was not substantially swayed by the error, [then] it is impossible to conclude that substantial rights were not affected."[47]

[B] Constitutional Trial Error: The *Chapman* Rule

Few broad doctrines of constitutional criminal procedure are more important than the constitutional harmless-error doctrine or, for short, *Chapman*[48] rule.

Until the 1960s, most courts believed that if any constitutional error occurred during a trial, *e.g.*, evidence obtained in violation of the Fourth Amendment was admitted, the subsequent conviction had to be overturned. In *Chapman v. California*, however, the Supreme Court held that a conviction need not be overturned because of a constitutional error if no prejudice resulted from the mistake.

Under the rule announced in *Chapman*, "the beneficiary of a constitutional error" — the government — must prove beyond a reasonable doubt that the error was harmless, *i.e.*, "that the error complained of did not contribute to the verdict

---

[43] *See generally* Goldberg, *Harmless Error: Constitutional Sneak Thief,* 71 J. Crim. L. & Criminology 421 (1980); Mause, *Harmless Constitutional Error: The Implications of Chapman v. California,* 53 Minn. L. Rev. 519 (1969); Saltzburg, *The Harm of Harmless Error,* 59 Va. L. Rev. 988 (1973); Stacy & Dayton, *Rethinking Harmless Constitutional Error,* 88 Colum. L. Rev. 79 (1988).

[44] United States v. Hasting, 461 U.S. 499, 508–09 (1983).

[45] 28 U.S.C. § 391.

[46] FRCP 52(a).

[47] Kotteakos v. United States, 328 U.S. 750, 765 (1946). A nonconstitutional error that occurs in the pre–trial context is "harmless unless the court concludes from the record as a whole that the error may have had a 'substantial influence' on the outcome of the proceedings." United States v. Montalvo–Murillo, 110 S.Ct. 2072, 2080 (1990); *see also* Bank of Nova Scotia v. United States, 487 U.S. 250, 256 (1988). For further discussion of nonconstitutional harmless–error doctrine, *see* Saltzburg, n. 43 *supra*, at 998–1012.

[48] Chapman v. California, 386 U.S. 18 (1967).

obtained." In other words, a conviction will be upheld, notwithstanding the constitutional error(s) at trial, if the prosecutor convinces the appellate court to a moral certainty[49] that, but for the error(s), the same verdict would have been obtained.

The *Chapman* rule is grounded on the view that a defendant in a criminal trial is entitled "to a fair trial, not a perfect one," and "that the central purpose of a criminal trial is to decide the factual question of the defendant's guilt or innocence."[50] If overwhelming error–free evidence exists of the defendant's guilt, the trial has fulfilled its mission and, therefore, the conviction should not be reversed.

Although the *Chapman* rule applies to most constitutional trial errors,[51] it is a controversial doctrine. Among the criticisms of it are the following. First, one supposed benefit of the rule — more efficient use of judicial resources — is largely illusory because a conscientious court must expend considerable resources carefully inspecting the record in order to determine whether the trial errors were harmless.

Second, *Chapman* assumes that appellate courts can "reconstruct the world of the criminal trial"[52] by subtracting the constitutionally inadmissible evidence that the violation produced and/or by adding to the trial testimony the evidence that the constitutional violation kept from the factfinder, so as to determine whether the violation(s) contributed to the verdict. But, such reconstruction requires a court to speculate regarding a counter–factual reality. How can a court say with confidence what a jury would have done in that entirely different and non–existent world?

Third, as the latter criticism suggests, the *Chapman* rule requires appellate courts to function as an appellate jury, a role for which it is particularly ill–suited. Critics argue that appellate courts should only be expected to focus "on the *process* used at trial rather than on the *evidence* that process produced."[53]

Finally, the *Chapman* rule acts like a "constitutional sneak thief."[54] The gist of the criticism is that the harmless–error rule, by focusing on the reliability of the verdict, de–emphasizes the importance of enforcing the constitutional rights that were violated and of deterring future violations. In effect, the harmless–error

---

[49] Basically, this is what is meant by "proof beyond a reasonable doubt." J. Dressler, at § 7.03[C].

[50] Delaware v. Van Arsdall, 475 U.S. 673, 681 (1986).

[51] *E.g.*, Delaware v. Van Arsdall, 475 U.S. 673 (1986) (confrontation clause error); United States v. Hasting, 461 U.S. 499 (1983) (impermissible prosecutorial comment on *D*'s silence, in violation of the Fifth Amendment self–incrimination clause); Moore v. Illinois, 434 U.S. 220 (1977) (introduction at trial of a pre–trial identification procedure conducted in violation of *D*'s right to counsel); Rushen v. Spain, 464 U.S. 114 (1983) (right to be present at trial); Milton v. Wainwright, 407 U.S. 371 (1972) (introduction at trial of a confession obtained in violation of *D*'s right to counsel); Chambers v. Maroney, 399 U.S. 42, *reh'g denied*, 400 U.S. 856 (1970) (introduction of evidence obtained in violation of the Fourth Amendment).

[52] Weisberg, *Criminal Procedure Doctrine: Some Versions of the Skeptical*, 76 J. Crim. L. & Crimin. 832, 846 (1985).

[53] *The Supreme Court – Leading Cases*, 100 Harv. L. Rev. 100, 116 (1986).

[54] Goldberg, n. 43 *supra*, at 421.

doctrine, which is not expressed in the Constitution, trumps explicit constitutional rights.

[C] *Per Se* Prejudicial Constitutional Error

Some constitutional rights are considered so basic to a fair trial that their violation is never treated as harmless error, *i.e.*, in such cases the *Chapman* harmless–error rule does not apply.

An error is prejudicial *per se* in two classes of situations. First, the *per se* rule is invoked when the trial error itself makes it very difficult to determine whether the defendant was prejudiced. For example, if *D* is denied an attorney at trial[55] or is represented by a lawyer with an active conflict of interest,[56] it is nearly impossible to gauge what would have occurred if *D* had been provided a conflict–free attorney.

Second, *Chapman* does not apply if the likelihood of prejudice is so great that it is wasteful of judicial resources to invoke harmless–error analysis. Examples are: the introduction of a coerced confession at trial;[57] adjudication by a biased judge;[58] and selection of a jury by a judge without jurisdiction to preside over the procedure.[59]

§ 14 Supervisory Power[60]

When a federal court renders a decision in the field of criminal procedure, its source of authority is usually the Constitution, a federal statute, or a provision of the Federal Rules of Criminal Procedure. Occasionally, however, the Supreme Court and lower federal courts exercise their so–called "supervisory power" or "supervisory authority" over the federal courts.

This power was first invoked by the Supreme Court in 1943 in *McNabb v. United States*.[61] In *McNabb*, the justices were troubled because federal law

---

[55] Gideon v. Wainwright, 372 U.S. 335 (1963); *see also* Geders v. United States, 425 U.S. 80 (1976) (direct interference with the defendant's counsel, such as by ordering *D* not to consult with his attorney during an overnight recess, constitutes *per se* error); McKaskle v. Wiggins, 465 U.S. 168 (1984) (denial of *D*'s constitutional right of self–representation constitutes *per se* error).

[56] Holloway v. Arkansas, 435 U.S. 475 (1978).

[57] Payne v. Arkansas, 356 U.S. 560 (1958). This prejudicial-error rule was recently called into question. *See* Arizona v. Fulminante, 161 Ariz. 237, 778 P.2d 602 (1989), *cert. granted*, 110 S. Ct. 1522 (1990) (89-839). An issue raised in *Fulminante* is: "Can [an] erroneous admission of [an] involuntary confession be subjected to harmless error analysis in [a] case in which there is overwhelming evidence of guilt. . . ." 58 U.S.L.W. 3614 (Mar. 26. 1990).

[58] Tumey v. Ohio, 273 U.S. 510 (1927).

[59] Gomez v. United States, 109 S.Ct. 2237 (1989).

[60] *See generally* Beale, *Reconsidering Supervisory Power in Criminal Cases: Constitutional and Statutory Limits on the Authority of the Federal Courts*, 84 Colum. L. Rev. 1433 (1984); Dix, *Nonconstitutional Exclusionary Rules in Criminal Procedure*, 27 Am. Crim. L. Rev. 53 (1989); Hill, *The Bill of Rights and the Supervisory Power*, 69 Colum. L. Rev. 181 (1969); Note, *The Supervisory Power of the Federal Courts*, 76 Harv. L. Rev. 1656 (1963).

[61] 318 U.S. 332, *reh'g denied*, 319 U.S. 784 (1943).

enforcement agents were regularly violating a statute that required them to take arrested persons before the nearest available federal magistrate "without unnecessary delay."[62] Although the statute provided no remedy for its violation, the justices, exercising their supervisory authority, held that any confession obtained by the police during an unlawful detention was inadmissible at trial even if it was obtained voluntarily.

Since then, exercise of the supervisory power has become commonplace, particularly in the lower federal courts.[63] For example, federal circuit courts and district judges have suppressed evidence obtained by prosecutors in violation of ethical canons,[64] have restricted use of hearsay evidence in grand jury proceedings,[65] have recognized new evidentiary privileges at trial,[66] and have developed procedures for taking guilty pleas.[67]

It is important to distinguish constitutional decisionmaking from supervisory rulings. The Supreme Court's constitutional jurisprudence has national scope; the supervisory authority extends only within the federal system. Similarly, a circuit court's supervisory power cannot extend beyond the district courts in its circuit. It is also easier to repeal a supervisory rule: not only may the court that promulgated it change its mind (or a higher federal court overrule it), but because it is not based on constitutional principles a supervisory ruling may be revised or negated by Congress.[68]

Courts and commentators have questioned the source of the federal courts' supervisory authority. The Supreme Court once suggested that the power emanates from a federal statute,[69] but this view is no longer generally accepted. Instead, the power apparently arises from article III of the Constitution, which confers general judicial power on the federal courts.[70] Although article III does not expressly grant federal courts supervisory authority, advocates of the use of the power argue that it is implied or inherent in the judicial role.

One constitutional law scholar, Professor Sara Beale, believes that "[s]upervisory power as such does not exist,"[71] although she believes that some judicial exercises of authority under the "supervisory power" label are legitimate on other grounds. She doubts that circuit courts have authority to establish procedural rules for the district courts, and she contends that the Supreme Court, in the absence of statutory authority, has inherent power only to develop rules that relate to the

---

[62] The statutory requirement is now incorporated in FRCP 5(a).

[63] *See* Beale, n. 60 *supra*, at 1448–64.

[64] *See* United States v. Hammad, 858 F.2d 834 (2d Cir. 1988); United States v. Thomas, 474 F.2d 110 (10th Cir.), *cert. denied*, 412 U.S. 932 (1973); United States v. Howard, 426 F. Supp. 1067 (W.D.N.Y. 1977).

[65] United States v. Estepa, 471 F.2d 1132 (2d Cir. 1972).

[66] Mullen v. United States, 263 F.2d 275 (D.C. Cir. 1958).

[67] Moody v. United States, 497 F.2d 359 (7th Cir. 1974).

[68] For example, Congress responded to the *McNabb* rule by enacting 18 U.S.C. § 3501(c), which provides in part that "a confession . . . shall not be inadmissible solely because of delay in bringing such person before a [magistrate]. . . ."

[69] La Buy v. Howes Leather Co., 352 U.S. 249, 259, *reh'g denied*, 352 U.S. 1019 (1957) (invoking the All Writs Act, 28 U.S.C. § 1651).

[70] Beale, n. 60 *supra*, at 1464.

[71] *Id.* at 1520.

efficiency and reliability of the judicial process (*e.g.*, rules that reduce the risk of perjured testimony). Supervisory rulings intended to influence the police and other extrajudicial parties are improper, according to Beale.

Although the Supreme Court continues to exercise its claimed supervisory authority on occasion, it has sent a clear message to lower courts that they may not use the power to undercut the high court's constitutional jurisprudence. Two cases demonstrate the Court's modern view.

In *United States v. Payner*,[72] Internal Revenue Service agents hired a private investigator to search for and photograph the contents of a bank official's briefcase, which resulted in incriminating evidence against a third person, *D*. Under Fourth Amendment "standing" law, D could not object to the search, although it was unconstitutional, because it was the bank official's, and not *D*'s, briefcase that was searched.

The district court found that the I.R.S. not only knew of the illegal activity but counseled its agents on how to use standing rules to avoid Fourth Amendment strictures. Troubled by this, the trial court exercised supervisory power to exclude the evidence obtained from the briefcase, in spite of standing rules.

The Supreme Court reversed this action. Although it stated that it understood the court's "commendable desire" to deter deliberate lawless activities by government agents, the Court held that lower courts are not permitted to upset the "careful balance of interests" embodied in previous constitutional decisions, even in the context of nonconstitutional supervisory law.

In a second case, *United States v. Hasting*,[73] a federal circuit court, concerned that prosecutors repeatedly were violating a constitutional rule announced by the Supreme Court, used its supervisory power to reverse a conviction without consideration of whether the violation in the case was prejudicial under the harmless–error rule.

The Supreme Court reversed the circuit court's actions on grounds similar to *Payner*. It ruled that lower courts may not invoke their supervisory authority "in a vacuum." In particular, a reviewing court may not ignore constitutional harmless–error doctrine in the exercise of its supervisory power.[74]

§ 15   Prophylactic Rules[75]

The Supreme Court occasionally identifies a rule that it has promulgated as "prophylactic" in nature, although it has not defined this term. The most

---

[72] 447 U.S. 727, *reh'g denied*, 448 U.S. 911 (1980).

[73] 461 U.S. 499 (1983).

[74] *See also* Bank of Nova Scotia v. United States, 487 U.S. 250 (1988) (a federal court may not invoke its supervisory power to circumvent harmless error inquiry prescribed by FRCP 52(a)).

[75] *See generally* Grano, *Prophylactic Rules in Criminal Procedure: A Question of Article III Legitimacy*, 80 Nw. U. L. Rev. 100 (1985); Monaghan, *Constitutional Common Law*, 89 Harv. L. Rev. 1 (1975); Strauss, *The Ubiquity of Prophylactic Rules*, 55 U. Chi. L. Rev. 190 (1988).

well–known example of a "prophylactic" rule is the *Miranda*[76] doctrine, which requires the police to inform suspects in custody of various constitutional rights before they undergo interrogation.

Commentators disagree as to whether a prophylactic rule ought to be considered constitutional in nature. Professor Joseph Grano defines a prophylactic rule as one "that functions as a preventive safeguard to insure that constitutional violations will not occur."[77] In his taxonomy, a "prophylactic constitutional rule" is not a "true constitutional rule" because it is possible to violate a prophylactic rule without actually violating the Constitution itself. Grano's analysis finds support in Supreme Court language relevant to the *Miranda* rule.[78]

If Professor Grano's analysis is correct, the identification of a rule as "prophylactic" in nature has two potentially broad implications. First, if a prophylactic rule is not constitutional in nature, it arguably should not apply to the states. Yet, the Supreme Court continues to enforce prophylactic rules in appeals from state convictions. Second, Congress might have authority to override judicially–developed prophylactic rules.

Not all commentators agree with Grano's analysis. Some view prophylactic rules as a form of constitutional common law, in which the Court develops "a substructure of. . . rules drawing their inspiration and authority from, but [which are] not required by, various constitutional provisions."[79] Based on this understanding, prophylactic rules are constitutional in nature, apply to the states, and cannot be overruled by Congress.

However this debate is ultimately resolved, the identification of a rule as "prophylactic" has at least one significant practical legal implication. As discussed elsewhere in this text,[80] evidence that would be inadmissible at trial if it were the product of a pure constitutional violation may, in some circumstances, be introduced at trial if it was the fruit of a violation of a prophylactic rule.

---

[76] Miranda v. Arizona, 384 U.S. 436, *reh'g denied*, 385 U.S. 890 (1966).

[77] Grano, n. 75 *supra*, at 105 (footnote deleted).

[78] *See* Oregon v. Elstad, 470 U.S. 298, 306 (1985) ("The *Miranda* exclusionary rule . . . serves the Fifth Amendment and sweeps more broadly than the Fifth Amendment itself. *It may be triggered even in the absence of a Fifth Amendment violation.*") (footnote deleted) (emphasis added).

[79] Monaghan, n. 75 *supra*, at 2–3.

[80] *See* §§ 147[C][3], 155[D], *infra* .

CHAPTER **5**

FOURTH AMENDMENT: OVERVIEW

This chapter should be read by students before beginning the study of the Fourth Amendment. All of the matters considered here are covered in greater depth in chapters 6–21.

§ 16 Fourth Amendment: The Text[1]

The Fourth Amendment to the United States Constitution is 54 words long. It reads:

> The right of the people to be secure in their persons, houses, papers, and effects, against unreasonable searches and seizures, shall not be violated, and no Warrants shall issue, but upon probable cause, supported by Oath or affirmation, and particularly describing the place to be searched, and the persons or things to be seized.

As one commentator has stated, the amendment is "brief, vague, general, [and] unilluminating."[2] For almost a century the text remained "largely unexplored territory."[3] It did not take "full flower"[4] until 1961, when the Supreme Court extended the provision's judicially–implied exclusionary rule to the states.[5]

Perhaps due to the generalities of the Fourth Amendment, "the course of true law pertaining to [it] . . . has not . . . run smooth."[6] The single sentence that constitutes the Fourth Amendment has resulted in billions of words of interpretive text by the Supreme Court, state and lower federal courts, and commentators. As

---

[1] By far the best Fourth Amendment research source is Professor Wayne LaFave's 4–volume treatise on the subject (*see* Frequent Sources, for a full citation).

For shorthand purposes, this text speaks of the provisions of the Fourth Amendment as if they applied directly to the states, although it is the Fourteenth Amendment due process clause that recognizes the fundamental right to be secure from unreasonable searches and seizures by state agents. Wolf v. Colorado, 338 U.S. 25 (1949), *overruled on other grounds*, Mapp v. Ohio, 367 U.S. 643 (1961).

[2] Amsterdam, at 353–54.

[3] J. Landynski, Search and Seizure and the Supreme Court; A Study in Constitutional Interpretation 49 (Johns Hopkins 1966).

[4] LaFave, *The Fourth Amendment Today: A Bicentennial Appraisal*, 32 Vill. L. Rev. 1061, 1064 (1987).

[5] Mapp v. Ohio, 367 U.S. 643, *reh'g denied*, 368 U.S. 871 (1961).

[6] Chapman v. United States, 365 U.S. 610, 618 (1961) (Frankfurter, J., concurring).

45

a result, the Fourth Amendment today looks to some like a Rorschach blot;[7] its jurisprudence has been described as the "Supreme Court's tarbaby."[8]

§ 17 Historical Purposes of the Fourth Amendment

The evils that the framers of the Fourth Amendment had foremost in their mind — the "aboriginal subject of the fourth amendment"[9] — were the so-called "general warrants" that issued in England, and their counterpart, the "writs of assistance," enforced in the colonies, that gave the government indiscriminate authority to search people's homes and property.[10]

Specifically, general warrants authorized government agents to enter and search houses for books and papers for use in seditious libel prosecutions. Writs of assistance empowered customs officers to search houses and other places at will, and to break open containers found during their searches, whenever they suspected uncustomed goods inside.

Although general warrants and writs of assistance constituted the immediate evils that the framers sought to prohibit, the Supreme Court has concluded "that the evil the Amendment was designed to prevent was broader than the[se] abuse[s]."[11]

The original interpretation of the Fourth Amendment was that it was intended to prevent violations of the "sacred and incommunicable" right to private property, which was described as "[t]he great end for which men entered into society."[12] The more recent view of the amendment is that the framers intended to protect people's legitimate expectations of privacy, rather than property rights *per se*.[13] Under both historical interpretations, "physical entry of the home is the chief evil against which the . . . Fourth Amendment is directed."[14]

§ 18 Standing to Raise Fourth Amendment Claims

A defendant in a criminal prosecution may not raise a claim of a Fourth Amendment violation unless she is the alleged victim of the unreasonable search or seizure. In other words, Fourth Amendment rights are personal; they may not be vicariously asserted.

---

[7] Amsterdam, at 375.

[8] Bradley, *Two Models of the Fourth Amendment*, 83 Mich. L. Rev. 1468, 1468 (1985) (the case law is "a mass of contradictions and obscurities that has ensnared the 'Brethren' in such a way that every effort to extract themselves only finds them more profoundly stuck.").

[9] Amsterdam, at 363.

[10] *See* Warden v. Hayden, 387 U.S. 294 (1967); Payton v. New York, 445 U.S. 573 (1980).

[11] Payton v. New York, 445 U.S. at 585.

[12] Boyd v. United States, 116 U.S. 616, 627 (1886) (*quoting* Lord Camden).

[13] *See* Katz v. United States, 389 U.S. 347 (1967).

[14] United States v. United States District Court, 407 U.S. 297, 313 (1972).

As a conceptual matter, "standing" to raise a Fourth Amendment claim is a threshold issue. That is, a defense lawyer who wishes to have evidence that was seized by the police suppressed at trial under the Fourth Amendment "exclusionary rule" (*see* § 19) must first demonstrate that her client is the alleged victim of the unreasonable search or seizure.

The Supreme Court no longer treats the issue of standing separately from the substantive merits of the defendant's Fourth Amendment claim. Nonetheless, it remains preferable to treat standing as a distinct inquiry, because it is possible to have standing to raise a claim that will ultimately be lost on the merits, just as there are cases in which Fourth Amendment interests have been violated, but the particular person who wishes to raise the claim is not the victim of the violation.

§ 19   Exclusionary Rule

The issue of the scope of the Fourth Amendment — *i.e.*, what constitutes an "unreasonable search or seizure" — must be distinguished from the question of what remedy is available to a victim of a Fourth Amendment violation.

In a criminal trial, the Fourth Amendment remedy is the so–called "exclusionary rule." This rule generally provides that evidence seized by the police in violation of the Fourth Amendment may not be introduced in a criminal trial of the victim of the unreasonable search or seizure.

Although the remedy of exclusion of evidence is not expressly provided for in the federal Constitution, the Supreme Court determined in 1914 that it was an implied component of the Fourth Amendment.[15] Although the exclusionary rule was originally employed only in federal trials involving improper conduct by federal agents, the rule's reach was extended to the states in 1961.[16]

The exclusionary rule is controversial because its effect is to suppress reliable evidence of a defendant's guilt. As a result, in recent years the Supreme Court has significantly limited the scope of the remedy. Those limits, and the controversies surrounding the rule, are surveyed in chapter 21.

§ 20   "Private" Searches and Seizures[17]

The Fourth Amendment does not extend to searches or seizures, no matter how unreasonable, that are conducted by private persons on their own initiative.[18] For example, if a private security guard searches an office or detains and searches a person in the building, these activities, even if they are unreasonable, do not violate the Fourth Amendment.

On the other hand, the Fourth Amendment applies if a private person acts "as an instrument or agent of the Government."[19] For example, a Fourth

---

[15] Weeks v. United States, 232 U.S. 383 (1914).

[16] Mapp v. Ohio, 367 U.S. 643, *reh'g denied*, 368 U.S. 871 (1961).

[17] *See generally* 1 W. LaFave, at § 1.8.

[18] *See* Skinner v. Railway Labor Executives' Ass'n, 109 S.Ct. 1402 (1989); Burdeau v. McDowell, 256 U.S. 465 (1921).

[19] *Skinner*, 109 S.Ct. at 1411; *see* United States v. Jacobsen, 466 U.S. 109, 113–14 (1984).

Amendment violation may be found if a private individual conducts surveillance of a citizen, or opens a package belonging to another, at the behest of a police officer. Whether a private person is an agent of the government is determined by the totality of the circumstances.[20]

Although most Fourth Amendment litigation involves searches and seizures by police officers, the amendment applies to other public employees, such as public school teachers[21] and housing inspectors.[22]

§ 21 Extra-Territorial Searches and Seizures[23]

The Supreme Court concluded in *United States v. Verdugo–Urquidez*[24] that the words "the people" in the Fourth Amendment text "refer[] to a class of persons who are part of a national community or who have otherwise developed sufficient connection with this country to be considered part of that community."

In general, under this interpretation of the Fourth Amendment, nonresident aliens not in the United States or its territories, as well as those aliens who are temporarily and involuntarily in the country, are not entitled to the protections of the Fourth Amendment.

For example, the Court held in *Verdugo–Urquidez* that *D*, a nonresident alien, could not object to a warrantless search of his Mexican property conducted by agents of the United States Drug Enforcement Agency. Likewise, an alien brought to this country against his will, and temporarily here in jail pending deportation, is not among "the people" referred to in the Fourth Amendment.

The Court has not determined whether illegal aliens living voluntarily in the United States and who "presumably have accepted some societal obligations" are among "the people" protected by the Fourth Amendment. The Court has also left for another day the question of whether a nonresident alien, whose involuntary presence in the country is prolonged (such as an alien inmate in a state or federal prison) obtains sufficient connection with the country to be entitled to raise Fourth Amendment claims.

§ 22 Abandonment of Houses, Papers, or Effects[25]

Although "persons, houses, papers, and effects" are constitutionally protected interests, *abandoned* houses, papers, and effects are not protected by the Fourth Amendment.

---

[20] *Skinner*, 109 S.Ct. at 1411.

[21] *E.g.*, New Jersey v. T.L.O., 469 U.S. 325 (1985).

[22] *E.g.*, Camara v. Municipal Court, 387 U.S. 523 (1967).

[23] *See generally* Note, *The Extraterritorial Applicability of the Fourth Amendment*, 102 Harv. L. Rev. 1672 (1989).

[24] 110 S.Ct. 1056, *reh'g denied*, 110 S.Ct. 1839 (1990).

[25] *See generally* 1 W. LaFave, at § 2.6(b); Mascolo, *The Role of Abandonment in the Law of Search and Seizure: An Application of Misdirected Emphasis*, 20 Buff. L. Rev. 399 (1971).

Three alternative explanations are sometimes offered by courts for the abandonment rule. First, a person has no legitimate expectation of privacy in abandoned property; therefore, the police activity in its regard is not a "search," as the latter term has been defined.[26] Second, when a person abandons her property, it is her own act, and not a "seizure" by the police, that discloses its contents.[27] Third, a search or seizure of abandoned property is reasonable *per se.*[28]

In general, property is considered "abandoned" if, in discarding personal property or departing from real property, the property–holder intends to forego any interest in it, or if in doing so she should realize that observation or use of the property by another person is likely.

For example, *D* has abandoned an object if she throws it out of the window of her car or discards it in a trash receptacle on a public street after she observes police officers in the vicinity. Property is not considered abandoned for Fourth Amendment purposes, however, if it is discarded as the result of unlawful police conduct such as when *D* throws away an object because she was unlawfully seized by the police.[29]

§ 23 Fourth Amendment Issue Checklist

Numerous issues arise in Fourth Amendment litigation. There is no foolproof way to tackle search–and–seizure questions. However, it is useful to have a checklist of potential issues to consider.

In criminal prosecutions, Fourth Amendment issues arise in an evidentiary context: Should a particular material object or oral statement secured by the government, which the prosecutor intends to introduce into evidence at trial against the defendant, be excluded because it was obtained in violation of the Fourth Amendment?

In answering this question, the student or lawyer should focus on the police activity that resulted in the discovery of the particular evidence at issue, and consider as many of the following questions as are relevant, although not necessarily in the order suggested below. Because of the "fruit–of–the–poisonous–tree" doctrine,[30] it is preferable to consider the admissibility of evidence in chronological order, that is, in the order in which the objects were secured by the police.

1. *Does D have standing to raise a Fourth Amendment challenge to the evidence in question?* In a multi–party criminal prosecution, the student should analyze the challenged evidence separately for each defendant. One person might have standing to raise the claim, while another other does not.

2. *Did the police activity in question implicate a "person, house, paper, or effect"?* The Fourth Amendment only protects these specified interests from unreasonable searches and seizures. This constitutional phrase rarely results in litigation.

---

[26] People v. Romano, 181 Mich. App. 204, 448 N.W.2d 795 (1989).

[27] Brower v. Inyo County, 489 U.S. 593 (1989); *see* Hester v. United States, 265 U.S. 57 (1924).

[28] City of St. Paul v. Vaughn, 306 Minn. 337, 346, 237 N.W.2d 365, 371 (1975).

[29] Hawkins v. State, 758 S.W.2d 255, 258–59 (Tex.Cr.App. 1988).

[30] *See* § 125 *infra.*

3. *Did the police activity constitute a "search" and/or "seizure"?* The words "search" and "seizure" have specialized meanings in Fourth Amendment jurisprudence. If the police activity in question does not constitute either a search or seizure, the Fourth Amendment does not apply.

4. *If a search and/or seizure occurred, did the officer have adequate grounds to conduct it?* Essentially, this question has two components to it: what degree of suspicion is legally required to justify the search or seizure?; and, did the officer in fact have the requisite degree of suspicion?

Warrants must be founded on "probable cause," a term of legal art. However, some searches and seizures that are less–than–ordinarily intrusive are permitted on the basis of the less demanding standard of "reasonable suspicion." Occasionally, suspicionless searches and seizures are allowed, in which case this issue evaporates.

5. *Did the officer have a warrant? If not, was there a valid reason not to secure one?* The Supreme Court often says that warrantless searches are *per se* unreasonable. All this really means is that the warrantless conduct must fall within one of the recognized exceptions to the warrant requirement, so as to constitute a reasonable search and seizure.

6. *If a warrant was secured, was it obtained in proper manner and is it in the proper form?* To be valid, warrants may only be issued by a "neutral and detached magistrate," based on information "supported by Oath or affirmation." Further, the warrant issued must describe in particularity "the place to be searched, and the persons or things to be seized." A warrant that is faulty on any one of these counts is invalid.

7. *Assuming that the preceding questions justify the conclusion that the police conducted an unreasonable search or seizure in violation of D's rights, what evidence, if any, must be excluded from the criminal trial?* This question considers the scope of the Fourth Amendment exclusionary rule, a matter of considerable complexity. In most cases, the evidence obtained in direct violation of the Fourth Amendment will be excluded. Secondary evidence, *i.e.*, evidence indirectly secured as a result of the original illegality, is sometimes inadmissible as a "fruit of the poisonous tree."

CHAPTER 6

FOURTH AMENDMENT: "PERSONS, HOUSES, PAPERS, AND EFFECTS"

§ 24 Significance of the Constitutional Phrase

The Fourth Amendment guarantees the "right of the people to be secure in their *persons, houses, papers, and effects,* against unreasonable searches and seizures."[1]

There are two plausible ways to interpret the relationship between the italicized words and the prohibitory phrase, "unreasonable searches and seizures." First, it may be argued that the Fourth Amendment only prohibits "unreasonable searches or seizures" of "persons, houses, papers, or effects." That is, the latter quoted phrase identifies the interests protected by the Fourth Amendment, whereas the former quoted phrase indicates what those interests are protected from.

Alternatively, the text could be interpreted to mean that government activity that does not impinge upon a "person, house, paper, or effect" is not a "search" or "seizure" within the meaning of the Fourth Amendment.

Both interpretations have case law support.[2] Either approach, however, leads to the same conclusion: police activity that does not affect "persons, houses, papers, or effects," whether reasonable or unreasonable, whether conducted with or without a warrant, and whether supported by probable cause, reasonable suspicion, or no credible evidence at all, is lawful under the Fourth Amendment.

Few cases turn on the meaning of this phrase. However, on a few occasions, the Supreme Court has defined components of the phrase narrowly, and thus ruled that police action did not intrude on a "constitutionally protected area."[3]

§ 25 "Persons"

The word "person" in the Fourth Amendment phrase "persons, houses, papers, and effects" includes: (1) *D*'s body, as a whole, such as when he is arrested;[4] (2) the exterior of *D*'s body (including his clothing), as when he is patted down for

---

[1] Emphasis supplied.

[2] *Compare* Olmstead v. United States, 277 U.S. 438 (1928), *overruled in* Katz v. United States, 389 U.S. 347 (1967) (oral communication is not a "person, house, paper, or effect"; therefore, the tapping of telephone wires outside of a speaker's house or office is not a "search" or "seizure" of the conversation) *with* Oliver v. United States, 466 U.S. 170 (1984) (discovery of contraband in an open field is lawful because an "open field" is not a "person, house, paper, or effect"; and, alternatively, entry into it is not a "search").

[3] Silverman v. United States, 365 U.S. 505, 512 (1961).

[4] *See, e.g.*, Chimel v. California, 395 U.S. 752, *reh'g denied*, 396 U.S. 869 (1969).

weapons or the contents of his clothing are searched;[5] and (3) the interior of *D*'s body, such as when blood is extracted to test for alcohol content.[6]

Early in the twentieth century, the Supreme Court held that the Fourth Amendment applied only to searches and seizures of material things. Based on that interpretation, oral communication was not a "person, house, paper, or effect"; therefore, warrantless electronic surveillance of conversations did not violate the Fourth Amendment.[7] The Court subsequently reversed itself[8] and construed the amendment's protection of "persons" to encompass electronic eavesdropping of their conversations.

§ 26 "Houses"

The word "houses" is broadly construed to include virtually all structures that people commonly use as a residence, whether on a temporary basis, such as a hotel room,[9] or a long–term basis, such as an apartment.[10] It also encompasses buildings connected to the residence, such as a garage.[11]

For constitutional purposes, the word "house" also includes the "curtilage" of the home, that is, "the area to which extends the intimate activity associated with the 'sanctity of a man's home and the privacies of life.' "[12] However, so–called "open fields," or unoccupied and undeveloped real property outside the curtilage of a home, are not included.[13]

Offices, stores, and other commercial buildings are included within the term,[14] a conclusion that the Supreme Court has stated has "deep roots in the history of the Amendment."[15]

§ 27 "Papers and Effects"

The term "papers" encompasses personal items, such as letters and diaries, as well as impersonal business records.[16]

---

[5] *See, e.g.*, Terry v. Ohio, 392 U.S. 1 (1968).

[6] *See, e.g.*, Schmerber v. California, 384 U.S. 757 (1966).

[7] Olmstead v. United States, 277 U.S. 438 (1928).

[8] Katz v. United States, 389 U.S. 347 (1967).

[9] *See, e.g.*, Stoner v. California, 376 U.S. 483, *reh'g denied*, 377 U.S. 940 (1964).

[10] *See, e.g.*, Clinton v. Virginia, 377 U.S. 158 (1964) (*per curiam*).

[11] *See, e.g.*, Taylor v. United States, 286 U.S. 1 (1932).

[12] Oliver v. United States, 466 U.S. at 180 (*quoting* Boyd v. United States, 116 U.S. 616, 630 (1886)).

[13] Hester v. United States, 265 U.S. 57 (1924); Oliver v. United States, 466 U.S. 170 (1984). For discussion of how to distinguish a "curtilage" from an "open field," *see* § 33[B] *infra*.

[14] *See, e.g.*, See v. City of Seattle, 387 U.S. 541 (1967).

[15] Oliver v. United States, 466 U.S. at 178 n.8.

[16] *See, e.g.*, Andresen v. Maryland, 427 U.S. 463 (1976) (business records).

The word "effects" constitutes the residual component of the constitutional phrase. For example, "effects" include automobiles, luggage and other containers, clothing, weapons, and even the fruits of a crime.[17]

The word "effects" is a less inclusive term than the word "property." In that light, the Supreme Court has determined that "open fields," which are not "houses," also are not "effects."[18]

---

[17] *See, e.g.*, Chambers v. Maroney, 399 U.S. 42, *reh'g denied*, 400 U.S. 856 (1970) (automobile); United States v. Chadwick, 433 U.S. 1 (1977) (luggage); United States v. Edwards, 415 U.S. 800 (1974) (clothing); Warden v. Hayden, 387 U.S. 294 (1967) (weapons, money from a robbery).

[18] Oliver v. United States, 466 U.S. at 177.

CHAPTER 7

FOURTH AMENDMENT TERMINOLOGY: "SEARCH"

§ 28 Constitutional Significance of the Term "Search"

The Fourth Amendment prohibits "unreasonable searches and seizures." This chapter considers the meaning of the word "search," and answers the question: When is a search not a "search"?[1]

"Search" is a term of art in Fourth Amendment jurisprudence. The word is not employed by lawyers in its ordinary and popular sense. At times, the difference between the usual meaning and the legal version of the word is so great that it is difficult even for lawyers, including those sitting on the Supreme Court, to avoid describing police activity as a "search," even as it is judged to be a "non–search" in the Fourth Amendment context.[2]

The legal significance of identifying police conduct as a "search" is great. A "search" may be reasonable or unreasonable — *i.e.*, the Fourth Amendment may be satisfied or not satisfied — but if the search is not a "search" in Fourth Amendment parlance, the Fourth Amendment is inapplicable to the case (assuming, also, that no "seizure" occurred).

Put differently, in evaluating police activity, if no "search" or "seizure" occurred, Fourth Amendment analysis ceases. It is not necessary to determine whether the officer had probable cause or a warrant, or whether her actions were otherwise reasonable. As one judge bluntly put it, "the law does not give a [Fourth Amendment] constitutional damn" about "non–search" and "non–seizure" police activity.[3]

Consequently, in considering the law discussed in this chapter, the reader should not confuse the question of whether particular warrantless police conduct should be permitted with the more basic issue of whether it is even a matter governed by the Fourth Amendment. One can answer the second question affirmatively — the conduct is a "search" and, therefore, is governed by the Fourth Amendment — and yet still determine that the search was reasonable and, thus, constitutionally permissible.

---

[1] *See* Burkoff, *When Is a Search Not a "Search?": Fourth Amendment Doublethink*, 15 U. Toledo L. Rev 515 (1984).

[2] *See, e.g.*, Oliver v. United States, 466 U.S. 170, 173 (1984) (in which the Court framed the issue to be whether the "open fields" doctrine "permits police officers to . . . search a field," although the doctrine asserts that inspection of an open field is not a Fourth Amendment "search").

[3] Moylan, *The Fourth Amendment Inapplicable Vs. The Fourth Amendment Satisfied: The Neglected Threshold of "So What?"*, 1 So. Ill. U.L.J. 75, 75–76 (1977).

§ 29 "Search": Original Pre-*Katz* Analysis

Fourth Amendment "search" analysis is divisible into two historical periods. In the first period, which ended in 1967 when the Supreme Court announced its landmark decision in *Katz v. United States*,[4] the justices generally treated Fourth Amendment issues as a property–focused inquiry.

Boyd v. United States,[5] the first Supreme Court case seriously to consider the nature of the Fourth Amendment, laid the seeds of the property–rights interpretation of the amendment.[6] According to *Boyd*, the odious English practice of issuing general warrants, which authorized officials of the Crown to search and, often, ransack houses, was "fresh in the memories" of the drafters of the Fourth Amendment. The Court quoted extensively from the "memorable discussion" and condemnation of general warrants in *Entick v. Carrington*,[7] in which Lord Camden stated that "every invasion of private property, be it ever so minute, is a trespass."

According to Lord Camden, as quoted in *Boyd*, "[t]he great end for which men entered into society was to secure their property. That right is preserved sacred and incommunicable in all instances where it has not been taken away . . . by some public law for the good of the whole." The Court in *Boyd* concluded from these remarks that "[i]t is not the breaking of his doors, and the rummaging of his drawers, that constitutes the essence of the [Fourth Amendment] offence; but it is the invasion of his indefeasible right of personal security, personal liberty, and private property. . . ."

Based on *Boyd*, the pre–*Katz* Supreme Court held that the Fourth Amendment did not apply in the absence of a physical intrusion — a trespass — into a "constitutionally protected area,"[8] most especially into a "house," as that term received its meaning in the constitutional phrase, "persons, houses, papers, and effects."

Olmstead v. United States,[9] provides the most famous example of the Court's pre–*Katz* property rights/trespass approach to the Fourth Amendment. In *Olmstead*, federal officers, without obtaining a search warrant, used wiretaps to intercept the conversations of *D* and others conducted by telephone from their homes and offices. The Court, per Chief Justice Taft, ruled that this conduct fell outside the scope of the Fourth Amendment.

The explanatory portion of the opinion was brief and unrevealing. The reasoning, however, came down to this: conversations are not "persons, house, papers, or effects," so they are unprotected; the houses and offices from which the conversations arose *are* protected by the Fourth Amendment, but only from physical intrusions or trespasses; eyes and ears cannot "search" or "seize," as

---

[4] 389 U.S. 347 (1967).

[5] 116 U.S. 616 (1886).

[6] Ironically, *Boyd* also provided support for the privacy–oriented view of the Fourth Amendment that ultimately developed. *See* Note, *A Privacy–Based Analysis for Warrantless Aerial Surveillance Cases*, 75 Calif. L. Rev. 1767, 1789–91 (1987).

[7] 19 Howell St. Tr. 1029, 1066 (1765) (Eng.).

[8] Lanza v. United States, 370 U.S. 139, 142 (1962).

[9] 277 U.S. 438 (1928), *overruled in* Katz v. United States, 389 U.S. 347 (1967).

neither can trespass; and, the wiretaps used to listen to the conversations, which can trespass, did not do so because they were installed on telephone lines outside *D*'s property.

In other pre–*Katz* decisions applying the trespass doctrine, the Supreme Court concluded that the use of a searchlight was not a "search," in essence because light cannot trespass.[10] It also held that it was not a "search" for an undercover agent consensually to enter a suspect's premises with a hidden transmitter[11] or tape recorder[12] on his body, and there engage the suspect in incriminating conversations, since the invited agent was not a trespasser.[13]

On the other hand, in *Silverman v. United States*,[14] a "search" occurred when a spike–microphone inserted into a party wall intruded minutely into the speakers' premises. In dictum, however, the Court observed that the decision was not based on the fact that there was a "technical trespass under . . . local property law." The property–rights/trespass conception of Fourth Amendment "search" law was eroding.

§ 30   "Search": The Modern *Katz v. United States* Analysis[15]

[A]   The Fall of the Trespass Doctrine

Katz v. United States[16] is the seminal case in modern "search" law, indeed in Fourth Amendment jurisprudence generally. Although critics of recent Supreme Court cases, including some members of the Court, have accused the justices of abandoning *Katz*'s underlying principles,[17] contemporary Fourth Amendment analysis begins (if it does not end) with *Katz*, rather than with the property–rights/ trespass approach discussed in the preceding section of this chapter.

In *Katz*, *D* was subjected to warrantless surveillance of his conversations by federal officers, who attached an electronic listening device to the outside of a telephone booth from which he conducted conversations. In light of the Court's original jurisprudence, the parties pressed their Fourth Amendment claims in terms of whether the telephone booth, like a house, was a "constitutionally protected area," and whether a physical intrusion of it was necessary to raise a "search" claim.

---

[10] United States v. Lee, 274 U.S. 559 (1927).

[11] On Lee v. United States, 343 U.S. 747, *reh'g denied*, 344 U.S. 848 (1952).

[12] Lopez v. United States, 373 U.S. 427, *reh'g denied*, 375 U.S. 870 (1963).

[13] The Court treated as frivolous the claim that the electronic device trespassed since it was uninvited. On Lee v. United States, 343 U.S. at 752.

[14] 365 U.S. 505 (1961).

[15] *See generally* Burkoff, n. 1 *supra*; Kitch, *Katz v. United States: The Limits of the Fourth Amendment*, 1968 Sup. Ct. Rev. 133; Tomkovicz, *Beyond Secrecy for Secrecy's Sake: Toward an Expanded Vision of the Fourth Amendment Privacy Province*, 36 **Hastings** L.J. 645 (1985); Note, *A Reconsideration of the Katz Expectation of Privacy Test*, 76 **Mich.** L. Rev. 154 (1977).

[16] 389 U.S. 347 (1967).

[17] *See* Florida v. Riley, 488 U.S. 445, 457, *reh'g denied*, 109 S.Ct. 1659 (1989) (Brennan, J., dissenting, with whom Marshall and Stevens, JJ. joined, observing that the plurality opinion "reads almost as if *Katz* . . . had never been decided.")

The Court rejected this line of analysis. With the advent of modern technology, and thus the ability of the government electronically to intercept conversations without entering a person's property, the Court arrived at the view that the trespass doctrine constituted "bad physics as well as bad law."[18] Consequently, the Court announced in *Katz* that the property–rights premise of the Fourth Amendment was fully discredited, and that the trespass doctrine was no longer controlling.

[B] In Search of a New Test

One commentator described Justice Stewart's opinion for the Court in *Katz* as an "efficient dismantler, but neglectful reconstructor."[19] That is, *Katz* buried the "trespass" doctrine, but no new test was born in its place. Although *Katz* "bestowed a controlling role upon privacy,"[20] Justice Stewart rejected "privacy" as a new talisman. He warned that the Fourth Amendment represents both more and less than a general right of privacy.

Justice Stewart stated that "the Fourth Amendment protects people, not places." This observation, however, is not helpful in determining the scope of the Fourth Amendment. The constitutional provision obviously is intended to benefit people. But, as Justice Harlan observed in his concurring opinion, "[t]he question . . . is what protection it affords to those people. Generally, . . . the answer to that question requires reference to a 'place.' "

Although Justice Stewart offered no bright–line definition of a "search," he did state in language that has proven important in post–*Katz* cases, that "[w]hat a person knowingly exposes to the public, even in his own home or office, is not a subject of Fourth Amendment protection," whereas "what he seeks to preserve as private, even in an area accessible to the public, may be constitutionally protected."

In this "knowing public exposure"/"seek to preserve as private" context, Justice Stewart distinguished between the uninvited ear (the electronic bug) and intruding eyes. Because the telephone booth was made of glass, *D*'s physical actions were knowingly exposed to the public, but what he sought to exclude when he entered the booth was the uninvited ear. Therefore, by shutting the door on the booth and paying the toll, *D* was "surely entitled to assume that the words he utter[ed] . . . [would] not be broadcast to the world." As a result, "the Government's activities . . . violated the privacy upon which he justifiably relied. . . ."

[C] "Reasonable Expectation of Privacy" Test

Justice Stewart's opinion was devoid of a definition of a Fourth Amendment "search." In his concurring opinion, Justice Harlan filled the void. He interpreted the case "to hold only" that a telephone booth, like a home, and unlike an open field, is an area in which a person has a constitutionally protected "reasonable expectation of privacy." Although Justice Harlan asserted that this holding "emerged from prior decisions," it is this language from *Katz* that has survived

---

[18] *Katz*, 389 U.S. at 362 (Harlan, J., concurring).
[19] Tomkovicz, n. 15 *supra*, at 650–51.
[20] *Id.* at 651.

as the operative definition — the new talisman — of a Fourth Amendment "search."

Justice Harlan's test has a subjective and an objective component. First, the individual must have manifested an actual, or subjective, expectation of privacy. Second, she must prove[21] that the expectation she exhibited is one that "society is prepared to recognize as 'reasonable' " or — to use the Court's variants — "legitimate"[22] or "justifiable."[23]

Police activity does not constitute a "search" if either prong of the test is lacking. For example, as Justice Harlan observed, if *D* in *Katz* had spoken "in the open" where he could have been overheard, rather than in the closed telephone booth that shut out the uninvited ears of others,[24] *D*'s expectation of privacy would not have been reasonable under the circumstances. Therefore, *D* could not have claimed successfully that he was "searched."

Similarly, it is likely *D* would not have had a valid "search" claim if he had surmised that the telephone booth was bugged, perhaps because he saw the tap and realized its significance.[25] Thus, although people *in general* may have a legitimate expectation of privacy in their telephone conversations, *D*'s subjective realization that his conversations were not private would have undermined his Fourth Amendment claim.

---

[21] *Katz* did not consider who had the burden of proof in "search" cases. However, in Florida v. Riley, 488 U.S. 445 (1989), four justices inferentially, and a fifth justice (Justice O'Connor) expressly, held that the defendant must prove that her expectation of privacy was reasonable. Four justices dissented on this issue.

[22] *E.g.*, Illinois v. Andreas, 463 U.S. 765, 771 (1983).

[23] Smith v. Maryland, 442 U.S. 735, 740; *see also Katz*, 389 U.S. at 353 ("The Government's activities . . . violated the privacy upon which [*D*] justifiably relied. . . .").

[24] Suppose that *X*, a lip reader hired by the government, had stood outside the booth and "listened" to *D*'s conversation? If *D* had observed *X* watching his lips, would he have had a reasonable expectation of privacy regarding this mode of interception of his conversation?

Perhaps not, at least if *D* had understood that *X* was reading his lips. Under such circumstances, *D* "knowingly exposed" (to use Justice Stewart's language) his words to *X*; his conversations were "in the open" (to use Justice Harlan's words) insofar as *X* was concerned. As well, Stewart explicitly distinguished between "intruding eyes" and "uninvited ears."

One could reason, therefore, that *Katz* stands for the proposition that a person may have a reasonable expectation of privacy regarding one mode of intrusion, and yet have none if the same information is intercepted in another manner. Some post–*Katz* decisions, however, conflict with this interpretation. *See e.g.*, § 33 *infra*.

[25] Or, for example, consider the case of a person who uses a "telecommunications device for the deaf" (T.D.D.) to call a deaf person. A T.D.D. prints a transcript of the caller's words. Is it a "search" if the police look at the transcript? Perhaps not, as the caller knows that the T.D.D. leaves this physical evidence. *See* Margolick, *Testing Privacy Rights in the World of the Deaf*, New York Times, March 30, 1990, B10, col. 3.

[D] Analysis and Critique of the New Test

[1] Do We Need a New Test?

Should Justice Harlan have provided a new "search" definition? One critic has observed that Justice Stewart's opinion "was written to resist captivation in any formula."[26] The Court dismantled the prior law because it had become too rigid: thoughtful analysis had given way to formulas and talismans, such as "trespass." Therefore, according to this criticism, Harlan's "search" test violated the essence of *Katz* because it substituted one talisman for another.

Justice Harlan came to agree in part with this criticism. He later acknowledged that his expectations formula, although "an advance over the unsophisticated trespass analysis of the common law," also had its "limitations and can, ultimately, lead to the substitution of words for analysis."[27]

[2] Should We Have the Subjective Prong?

Many commentators fault Justice Harlan for including a subjective prong in the expectations formula.[28] Their thesis is that if the subjective component is taken seriously, the government can eliminate privacy expectations by the simple act of announcing its intention to conduct Orwellian surveillance. Once people know that the government is reading their mail, listening to their conversations, and generally intruding on their privacy, they will have no subjective expectation of privacy.

Beyond this, *non*–government intrusions can undermine our right to be free of government intrusions. For example, technology makes it possible for private parties to track our movements electronically, as well as for corporations to discover private information about us by computer. Moreover, increased crime and urbanization accustom us to a less private way of life. With these lesser expectations of privacy, the scope of our Fourth Amendment protections narrows, which further increases the government's ability to invade our privacy.

Justice Harlan ultimately agreed with this criticism of his test. He concluded that the critical focus should be on objective expectations. Privacy analysis, he concluded, should "transcend the search for subjective expectations" because "[o]ur expectations . . . are in large part reflections of laws that translate into rules the customs and values of the past and present."[29] The task of the law, he noted, is "to form and project, as well as mirror and reflect."

The Court as a whole has also acknowledged the potential for danger inhering in the subjective prong. It has stated that if the situation should ever occur that a person's subjective expectations were " 'conditioned' by influences alien to well–recognized Fourth Amendment freedoms," — whatever that means — the subjective element "obviously could play no meaningful role."[30]

---

[26] Amsterdam, at 385.

[27] United States v. White, 401 U.S. 745, 786, *reh'g denied*, 402 U.S. 990 (1971).

[28] *E.g.*, Amsterdam, at 384; Burkoff, n. 1 *supra*, at 537–39; LaFave, *The Fourth Amendment Today: A Bicentennial Appraisal*, 32 Vill. L. Rev. 1061, 1080–81 (1987); Note, n. 15 *supra*, at 157–58.

[29] United States v. White, 401 U.S. at 786 (dissenting opinion).

[30] Smith v. Maryland, 442 U.S. at 740 n.5.

[3] The Objective Prong: What *Precisely* Is It?

Justice Harlan used the term "reasonable" in the expectation–of–privacy test. Justice Stewart used the word "justifiable" in talking about the privacy *D* relied on in the telephone booth.[31] Some post-*Katz* cases use the word "justifiable," but still others use the word "legitimate." Are these words — "reasonable," "justifiable," and "legitimate" — interchangeable, as the Supreme Court seems to believe?

To say that a person's belief is "reasonable" ordinarily means that it is one that a reasonable person in *D*'s situation would hold. In the privacy context, this would mean that an expectation of privacy is "reasonable" when a reasonable person would not expect her privacy to be invaded.

In contrast, to say that *D* has a "legitimate" or "justifiable" expectation of privacy is to draw a normative conclusion that she has a right to that expectation.[32] Or, as one court has put it, the privacy protected by the Fourth Amendment under this view "is not the privacy that one reasonably *expects* but the privacy to which one has a *right*."[33]

Based on this distinction, a privacy expectation might empirically be "reasonable" and yet normatively be "illegitimate" or "unjustifiable"; on the other hand, an "unreasonable" expectation of privacy might be "justifiable" or "legitimate."

For example, suppose that *D* commits a crime in a secluded spot in a park during the middle of the night after carefully ascertaining that the area is virtually never frequented at that hour. Based on this information, D expects that her actions will not be observed. That expectation might be "reasonable" in the sense that a reasonable person would expect to be free from observation.

Nonetheless, if a police officer happens by and observes the criminal conduct, most commentators agree that *D*'s subjective privacy expectation will not be protected.[34] If this is so, it is because *D*'s expectation, although perhaps "reasonable," was "unjustifiable" or "illegitimate." That is, as a normative matter, people have no right to expect privacy if they conduct crime in the open, no matter how unlikely it is that they will be discovered.

On the other hand, suppose that *D* lives in a high–crime area in which burglaries are very common. As a matter of foreseeability, it might be unreasonable for *D* to expect privacy in her home. As a normative matter, however, a court could readily conclude that a person living in such an environment may "legitimately" or "justifiably" expect privacy.

---

[31] *See* n. 23 *supra*.

[32] Note, n. 15 *supra*, at 155–56.

[33] State v. Campbell, 306 Or. 157, 164, 759 P.2d 1040, 1044 (1988) (applying state constitution).

[34] *E.g.*, Note, *From Private Places to Personal Privacy: A Post–Katz Study of Fourth Amendment Protection*, 43 N.Y.U. L. Rev. 968, 983 (1968); LaFave, n. 28 *supra*, at 1081. This conclusion follows from Justice Harlan's remark in *Katz* that "conversations in the open would not be protected against being overheard, for the expectation of privacy under the circumstances would be unreasonable." As the words are being used in the text, Harlan should have said that the expectation would be "unjustifiable" or "illegitimate."

Which expectational analysis did Justice Harlan intend by his test? His concurring opinion in *Katz* does not provide a definitive answer. However, he described the objective component in terms of an expectation "that *society is prepared to recognize* as 'reasonable'." His use of the italicized words appears to connote a normative inquiry.

Harlan's view of the issue became clearer after *Katz*. In one reflective post–*Katz* opinion he placed himself definitively on the side of a normative interpretation of the objective prong. He stated that judges must determine "the desirability of saddling" people with particular risks to their privacy. He wrote that "[t]he critical question . . . is whether under our system of government, as reflected in the Constitution, we should impose on our citizens . . . [particular privacy] risks . . . without at least the protection of a warrant requirement."[35]

Justice Harlan's views notwithstanding, the Court's approach to the issue is mixed. At times, it has stated that a normative inquiry is proper.[36] Many other times, however, the Court has treated the empirical fact of privacy incursions — *e.g.*, that people trespass on property, conduct aerial surveillance of residential backyards, or look through other people's trash — as a justification for concluding that people's subjective expectations of privacy are unreasonable. In such cases, the Court has not explicitly considered whether such expectations, although perhaps "unreasonable," are normatively legitimate.

§ 31 Post-*Katz* "Search" Cases: An Overview[37]

[A] Factors in "Search" Analysis

Many legal observers expected the Supreme Court to interpret the Fourth Amendment broadly after *Katz*. In fact, however, it has applied the reasonable–expectation–of–privacy test strictly: it has frequently concluded that police activity is not a "search" and that, therefore, it falls outside the protections of the Fourth Amendment. It has usually reached this conclusion by determining that the objective prong of the privacy test was lacking, *i.e.*, that the defendant's expectation of privacy was unreasonable.

Three factors have proved particularly important in post–*Katz* "search" jurisprudence. First, the nature of the property inspected or discovered is critical. Some property is linked more directly to activities that the Court wishes to protect from scrutiny than others. For example, "open fields" fall outside the protection of the Fourth Amendment, whereas the "curtilage" of a person's home is entitled to protection.

---

[35] United States v. White, 401 U.S. at 786 (dissenting opinion).

[36] *E.g.*, Smith v. Maryland, 442 U.S. at 740 n.5.

[37] *See generally* Burkoff, n. 1 *supra*; Junker, *The Structure of the Fourth Amendment: The Scope of the Protection*, 79 J. Crim. L. & Crimin. 1105 (1989); Katz, *In Search of a Fourth Amendment for the Twenty–first Century*, 65 Ind. L.J. 549 (1990); Maclin, *Constructing Fourth Amendment Principles From the Government Perspective: Whose Amendment Is It, Anyway?*, 25 Am. Crim. L. Rev. 669 (1988); Serr, *Great Expectations of Privacy: A New Model for Fourth Amendment Protection*, 73 Minn. L. Rev. 583 (1989); Tomkovicz, n. 15 *supra*; Wilkins, *Defining the "Reasonable Expectation of Privacy": An Emerging Tripartite Analysis*, 40 Vand. L. Rev. 1077 (1987).

Second, the extent to which a person has taken measures to keep information, property, or an activity private is important. In this context, two rules are frequently asserted: (1) a person cannot have a reasonable expectation of privacy in that which she knowingly exposes to the public or is in open view; and (2) one who voluntarily conveys information or property to another person assumes the risk that the latter individual will transmit the information or hand over the property to the government. The effect of the latter "limited exposure" doctrine is that "the fourth amendment is eliminated from a great many aspects of modern life. The Court requires the individual who seeks full . . . protection to live an isolated life within his house with the shades drawn."[38]

Third, the Court is concerned with the degree of intrusion caused by the police activity. At times, the justices' analysis of this factor is reminiscent of pre–*Katz* jurisprudence. For example, as discussed in § 35 below, the issue of whether very low–altitude aerial surveillance of the backyard of a person's home constitutes a "search" may depend on whether the noise and dust caused by the surveillance disrupts legitimate activities.

[B]   Lurking Issues In "Search" Cases

At least three broad, interrelated "search" question are worthy of consideration in evaluating the Supreme Court's post–*Katz* jurisprudence. First, how should the Court resolve the issue raised earlier[39] regarding the potential difference between an empirically "reasonable" expectation of privacy and a normatively "legitimate" or "justifiable" one?

Second, to what extent should the manner of the intrusion matter to the "search" determination? May we have a reasonable expectation of privacy regarding one form of intrusion or mode of surveillance, but not of another? For example, suppose that two persons are performing a sexual act in an open stall in a public restroom. Should we conclude that they have no reasonable expectation of privacy if an officer enters and observes them, but that they maintain a legitimate expectation that the government will not observe them from a more clandestine vantage point, such as through a peephole in the back wall or by use of a hidden overhead camera?[40]

Third, should we say that a person may have a legitimate expectation of privacy from government intrusion, even though she may not have a similar expectation of freedom from private invasions?[41] For example, should we be permitted to assume that government agents will not inspect our garbage without a warrant, even if we know that our neighbors or the homeless sift through our trash?

---

[38] *Katz*, n. 37 *supra*, at 568.

[39] *See* § 30[D][3] *supra*.

[40] *E.g.*, People v. Triggs, 8 Cal.3d 884, 106 Cal.Rptr. 408, 506 P.2d 232 (1973), *overruled on other grounds*, People v. Lilienthal, 22 Cal.3d 891, 150 Cal.Rptr. 910, 587 P.2d 706 (1978).

[41] *See, e.g.*, State v. Campbell, 306 Or. 157, 171, 759 P.2d 1040, 1048 (1988) (defining "search" under Oregon law as a particular surveillance technique, which "if engaged in wholly at the discretion of the government, will significantly impair 'the people's' freedom from scrutiny.").

§ 32 Surveillance of Conversations By "False Friends"[42]

[A] "False Friends" versus *Katz*

Katz involved government monitoring of private conversations to which none of the speakers consented. That is, while *D* and *X* spoke on the telephone, unbeknownst to either, government agents listened in to their conversations. *Katz* concluded that the speakers had a reasonable expectation of privacy in their telephone conversations. Therefore, the government was required to conduct the search in a constitutionally reasonable manner, by obtaining a search warrant before tapping the wires.[43]

Katz must be distinguished from cases in which the police acquire a suspect's statements without electronically monitoring her conversations or by monitoring them with the consent of the other party.

Two categories of cases of the latter sort are the subject of this section. Both involve situations in which *X*, a police informant or covert ("undercover") police agent insinuates herself into *D*'s confidence in order to elicit incriminating information from her. In such circumstances, *X* might be termed a "false friend" of *D*, essentially a visible "bug" with an invisible purpose.

In the first category of false–friend cases — the pure version — *D* makes statements to *X*, or makes statements to another person in *X*'s known presence. *X* gathers the information from *D* by listening, and then reports the statements to other police officers, so that the government may use the statements at *D*'s criminal trial.

---

[42] *See generally* Steinberg, *Making Sense of Sense–Enhanced Searches*, 74 Minn. L. Rev. 563 (1990); Stone, *The Scope of the Fourth Amendment: Privacy and the Police Use of Spies, Secret Agents, and Informers*, 1976 Am. B. Found. Res. J. 1193.

[43] As the result of *Katz* and Berger v. New York, 388 U.S. 41 (1967), which struck down a statute because of its "blanket grant of permission to eavesdrop . . . without adequate [judicial] supervision or protective procedures," Congress passed Title III of the Omnibus Crime Control and Safe Streets Act of 1968, § 18 U.S.C. §§ 2510–2520 (now through § 2521).

Title III regulates only nonconsensual electronic surveillance, that is, "the aural acquisition of the contents of any wire or oral communication through the use of any electronic, mechanical, or other device," without the knowledge or consent of any of the participants of the conversation. § 2518(1).

Under the law, except in limited emergency situations, the government may not conduct nonconsensual electronic surveillance in the absence of prior judicial authorization. The surveillance must be conducted so to minimize the interception of communications that are not included in the warrant authorization, and must "terminate upon attainment of the authorized objective, or in any event in thirty days." The authorization, however, may be renewed. § 2518(5).

For discussion of the federal wiretap statute, *see* Fishman, *The "Minimization" Requirement in Electronic Surveillance: Title III, The Fourth Amendment, and the Dred Scott Decision*, 28 Am. U. L. Rev. 315 (1979); Goldsmith, *The Supreme Court and Title III: Rewriting the Law of Electronic Surveillance*, 74 J. Crim. L. & Criminology 1 (1983); Greenawalt, *The Consent Problem in Wiretapping & Eavesdropping: Surreptitious Monitoring With the Consent of a Participant in a Conversation*, 68 Colum. L. Rev. 189 (1968).

The second category might be termed the "wired false friend" cases, which differ from the first scenario only in that the "friend," X, also has in her possession a hidden transmitter that permits the police simultaneously to monitor the conversations, or has with her a hidden tape recorder that registers D's words.

[B] "False Friends"

No "search" occurs if X, a police informant or undercover agent who is visibly present but is masquerading as D's friend, acquaintance, or business associate, listens to and reports to the government D's statements to X or to another person in X's presence.[44] Prior to *Katz*, the justices invoked an "assumption of the risk" doctrine to reach this conclusion; after *Katz*, they reaffirmed this rule but framed their reasoning in expectation–of–privacy terms.

In the leading pre–*Katz* false–friend case, *Hoffa v. United States*,[45] D conversed with X in D's hotel suite. X was an acquaintance of D, but at the time of their conversations the Supreme Court assumed that X was serving as a paid government informant.

The Court rejected D's claim that his statements were obtained in violation of the Fourth Amendment. The justices held that although the hotel room in which the conversations arose was a constitutionally protected area, "no interest legitimately protected by the Fourth Amendment [was] involved" because D "was not relying on the security of the hotel room; he was relying upon his misplaced confidence that [X] would not reveal his wrongdoing."

The lesson of *Hoffa* is that when a person voluntarily speaks to another, *i.e.*, deliberately reveals her mental impressions to a second person, she assumes the risk that the listener is not who she claims to be — a friend — or is a friend who will ultimately betray her. According to the Court, such a possibility is "inherent in the conditions of human society. It is the kind of risk we necessarily assume whenever we speak."

Hoffa was reaffirmed after *Katz* in *United States v. White*.[46] *White* stated that *Katz* left the holding of *Hoffa* "undisturbed," but the Court restated *Hoffa* in "*Katz*ian" terms, stating that a person does not have "a justifiable and constitutionally protected expectation that a person with whom he is conversing will not then or later reveal the conversation to the police."

Hoffa and *White* are defensible on this ground: whereas a person can control the extent to which she gives up her privacy in her home, she cannot similarly control her privacy regarding her thoughts once she has disclosed them to another. That is, D can admit X into her home, and yet remain fully protected from unreasonable entries by others. When D discloses her thoughts to X, however, she cannot selectively surrender them. She "necessarily entrust[s] the recipient with complete control over their dissemination, relying wholly on [the] listener's discretion."[47]

---

[44] Under some circumstances, however, such conduct will violate D's Sixth Amendment right to counsel. *See* § 149 *infra*.

[45] 385 U.S. 293, *reh'g denied*, 386 U.S. 940 (1967).

[46] 401 U.S. 745, *reh'g denied*, 402 U.S. 990 (1971) (plurality opinion).

[47] Uviller, at 1198.

Despite this justification, the Court's holdings in *Hoffa* and *White* are controversial for various reasons. First, people doubtlessly assume the risk that their friends will later betray them, as such a possibility always exists in interpersonal relations. It does not necessarily follow, however, that people should be expected to assume the risk in a free society that their "friends" are government agents at the moment they speak.

Second, one critic has argued that the false–friend rule jeopardizes the conversational confidentiality "necessary for the maintenance of personal autonomy and the development of creative individuality."[48] If a person must assume the risk of disclosure of her private comments, she cannot "discard [her] social mask, blow off steam, and disregard minor social conventions." Intimacy is lost, for its essence is the sharing of feelings and ideas not revealed to the public as a whole. Arguably, therefore, government–initiated seizure of conversations should ordinarily be forbidden unless a search warrant is obtained.

Notwithstanding these criticisms, as well as the risk that some police informants will fabricate conversations,[49] the Supreme Court has consistently upheld the use of covert government agents to conduct conversational surveillance. The justices' tolerance of this investigative technique is probably based on their pragmatic recognition of the fact that it is essential to the detection of otherwise inaccessible information about crime.[50]

[C] "Wired" False Friends

Prior to *Katz*, the fact that a false friend was "wired" with a transmitter or tape recorder was irrelevant to "search" analysis. As long as the agent did not trespass, no search occurred.[51]

Katz did not affect the Court's conclusion regarding this matter, although the trespassory analysis no longer applies. In *United States v. White*[52] the Court held

---

[48] *See* Stone, n. 42 *supra*, at 1233; *see also* Fried, *Privacy*, 77 Yale L.J. 475 (1968) (arguing that privacy is a prerequisite to love, friendship, and trust).

[49] The risk is not a small one because, as one prosecutor observed about informants (as distinguished from ordinary police officers working undercover), "[t]hey are scum, the underbelly of the system. Informants will not testify because they are nice guys. . . . [W]e are trading something for something." Reinhold, *California Shaken Over an Informer*, New York Times, Feb. 17, 1989, p. 1, col. 2 (news story reporting that one informant, who had provided testimony in 140 criminal prosecutions over ten years, confessed that he had fabricated many conversations).

[50] Uviller, at 1199. In a companion case to *Hoffa*, the Supreme Court ruled that the Fourth Amendment was not violated when *X*, a federal agent, misrepresented his identity and purpose in order to obtain an invitation to *D*'s home, where an illegal narcotics sale occurred. Lewis v. United States, 385 U.S. 206, *reh'g denied*, 386 U.S. 939 (1967).

The Court held that *X*'s testimony regarding the sale was admissible because his activities inside *D*'s premises remained within the scope of *D*'s invitation. Chief Justice Warren observed that "[w]ere we to hold the deceptions of the agent in this case constitutionally prohibited, we would come near to a rule that the use of undercover agents in any manner is virtually unconstitutional *per se*." For a history of covert surveillance, as well as a balanced discussion of the practical and moral issues regarding the technique, *see* G. Marx, Undercover: Police Surveillance in America (U. of California 1988).

[51] *See* ns. 11–13 and accompanying text *supra*.

[52] 401 U.S. 745, *reh'g denied*, 402 U.S. 990 (1971) (plurality opinion).

that there is no constitutional difference between the pure false–friend case, in which *X* converses with *D* and then testifies at trial as to her recollection of the conversations, and the situation in which *X* uses the more reliable technique of recording the conversations, or where she carries a microphone that transmits the conversations to other agents who can then corroborate *X*'s testimony.

Justice Harlan dissented in *White*. He believed that the practice of monitoring conversations undermined "that confidence and sense of security with one another that is characteristic of individual relationships between citizens in a free society" and goes "beyond the impact on privacy occasioned by the ordinary type of 'informer' investigation upheld in . . . *Hoffa*."

Justice Harlan reasoned that people will measure their words more carefully if they fear that their conversations are being transmitted to third persons (or, perhaps, if they are recorded), than they will in the pure false–friend situation. The fear of bugging, he predicted, will "smother that spontaneity — reflected in frivolous, impetuous, sacrilegious, and defiant discourse — that liberates daily life."

§ 33   Open-Fields Doctrine

[A]   Rule

Entry into and exploration of so–called "open fields" does not amount to a "search" within the meaning of the Fourth Amendment. This "open–fields doctrine," first announced by the Supreme Court prior to *Katz*,[53] was reaffirmed by it in *Oliver v. United States*.[54]

Oliver involved two cases in which federal officers without search warrants entered private property on foot, ignored "No Trespassing" signs, and walked around either a locked gate or a stone wall, where they observed marijuana plants that were not visible from outside the owners' property.

The Supreme Court, per Justice Powell, held that people do not have a reasonable or legitimate expectation of privacy in activities occurring in open fields, even if the activity could not be observed from the ground except by trespassing in violation of civil or criminal law.[55]

According to *Oliver*, the Fourth Amendment reflects the constitutional framers' belief that certain "enclaves," such as a house, should be free from governmental interference. In contrast, "open fields do not provide the setting for those intimate activities that the Amendment is intended to shelter from government interference or surveillance."

---

[53] Hester v. United States, 265 U.S. 57 (1924).

[54] 466 U.S. 170 (1984).

[55] The Supreme Court has not determined whether a person retains a reasonable expectation of privacy regarding the interior of a structure, such as a barn, found in an open field. The Court has assumed *arguendo*, but never held, that a "search" occurs if a police officer, while in an open field, enters a structure, where she then observes activities not visible from outside. United States v. Dunn, 480 U.S. 294, *reh'g denied*, 481 U.S. 1024 (1987).

Furthermore, as a practical matter, open fields usually are accessible to the public and the police in ways that homes and offices are not. "No Trespassing" signs do not effectively bar intruders. And, the same activities that police officers observe by trespassing can be observed lawfully by air.

[B] "Open Field" versus "Curtilage"

The Supreme Court in *Oliver* did not define the term "open field," but it did state that it "may include any unoccupied or undeveloped area outside the curtilage." It also stated that it "need be neither 'open' nor a 'field' as those terms are used in common speech."

As distinguished from an "open field," the "curtilage," which is entitled to Fourth Amendment protection, is "the land immediately surrounding and associated with the home . . . to which extends the intimate activity associated with the 'sanctity of a man's home and the privacies of life.' "[56]

As set out in *United States v. Dunn*,[57] four factors are relevant in determining whether land falls within the curtilage:[58] (1) the proximity of the area in question to the home; (2) whether the area is included within enclosures surrounding the house; (3) the nature of the use to which the area is put; and (4) the steps taken by the resident to protect the area from observation.

For example, in *Dunn*, D owned a ranch enclosed by a fence. Another fence surrounded D's ranch house. Approximately 50 yards outside the latter fence were two barns, each enclosed by its own fence. A federal officer, who had received information that D was producing illegal drugs on his property, climbed over D's perimeter fence and an interior fence. The officer smelled an acidic odor commonly associated with drug production emanating from the barns. He climbed over the barn fences and, without entering the structures, peered in. He observed incriminating evidence in one barn.

The Court determined that the barns were not within the curtilage of the ranch house: they were 60 yards from it, and 50 yards outside the fence surrounding the house; the officer had objective evidence that the barns were not being used for intimate, home–related, activities; and the Court did not believe that D took sufficient steps to prevent observation into the barn from the open–field vantage point.

[C] Criticism of the Doctrine

Oliver is a controversial decision.[59] Various criticisms of the opinion merit note, especially because they raise broader questions about the Court's Fourth Amendment "search" analysis.

---

[56] *Oliver*, 466 U.S. at 180 (*quoting* Boyd v. United States, 116 U.S. 616, 630 (1886)).

[57] 480 U.S. 294, *reh'g denied*, 481 U.S. 1024 (1987).

[58] Arguably, a gap could exist between an "open field" and a "curtilage." That is, property might fall outside the curtilage and yet be "occupied" and "developed" and, thus, apparently not be an open field. To date, however, the Court has not recognized such a gap.

[59] At least one state court has rejected the doctrine on the basis of its own constitution. State v. Dixson, 307 Or. 195, 766 P.2d 1015 (1988); *see also* Barnard v. State, 155 Miss. 390, 124 So. 479 (1929) (the word "possession" in the state constitution protects unenclosed lands); Welch v. State, 154 Tenn. 60, 289 S.W. 510 (1926) (same).

First, the Court resolved the issue by providing a bright–line rule — *i.e.*, an expectation of privacy in an open field is never legitimate. It might have chosen to resolve the question on a case–by–case basis, by holding that a person may have a legitimate expectation of privacy in an open field in some cases, depending on the circumstances. The justices rejected this approach because they believed it would provide insufficient guidance to police officers.

However, even if a bright–line rule is preferable to case–by–case adjudication,[60] the Court could have drawn an alternative bright line. For example, the dissenters suggested that a better rule would have been: "Private land marked in a fashion sufficient to render entry thereon a criminal trespass under the law of the state in which the land lies is protected by the Fourth Amendment. . . ." Under this rule, officers could enter such fields if they had a search warrant or reasonable grounds not to secure one.

Second, the Court justified its conclusion that expectations of privacy in open fields are illegitimate in part on the basis that people frequently trespass on them. But, this raises a more basic question: Should the foreseeability of such wrongdoing undercut privacy rights? At the least, perhaps the appropriate question ought to be whether people have a legitimate right to expect that law enforcement officers, as distinguished from private persons, will obey criminal laws and respect property rights.

Third, *Oliver* is based in part on the ground that, since the police may observe an open field lawfully from the air, the Fourth Amendment is not violated by unlawful entry on foot. In short, the Court does not distinguish between the *means* of intrusion. Yet, such a distinction might have been intended in *Katz* when Justice Stewart distinguished between "the intruding eye . . . [and] the uninvited ear."

§ 34   Technological Information–Gathering[61]

[A]   Pen Registers

The Supreme Court held in *Smith v. Maryland*[62] that the installation and use of a pen register[63] by the telephone company, at the behest of the government, in order to record the numbers dialed on a telephone, is not a "search" within the meaning of the Fourth Amendment.

Smith distinguished *Katz* on the ground that wiretaps and bugs permit the police to acquire the *contents* of communications, whereas pen registers do not.

---

[60] This is a controversial issue. *See* § 73, *infra*.

[61] *See generally* Fishman, *Technologically Enhanced Visual Surveillance and the Fourth Amendment: Sophistication, Availability, and the Expectation of Privacy*, 26 Am. Crim. L. Rev. 315 (1988); Steinberg, n. 42 *supra*.

[62] 442 U.S. 735 (1979); *contra*, applying state constitutions, People v. Sporleder, 666 P.2d 135 (Colo. 1983); State v. Thompson, 114 Idaho 746, 760 P.2d 1162 (1988); Commonwealth v. Melilli, 521 Pa. 405, 555 A.2d 1254 (1989).

[63] A "pen register" records the numbers dialed on a telephone by monitoring electrical impulses. It does not overhear conversations and does not indicate whether the calls were actually completed.

Telephone users have a legitimate expectation of privacy regarding their conversations; however, according to *Smith*, they do not possess a similar expectation that the telephone numbers that they dial will not be recorded by the telephone company and furnished to the government without a search warrant.

The Court in *Smith* discussed both elements of the reasonable–expectation–of–privacy test. First, the Court doubted "that people in general entertain any actual expectation of privacy in the numbers they dial." The justices reasoned that telephone users know that they convey the telephone numbers they are dialing to the telephone company, that the latter has the capacity to record this information, and that it does so in some circumstances (such as when it bills users for long–distance calls and investigates harassing calls). From this, the Court concluded that, "[a]lthough subjective expectations cannot be scientifically gauged, it is too much to believe" that persons harbor subjective privacy expectations regarding the numbers that they call.

Second, the Court concluded that even if the defendant in this case did harbor some subjective expectation that the phone numbers he dialed remained private, this expectation of privacy was not reasonable. Citing the false–friend conversational surveillance cases[64] and *United States v. Miller*,[65] it held that a person has no legitimate expectation of privacy in any information that she voluntarily turns over to third parties. By knowingly exposing the information to the third party, she assumes the risk that it will be transmitted to law enforcement agents.

The dissenters sought to distinguish the false–friend cases from pen registers. They argued that a person can "exercise some discretion in deciding who should enjoy his confidential communications." It is fair, therefore, to require them to assume the risk of their decision. In contrast, people have no choice regarding the use of telephones, a modern necessity.

[B] Electronic Tracking Devices

Police officers increasingly use "beepers" to track the movement of suspects. A "beeper" is a small battery–operated device that can be installed in a suspect's vehicle or in some object that the suspect will have in her possession, which emits periodic radio signals that can be picked up by officers in police vehicles, airplanes, or helicopters. Installation of such devices in or on the suspect's property raises a "seizure" issue.[66] Use of the device to monitor the suspect's movements raises a "search" question.

United States v. Knotts[67] holds that the use of a beeper to monitor a person's movements is not a "search" if the only information that it reveals is available to the world at large, or at least to people who theoretically could obtain the information from a lawful vantage point.

---

[64] *See* § 32[B] *supra*.

[65] 425 U.S. 435 (1976). In *Miller*, the Court held that a bank customer has no legitimate expectation of privacy in financial information that he "voluntarily conveys" to bank employees in the ordinary course of business. No "search" occurs, therefore, if the bank hands over the customer's financial records to the government.

[66] *See* § 39[B] *infra*.

[67] 460 U.S. 276 (1983).

In *Knotts*, federal officers suspected *D* of manufacturing drugs. Without obtaining a warrant, they installed a beeper in a chemical drum that they knew would be sold to *D*. With the assistance of the beeper, the officers followed *D*'s automobile as he drove from one state to another. At one point, due to *D*'s evasive maneuvers, the police ended visual surveillance of the vehicle. They also temporarily lost the signal from the beeper, but they later regained contact with it by helicopter. The signal indicated that the chemical drum was located outside a certain cabin. Based on this information, the police secured a warrant to search the cabin.

The Supreme Court held that this surveillance did not constitute a "search."[68] Two related factors were of significance to the Court. First, the beeper did not provide the police with any information that they could not have secured by visual surveillance from public places along the route. In essence, *D* knowingly exposed to others the information of his movements by driving on public roads. The fact that a beeper was used instead of visual surveillance did not alter the analysis. Second, the beeper had "limited use" in this case: it did not reveal information as to *D*'s movements within any private place, such as within the cabin.

The latter distinction proved significant in *United States v. Karo*.[69] In *Karo*, the beeper allowed the police to monitor the movement of a container of chemicals inside various houses as well as in public places. The information secured was used to obtain a warrant to search a house for drug–related evidence. The Court held that "[i]ndiscriminate monitoring of property that has been withdrawn from public view would present far too serious a threat to privacy interests in the home to escape entirely some sort of Fourth Amendment oversight."

Knotts and *Karo* raise intriguing questions about Fourth Amendment "search" analysis generally. First, the implication of *Knotts* is that as long as monitoring is limited to movements of persons in non–private areas, the government is free to conduct constant surveillance of citizens' movements. The justices in *Knotts* were aware of this implication, noting that "if such dragnet–style . . . practices . . . should eventually occur, there will be time enough then to determine whether different constitutional principles may be applicable."[70]

Second, the Court's suggestion in *Knotts* that *D* did not have a legitimate expectation of privacy because the officers could have obtained the same information by visual surveillance, obscures the fact that "to learn what the beeper revealed . . . would have taken an army of bystanders in ready and willing communication with one other" along the route traveled.[71] The implication of *Knotts* is that as long as it is hypothetically conceivable, albeit unlikely as a practical matter, for people to obtain information in a non–technologically–enhanced manner, it is irrelevant that an electronic tracking device is used by the government.

---

[68] *Contra*, State v. Campbell, 306 Or. 157, 759 P.2d 1040 (1988) (based on the state constitution).

[69] 468 U.S. 705, *reh'g denied*, 468 U.S. 1250 (1984).

[70] One commentator was not impressed, suggesting that this is "hardly a comforting response — we'll deal with Orwellian excess when and if and *after* they occur!" Burkoff, n. 1 *supra*, at 540.

[71] LaFave, n. 28 *supra*, at 1082.

On the other hand, assuming that *Knotts* is properly decided, a plausible argument can be made that the monitoring that arose in *Karo* should not have been condemned. The difference between the two cases might come down to little more than that the chemical drum in *Knotts* was placed outside the cabin rather than inside or, at least, that the signals from the *Knotts* beeper were inadvertently lost while the drum was inside the cabin. If the only information that the beeper provides to the police is its geographical position, it is hard to see why the fortuity of its placement inside a dwelling, rather than next to it, significantly affects the citizen's privacy interest in the dwelling.

§ 35 Aerial Surveillance[72]

[A] Rule

As explained more fully below, non–technologically–enhanced aerial surveillance by the government of activities occurring within the curtilage[73] of a house does not constitute a "search" if the surveillance: (1) occurs from public navigable airspace; and (2) is conducted in a physically nonintrusive manner.[74] Police use of devices to enhance their vision of the activities within the curtilage does not constitute a "search" except, perhaps, if the device used is highly sophisticated and not generally available to the public.[75]

[B] Surveillance by Airplanes

Aerial surveillance of the curtilage of a house was first upheld by the Supreme Court in *California v. Ciraolo*.[76] In *Ciraolo*, *O*, a police officer, received an anonymous tip that *D* was growing marijuana in his backyard. *O*'s attempt to observe *D*'s yard from ground level failed because of a six–foot–high outer fence and a ten–foot–high inner fence. Therefore, *O* obtained a private plane to fly over the backyard at an altitude of approximately 1,000 feet, which was within public navigable airspace under Federal Aviation Administration (F.A.A.) regulations. From that vantage point, *O* observed marijuana plants in *D*'s backyard.

The Court held that even if *D* possessed a subjective expectation of privacy regarding his "unlawful gardening pursuits" in the curtilage, which it questioned but assumed that he did, this expectation was not a reasonable one. Applying the *Katz* principle, the Court stated that the police need not shield their eyes from objects or activities which are knowingly exposed to them, even in the curtilage.

---

[72] *See generally* Fishman, n. 61 *supra*; Steinberg, n. 42 *supra*; Comment, *A Privacy–Based Analysis For Warrantless Aerial Surveillance Cases*, 75 Calif. L. Rev. 1767 (1987).

[73] For discussion of the meaning of term "curtilage," *see* § 33[B] *supra*.

[74] California v. Ciraolo 476 U.S. 207, *reh'g denied*, 478 U.S. 1014 (1986); Florida v. Riley, 488 U.S. 445, *reh'g denied*, 109 S.Ct. 1659 (1989).

[75] Dow Chemical Co. v. United States, 476 U.S. 227, 238 (1986) (use of a "standard, floor–mounted, precision aerial mapping camera" costing $22,000.00 to conduct surveillance of a constitutionally protected area is not a "search"; use of satellite technology might require prior judicial authorization).

[76] 476 U.S. 207, *reh'g denied*, 478 U.S. 1014 (1986).

And, the fact that a person has taken measures to restrict some views of her activities within the curtilage does not preclude the police from observing them from a public vantage point where they have a right to be.

According to *Ciraolo*, a person is not entitled to assume that what she grows in the backyard will not be observed in a nonintrusive manner by a passing aircraft in public navigable airspace or, for that matter, "by a power company repair mechanic on a pole overlooking the yard." The Court stated that "[i]n an age where private and commercial flights in the public airways is routine," it is unreasonable for *D* to expect privacy from the air.

Ciraolo has been criticized on various grounds. First, the Court concluded that *D* could not have a reasonable expectation of privacy in his backyard because airplane flights over private property are common. This fact of modern life, however, ignores the issue of whether persons should have a *right* to expect privacy in this regard, at least from government surveillance as distinguished from the unfocused, momentary observations of private persons in commercial airplanes. In short, the Court applied the "crude approach"[77] of empiricism rather than attempting to make a normative judgment, which some commentators and justices believe *Katz* requires.[78]

Second, as Justice O'Connor has complained,[79] a possible implication of *Ciraolo* is that people who wish to retain Fourth Amendment privacy rights in their backyards and patios can do so only by completely covering and enclosing them, which in many cases will mean that they must give up their enjoyment of those areas.

[C] Surveillance by Helicopters

In *Florida v. Riley*,[80] the Supreme Court applied the reasoning of *Ciraolo* to aerial inspections by helicopters. In *Riley*, *O*, an officer in a police helicopter, observed marijuana plants growing in *D*'s within–the–curtilage greenhouse, which was missing two roof panels. In order to observe the inside of the structure, *O* descended to an altitude of 400 feet, which would have been impermissible under F.A.A. regulations if the flight had occurred in a fixed–wing aircraft, but which was lawful for helicopter flights.

The Supreme Court held, 5–4, that the police action was not a "search." Justice White, in a short opinion for a four–justice plurality, stated that *D* knowingly exposed his greenhouse to the surveillance because private and commercial helicopter flights are routine in public airways, and *D* offered no evidence "that such flights [were] unheard of" in the vicinity of his house.

The plurality indicated it "would have [been] a different case if flying at that altitude had been contrary to law or regulation." The implication of this remark is that the police action might have constituted a "search" if an airplane rather than a helicopter had surveyed *D*'s greenhouse from precisely the same vantage

---

[77] Note, *Supreme Court, Leading Cases*, 100 Harv. L. Rev. 100, 142 (1986).

[78] *See* § 30[D][3] *supra*.

[79] Florida v. Riley, 488 U.S. at 454 (concurring opinion).

[80] 488 U.S. 445, *reh'g denied*, 109 S.Ct. 1659 (1989).

point. In short, the mode of intrusion — the type of flying machine used — might matter, at least if one form is lawful and the other is not.[81]

Justice White also warned that "an inspection of the curtilage of a house from an aircraft will [not] always pass muster under the Fourth Amendment simply because the place is within navigable airspace specified by law." He suggested that the result might have been different in the case if there had been "any intimation that the helicopter interfered with [D's] normal use of the greenhouse or of other parts of the curtilage." The plurality considered it significant that the record did not reveal that "intimate details connected with the use of the home or curtilage were observed, and there was no undue noise, no wind, dust, or threat of injury."

This language is intriguing. Why should it matter whether the officer spots marijuana crops or, instead, observes "intimate" activities? Can the Court possibly mean that if the same helicopter had observed the contents of the greenhouse as well as consensual but illegal sexual acts in the backyard, the surveillance would have been a "search" of one but not of the other activity? If so, this conclusion would run counter to the often–expressed statement of the Court that the police need not shield their eyes to activities visible to them from vantage points where they have a right to be.

Nor is it clear why helicopter–caused dust, as an example, triggers a privacy right that is not otherwise implicated. This harkens back, as the dissenters pointed out, to the pre–*Katz* "intrusion" and "trespass" concepts of the Fourth Amendment.

Justice O'Connor, who concurred in the judgment, and the four dissenters in *Riley* minimized the significance of the lawfulness of the helicopter flight. The issue to them was not whether the flight was lawful, or even whether police helicopter flights at 400 feet were common, but rather whether, as Justice O'Connor phrased the issue, "members of the public travel with sufficient regularity [at such low altitudes] that [D's] expectation of privacy from aerial observation was not one that society is prepared to recognize as 'reasonable.' "[82] In other words, a majority of justices in *Riley* apparently believed that a person may have a reasonable expectation of privacy regarding police aerial surveillance, even if the latter form of intrusion is common, if non–police aerial surveillance is rare.

§ 36   Testing for Contraband[83]

[A]   Dog Sniffs

In *United States v. Place*,[84] Drug Enforcement Agency (D.E.A.) agents seized luggage belonging to *D*, a deplaning airline passenger whom they suspected of drug

---

[81] Yet, that distinction does not seem to matter in the open–fields context, *see* § 33 *supra*, in which the Court justified trespassing by the police in open fields on the ground that they could have observed the same activities lawfully from the air.

[82] *Riley*, 488 U.S. at 454 (*quoting Katz*, 389 U.S. at 361).

[83] *See generally* Steinberg, n. 42 *supra*.

[84] 462 U.S. 696 (1983).

possession, and subjected it to a "sniff test" by a dog trained to discover narcotics. The dog "reacted positively" to one of the pieces of luggage.

The Supreme Court declared that the dog sniff was not a "search." Its conclusion was based on two facts. First, the information was secured in a comparatively nonintrusive manner: the luggage, which was in a public place when it was sniffed, was not opened and, thus, noncontraband items were never exposed to the public eye.

Second, the information revealed by the test was extremely limited, as it disclosed only the presence or absence of narcotics, a contraband item. The Court observed that "the canine sniff is *sui generis*. We are aware of no other investigative procedure that is so limited both in the manner in which the information is obtained and in the content of the information revealed by the procedure."

[B] In-the-Field Chemical Tests

Dog sniffs proved not to be *sui generis*. In *United States v. Jacobsen*,[85] a D.E.A. agent conducting a drug investigation came upon white powder in a plastic bag belonging to *D*. Because the agent suspected that it was cocaine, he conducted an on-the-scene test: he placed a small amount of the powder in three test tubes containing liquids; the liquids took on a certain sequence of colors, which confirmed that the powder was cocaine.

The Supreme Court, in a conclusion "dictated" by *Place*, ruled that any chemical test that "merely discloses whether or not a particular substance is cocaine does not compromise any legitimate interest in privacy." As Congress has determined that private possession of certain items is illegitimate, "government conduct that can reveal whether a substance is [contraband], and no other arguably 'private' fact, compromises no legitimate privacy interest."[86]

§ 37 Inspection of Garbage

The Supreme Court in *California v. Greenwood*[87] held, 7–2, that a person has no reasonable expectation of privacy in garbage enclosed in a bag left for collection outside the curtilage of a home. No search arises, therefore, when an officer opens a trash bag left at the curb and sifts through its contents.[88]

In *Greenwood*, the Court conceded that *D*, the homeowner whose garbage was inspected by the police, might have had a subjective expectation that the trash

---

[85] 466 U.S. 109 (1984).

[86] In contrast, if a substance is not tested to determine if it is contraband, but rather to find out whether it contains evidence of the use of contraband, the test is a "search." Skinner v. Railway Labor Executives' Ass'n, 489 U.S. 602 (1989) (tests of blood and urine for evidence of drug usage is a "search").

[87] 486 U.S. 35 (1988).

[88] *Contra*, State v. Hempele, 120 N.J. 182, 576 A.2d 793 (1990) (under the New Jersey constitution, police may *seize* a garbage bag left for collection without a warrant or probable cause, but a warrant is required to *search* its contents); State v. Boland, 115 Wash.2d 571, 800 P.2d 1112 (1990) (under the state constitution, a warrant is required to open and search curbside garbage bags).

bag would not be opened by the police or the public. However, it concluded that *D*'s Fourth Amendment claim failed on objective grounds, because "it is common knowledge" that plastic garbage bags left on the curb for pickup "are readily accessible to animals, children, scavengers, snoops, and other members of the public."

In light of this common knowledge, the Court invoked two related "search" rules. First, applying *Katz* and the aerial surveillance decisions, it stated that the Fourth Amendment does not protect information knowingly exposed to the public. Second, citing *Smith v. Maryland*,[89] the pen register case, it noted that one cannot have a reasonable expectation of privacy in information voluntarily turned over to others.

However, *Greenwood* goes further than the cases the Court cites. In those cases, the individuals exposed *information* to others (by conducting activities in an area visible to aircraft, and by making telephone calls, the numbers of which were being recorded by the telephone company). In *Greenwood*, *D* only knowingly exposed the *container* that enclosed the information. As the dissent pointed out, *D* did not "flaunt[] his intimate activity" by exposing the contents of his trash. Nor was this a case in which a private party invaded *D*'s privacy by tearing open the container and exposing the contents to anyone else who might happen by.

Under *Greenwood*, *D*'s expectation of privacy is illegitimate because of the "mere *possibility* that unwelcome meddlers [might] open and rummage through the containers." That is, because private persons *might* snoop, individuals have no constitutionally recognized "reasonable expectation of privacy" when and if the police *in fact* snoop. But if that is enough to render the Fourth Amendment inapplicable, the *Greenwood* dissenters asked rhetorically, would the Court suggest that "the possibility of a burglary negates an expectation of privacy in the home[?]"

---

[89] 442 U.S. 735 (1979), discussed at § 34[A] *supra.*

CHAPTER 8

FOURTH AMENDMENT TERMINOLOGY: "SEIZURE"

§ 38   Constitutional Significance of the Term "Seizure"

This chapter defines the term "seizure." Unlike the term "search," which has a single definition, the word "seizure" has two definitions, one relating to "seizures" of property and the other to "seizures" of persons. As is the case with the term "search," the issue of whether a particular act by the police constitutes a "seizure" is a matter of threshold significance: unless the police action is a "seizure" (or a "search"), the Fourth Amendment does not apply.

In the case of property, if the determination is made that the police action constitutes a "seizure," then it must occur in a constitutionally reasonable manner, which often means that the police must have a search warrant, based on "probable cause," or a justification for not securing the warrant.

In the case of persons, the police must have adequate cause to seize a person ("probable cause" or, sometimes, "reasonable suspicion," a lesser standard); in the case of arrests, one form of "seizure" of a person, they sometimes must have an arrest warrant, as well.

§ 39   "Seizure" of Property

[A]   General Rule

In contrast to a search, which affects a person's privacy interest, a "seizure" of property invades an individual's possessory interest in that property.[1] Tangible[2] property is "seized" in Fourth Amendment terms "when there is some meaningful interference with an individual's possessory interest in that property."[3]

A "seizure" uncontroversially occurs when a police officer exercises control over *D*'s property by destroying it,[4] or by removing it from *D*'s actual or constructive possession.[5] A house or office and its contents apparently are "seized" when an

---

[1] Texas v. Brown, 460 U.S. 730, 747 (1983) (Stevens J., concurring).

[2] The Supreme Court originally ruled that the Fourth Amendment applied only to searches and seizures of material things, which excluded conversations; but the word "person" in the constitutional phrase "persons, houses, papers and effects" is now interpreted to encompass conversations. *See* § 30 *supra*. Over strong dissent, the Court has assumed that the act of monitoring a conversation constitutes both a "search" and a "seizure" of the words. *See* Berger v. New York, 388 U.S. 41 (1967).

[3] United States v. Jacobsen, 466 U.S. 109, 113 (1984); *see also* Hale v. Henkel, 201 U.S. 43, 76 (1906) ("a seizure contemplates a forcible dispossession of the owner. . . .").

[4] United States v. Jacobsen, 466 U.S. at 124-25.

[5] *See* United States v. Place, 462 U.S. 696, 707 (1983).

officer secures the premises, *i.e.*, prevents persons from entering and taking away personal property.[6] On the other hand, no "seizure" occurs when an officer merely picks up an object to look at it or moves it a small distance, because any interference with *D*'s possessory interest in such circumstances is not "meaningful."[7]

[B] Installation of Electronic Devices On or In Property

The installation of an electronic device, such as a "beeper" to monitor a person's movements or a "bug" to intercept conversations, in or on a person's personal property, raises controversial "seizure" issues.[8]

At least in some contexts, installation of an electronic device is not a "seizure," as evidenced by *United States v. Karo*.[9] In *Karo*, federal agents learned that *D* intended to obtain ether from *X*, a merchant, for use in the production of drugs. Therefore, with *X*'s consent, they installed a beeper inside an ether can that *X* agreed to transfer to *D*, so that the agents could monitor the latter's movements.

The Court held that the placement of the beeper in the can was not a "seizure" since the container at that time did not belong to *D*, and thus did not invade his possessory interests. It also held that no "seizure" occurred when the "bug"-infested can was transferred to *D* by *X*. According to the Court, "[a]lthough the can may have contained an unknown and unwanted foreign object, it cannot be said that anyone's possessory interest was interfered with in a meaningful way."

Justice Stevens, joined by Justices Brennan and Marshall, dissented from this conclusion. They contended that a possessory interest in property includes the right to exclude others from it, which was meaningfully interfered with the moment the can was transferred to *D*. As the dissent put it, "the character of the property is profoundly different when infected with an electronic bug than when it is entirely germ free."

---

[6] *See* Segura v. United States, 468 U.S. 796, 805-06 (1984) (in which the Court assumed *arguendo* that the act of securing premises is a "seizure").

[7] *See, e.g.*, Texas v. Brown, 460 U.S. 730 (1983) (officer moved a balloon a few feet in order to better view its contents: no "seizure" issue raised); New York v. Class, 475 U.S. 106 (1986) (officer slightly moved a piece of paper in *D*'s automobile to see underneath: no "seizure" issue raised); Arizona v. Hicks, 480 U.S. 321 (1987) (officer slightly moved stereo equipment in order to read a serial number on the back: no "seizure" issue raised).

[8] Use of the device after it is installed also raises "search" issues. *See* § 34[B] *supra*.

[9] 468 U.S. 705 (1984).

§ 40 "Seizure" of Persons [10]

[A] General Rule

A "seizure" of a person occurs when a police officer, by means of physical force or show of authority, intentionally [11] restrains the individual's liberty in such a manner that, in view of all the circumstances surrounding the incident, a reasonable person would believe that he is not free to leave. [12]

For example, D is "seized" by an officer when he is: physically restrained so that he can be frisked; [13] placed under arrest; [14] intentionally shot by the officer; [15] taken into custody and brought to a police station for questioning [16] or fingerprinting; [17] ordered to pull his automobile off the highway for questioning or to receive a traffic citation; [18] or intentionally forced to stop his vehicle by means of a roadblock. [19]

Occasionally, the "seizure" issue is controversial because D believes that he was not free to leave, whereas the officer asserts that he was. As the definition of "seizure" indicates, however, the subjective impressions of the person accosted are irrelevant, as are the uncommunicated intentions of the officer. [20] The question is always whether a reasonable person in D's place would have believed that his freedom of movement was restricted.

Although each case must be decided on its own facts, Professor Wayne LaFave has concluded that a police-citizen confrontation does not amount to a "seizure" unless the officer adds to the pressures inherent in the situation "by engaging in conduct significantly beyond that accepted in social intercourse." [21] Among the factors that tend to support the conclusion that D was "seized" are that: a police

---

[10] See generally 3 W. LaFave, at § 9.2(h); LaFave, *"Seizures" Typology: Classifying Detentions of the Person to Resolve Warrant, Grounds, and Search Issues*, 17 U. Mich. J.L. Ref. 417, 420-26 (1984); Maclin, *The Decline of the Right of Locomotion: The Fourth Amendment on the Streets*, 75 Cornell L.Rev. 1258 (1990); Williamson, *The Dimensions of Seizure: The Concepts of "Stop" and "Arrest"*, 43 Ohio St. L.J. 771 (1982).

[11] According to Brower v. Inyo County, 489 U.S. 593 (1989), the police action that restricts the person's liberty must be by "means intentionally applied by the officer." For example, as the Court explained, D, a person for whom an arrest warrant is outstanding, is not "seized" if by accident he is pinned under a parked police vehicle that slips its brakes, or if, while being pursued by the police in a high-speed car chase, he loses control of his vehicle and crashes into a tree. In both cases, the person is no longer free to move as the result of police action, but the means by which the police obtained physical control was unintentionally applied.

[12] United States v. Mendenhall, 446 U.S. 544, *reh'g denied*, 448 U.S. 908 (1980) (plurality opinion); I.N.S. v. Delgado, 466 U.S. 210 (1984).

[13] Terry v. Ohio, 392 U.S. 1 (1968).

[14] See Henry v. United States, 361 U.S. 98 (1959).

[15] Tennessee v. Garner, 471 U.S. 1 (1985).

[16] Dunaway v. New York, 442 U.S. 200 (1979).

[17] Hayes v. Florida, 470 U.S. 811 (1985).

[18] United States v. Hensley, 469 U.S. 221 (1985).

[19] Brower v. Inyo County, 489 U.S. 593 (1989).

[20] Michigan v. Chesternut, 486 U.S. 567, 574-75 (1988).

[21] 3 W. LaFave, § 9.2(h) at 412.

officer displayed a weapon; *D* was encircled by the police; *D* was roughly touched by an officer;[22] or the tone of the officer's voice "indicat[ed] that compliance with [his] . . . request might be compelled."[23]

[B] "Seizure" by Questioning?

Rather clearly, "not all personal intercourse between policemen and citizens involves 'seizures' of persons."[24] If an officer asks a person on the street for the time of day, for example, no reasonable person would believe that his freedom of movement is restricted because of the question.

Even if police questioning relates to suspected criminal activity, the Supreme Court has indicated that questioning by itself is unlikely ever to amount to a "seizure."[25] From a Fourth Amendment perspective, an officer has the same right as anyone to ask questions of another person, and the citizen ordinarily has the right to refuse to submit to interrogation and walk away.

More specifically, the Supreme Court has held that "interrogation relating to one's identity or a request for identification by the police does not, by itself, constitute a Fourth Amendment seizure."[26] A "seizure" does not arise in such circumstances unless there are abnormally intimidating conditions present.[27] For example, a "seizure" occurs if an officer frisks *D*, or applies other force upon him, because *D* is uncooperative.[28]

The most difficult seizure-by-questioning cases have arisen in the context of airport interrogations, in which passengers embarking or deplaning, were unthreateningly confronted and questioned by law enforcement officers regarding suspected drug activity. The line between "non-seizure" interrogation and a "seizure" in this context is a thin one, and one that has sharply divided the Court. For example, compare the somewhat-similar facts but dissimilar holdings in *United States v. Mendenhall*[29] and *Florida v. Royer.*[30]

In *Mendenhall*, federal agents confronted *D* in an airport as she deplaned, identified themselves, and asked to see her identification and plane ticket. Justice Stewart, in an opinion of the Court in which only Justice Rehnquist joined,[31] concluded that a reasonable person in *D*'s situation would have believed that she was free to end the conversation at that time and move on; therefore, *D* was not

---

[22] However, a mere tap on the shoulder, as might be applied by any person to gain another's attention, does not constitute a "seizure." *Id.* at 413.

[23] United States v. Mendenhall, 446 U.S. at 554.

[24] Terry v. Ohio, 392 U.S. at 19 n.16.

[25] I.N.S. v. Delgado, 466 U.S. at 216.

[26] *Id.*

[27] *See generally* the factors set out in text following note 21 *supra*.

[28] *E.g.*, Brown v. Texas, 443 U.S. 47 (1979).

[29] 446 U.S. 544, *reh'g denied*, 448 U.S. 908 (1980).

[30] 460 U.S. 491 (1983).

[31] Chief Justice Burger and Justices Powell and Blackmun believed that the "seizure" question was a close one, but they concluded that even if it were a seizure, it was a reasonable one. Justices White, Brennan, Marshall, and Stevens concluded that *D* was seized.

"seized."[32] In defense of this position, Justice Stewart pointed out that the encounter took place in public, the agents were not in uniform, they did not display weapons, and they requested, but never demanded, to see D's identification.

In *Royer*, two detectives accosted D, an embarking airline passenger, identified themselves, and asked to see his ticket and driver's license, which he handed over. When the officers spotted a discrepancy in the documents, they informed him that he was suspected of transporting narcotics. Without returning his ticket and license, they requested that he accompany them to a small nearby room, which D did.

The Supreme Court held that the initial encounter — when the officers asked D for identification — was not a "seizure," but that he was "seized" when he was asked to accompany them to the room. The Court reasoned that because the officers retained D's ticket and driver's license without indicating that he was free to depart, a reasonable person in D's situation would have believed that he was not free to leave.

[C]　"Seizure" by Pursuit?

Nearly all Fourth Amendment "seizure" cases involve actual restraint of an individual by the police. However, may the mere act of pursuit of a suspect ever constitute a "seizure," even if the person is not immediately apprehended?

Although the answer to the question is not absolutely clear,[33] language in *Michigan v. Chesternut*[34] suggests that a police pursuit that does not result in apprehension can constitute a "seizure." In *Chesternut*, D, standing on a corner, fled by foot when he observed a marked police vehicle. Suspicious of D's flight, the officers caught up to him in their vehicle and followed alongside him a short distance. Although D was later arrested, at no time during this initial pursuit was he stopped by the police. However, during this time, he discarded some drugs,

---

[32] Is this conclusion realistic? Consider in this context I.N.S. v. Delgado, 466 U.S. 210 (1984), in which Immigration and Naturalization Service officers conducted a "factory survey" by entering a factory *en masse*, placing armed agents at the exits, displaying their badges, carrying walkie-talkies, and going about the plant asking workers for identification, in order to determine if they were lawfully in the country.

The Court ruled that this procedure did not result in the seizure of the employees *en masse*. It reasoned that the workers' freedom of movement, by the nature of the employment contract, was already restricted to the factory area. In no way were the employees placed in "reasonable fear that [they] were not free to continue working or to move about the factory."

But, is that really the appropriate question? Many people — for example, factory employees, college professors, and professional basketball players — expect to remain in a fairly small, confined area during work time, but it seems unduly restrictive to describe their freedom of movement in such narrow terms. They *are* ordinarily free to leave, even though the act may carry with it negative employment consequences. But, that is the point of freedom: they can choose to accept those consequences. But, were the factory workers in *Delgado* similarly free to choose to leave the factory, if they were willing to risk dismissal?

[33] *See* n. 35 *infra*.

[34] 486 U.S. 567 (1988).

so the issue arose as to whether the police retrieval of the contraband was the fruit of an unlawful seizure of *D*.

The Court, per Justice Blackmun, unanimously concluded that no "seizure" occurred on these facts. In reaching this conclusion, it rejected two conflicting bright-line rules submitted to them by the parties: it rejected *D*'s proposition that all police chases are "seizures," whether or not the suspect is apprehended; and it also refused to abide by the state's claim that a "seizure" can never occur, no matter how coercive, as long as the police are unsuccessful in apprehending the individual.

Instead, Justice Blackmun applied the usual "seizure" test and concluded that the police action in this case, although "somewhat intimidating," was insufficient to communicate to a reasonable person "an attempt to capture or otherwise intrude upon [*D*'s] freedom of movement." The Court suggested that the result might have been different if the officers had used their siren, drawn their guns, or had "operated the car in an aggressive manner to block [*D*'s] course or otherwise control the direction or speed of his movements."

Justices Kennedy and Scalia, although concurring, stated that they did not interpret the opinion they joined to foreclose a ruling, which they described as "at least plausible," that a "seizure" does not occur unless the police "achieve a restraining effect." However, the Court's rejection of the government's proposed "no apprehension, no seizure" bright-line rule, its use of the "attempt to capture" language, and its suggestion that a "seizure" might occur if the police "control the direction or speed" of a suspect's movements, reinforces the view that the concurring justices' suggested ruling is inconsistent with *Chesternut*.[35]

---

[35] The significance of *Chesternut* was cast into some doubt by the Court in Brower v. Inyo County, 489 U.S. 593 (1989). In *Brower*, the Court stated that "[v]iolation of the Fourth Amendment requires an intentional *acquisition of physical control*." (Emphasis added.) The italicized language might imply that a seizure cannot occur in the absence of a successful detention of a suspect. However, *Brower* did not involve an unsuccessful pursuit, so the seizure-by-pursuit issue was not before the Court; nor was *Chesternut* cited, much less expressly called into question, in either the majority or dissenting opinions. *See* State v. Lemmon, 318 Md. 365, 568 A.2d 48 (1990) (concluding that *Brower* does not "refine" *Chesternut*).

The meaning of *Chesternut* in light of *Brower* may soon be explained by the Supreme Court. In *California v. Hodari D*, 216 Cal. App.3d 795, 265 Cal. Rptr. 79 (1989), *cert. granted*, 111 S. Ct. 38 (1990) (No. 89-1632), one of the questions presented is: "Is physical restraint required for [a] seizure of [a] person under the Fourth Amendment?"

CHAPTER 9

FOURTH AMENDMENT: "PROBABLE CAUSE"

§ 41   The Constitutional Role of "Probable Cause"

One clause of the Fourth Amendment provides that "no Warrants shall issue, but upon probable cause." Another clause prohibits "unreasonable searches and seizures." The interrelationship of these two clauses is a matter of considerable dispute,[1] but what is not in dispute is that "probable cause" is a key element of the Fourth Amendment.

The Supreme Court has observed that the "rule of probable cause is a practical, nontechnical conception affording the best compromise that has been found for accommodating [the] often opposing interests" of "safeguard[ing] citizens from rash and unreasonable interferences with privacy and from unfounded charges of crime" and of "giv[ing] fair leeway for enforcing the law in the community's protection."[2]

The importance of "probable cause" in Fourth Amendment jurisprudence is evident in two constitutional principles: (1) an arrest is never constitutionally reasonable in the absence of probable cause;[3] and (2) subject to various "well–defined" exceptions, a search or seizure of property is unreasonable unless it is accomplished pursuant to a warrant based upon probable cause.[4] Even when a warrant is not required, probable cause to conduct the search usually is required.

§ 42   Probable Cause: General Principles[5]

[A]   "Probable Cause": Definition

"Probable cause" exists when the facts and circumstances within an officer's knowledge and of which she has reasonably trustworthy information are sufficient in themselves to warrant a person of reasonable caution in the belief that: (1) in the case of an arrest, an offense has been committed and the person to be arrested committed it; and (2) in the case of a search, seizable evidence will be found in the place to be searched.[6]

---

[1] *See* § 49 *infra*.

[2] Brinegar v. United States, 338 U.S. 160, 176, *reh'g denied*, 338 U.S. 839 (1949).

[3] Dunaway v. New York, 442 U.S. 200 (1979).

[4] Skinner v. Railway Labor Executives' Ass'n, 489 U.S. 602 (1989).

[5] *See generally* 1 W. LaFave, at § 3.1.

[6] *Brinegar*, 338 U.S. at 175–76; Carroll v. United States, 267 U.S. 132, 162 (1925).

[B] "Probable Cause": Objective versus Subjective

"Probable cause" is an objective concept. An officer's belief, no matter how sincere, that she has sufficient cause to arrest a person or to conduct a search or seizure does not in itself constitute probable cause.[7] Moreover, an officer's lack of subjective belief that she has probable cause does not foreclose a finding to the contrary.[8]

On the other hand, the "person of reasonable caution" may take into account the specific experiences and expertise of the officer whose actions are under scrutiny. For example, an officer's specialized knowledge of the appearance or odor of a narcotic is relevant in determining whether an arrest based on that knowledge was valid.[9]

[C] "Probable Cause": Arrests versus Searches

The methodology for making a probable–cause determination is the same for arrests as it is for searches. However, the result need not be the same in a specific case: that is, an officer might have probable cause to arrest a person but not to search, or vice–versa.

For example, *O*, an officer, might have probable cause to believe that she will find contraband in *D*'s automobile, and yet lack probable cause to arrest *D*, because she may lack sufficient evidence that *D* is aware of the contraband. Conversely, *O* might possess probable cause to arrest *D* for manufacturing drugs, but if *D*'s arrest arises at *X*'s house, about which *O* has no evidence of drug production, she might lack probable cause to search *X*'s residence for drugs.

Furthermore, evidence that would justify a search is apt to become "stale" sooner than information that is used to justify an arrest. For example, information obtained on January 1 that a small quantity of drugs will be found in *D*'s bedroom might be insufficient to warrant a search one month later because the drugs might have been moved or consumed by then.

In contrast, if an officer has probable cause to arrest *D* for possession of drugs on January 1, the arrest will be valid a month later — the "probable cause" is still fresh — unless intervening information casts doubt on the trustworthiness of the earlier information. For example, "probable cause" might no longer exist if the officer subsequently learned that the informant who implicated *D* had a motive to lie.

[D] "Probable Cause": With or Without Warrants

A central feature of Fourth Amendment jurisprudence is that the constitutionally preferable arbiter of probable cause is a "neutral and detached magistrate" rather than a police officer "engaged in the often competitive enterprise of ferreting out crime."[10] Therefore, a police officer ordinarily should seek judicial authorization for a search or seizure.

---

[7] *See* Beck v. Ohio, 379 U.S. 89 (1964).
[8] Florida v. Royer, 460 U.S. 491, 507 (1983).
[9] *E.g.*, Johnson v. United States, 333 U.S. 10 (1948).
[10] *Id.* at 13–14.

Even in cases in which the police are justified in acting without prior judicial authorization, "probable cause" usually is required. If an officer acts without a warrant, a court that is subsequently called on to determine whether her actions were reasonable must determine whether the officer had probable cause at the time of the Fourth Amendment activity — *i.e.*, whether a magistrate *would* have issued a warrant if one had been sought.

Because warrants are constitutionally preferred, the Supreme Court has indicated that Fourth Amendment requirements "surely cannot be less stringent"[11] in cases of warrantless conduct than when an officer seeks prior judicial approval. Therefore, "[i]n doubtful or marginal cases," a search under warrant might be upheld where without one it would not be.[12]

[E] "Probable Cause": Search For and Seize What?

[1] "Mere Evidence" Rule

Originally, a search was unjustifiable unless there was probable cause to believe that it would result in the seizure of one of three types of evidence: (a) a "fruit" of a crime (*e.g.*, the money obtained in a robbery); (b) an instrumentality of a crime (*e.g.*, the gun used to commit a robbery); or (c) contraband (*e.g.*, narcotics). So–called "mere evidence," that is, items that have only evidentiary value in the apprehension or conviction of a person for a criminal offense, could not be seized.[13]

The so–called "mere evidence rule" was founded on property–rights concepts consistent with the original understanding of the Fourth Amendment. The justification of the rule was that the government could search for and seize property only if it asserted an interest in the property superior to that of the person from whom it would be taken. Such a superior right was thought to exist in relation to fruits, instrumentalities, and contraband, but not as to "mere evidence."

The superior–interest theory was largely a fiction, but it was based on the following assumptions. In the case of fruits, the government, representing a private complainant, had a greater interest in the stolen items than did the alleged criminal. Regarding contraband, the government had a superior property right to it because a private person has no right whatsoever to possess such property. In the case of a criminal instrumentality, the property was considered forfeited to the government because of its use in criminal activities. Regarding evidence of crime, however, no justification existed for subordinating the individual's property rights to the government.

[2] Abolition of the "Mere Evidence" Rule

The mere–evidence rule was abolished by the Supreme Court in *Warden v. Hayden*.[14] Police officers may now seize "mere evidence," as well as fruits, instrumentalities, and contraband, as long as there is a "nexus" between the

---

[11] Wong Sun v. United States, 371 U.S. 471, 479 (1963).
[12] United States v. Ventresca, 380 U.S. 102, 106–07 (1965).
[13] Gouled v. United States, 255 U.S. 298 (1921).
[14] 387 U.S. 294 (1967).

evidence and criminal activity. According to *Hayden*, this nexus exists if there is probable cause "to believe that the evidence sought will aid in a particular apprehension or conviction."[15]

The Supreme Court in *Hayden* abolished the mere–evidence rule because it believed that the doctrine was indefensible in light of modern Fourth Amendment privacy principles. It concluded that a search for evidence disturbs privacy no more than one directed at fruits, instrumentalities, or contraband because, in all of these cases, a magistrate can intervene, "and the requirements of probable cause and specificity [in the warrant] can be preserved intact."

The Court also concluded that nothing in the nature of property seized as "mere evidence" is more private than other forms of property. Indeed, the same item that constitutes evidence in one case might be a fruit or instrumentality in another. For example, a diary might be seized in one case because it includes evidence that ties the defendant to the crime, but a diary might also be a fruit of a crime.[16]

In general, the reasoning of *Hayden* is unexceptionable. Nonetheless, abolition of the mere–evidence rule is not without some significant privacy repercussions. First, those who possess the fruits of a crime, criminal instrumentalities, or contraband usually are guilty of wrongdoing. Innocent persons, however, may unwittingly come into possession of evidence that relates to a criminal investigation. As a practical matter, therefore, *Hayden* enlarges the class of persons who may be subjected to searches.[17]

Second, although *Hayden* involved the seizure of clothing rather than of papers that might provide evidence of a crime, the implication of the case is that private papers are no longer immune from search and seizure as "mere evidence." Yet, as the Supreme Court has acknowledged, there are "grave dangers inherent in executing a warrant authorizing the search and seizure of a person's papers that are not necessarily present in executing a warrant for physical objects whose relevance is more easily ascertainable."[18]

The special problem is that in searching for evidentiary papers, the police must often examine innocent–but–private documents in order to find the incriminating items. Despite this danger, the Supreme Court has approved the seizure of business records as long as the police seek to minimize unwarranted intrusions on privacy,[19] and there is no reason to believe that it will devise any greater protections for more personal papers, such as diaries and letters.[20]

---

[15] Some jurisdictions also provide for warrants to be issued to search for and seize any "person . . . who is unlawfully restrained." *E.g.*, FRCP 41(b). This provision, based on the American Law Institute's Model Code of Pre–Arraignment Procedure § 210.3(1)(d) (Proposed Official Draft, 1975), is justified on the ground that the person to be seized, such as a kidnap victim, is evidence of a crime.

[16] *E.g.*, Matthews v. Correa, 135 F.2d 534 (4th Cir. 1943).

[17] *See* Zurcher v. Stanford Daily, 436 U.S. 547, *reh'g denied*, 439 U.S. 885 (1978) (in which the police obtained a warrant to search the files of a newspaper organization for photographs revealing the identity of persons who attacked police officers during a demonstration).

[18] Andresen v. Maryland, 427 U.S. 463, 482 n.11 (1976).

[19] *Id.*

[20] One possible protection, other than to prohibit seizure of private papers as "mere evidence," would be to require a heightened level of probable cause. *See* Grano, *Perplexing*

§ 43 How Probable Is "Probable Cause"?[21]

[A] Governing Law

Suppose that *O*, a police officer, observes *A* and *B* standing over *V*'s body. She has reason to believe, nearing one hundred percent certainty, that *A* or *B*, but not both, murdered *V*; the odds, however, are equal as to which one is guilty.[22] May *O* constitutionally arrest both suspects?[23] Is the answer different if three, rather than two, suspects are at the scene, and only one is guilty?

The question raised is: How probable is "probable cause"? Put another way: How certain must the person of reasonable caution be before she arrests a suspect or conducts a search and seizure, or before a magistrate authorizes such activity?

The Supreme Court has never quantified "probable cause." To the contrary, in its fullest explication of the matter,[24] the justices described probable cause as a "fluid concept" that turns on "assessment of probabilities in particular factual contexts" and, therefore, is "not readily, or even usefully, reduced" to a mathematical formula. The Court used phrases such as "fair probability" and "substantial basis" to articulate the quantum of evidence necessary to prove "probable cause."

While the Court eschews a precise quantification of "probable cause," this much is evident: less evidence is required to justify an arrest or search than to convict a person at trial, but more is required than "bare" or "mere" or even "reasonable suspicion."[25] More specifically, the Court has stated that the "probable cause" standard does not "demand any showing that such a belief be correct or more likely true than false."[26] In other words, "probable cause" involves less than a fifty–percent–plus likelihood of accuracy.

Consequently, in the hypothetical described above, O has "probable cause" to arrest *A* and *B* for murder, although she knows that one of the suspects is innocent.[27] On the other hand, Supreme Court dictum implies that the arrest of

---

Questions About Three Basic Fourth Amendment Issues: Fourth Amendment Activity, Probable Cause, and the Warrant Requirement, 69 J. Crim. L. & Crimin. 425, 452 (1978).

[21] *See generally* Grano, *Probable Cause and Common Sense: A Reply to the Critics of Illinois v. Gates*, 17 U. Mich. J.L. Ref. 465 (1984).

[22] If it were reasonable for *O* to believe that *A* and *B* acted jointly, the problem raised in the text would disappear.

[23] This hypothetical is based on Restatement (Second) of Torts, § 119, illus. 2 (1965), *quoted in* Model Code, n. 15 *supra*, § 120 commentary at 295.

[24] *See* Illinois v. Gates, 462 U.S. 213, *reh'g denied*, 463 U.S. 1237 (1983).

[25] *Brinegar*, 338 U.S. at 175 ("bare suspicion"); Mallory v. United States 354 U.S. 449, 454 (1957) ("mere suspicion"). "Reasonable suspicion" is a term of art that justifies certain less–intrusive searches and seizures. *See* chapter 18 *infra*.

[26] Texas v. Brown, 460 U.S. 730, 742 (1983); *see also* Illinois v. Rodriguez, 110 S.Ct. 2793, 2799 (1990) ("[W]hat is generally demanded of the many factual determinations that must regularly be made by agents of the government . . . is not that they always be correct, but that they always be reasonable.").

[27] *See Gates*, 462 U.S. at 235 (citing with approval Model Code, n. 15 *supra*, § 120, which framed the hypothetical and recommended a finding of "reasonable cause" under the circumstances).

three persons, only one of whom is guilty, is unconstitutional for want of probable cause.[28]

[B] Reflections on the Issue

Precedent and dictum aside, is the Court justified in permitting arrests and searches[29] on less than a preponderance of the evidence? One quite plausible answer is, "It depends." That is, "probable cause" might be determined on a sliding scale, in which the degree of suspicion required would depend on the individual and societal interests implicated in the specific case.

Sliding–scale "probable cause," a doctrine not explicitly authorized by the Supreme Court, is discussed in § 48 of this chapter. However, even if the degree of "probable cause" were to vary depending on the circumstances involved, the question at hand would remain: How probable should "probable cause" be in the average, unexceptional case?

Ideally, problems such as that hypothesized in part [A] would not occur. For example, the officer might be able to avoid the dilemma by temporarily detaining both suspects rather than arresting them, and questioning them long enough to determine which person is more likely guilty. But, even if she were to do so, the suspects might refuse to answer her questions, or their answers might not assist her to focus suspicion on one of them, in which case the officer would be back where she started.

The question that ultimately must be answered — one that does not provide an easy or uncontroversial solution — is whether it is better that both persons, one of whom is a murderer, go free at least temporarily, than that she arrest them both, one of whom is innocent, and seek to obtain post–arrest evidence that would incriminate one or exculpate the other.

The conclusion that O, the officer in the hypothetical, may arrest two persons for a crime knowing that one of them is innocent, is troubling, but arguably is correct. To permit O to arrest both suspects provides her and society needed leeway without "leav[ing] law–abiding citizens at the mercy of the officers' whim or caprice."[30] An officer who acts on a fifty percent probability that the person arrested is a guilty party arguably has conducted a "reasonable" seizure (an arrest is a "seizure" of a person), at least if the alternative is to arrest neither suspect, and thus knowingly release a murderer.[31]

Even if an arrest or search based on a fifty percent likelihood of accuracy is constitutionally reasonable, this only shifts the debate to the more difficult question: How improbable are we willing to let "probable cause" be? That is, how much lower are we prepared to reduce the odds of accuracy before we conclude

---

[28] *See* Mallory v. United States, 354 U.S. at 456 (condemning "arrests at large," in which one of three suspects was arrested in order to interrogate him).

[29] Although the discussion in the text focuses on arrests, the issue applies to searches. For example, if an officer has reason to believe that a suspect is hiding in one of two (or three) houses, should she be permitted to search both (or all three) houses?

[30] *Brinegar*, 338 U.S. at 176.

[31] Of course, the officer has another alternative: arrest one of the two suspects, perhaps by flipping a coin, but is this preferable?

that the interest in protecting the community must give way to the Fourth Amendment interest in safeguarding citizens from rash and unreasonable interferences with privacy?

One commentator, Professor Joseph Grano, would go at least as far as to say that an officer who suspects ten persons of a crime but has no way of distinguishing among them should be permitted in some circumstances to arrest all ten and then seek evidence to clear the nine innocent persons.[32] To Grano, focusing exclusively on the ten percent accuracy figure "distorts our perspective." He would concentrate on the fact that the police successfully narrowed their investigation "from the universe of all possible suspects, which may include much of the population, to ten individuals."

What about the nine innocent persons? Why are they not justified in demanding that the police narrow their investigation further before they are arrested? Professor Grano's answer is that we should construct a "community model" of criminal justice that is premised on the view that individuals cannot act "oblivious to the community's needs." According to this model, even in a society "traditionally and properly dedicated to individual rights," the community may legitimately demand that the nine innocent persons sacrifice "some liberty or privacy in order to unmask the offender."

All models of criminal justice are controversial in their value judgments. However, Grano's view of the proper balance between the individual and society — at least, in a system that he concedes is properly dedicated to individual rights — is one that many people would reject on the ground that it unduly minimizes the interests of the nine innocent persons arrested. Their arrests entail more than "some" liberty and privacy loss: an arrest (here, multiplied times nine innocent persons) results in loss of liberty, stigmatization, possible humiliation (such as when the arrestee is compelled to undergo a strip search prior to incarceration), any trauma that might occur in the jails, and collateral harm, such as legal fees, possible loss of employment, and a permanent arrest record.

In any case, how far might Professor Grano's reasoning take us? Suppose that it could statistically be proved that during a specified range of hours at night, in a particular urban area, ten percent of all males on the street between the ages of sixteen and twenty–five are in possession of illegal narcotics.[33] During the hours and in the geographical region specified, may O, an officer, arrest every male in the appropriate age bracket, because the chance of finding a guilty person is ten percent?

Grano would not permit such arrests, distinguishing them from the first case. In the original hypothetical the police developed cause to suspect ten specific individuals of a crime; in the present case no individualized suspicion is involved. The society may require personal sacrifice in the former case, Grano argues, but

---

[32] See Grano, n. 21 supra, at 496–97. Apparently, he would allow the police to hold the suspects until their first appearance before a magistrate, which usually occurs within a day after arrest, except on weekends, see § 3[C][3] supra, or until a preliminary hearing is conducted, usually within two weeks after the first appearance, at which time the prosecutor would be required to meet a higher standard of proof.

[33] See Alschuler, Bright Line Fever and the Fourth Amendment, 45 U. Pitt. L. Rev. 227, 246 (1984).

not "when no cause whatsoever exists to believe that the individual, as opposed to anyone else, is involved with crime."[34]

But why should that be the case? If it is fair to demand sacrifice by innocent persons in the first example, why is it not fair in the second? His assertion to that effect hardly makes his conclusion inevitable. As with any other normative judgment, once we are prepared to say that the community has a right to demand that the nine innocent people sacrifice their liberty for awhile in order to permit the police to attempt to discover the guilty tenth person, it is a very small step to demand that nine innocent urban youths give up some liberty and privacy in order to attack the scourge of narcotics in their community. If we are troubled by the arrests in the second case — as we should be — we ought to be concerned with the first ones as well.

§ 44 Determining "Probable Cause": Overview

[A] Types of Information: In General

When a magistrate determines whether probable cause exists to arrest a person or to conduct a search, she must ask herself two questions: (1) Is the information being tendered sufficiently trustworthy to be considered?; and (2) If it is, is the quantum of evidence proffered sufficient to constitute probable cause? The latter question was considered in the immediately preceding chapter section. The first question is the subject of this section and the two that follow.

In general, an officer might furnish the magistrate with two types of information when she applies for a warrant: (1) "direct information," *i.e.*, information she secured by personal observation; and (2) "hearsay information," *i.e.*, information she received from another person who is not available for questioning by the magistrate. Because the officer provides her information under oath by affidavit, she is commonly described in probable–cause nomenclature as the "affiant," whereas the person whose hearsay information is tendered in the affidavit is described as the "informant."

Regarding hearsay, although the Supreme Court once stated that a warrant "may issue only upon evidence which would be competent in the trial,"[35] it is now clear that for purposes of determining "probable cause" a magistrate may consider hearsay, even if it is inadmissible at trial, as long as it is reasonably trustworthy.[36]

Moreover, the informant's identity need not be disclosed to the magistrate in the warrant application process unless the magistrate doubts the credibility of the affiant regarding the hearsay.[37] For example, disclosure may be compelled if the magistrate has reason to believe that the affiant lied regarding the informant's existence or misstated the nature of the information received.[38]

---

[34] Grano, n. 21 *supra*, at 498.

[35] Grau v. United States, 287 U.S. 124, 128 (1932).

[36] *Brinegar*, 338 U.S. at 173–74.

[37] *See* McCray v. Illinois, 386 U.S. 300, *reh'g denied*, 386 U.S. 1042 (1967).

[38] *See* People v. Thomas, 174 Mich. App. 411, 436 N.W.2d 687 (1989).

[B] "Bald and Unilluminating" Assertions

"Bald and unilluminating assertions of suspicion" are entitled to no weight in the probable–cause determination.[39] For example, a magistrate may not consider an affiant's assertion that she "has cause to suspect and does believe" that seizable articles will be found in a particular place, unless the affiant provides the reasons for her belief.[40] Similarly, the magistrate should give no weight to an unsupported claim by the affiant that she has information that *D* "is known [to others] as a gambler."[41]

This rule applies because it is the magistrate rather than the officer who should determine whether probable cause exists. If a magistrate were to consider wholly conclusory statements made in an affidavit, she "would be serving simply as the rubber stamp of the source's conclusion."[42]

[C] Direct Information

Unless a magistrate has reason to believe that the affiant has committed perjury or recklessly misstated the truth,[43] she may consider all direct information (as distinguished from "bald and unilluminating" assertions) provided by the affiant. The affiant's information is considered reasonably trustworthy because the oath she takes affirms her honesty, and the fact that the information was personally observed by her attests to the basis of her knowledge.[44]

Of course, the fact that the magistrate is allowed to consider direct information provided by the affiant does not mean that there is probable cause to issue a warrant based on it. The magistrate must still determine whether the information, alone or in conjunction with any trustworthy hearsay information that is tendered, satisfies the probable–cause standard.[45]

[D] Hearsay ("Informant") Information

An informant's assertions are not always trustworthy. The difficulty with hearsay is not just that it is second–hand in nature, but that it often comes from untrustworthy sources. As one commentator has observed, the ordinary police informant is not a former Boy Scout and present–day prince of the church.[46] Typically, an informant is one involved in criminal activities, perhaps as a small–time drug pusher or as a middle– or even high–level member of an organized crime syndicate, and, therefore, not from a trustworthy milieu.[47]

---

[39] Nathanson v. United States, 290 U.S. 41 (1933); Spinelli v. United States, 393 U.S. 410 (1969); Illinois v. Gates, 462 U.S. at 239 (reaffirming *Nathanson*).

[40] Nathanson v. United States, 290 U.S. 41 (1933).

[41] *Spinelli*, 393 U.S. 410 (1969).

[42] Moylan, *Illinois v. Gates: What It Did and What It Did Not Do*, 20 Crim. L. Bull. 93, 101 (1984).

[43] *See* § 52 *infra*.

[44] *Spinelli*, 393 U.S. at 423 (White, J., concurring).

[45] If the direct evidence alone constitutes probable cause, hearsay information is "redundant and can simply be factored out." Moylan, n. 42 *supra*, at 101.

[46] *See* Moylan, *Hearsay and Probable Cause: An Aguilar and Spinelli Primer*, 25 Mercer L. Rev. 741, 758 (1974).

[47] When the victim of the crime or an eyewitness to it serves as an informant, she is considered reasonably trustworthy. *See* n. 58 *infra*.

Frequently, as well, the tipster provides the information in consideration for some benefit from the police or the prosecutor, which calls into question her motives.[48]

Not only are some informants untrustworthy by nature, but the source of *their* information varies. In some cases, the informant's "knowledge" of the facts that she relates to the officer arises from first–hand participation in the criminal activities reported, but in other cases she may be relating no more than a vague rumor that she has heard on the streets.

The difficult question that must be answered in probable–cause determinations, then, is this: Under what circumstances is information obtained from an informant sufficiently trustworthy to justify its consideration?

The Supreme Court has wrestled mightily with this question. At one time it applied the so–called "*Aguilar* two–pronged test." In 1983, it abandoned that test in favor of the *Gates* "totality–of–the–circumstances test." However, the full import of the prevailing *Gates* test cannot be appreciated without an understanding of the *Aguilar* test. The old and new tests are discussed in the two sections that follow.

§ 45 The *Aguilar* Two-Pronged Test[49]

[A] In General

The two–pronged test for determining the trustworthiness of hearsay ("informant") information was stated in *Aguilar v. Texas*,[50] a case in which the validity of a warrant to search for drugs was at issue:

> Although an affidavit may be based on hearsay information and need not reflect the direct personal observations of the affiant, . . . the magistrate must be informed of some of the underlying circumstances from which the informant concluded that the narcotics were where he claimed they were, and some of the underlying circumstances from which the officer concluded that the informant . . . was "credible" or his information "reliable."

This statement, as explained in *Spinelli v. United States*,[51] suggests two inquiries regarding hearsay evidence: (1) "How did the informant get the information?"; and (2) "Why should I [the magistrate] believe this person?" These two questions represent the two prongs of *Aguilar*: (1) the *basis of knowledge* prong; and (2) the *veracity* prong, of which there are two alternative spurs, the "credibility-of-the-informant spur" and the "reliability-of-the-information spur."[52]

Under *Aguilar*, if both prongs of the test are satisfied, the informant's assertions are sufficiently trustworthy to be considered by the magistrate in her

---

[48] *E.g.*, the police might agree not to bring charges against the informant for her own criminal activities, or they may pay her for her information, which she may then use to finance a drug or alcohol habit.

[49] *See generally* LaFave, *Probable Cause From Informants: The Effects of Murphy's Law on Fourth Amendment Adjudication*, 1977 U. Ill. L.F. 1; Moylan, n. 46 *supra*.

[50] 378 U.S. 108 (1964).

[51] 393 U.S. 410 (1969)

[52] Moylan, n. 46 *supra*, at 755.

probable–cause determination. If either of the prongs is lacking, however, the hearsay evidence standing alone is insufficiently trustworthy to be considered. Its trustworthiness, however, may be "resuscitated" by at least partial corroboration of the informant's tip.

[B] Basis-of-Knowledge Prong

[1] In General

The point of the basis–of–knowledge prong — "How did the informant get the information?" — is that the tipster might be passing along information based on her personal knowledge, which is good, but it is also possible that she is reporting nothing more reliable than "an offhand remark heard at a neighborhood bar."[53]

This *Aguilar* prong is satisfied if the informant explicitly states that she personally observed the reported facts. For example, the basis–of–knowledge is proved if *I*, the informant, tells *O*, the officer–affiant, that "*D* is using her house to sell drugs. *I know this because I bought drugs from her at her house yesterday*." The italicized words demonstrate *I*'s first–hand knowledge.[54]

On the other hand, suppose that *I* tells *O*, "A friend of mine told me that *D* is selling drugs in her house." Here, *I* has her own informant. In that case, under *Aguilar*, the two–pronged test must be applied one step further down the hearsay chain, and the magistrate must ascertain how *I*'s informant got *her* information, and how reliable *that* informant is.

[2] "Self-Verifying Detail"

If an informant does not indicate how she obtained her information and the officer fails to question her regarding this omission, the officer might be unable to satisfy the magistrate's need under *Aguilar* for sufficient underlying information to ascertain the basis of the informant's knowledge. For example, if *I* tells *O* only that "*D* is using her house to sell drugs," neither *O* nor the magistrate can ascertain the basis of *I*'s knowledge. Without clarification, the basis–of–knowledge prong is not met.

In some circumstances, however, the basis–of–knowledge prong may be proved indirectly on the basis of what has been described as "self–verifying detail,"[55] of which the facts in *Draper v. United States.*[56] are said to "provide a suitable benchmark."[57]

In *Draper*, *I*, without stating how he obtained his information, told police that *D* had gone to Chicago on a specified date by train, that he would return by train with three ounces of heroin on one of two particular dates, that he would be wearing particularly described clothing, that he would carry a tan zipper bag, and that he walked "habitually fast."

---

[53] *Spinelli*, 393 U.S. at 417.

[54] Of course, the informant could be lying, but this goes to the issue of veracity, the other prong.

[55] Moylan, n. 46 *supra*, at 749.

[56] 358 U.S. 307 (1959).

[57] *Spinelli*, 393 U.S. at 416.

The Supreme Court in *Draper* considered *I*'s information trustworthy. *Spinelli* explained *Draper*, which was a pre–*Aguilar* decision, this way: "the tip describe[d] the accused's criminal activity in sufficient detail that the magistrate may know that he is relying on something more substantial than a casual rumor . . . or an accusation based merely on an individual's general reputation." In other words, *I*'s information was so rich in detail that it was reasonable to conclude that he obtained the information first hand.

This reasoning is not entirely persuasive. Even if *I* did not make up the story (a veracity issue), the detail demonstrates at most that *someone* apparently had first–hand knowledge of *D*'s plans. *I* might have been passing along the detailed information of *X*, a third person, whose own veracity would then be at issue. In light of the importance of the warrant procedure, perhaps a magistrate should not have assumed on an ambiguous record that *I* was reporting first–hand information.

[C] Veracity Prong

Even if an informant states that her information was obtained first hand, she may be lying or her information–gathering skills might be poor. For these reasons, evidence is required to demonstrate either that I is a credible person (the credibility spur of the veracity prong) or, if that cannot be shown, that her information in the present case is reliable (the reliability spur).[58]

The Supreme Court has provided little guidance regarding how the affiant should demonstrate an informant's veracity. Lower federal and state courts have exercised primary responsibility to fashion an answer.[59] *Aguilar* itself states only that reliability cannot be proved on the ground of a mere assertion by the affiant that the informant is reliable.

Typically, an affiant proves the informant's veracity by providing the magistrate with the informant's "track record" or "batting average." For example, an assertion that the informant's prior tips have led to arrests culminating in convictions is an especially suitable way to prove *I*'s credibility.[60] Of course, if the affiant informs the magistrate regarding the tipster's successes, she should also report any failures. That is the only way to measure the informant's batting average.

The veracity prong may also be satisfied through the reliability–of–the–information spur. This approach is apt to be fruitful in circumstances in which the informant has a questionable (or no) track record. A statement by *I* that constitutes a declaration against her penal interest may be adequate under this spur.

---

[58] Courts do not carefully attend to the veracity prong if the informant was the victim of the offense or an ordinary citizen who witnessed the crime. Although such persons are "informants" (they are sometimes called "citizen–informers" in an effort to distinguish them from the unsavory characters who ordinarily provide tips), courts assume their reliability absent special circumstances. Arguably, their veracity is reasonably assured by the fact that by coming forward they open themselves up to prosecution for providing false information.

[59] *See generally* 1 W. LaFave, at § 3.3(b).

[60] *See* McCray v. Illinois, 386 U.S. 300, *reh'g denied*, 386 U.S. 1042 (1967).

For example, when an affiant reports that the informant "has personal knowledge of and has purchased illicit whisky from within the residence described, for a period of more than two years, and most recently within the past two weeks,"[61] this statement might be sufficient to satisfy both prongs, as it states the basis of the informant's knowledge, and the claim constitutes an admission of a crime by the tipster, which tends to make the other assertions more believable.

[D] Corroboration

A tipster's information that would not otherwise satisfy the two–pronged *Aguilar* test may be considered by a magistrate if the affiant or other officers verify aspects of the informant's facts, as long as it can "fairly be said that the [corroborated] tip . . . is as trustworthy as a tip which would pass *Aguilar*'s test without independent corroboration."[62]

Draper again provides a benchmark. In that case, after *I* provided the detailed information regarding *D*'s activities, the police corroborated some of *I*'s assertions, including *D*'s presence at the train station on one of the dates predicted, his clothing, and his fast gait. As one commentator put it, the verification in this case "is simply the present–tense equivalent of a good past track record."[63]

In contrast, in *Spinelli* the police "corroborated" an informant's claim that *D* was a gambler using a particular residence for bookmaking by learning independently that the residence had two telephone numbers. The corroboration of this "one small detail" was deemed insufficient.

§ 46   The *Gates* "Totality of the Circumstances" Test[64]

[A] Nature of the Test

In *Illinois v. Gates*,[65] the police received an anonymous letter that accused a married couple of selling drugs at a specified address. The letter described in detail the couple's alleged *modus operandi*, including the fact that they usually bought drugs in Florida and brought them to Illinois by car. The letter writer also stated that on a specific date the wife would drive to Florida, the husband would fly down, and that he would drive back with a large quantity of drugs in the trunk. The police verified some of the facts alleged in the letter, including the Florida trip, and secured a warrant to search the suspects' automobile and home.

---

[61] *See* United States v. Harris, 403 U.S. 573 (1971).

[62] *Spinelli*, 393 U.S. at 415.

[63] Moylan, n. 42 *supra*, at 101.

[64] *See generally* 1 W. LaFave, at § 3.3; Grano, n. 21 *supra*; Hanson, *The Aftermath of Illinois v. Gates and United States v. Leon: A Comprehensive Evaluation of Their Impact Upon the Litigation of Search Warrant Validity*, 15 Western State U.L.Rev. 393 (1988); Kamisar, *Gates, "Probable Cause," "Good Faith," and Beyond*, 69 Iowa L. Rev. 551 (1984); Moylan, n. 42 *supra*.

[65] 462 U.S. 213, *reh'g denied*, 463 U.S. 1237 (1983).

The anonymous tip standing alone did not meet either prong of the *Aguilar* standard,[66] although arguably the police department's corroboration was sufficient to permit a finding of probable cause under *Aguilar*. Nonetheless, Justice Rehnquist, writing for five justices, abandoned *Aguilar* and what he described as "the elaborate set of legal rules" that developed from it, and in its place substituted "the totality–of–the–circumstances analysis that traditionally has informed probable–cause determinations."

Under *Gates*, a magistrate must conduct a "balanced assessment of the relative weights of all the various indicia of reliability (and unreliability) attending an informant's tip." The factors enunciated in *Aguilar* — basis–of–knowledge and veracity — remain "highly relevant" in determining the value of an informant's tip. However, the prongs are no longer treated as separate, independent requirements. Now, the strength of one prong or some other indicia of reliability may compensate for weakness in the other prong.

The Court justified the abandonment of *Aguilar* on the ground that probable cause is a "fluid," nontechnical, common sense conception, based on "the factual and practical considerations of everyday life on which reasonable and prudent men, not legal technicians, act." According to *Gates*, "probable cause" is not "reduc[ible] to a neat set of legal rules," such as developed under *Aguilar*.

Justice Rehnquist also defended the change on the ground that the earlier test's rigidity seriously impeded effective law enforcement. He also contended that *Aguilar*'s inflexibility tempted police officers to avoid the warrant process entirely, thereby reducing the desired influence of magistrates in the search–and–seizure process.[67]

[B] The Practical Effect of *Gates*

Gates warns magistrates to avoid a "grudging or negative attitude toward warrants," and to interpret warrant applications in a non–technical, common sense fashion. Presumably, therefore, more warrant applications should be granted under *Gates* than occurred under *Aguilar*'s "rigid" requirements.

Has this occurred? One study of lower court cases in the first five years following *Gates* suggests that its impact has not been substantial.[68] Among the reasons for this appear to be that many "*Gates* cases" would also have satisfied the *Aguilar* test, some courts tended to interpret *Aguilar* loosely even before *Gates*, and some courts continue to apply *Aguilar* under their own state constitutions.[69]

---

[66] The letter writer was unknown to the police, so there was no way to judge his or her veracity. The Court also stated that the letter gave "absolutely no indication of the basis for the writer's predictions regarding the criminal activities."

[67] Does this mean that *Gates* does not apply if the officer does *not* seek a warrant, but only seeks to defend her probable–cause determination after the fact? Lower courts have consistently answered the question in the negative. *E.g.*, United States v. Figueroa, 818 F.2d 1020 (1st Cir. 1987); United States v. Gonzalez, 835 F.2d 449 (2d Cir. 1987); United States v. Love, 767 F.2d 1052 (4th Cir. 1985), *cert. denied*, Love v. United States, 474 U.S. 1081 (1986); State v. Espinosa–Gamez, 139 Ariz. 415, 678 P.2d 1379 (1984); People v. Mitchell, 123 Ill.App.3d 868, 79 Ill.Dec. 310, 463 N.E.2d 864 (1984); Malcolm v. State, 314 Md. 221, 550 A.2d 670 (1988).

[68] Hanson, n. 64 *supra*, at 396–97.

[69] On the latter possibility, *see* n. 72 *infra*.

Gates's impact should also be seen at the appellate stage, in the form of fewer reversals of magistrates' determinations. According to *Gates*, a magistrate's decision regarding probable cause is entitled to great deference. Furthermore, an appellate court cannot easily overturn a magistrate's finding on the basis of precedent because, as *Gates* observed, "[t]here are so many variables in the probable cause equation [under the totality–of–the–circumstances test] that one determination will seldom be a useful 'precedent' for another."

[C] Criticism of *Gates*

[1] Is the "Message" of *Gates* a Good One?

Gates has been criticized by many,[70] but not all,[71] commentators and by some courts.[72] Some critics of *Gates* are troubled by what they perceive to be its implicit message to magistrates that they can afford to be lenient in their probable–cause determinations. The result, they fear, will be even more cursory oversight of warrant applications than existed prior to *Gates*.[73]

[2] Can One Prong Logically Compensate for Another?

Critics of *Gates* question the essence of the opinion, which is that the two–pronged *Aguilar* test "relied too much on logic and not enough on experience to decide what the reasonably cautious police officer would and should do under the circumstances."[74]

Specifically, many critics disagree with *Gates* that the strength of one prong can logically compensate for the weakness of the other. In this context, consider two examples provided by Justice Rehnquist in support of his view that either prong of *Aguilar* may compensate for the other.

First, according to Justice Rehnquist, if *I*, an informant, is "known for the unusual reliability of his predictions . . . his failure, in a particular case, to thoroughly set forth the basis of his knowledge surely should not serve as an absolute bar to a finding of probable cause based on his tip." Great strength in the veracity prong, in other words, may make up for lack of evidence regarding the informant's basis of knowledge.

But, this conclusion is highly debatable. Consider that information reported to a magistrate by a pillar of the church, who obtained it from a pathological liar, is no more trustworthy than the liar whose information was filtered through the church member. Moreover, as Justice White argued in his concurring opinion in *Gates*, if Justice Rehnquist is correct in the view that the veracity of an informant may compensate for the lack of information regarding the tipster's basis of

---

[70] *E.g.*, 1 W. LaFave, at § 3.3; Kamisar, n. 64 *supra*.

[71] *E.g.*, Grano, n. 21 *supra*.

[72] As of 1990, at least eight states (Alaska, Connecticut, Massachusetts, Michigan, New York, Oregon, Tennessee, and Washington) had rejected *Gates* on the basis of a state statute or a judicial interpretation of the state constitution. *See* Hanson, n. 64 *supra*, at 439–44 (citations provided therein); *see also* State v. Jacumin, 778 S.W.2d 430 (Tenn. 1989).

[73] *See Gates*, 462 U.S. at 290 (Brennan, J., dissenting). Even before *Gates*, magistrates often failed to provide substantial oversight of warrant applications. *See* § 50 *infra*.

[74] Grano, n. 21 *supra*, at 469.

knowledge, then it follows that a similar conclusory assertion by an honest and experienced police officer should also be acceptable. Yet, the Supreme Court has repeatedly held that the unsupported assertions of an officer do not satisfy the probable–cause requirement.[75]

Defenders of *Gates* respond that if an informant has provided, for example, ten reliable reports in the past, but in the present case does not indicate how he obtained his information, "it may be reasonable to infer that he . . . does not report information unless it has been reliably obtained."[76]

Perhaps the defenders are correct, but in light of the constitutional interests at stake, it may be preferable for courts to require magistrates to question affiants carefully to determine the source of their information and, likewise, for officers to question their informants, so that magistrates later are not tempted to infer a reliable basis of knowledge that might not actually exist.

Whether one agrees with Justice Rehnquist or his critics on this matter, the *Gates* majority is probably wrong in its other assertion, namely, that strength in the basis–of–knowledge prong logically can make up for weakness in the informant's veracity. On this matter, Justice Rehnquist states: "[E]ven if we entertain some doubt as to an informant's motives, his explicit and detailed description of alleged wrongdoing, along with a statement that the event was observed firsthand, entitles the tip to greater weight than might otherwise be the case."

Even taking into consideration the soft language used — "entitles the tip to *greater* weight than *might* otherwise be the case" — Justice Rehnquist provides no case support whatsoever for a notion that one commentator has described as "bizarre."[77] A liar can just as easily provide specific non–existent "details" as she can give a more general statement. Indeed, it is probably reasonable to assume that the liar, to appear more credible, will be as specific as her creativity allows. If this criticism is fair, it follows that an informant's claims should not be considered by a magistrate unless the veracity prong is independently satisfied.

§ 47 Balancing Competing Interests: The *Camara* Principle[78]

The Fourth Amendment was once considered a "monolith."[79] That is, a "search" was an all–or–nothing matter: there were no degrees of searches. It was assumed as well that all searches required probable cause, and that "probable cause" had the same meaning in every context.

---

[75] *See* § 44[B] *supra.*

[76] Grano, n. 21 *supra*, at 513.

[77] 1 W. LaFave, § 3.3(a) at 622.

[78] *See generally* Bacigal, *The Fourth Amendment in Flux: The Rise and Fall of Probable Cause*, 1979 U. Ill. L.F. 763; LaFave, *Administrative Searches and the Fourth Amendment: The Camara and See Cases*, 1967 Sup. Ct. Rev. 1; Sundby, *A Return to Fourth Amendment Basics: Undoing the Mischief of Camara and Terry*, 72 Minn. L. Rev. 383 (1988).

[79] Amsterdam, at 388.

Such a monolith no longer exists, if it ever did. Not all searches require probable cause.[80] And, it is now fair to say in light of *Camara v. Municipal Court*[81] that "probable cause" is a "somewhat variable concept."[82]

At least in the context of so–called "administrative" searches, as distinguished from searches conducted in criminal investigations, "probable cause" exists, quite simply, if the search is "reasonable," and a search is "reasonable" if the administrative reasons for conducting it outweigh the individual's Fourth Amendment privacy interests.

In *Camara*, housing inspectors sought to conduct a routine annual administrative inspection of *D*'s apartment in order to ascertain whether the municipal housing code was being honored. The inspectors lacked suspicion of any criminal law or administrative code violation on *D*'s premises. Application of traditional "probable cause" standards, therefore, would have prevented their entry onto *D*'s premises without his consent, which he refused to grant. It would also have frustrated the enforcement of countless other administrative regulations.

The Supreme Court's response to this situation was to retain the Fourth Amendment warrant requirement in this case,[83] but to recognize a different kind of "probable cause" for issuance of a search warrant in the administrative–search area. In the latter case, the Court stated, the probable–cause standard must be "tested against the constitutional mandate of reasonableness." In turn, "there can be no ready test for determining reasonableness other than by balancing the need to search against the invasion which the search entails."

The Court balanced the competing interests. On the side of permitting housing–code inspections was the public's long acceptance of such programs, and the Court's realization that their effectiveness would be seriously threatened if inspectors could not readily enter personal premises in order to check for violations not visible from public vantage points. Weighed against this (according to *Camara*) was "a relatively limited invasion of the urban citizen's privacy," because such inspections "are neither personal in nature nor aimed at the discovery of evidence of crime."

Therefore, the Court concluded, "probable cause" exists to issue a warrant to inspect premises for administrative code violations as long as there are "reasonable legislative or administrative standards for conducting an area inspection [that] are satisfied with respect to a particular dwelling." In other words, unlike traditional "probable cause," which requires individualized suspicion that criminal evidence will be found in the area to be searched, administrative "probable cause" may be founded on the basis of general factors, such as passage of time since the last inspection, the nature of the building in question, and the condition of the entire area to be searched.

The significance of *Camara* in Fourth Amendment jurisprudence far exceeds its role in justifying administrative searches. By defining "probable cause" in terms

---

[80] *See, e.g.,* §§ 93–94, 106–108 *infra.*

[81] 387 U.S. 523 (1967).

[82] LaFave, *The Fourth Amendment Today: A Bicentennial Appraisal,* 32 Vill. L. Rev. 1061, 1070 (1987).

[83] Warrants are not required for all administrative searches. *See* § 104 *infra.*

of "reasonableness," *Camara* brought a balancing approach to the Fourth Amendment, albeit "through the portal of probable cause."[84] This balancing approach is now a part of traditional Fourth Amendment analysis in criminal investigations, even outside the realm of "probable cause."[85]

§ 48   "Probable Cause": A Sliding Scale?

[A]   *Is* There a Sliding Scale?

Camara v. Municipal Court[86] demonstrated that there are different *kinds* of "probable cause," one that applies to criminal investigations and another that is used in administrative search cases. But, are there also different *degrees* of "probable cause"? Is it the case that a greater — or lesser — quantum of evidence is required to satisfy the probable–cause standard in some cases than in others? Is there, in other words, a sliding scale of "probable cause"?

The Supreme Court has expressly rejected such a concept, preferring instead to retain the "single, familiar standard"[87] of probable cause. However, although it is unwilling to acknowledge different degrees of probable cause, it has developed an alternative sliding–scale approach to searches and seizures.

In the watershed case of *Terry v. Ohio*,[88] the Supreme Court held that searches and seizures that are less–than–ordinarily intrusive may be conducted on the basis of a lesser quantum of evidence than "probable cause." That lesser amount is generally termed "reasonable suspicion." Furthermore, in certain circumstances, where the intrusion on a person's privacy is slight, and the society's interest in permitting the Fourth Amendment activity is substantial, the police may act without any individualized suspicion whatsoever.[89]

Does the sliding–scale slide in the other direction? Do *more*–than–ordinarily intrusive searches and seizures require a quantum of evidence greater than probable cause? Logic, if not the laws of gravity, would suggest that they should, but the Supreme Court, although given various opportunities to do so, has never acknowledged such a concept.

For example, in *Zurcher v. Stanford Daily*,[90] the Court justified the search of a newspaper office for photographic evidence of a crime on the basis of ordinary probable cause, although heightened probable cause might have been required on either of two grounds: that the search was of the premises of persons not personally suspected of crime;[91] or that the police conduct threatened First Amendment values.[92]

---

[84] Sundby, n. 78 *supra*, at 399.
[85] *See* chapter 18 *infra*.
[86] 387 U.S. 523 (1967). *See* § 47 *supra*.
[87] Dunaway v. New York, 442 U.S. 200, 213 (1979).
[88] 392 U.S. 1 (1968). *See generally* chapter 18 *infra*.
[89] Michigan Dept. of State Police v. Sitz, 110 S.Ct. 2481 (1990). *See* § 102 *infra*.
[90] 436 U.S. 547 (1978).
[91] *Id.* at 577 (Stevens, J., dissenting).
[92] Grano, n. 20 *supra*, at 450–52; *see also* New York v. P.J. Video, Inc., 475 U.S. 868 (1986) (providing that a warrant application authorizing the seizure of materials presump-

Similarly, the Supreme Court does not require the police to have heightened probable cause before they conduct a surgical intrusion beneath a person's skin. For example, in *Schmerber v. California*,[93] at the direction of a police officer, a physician extracted blood from a suspect to test for alcohol content. This intrusion "implicated . . . [the] most personal and deep–rooted expectations of privacy."[94] Yet, the Court held only that the intrusion required "a clear indication," rather than "mere chance," that the evidence would be found. The precise meaning of the phrase "clear indication" is in doubt, but subsequent cases suggest that bodily intrusions do not require more than probable cause, and might even require less, in some circumstances.[95]

[B] *Should* There Be a Sliding Scale?

As indicated in the last subsection, although the Supreme Court has not expressly implemented a sliding–scale of "probable cause," it has developed a downward–directed sliding–scale of "reasonable" searches and seizures, *i.e.*, those that require probable cause, and those that require less than probable cause ("reasonable suspicion" or no individualized suspicion).

The lingering question is: Should the Court expressly recognize a sliding–scale of "probable cause" — presumably, one that slides in *both* directions — either in conjunction with the standards now in existence or in their place?

Justice Jackson once advocated a sliding–scale view of probable cause.[96] He conceded, for example, that he would "strive hard" to justify a roadblock around a neighborhood in which all outgoing automobiles were searched if its purpose was to prevent a kidnapper from leaving with his victim, but that he would not justify the same conduct, based on the same information, in order "to salvage a few bottles of bourbon and catch a bootlegger."

Or, consider the case in which the police have reason to believe that a bomb is set to explode in a locker in a busy airport.[97] Although the odds might be small that the bomb will be found in any particular locker, it is intuitively appealing to permit the police to conduct warrantless searches of each locker until the bomb is found, even though we would not permit searches of the same lockers, based

---

tively protected by the First Amendment is evaluated by traditional standards of "probable cause").

[93] 384 U.S. 757 (1966).

[94] Winston v. Lee, 470 U.S. 753, 760 (1985).

[95] *Compare id.*, (in which the Court stated that *Schmerber* "noted the importance of probable cause") *with* United States v. Montoya de Hernandez, 473 U.S. 531 (1985) (in which the Court observed that the words "clear indication" in *Schmerber* "were used to indicate the necessity for particularized suspicion that the evidence sought might be found within the body of the individual.").

The Court has indicated that a "more substantial justification" is required to "intrude upon an area in which our society recognizes a significantly heightened privacy interest." Winston v. Lee, 470 U.S. at 760. Thus, before government–ordered surgery is permitted, the state must not only prove that there is a clear indication that the evidence sought will be secured by the surgery, but it must demonstrate a "compelling need" for the evidence.

[96] *Brinegar*, 338 U.S. at 182–83 (Jackson, J., dissenting).

[97] Alschuler, n. 33 *supra*, at 246–47.

on the same degree of likelihood of success, to search for small quantities of marijuana.

But, there are dangers inherent in sliding–scales, which have been articulated well by Professor Anthony Amsterdam. Once a sliding–scale approach to "probable cause" is recognized, the Fourth Amendment becomes "one immense Rorschach blot,"[98] in which police conduct ultimately is measured by a general, amorphous standard of "reasonableness."[99]

One potential effect of the sliding–scale, troubling to persons interested in an efficient criminal justice system, is a "graduated fourth amendment . . . splendid in its flexibility, [but] awful in its unintelligibility, unadministrability, unenforcibility and general ooziness."[100]

Given its "ooziness," a second effect of a sliding–scale, disturbing to civil libertarians, is that it "produce[s] more slide than scale," i.e., "courts are seldom going to say that what [the police] did was unreasonable."[101]

---

[98] Amsterdam, at 393.

[99] This is, of course, precisely what the Supreme Court allowed "probable cause" to become in *Camara*, *see* § 47, *supra*; and, it was the principle of *Camara* that justified the Court's later decisions to justify searches and seizures on less than probable cause, *see* Chapter 18, *infra*.

[100] Amsterdam, at 415.

[101] *Id.* at 394.

CHAPTER 10

SEARCH WARRANTS: IN GENERAL

§ 49   The Constitutional Role of the Search Warrant[1]

[A]   Nature of the Constitutional Debate

The first clause of the Fourth Amendment (the "reasonableness" clause) provides that persons shall "be secure . . . against unreasonable searches and seizures." The amendment's second clause (the warrant clause) states that "no Warrants shall issue, but upon probable cause, supported by Oath or affirmation, and particularly describing the place to be searched, and the persons or things to be seized." The interrelationship of these two clauses is a "syntactical mystery"[2] and a subject of ongoing controversy.

The constitutional issue is this: Does the warrant clause imply that a search or seizure is unreasonable — and, thus, violative of the reasonableness clause — if it is conducted without a warrant, or do the particulars in the warrant clause (*i.e.*, probable cause, oath or affirmation, particularity) only govern searches and seizures conducted under warrants, but imply nothing regarding whether warrants are required in all instances?[3] As is discussed immediately below, the Supreme Court's answer of this question has been inconsistent.

[B]   Competing Rules and Policy

[1]   The "Warrant Requirement" Rule

The dominant position of the Supreme Court during the 1950s and 1960s was that expressed by Justice Stewart[4] in *Katz v. United States*:[5] "searches conducted

---

[1] *See generally* Bradley, *Two Models of the Fourth Amendment*, 83 Mich. L. Rev. 1468 (1985); Goldstein, *The Search Warrant, the Magistrate, and Judicial Review*, 62 N.Y.U. L. Rev. 1173 (1987); Grano, *Rethinking the Fourth Amendment Warrant Requirement*, 19 Am. Crim. L. Rev. 603 (1982); Strossen, *The Fourth Amendment in the Balance: Accurately Setting the Scales Through the Least Intrusive Alternative Analysis*, 63 N.Y.U. L. Rev. 1173 (1988); Uviller, *Reasonability and the Fourth Amendment: A (Belated) Farewell to Justice Potter Stewart*, 25 Crim. L. Bull. 29 (1989); Wasserstrom, *The Court's Turn Toward a General Reasonableness Interpretation of the Fourth Amendment*, 27 Am. Crim. L. Rev. 119 (1989) (hereafter, Wasserstrom, *Court's Turn*); Wasserstrom, *The Incredible Shrinking Fourth Amendment*, 21 Am. Crim. L. Rev. 257 (1984) (hereafter, Wasserstrom, *Shrinking Fourth Amendment*; Wasserstrom & Seidman, *The Fourth Amendment as Constitutional Theory*, 77 Geo. L.J. 19 (1988).

[2] Uviller, n. 1 *supra*, at 33.

[3] *See* Wasserstrom, *Shrinking Fourth Amendment*, n. 1 *supra*, at 281-82.

[4] Justice Stewart was the leading spokesman for the warrant requirement during the Warren Court era and until his departure in 1981. *See* Uviller, n. 1 *supra*. Previously,

outside the judicial process, without prior approval by judge or magistrate, are per se unreasonable under the Fourth Amendment — subject only to a few specifically established and well-delineated exceptions." This constitutes the "warrant requirement" rule.

Advocates of this rule believe that exceptions to the warrant requirement should be "jealously and carefully drawn,"[6] and permitted only on "a showing . . . that the exigencies of the situation made that course imperative."[7] Accordingly, the burden of proof is on the government to demonstrate the need for any warrant exception.[8]

Historical, textual, and policy arguments support the rule. First, evidence exists that the constitutional framers sought to ensure that the power to search would not exclusively rest in the hands of the executive branch of the government, but that it would be shared with the judiciary through the warrant process.[9]

Second, if the Fourth Amendment does not require search warrants in at least some cases, a legislature could abolish them, in which case the amendment's warrant clause would be superfluous.[10]

Finally, the search warrant process is desirable in a society that values privacy, because it authorizes a judicial officer ("a neutral and detached magistrate") rather than a police officer or prosecutor (someone "engaged in the often competitive enterprise of ferreting out crime") to determine "[w]hen the right of privacy must reasonably yield to the right of search."[11] Under this view, the warrant requirement is intended to guarantee "the citizen that the intrusion is authorized by law, and that it is narrowly limited in its objectives and scope."[12]

[2] The "Reasonableness" Rule

The competing position, expressed in recent years most often by Justices Rehnquist and White,[13] is that the preference for search warrants was "judicially created"[14] and is not constitutionally compelled. Under this view, the constitutional test "is not whether it is reasonable to procure a search warrant, but whether the search was reasonable."[15] This is the "reasonableness" rule of the Fourth Amendment.

Justice Frankfurter was the key exponent of the rule, usually as a dissenter. *See, e.g.,* United States v. Rabinowitz, 339 U.S. 56, 68-86 (1950) (Frankfurter, J., dissenting), *overruled by* Chimel v. California, 395 U.S. 752 (1969).

[5] 389 U.S. 347, 357 (1967).

[6] Jones v. United States, 357 U.S. 493, 499 (1958).

[7] McDonald v. United States, 335 U.S. 451, 456 (1948); *see also id.* at 455 (a warrant is required "absent some grave emergency").

[8] United States v. Jeffers, 342 U.S. 48 (1951).

[9] *See* Grano, n. 1 *supra*, at 613-21.

[10] *See* Robison v. Miner & Haug, 68 Mich. 549, 557, 37 N.W. 21, 25 (1888).

[11] Johnson v. United States, 333 U.S. 10, 14 (1948).

[12] Skinner v. Railway Labor Executives' Ass'n, 109 S.Ct. 1402, 1415 (1989).

[13] For a full exposition of Justice White's debate with Justice Stewart on this issue, *see* Uviller, n. 1 *supra*.

[14] Robbins v. California, 453 U.S. 420, 438, *reh'g denied*, 453 U.S. 950 (1981) (Rehnquist, J. dissenting), *overruled by* United States v. Ross, 456 U.S. 798 (1982).

[15] United States v. Rabinowitz, 339 U.S. at 66.

Under the reasonableness clause of the Fourth Amendment, "there is 'no ready test for determining reasonableness other than by balancing the need to search [or seize] against the invasion which the search [or seizure] entails.' "[16] Accordingly, the failure of an officer to obtain a warrant when it was practicable to do so is *at most* a factor relevant in the balancing test.[17]

Proponents of the "reasonableness" rule believe that the competing rule historically stands "the fourth amendment on its head."[18] As they read constitutional history, it was the abusive use of the warrant power — *i.e.*, general warrants and writs of assistance — rather than the framers' fear of police officers' inherent power to search and seize without a warrant that precipitated the Fourth Amendment.[19] Textually, as well, "[t]he terms of the Amendment simply mandate that the people be secure from unreasonable searches and seizures, and that any warrants which *may* issue shall only issue upon probable cause. . . ."[20]

As a matter of policy, proponents of the "reasonableness" rule argue that the warrant requirement unduly frustrates law enforcement goals. To the extent that an officer must seek prior approval from a magistrate, society runs the risk that evidence will be lost in the interim.

[3] Which Theory Has "Won"?

In terms of rhetoric, the Supreme Court, even in recent years, has often stated that warrantless searches and seizures are presumptively unreasonable.[21] However, Professor Silas Wasserstrom appears to be correct when he states that it "is now evident" that the Court has "turn[ed] away from the specific commands of the warrant clause and toward a balancing test of general reasonableness."[22] In view of recent personnel changes on the Court,[23] it is unlikely that this trend will be aborted in the near future.

The movement toward the reasonableness rule has been gradual. Over time, the "few specifically established and well-delineated exceptions"[24] to the warrant requirement became more numerous and not nearly as "well-delineated" or as "jealously and carefully drawn"[25] as they were in the Warren Court era. The Court

---

[16] Terry v. Ohio, 392 U.S. 1, 21 (1968) (*quoting* Camara v. Municipal Court, 387 U.S. 523, 536-37 (1967)).

[17] Wasserstrom, *Shrinking Fourth Amendment*, n. 1 *supra*, at 281.

[18] Coolidge v. New Hampshire, 403 U.S. 443, 492, *reh'g denied*, 404 U.S. 874 (1971) (Harlan, J., concurring) (*quoting* T. Taylor, Two Studies in Constitutional Interpretation 23-24 (Ohio State 1969)); *but see* Grano, n. 1 *supra*, at 616 (observing that a full reading of Taylor's book "discloses that Taylor's thesis may have been more narrow than is usually assumed.").

[19] Payton v. New York, 445 U.S. 573, 608 (1980) (White, J., dissenting).

[20] Robbins v. California, 453 U.S. at 438 (Rehnquist, J., dissenting).

[21] *E.g.*, *Skinner*, 109 S.Ct. at 1414 ("Except in certain well-defined circumstances, a search or seizure . . . is not reasonable unless it is accomplished pursuant to a judicial warrant issued upon probable cause.").

[22] Wasserstrom, *Court's Turn*, n. 1 *supra*, at 129.

[23] *See* § 4[E] *supra*.

[24] Katz v. United States, 389 U.S. at 357.

[25] Jones v. United States, 357 U.S. at 499.

now says only that "normally,"[26] "usually,"[27] "ordinar[ily],"[28] "as a general matter,"[29] or "[i]n most criminal cases, we strike th[e] balance in favor of the procedures described by the Warrant Clause. . . ."[30]

If the warrant-requirement rule remains significant today, it is primarily because the Court now recognizes a "free-floating"[31] "reasonableness" exception to it. As a consequence, the overwhelming majority of lawful searches today occur in the absence of a warrant.[32]

§ 50   The Warrant Application Process[33]

A primary purpose of the Fourth Amendment warrant clause is to reduce the risk that the police will search or seize "persons, houses, papers, and effects" without probable cause. The premise of the warrant requirement is that magistrates are more likely to make neutral and detached probable-cause determinations than are the police officers "engaged in the often competitive enterprise of ferreting out crime."[34] Therefore, a brief summary of the warrant-application process is worthwhile.

When an investigating officer seeks a warrant, he prepares an application for it, an affidavit (in which, under oath or by affirmation, he sets out the facts that he believes justifies the warrant), and the warrant itself. The officer then seeks approval of the documents from a supervisor or, in some jurisdictions, an assistant prosecutor.

Once approval is obtained, the officer goes to the courthouse or, if necessary, to the home of a judge.[35] When choices are available, such as in large urban areas, judge-shopping is common: the officer seeks a judge[36] known to issue warrants liberally. During the daytime, the officer ordinarily presents the application to the judge while he is on the bench, during a court recess.

In theory, the judge carefully reads the officer's documents and questions him regarding any ambiguous matters. When the application includes hearsay information, which is common, the judge is expected to question the officer closely to ensure that the informant's basis of knowledge was good and his veracity high. The judge may also require the informant to be identified or produced, if necessary to the probable-cause determination.[37]

---

[26] Arkansas v. Sanders, 442 U.S. 753, 758 (1979).

[27] Griffin v. Wisconsin, 483 U.S. 868, 873 (1987).

[28] Illinois v. Rodriguez, 110 S.Ct. 2793, 2799 (1990).

[29] Nat'l Treasury Employees Union v. Von Raab, 109 S.Ct. 1384, 1390 (1989).

[30] *Skinner*, 109 S.Ct. at 1414.

[31] Illinois v. Rodriguez, 110 S.Ct. at 2806 (Stevens, J., dissenting).

[32] R. Van Duizend, *et al.*, at 19.

[33] *See generally* R. Van Duizend, *et al.*; Goldstein, n. 1 *supra*.

[34] Johnson v. United States, 333 U.S. at 14.

[35] In a few jurisdictions, a warrant may be issued on sworn oral testimony via telephone. *E.g.*, FRCP 41(c)(2)(A).

[36] In most states, all judges — from the lowest level magistrate to the justices of the state supreme court — are authorized to issue warrants, but in practice the authority is exercised by felony and misdemeanor court judges.

[37] McCray v. Illinois, 386 U.S. 300, *reh'g denied*, 386 U.S. 1042 (1967).

In reality, warrant proceedings are brief. According to one study, the average time taken by a reviewing magistrate to consider an application was two minutes, 48 seconds; the median time was two minutes, 12 seconds. Ten percent of all applications were reviewed in less than one minute. Fewer than ten percent of all applications were rejected.[38]

After a warrant is approved and signed by the judge, he gives the original warrant and a copy to the officer, and retains a copy and the supporting documentation. Frequently, a clerk will establish a file for the case. After execution of the warrant, the officer files a "return" with the court, indicating when the search occurred and what, if anything, was seized.

§ 51 "Neutral and Detached Magistrate"[39]

Warrants may be issued only by "neutral and detached magistrates."[40] This requirement is not met if the person issuing the warrant is a member of the executive branch, such as the state attorney general.[41]

Even if the warrant is issued by a member of the judiciary, he must be "neutral and detached," rather than a "rubber stamp for the police."[42] Thus, an unsalaried magistrate who receives a fee for each warrant issued, but no compensation for applications denied, lacks the requisite detachment.[43]

A warrant is also invalid if the issuing magistrate, by his behavior in a particular case, manifests a lack of neutrality. For example, a judge who accompanies officers to a bookstore suspected of selling obscene material, and who there inspects the materials to determine which ones are obscene, is "not acting as a judicial officer but as an adjunct law enforcement officer."[44]

On the other hand, the magistrate need not be a judge[45] and, perhaps, not even be a lawyer. In *Shadwick v. City of Tampa*,[46] the Supreme Court approved the issuance of misdemeanor arrest warrants by non-lawyer court clerks. Although the case dealt only with misdemeanor arrests, the Court's language was broad, and cited search warrant cases in support. Various commentators, however, doubt that *Shadwick* will be extended beyond the narrow facts of the case.[47]

---

[38] R. Van Duizend, *et al.*, at 25-32.

[39] *See generally* 2 W. LaFave, at § 4.2.

[40] Johnson v. United States, 333 U.S. at 14.

[41] Coolidge v. New Hampshire, 403 U.S. 443, *reh'g denied*, 404 U.S. 874 (1971).

[42] United States v. Leon, 468 U.S. 897, 914, *reh'g denied*, 468 U.S. 1250 (1984) (*quoting* Aguilar v. Texas, 378 U.S. 108, 111 (1964)).

[43] Connally v. Georgia, 429 U.S. 245 (1977).

[44] Lo-Ji Sales, Inc. v. New York, 442 U.S. 319, 327 (1979).

[45] When the Court uses the phrase "judicial officer" to describe the person who issues a search warrant it means only that the individual serves in a "judicial" capacity. Goldstein, n. 1 *supra*, at 1183 n.38.

[46] 407 U.S. 345 (1972).

[47] *E.g.*, 2 W. LaFave, § 4.2(c) at 158-59; Goldstein, n. 1 *supra*, at 1183-84.

§ 52 "Oath or Affirmation"[48]

Warrants may not be issued unless they are "supported by Oath or affirmation." Therefore, a warrant that is defective for want of probable cause cannot be saved by post-warrant proof that the affiant had additional information that he failed to disclose to the judge.[49]

A more complex situation arises when an officer provides false information to the magistrate. Under limited circumstances outlined in *Franks v. Delaware*,[50] a defendant may mount a post-search attack on a facially valid warrant on the ground that, but for the falsity in the affidavit, a warrant would not have been issued.

According to *Franks*, an affidavit supporting a search warrant is presumed valid. A defendant is not entitled to a hearing to attack the affidavit (and, thus, the warrant) unless he makes a "substantial preliminary showing"[51] that: (1) a false statement was included in the affidavit; (2) the affiant made the false statement "knowingly and intentionally" or with reckless disregard for the truth;[52] and (3) the false statement was necessary to the magistrate's finding of probable cause.

If these allegations are proved by a preponderance of the evidence, the false statements must be excised from the affidavit. If the remaining allegations do not satisfy the probable-cause standard, the warrant is void, and the fruits of the search must be excluded from evidence at the criminal trial. As stated in *Franks*, "it would be an unthinkable imposition upon the [the magistrate's] authority if a warrant affidavit, revealed after the fact to contain a deliberately or recklessly false statement, were to stand beyond impeachment."

The scope of the *Franks* rule should be carefully observed. First, it applies if the defendant can show that the affiant lied. For example, if the affiant's allegations were necessary to the finding of probable cause, a warrant would be void if it were proved that the affiant did not observe the events that he swore that he saw, did not have the conversations that he claimed to have had, or fabricated the existence of a confidential informant and the details supposedly received from him.[53] A warrant could also be invalidated if, for example, it were shown that an officer recklessly provided false information regarding the prior reliability of a genuine informant.

---

[48] *See generally* 2 W. LaFave, at §§ 4.3-4.4.

[49] Whiteley v. Warden, 401 U.S. 560 (1971).

[50] 438 U.S. 154 (1978).

[51] Such a showing is made in the form of specific allegations and an offer of proof, including the use of affidavits or other reliable statements of witnesses.

[52] In a different context the Court has defined "reckless disregard for the truth" to mean that the person "in fact entertained serious doubts as to the truth" of the statement made. St. Amant v. Thompson, 390 U.S. 727, 731 (1968) (definition of "constitutional malice" in defamation actions).

[53] *E.g., see* Gold, *Dead Officer, Dropped Charges: a Scandal in Boston*, New York Times, Mar. 20, 1989, at A9, col. 1 (reporting that charges were dropped in a homicide case due to "egregious misconduct" by the prosecutor and the police, including the fact that a police officer applied for several warrants based on hearsay "information" of "John," who did not exist).

On the other hand, *Franks* does not permit the impeachment of a "nongovernmental informant."[54] Therefore, a warrant will not be voided if an informant lies to the affiant, who then innocently or negligently (rather than recklessly) passes this false information along to the magistrate.

§ 53　Search Warrant "Particularity"[55]

[A]　In General

The Fourth Amendment provides that warrants must "particularly describ[e] the place to be searched, and the persons or things to be seized." Particularity is required in order to avoid the abuses, exemplified by general warrants and writs of assistance, that occurred under the English and colonial common law. A warrant that lacks particularity permits police officers too much discretion in its execution and undercuts the probable-cause requirement.

[B]　"Place to be Searched"

The place to be searched, whether a building, a vehicle, or even a person, must be described in the warrant in a manner sufficiently precise that the officer executing the warrant can identify it with reasonable effort.[56] For example, it is sufficient if the search warrant provides the street address of a single-unit house to be searched. If the structure is a multiple-unit building, additional information — *e.g.*, an apartment number — is required.

If the officer who applies for the warrant has reason to believe that the building to be searched is a single-unit structure — so that a street address is sufficient — but the officer executing the warrant learns that the structure contains multiple units, the warrant itself is not invalid for want of particularity, because its validity "must be assessed on the basis of the information that the officers disclosed, or had a duty to discover and to disclose, to the issuing magistrate."[57]

The more difficult problem in such cases relates to the *execution* of the facially valid warrant. If the warrant directs officers to search "the home belonging to *D*, who lives at 123 Main Street," and upon arriving there they learn (or should have learned) that the building at that address is a duplex, the officers are obligated to limit their search to *D*'s unit, which they can ascertain by reasonable effort, such as by checking names on the mailbox or by asking neighbors.[58]

---

[54] The Court did not explain the meaning of the adjectival limitation. It may mean that it would be permissible to impeach another police officer who, although not the affiant, provided information that went into the affidavit.

[55] *See generally* 2 W. LaFave, at §§ 4.5-4.6.

[56] Steele v. United States, 267 U.S. 498 (1925).

[57] Maryland v. Garrison, 480 U.S. 79, 86 (1987) (footnote omitted).

[58] However, a "wrong" search can nevertheless be "reasonable." In *Garrison, id.*, the officers executed a warrant of a "third floor apartment" at a particular address. The officers did not learn (and had no reason to know) until after they had entered the "third floor apartment" and seized the evidence for which they were searching, that the premises actually were a two-apartment unit, and that they were in the wrong apartment. The Court upheld the search and seizure as reasonable, observing that it must "allow some latitude

Warrants to search automobiles are rare,[59] but when they are sought it is sufficient to describe the vehicle in a manner that will make it easy for the officer to determine what car may be searched. For example, the license or vehicle identification number of the vehicle, like the address of a house, is adequate. So, too, it could be sufficient simply to identify it by its location, if the location is a one-car garage, but not if it is a public parking lot. In the latter case, even if only one automobile were found at the scene at the time that the warrant were executed, the officers would have no way of knowing if that was the vehicle described in the warrant.

Although rarely used, warrants to search persons may be obtained like any other search warrant, in which case it is necessary only to describe adequately the person to be searched. It is not necessary to identify the place where the search will occur.

Whenever a search warrant adequately describes the place to be searched, the authority to search includes the entire area in question, including containers found within it, if they are large enough to contain the object of the search.[60]

[C] "Persons or Things to be Seized"

The Fourth Amendment phrase, "persons . . . to be seized" primarily relates to arrest warrants, because an arrest is a seizure of a person.[61]

The "things to be seized" should be described in search warrants with sufficient particularity that, in the words of the Supreme Court, "general searches under [warrants are] . . . impossible and . . . seizure of one thing under a warrant describing another [cannot occur]. As to what is to be taken, nothing is left to the discretion of the officer executing the warrant."[62] In practice, however, neither the Supreme Court nor lower courts have applied such a strict test.

In his treatise, Professor Wayne LaFave has helpfully summarized the general principles that he has distilled from the numerous cases in the field.[63] Among the principles he identified are: (1) vagueness in the warrant description is tolerated to a greater degree when the police have described the item with as much particularity as can reasonably be expected;[64] and (2) less specificity is required

---

for honest mistakes that are made by officers in the dangerous and difficult process of making arrests and executing search warrants." Once they became aware of their error, however, the officers were required to desist from searching the apartment further.

[59] Ordinarily, automobiles may be searched without a warrant. *See* chapter 14 *infra*.

[60] United States v. Ross, 456 U.S. 798, 820-21 (1982).

[61] Some jurisdictions permit the seizure of a person "who is unlawfully restrained," such as a kidnap victim, as "evidence" of the crime. *E.g.*, FRCP 41(b).

[62] Marron v. United States, 275 U.S. 192, 196, *reh'g denied*, 277 U.S. 613 (1928). Once the articles particularly described in the warrant are discovered and seized, the search must cease. Horton v. California, 110 S.Ct. 2301, 2310 (1990).

[63] 2 W. LaFave, § 4.6(a) at 238-41.

[64] *E.g.*, Andresen v. Maryland, 427 U.S. 463 (1976) (a warrant authorizing the seizure of items pertaining to real estate fraud, but which included a residual clause authorizing the seizure of "fruits, instrumentalities of crime at this [time] unknown," was upheld by the Court in part because of the complexity of the real estate scheme and the inability of the police to be more specific).

regarding contraband[65] than is required regarding stolen goods[66] or items, such as books and papers, that retain special First Amendment protection.[67]

§ 54   Execution of Search Warrants[68]

[A]   Time of Execution

Statutes and rules of procedure in many states set limits on the execution of search warrants. For example, some jurisdictions require that search warrants be executed within a specified period of time from the date that the warrant was signed by the magistrate, often within ten days.[69]

Some jurisdictions prohibit nighttime execution of warrants, "unless the issuing authority, by appropriate provision in the warrant, and for reasonable cause shown" authorizes it.[70] The Supreme Court has not determined the constitutionality of non-exigent nighttime warrant executions.[71]

[B]   Mode of Entry

At least since the early nineteenth century,[72] the common law rule has been that, absent special circumstances, an officer may not forcibly enter a home to execute a warrant unless he knocks at the door (or otherwise indicates his presence), identifies himself as an officer, states his purpose for entering, requests admittance, and is refused entry.[73]

Request for admittance is not required at common law in three circumstances: (1) if the occupants are already aware of the officers' presence and purpose; (2) if the officer has reason to believe, based on the facts of the particular case,[74] that

---

[65] *E.g.*, it is satisfactory for the warrant to direct the officers to seize "gambling paraphernalia," "controlled substances," or "drugs unlawfully possessed."

[66] *E.g.*, it is insufficient to describe the item to be seized as "the stolen automobile" or "the jewelry," if a more specific description is possible.

[67] *See* Stanford v. Texas, 379 U.S. 476, 485, *reh'g denied*, 380 U.S. 926 (1965) ("The constitutional requirement [of particularity] . . . is to be accorded the most scrupulous exactitude when the 'things' are books, and the basis for their seizure is the ideas which they contain.").

[68] *See generally* 2 W. LaFave, at §§ 4.7-4.10; R. Van Duizend, *et al.*, at 45-54.

[69] *E.g.*, FRCP 41(c)(1).

[70] *Id.*

[71] *But see* Gooding v. United States, 416 U.S. 430 (1974) (in a case involving the interpretation of a statute, the Court approved the execution of a nighttime search authorized in a warrant without a showing of need; the constitutionality of the statute was not addressed in the case).

[72] Bell v. Clapp, 10 Johns.R. 263 (N.Y.Sup.Ct. 1813)

[73] Federal law provides that an officer may break open any outer or inner door or window of a house in order to execute a search warrant "if, after notice of his authority and purpose, he is refused admittance or when necessary to liberate himself or a person aiding him in the execution of a warrant." 18 U.S.C. § 3109.

[74] Some jurisdictions apply a "blanket rule": the officers may enter without notice if the type of evidence to be seized is generally susceptible to easy destruction, such as narcotics that can be flushed down a toilet, although there might be no evidence of such a risk in the particular case. Many jurisdictions reject this rule. *See* 2 W. LaFave, § 4.8(d) at 280.

the evidence to be seized is being or will be destroyed imminently;[75] or (3) if notice would jeopardize the safety of the officer or persons inside the dwelling.

[C] Search of Persons While Executing a Warrant

[1] In Premises Open to the Public

A warrant may properly authorize the search of particular individuals who are expected to be found on the premises to be searched. On the other hand, a warrant authorizing the search of "all persons found on the premises," without identifying the individuals, is unconstitutionally broad except in the unlikely event that there is probable cause to believe that anyone who might be on the premises at the time of the search would be in possession of seizable evidence.

The more difficult issue is under what circumstances, if any, may an officer executing a valid search warrant of premises search persons found at the scene, if the warrant is silent as to the matter. *Ybarra v. Illinois*[76] provides the guidelines by which to determine the scope of an officer's authority to search persons while executing a search warrant of premises open to the public.

In *Ybarra*, officers had a warrant to search a tavern, and a specifically named bartender, for heroin. Eight officers executing the warrant entered the bar while it was open to the public and frisked each of the customers for weapons. One of the customers, *D*, who had not acted suspiciously, was frisked while he was standing at a pinball machine. The officer felt something in *D*'s pocket, which seemed to him to be "a cigarette pack with objects in it." Although he did nothing immediately, the officer returned a few minutes later, pulled out the object, which was a cigarette pack as predicted, and opened it to find tin foil packets of heroin.

The Supreme Court concluded that "a person's mere propinquity to others independently suspected of criminal activity does not, without more, give rise to probable cause to search that person." Every customer at the bar had personal Fourth Amendment protection. The officers' authority to search the bartender and the premises, therefore, did not justify a full search of the customers.

Based on the principles of *Terry v. Ohio*,[77] however, the Court in *Ybarra* held that, at least in circumstances similar to this case, it is reasonable for the police to frisk an occupant for weapons (but not for contraband) if they have a reasonable suspicion, based on specific, articulable facts, that he is armed and dangerous. If the officer conducting the pat-down feels what appears to be a weapon, then (but only then) may he conduct a full search in order to seize the weapon.

---

[75] In Ker v. California, 374 U.S. 23 (1963), a four-justice plurality approved a no-knock entry on the ground that the officers had a reasonable belief that the occupants knew the officers were coming and, therefore, that the narcotics "could be quickly and easily destroyed"; four dissenters hinted that they would only permit entry to prevent the destruction of evidence if the occupants were actually engaged in activities to destroy the evidence. Subsequent cases suggest that imminent destruction of evidence justifies unrequested entry of a home. *E.g.*, Minnesota v. Olson, 110 S.Ct 1684 (1990) (justifying warrantless entry into a house in order to make an arrest, if there is probable cause to fear imminent destruction of evidence). *See* § 65 *infra*.

[76] 444 U.S. 85 (1979), *reh'g denied*, 444 U.S. 1049 (1980).

[77] 392 U.S. 1 (1968). *See* § 94 *infra*.

[2] In Private Homes

Ybarra involved the execution of a search warrant on premises open to the general public, in which there was no evidence that any customer was linked to the criminal activities that brought the officers to the tavern. The analysis in *Ybarra* possibly does not apply when a search warrant is executed on a private home.

A private home "does not attract casual visitors off the street."[78] Police officers in a home, therefore, have more reason to believe that occupants are connected to the suspected criminal activity going on in the home or, at least, have the incentive to protect the interests of the residents of the home. Therefore, some courts permit the police to conduct a weapons-frisk of the occupants of a home without particularized suspicion that the persons being frisked are armed and dangerous, while a search warrant is being executed.[79]

[D] Detention of Persons During Searches

Suppose that in *Ybarra*, *D*, one of the customers in the tavern, had tried to leave when the officers entered for the purpose of searching the premises for narcotics. Could the officers have detained him while they conducted the search?

This issue arose in the context of a warrant to search a home in *Michigan v. Summers*.[80] In *Summers*, police officers encountered *D* as he descended the front steps of a house that the officers had a warrant to search for narcotics. They requested and obtained *D*'s assistance in entering the premises, after which they forcibly detained — "seized" — him while they searched the house.

The search proved fruitful. After the officers learned that *D* was the owner of the house, they arrested and searched him incident to the arrest. More drugs were found on his person, and it was this evidence that *D* sought to exclude at his trial on the ground that it was a fruit of an unlawful detention in the home.

The Court held that the temporary seizure of *D* was reasonable. It noted various justifications for the detention of persons during the execution of search warrants: (1) to avoid the risk that an occupant might leave with the evidence sought; (2) to reduce the risk of bodily harm to the officers or others; and (3) to facilitate the search, by inducing the detained occupants to open locked containers or doors.

Although the police did not prove that any of the above-stated reasons applied in *Summers*, the Court chose to provide a bright-line rule. The bright-line rule of *Summers* is: a warrant to search for contraband includes the limited authority to detain all occupants of the premises to be searched while it is executed.

The potential limits of *Summers* should be noted. First, the Court did not determine whether the rule announced in the case also applies to warrantless searches. The Court stated in a footnote, however, that its holding does not

---

[78] People v. Thurman, (1989) 209 Cal.App.3d 817, 257 Cal.Rptr 517, 520.

[79] 2 W. LaFave, § 4.9(d) at 302. Also, in this regard, consider Maryland v. Buie, 110 S.Ct. 1093 (1990), in which the Court held that the Fourth Amendment permits a properly limited "protective sweep" of a home for persons who might constitute a danger to the officers while conducting an *arrest* in the home. *See* §§ 67[A], 100 *infra*.

[80] 452 U.S. 692 (1981).

"preclude the possibility that comparable police conduct may be justified by exigent circumstances in the absence of a warrant."

Second, the *Summers* rule is limited to searches for contraband. In a footnote, the Court left open the issue of whether persons may be detained during searches for mere evidence. Apparently, therefore, the term "contraband" is used broadly to include the fruits and instrumentalities of criminal activity. In any case, there is no persuasive reason to distinguish between contraband and mere evidence.

Third, the Court used the word "occupants" in the holding and in other places in the opinion. At least once, however, it used the word "residents," and observed in that context that "we may safely assume that most citizens . . . would elect to remain in order to observe the search of their possessions."

A question, therefore, remains: Does the Court intend to limit the scope of its holding to persons — whether called "occupants" or "residents" — who have a possessory connection to the premises searched, or may the police detain any person present at the time the warrant is executed? The Court has not answered this question, although one expert believes that "it would seem that the word 'occupants' is not to be loosely construed as covering anyone present. . . ."[81]

---

[81] 2 W. LaFave, § 4.9(e) at 309. If this assumption is correct, the officers in *Ybarra* would not have had a *per se* right to detain *D* or other customers who chose to leave the tavern when the officers entered.

CHAPTER 11

ARRESTS

§ 55 Nature of an "Arrest"

The term "arrest" is often used in court opinions and statutes, but is almost never defined. Indeed, the word "arrest" is sometimes modified by adjectives such as "formal,"[1] "custodial,"[2] and "traditional,"[3] which suggests that some "arrests" are "informal," "noncustodial," and "nontraditional."

In general, a person is "arrested" when she is taken into custody by lawful authority, ordinarily by the police, for the purpose of holding her in order to answer a criminal charge against her. In constitutional terms, an arrest constitutes a "seizure" of the person, as the latter term is defined in Fourth Amendment jurisprudence.

One should be careful to note that not all Fourth Amendment "seizures" are "arrests," at least in the "traditional" sense of the latter term. An "arrest" implies that the individual's freedom of movement has been significantly curtailed, whereas a person can be detained against her will for a brief time — and, thus, be "seized" — without being arrested.[4] Nonetheless, some statutes characterize as an "arrest" the temporary detention that occurs when a person is stopped in her automobile in order to receive a traffic citation.[5] The best that can be said of this use of the term is that it states an "informal," "noncustodial," and "nontraditional" version of an "arrest."

§ 56 Common Law and Statutory Arrest Rules

At common law[6] and by statute,[7] a police officer may arrest a person for an offense if she has reasonable grounds to believe that a crime has been committed and that the person to be arrested committed it. The common law phrase "reasonable grounds" is equivalent to the constitutional term "probable cause."[8]

Under common law and statutory principles, a warrant is not required for a felony arrest, but is required for a misdemeanor arrest unless the offense occurred

---

[1] *E.g.*, Cupp v. Murphy, 412 U.S. 291, 294 (1973); Berkemer v. McCarty, 468 U.S. 420, 425 (1984).

[2] *E.g.*, United States v. Robinson, 414 U.S. 218, 235 (1973).

[3] *E.g.*, Dunaway v. New York, 442 U.S. 200, 212 (1979).

[4] *See* § 94 *infra.*

[5] 2 W. LaFave, § 5.2(h) at 466.

[6] *See generally* J. Dressler, § 21.02[B][1]; 2 W. LaFave, at § 5.1(b).

[7] *See generally* 1 C. Wright, at § 77.

[8] Draper v. United States, 358 U.S. 307, 310 n.3 (1959).

in the officer's presence.[9] However, as discussed below, in some circumstances warrantless arrests are unconstitutional, notwithstanding statutory and common law precedent.

§ 57   Arrests: Constitutional Law Overview

[A]   General Rules

Without exception, all traditional arrests must be founded on probable cause.[10] An arrest not based on probable cause constitutes an unreasonable seizure of the person, in violation of the Fourth Amendment.

Regarding arrest warrants, as a constitutional matter, a police officer: (1) may arrest a person in a public place without a warrant, even if it is practicable for her to secure one; (2) may not arrest a person in her home without an arrest warrant, absent exigent circumstances or valid consent; and (3) may not arrest a person in another person's home without a search, and perhaps an arrest, warrant, absent exigent circumstances or valid consent.

[B]   How Arrest-Warrant Issues Arise

An arrest that is invalid because it was made without a warrant does not render unlawful the continued custody of the suspect and, therefore, does not in itself void a subsequent conviction.[11]

Instead, the constitutionality of a warrantless arrest arises as an issue in a criminal prosecution in an evidentiary context, that is, when the arrest results in the seizure of evidence to be used against the arrestee at her criminal trial.

For example, if the police seek to justify a warrantless search for property on the basis that it was an incident to a lawful arrest, or that the seizure of the property was in lawful "plain view" at the time of the arrest, the lawfulness of the arrest that gave rise to the search is brought into question. Similarly, the admissibility of a post-arrest confession depends in part on the constitutionality of the arrest that triggered the statement.[12]

§ 58   Arrests in Public Places: the *Watson* No-Warrant Rule

In *United States v. Watson*,[13] D was arrested by federal postal inspectors in a restaurant, on suspicion of possession of stolen credit cards. The arrest, although apparently based on probable cause, was made without a warrant, under authority

---

[9] For the common law meaning of the phrase "in the presence," *see* 2 W. LaFave, at § 5.1(c).

[10] Dunaway v. New York, 442 U.S. 200 (1979).

[11] *See* United States v. Crews, 445 U.S. 463 (1980); Gerstein v. Pugh, 420 U.S. 103 (1975); Frisbie v. Collins, 342 U.S. 519, *reh'g denied*, 343 U.S. 937 (1952); *see also* New York v. Harris, 110 S.Ct. 1640, 1650 (1990).

[12] *See* §§ 68[B] (search incident to lawful arrest), 81[A] (plain view), 125[C][4] (admissibility of post-arrest confessions) *infra*.

[13] 423 U.S. 411, *reh'g denied*, 424 U.S. 979 (1976).

of a federal statute similar to those in nearly all states that permits warrantless arrests on the basis of probable cause that the suspect "has committed or is committing a felony."

The Court, by a 6-2 vote, upheld the constitutionality of the statute in the context of arrests in public places.[14] The ruling was grounded largely on history. The majority observed that warrantless felony arrests were permitted at common law, and that this rule "survived substantially intact" in nearly all states, as well as in the federal system.

Of particular note to the Court was the enactment by the 1792 Congress of a law providing federal marshals with, in the words of the original statute, "the same powers in executing the laws of the United States, as sheriffs and their deputies in the several states have by law." Since sheriffs at that time had the authority to arrest felons without a warrant, this legislation demonstrated that contemporaries of the drafters of the Constitution saw no inconsistency between the Fourth Amendment and legislation authorizing warrantless felony arrests.

Justice Powell concurred in the opinion, but with reservations. He conceded that the holding of the Court "created a certain anomaly." The anomaly is that seizures of persons — arrests — in public places are subject to less judicial scrutiny than searches and seizures of property. As he observed:

> There is no more basic constitutional rule in the Fourth Amendment area than that which makes a warrantless search unreasonable except in a few "jealously and carefully" drawn exceptional circumstances. . . .

> Since the Fourth Amendment speaks equally to both searches and seizures, and since an arrest, the taking hold of one's person, is quintessentially a seizure, it would seem that the constitutional provision should impose the same limitations upon arrests that it does on searches. Indeed, as an abstract matter an argument can be made that the restrictions upon arrest should be greater. A search may cause only annoyance and temporary inconvenience to the law-abiding citizen. . . . An arrest, however, is a serious personal intrusion regardless of whether the person seized is guilty or innocent. . . .

> But logic sometimes must defer to history and experience.

The dissenters questioned the Court's reliance on common law authority. They pointed out that only the most serious crimes were identified as felonies at common law; many modern-day felonies, such as assault with the intent to commit murder, were common law misdemeanors and, therefore, required an arrest warrant. The holding in *Watson*, therefore, "result[ed] in contravention of the common law."

---

[14] Although warrantless arrests in public places are constitutional, the Fourth Amendment requires that a person arrested in such a manner be provided with "a fair and reliable [judicial] determination of probable cause as a condition for any significant pretrial restraint of liberty." Gerstein v. Pugh, 420 U.S. 103, 125 (1975). *See* § 3[C][2] *supra.*

§ 59   Arrests in the Home: the *Payton* Warrant-Requirement Rule

In *Payton v. New York*[15] the Supreme Court held that the Fourth Amendment prohibits warrantless, nonconsensual entry into a suspect's home in order to make a "routine" felony[16] arrest.

In *Payton*, police officers had probable cause to arrest *D1* for a felony. They went to *D1*'s home to arrest him without a warrant. They heard music playing inside the home, and knocked, but received no reply. They then broke in with the assistance of a crow bar. Nobody was inside, but they seized evidence in plain view. In a companion case, the police knocked at *D2*'s door, his three-year-old son opened it, and the officers, observing *D2* inside, entered and arrested him without a warrant.

The Court held, 6-3, that the Fourth Amendment prohibited the police conduct in these two cases. The majority held that, absent exigent circumstances, which it did not define,[17] entry into a suspect's home in order to make an arrest requires an arrest warrant and "reason to believe the suspect is within," or legally recognized consent to the entry. If the officer is armed with a warrant, however, she has implicit authority to search anywhere in the home that the person named in the warrant might be found until she is taken into custody.[18]

The Court justified the warrant requirement primarily on the ground that "physical entry of a home is the chief evil against which the wording of the Fourth Amendment is directed." The purpose of the arrest warrant, in other words, is not to protect the suspect's bodily integrity, but rather is to safeguard the physical integrity of the home from entry in the absence of a prior determination of probable cause by a magistrate.[19]

According to *Payton*, although general warrants and writs of assistance were the immediate evils that motivated the adoption of the Fourth Amendment, the broader reason for the amendment was to protect against government intrusion of "the sanctity of a man's home and the privacies of life." Although the Fourth Amendment protects persons in various settings, the *Payton* Court concluded that "[i]n none is the zone of privacy more clearly defined than when bounded by the unambiguous physical dimensions of an individual's home."[20]

---

[15] 445 U.S. 573 (1980).

[16] Although *Payton* concerned felony arrests, and the rule was consequently stated in those terms, the doctrine applies to misdemeanor arrests in the home as well. *See* Welsh v. Wisconsin, 466 U.S. 740 (1984).

[17] *See* § 60[B] *infra*.

[18] Maryland v. Buie, 110 S.Ct. 1093, 1096 (1990). Under limited circumstances, arresting officers may also conduct a "protective sweep" of the home for other persons who might pose a danger to the officers or others. *See* § 100 *infra*.

[19] *See* Minnesota v. Olson, 110 S.Ct. 1684, 1687 (1990).

[20] The dissenters found the majority's historical argument faulty. They argued that at the time of the adoption of the Fourth Amendment law enforcement officers had broad inherent power to arrest. General warrants and writs of assistance *expanded* on this authority, and it was this expansion, not the officers' inherent power to make warrantless arrests, that the constitutional framers sought to prohibit.

§ 60 Scope of the *Payton* Rule

[A] *Payton* vs. *Watson*: "Home" versus "Public Place"

Although an arrest warrant is required (absent consent) for a routine arrest in a home (*Payton*), warrantless arrests in public places are constitutionally permitted (*Watson*). It is critical, therefore, to distinguish between a "home" and a "public place" for Fourth Amendment arrest purposes.

Clearly, an arrest on the street, in a public park, or on or in any other public site, falls within the *Watson* "public place" no-warrant-requirement rule. It is also clear that "public place" includes the inside of a privately owned commercial building open to the public, since the arrest in *Watson* occurred in a restaurant during working hours. Uncertain — lower court case law is divided[21] — is whether *Watson* or *Payton* applies to an arrest in a commercial structure closed to the general public at the time of the police entry.

The *Payton-Watson* distinction can be difficult to draw, even when an arrest occurs in the context of an arrestee's home. For example, in *United States v. Santana*,[22] the arresting officer testified that he found D standing directly in the doorway of her house when he arrived without a warrant to arrest her. The Court stated that "one step forward would have put her outside [the house], one step backward would have put her in the vestibule of her residence."

The Court held that although the threshold of her dwelling is "private" in the same way that her yard is, for purposes of the arrest-warrant rule, D was standing in a "public place." According to the Court, she was standing in open view; as such, she was "as exposed to view, speech, hearing, and touch as if she had been standing completely outside her house."

In *Santana*, D retreated into her house after she spotted the officers, who followed her inside. The Court justified the entry on the grounds of hot pursuit, an exception to *Payton* discussed in the next subsection. However, if D had stood motionless in the doorway, her warrantless arrest would have been constitutional, as much so as if she had been on a public street. And, although lower courts are divided on the matter,[23] the same result would probably have applied if D had been one foot inside her home, as long as the officer made the arrest without entering the house.

In contrast, *Payton* requires that an officer obtain an arrest warrant (consent and exigencies aside) if she must enter the dwelling, even slightly, to arrest the suspect. This conclusion follows from the facts of one of the appeals heard in *Payton* itself, in which the officers knocked, a young child opened the door, and the officers observed D2 inside. Because the officers entered, a warrant was required.

[B] Exigencies Justifying Warrantless Entry

The existence of certain emergencies or dangerous situations — what the Court describes in Fourth Amendment jurisprudence as "exigent circumstances" —

---

[21] 2 W. LaFave, § 6.1(c) at 583-84.

[22] 427 U.S. 38 (1976).

[23] 2 W. LaFave, § 6.1(e) at 589-90.

justifies warrantless entry of a home in order to arrest a suspect, just as exigencies justify warrantless entry of a home in order to search for property.[24] The Court in *Payton* did not have occasion to consider the "exigency" issue, but it has explained the concept in subsequent cases.

[1] Hot Pursuit

Warrantless entry of a home is permitted in "hot pursuit" of a fleeing felon. As the Court explained in *United States v. Santana*,[25] "hot pursuit" involves "some sort of chase [of the suspect], but it need not be an extended hue and cry 'in and about [the] public streets.' "

For example, in *Santana*, police officers had probable cause, but no warrant, to arrest *D* for a felony. They drove to D's house, where they observed her standing in the doorway. Constitutionally speaking, this placed her in a "public place." When she observed the officers, she retreated into the house, although she left the door open. The officers entered to arrest her.

The entry into the home took the case outside the *Watson* "public places" rule. Nonetheless, the Court justified the entry and the warrantless arrest under the "hot pursuit" doctrine: that is, the pursuit to arrest began in a public place and ended, albeit quickly, in the privacy of the home.[26]

[2] Other Exigencies

The Supreme Court in *Minnesota v. Olson*[27] stated that, hot pursuit issues aside, the "essentially, correct standard" for determining whether a warrantless entry of a home is justified under the exigent-circumstances exception is whether the officers have probable cause to believe that if they do not enter immediately: (1) evidence will be destroyed; (2) the suspect will escape; or (3) harm will occur to the police or others, either inside or outside the dwelling. In assessing the exigency, the gravity of the crime and the likelihood that the suspect is armed must be considered.

The gravity of the crime for which the person will be arrested is sometimes a critical factor. As the Supreme Court indicated in *Welsh v. Wisconsin*,[28] the less serious the offense, the less likely the warrantless entry can be justified on grounds of exigency.

In *Welsh*, officers received reliable information that, minutes earlier, *D* had driven his automobile under the influence of alcohol, which constituted a civil

---

[24] Regarding the latter issue, *see* § 65 *infra*.

[25] 427 U.S. 38 (1976).

[26] *See also* Warden v. Hayden, 387 U.S. 294 (1967), in which the police had probable cause to believe that *D* had committed an armed robbery moments earlier and had entered a particular house. The Court upheld the warrantless entry of the house to search for and arrest *D* on the basis of the "exigencies of the situation." Because the officers did not chase *D* from the streets into the house, *Hayden* did not "involve a 'hot pursuit' in the sense that that term would normally be understood." *Santana*, 427 U.S. at 42 n.3. Nonetheless, the Court often treats *Hayden* as if it were a "hot pursuit" case. *E.g.*, Welsh v. Wisconsin, 466 U.S. at 750.

[27] 110 S.Ct. 1684 (1990).

[28] 466 U.S. 740 (1984).

offense for first-time offenders and a misdemeanor for subsequent violators.[29] The police proceeded to D's residence, and entered without consent or a warrant to arrest him.

The state defended the warrantless entry in part on the ground that the evidence of the offense — the alcohol in D's bloodstream — would have been imminently "destroyed" by bodily processes if the police had been required to seek an arrest warrant.[30] The Court rejected the argument because of the petty nature of the offense.

The Court stopped short of deciding whether the Constitution "impose[s] an absolute ban on warrantless home arrests for certain minor offenses." However, it observed that "it is difficult to conceive of a warrantless home arrest that would not be unreasonable . . . when the underlying offense is extremely minor."

Even when an offense is a grave one, the Court is strict in its application of the exigency exception. For example, in *Olson*, the Court did not disturb the trial court's finding that no exigency existed for entering a home to arrest the driver of the getaway car in a murder-robbery, although the police had reason to believe that two women were in the house with him. No exigency existed because the murder weapon had already been seized, there was no reason to believe that the suspect posed a threat to the other occupants of the home, and the police had surrounded the area, so that flight was not a realistic possibility.

[C]   Entry Into a Third Person's Home

When the police seek to enter D's home in order to arrest her, they must have an *arrest* warrant, although the primary reason for the warrant is to safeguard the sanctity of the home, which would ordinarily be protected by a *search* warrant.

Suppose, however, that the police have reason to believe that D is not at home but is a guest in X's house. Does the arrest warrant provide the police with the limited authority to enter and search X's residence for D, or is a search warrant required? *Payton* left the question open. *Steagald v. United States*[31] answered it.

In *Steagald*, police had information that D, for whom they had an arrest warrant, could be "reached during the next 24 hours" at X's home. The officers did not go to X's home for a few days. When they did, they entered without consent, did not find D, but observed illegal drugs that resulted in X's arrest.

The Supreme Court held that the warrant for D's arrest was an inadequate safeguard of X's independent Fourth Amendment right to privacy in his home. It reasoned that the arrest warrant in this case primarily served to prevent D's arrest on less than probable cause; it did not protect X's right to reasonable security in his home.

The Court ruled that a person whose home is searched for the presence of a guest is entitled, absent exigencies or consent, to a prior judicial determination of

---

[29] D had a prior conviction, but the officers did not know this, so the Court analyzed the case as if they were arresting a first-time offender.

[30] The state also defended the warrantless entry on hot-pursuit grounds, but the Court rejected this argument because "there was no immediate or continuous pursuit of [D] . . . from the scene of the crime."

[31] 451 U.S. 204 (1981).

probable cause to search the premises for the person to be arrested.[32] Without this protection, the Court pointed out, there would be a "significant potential for abuse," in that the police, armed only with an arrest warrant, "could search all the homes of that individual's friends and acquaintances."

Steagald raises line-drawing problems. When the residence that is entered is, as *Payton* put it, the "dwelling in which the suspect lives," an arrest warrant is required, but a search warrant need not be obtained. When *D* is a "guest" in another person's home, however, a search warrant (at a minimum[33]) is required. The line between a householder (*Payton*) and a guest (*Steagald*) is a thin one.

Some cases are easy to decide. After all, in *Payton* itself, other people — *D*'s family — lived with *D*. *Their* privacy rights were threatened, but the arrest warrant was sufficient. It follows, therefore, that where *D* and *X* are co-residents of a home, *Payton* applies. At the other extreme, *Steagald* applies if *D* is merely a one-day daytime-only guest in *X*'s home.

What about an overnight guest? In *Steagald*, *D* was expected to be at *X*'s house "during the next 24 hours," which would seem to have made him an overnight guest. Furthermore, the police did not enter for a few more days, which suggests that they were acting on the supposition that his guest status had not yet terminated. On these facts, a search warrant was required. From this one could conclude that *Steagald* applies when a person is an overnight guest in another person's residence.[34]

§ 61 Use of Unreasonable Force in Making an Arrest[35]

[A] Deadly Force

Until the fourteenth century, use of deadly force to kill fleeing felons was justifiable, regardless of the felony, and regardless of whether the force was necessary in order to prevent the escape. Eventually a necessity component was added to the rule, but it remained the case that deadly force was permissible to prevent any felon, even a non-violent one, from avoiding arrest.[36]

---

[32] *Steagald* does not indicate whether an arrest warrant, obtained in this case, is also required. Although the Court pointed out that the police can easily obtain a search warrant "when they obtain an arrest warrant," a search warrant ought to be adequate if the magistrate also determines that there is probable cause to arrest the suspect who is the object of the search. 2 W. LaFave, § 6.1(b) at 576.

[33] *See* the immediately preceding footnote.

[34] However, in Minnesota v. Olson, 110 S.Ct. 1684 (1990), the Supreme Court agreed with a state court that *Payton* applied to a warrantless arrest of an overnight guest in a friend's home, "because he had sufficient connection with the premises to be treated like a householder."

Olson's relevance to the *Payton-Steagald* distinction is not clear, however. The case was argued and decided below on the issue of standing, as it apparently was at the high court level. In that context, the Court stated that "[w]e need go no further than to conclude . . . that [*D*'s] status as an overnight guest is alone enough to show that he had a[] [legitimate] expectation of privacy in the home. . . ."

[35] *See generally* Uviller, *Seizure by Gunshot: The Riddle of the Fleeing Felon*, 14 N.Y.U. Rev. L. & Soc. Change 705 (1986).

[36] *See* J. Dressler, at § 21.03[B][2].

In *Tennessee v. Garner*,[37] the Supreme Court held that this common law rule, codified in many states, is unconstitutionally broad.[38] In *Garner*, an officer was dispatched to a home on a "prowler inside call." He observed a person, *D*, fleeing in the direction of a six-foot-high chain-link fence. By use of his flashlight, the officer determined that *D* was young, 5′5″ to 5′7″ tall, and apparently unarmed. He ordered *D* to halt; when the youth began to scale the fence, the officer shot and killed him.

The Supreme Court, per Justice White, held that the use of deadly force to prevent the escape of the apparently unarmed felon constituted an "unreasonable seizure." It stated that "[t]he use of deadly force to prevent the escape of all felony suspects, whatever the circumstances, is constitutionally unreasonable. It is not better that all felony suspects die than that they escape."

Under *Garner*, use of deadly force to make an arrest is unreasonable unless the police officer: (1) reasonably believes that deadly force is necessary to prevent the suspect's escape; and (2) has probable cause to believe that the suspect constitutes a threat to cause serious bodily harm to the officer or others if she is not immediately arrested. According to the Court, an officer would have a right to use deadly force if the suspect threatened her with a deadly weapon or if the officer had probable cause to believe that the suspect had committed a felony involving the actual or threatened use of deadly force.

Garner raises two intriguing questions regarding its scope. First, what does the Court mean by use of the term "deadly force"? Although it does not say so, it may intend to invoke the common law definition, namely "force likely to cause death or grievous bodily injury."[39] If so, this would mean that the *Garner* rule is implicated if an officer "brings down" (but does not kill) a non-violent felon with a hard blow to the head with a club.

Second, at various places in the *Garner* opinion, the Court uses the phrase "*threat of* deadly force" as if it were synonymous with "deadly force." Does this mean that an officer has seized a non-violent felon "unreasonably" by getting her to stop by calling out, "Stop, or I'll shoot," or by purposely firing a shot well over her head? At least as long as the officer's threat is a bluff, it seems unconvincing to argue that such conduct is unreasonable.

---

[37] 471 U.S. 1 (1985).

[38] In most cases, as in *Garner*, the issue of the alleged use of unnecessary force will arise in the context of a civil suit against the officer for the wrongful death of the suspect or, less often, for the violation of her constitutional rights under 42 U.S.C. § 1983, or in a prosecution of the officer for criminal homicide.

The rule announced in *Garner* raises potential Fourth Amendment exclusionary rule issues if a non-violent suspect survives the "deadly force" and evidence is secured from her as the result of the unreasonable arrest. Although the Court has not had the occasion to say so, the exclusionary rule should apply in such circumstances. That is, although an officer has probable cause to arrest D, the unreasonable means used to effectuate the arrest should render evidence obtained pursuant to it inadmissible, at least if *D* would not have been seized non-violently.

[39] J. Dressler, at § 18.02[B][1].

[B] Non-Deadly Force

Garner dealt with the use of deadly force. However, as at least one commentator observed shortly after *Garner* was announced,[40] its reasoning supports a constitutionally-based proportionality rule applicable to arrest procedures in general. That is, if the use of deadly force is unreasonable in the case of some fleeing felons, the use of non-deadly force to arrest a petty criminal might also be excessive in some circumstances.

Indeed, the Court has subsequently acknowledged *Garner*'s relevance to cases involving the use of non-deadly force. In *Graham v. Connor*,[41] the Court — stating that it was making "explicit what was implicit in *Garner*'s analysis" — held "that *all* claims that law enforcement officers have used excessive force — deadly or not — in the course of an arrest, investigatory stop, or other 'seizure' of a free citizen should be analyzed under the Fourth Amendment . . . 'reasonableness' standard." Presumably, one factor in determining whether the force used in an arrest was "reasonable" or, on the other hand, "excessive" is the seriousness of the offense for which the suspect was seized.

---

[40] *See* Uviller, n. 35 *supra*, at 709-10.
[41] 109 S.Ct. 1865 (1989).

CHAPTER 12

WARRANTLESS SEARCHES: EXIGENT CIRCUMSTANCES

§ 62   Nature of the Warrant Exception

Most exceptions to the warrant requirement of the Fourth Amendment are based on exigent circumstances, that is, on the ground that it is impracticable for the officer to secure a warrant. Because an exigency is a situation that requires immediate action, it is reasonable for the officer to search without a warrant.

Certain types of exigent circumstances commonly recur. For example, an arrest triggers a threat to the police officer that the arrestee might use a concealed weapon or destroy evidence hidden on his person or in the area of his immediate control before the officer can obtain a search warrant. Similarly, the mobility of an automobile makes it difficult to secure a warrant to search a car stopped on the highway.

Because of the frequent nature of certain types of exigent circumstances, courts and commentators treat them as if they involve separate categories of exceptions to the search warrant requirement, identifying them, for example, as the "search incident to a lawful arrest" and "automobile" exceptions.

Other exigencies occur less frequently or occur in such disparate factual circumstances that courts have not classified them under a specific warrant exception. Therefore, these cases tend to be grouped together under the general umbrella of an "exigency exception" or "emergency exception" to the search-warrant requirement.

Although the circumstances that fall within this "exception" vary, three generalizations are possible. First, by definition, the exception applies when emergent circumstances make it impracticable or unreasonable for the officer to obtain a warrant prior to conducting the search.

Second, the emergency that justifies the police action usually defines the appropriate scope of the search. For example, if the emergency is that a bomb might explode in a particular house, the right to search will extend to those places in the house that could reasonably conceal the bomb.

Third, although an exigency justifies the absence of a search warrant, it does not dispense with any underlying probable-cause requirement that otherwise exists.

Examples of warrantless searches that have been, or may be, justified on the basis of exigent circumstances are discussed in the following sections.

§ 63 Intrusion Into the Human Body

In *Schmerber v. California*,[1] *D* was arrested at a hospital for driving under the influence of alcohol. On the order of the arresting officer, a physician took a blood sample from *D* to test for alcohol content. Although the Court stated that there was "plainly probable cause" for the arrest, the search and seizure were without a warrant.

Because the search involved an intrusion into the body of the arrestee, the Court determined that ordinary rules regarding searches incident to lawful arrests did not apply. Nonetheless, the Court held that the warrantless search was justifiable on the ground that the evidence — *i.e.*, the alcohol in the bloodstream — would have been lost if the police had been required to obtain a warrant, because it was in the process of being "destroyed," as *D*'s body eliminated it from his system.

Although the Court held that the warrantless search was permissible, it also ruled that the police could intrude into *D*'s body only if: (1) they were justified in requiring *D* to submit to the test; and (2) the means and procedures employed were reasonable.

The first requirement was met in this case: the officer had "plainly probable cause" to arrest *D* for driving under the influence of alcohol; and the test was not conducted "on the mere chance" that alcohol would be found in the bloodstream, but rather on the basis of a "clear indication" that such evidence would be discovered.[2]

The second requirement was also met. The test chosen — the extraction of blood — is highly effective, commonplace, and rarely painful or traumatic. Also, the test was performed in a reasonable manner: by a physician, in a hospital environment, under accepted medical practices.

§ 64 External Search of the Body

In *Cupp v. Murphy*,[3] the police had probable cause to arrest *D* for the strangulation murder of his wife. Rather than arrest him, the police requested that he respond to questions at the police station, which he agreed to do, after which he was released.

During the questioning, the officers observed a "dark spot" on *D*'s finger, which they suspected was dried blood from the murder. When they asked for permission to take a small scraping for testing, *D* refused and rubbed his fingers together. He then put his hands in his pocket, which produced a "metallic sound, such as keys or change rattling," which further suggested that *D* was attempting to destroy the

---

[1] 384 U.S. 757 (1966).

[2] In light of this language as well as the underlying reasoning of *Schmerber*, many courts and commentators interpret the case to require probable cause for any nonconsensual intrusion into a person's body. However, the Court has cast some doubt on this proposition. *Compare* Winston v. Lee, 470 U.S. 753 (1985) (*Schmerber* "noted the importance of probable cause") *with* United States v. Montoya de Hernandez, 473 U.S. 531 (1985) (*Schmerber* "indicate[d] the necessity for particularized suspicion").

[3] 412 U.S. 291 (1973).

evidence on his hands connecting him to the crime. Therefore, an officer forcibly took scrapings from *D*'s fingernails.

The Supreme Court approved the warrantless search on the basis of "search incident to lawful arrest" principles. The Court pointed out that arrestees may be searched without a warrant because it is reasonable for an officer to expect that a person taken into custody will use any weapon that he might possess and destroy any evidence on his person. In this case, because *D* was not under arrest and knew that he was going to be released, the Court reasoned that he was likely to "be less hostile to the police and less likely to take conspicuous, immediate steps to destroy incriminating evidence on his person."

Based on the difference between the facts of this case and the typical arrest, the Court held that it would have been inappropriate for the police to conduct a full search of *D*. On the other hand, in view of "the existence of probable cause, the very limited intrusion undertaken . . . , and the ready destructibility of the evidence," the police action here was reasonable.

As *D* was not arrested incident to the search, *Murphy* is easier to justify on straightforward exigency principles. Indeed, analyzed as an exigent search, the Court might have been too stringent in its analysis. After all, the fact that *D* knew that he was going to be released only shows that the officers had little reason to fear for their safety. However, they had at least as much reason as in the arrest context to fear that, on release, *D* would destroy *any* evidence on his person that tied him to the murder, not simply that which might have been on his fingers. A full search of *D*'s person, therefore, might have been reasonable.

§ 65   Entry and Search of a Home[4]

The Supreme Court has stated in ringing terms that "physical entry of a home is the chief evil against which the wording of the Fourth Amendment is directed."[5] Nonetheless, warrantless entry of a dwelling due to exigent circumstances is sometimes constitutionally reasonable.

The Court has had little occasion to identify the exigencies that justify a warrantless entry of a home for the purpose of arresting an occupant[6] or searching for evidence. However, in *Minnesota v. Olson*,[7] the Court stated that a state court "applied essentially the correct standard" when it identified the following exigencies as justifying the warrantless entry of a home: (1) hot pursuit of a fleeing felon; (2) imminent destruction of evidence;[8] (3) the need to prevent a suspect's escape;

---

[4] *See generally* 2 W. LaFave, at § 6.5; Salken, *Balancing Exigency and Privacy in Warrantless Searches to Prevent Destruction of Evidence: The Need For a Rule*, 39 Hastings L.J. 283 (1988).

[5] United States v. United States District Court, 407 U.S. 297, 313 (1972).

[6] Regarding warrantless entries of a home in order to make an arrest, *see* § 60[B] *supra*.

[7] 110 S.Ct. 1684 (1990).

[8] In dictum, the Court has suggested that the police may guard (even from within) *unoccupied* premises for a reasonable period of time until a search warrant can be secured, if the officers have probable cause to believe that the premises contain destructible evidence, although such evidence is not in imminent threat of destruction. *See* Mincey v.

and (4) the risk of harm to the police or to others, inside or outside the dwelling. In the latter three circumstances, there must be probable cause to believe that one or more of the factors justifying the entry exist.

Warden v. Hayden[9] provides a good example of how an entry into a home and a full-scale search of the premises may be justified on grounds of exigency. In the case, police officers had probable cause to believe that a man involved in an armed robbery had moments earlier entered a particular house. An unspecified number of officers hurried to the address, knocked at the door, and were allowed to enter "without objection" by a woman living in the house.

The officers spread out throughout both floors of the house and the basement looking for the suspect. *D* was found feigning sleep in his bedroom, where he was arrested. At approximately the same time other officers came upon and seized items related to the crime in other parts of the house. A shotgun and a pistol were found in an adjoining bathroom flush tank, which an officer opened because of the noise of running water; a jacket and trousers fitting the description of those worn by the robber were found by an officer who was "looking for a man or the money" in a washing machine in the basement; and various items were discovered under *D*'s bed mattress and in a bureau drawer in the bedroom.

The police officers' warrantless conduct was justified by the Supreme Court on the basis that "the exigencies of the situation made the course imperative." The officers were in hot pursuit[10] of an armed robber and speed was essential. This justified their warrantless entry into *D*'s house. Once they entered and began their search for him, "only a thorough search of the house for persons and weapons could have insured that [*D*] was the only man present and that the police had control of all weapons which could be used against them or to effect escape."

In short, the exigency justified the warrantless conduct, and the nature of the exigency defined the legitimate scope of this search: a search of any place in the home where the armed robber, anyone else who might interfere with the arrest,[11] and/or weapons, might be found.

Arizona, 437 U.S. 385 (1978) (the fact that a homicide occurred in a house is not, in itself, an exigency justifying the warrantless search of the premises for evidence; but the Court mentioned, with apparent favor, the presence of a police guard who minimized the possibility of the loss, destruction, or removal of any evidence); Segura v. United States, 468 U.S. 796 (1984) (dictum of two-justice plurality approved the warrantless entry into a home, and a 19-hour occupation of it, in order to prevent the destruction or removal of evidence while a warrant was secured). *Segura* is criticized in Dressler, *A Lesson in Incaution, Overwork, and Fatigue: The Judicial Miscraftsmanship of Segura v. United States*, 26 Wm. & Mary 375 (1985).

[9] 387 U.S. 294 (1967).

[10] *Hayden* did not use the term "hot pursuit," but the entry by the officers was subsequently explained by the Court in those terms. *E.g.*, Welsh v. Wisconsin, 466 U.S. 740, 750 (1984).

[11] The police had no reason to believe that the robbery involved more than one person, and they told the woman at the front door that they were looking for a "robber" — singular — in the house. Nonetheless, the Court stated that the police were entitled to insure themselves that *D* "was the only man present" in the house.

This language might suggest that officers otherwise legitimately on premises may automatically conduct a protective sweep of a house for persons who might threaten their safety. However, the Supreme Court has more recently held that a protective sweep through a home while making a valid arrest is only permitted if the arresting officers have reasonable suspicion that the area to be swept harbors a person posing a danger to them or others. Maryland v. Buie, 110 S.Ct. 1093 (1990). *See* § 100 *infra.*

CHAPTER 13

SEARCHES INCIDENT TO LAWFUL ARRESTS

§ 66 Chapter Overview

"Search incident to a lawful arrest" is the long, and somewhat awkward, label attached to one of the most frequently asserted exceptions to the Fourth Amendment warrant requirement.[1] For short, the exception is sometimes called (based on the primary case on the subject) the "*Chimel* rule," or, simply, the "search-incident" rule. The general principles of the exception are laid out in §§ 67-69 below.

The Supreme Court's treatment of the search-incident exception is also helpful in understanding Fourth Amendment jurisprudence generally, because many of the issues relating to the amendment have been played out in the Court's search-incident cases. Therefore, the leading cases in the field are considered in §§ 70-72 below. Furthermore, two important overarching Fourth Amendment controversies with special pertinence to the subject of this chapter are discussed in §§ 73-74 below.

§ 67 Nature of the Search Warrant Exception: In General

[A] Rule

Subject to clarification in subsequent sections of this chapter, a police officer who makes a lawful custodial arrest may conduct a warrantless search of: (1) the arrestee's person; and (2) the area within the arrestee's immediate control (the so-called "grabbing area").[2] If the arrest occurs in a home, the officer may, as a precautionary matter, also search for persons "in closets and other spaces immediately adjoining the place of arrest from which an attack could be immediately launched."[3]

[B] Rationale of the Warrant Exception

The justification for the warrant exception is that a custodial arrest provides the suspect with the incentive to use any available weapon to resist the officer or to flee, and to destroy or conceal evidence of the crime. Further, an in-home arrest "puts the officer at the disadvantage of being on his adversary's 'turf,' "[4] that is,

---

[1] *See* T. Taylor, Two Studies in Constitutional Interpretation 48 (Ohio State Press 1969); R. Van Duizend, *et al.*, at 21.

[2] Chimel v. California, 395 U.S. 752, *reh'g denied*, 396 U.S. 869 (1969).

[3] Maryland v. Buie, 110 S.Ct. 1093, 1098 (1990).

[4] *Id.*

the arrest creates the risk that an accomplice or relative of the suspect will ambush the officer.

In light of these risks, therefore, it is reasonable to allow the officer immediately to search the suspect and her "grabbing area" for weapons or evidence, as well as to search the adjoining area for dangerous persons who might be hidden.

[C]   The Probable-Cause Requirement

Although searches ordinarily require a warrant founded on probable cause, the existence of an exception to the warrant requirement does not necessarily dispose of the probable-cause obligation.

However, in the context of searches incident to lawful arrests, the right of an officer to search the person of the arrestee for weapons and evidence, and to search the adjoining area for persons who might launch an attack, flows automatically from the arrest itself.[5] Although there is no Supreme Court holding directly on point, there is little doubt that the officer's right to search the area within the arrestee's immediate control is also automatic.[6] In short, neither "probable cause" nor any lesser standard of suspicion is required to justify the warrantless search.

[D]   Seizure of Evidence During the Search

Although the purpose of a warrantless search incident to a lawful arrest is to find weapons or evidence related to the crime or a hidden person who represents a danger to the officer, the officer may *seize* without a warrant any article found during the search, if she has probable cause to believe that it is evidence of a crime.[7] Thus, the officer need not have probable cause to conduct the search, but she must have probable cause to seize the evidence found in the search.

It does not matter whether the article discovered is related to the offense for which the person was arrested or to a different crime. For example, if an officer arrests *D* for bank robbery, and the search incident to the arrest turns up the money taken in the robbery and also, unexpectedly, illegal narcotics, both the fruits of the robbery and the contraband may be seized.[8]

§ 68   Prerequisites to the Use of the Warrant Exception

[A]   "Custodial" Arrest

The search-incident rule applies to full-scale arrests, that is, to arrests in which the officer takes the suspect into custody and transports her to the station for booking.

---

[5] United States v. Robinson, 414 U.S. 218 (1973) (search of the arrestee); Maryland v. Buie, 110 S.Ct. 1093 (1990) (search of the adjoining area for dangerous persons).

[6] *See* 3 W. LaFave, § 7.1(b) at 8-9.

[7] *See* Warden v. Hayden, 387 U.S. 294, 307 (1967) (stating that there must be "a nexus . . . between the item to be seized and criminal behavior"); Arizona v. Hicks, 480 U.S. 321 (1987) (officer must have probable cause to seize items found in plain view).

[8] *See* United States v. Robinson, 414 U.S. 218 (1973) (the officer properly seized heroin discovered during the search of a traffic violator).

The Court has not considered the applicability of the search-incident rule to the situation in which an officer issues a citation, which sometimes is described as an "arrest,"[9] but does not take the person into custody, such as is the case of a routine traffic violation. However, in view of the usual rule that full searches of persons temporarily detained by the police are impermissible in the absence of probable cause,[10] it is unlikely that the search-incident exception, which justifies a full search, applies to non-custodial "arrests."

[B] Lawfulness of the Arrest

The search-incident rule applies only to searches that are an incident to a *lawful* arrest. Thus, although probable cause for a search incident to a lawful arrest is not required, probable cause for the arrest that triggers the search is required, as is an arrest warrant in some circumstances. Therefore, although the unlawfulness of an arrest itself does not bar further criminal proceedings,[11] an arrestee may challenge the lawfulness of her arrest in order to suppress evidence seized incident to it.[12]

[C] Contemporaneousness of the Search

[1] Area Within Arrestee's Immediate Control

An officer's right to conduct a search of the area within the immediate control of the arrestee is limited to searches reasonably contemporaneous to the arrest. For example, if an officer arrests the driver of an automobile, but does not search the car until after she tows it to the police garage, the search cannot be justified under the search-incident warrant exception.[13] It is no longer an "incident" to the arrest.

This limitation on the warrant exception is reasonable in light of the rule's purpose: once the arrestee is separated from the vehicle there is no risk that she can grab any weapons or destroy any evidence that previously were in her grabbing area.

[2] Of the Person

The contemporaneousness limitation does not always apply to searches of the person or, at least, the search-incident exception will merge nearly imperceptibly into another warrant exception in many cases.

For example, consider *United States v. Edwards*:[14] *D* was arrested at night and jailed for an attempted burglary of a local Post Office. Soon after the arrest the police learned that the burglar had attempted to enter the building by prying open

---

[9] *See* § 55 *supra.*

[10] *See* Terry v. Ohio, 392 U.S. 1 (1968). *See* § 94 *infra.*

[11] Frisbie v. Collins, 342 U.S. 519 (1952).

[12] If the police possess probable cause to arrest *X*, but they mistakenly arrest *D* whom they reasonably believe is *X*, *D*'s arrest is lawful. Therefore, a search incident to the arrest is lawful; if criminal evidence is found on *D*, it may be introduced against her at a subsequent trial. *See* Hill v. California, 401 U.S. 797 (1971).

[13] Preston v. United States, 376 U.S. 364 (1964).

[14] 415 U.S. 800 (1974).

a window. Therefore, the police suspected that paint chips might be found on *D*'s clothing. The next morning, approximately ten hours after the arrest, the police purchased new clothing for D and seized what he was wearing, which they inspected and held as evidence of the crime.

The Supreme Court justified the warrantless search. Although its holding appears to be based on various warrant-exception rules,[15] the Court apparently had the search-incident rule in mind when it stated that a search of a person "that could be made on the spot at the time of arrest may legally be conducted later when the accused arrives at the place of detention."

Edwards is controversial. In support of the holding is the fact that, as the Court said, *D* "was no more imposed upon than he could have been at the time and place of arrest or immediately upon arrival at the place of detention." If the police could have inspected his clothing, even vacuumed it, at the scene of the crime, *D*'s privacy was not invaded any more because the search occurred ten hours later. Furthermore, any paint chips that were on *D*'s clothing remained in his grabbing area, and the incentive to conceal or destroy the evidence existed throughout the night. Finally, the delay in the search was reasonable, as the police needed time to obtain replacement clothing.

On the other hand, the police had ten hours to secure a warrant, which distinguishes *Edwards* from the ordinary search-incident case. Moreover, to the extent that *D* had the inclination to destroy evidence on his clothing, he already had time to do so.

Cases like *Edwards* are rare. As a practical matter, when an arrestee is incarcerated, the right to search her person incident to the arrest is followed quickly by the right of the police to conduct an arrest inventory that is likely to be as or more thorough than the search incident to the arrest.

§ 69 Scope of the Warrant Exception

[A] Search of the Person

The right to search a person incident to a lawful arrest includes the right to search the pockets of the arrestee's clothing and to open containers found therein,[16] as well as to search containers "immediately associated"[17] with the person, such as a purse or shoulder bag, as long as the containers are large enough to conceal a weapon or evidence of the crime.

The right to search the arrestee is not unlimited in scope. For example, because it implicates the "most personal and deep-rooted expectations of privacy,"[18] a

---

[15] Some language in *Edwards* supports the proposition that the search could be justified on principles analogous to the "arrest inventory" exception to the warrant requirement. *See* § 87 *infra.* The Court said that another "closely related consideration" that justified the examination of the clothing was the plain-view principle that "the police . . . are normally permitted to seize evidence of crime when it is lawfully encountered."

[16] *E.g.*, United States v. Robinson, 414 U.S. 218 (1973) (cigarette package in pocket of arrestee).

[17] United States v. Chadwick, 433 U.S. 1, 15 (1977).

[18] Winston v. Lee, 470 U.S. 753, 760 (1985).

warrantless search that involves penetration of the surface of the body, such as a search of a person's blood for evidence of alcohol, may not be justified under ordinary search-incident doctrine, although it may be justifiable on other grounds.[19]

The Court has not determined under what circumstances, if any, strip searches and body-cavity searches incident to arrests are constitutional.[20] However, searches incident to arrest and incarceration must not "violate the dictates of reason . . . because of . . . their manner of perpetration."[21]

[B] Area Within the Immediate Control

[1] In General

The "area within the immediate control" of the arrestee is the area from within which the person might grab a weapon or destructible evidence. The precise scope of the grabbing area depends on the circumstances of the individual case.

For example, the arrest of a person in her home does not justify a search of the entire premises,[22] but it could justify the search of the entire room in which the arrest occurs, including all containers found in it that could harbor a weapon or evidence.[23] Among the factors that may properly[24] affect the size of the arrestee's grabbing area are: whether she is handcuffed (and, if so, whether she is cuffed in front of or behind her back); the size of the room; whether the containers in the room are open or shut, and if shut, whether they are locked or unlocked;[25] and the relative number of officers to suspects.

The "area within the immediate control" of a suspect changes if the arrestee's grabbing area necessarily changes. The Supreme Court has held that it is not

---

[19] *See* Schmerber v. California, 384 U.S. 757 (1966) (upholding a blood test of a person arrested for driving under the influence of alcohol, on search-incident grounds, but requiring that there be a "clear indication" that the test will discover alcohol, and that the search be performed in a reasonable manner). The case is more easily treated as falling within the general "exigency" exception to the warrant requirement. *See* § 63 *supra*.

[20] Strip searches of pre-trial detainees who have had contact with visitors from outside the jail are reasonable under the Fourth Amendment if they are conducted in a reasonable manner. Bell v. Wolfish, 441 U.S. 520 (1979).

[21] United States v. Edwards, 415 U.S. at 808 n.9 (*quoting* Charles v. United States, 278 F.2d 386, 389 (9th Cir. 1960)).

[22] Chimel v. California 395 U.S. 752, *reh'g denied*, 396 U.S. 869 (1969).

[23] Many courts apply a bright-line "one-room rule" and permit the search of the entire room in which the arrest occurs, regardless of its size or other circumstances. 2 W. LaFave, § 6.3(c) at 627. This approach is inappropriate under *Chimel*, as is discussed in the text immediately *infra*.

[24] Improperly, but commonly, some courts treat an arrestee as "a combination acrobat and Houdini," whose grabbing area is quite large. 2 W. LaFave, § 6.3(c) at 628; *but see* United States v. Vasey, 834 F.2d 782, 787 (9th Cir. 1987) ("*Chimel* does not allow the officers to presume that an arrestee is superhuman.").

[25] Although closed containers ordinarily are entitled to full Fourth Amendment protection, United States v. Chadwick, 433 U.S. 1 (1977), courts sometimes fail to distinguish between the container itself, which might be in the grabbing area, and the *interior* of the container — where a weapon or evidence might be held — which might not be in the grabbing area if it is locked. *See* 2 W. LaFave, at § 5.5(a).

unreasonable for an officer, "as a matter of routine, to monitor the movements of an arrested person, as his judgment dictates, following the arrest."[26] For example, if *D* is arrested in her bathrobe in the living room of her house, it is not unreasonable for the officer to allow her to enter the bedroom to get dressed in order to go to the police station. In such circumstances, the officer has "a right to remain literally at [*D's*] elbow,"[27] and to search the new grabbing area.

[2] Automobiles

In order to assist the police in determining the legally recognized grabbing area of a person arrested in her automobile, the Supreme Court in *New York v. Belton*[28] devised a bright-line rule.

The *Belton* rule states that a police officer may, contemporaneous to the arrest of an occupant of an automobile, search the passenger compartment of the vehicle and all containers found therein, whether the containers are open or closed, as an incident of the arrest. For purposes of the rule, a "container" is "any object capable of holding another object."

Under this rule, the glove compartment, consoles "or other receptacles," as well as luggage, clothing, boxes, "and the like" found in the passenger portion of the vehicle are subject to a warrantless search incident to the arrest. The trunk and engine compartment, because they are not in the interior of the passenger compartment of the vehicle, fall outside the bright-line *Belton* rule.

Various observations regarding the scope of the rule are possible. First, it applies only if the arrestee was an "occupant" of the vehicle — *i.e.*, the driver or a passenger — immediately prior to the arrest. If the arrestee was merely standing near an automobile, ordinary search-incident doctrine applies.

Second, the physical proximity of the arrestee to the automobile, as long as she and the vehicle are still at the scene, is immaterial. Nor does it matter whether the automobile doors are open or shut, or even whether the arrestee is handcuffed or in the police vehicle.

Third, although *Belton* involved four arrestees and a single officer to guard them, the bright-line nature of the rule suggests that it applies regardless of the relative number of officers and arrestees.

Less clear is whether the rule, which permits the police to open "shut" containers applies as well to *locked* shut containers. It strains credulity to believe that an arrestee, perhaps handcuffed in the police vehicle, would be able to grab a weapon or evidence in a locked glove compartment or suitcase in the backseat of the car. Moreover, if the Court merely wishes to retain the bright-line nature of the *Belton* rule, it could do so by declaring locked containers off-limits. However, in view of the Court's current tendency to provide leeway to law enforcement officers, an opposite bright-line is more predictable.

---

[26] Washington v. Chrisman, 455 U.S. 1, 7 (1982).

[27] *Id.* at 6.

[28] 453 U.S. 454, *reh'g denied*, 453 U.S. 950 (1981).

[C] Protective Searches for Dangerous Persons

Although the traditional purpose of a search incident to a lawful arrest is to look for weapons or evidence that the arrestee might grab, the Supreme Court declared in *Maryland v. Buie*[29] that as an incident to the arrest, officers may also search "closets and other spaces immediately adjoining the place of arrest" large enough to contain a person who might threaten them while they are making an arrest and before they have time to depart.[30]

The *Buie* opinion sheds no clues as to the meaning of the phrase "immediately adjoining the place of arrest." Nor does it indicate what the officer may do if she finds a person during such a protective search, *i.e.*, whether she may automatically search the person for weapons, or whether she may only search the person discovered if she has individualized suspicion that the latter constitutes a threat.

§ 70   *Chimel v. California*: Setting the Rule's Contours

Chimel v. California[31] is the benchmark search-incident case. In *Chimel*, the police, armed with an arrest warrant but without a search warrant, arrested D in his home for burglary. After the arrest, they searched the house for evidence connected to the crime. Various items were seized. The police defended their warrantless search on the ground that it fell within the search-incident exception to the warrant requirement, whereas *D* said that the search exceeded the lawful scope of the exception.

The Court, per Justice Stewart, conceded that the Court's prior law bearing on the issue was "far from consistent." It detailed the Court's four decades of "twists and turns,"[32] including twists in which it authorized searches as broad in scope as that which occurred in *Chimel*.[33]

In *Chimel*, however, the Court took another turn: it ruled, 7-2, that the police may, incident to an arrest, conduct a warrantless search of the person and the area in the suspect's immediate control, but that they may not search the entire house without a warrant.

The majority's treatment of the search-incident issue is illustrative of the Supreme Court's approach to search warrant cases generally in the 1960s and early 1970s, just as the dissent's response to it represents the now-dominant view of the Court in relation to Fourth Amendment warrant-clause jurisprudence.

The majority's analysis centered around the Fourth Amendment warrant clause and its belief that, in general, "the Constitution requires a magistrate to pass on

---

[29] 110 S.Ct. 1093 (1990).

[30] Under limited circumstances, they may also do a protective sweep of other parts of the home, but this action is not based on the search-incident exception to the warrant requirement. *See* § 100 *infra*.

[31] 395 U.S. 752 *reh'g denied*, 396 U.S. 869 (1969).

[32] LaFave, *Warrantless Searches and the Supreme Court: Further Ventures Into the "Quagmire"*, 8 Crim. L. Bull. 9, 11 (1972).

[33] *E.g.*, Harris v. United States, 331 U.S. 145, *reh'g denied*, 331 U.S. 867 (1947); United States v. Rabinowitz, 339 U.S. 56 (1950). Both cases were overruled by *Chimel*.

the desires of the police before they violate the privacy of the home."[34] Accordingly, under this view, warrantless conduct is prohibited unless the government demonstrates that the exigencies of the situation made the warrantless conduct imperative.

The *Chimel* Court also stated that when a warrant exception is recognized, it "must be 'strictly tied to and justified by' the circumstances which rendered its initiation permissible."[35] In short, in view of the importance of the warrant requirement, the scope of any exception to it should be defined as narrowly as possible, and the exception should not apply if the justification for it — the exigency — is not present in the case under adjudication.

In the case of a search incident to an arrest, the Court concluded that a warrantless search of the person of the arrestee is justified in order to remove any weapons that she might seek to use in order to resist arrest or to effect an escape, as well as to seize any evidence that might be destroyed or concealed. For the same reasons, the scope of the search must include the "area within the immediate control" of the arrestee, which the Court defined as "the area into which an arrestee might reach in order to grab a weapon or evidentiary items."

On the other hand, the Court concluded that it is unreasonable to expand the scope of the search to the remainder of the premises on which a suspect is arrested. Such a rule would expand the exception beyond its stated justification of protecting the arresting officer from harm, and of preventing the destruction of evidence by the person arrested.

Justice White, with whom Justice Black joined, dissented. He believed that the "reasonableness" clause of the Fourth Amendment ("the right of the people to be secure . . . against unreasonable searches and seizures") governed the case, rather than the warrant clause. In his view, therefore, the proper issue raised by the case was not whether an exigency made it impracticable to secure a warrant, but rather was whether a search beyond the area of the arrestee's immediate control, if founded on probable cause, was reasonable.

The dissent argued that a search of the arrestee's home incident to an arrest, if founded on probable cause, is reasonable, because an arrest in a home often creates exigent circumstances, including the risk that a family member (for example, *D*'s wife, who was present at the time of his arrest) or an accomplice will destroy evidence after the police depart. "This must so often be the case," Justice White concluded, that a general rule authorizing such searches is appropriate.

---

[34] *Chimel, quoting* McDonald v. United States, 335 U.S. 451, 455-56 (1948).
[35] *Chimel, quoting* Terry v. Ohio, 392 U.S. 1, 19 (1968).

§ 71 *United States v. Robinson*: The Traffic Arrest Case[36]

[A] Holding

Four years after *Chimel*, but also after four changes in personnel on the Supreme Court, the high court decided *United States v. Robinson*,[37] a case that focused on the issue of whether the police, incident to a lawful custodial arrest for a routine traffic violation, may search a person although they have no reason to believe that weapons or evidence of the crime will be found on the arrestee.

In *Robinson*, a District of Columbia police officer observed *D* driving his automobile on a public road. Based on prior information, he had probable cause to believe that *D* was driving his vehicle without an operator's permit, an offense that required *D*'s custodial arrest.

Because D.C. police procedures required the officer to conduct a full search of *D*, he patted down the outside of *D*'s clothing. He felt an object in *D*'s breast pocket that he could not identify, but which he pulled out. It was a crumpled up cigarette package, inside of which were objects that did not feel like cigarettes. He opened the package and found fourteen gelatin capsules that contained heroin, which he seized.

The Court of Appeals ruled that the officer acted unconstitutionally by conducting the full search. It reasoned that the officer had no basis to believe that *D* was in possession of evidence related to the traffic violation, as such evidence did not realistically exist. Furthermore, any concern that he might have had for his safety could have been satisfied by a pat-down of *D* to feel for weapons. As the pat-down that occurred here did not disclose any object that felt like a weapon, the Court of Appeals determined that the subsequent full searches (pulling out the cigarette package, and then opening it) were impermissible.

The Supreme Court, per Justice Rehnquist, rejected this analysis. It treated as speculative the assumption that persons who violate traffic laws are less likely to possess dangerous weapons than those arrested for more serious crimes. However, its "more fundamental disagreement" with the lower court was with the latter's view that, as the Supreme Court put it, "there must be litigated in each case the issue of whether or not there was present one of the reasons supporting the authority for a search of the person incident to a lawful arrest."

Under *Robinson*, the authority to search the person incident to a lawful custodial arrest does not depend on "what a court may later determine was the probability in a particular arrest situation that weapons or evidence would in fact be found upon the person of the suspect." That is, if the custodial arrest itself is lawful, a search of the person incident to it requires no additional justification.

---

[36] *See generally* Alschuler, *Bright Line Fever and the Fourth Amendment*, 45 U. Pitt. L. Rev. 227, 256-60 (1984); LaFave, *"Case-by-Case Adjudication" Versus "Standardized Procedures": The Robinson Dilemma*, 1974 Sup. Ct. Rev. 127; Salken, *The General Warrant of the Twentieth Century? A Fourth Amendment Solution to Unchecked Discretion to Arrest for Traffic Offenses*, 62 Temple L.Q. 221 (1989); White, *The Fourth Amendment As a Way of Talking About People: A Study of Robinson and Matlock*, 1974 Sup. Ct. Rev. 165.

[37] 414 U.S. 218 (1973).

[B] *Robinson* versus *Chimel*

The holding of *Robinson* is not inconsistent with that of *Chimel*. *Chimel* was concerned with the scope of the search-incident warrant exception; the Court was not called upon in that case to determine whether probable cause (or any other level of suspicion) was required for searches that occurred within the scope of the exception. Nonetheless, the Court's Fourth Amendment analysis in *Robinson* differs appreciably from the *Chimel* Court's reasoning and, therefore, is worthy of some attention.

In *Chimel*, the Court focused on the warrant clause of the Fourth Amendment, placed the burden of proof on the government to justify any exception to the warrant requirement, and, in light of the presumption against warrantless searches, refused to announce a search-incident exception broader than necessary to meet the circumstances of the case. The fact that, as the dissent in *Chimel* pointed out, arrests in homes often create exigent circumstances, did not justify a warrantless search where the exigency was not proved.

In contrast, the *Robinson* Court focused more on the reasonableness clause of the Fourth Amendment, and held that a full search of a person arrested for a traffic violation is a reasonable search. Because its analysis was not tied to the warrant clause, the Court saw no reason to prohibit a warrantless search in a case in which there were no facts that justified dispensing with the warrant requirement.

In the same vein, notice how the *Robinson* Court gave short shrift to the search of *D*'s cigarette package after it was removed from his pocket. That is, even granting the right of officers to search all arrestees for weapons and evidence, a remaining question is whether a police officer should have the automatic right to open containers found on the person of the arrestee.

Again, if warrant exceptions are tied to the exigencies that justify them (as *Chimel* said), an officer should *seize* such containers without a warrant, place them in a safe place outside the arrestee's grabbing area, and thereby avoid the additional privacy intrusion of a warrantless *search* of the container. Justice Rehnquist's analysis of this issue in *Robinson* consisted simply of the statement that "the Fourth Amendment does not require [the officer's judgment] to be broken down in each instance into an analysis of each step in the search."

§ 72 *New York v. Belton*: Bright Lines for Automobiles[38]

In *New York v. Belton*,[39] a police officer arrested four occupants of an automobile that he had stopped for speeding, after he smelled burnt marijuana in the vehicle and observed an envelope on the floor of the car marked "Supergold," a term that he associated with marijuana.

The four occupants were removed from the car and separated from each other "so they would not be in physical touching area of each other." The officer returned to the vehicle, opened the envelope, and discovered marijuana. He then searched

---

[38] *See generally*, Alschuler, n. 36 *supra*, at 272-85.
[39] 453 U.S. 454, *reh'g denied*, 453 U.S. 950 (1981).

the remainder of the passenger compartment of the car. In the backseat he found a jacket. He unzipped a pocket of it, in which he found cocaine.

In an opinion written by Justice Stewart, the author of *Chimel*, the Court approved the warrantless police search, including that of the jacket, as incident to the lawful arrest of the occupants. The Court lamented the lack of a "straightforward rule" respecting the question of what constitutes the grabbing area of persons arrested in automobiles. Therefore, the Court generated a bright-line rule: in all cases, an officer may conduct a contemporaneous warrantless search of the passenger compartment of a vehicle incident to a lawful arrest.[40]

It is almost impossible to rationalize *Belton* in light of *Chimel*, and particularly perplexing that Justice Stewart authored both opinions. As discussed earlier, *Chimel* applied the principle that, in view of the constitutional importance of warrants, the scope of a search should be "strictly tied" to the circumstances that render the warrantless action permissible. In *Belton*, however, the bright-line rule clearly permits the police to dispense with the warrant requirement in cases in which no genuine exigency exists.

If the passenger compartment of an automobile whose doors are closed is within the grabbing area of an arrestee sitting handcuffed in a police car — as the *Belton* bright-line rule suggests — then it would not seem difficult to argue that the search that occurred but was condemned in *Chimel* was legitimate. At the least, a bright-line "one room" or "one floor" rule, rather than the vaguer "area of immediate control" rule, could easily be defended after *Belton*. In short, if *Belton* is right, *Chimel* is hard to justify. If *Chimel* is right, *Belton* is hard to fathom.[41]

Even if bright-line rules generally are desirable,[42] a controversial matter, a strong case can be made that *Belton* is not the right bright-line rule. Bright-line rules ought to produce results similar to those that would occur by case-by-case adjudication.[43] It is implausible to believe that in the majority of cases in which an automobile occupant is arrested, the entire passenger compartment of the vehicle is in the arrestee's grabbing area after the arrestee is removed from the vehicle.

Assuming that the facts described in lower court cases are typical, the usual scenario after an occupant of an automobile is arrested is that she is removed from the vehicle, handcuffed, and placed in the police car. In light of this, it makes more sense, if a bright-line rule is needed, to declare that the interior of a vehicle is never in the arrestee's immediate control once she is removed from it or, at least, once she is handcuffed or placed in the police car.

---

[40] The scope of this rule is discussed at § 69[B][2] *supra*.

[41] On remand, the New York Court of Appeals, interpreting its own constitution, rejected the Supreme Court's bright-line rule in favor of a *Chimel*-like test. People v. Belton, 55 N.Y.2d 49, 432 N.E.2d 745, 447 N.Y.S.2d 873, *reh'g denied*, 56 N.Y.2d 646, 436 N.E.2d 196, 450 N.Y.S.2d 1026 (1981).

[42] *See* § 73 *infra*.

[43] LaFave, The Fourth Amendment in an Imperfect World: On Drawing "Bright Lines" and "Good Faith", 43 U. Pitt. L. Rev. 307, 325-26 (1982).

§ 73 Bright Line Rules vs. Case-by-Case Adjudication[44]

A significant issue in the search-incident cases, but one that permeates Fourth Amendment jurisprudence (indeed, criminal procedure) generally is this: Is it better for courts to develop bright-line rules or for them to formulate "no line" or "fuzzy line" rules, the implementation of which requires case-by-case adjudication?

Consider the ultimate fuzzy-line Fourth Amendment rule, as suggested by one commentator: "A search or seizure must be reasonable, considering all relevant factors on a case-by-case basis. If it is not, the evidence must be excluded."[45]

Of course, the Court has not invoked this rule but it has announced fuzzy-line rules in some contexts. For example, the search-incident-to-a-lawful-arrest rule enunciated in *Chimel v. California*[46] is fuzzy to the extent that it invites courts to adjudicate on a case-by-case basis the meaning of the phrase "area within the arrestee's immediate control."

Similarly, in the Fifth Amendment context, the Court has held that involuntarily-secured confessions are inadmissible in criminal trials, but it has provided "no talismanic definition of 'voluntariness.' "[47] Instead, the Court assesses voluntariness on a case-by-case basis, on the totality of the circumstances.

In contrast to rules that require case-by-case adjudication, the Court frequently devises bright-line rules. An alternative to the fuzzy Fourth Amendment rule noted above could be: "All warrantless searches and seizures are prohibited." And, an alternative to the fuzzy "voluntariness" confession rule is the bright-line *Miranda*[48] rule that excludes any confession obtained as the result of a custodial interrogation that was not preceded by "*Miranda* warnings."

Similarly, in the search-incident field, the fuzzy line drawn in *Chimel* was followed by the Court's bright-line rules of *Robinson*[49] and *Belton*,[50] which instruct police officers, respectively, that they may search all arrestees whether or not they have reason to fear for their safety or the destruction of evidence, and that they may search the passenger compartments of all vehicles and all containers found therein, regardless of the proximity of the arrestees to their cars.

Which approach to rule-making is preferable? Advocates of case-by-case adjudication argue that their approach is more apt to lead to the "correct" result, *i.e.*, to the result that is consistent with the underlying justification of the rule. They contend that bright-line rulemaking can do no more than be right most of the time, whereas the goal of case-by-case adjudication is to be correct all of the time.

For example, the justification for warrantless searches incident to arrests is to protect the officer's safety and to prevent the destruction of evidence in the

---

[44] *See generally* Alschuler, n. 36 *supra*; Bradley, *Two Models of the Fourth Amendment*, 83 Mich. L. Rev. 1468 (1985); LaFave, n. 36 *supra*; LaFave, n. 43 *supra*.
[45] Bradley, n. 44 *supra*, at 1471.
[46] 395 U.S. 752, *reh'g denied*, 296 U.S. 869 (1969). *See* § 70 *supra*.
[47] Schneckloth v. Bustamonte, 412 U.S. 218, 224 (1973).
[48] Miranda v. Arizona, 384 U.S. 436, *reh'g denied*, 385 U.S. 890 (1966).
[49] United States v. Robinson, 414 U.S. 218 (1973). *See* § 71 *supra*.
[50] New York v. Belton, 453 U.S. 454 (1981). *See* § 72 *supra*.

arrestee's proximity. The *Chimel* rule fits this justification by allowing the police to search the suspect's grabbing area, but to go no further. But, when that principle is converted to a bright-line rule, as it was in *Belton*, the police are permitted to conduct warrantless searches in many cases in which the need for the exception to the warrant requirement is absent.

In response, advocates of bright lines argue that fuzzy-line rules lead to incorrect results more often than do bright-line rules. They point out that law enforcement officers must make split-second constitutional determinations. To do their job properly, therefore, they need clear guidance, rather than rules that are "qualified by all sorts of ifs, ands, and buts [that] . . . requir[e] the drawing of subtle nuances and hairline distinctions."[51]

Professor Anthony Amsterdam has pointed out that a fuzzy-line rule may be "splendid in its flexibility," but is apt to be "awful in its unintelligibility, unadministrability, and . . . general ooziness."[52] Therefore, the argument proceeds, it is preferable to have a clear rule that can be obeyed nearly all of the time by police, even if it will lead to a correct result in, perhaps, only ninety percent of the cases, than it is to implement fuzzy rules that should lead to the correct result all of the time, but which well-intentioned officers are able to apply correctly in only seventy-five percent of the cases.[53]

However, even assuming their virtue, do bright-line rules remain bright? Justice Rehnquist has observed that lawyers are "trained to attack 'bright lines' the way hounds attack foxes."[54] They want rules to be "responsive to every relative shading of every relevant variation of every relevant complexity" that might arise in a criminal case.[55] The tendency of judges who are forced to attack real-world issues of gray with black-and-white rules is to develop hairline distinctions that complicate the law.

Some commentators take a middle position in the debate:[56] they favor bright lines, but only if three conditions are met. First, a bright-line rule should be implemented only when there is evidence of a genuine need for it, *i.e.*, when case-by-case adjudication has resulted in inadequate guidance to those who must enforce the law.

Second, assuming good-faith on the part of the person applying the rule, the bright-line rule should parallel the result in case-by-case adjudication in a high percentage of cases. Third, the rule should not be readily susceptible to abuse by the police. The latter issue is discussed immediately below.

---

[51] LaFave, n. 36 *supra*, at 141.

[52] Amsterdam, at 425.

[53] LaFave, n. 43 *supra*, at 321.

[54] Robbins v. California, 453 U.S. 420, 443, *reh'g denied*, 453 U.S. 950 (1981).

[55] Amsterdam, at 375.

[56] *E.g.*, LaFave, n. 43 *supra*, at 325-33.

§ 74 Pretextual Police Conduct[57]

So-called "pretextual" police conduct is a matter of concern in criminal procedure generally, and in the search-and-seizure field in particular. A police officer acts on a pretext when the justification she gives for her conduct, although objectively valid, is a subterfuge for her true, and illegitimate, purpose for the activity.

For example, the rule handed down in *United States v. Robinson*,[58] namely that a police officer may automatically search any traffic violator she takes into custody, invites the possibility of a pretextual arrest. With only a slight embellishment on the facts of that case, the problem is quickly seen.

Suppose that the officer in *Robinson* ordinarily overlooked minor driving violations, but that he had a hunch (but lacked probable cause to believe) that *D* was a drug pusher and, therefore, he wanted to see if he could find evidence of narcotics in *D*'s possession. In view of the holding in *Robinson*, the officer could arrest *D* for the minor driving offense simply so that he could search him.[59]

What should a court do about the risk of pretextual conduct? The most obvious way to deal with the concern is to consider claims of pretext on a case-by-case basis, and to exclude evidence from a criminal trial if it is proved that the officer acted for illegitimate reasons. This may be termed the "secret motivation" approach to pretextual conduct.

The primary difficulty with the secret-motivation approach is that "the catch is not worth the trouble of the hunt when courts set out to bag the secret motivations of police. . . ."[60] People rarely act of a single mind: conflicting motivations, some proper and others not, often inspire action. Even the most truthful officer may be unable to testify with certainty regarding her genuine motivations, while the overzealous officer would have a strong incentive to lie if her subjective beliefs controlled the admissibility of the evidence. Furthermore, it is likely that a judge, forced to divine a police officer's motivation, will usually assume that she acted non-pretextually.

Alternatively, the Supreme Court might devise its Fourth Amendment rules so as to limit police power in those classes of cases in which the risk of pretext is especially high. This is the "power-limitation" approach.

For example, in *Robinson*, using the power-limitation approach, the Court might have announced a different bright-line rule than it did: that officers may

---

[57] *See generally* Burkoff, *The Pretext Search Doctrine Returns After Never Leaving*, 66 U. Det. L. Rev. 363 (1989); Burkoff, *The Pretext Search Doctrine: Now You See It, Now You Don't*, 17 U. Mich. J.L. Ref. 523 (1984); Haddad, *Pretextual Fourth Amendment Activity: Another Viewpoint*, 28 U. Mich. J.L. Ref. 639 (1985).

[58] 414 U.S. 218 (1973). *See* § 71 *supra*.

[59] Other examples abound: an officer enters a house pursuant to a warrant to search for evidence of a minor crime, for which she has probable cause to search, as a pretext to look for evidence of a more serious crime, for which she lacks probable cause to search; or an officer enters a home without a warrant in hot pursuit of the felon, as a pretext to seize items she knows she will find in plain view. *See* Horton v. California, 110 S.Ct. 2301, 2313-14 (1990) (Marshall, J., dissenting) (discussing these examples).

[60] Amsterdam, at 436 (footnote deleted).

pat-down the outside of the clothing of arrested traffic-violators for weapons, but that they may not fully search them. Such a bright-line rule would have reduced the incentive for officers to act pretextually. And, in contrast to the secret-motivation approach, trial courts would not be forced to determine why an officer acted as she did, only that she deviated from the constitutional rule.[61]

The Supreme Court is disinclined to follow the secret-motivation approach in cases involving alleged pretextual conduct. This seems to be the gist of *Scott v. United States*,[62] in which the Court stated:

> [T]he fact that [an] officer does not have a state of mind which is hypothecated by the reasons which provide the legal justifications for the officer's actions does not invalidate the action taken as long as the circumstances, viewed objectively, justify that action.[63]

However, the Court is willing, at least infrequently, to limit the Fourth Amendment authority of the police in cases in which the risk of pretext is great. For example, in *Steagald v. United States*,[64] the Court held that an officer may not ordinarily enter a person's home to arrest a guest, even if the officer has an arrest warrant, unless she is also armed with a warrant to search the premises. One reason given by the Court for this limitation on police power was that if a search warrant were not required, an arrest warrant might "serve as the pretext for entering a home in which the police have a suspicion, but not probable cause to believe, that illegal activity is taking place."[65]

---

[61] *See* 1 W. LaFave, § 1.4(e) at 94.

[62] 436 U.S. 128, *reh'g denied*, 438 U.S. 908 (1978).

[63] The Court recently reaffirmed this point. *See* Horton v. California, 110 S.Ct. at 2308-09 (1990) (in which Justice Stevens, writing for seven justices, stated that "even-handed law enforcement is best achieved by the application of objective standards of conduct, rather than standards that depend upon the subjective state of mind of the officer").

[64] 451 U.S. 204 (1981).

[65] *See also* Maine v. Moulton, 474 U.S. 159, 180 (1985) ("To allow the admission of evidence obtained from the accused in violation of his Sixth Amendment rights whenever the police assert an alternative, legitimate reason for their surveillance invites abuse . . . in the form of fabricated investigations. . . .").

CHAPTER 14

SEARCHES OF CARS AND CONTAINERS THEREIN

§ 75 Automobile Search-Warrant Exception: General Rules [1]

[A] Overview

The so-called "automobile exception" to the Fourth Amendment search-warrant requirement has broadened over time. The Supreme Court once stated that "[t]he word 'automobile' is not a talisman in whose presence the Fourth Amendment fades away and disappears." [2] Today, however, it is closer to the truth to state that, as the Court recently did, "[a] citizen does not surrender *all* the protections of the Fourth Amendment by entering an automobile." [3]

The current scope of the "automobile exception" is described in the following two subsections. [4] The leading "car cases" are considered in detail in the subsequent sections of this chapter.

[B] Searches "At the Scene"

A police officer may conduct a warrantless contemporaneous search of an automobile [5] that he has probable cause to believe contains criminal evidence if: (1) he stops the car while it is being used on the highway; or (2) the car is readily capable of use on the highway, but is discovered in a stationary position in a place not regularly used for residential purposes. [6]

For example, the "automobile exception" applies if an officer, based on probable cause, stops a car on a public road and immediately searches it, [7] or if he discovers

---

[1] *See generally* 3 W. LaFave, at § 7.02(a)-(c); Gardner, *Searches and Seizures of Automobiles and Their Contents: Fourth Amendment Considerations in a Post-Ross World,* 62 Neb. L. Rev. 1 (1983); Grano, *Rethinking the Fourth Amendment Warrant Requirement,* 19 Am. Crim. L. Rev. 603 (1982); Katz, *United States v. Ross: Evolving Standards for Warrantless Searches,* 74 J. Crim. L. & Criminology 172 (1983); Note, *Warrantless Searches and Seizures of Automobiles,* 87 Harv. L. Rev. 835 (1974).

[2] Coolidge v. New Hampshire, 403 U.S. 443, 461, *reh'g denied,* 404 U.S. 874 (1971).

[3] New York v. Class, 475 U.S. 106, 112 (1986) (emphasis added).

[4] Two other search-warrant exceptions expressly relate to cars: searches incident to a lawful arrest, *see* § 69[B][2] *supra*; and automobile inventories, *see* §§ 84-86 *infra.*

[5] The word "automobile" in the warrant exception discussed in this chapter applies to all motorized vehicles, including trucks, airplanes, motor homes, and motor boats. *See* California v. Carney, 471 U.S. 386, 393 n.2 (1985).

[6] *Id.* at 390-93.

[7] *E.g.,* Carroll v. United States, 267 U.S. 132 (1925).

the vehicle off the highway, for example, at a gas station,[8] or parked in a public place, such as in a parking lot[9] or on the street,[10] and searches it at the scene.

In contrast, the exception does not justify a warrantless search of an unoccupied car parked in the user's driveway or garage, at least if the police have time to secure a warrant prior to the search.[11]

[C] Searches "Away From the Scene"

A warrantless search of an automobile that would be valid if it were conducted at the scene, *i.e.*, at the place where it was stopped or first discovered, is also permitted if it takes place shortly thereafter away from the scene.[12]

In other words, if the police wish to do so, and regardless of the reason for their decision,[13] they may choose to seize a car without searching it, move it to another site (such as a police impoundment lot), and search it there without a warrant, on the day of the seizure,[14] or even a day[15] or a few days[16] later. On the other hand, a delay of a year to search an impounded vehicle without a warrant is unreasonable.[17]

§ 76 *Carroll v. United States*: The "Mobility" Rationale

In *Carroll v. United States*,[18] the Supreme Court first enunciated an "automobile exception" to the Fourth Amendment warrant requirement. In *Carroll*, federal officers stopped *D*'s automobile on the highway and searched it without a warrant for "bootleg" liquor. At the time *D*'s car was stopped, the officers had probable cause to search it for the contraband, but they lacked statutory authority to arrest the occupants of the car until the goods were found.

The Court upheld the warrantless search. It stated that "a necessary difference [exists] between a search of a . . . dwelling house or other structure of which a

---

[8] *E.g.*, Colorado v. Bannister, 449 U.S. 1 (1980) (*per curiam*).

[9] *E.g.*, California v. Carney, 471 U.S. 386 (1985).

[10] *E.g.*, United States v. Bagley, 772 F.2d 482 (9th Cir. 1985), *cert. denied*, 475 U.S. 1023 (1986).

[11] *E.g.*, Coolidge v. New Hampshire, 403 U.S. 443, *reh'g denied*, 404 U.S. 874 (1971) (plurality opinion).

[12] Chambers v. Maroney, 399 U.S. 42, *reh'g denied*, 400 U.S. 856 (1970); United States v. Ross, 456 U.S. 798, 807 n.9 (1982).

[13] Texas v. White, 423 U.S. 67, *reh'g denied*, 423 U.S. 1081 (1976) (*per curiam*).

[14] *E.g.*, Chambers v. Maroney, 399 U.S. 42, *reh'g denied*, 400 U.S. 856 (1970).

[15] *E.g.*, Cardwell v. Lewis, 417 U.S. 583 (1974) (plurality opinion).

[16] *E.g.*, United States v. Johns, 469 U.S. 478 (1985) (three-day delay was reasonable; however, the Court did not "foreclose the possibility" that a delay of that length could be deemed unreasonable if the owner proved that the delay "adversely affected [his] . . . privacy or possessory interest" in the car or its contents).

[17] *E.g.*, Coolidge v. New Hampshire, 403 U.S. 443 (1971) (after a timely search, the car was re-searched more than a year after its seizure); United States v. Johns, 469 U.S. at 487 (citing *Coolidge*, the Court observed that "police officers may [not] indefinitely retain possession of a vehicle and its contents before they complete a vehicle search.").

[18] 267 U.S. 132 (1925).

warrant readily may be obtained" and an automobile that "can be quickly moved out of the locality" while the warrant is sought.

The result in *Carroll* is unsurprising. The automobile was clearly mobile: it was in transit when it was stopped. And, because the occupants could not be arrested, the police had no way to search the car without conducting one type of warrantless Fourth Amendment activity or another. That is, either they had to search the car immediately without a warrant, or they had to seize it (so as to prevent the occupants from driving away) until a warrant could be secured some time later.

§ 77　*Chambers v. Maroney*: The Mobility Rationale Is Undermined

In *Chambers v. Maroney*,[19] police officers stopped *D*'s car on the highway because it fit the description of one involved in a robbery in the vicinity an hour earlier. When the officers approached the car and saw that its occupants fit the description of the robbers, they lawfully arrested them.

The police then drove the vehicle and the arrestees to the police station. Shortly thereafter, while the occupants were in jail, the police searched the car without a warrant, and found weapons and evidence of the crime concealed under the dashboard.

The Court, per Justice White, upheld the warrantless search, ostensibly on the basis of *Carroll*. It observed that although a warrantless search of an automobile is not justified "in every conceivable circumstance . . . [t]he circumstances that furnish probable cause to search . . . are most often unforeseeable; moreover, the opportunity to search is fleeting since a car is readily movable."

The Court reasoned that when an automobile is stopped on the highway, an effective search is possible only if the police search the car on the scene, or seize it without a warrant and hold it until one is obtained. Justice White conceded that "arguably," in view of the preference for a magistrate's determination of probable cause, the latter option should have been followed in the case, on the ground that "the 'lesser' intrusion [of the seizure] is permissible until the magistrate authorizes the 'greater' [intrusion of the search]."

But, the Court rejected this "arguable" claim. It stated that the question of which is the greater intrusion — the seizure of the car, or the search of its contents — "is itself a debatable question . . . the answer [to which] may depend on a variety of circumstances." Consequently, the Court concluded, there is no constitutional difference between the options.

But, the police in *Chambers* followed neither of these paths: they did not search the car at the scene without a warrant; and they did not seize it without a warrant and then submit the issue of probable cause to search to a magistrate. Instead, they seized the car without a warrant and searched it — again without a warrant — at the station.

The Court justified the latter action on the ground that, "unless the Fourth Amendment permits a warrantless seizure of the car and the denial of its use to anyone until a warrant is secured," the car retained its mobility at the police

---

[19] 399 U.S. 42, *reh'g denied*, 400 U.S. 856 (1970).

station. Therefore, the officers' practical options at the stationhouse were the same as they were on the highway: search it immediately; or deny its use to others until a warrant could be obtained. Again, the Court ruled that there was no significant difference between these choices.

Two critical observations of *Chambers* are in order.[20] First, "mobility," as it existed in *Carroll*, plainly was absent in *Chambers*. In *Carroll*, the police were unable to arrest the occupants until they searched the vehicle. In *Chambers*, the occupants were already under arrest prior to the search; therefore, there was no risk that the car would be quickly moved out of the jurisdiction or hidden. Nor did the government present any evidence to the court that anyone who had a right to the car sought to take it while it was at the station.

Second, the Court was probably wrong when it concluded that there was no constitutional difference between the warrantless search of *D*'s car in *Chambers*, on the one hand, and its warrantless seizure until a magistrate could make a probable-cause determination, on the other hand. Almost certainly, the latter option involved a lesser intrusion.

When a car is stopped by police on the highway, three Fourth Amendment interests are at stake.[21] First, the occupants of the car have an interest in being permitted to continue their travel unimpeded. Second, the car owner has a possessory interest in his vehicle. Third, at least some of the occupants of the car have a privacy interest in its contents.

On the facts in *Chambers*, *D* was not in a position to protect either of the first two interests. As he was already in custody, his interest in uninterrupted travel had lapsed. Nor could he realistically expect the police to leave the car on the highway; the officers' caretaking function probably required them to move it to a safer site, thus impairing his right to control the use of his car. Thus, *D*'s only substantial Fourth Amendment concern was his privacy interest in the contents of the car, which could only be protected by the requirement that the police apply for a search warrant.[22]

§ 78 From *Cady* to *Cardwell* to *Carney*: The "Privacy" Rationale

Chambers purported to apply the *Carroll* mobility principle when in fact it distorted it. It was difficult for the Court in subsequent cases to defend *Chambers* on that basis. By 1982, it conceded in *Michigan v. Thomas*[23] that the right to search a car without a warrant "does [not] . . . depend upon a reviewing court's assessment of the likelihood in each particular case that the car would have been

---

[20] Many scholars have criticized *Chambers*. E.g., 3 W. LaFave, § 7.2(a) at 26-27; Grano, n. 1 *supra*, at 605, 642-46; Note, n. 1 *supra*, at 837-45.

[21] *See* Note, n. 1 *supra*, at 840-45.

[22] In contrast, in a pre-arrest situation such as in *Carroll*, all three interests come into play. As in *Chambers*, a driver's privacy interest in the contents of his car favors a search warrant. On the other hand, unlike *Chambers*, his interests in continuing his trip unimpeded and in maintaining possession of his car point in the direction of a warrantless on-the-scene search.

[23] 458 U.S. 259 (1982) (*per curiam*).

driven away, or that its contents would have been tampered with, during the period required for the police to obtain a warrant."

The Court needed a new theory to explain its willingness to permit warrantless searches of cars not readily mobile. The seeds of the new theory were sown in *Cady v. Dombrowski.*[24] In *Cady*, a car rented and driven by *D*, an off-duty police officer, was involved in a traffic accident. *D* was arrested for drunk driving, and the car was towed to a privately owned garage. Shortly thereafter, officers investigating the accident learned that *D*'s service revolver was probably still in the car. Because the gun was vulnerable to theft in the parking lot, the police searched the car in the middle of the night. Inadvertently, they discovered evidence that tied *D* to a homicide.

In a 5-4 opinion, the Court held that the warrantless search — "standard police procedure" in the department under such circumstances — was reasonable. However, *Cady*'s long-term significance is found in the Court's discussion of the "automobile exception."

It conceded that although the original justification for the exception "was the [car's] vagrant and mobile nature," subsequent warrantless searches were upheld in cases in which mobility was "remote, if not non-existent." *Cady* provided another explanation of why, mobility aside, automobiles *qua* automobiles are different from houses:

> Because of the extensive regulation of motor vehicles and traffic, and also because of the frequency with which a vehicle can become disabled or involved in an accident on public highways, the extent of police-citizen contact involving automobiles will be substantially greater than police-citizen contact in a home or office.

A year later, in *Cardwell v. Lewis*,[25] a four-justice plurality developed this argument further. After noting the mobility feature of cars, the Court stated that "there is still another distinguishing factor," which was that:

> [o]ne has a lesser expectation of privacy in a motor vehicle because its function is transportation and it seldom serves as one's residence or the repository of personal effects. A car has little capacity for escaping public scrutiny. It travels public thoroughfares where its occupants and its contents are in plain view.

Ultimately, the lesser-expectation-of-privacy rationale was accepted by a majority of justices in *California v. Carney*,[26] when the Supreme Court expressly applied both rationales of the "automobile exception" in order to uphold a warrantless vehicle search in a criminal investigation.

Carney involved a search of a motor home that the Court stated "possessed some, if not many of the attributes of a home." The vehicle was parked in a city lot near a courthouse where a warrant could have been secured. There was no indication that the vehicle was about to depart and it was under constant police surveillance.

---

[24] 413 U.S. 433 (1973).
[25] 417 U.S. 583 (1974).
[26] 471 U.S. 386 (1985).

The Court provided lip service to the mobility principle. It stated that the "motor home was readily mobile. Absent the prompt search and seizure, it could readily have been moved. . . ." This statement, however, was true only in the sense that the motor home had the capacity for transportation; if that capacity had been utilized while an officer was seeking a warrant, the vehicle would have been stopped.

However, the Court went on to state that even when an automobile is not "immediately mobile, the lesser expectation of privacy resulting from its use . . . justifie[s] application of the vehicular exception." The Court emphasized the latter rationale regarding the mobile home:

> [T]he vehicle was licensed to "operate on public streets; [was] serviced in public places; . . . and was subject to extensive regulation and inspection."
> . . . And the vehicle was so situated that an objective observer would conclude that it was being used not as a residence, but as a vehicle.[27]

The lesser-expectation-of-privacy rationale in the context of automobile searches has been criticized by some scholars.[28] They argue that the fact that a car is visible to the public on the road (a matter noted in *Cardwell*) does not distinguish it from any object that a person might carry on a public road, for example, a suitcase or valise.

Nor was the Court in *Cardwell* accurate in stating that an automobile "seldom serves as one's residence or the repository of personal effects." The motor home in *Carney* belies this observation. Moreover, people commonly use their cars, especially the trunk and glove compartment, to transport articles of considerable importance and of a personal nature. Although the car serves in such cases as only a temporary repository of these items, a car is no less important a source of privacy than a hotel room, which receives full Fourth Amendment protection.[29]

Finally, the fact that cars are the object of extensive governmental regulation, although true, does not distinguish them from "fully" protected houses and offices, which are the subject of building, safety, and health code regulations and nonconsensual inspections.[30] Perhaps in view of the fact that the government regulates so many aspects of our lives — and, therefore, reduces our "reasonable expectations" — the issue regarding cars ought to be whether we have a right to an expectation of privacy in our cars, regardless of the heavily regulated nature of automobile usage.

---

[27] The Court did not determine whether or when a warrant might be required to search a "motor home that is situated in a way or place that objectively indicates it is being used as a residence." According to *Carney*, among the factors that might be relevant in such a case would be whether the motor home: is readily movable or, instead, is elevated on blocks; is licensed as a vehicle; is connected to utilities; and/or has convenient access to a public road.

[28] *E.g.*, Grano, n. 1 *supra*, at 629-38; Katz, n. 1 *supra*.

[29] The Court appears to have accepted this latter point. It has conceded that "[c]ertainly the privacy interests in a car's trunk or glove compartment may be no less than those in a movable container." United States v. Ross, 456 U.S. at 823.

[30] *See* § 104 *infra*.

§ 79   Special Problem: Search of Containers in Cars[31]

[A]   Clarification of the Issue

Courts generally agree that the right to search a car pursuant to the "automobile exception" extends to the entire vehicle and not simply to a portion of it (*e.g.*, the trunk or passenger compartment), as long as the object of the search is small enough to be found in the area of the car searched.

A separate issue is whether an officer, while conducting an otherwise valid warrantless search of an automobile, may also open containers found in the car. For Fourth Amendment purposes, a "container" is an any object "capable of holding another object."[32] This issue is discussed in the following subsections.

[B]   Are There Containers "Unworthy" of Protection?

Containers are not all alike. Some containers are simple, such as a paper bag, whereas others are sophisticated, such as an executive's attache case.[33]

Furthermore, people protect their privacy in the contents of containers in different ways. One person with a paper bag might leave it open, another might fold it closed, and still another could staple it shut; the briefcase might be unlocked, locked, or even double-locked.

Should all containers, despite these differences, be treated alike for Fourth Amendment purposes? Or, does a person have a less reasonable expectation of privacy — or none at all — in some containers?

The Supreme Court considered this question for the first time in *Arkansas v. Sanders*,[34] a case involving the warrantless search of an obviously "worthy" container, *i.e.*, a closed suitcase found in a taxicab. In a footnote, the Court, per Justice Powell, observed that "[n]ot all containers and packages found by police during the course of a search . . . deserve . . . protection of the Fourth Amendment."

The Court explained that some containers — its examples were a kit of burglar tools and a gun case — "by their very nature cannot support any reasonable expectation of privacy because their contents can be inferred from their outward appearance." It also suggested that some containers do not deserve protection because their contents are open to plain view.

The Court clarified these remarks in *Robbins v. California*.[35] In *Robbins*, the police opened two packages they discovered in a car, each of which was wrapped in green opaque plastic, and was sealed. The containers were described as "roughly resembl[ing] an oversized, extra-long cigar box with slightly rounded corners and

---

[31] *See generally* 3 W. LaFave, at § 7.2(c)-(d); Gardner, n. 1 *supra*; Katz, n. 1 *supra*.

[32] New York v. Belton, 453 U.S. 454, 460 n.4. In theory, a person is a "container." Under the "automobile exception," however, the right to search the contents of a car does not extend to a search of its occupants. United States v. Di Re, 332 U.S. 581 (1948).

[33] United States v. Ross, 456 U.S. at 822.

[34] 442 U.S. 753 (1979).

[35] 453 U.S. 420, *reh'g denied*, 453 U.S. 950 (1981), *overruled on other grounds in* United States v. Ross, 456 U.S. 798 (1982).

edges." Each package contained fifteen pounds of marijuana. A California trial court concluded that the packages fell within the first category of "unworthy" containers noted in *Sanders*, which therefore placed them outside the protection of the Fourth Amendment warrant clause.

The Supreme Court disagreed, although the justices differed in their reasoning. Justice Powell, who authored *Sanders*, stated that courts should adjudicate the Fourth Amendment worthiness of containers on a case-by-case basis.[36] In this case, because the packages were securely wrapped and sealed, he concluded that the defendant's expectation of privacy in their contents was reasonable.

In contrast, Justice Stewart, author of the Court's plurality opinion, contended that there are no objective criteria by which to distinguish between containers: "What one person may put into a suitcase, another may put into a paper bag." Therefore, the plurality determined that a bright-line rule was required.

The bright-line rule announced in *Robbins*, which it believed was consistent with *Sanders*, was that all containers are entitled to Fourth Amendment protection except those whose contents are, in some sense, in plain view. This rule was reaffirmed in a majority opinion a year later.[37]

Under *Robbins*, the contents of a container are in "plain view" (and, therefore, the container is not entitled to Fourth Amendment protection) if the container is open, transparent, or, as with a kit of burglar tools or a gun case, its "distinctive configuration . . . proclaims its contents."[38] Perhaps, as well — the Court has subsequently left the issue open[39] — one may not possess a reasonable expectation of privacy in a container the contents of which can be determined by its odor.

[C] When Are "Worthy" Containers in Cars Protected?

[1] Overview

Containers worthy of Fourth Amendment protection, but which are found by the police in an automobile, may be searched without a warrant under certain circumstances.

The Court has developed two contrasting lines of "container-in-car" cases, which are discussed more fully below. In one line of cases that might be coined

---

[36] Relevant to the inquiry would be the "size, shape, material, and condition of the exterior [of the container], the context within which [it was] discovered, and whether the possessor had taken some significant precaution, such as locking, securely sealing or binding the container[]."

[37] United States v. Ross, 456 U.S. 798 (1982).

[38] Another example of a "distinctive configuration that proclaims its contents" might be an uninflated balloon, tied at its neck, with a substance inside it. In Texas v. Brown, 460 U.S. 730 (1983), an officer discovered such a container in *D*'s vehicle. Based on his knowledge that drugs are commonly packaged this way, he opened the balloon without a warrant. In a plurality opinion, Justice Rehnquist stated that the "distinctive character of the balloon itself spoke volumes as to its contents — particularly to the trained eye of the officer." Three dissenters were prepared to agree that *D* lacked a legitimate expectation of privacy in the container if it were shown that a "balloon of this kind might be used only to transport drugs."

[39] United States v. Johns, 469 U.S. 478 (1985).

the "container-coincidentally-in-a-car" line, the Court has determined that if the police have independent probable cause to search a particular container, they must, time permitting, obtain a warrant to search it. The fact that the container is found in an automobile does not negate the warrant requirement.

These cases must be distinguished from the "car-with-a-coincidental-container" line of cases. This line holds that if, while the police are conducting a lawful car search, they come across a container, their right to search the car without a warrant extends to the container, as long as it is large enough to hold the object of their search.

[2] Requiring A Warrant: The *Chadwick-Sanders* Doctrine

In two cases in which the Court invalidated a warrantless search of a container found in a car, the warrant issue arose in a narrow factual context: the officers had probable cause to search a specific container before it was placed in a vehicle; and they had the opportunity to seize it before it was put in the car, but they failed to do so.

In *United States v. Chadwick*,[40] Amtrak officials observed two men load an unusually heavy footlocker onto a train. One of the men fit a profile used to spot drug traffickers, and the footlocker was leaking talcum powder, a substance often used to mask the odor of illegal narcotics. The railroad employees transmitted this information to federal narcotics agents.

The agents put the suspects under surveillance when they got off the train two days later. Although the agents did not have a search or arrest warrant, they came with a dog trained to detect marijuana. While the footlocker was sitting on the floor in the train station, the dog signaled the presence of an illegal narcotic inside.

The agents then watched as D and two other men lifted the double-locked footlocker into the trunk of a car. Before the car was started, however, the officers arrested the three men, seized the footlocker, transported it to their headquarters, and searched it without a warrant.

The government sought to justify the warrantless search on various grounds at various stages of the trial and appellate process.[41] One theory it did *not* raise at the Supreme Court stage, however, was that the search fell within the "automobile exception," apparently because, as the Court put it, "the relationship between the footlocker and [D's] automobile [w]as merely coincidental."

The government did argue, however, that the footlocker was analogous to an automobile. Essentially, it reasoned that the footlocker, like a car, is capable of being moved; therefore, assuming probable cause for the search, a container

---

[40] 433 U.S. 1 (1977).

[41] The government argued that the search was justifiable on the ground that it was a search incident to a lawful arrest, but this theory was rejected because the footlocker was searched at a time and place remote from the arrest. If the footlocker had been found in the passenger compartment of the car rather than in the trunk, and if it had been searched at the scene immediately after the arrest, the search might have been permitted as a search incident to a lawful arrest.

should be subject to a warrantless search at the scene or, as in *Chambers*,[42] at police headquarters shortly thereafter.

The Court rejected this argument. It held that the warrantless seizure of *D*'s footlocker was permissible, but that the subsequent warrantless search of it was unconstitutional, as no exigency existed at the time of the search. In essence, unlike its reasoning in *Chambers*, the Court concluded that a warrantless search of a container is a greater Fourth Amendment intrusion than its warrantless seizure; therefore, only the latter was permissible.

The Court distinguished the automobile cases on the ground that "a person's expectations of privacy in personal luggage are substantially greater than in an automobile." Therefore, as there was no risk that the footlocker would be moved once it was seized, and no other exigency existed (such as a concern that the container possessed an explosive), a warrant to search it should have been sought.

The Court applied the same analysis in *Arkansas v. Sanders*.[43] In *Sanders*, law enforcement officers had probable cause to believe that *D* would disembark from an airplane in possession of a green suitcase containing marijuana. The officers, who did not have a warrant, went to the airport and observed *D* disembark, retrieve a green suitcase, and place it in the trunk of a taxicab. After the taxi drove away, the officers gave pursuit, stopped the cab a few blocks away, seized the suitcase, and opened it immediately. The government defended the officers' warrantless activity on the ground that it was permissible under the "automobile exception."

The Court disagreed with the government's reasoning. It concluded that *Chadwick*, rather than the car cases, applied. According to the Court, neither rationale of the "automobile exception" — lesser-expectation-of-privacy or mobility — pertained to the facts of the case.

First, it concluded that a person's expectation of privacy in a suitcase is not reduced merely because it is placed in an automobile. Indeed, as the justices pointed out, suitcases serve "as a repository for personal items when one wishes to transport them."

Second, although the Court agreed that a suitcase in the trunk of an automobile is as mobile as the vehicle itself, it stated that "the exigency of mobility must be assessed at the point immediately before the search — after the police had seized the object to be searched and have it securely within their control." As the suitcase was in the officers' control when it was searched, it was not mobile.[44]

---

[42] Chambers v. Maroney, 399 U.S. 42, *reh'g denied*, 400 U.S. 856 (1970). *See* § 77 *supra.*

[43] 442 U.S. 753 (1979).

[44] Of course, this reasoning could have been applied to the facts in *Chambers* to reach a contrary result in that car case: once the occupants of the vehicle were arrested, and the car was at the police station, the vehicle was no longer mobile.

The *Sanders* Court's "answer" to this point was that "the difficulties in seizing and securing automobiles have led the Court to make special allowances for their search." That is, if the rule were that police could seize, but not search, cars found on the highway without a warrant, police departments would have to secure equipment and personnel to transport cars from the highway to impoundment lots. According to the Court, this rule would "impose[] severe, even impossible burdens on many police departments."

[3] Not Requiring a Warrant: The *Ross* Doctrine

Chadwick and *Sanders* involved searches of containers that the police had probable cause to seize and search before they were placed in a car. In that sense, the containers were only — to use the language of *Chadwick* — "coincidentally" in a vehicle.

Nonetheless, in language broader than was required to decide the case, the Court in *Sanders* stated that "as a general rule there is no greater need for warrantless searches of luggage taken from automobiles than of luggage taken from other places." The implication of this dictum was that containers found in cars never fall within the scope of the "automobile exception."

Did the Court mean this? In its first opportunity to answer the question, it demonstrated that it did. In *Robbins v. California*,[45] the police stopped *D* in his automobile because he was driving erratically. They smelled marijuana smoke, which ultimately led to *D*'s arrest. In a subsequent search of a "recessed luggage compartment" in the vehicle,[46] the officers discovered two packages, which they opened without a warrant. The Court held that *Chadwick* and *Sanders* "made clear . . . that a closed [container] . . . found in a lawfully searched car is constitutionally protected to the same extent as are closed [containers] . . . found anywhere else."

A year later the Court overruled *Robbins* on this matter in *United States v. Ross*.[47] In *Ross*, the police had probable cause to search an entire car for contraband. During the search, they discovered a closed paper bag in the trunk, which they opened without a warrant.

The Court ruled that the latter search was constitutional. It stated that "[i]f probable cause justifies the search of a lawfully stopped vehicle [under the 'automobile exception'], it justifies the search of every part of the vehicle and its contents that may conceal the object of the search."

The Court compared the scope of a search of an automobile to that of a home. In the latter case, a warrant, founded on probable cause, and which meets the particularity requirements of the Fourth Amendment, ordinarily is required. However, once the warrant is authorized, the police may search "the entire area in which the object of the search may be found and is not limited by the possibility that separate acts of entry or opening may be required to complete the search." For example, the right to search a bedroom in a house includes the right to open and search chests, drawers, and other containers found within it, as long as they are large enough to contain the criminal articles that are the object of the search.

The same analysis applies to the search of an automobile, according to *Ross*. Although a warrant is not required for the search of a car because of its mobility, the scope of the search should include all areas in the car that a magistrate, if it had been practicable to request a warrant, could have authorized.

---

[45] 453 U.S. 420 (1981).

[46] The officers could only reach the compartment by opening the tailgate of the station wagon. Consequently, the government did not allege that the search was incident to a lawful arrest.

[47] 456 U.S. 798 (1982).

Thus, subject to the principles of *Chadwick* and *Sanders*, which *Ross* does not expressly overrule, all containers large enough to hold the object of the search may be opened without a warrant during an automobile search. And, as the Court has subsequently held, if the container may be searched at the scene, it may also be seized and searched without a warrant shortly thereafter, at the police station.[48]

Ross is sensible in light of *Chambers*.[49] That is, in terms of mobility, there is no difference between, on the one hand, a search at the police station of the glove compartment or trunk of an automobile (which, after all, are themselves containers inside a container) and, on the other hand, the search of a movable container found in an automobile. As warrants are not required in the former case, there is no reason based on mobility to require them in the latter situation.

On the other hand, *Ross* is on weaker ground if one emphasizes the lesser-expectation-of-privacy rationale of the car cases. A critical premise of those cases — and the key distinguishing feature of *Chadwick* and *Sanders* — is that people possess a greater expectation of privacy in containers than they do in cars.

[4] Making Sense of It All: Some Examples

Because the line between *Chadwick* and *Sanders*, on the one hand, and *Ross*, on the other, is a thin one,[50] examples may clarify the situation.[51]

Example 1. Police officers receive trustworthy information from an informant (sufficient to constitute probable cause to believe) that *D* will leave town in a few minutes by automobile with a large cache of illegal drugs. Because they lack time to obtain a warrant, the officers rush to *D*'s house. When they arrive, they see a large box sitting on the sidewalk next to *D*'s car, which is parked on the street. Just as *D* appears ready to place the box in the car, police seize and immediately search the container. They find drugs in it, and thereupon arrest *D*. Assuming that the police had probable cause, was the warrantless search permissible?

Probably not. As the box was not in the automobile, *Chadwick* applies. Indeed, even it had been placed in the car, *Chadwick* applies. Absent exigent circumstance not alleged in these facts, a warrant, supported by probable case, was required to search the container, although the warrantless seizure was lawful.[52]

Example 2. The facts are the same as in Example 1, except that the police arrive at *D*'s house a moment later, as he is driving away in his vehicle. They stop the car and search it. During the search, they come upon the box in the back seat.

Ross applies. When they stopped the vehicle they had probable cause to search the car for drugs, based on the information from the informant. They did not know

---

[48] United States v. Johns, 469 U.S. 478 (1985).

[49] Of course, *Chambers* might have been wrongly decided. *See* nn. 20-22 and accompanying text *supra*.

[50] Is the line between these cases so thin as not to exist? Although the Supreme Court has never so suggested, it recently granted certiorari in a case in which one of the questions raised is whether *Ross* implicitly overrules or limits *Chadwick*. People v. Acevedo, 216 Cal. App.3d 586, 265 Cal. Rptr. 23 (1989), *cert. granted*, 111 S. Ct. 39 (1990). The assumption in the text that follows is that *Ross* does not have this effect.

[51] The examples are inspired by Katz, n. 1 *supra*, at 202-03.

[52] If the police had properly arrested *D prior* to the seizure of the box, they probably could have searched it as an incident to the arrest.

about the box until they found it during the search. Therefore, the right to search the vehicle (under *Carroll-Chambers*) entitles them to open the container when it is found.

Example 3. The facts are the same as in Example 2, except that when the police find the container, they observe talcum powder seeping from it, which provides them with independent probable cause to believe that contraband will be found inside the box.

These facts are not "on all fours" with *Ross*. Notice the difference: in *Ross*, the officers had probable cause to search the car, but they did not possess independent probable cause — before or during the search — to believe that the container they found in the vehicle had contraband in it. Here, however, once the search turned up the container, they had independent cause to search it. Thus, simultaneously, they had probable cause to search the remainder of the vehicle (*Ross*) and to search the container (*Chadwick*).

Despite this difference, *Ross* applies, based on the holding of *United States v. Johns*.[53] In *Johns*, the police lawfully stopped a pickup truck, and immediately smelled marijuana. This gave them probable cause to search the vehicle. At about the same time, they spotted containers wrapped in a manner typical of smuggled marijuana. This provided them with probable cause to search the containers. The Court justified the warrantless search of the latter packages on the basis of *Ross*, without consideration of whether the police conducted any further search of the vehicle itself.

Example 4. The facts are the same as in Example 2, except that the officers find the box after the search of the remainder of the car has turned up no drugs.

This is a tougher case. It could be argued that *Chadwick* applies because the car search is over, and only a container remains. Nonetheless, *Ross* probably applies. After all, *Ross* applied when the search began. Had the officers found the box at any time prior to the completion of the car search, they could have opened it (Example 2). The fact that they discovered it at the end of the car search should not affect *Ross*'s bright-line rule.

Example 5. The facts are the same as in Example 2, except that the informant indicates that *D* will be leaving with the drugs in his automobile, "and that some of the drugs will be in a box," which the informant specifically describes. The officers stop the vehicle on the road.

Here, we have a combination of *Ross* and *Chadwick*. That is, before — not after — the search is commenced, the officers have probable cause to search the car *and* probable cause to search that particular container, wherever it is found.

Chadwick arguably applies. The argument for this position is that, had they found *D* (as in Example 1) before he put the box in the car, they could have searched the car pursuant to *Ross*, but they would have needed a warrant to search the container (*Chadwick*). The fact that they came a few seconds too late should not diminish *D*'s legitimate privacy interest in the container.

---

[53] 469 U.S. 478 (1985).

This argument has not persuaded many lower courts, for good reason.[54] Notice the anomaly if *Chadwick* were to apply to these facts: they could search (without a warrant) all of the containers found inside the vehicle (per *Ross*) except the very one for which they had probable cause to believe contained contraband!

---

[54] *E.g.*, United States v. Sanchez, 861 F.2d 89 (5th Cir. 1988); *see* 3 W. LaFave, § 7.2(d) at 58 n.128.

CHAPTER **15**

THE "PLAIN VIEW" DOCTRINE

§ 80   General Principles[1]

An object of an incriminating nature may be seized without a warrant if it is in the plain view of a police officer lawfully present at the scene.

"Plain view" is a constitutional term of art. As explained more fully in the next chapter section, an article is in "plain view," and subject to warrantless seizure by a police officer, if: (1) she observes it from a lawful vantage point; (2) she has a right of physical access to it from the lawful vantage point; and (3) its nature as an article subject to seizure (*i.e.*, that it is contraband or a fruit, instrumentality, or evidence of a crime) is immediately apparent when she views it.[2]

For example, suppose that O, a police officer, has a valid warrant to search D's garage for drug paraphernalia and illegal narcotics. As she is searching the garage pursuant to the warrant, she observes an automobile that, to her surprise, fits the description of one recently used in an unrelated murder. Therefore, O seizes the car as evidence of the murder, although her warrant does not authorize her to do so.

Under the plain-view doctrine, the warrantless seizure of the car would be permissible because: (1) her entry into the garage was proper, as it was authorized by the warrant; (2) her physical access to the car was lawful, as it was parked in the area that she had a right to search pursuant to the warrant; and (3) when she observed the vehicle it was immediately apparent to her that it was subject to seizure as evidence of a crime.

The warrantless seizure of the vehicle in this example is not inconsistent with the purposes of the Fourth Amendment warrant clause. As Justice Stewart explained in *Coolidge v. New Hampshire*,[3] the warrant clause is intended to guarantee that police officers, whenever practicable, seek a prior judicial determination of probable cause in order "to eliminate altogether searches not based on probable cause," as well as to prevent exploratory or general searches. In the example, O obtained a prior judicial determination of probable cause to search the garage. Furthermore, the search did not devolve into an exploratory one merely because she seized the automobile: her presence in the garage was authorized by the warrant; and the seizure of the car did not expand on the lawful scope of the search.

---

[1] *See generally* 2 W. LaFave, at § 4.11.

[2] Horton v. California, 110 S.Ct. 2301 (1990); *see* Coolidge v. New Hampshire, 403 U.S. 443, *reh'g denied*, 404 U.S. 874 (1971); Arizona v. Hicks, 480 U.S. 321 (1987); Texas v. Brown, 460 U.S. 730 (1983).

[3] 403 U.S. 443, *reh'g denied*, 404 U.S. 874 (1971).

Under such circumstances, as Justice Stewart stated, a warrantless seizure of an article discovered in plain view is only a "minor peril to Fourth Amendment protections, [but] . . . a major gain in effective law enforcement." To require an officer to obtain a warrant to seize what she discovers in plain view would be a "needless inconvenience, and sometimes [might be] dangerous — to the evidence or to the police themselves."

§ 81 "Plain View": Examining the Elements

[A] Element 1: Lawful Vantage Point

The first element of the plain-view doctrine is that the officer must observe the article from a lawful vantage point. As the Supreme Court has observed, "it is important to keep in mind that, in the vast majority of cases, *any* evidence seized by the police will be in plain view, at least at the moment of seizure."[4] Therefore, "an essential predicate to any valid warrantless seizure of incriminating evidence [is] that the officer did not violate the Fourth Amendment in arriving at the place from which the evidence could be plainly viewed."[5]

Generally speaking, there are four ways in which an officer may "arrive" at the place from which the evidence is in plain view. First, she may discover the article during a search that is justified by a warrant, such as in the example discussed in the last chapter section.

Second, the evidence may come into view during an in-home arrest pursuant to a warrant. For example, an officer who enters *D*'s house armed with an arrest warrant may seize an incriminating article she observes sitting in plain view on a nearby table, even if it is not within *D*'s area of immediate control.

Third, an incriminating article might be discovered by an officer during a search justified under an exception to the warrant requirement. For example, an officer might come across an article of evidence while she is in a house in hot pursuit of a felon or while she is conducting a warrantless consent search. In such circumstances, the *search* that turned up the evidence is justified by an independent warrant exception; the plain-view doctrine justifies the warrantless *seizure* of the evidence found.

Fourth, an officer's view of an incriminating article may arise from activity that does not constitute a search or seizure, and, therefore, falls outside the Fourth Amendment's restrictions. For example, trespass by an officer in an open field is not a Fourth Amendment "search";[6] therefore, marijuana discovered in plain view in the field may be seized.

[B] Element 2: Right of Access to the Object

Not only must a police officer observe the incriminating article from a lawful vantage point, but "she must also have a lawful right of access to the object itself."[7]

---

[4] *Id.* at 465.
[5] *Horton*, 110 S.Ct. at 2308.
[6] *See* § 33 *supra.*
[7] *Horton*, 110 S.Ct. at 2308.

For example, *O*, a police officer, has a lawful right to observe marijuana hidden behind a large fence in *D*'s backyard if she observes it while flying in a helicopter in public navigable airspace. Nonetheless, the plain-view doctrine does not justify her to land the helicopter in *D*'s backyard in order to seize the contraband. Access to the backyard requires a search warrant or some independent search-warrant exception.

Likewise, an officer standing on the sidewalk is justified in observing a marijuana plant sitting in the window sill of a person's home. This observation could constitute probable cause to seize the plant, but it does not justify a warrantless entry of the house to seize it.[8]

On the other hand, if the officer has a Fourth Amendment justification — other than that the article is visible to her — to enter the house, she may do so. For example, in *Washington v. Chrisman*,[9] *O* arrested *D*, a college student, in a public place for underage possession of alcohol. *D* claimed that he was over the minimum age for possession of the liquor and, therefore, asked permission to retrieve his identification from his dormitory room. *O* agreed and followed him to the room. While *D* was inside, *O* remained just outside the door, but from that spot he observed marijuana and drug paraphernalia inside the room. He entered and seized the items.

Because an arresting officer has the right to remain at an arrestee's elbow,[10] *O* had the right from the outset to enter the dormitory room. Consequently, the Court held that *O*'s warrantless entry after the articles came into his view was permissible. If the result were otherwise, the Court said, the "perverse effect" would be to "penaliz[e] the officer for exercising more restraint than was required under the circumstances."

[C] Element 3: Seizability is "Immediately Apparent"

A police officer may not seize an article without a search warrant merely because she has a right of access to the object from a proper vantage point. For example, the fact that *O* is lawfully in *D*'s living room in order to make an arrest does not justify the seizure of every article that *O* observes in the room, regardless of its innocent character.

The Supreme Court stated in *Coolidge v. New Hampshire*[11] that seizure of an article in plain view is "legitimate only where it is immediately apparent to the police that they have [criminal] evidence before them." The Court explained in *Arizona v. Hicks*[12] that "immediately apparent" means no more, but also no less, than that the officer has probable cause to seize the article in plain view.

The "immediately apparent" — or probable-cause — requirement is consistent with the underlying purposes of the plain-view rule. That is, the doctrine is intended merely to free an officer from the inconvenience of securing a warrant to seize that which is found in plain view during an otherwise lawful intrusion.

---

[8] *See Coolidge*, 403 U.S. at 468.

[9] 455 U.S. 1 (1982).

[10] *See* § 69[B][1] *supra*.

[11] 403 U.S. 443, *reh'g denied*, 404 U.S. 874 (1971).

[12] 480 U.S. 321 (1987).

It does not purport to dispense with the probable-cause requirement for the seizure.

§ 82   Application of the Plain-View Doctrine: *Arizona v. Hicks*

Although application of the plain-view doctrine is often straightforward, sometimes it is not. *Arizona v. Hicks*[13] provides a good, but controversial, example of the interrelationship of the elements of the rule.

In *Hicks*, the police entered *D*'s apartment without a search warrant because a bullet had been fired through *D*'s floor into an apartment below it, injuring a person. The officers entered "to search for the shooter, for other victims, and for weapons."

While inside, *O* observed two sets of expensive stereo components that seemed out of place in *D*'s apartment. *O* reasonably suspected, but lacked probable cause to believe, that the equipment was stolen. Therefore, he either turned around or upside down one piece of the equipment — a turntable — in order to read and record its serial number. *O* immediately reported the number to police headquarters, which confirmed that it had been taken in a robbery. Therefore, *O* seized the turntable. Later, he secured a warrant to seize the remaining equipment.

The government sought to justify the warrantless seizure of the turntable on the basis of plain view. Clearly, the officers' warrantless entry into *D*'s apartment was proper due to the exigencies of the situation. Therefore, *O* had a right to be in a position in which the stereo was visible to him and within his physical access as he looked for persons and weapons. Nonetheless, by a 6-3 vote, the Supreme Court, per Justice Scalia, held that the seizure of the turntable was unconstitutional.

The route that the Court took in reaching its conclusion merits careful attention. The difficulty in this case in the application of the plain-view doctrine was with the requirement that the incriminating nature of the article be immediately apparent. To properly analyze this issue, and to see how it relates to the other elements of the plain-view doctrine, it is useful to consider not only what occurred in *D*'s house but also what could have happened.

For example, if it had been immediately apparent to *O* as he looked at (without touching) the stereo components that they were stolen, it would have been proper for him to seize them under the plain-view doctrine. But, as the circumstance actually arose, *O* did not have probable cause to believe that the equipment was stolen when he first spotted the turntable. More was needed to bring his suspicion to the level of probable cause: he needed the serial number.

If *O* could have read the serial number without touching the equipment, there would have been no constitutional problem. His action — merely observing that which was in open view from a place where he had a right to be — would not have constituted a search. Because the equipment, under this hypothesis, was not touched, there also would have been no seizure. Therefore, if this non-Fourth-Amendment activity — the non-search and non-seizure inspection of the serial

---

[13] *Id.*

number — had provided *O* with probable cause to believe that the turntable was the fruit of a crime, *O* would have been acting lawfully if he had seized it pursuant to the plain-view doctrine.

But, in *Hicks* the facts were not as hypothesized. The turntable had to be moved to observe its serial number. Therefore, the question that the Court had to answer was whether *this* action — physically trivial as it was — constituted a new "search" or "seizure" that required an additional justification.

The slight movement of the turntable, as it did not constitute a meaningful interference with *D*'s possessory interest in it, was not a "seizure" within the meaning of the Fourth Amendment. But, the act of moving it was another "search" because it exposed to *O* matters not previously visible to him. As Justice Scalia put it, "a search is a search, even if it happens to disclose nothing but the bottom of a turntable."

The issue, therefore, was whether this new search was justified. To resolve this question the Court needed to reconsider the first element of the plain-view doctrine. That is, in light of the original justification for the intrusion into the room (to look for the shooter, additional victims, and the weapon), was this additional search (moving the turntable to look underneath it) justified?

If the answer had been yes — *e.g.*, if *O* had moved the turntable to look for a gun that might have been hidden underneath — the new search would have been permissible and, as it resulted in the information that gave *O* probable cause to believe that the turntable was stolen, he could lawfully have seized it. However, the search was conducted for reasons unrelated to the initial intrusion. Therefore, *Hicks* held, *O* was unable to justify his actions on the basis of plain view.

Justice Scalia's analysis was controversial. The dissent argued that the act of moving the turntable was a "cursory inspection" rather than a "full-blown search." As such, it claimed, *O* should have been allowed to inspect it on the basis of "reasonable suspicion" (which he possessed) rather than "probable cause." The majority rejected this argument, however, because it was "unwilling to send police and judges into a new thicket of Fourth Amendment law, to seek a creature of uncertain description."

However, as Professor LaFave has pointed out,[14] the "cursory inspection" concept, if it had been recognized, would not have sent the police and courts into a new Fourth Amendment "thicket." The Court has already recognized the general principle that searches that are less than ordinarily intrusive, which the trivial act of moving the turntable surely was, may be conducted on less than probable cause.[15] Nor is a "cursory inspection" inevitably a "creature of uncertain description": it might be defined, as Professor LaFave has suggested, as the act of picking up or moving an object a short distance.

The better argument for the majority's objection to the dissent's position is found in Justice Scalia's remarks about the importance of probable cause in Fourth Amendment jurisprudence:

> [T]here is nothing new in the realization that the Constitution sometimes insulate[s] the criminality of a few in order to the protect the privacy of us

---

[14] 2 W. LaFave, at § 4.11(c).
[15] *See* chapter 18 *infra*.

all. Our disagreement with the dissenters pertain to where the proper balance should be struck; we choose to adhere to the textual and traditional standard of probable cause.

§ 83 "Inadvertent Discovery": The Plain-View Debate

In the typical case of a lawful plain-view seizure, *O*, an officer, conducting a valid search discovers incriminating evidence in plain view that she did not anticipate finding. In such circumstances, as discussed in this chapter, *O* may seize without a warrant the evidence inadvertently discovered.

Suppose, however, that *O* anticipated finding the evidence in plain view? For example, suppose that *O* has probable cause to search *D*'s premises for articles A and B. She obtains a warrant to seize article A, but she does not request authorization to seize article B, although she expects that she will find it during the search, and she intends to seize it if and when she discovers it. If *O* discovers article B during the execution of the warrant, may she seize it under the plain-view doctrine?

In *Coolidge v. New Hampshire*,[16] Justice Stewart, author of the Court's four-justice plurality opinion, answered the question in the negative. He stated that if an officer anticipates discovery of a particular article but she fails to request a warrant to seize it, or if she fails to mention it in her application for a warrant to search for other articles, the subsequent search is analogous to an exploratory search, and the seizure of the anticipated articles "fl[ies] in the face of the basic rule that no amount of probable cause can justify a warrantless seizure."

The inadvertency element of the plain-view doctrine announced by Justice Stewart in *Coolidge* was never accepted by a judgment supported by a majority of the members of the Supreme Court.[17] Nonetheless, after *Coolidge* was decided, the vast majority of states and lower federal courts endorsed the inadvertency requirement.[18]

In *Horton v. California*,[19] however, the Supreme Court "revisited" the issue. In *Horton*, *O*, a police officer, obtained a warrant to search *D*'s home for the proceeds from a robbery. *O* anticipated finding the weapons used in the crime during the search, and he intended to seize them, which he did, when they were discovered in open view in the home. *D* argued that the latter seizure was impermissible: the warrant did not provide for the seizure of the weapons; and, because their discovery was not inadvertent, the seizure of the weapons could not be justified under the plain-view doctrine, as set out in *Coolidge*.

The Supreme Court ruled, 7-2, that inadvertency, although "a characteristic of most legitimate 'plain view' seizures, . . . is not a necessary condition" of the doctrine. It concluded that "the absence of inadvertence was not essential to the

---

[16] 403 U.S. 443, *reh'g denied*, 404 U.S. 874 (1971).

[17] *See Hicks*, 480 U.S. at 330 (observation by White, J., concurring).

[18] Forty-six states, the District of Columbia, and twelve United States Courts of Appeals endorsed the requirement. *See Horton*, 110 S.Ct. at 2314-16 (Appendices A and B to the dissenting opinion of Brennan, J.).

[19] 110 S.Ct. 2301 (1990).

Court's rejection of the State's 'plain view' argument in *Coolidge*." In short, although the holding in *Coolidge* was binding precedent, its discussion regarding inadvertency was flawed.

As *Horton* pointed out, the inadvertency requirement is not necessary "to prevent the police from conducting general searches, or from converting specific warrants into general warrants." These Fourth Amendment evils are prevented by scrupulous adherence to the Fourth Amendment requirement that no warrant be issued unless it particularly describes "the place to be searched and the persons or things to be seized," and by the judicial rule that warrantless searches must "be circumscribed by the exigencies which justify its initiation." In other words, the area and duration of a search is limited by the latter requirements; the inadvertency element of the plain-view doctrine adds no additional privacy protection.

For example, in *Horton*, the inadvertency element would not have offered *D* any privacy protection that was not already guaranteed: the warrant entitled the officer to be in *D*'s home in order to search for the fruits of a robbery; and the weapons were found in those areas of the home to which the officer had a constitutional right of access under the warrant. Furthermore, if the proceeds of the crime had been found before the weapons had been discovered, which they were not, the search would have had to terminate at that time, so the omission of the weapons from the warrant did not increase the length of time the officers could legitimately stay on the premises.

The *Horton* majority also expressed its disinclination to apply a plain-view doctrine that requires courts to divine an officer's subjective state of mind. According to the Court, "evenhanded law enforcement is best achieved by the application of objective standards of conduct. . . ."

It pointed out that if an officer has knowledge approaching certainty that a certain article of evidence will be found during a search, there is no reason to believe that "she would deliberately omit a particular description of the item to be seized from the application for a search warrant."

On the other hand, if the officer has a warrant to search for one article, and merely suspects that she will find another item, whether or not the suspicion amounts to probable cause, the *Horton* majority did not believe that such a "suspicion should immunize the second item from seizure if it is found during a lawful search for the first." Borrowing from Justice White's dissent in *Coolidge*, the Court contended that there is no reason to draw a distinction between an article discovered inadvertently and one that is anticipated: the interference with the individual's possessory interest is the same in both cases, as is the inconvenience and danger of requiring the officer to depart and secure a warrant.

Justice Brennan, with whom Justice Marshall joined, dissented in *Horton*. The dissent agreed with the majority that the inadvertent-discovery requirement furthers no privacy interests. But, it argued, it does protect possessory interests: the message sent by the inadvertency requirement is that "we will not excuse officers from the general requirement of a warrant to seize if the officers know the location of the evidence, have probable cause to seize it, intend to seize it, and yet do not bother to obtain a warrant particularly describing that evidence." Exclusion of "evidence so seized will encourage officers to be more precise and complete in future warrant applications."

CHAPTER 16

INVENTORY SEARCHES

§ 84 Automobile Inventories: General Principles[1]

[A] Rule

In *South Dakota v. Opperman*[2] the Supreme Court determined for the first time that a warrantless, suspicionless automobile-inventory search is constitutional under the Fourth Amendment. In *Opperman*, the police towed an unoccupied car to a city impoundment lot after it had been ticketed twice in the same day for being illegally parked in a tow-away zone. At the lot, pursuant to standard procedures in the jurisdiction, the police unlocked the car, inventoried the contents of the passenger compartment, and removed them for safekeeping. During the inventory the police discovered marijuana in the unlocked glove compartment. *D*, the owner of the car, was prosecuted for possession of this contraband.

The Supreme Court held, 5-4, that a routine inventory of a lawfully impounded car by the police is reasonable under the Fourth Amendment, although it is conducted without a warrant and in the absence of probable cause to believe that evidence of a crime will be discovered.[3] Consequently, if the officers discover criminal evidence during the inventory process, they may seize it pursuant to the plain-view doctrine.

[B] Rationale of the Rule

The Court in *Opperman* reasoned that the "probable cause" concept, which in its traditional form is a standard for use in criminal investigations, is "unhelpful when analysis centers upon the reasonableness of routine administrative caretaking functions, particularly when no claim is made that the protective procedures are a subterfuge for criminal investigations."[4]

---

[1] *See generally* 3 W. LaFave, at §§ 7.4(a) and 7.5(e).

[2] 428 U.S. 364 (1976); *but see* State v. Opperman, 247 N.W.2d 673 (S.D. 1976) (under state constitution, warrantless automobile inventories are only permitted to secure articles within plain view).

[3] Although most of the opinion dealt with the "search" aspect of the inventory, the Court perfunctorily approved the prior impoundment, which constituted a seizure of *D*'s car. It observed that police are often required to remove and impound vehicles, either because they are disabled on the road or are in violation of parking ordinances. It described as "beyond challenge," the right "of police to seize and remove vehicles impeding traffic or threatening public safety and convenience."

[4] This conclusion was not inevitable. It might have formulated a different type of "probable cause" standard relevant to administrative inventory searches, much as the Court has done with other administrative inspections. *See* § 47 *supra*.

In turn, the Court disposed of the need for search warrants in inventory cases by noting that the warrant requirement is "linked . . . textually . . . to the probable-cause concept." That is, because the warrant clause provides that "no Warrants shall issue, but upon probable cause," there is no need for a warrant if there is no basis for determining probable cause. In view of the inapplicability of the warrant clause to inventories, the *Opperman* Court applied the general, Fourth Amendment "reasonableness" standard, *i.e.*, "[t]he right of the people to be secure . . . against unreasonable searches and seizures."

The Court stated that automobile inventories are a "response to three distinct needs": (1) to protect the owner's property while it is in police custody; (2) to protect the police against claims of lost or stolen property; and (3) to protect the police and the public from dangerous instrumentalities that might be hidden in the car. The Court concluded that these interests outweigh the owner's expectation of privacy in his automobile, which it described as "significantly less than that relating to one's home or office."[5] Therefore, as a general matter, warrantless automobile-inventory searches are reasonable.

Critics question the Court's analysis of the need for automobile inventories. They contend that the claim that inventories are required in order to protect the safety of the police and the public "borders on the ridiculous."[6] Cars rarely contain dangerous instrumentalities,[7] and there is no reason to believe that an unsearched automobile sitting in an impoundment lot constitutes a greater danger than one parked on the street or in a public parking lot. Yet, a non-impounded car may not be searched without reasonable cause.[8]

Protection of the police against claims of theft, although a weightier concern, probably does not justify warrantless inventories. Police departments, as involuntary bailees, usually have only limited liability for losses in such circumstances; and as Justice Powell conceded in his concurrence, inventories might not discourage false claims, because a person can fraudulently assert that an article was stolen prior to the inventory or was purposely left off the inventory list.

The strongest argument in support of automobile inventories is that they protect the owner's property from theft. But, it is not clear that they provide substantially greater protection than the simpler and less intrusive procedure of rolling up the windows of an impounded car, locking its doors, and placing it in a secure place.

Moreover, if the police are going to invade a car owner's privacy in order to protect his property, critics argue that it is not unreasonable to suggest, as the dissenters did in *Opperman*, that an inventory should only be conducted after "the

---

[5] The lesser-expectation-of-privacy thesis regarding cars is discussed at § 78 *supra*.

[6] 3 W. LaFave, § 7.4(a) at 105.

[7] Justice Powell, who concurred in *Opperman*, conceded that "[e]xcept in rare cases, there is little danger associated with impounding unsearched automobiles." However, he was unwilling to discount this factor entirely because the consequences are apt to be severe in the rare case in which the danger materializes, and there is no way to identify a high-risk automobile without searching it.

[8] *See* Cady v. Dombrowski, 413 U.S. 433 (1973) (pursuant to their "caretaking function," the police properly conducted a warrantless search of a non-impounded car towed to a private garage because they had reasonable cause to believe that it contained a gun that might be stolen by a vandal).

exhaustion and failure of reasonable efforts . . . to identify and reach the owner of the property in order to facilitate alternative means of security or to obtain his consent to the search."

The difficulty with the dissenter's suggestion, however, is that not all communities can afford to place impounded cars in guarded lots. Furthermore, according to the Court, "[t]he reasonableness of any particular governmental activity does not necessarily or invariably turn on the existence of alternative 'less intrusive' means. . . . [The Court] is not in a position to second-guess police departments as to what practical administrative method will best deter theft. . . ."[9]

§ 85   Elements of the Warrant Exception: Specifics

[A]   "Routine" Nature of the Inventory

[1]   In General

A warrantless search of an automobile lawfully in police custody is not justifiable merely because the police assert that it was conducted for inventory purposes rather than as part of a criminal investigation. The inventory must be a "routine" or "standard" procedure of the department conducting the search.[10] The purpose of this requirement is to reduce the risk that inventories will be conducted arbitrarily, discriminatorily, or as "a ruse for a general rummaging in order to discover incriminating evidence."[11]

[2]   Nondiscretionary Inventories

Ideally, the regulations authorizing an inventory should be similar to those involved in *Opperman*, namely, they should place no significant discretion in the hands of the individual officer. The procedures should require officers to "act more or less mechanically, according to a set routine."[12]

Nondiscretionary inventories are desirable because they "promote[] a certain equality of treatment. . . . [T]he minister's picnic basket and grandma's knitting bag [found in an automobile] are opened and inventoried right along with a biker's tool box and the gypsy's satchel."[13] They also are less likely to function as a ruse for a criminal investigation.

[3]   Discretionary Inventories

Inventories are problematic when they are conducted pursuant to regulations that allow individual officers discretion in determining whether to conduct the

---

[9] Illinois v. Lafayette, 462 U.S. 640, 647-48 (1983) (arrest inventory); *see also* Colorado v. Bertine, 479 U.S. 367, 374 (1987) ("[R]easonable police regulations . . . administered in good faith satisfy the Fourth Amendment, even though courts might as a matter of hindsight be able to devise equally reasonable rules requiring a different procedure.").

[10] Colorado v. Bertine, 479 U.S. at 374 n.6 ("Our decisions have always adhered to the *requirement* that inventories be conducted according to standardized criteria.").

[11] Florida v. Wells, 110 S.Ct. 1632, 1635 (1990).

[12] Commonwealth v. Sullo, 26 Mass. App. Ct. 766, 769, 532 N.E.2d 1219, 1222 (1989).

[13] State v. Shamblin, 763 P.2d 425, 428 (Utah App. 1988).

inventory and/or in deciding the scope of the search. With increased discretion comes the heightened risk of arbitrariness, discrimination, and the use of the inventory as a disguise for a criminal investigation.

Nonetheless, in recent years the Supreme Court has upheld inventories that permit some police discretion. First, in *Colorado v. Bertine*,[14] the Court upheld an inventory in which the regulations allowed officers in certain circumstances to choose whether to impound the automobile and conduct an inventory of it, on the one hand, or to park the car in a public parking lot and lock it, on the other hand.

The Court held that discretion regarding whether to conduct an inventory is allowed "as long as [it] . . . is exercised according to standard criteria and on the basis of something other than suspicion of evidence of criminal activity." The "standard criteria" in *Bertine* included provisions that prohibited officers from parking vehicles in lots vulnerable to theft or vandalism.

More recently, Chief Justice Rehnquist, in dictum for five justices in *Florida v. Wells*,[15] stated that "in forbidding uncanalized discretion to police officers conducting inventory searches, there is no reason to insist that they be conducted in a mechanical 'all-or-nothing' fashion."

Therefore, an inventory procedure is not unreasonable if it allows "sufficient latitude [to the individual officer] to determine whether a particular container should or should not be opened in light of the nature of the search and characteristics of the container." According to *Wells*, the Fourth Amendment is not violated by "[t]he allowance of the exercise of judgment based on concerns related to the purposes of an inventory search."

[B] Administrative Nature of the Search

In upholding specific automobile inventories, the Supreme Court has repeatedly stressed that they were not subterfuges for criminal investigations. The implication of this is that evidence found during an inventory is inadmissible in a criminal trial if the search was a pretext for a criminal investigation. This interpretation is plausible in view of the Court's reasoning in *Opperman* that the warrant clause is "unhelpful" in analyzing the reasonableness of "routine, administrative caretaking" activities by the police: pretextual inventory searches are not routine administrative police activities.

On the other hand, such a limitation conflicts with the view expressed by the Court in other contexts[16] that the validity of an officer's actions should be based only on objective factors, without regard to his underlying intent or motivation.

Furthermore, the no-criminal-investigation limitation, if indeed there is one, apparently only applies if, in the words of *Bertine*, the officer's "sole" purpose in conducting the inventory is to investigate crime. This would mean that an officer who hopes or even suspects that he will find criminal evidence during an inventory may nonetheless conduct one if he is doing so, at least in part, for legitimate

---

[14] 479 U.S. 367 (1987).
[15] 110 S.Ct. 1632 (1990).
[16] *See, e.g.,* §§ 74, 83 *supra*.

administrative reasons.[17] At least when the inventory is required in the particular case, it will be nearly impossible for the defendant to argue convincingly that the officer's sole purpose was to investigate a crime.

[C] Irrelevance of the Car Owner's Wishes

The right of the police to inventory an automobile does not depend on a finding that the car owner is unavailable to give his consent to the search, to take his belongings out of the car, or to waive any rights that he might have against the police for the theft of his property.

Originally, it was plausible to interpret *Opperman* narrowly to permit warrantless inventory searches only when it was unreasonable for the police to contact the car owner. For example, the majority in *Opperman* observed that the car owner in that case "was not present to make other arrangements for the safekeeping of his belongings."

Notwithstanding this language, the Court in *Bertine* upheld an inventory search although the vehicle owner was in police custody and, therefore, could have been given the opportunity to make other arrangements to protect his property. Quoting from *Illinois v. Lafayette*,[18] an arrest inventory case, the *Bertine* Court stated that although such an alternative was possible, "the real question is not what 'could have been achieved,' but whether the Fourth Amendment *requires* such steps." The Court stated that the Fourth Amendment does not require the police to act in the least intrusive fashion possible.

§ 86 Scope of an Inventory Search: Specifics

[A] Containers

The Supreme Court ruled in *Colorado v. Bertine*[19] that as part of a valid automobile-inventory search, the police may open containers found in the car without a warrant and in the absence of probable cause.

A majority of the justices in *Bertine* appeared to accept the premise that the police may open and search containers under the inventory exception only "if they are following standard police procedures that *mandate* the opening of such containers in *every* impounded vehicle."[20] However, subsequently in *Florida v. Wells*,[21] five members of the Court approved dictum that procedures that allow some discretion in determining which containers to open are permissible.[22]

---

[17] United States v. Frank, 864 F.2d 992, 1001 (3d Cir. 1988), *reh'g denied*, 109 S.Ct. 2442 (1989).

[18] 462 U.S. 640 (1983).

[19] 479 U.S. 367 (1987).

[20] *Id.* at 377 (Blackmun, Powell, and O'Connor JJ., concurring). Dissenting Justices Marshall and Brennan wanted to limit inventories of containers even further, so they would presumably have accepted the limiting language in the concurring opinion.

[21] 110 S.Ct. 1632 (1990).

[22] *See* § 85[A][3] *supra*. The shift was the result of the change of heart of Justice O'Connor, who concurred in *Bertine*, but who joined the five-justice dictum in *Wells* without explanation.

[B] Locked Portions of the Automobile

Opperman approved an inventory search of an unlocked glove compartment because it was a customary place for persons to store valuables. The Court did not consider, nor has it since, the justifiability of inventories of *locked* glove compartments or of automobile trunks, although most courts have authorized such searches when they are part of a routine inventory.[23]

The lower court trend is likely to receive the Court's approval when and if it considers the issue. The car in *Opperman* was locked (although the glove compartment was not), and yet the inventory was permitted; it is reasonable, therefore, to conclude that the fact that an interior compartment of an automobile or the trunk is locked is not constitutionally significant, as long as the standard procedure in the jurisdiction is to permit the officer to open the locked portions of the car.

[C] Inspection of Papers

The Supreme Court has not determined whether or to what extent the police may read papers and documents found during an otherwise valid inventory. However, a majority of the justices in *Opperman* expressed objection to the hypothetical reading of papers that touch upon intimate areas of a person's private life.

Justice Powell observed in *Opperman* that "[u]pholding [inventory] searches . . . provides no general license for the police to examine all the contents of such automobiles." In particular, he noted that there was no evidence in the case that the police, who found "miscellaneous papers," a checkbook, and a social security card, examined the contents of these personal papers. The four dissenters, as well, stated that the police "would not be justified in sifting through papers secured under the procedures employed here." This conclusion seems correct, as none of the reasons for an inventory search justifies reading personal papers.

Lower courts have frequently prohibited the introduction of evidence secured as the result of the inspection of private papers found during an inventory.[24] Line-drawing, however, is necessary. The police inevitably must handle papers found during an inventory, and they will often need to peruse them in order to identify them on an inventory sheet.[25] Therefore, although the police should not read the documents beyond what is necessary to complete the inventory, they cannot be expected to blind themselves to what they see in the process.

§ 87 Arrest Inventories[26]

In *Illinois v. Lafayette*[27] the Supreme Court held that the police may search an arrested person, as well as his personal effects, including containers, as part of a

---

[23] 3 W. LaFave, § 7.4(a) at 112-13. In *Opperman*, the regulations authorized a search of the trunk, but it was not done, because it was locked.

[24] *E.g.*, Commonwealth v. Sullo, 26 Mass.App.Ct. 766, 532 N.E.2d 1219 (1989).

[25] *See* People v. Hovey, (1988) 44 Cal.3d 543, 244 Cal. Rptr. 121, 749 P.2d 776, *cert. denied*, 488 U.S. 871 (1988) (arrest inventory case).

[26] *See generally* 2 W. LaFave, at § 5.3.

[27] 462 U.S. 640 (1983).

routine[28] inventory at a police station incident to his booking and jailing.[29] Neither a search warrant nor probable cause is required for an arrest inventory.

The Court's reasoning in *Lafayette* in support of arrest inventories parallels that pertaining to automobile inventories. The Court stated that inventories are needed to prevent theft of the arrestee's property by inmates and jail employees, to protect the police from theft claims, and to prevent the arrestee from carrying dangerous instrumentalities or contraband into the jail.

In practice, the scope of an arrest inventory will be broader than a search incident to an arrest. Searches that would be impractical or embarrassing at the scene of the arrest can be conducted at the stationhouse. For example, as part of an arrest inventory, authorities are entitled not only to search the arrestee's clothing, but also to take the clothing and keep it in official custody.[30] The Court in *Lafayette* also left open the question of "the circumstances in which a strip search may or may not be appropriate" as part of the inventory process.

---

[28] Regarding the requirement that inventories be routine, *see* § 85[A] *supra.*

[29] Prior to *Lafayette*, the Court held in United States v. Edwards, 415 U.S. 800 (1974), that the police were entitled in that case, "with or without probable cause," to seize, search, and keep in official custody the clothing worn by *D*, a jail inmate, when he was arrested. Although the clothing was not taken from *D* until ten hours after his arrest, the Court stated that the police "did no more . . . than they were entitled to do incident to the usual custodial arrest and incarceration." *Edwards*, however, did not strictly involve an inventory search. *See* § 68[C][2] *supra.*

[30] *See* United States v. Edwards, 415 U.S. 800 (1974).

CHAPTER 17

CONSENT TO SEARCH

§ 88   General Rule and Rationale[1]

Validly obtained consent justifies an officer in conducting a warrantless search, with or without probable cause. If the officer discovers evidence during a warrantless "consent search," she may seize it without a warrant pursuant to the plain-view doctrine. Perhaps as many as 98 percent of all warrantless searches are justified on the ground of consent.[2]

The underlying rationale for the consent rule has been a matter of some dispute. In comparatively early Supreme Court opinions, consent searches were apparently justified on waiver principles, that is, on the ground that, by consenting, a person waives any objection she might otherwise have to an intrusion on her Fourth Amendment rights.[3]

Another theory, expressed by three members of the Court in *Illinois v. Rodriguez*,[4] is "that a person may voluntarily limit his expectation of privacy by allowing others to exercise authority over his possessions." In effect, under this rationale, a consent search is not really a "search" at all.

Both of these theories were rejected by six members of the Court in *Rodriguez*. As Justice Scalia explained, "[t]o describe a consented search as a non-invasion of privacy and thus a non-search is strange in the extreme."[5] Nor does the Court now believe that the issue is one of waiver. Instead, "[t]here are various elements . . . that can make a search . . . 'reasonable' — one of which is the consent of the person" whose premises or effects will be searched.

Put simply, a search based on lawfully-obtained consent is a "search," but it is a reasonable one. Because a consent search is reasonable, the Fourth Amendment prohibition on "unreasonable searches" is not violated. As discussed below,[6]

---

[1] *See generally* 3 W. LaFave, at §§ 8.1-8.6.

[2] R. Van Duizend, *et al.*, at 21.

[3] *E.g.*, Johnson v. United States, 333 U.S. 10, 13 (1948) (consent is invalid if it is "granted in submission to authority rather than as an understanding and intentional waiver of a constitutional right"); Stoner v. California, 376 U.S. 483, 489, *reh'g denied*, 377 U.S. 940 (1964) (the right to be free of a warrantless search "was a right . . . which only the petitioner could waive by word or deed. . . .").

[4] 110 S.Ct. 2793, 2802 (1990) (Marshall, J., with whom Brennan and Stevens, JJ. joined, dissenting).

[5] This observation, however, might also be appropriate in regards to various other Supreme Court opinions in which it has held that specific police activity is not a "search." *E.g.*, Oliver v. United States, 466 U.S. 170 (1984) (entry onto, and inspection of, an "open field" is not a "search"). *See* §§ 28, 33 *supra*.

[6] *See* § 90 *infra*.

because the issue is not framed in terms of "waiver," ordinary waiver principles do not apply, including the requirement that the relinquishment of the constitutional right be knowing.

§ 89 The Nature of Lawful Consent: General Principles

[A] Requirement of Voluntariness

Consent is legally ineffective unless the party giving consent does so voluntarily, rather than as "the result of duress or coercion, express or implied."[7] The burden of proof is on the prosecutor to demonstrate that consent was freely given.[8]

There is "no talismanic definition of 'voluntariness.' "[9] It is an "amphibian"[10] notion, "reflect[ing] an accommodation of the complex of values implicated"[11] in the police conduct. In the case of consent searches, the competing values are "the legitimate need for such searches and the equally important requirement of assuring the absence of coercion."[12]

"Voluntariness" is a question of fact, to be determined from the totality of the circumstances of the individual case. As with other usages of the totality-of-the-circumstances test,[13] it is impossible to predict with a fair degree of certainty what factors will render consent involuntary in a specific case.[14]

Among the factors that may support a finding of coercion are: (1) a show of force by the police, such as a display of guns, that would suggest to the person that she is not free to refuse consent; (2) repetitive requests for consent after an initial refusal; and (3) evidence relating to the consenting person's age, level of education, emotional state, or mental condition, that makes it reasonable to infer that her will was overborne by the officer's conduct. Other pertinent factors are discussed immediately below.

[B] Claim of Authority by the Police

In *Bumper v. North Carolina*,[15] police officers told *X*, who was standing at the front door of her house, that they had a warrant to search her premises. *X* opened the door and said "go ahead." In the ensuing search, the police seized a rifle that connected *D*, who lived with *X*, to a crime. Because no warrant was ever proved to exist, the prosecutor defended the search on the ground of consent.

The Supreme Court held that a state may not meet its burden of proof that consent was voluntarily granted "by showing no more than acquiescence to a

---

[7] Schneckloth v. Bustamonte, 412 U.S. 218, 248 (1973).
[8] Bumper v. North Carolina, 391 U.S. 543 (1968).
[9] *Schneckloth*, 412 U.S. at 224.
[10] Culombe v. Connecticut, 367 U.S. 568, 605 (1961).
[11] *Schneckloth*, 412 U.S. at 224-25.
[12] *Id.* at 227.
[13] *See* § 133 *infra*; regarding the debate between bright-line rules and case-by-case adjudication, *see* § 73 *supra*.
[14] *See* Weinreb, *Generalities of the Fourth Amendment*, 42 U. Chi. L. Rev. 47, 57 (1974); *see* 3 W. LaFave, § 8.2(a) at 176.
[15] 391 U.S. 543 (1968).

claim of lawful authority." Specifically, consent is invalid when it "has been given only after the official conducting the search has asserted that he possesses a warrant." Such a situation "is instinct with coercion."

Bumper appears to provide a bright-line rule: if an officer asserts authority to conduct a search on the basis of a warrant, any consent granted thereafter is invalid. However, lower courts have not treated the rule as if it were categorical.[16] For example, if *D* indicates to the officer asserting authority, "I don't care about the warrant, go ahead anyway," the consent might be legally effective, on the ground that *D*'s statement indicates that her consent was not linked to the officer's claim of authority.

[C] Police Deception

Police officers sometimes use deception to obtain consent to a search. Perhaps most commonly, they deceive a person regarding the purpose of the requested search. For example, *O*, a police officer, might request consent to search *D*'s home for evidence relating to a recent jewelry theft, when in fact she is looking for a bloody shirt that is evidence of a recent murder. *D* might consent, knowing that she has no jewelry, and assuming that *O* will not understand the significance of the bloody shirt if it is discovered. Does *O*'s deception vitiate *D*'s consent?

The Supreme Court has said little on the matter, and state and lower federal courts have reached mixed results in deception cases. The law is sufficiently muddled that Professor LaFave has stated that "as unsettling as it may be to say," the test appears to be whether the police "deception is 'fair.' "[17]

Even if "fair deception" is not an oxymoron, the concept is obviously value-laden and, therefore, subjective. The test can be made somewhat more objective by asking the question: "Would the deceit have induced an ordinary law-abiding person in the same situation to grant consent to a search that she would not otherwise have approved?"

Even if police deception does not otherwise vitiate consent, a search may not exceed the scope of the consent granted. For example, suppose that *O* obtains consent to search *D*'s home on the fraudulent basis that she wants to look for a stolen refrigerator. In fact, *O* uses the opportunity to look in *D*'s dresser for evidence that would connect him to a rape.

Any evidence seized from the dresser ought to be ruled inadmissible at trial, but not necessarily on the grounds of deception: the most reasonable interpretation of *D* consent is that he gave *O* authority to search those places in the home in which a stolen refrigerator might be hidden; the search of dresser drawers, therefore, exceeded the scope of the consent granted.[18]

---

[16] 3 W. LaFave, § 8.2(a) at 178-79.

[17] *Id.*, § 8.2(n) at 233.

[18] *Accord*, Gouled v. United States, 255 U.S. 298 (1921) (*O* gained entry to an office for a "social visit;" inside, he surreptitiously searched for incriminating papers; the search was improper because it exceeded the scope of the consent granted).

§ 90 Special Issue: Awareness of the Right to Refuse Consent

In *Schneckloth v. Bustamonte*,[19] the Supreme Court held that knowledge of the right to refuse consent is not a necessary condition to establishing a voluntary consent by a person not in police custody, although the subject's lack of knowledge is a factor to be taken into account in the voluntariness determination. Subsequently, the rule announced in *Schneckloth* was extended to consent searches granted by persons under arrest "on a public street, not in the confines of the police station."[20]

In *Schneckloth*, the police stopped a car in which X and D were passengers, because a headlight was burned out. After the driver failed to produce his driver's license and only X could provide identification, an officer asked for permission to search the car. X, the brother of the absent vehicle owner, consented. During the search, the police discovered evidence that connected D to a crime.

In the ensuing prosecution, D asserted that X's consent to the car search was invalid.[21] Although the state courts found that X's consent was voluntary, a federal court ruled that the consent was not valid unless the government proved that X knew that he had the right to refuse to consent to the search.

The Supreme Court, per Justice Stewart, disagreed with the federal court's analysis. It framed the issue as follows: "[W]hat must the state prove to demonstrate that a consent was 'voluntarily' given[?]" To answer this question, Justice Stewart sought guidance from the Court's decisions regarding coerced confessions, his distillation of which indicated that awareness of a right to refuse to answer questions is not a prerequisite to a finding of voluntariness, although it is a factor to be taken into account in the determination. The Court concluded that the same rule applies to Fourth Amendment consent searches.

The Court justified its holding on policy grounds. It stated that a properly conducted consent search "is a constitutionally permissible and wholly legitimate aspect of effective police activity." It warned that in cases in which the police have evidence of criminal activity, but lack probable cause to search or make an arrest, a consent search "may be the only means of obtaining important and reliable evidence" of a person's guilt.

Furthermore, according to the Court, even if the police possess probable cause and thus could obtain a warrant, a consent search "may still be valuable." An immediate, warrantless search, if it proves fruitless, might convince the police of the suspect's innocence, thereby saving her from the ordeal of an unnecessary arrest.[22]

In view of the importance of consent searches, the Court concluded that it was unwilling to permit defendants to "effectively frustrate the introduction into

---

[19] 412 U.S. 218 (1973).

[20] United States v. Watson, 423 U.S. 411, 424, *reh'g denied*, 424 U.S. 979 (1976).

[21] The prosecutor did not argue that D lacked standing to object to the alleged violation of X's rights. Today, such a claim might have been successful. *See* § 115 *infra*.

[22] Is this the reason why officers seek consent rather than a warrant? Often not, as one officer has explained: "Actually there are a lot of warrants that are not sought because of the hassle. You just figure it's not worth [it]. . . . If I can get consent, I'm gonna do it." R. Van Duizend, *et al.*, at 21.

evidence of the fruits of [a consent] search by simply failing to testify that he in fact knew he could refuse to consent."

Many commentators are highly critical of the reasoning of *Schneckloth*, if not also of its ultimate holding.[23] The primary objection to the case is, as Justice Marshall argued in dissent, that the majority misstated the issue of the case. According to the critics, the issue was not whether *X*'s consent was voluntary, as Justice Stewart claimed, but rather whether *X* waived his constitutional right to be free from unreasonable searches and seizures.[24]

The distinction is a significant one. Under the traditional waiver principles enunciated in *Johnson v. Zerbst*,[25] the state must prove "an intentional relinquishment . . . of a *known* right or privilege." In *Schneckloth*, such knowledge was not proved; therefore, there was no "waiver" of Fourth Amendment rights under this test.

Justice Stewart discounted the relevance of the waiver rule to consent searches. He stated that "a 'waiver' approach to consent searches would be thoroughly inconsistent with [the Court's] decisions that have approved 'third party consents.' " That is, as explained in the next chapter section, a search is valid if it is based on the consent of a third party who possesses common authority over the property in question. This rule could not be correct, Justice Stewart maintained, if waiver principles applied, because it would be wrong to hold that one person, not an agent of the other, may waive another's constitutional rights.[26]

Furthermore, according to Justice Stewart, the Court's waiver decisions "do not reflect an uncritical demand for a knowing and intelligent waiver in every situation where a person has failed to invoke a constitutional protection."

The Court distinguished between, on the one hand, rights that protect a fair criminal trial, such as the right to counsel, which was at issue in *Zerbst*, and the rights guaranteed under the Fourth Amendment. In the former case, a "strict standard of waiver" is required because the reliability of the trial is at stake. In contrast, "[t]he [privacy] protections of the Fourth Amendment are of a wholly different order, and have nothing whatsoever to do with promoting the fair ascertainment of truth at a criminal trial."

---

[23] *See* 3 W. LaFave, § 8.1(a) at 152.

[24] Justice Marshall reasoned that the "voluntariness" case law was inapt. The interrogation cases concerned the scope of the Fifth Amendment right of a person not to be "compelled to be a witness against himself." As he pointed out, "no sane person would knowingly relinquish a right to be free from compulsion"; therefore, awareness of the Fifth Amendment right was not a significant issue in those cases.

[25] 304 U.S. 458 (1938). *See* § 12 *supra*.

[26] Justice Stewart conclusion in this regard is wrong. As the doctrine of third-party consent has been explained, *X*'s consent to a search of property over which she and *D* possess common authority is valid because she possesses her own right — independent of *D* — to permit the police to conduct the search; thus, she would be "waiving" her own right, not *D*'s.

§ 91 Third-Party Consent[27]

More than one person may have a privacy interest in real or personal property that the police want to search. A search of a residence, for example, will often intrude on the privacy of several persons who inhabit it; a search of a container intrudes on the privacy interests of anyone who uses it as a depository of private effects.

The issue of consent does not arise if X voluntarily consents to a search of premises or personal effects that also belong to D, as long as the evidence found during the search is introduced at trial only against X. The issue of "third-party consent" arises, however, when the person against whom the evidence is introduced (D) is not the one who granted the consent (X).

One of the earliest Supreme Court cases to consider the issue of third-party consent was *Stoner v. California.*[28] In *Stoner*, the police obtained consent from a hotel clerk to enter D's hotel room. The Court ruled that the consent was invalid, "[e]ven if it be assumed that a state law . . . gave a hotel proprietor blanket authority to authorize the police to search."

The Court stated that Fourth Amendment rights are "not to be eroded by strained applications of the law of agency" or by the "subtle distinctions" of property law. In language that suggested that third-party consent might never be valid, the Court indicated that "[i]t is important to bear in mind that it was [D's] constitutional right which was at stake here. . . . It was a right, therefore, which only . . . [D] could waive by word or deed, either directly or through an agent."

In *United States v. Matlock,*[29] however, the Court affirmed that a warrantless search is constitutionally valid if the police obtain the consent of a person who possesses common authority over the property searched. The burden of proof is on the government to establish common authority.[30]

In *Matlock*, D was arrested in the front yard of a home in which he shared a room with X. The officers received consent from X to search the room. D's consent was not requested. The Court declared the law to be "clear" that consent to a search "of one who possesses common authority over premises or effects is valid *as against the absent nonconsenting person* with whom the authority is shared."[31]

---

[27] *See generally* Coombs, *Shared Privacy and the Fourth Amendment, or the Rights of Relationships,* 75 Calif. L. Rev. 1593 (1987); Goldberger, *Consent, Expectations of Privacy, and the Meaning of "Searches" in the Fourth Amendment,* 75 J. Crim. L. & Crimin. 319 (1984); White, *The Fourth Amendment As a Way of Talking About People: A Study of Robinson and Matlock,* 1974 Sup. Ct. Rev. 165; Comment, *The Problem of Third-Party Consent in Fourth Amendment Searches: Toward a "Conservative" Reading of the Matlock Decision,* 42 Maine L. Rev. 159 (1990); Comment, *Third-Party Consent Searches, The Supreme Court, and the Fourth Amendment,* 75 J. Crim. L. & Crimin. 963 (1984).

[28] 376 U.S. 483, *reh'g denied,* 377 U.S. 940 (1964).

[29] 415 U.S. 164 (1974).

[30] Illinois v. Rodriguez, 110 S.Ct. at 2797.

[31] Emphasis added.

It stated that "common authority" rests on "mutual use of the property by persons generally having joint access or control for most purposes."[32]

The Court in *Matlock* justified third-party common-authority consent on the ground that "it is reasonable to recognize that any of the co-inhabitants has the right to permit the inspection in his own right and that the others have assumed the risk that one of their number might permit the common area to be searched." In short, each person with common authority over the property to be searched maintains her own right to consent to the search.

Because *Matlock* referred to "absent, nonconsenting persons," in its description of the third-party consent rule, there is a split of authority among lower courts regarding whether consent by one joint occupant is legally effective against another occupant who is present and who objects to the search.[33] Some courts have concluded that the consent of both parties is required when both are present, on the theory that one co-tenant's right to restrict access to the premises is not subordinated to the second person's right to grant consent, at least if the former contemporaneously asserts her objection.[34]

On the other hand, this limitation is inconsistent with the Court's reasoning in *Matlock* that each person with common authority over property possesses a personal right to consent to a search of it. That is, if *Matlock* is rightly decided, it should follow that by sharing her privacy with X, D assumes the risk that X will voluntarily[35] consent to a search of their joint property, even over her objection.[36]

§ 92   "Apparent Authority"

Is consent valid if it is based on "apparent authority"? That is, is a warrantless search constitutional if permission for the search is granted by a third person whom the police at the time reasonably, but wrongly, believed had authority to grant consent?

---

[32] One who shares premises with another person may retain exclusive control over a portion of the premises or over particular effects within them. For example, a particular room in an apartment shared by college roommates might be used exclusively by one person. Lower courts agree that as to such areas or personal effects, consent is ineffective unless it is granted by the person with exclusive control.

[33] *See* 3 W. LaFave, § 8.3(d) at 251-52.

[34] *E.g.*, State v. Leach, 113 Wash.2d 735, 782 P.2d 1035 (1989) (holding that the state had to prove, at the very least, that the defendant did not object to the search to which the joint occupant consented).

[35] As Professor Mary Coombs has argued, some relationships are sufficiently intimate "to permit a presumption that the parties would shelter one another's interests." Coombs, n. 27 *supra*, at 1653; *see* Weinreb, n. 14 *supra*, at 63 ("[O]rdinarily, persons with equal 'rights' in a place would accommodate each other by not admitting persons over another's objection while he was present."). In such circumstances, a trial court should be skeptical that X's consent was voluntary. Coombs, at 1661.

[36] *See also* Illinois v. Rodriguez, 110 S.Ct. at 2797 (in which the Court described the third-party consent rule to be, simply, that a warrantless search of premises is valid if "voluntary consent has been obtained . . . from a third party who possesses common authority over the premises.").

In *Stoner v. California*,[37] the Supreme Court stated that "the rights protected by the Fourth Amendment are not to be eroded . . . by unrealistic doctrines of 'apparent authority.'" Ten years later, however, in *United States v. Matlock*,[38] the Court expressly left open the issue of whether "apparent authority" constitutes effective consent.

In *Illinois v. Rodriguez*,[39] the Court resolved the issue left open in *Matlock*. It held, 6-3, that a warrantless entry of a residence is valid when it is based on the consent of a person whom the police, at the time of entry, reasonably believed had common authority over the premises.

In *Rodriguez*, X reported to the police that she had been severely beaten that day by D in a specified apartment. X stated that D was now asleep on the premises, and she offered to let the police in with her key so that they could arrest him. During her conversation with the police, X referred to D's apartment as "our" apartment, and she stated that she had clothing and furniture there. In fact, however, although she had once shared the apartment with D, she had vacated it weeks earlier and had taken the key without D's knowledge.

With X's consent, the police entered D's apartment. Inside, they observed drug paraphernalia and cocaine in plain view. D was arrested and charged with possession of illegal drugs. The trial court granted D's motion to exclude the evidence found in the apartment on the ground that X lacked common authority over the premises.

The Supreme Court reversed. It stated that "in order to satisfy the 'reasonableness' requirement of the Fourth Amendment, what is generally demanded of the many factual determinations that must regularly be made by agents of the government . . . is not that they always be correct, but that they always be reasonable."

According to *Rodriguez*, "what is at issue when a claim of apparent consent is raised is not whether the right to be free of searches has been *waived*, but whether the right to be free of *unreasonable* searches has been *violated*." In effect, a search based on a reasonable mistake of fact regarding the authority of the third person to give consent is a "reasonable" search within the meaning of the Fourth Amendment.

The consent determination, as with other factual determinations that arise under the Fourth Amendment, must be judged against an objective standard. It warned that an invitation by a person to conduct a search, even if accompanied by an explicit claim of authority to grant consent (*e.g.*, "I live here"), is insufficient to justify a consent search if "the surrounding circumstances [are] . . . such that a reasonable person would doubt its truth."

Specifically, the objective test announced in *Rodriguez* is: "[W]ould the facts available to the officer at the moment . . . 'warrant a man of reasonable caution in the belief' that the consenting party had authority over the premises?" If the answer is "no," then "warrantless entry without further inquiry is unlawful unless actual authority exists." If the answer is "yes," the warrantless search is valid.

---

[37] 376 U.S. 483, *reh'g denied*, 377 U.S. 940 (1964).
[38] 415 U.S. 164 (1974).
[39] 110 S.Ct. 2793 (1990).

CHAPTER **18**

MINIMALLY INTRUSIVE SEARCHES AND SEIZURES: THE *TERRY* PRINCIPLE

§ 93   *Terry v. Ohio*: An Overview [1]

The Fourth Amendment was once considered a monolith.[2] "Probable cause" had a single meaning, and "searches" and "seizures" were all-or-nothing concepts.

The monolith was cracked by the Supreme Court in *Camara v. Municipal Court*.[3] In *Camara*, the justices recognized a different form of "probable cause," applicable to administrative searches, that does not require individualized suspicion and that is based on a general standard of "reasonableness." To determine "reasonableness," the Court in *Camara* invoked a balancing test, in which the individual's and society's interests are weighed against each other.

If *Camara* cracked the Fourth Amendment monolith, *Terry v. Ohio*[4] broke it entirely. Although the issue in *Terry* was described by the Court as "quite narrow" — namely, "whether it is always unreasonable for a policeman to seize a person and subject him to a limited search for weapons unless there is probable cause to arrest" — the significance of the case to Fourth Amendment jurisprudence is exceeded, if at all, only by *Katz v. United States*.[5]

Briefly, the significance of *Terry* to search-and-seizure law is as follows. First, it transported *Camara*'s "reasonableness" balancing test from the realm of administrative searches to traditional criminal investigations, and used it to determine the reasonableness of a warrantless search and seizure, rather than merely to define "probable cause." The result has been a diminution in the role of the warrant clause in Fourth Amendment jurisprudence.

Second, *Terry* recognized that both searches and seizures can vary in their intrusiveness. As a result of *Terry*, the police may now conduct a wide array of searches and seizures that are less-than-ordinarily intrusive on the basis of "reasonable suspicion," a lesser standard of cause than "probable cause." Furthermore, some "full" searches are now permissible on the basis of "reasonable suspicion."[6]

---

[1] *See generally* 3 W. LaFave, at § 9.1; LaFave, *"Street Encounters" and the Constitution: Terry, Sibron, Peters, and Beyond*, 67 Mich. L. Rev. 39 (1968); Maclin, *The Decline of the Right of Locomotion: The Fourth Amendment on the Streets*, 75 Cornell L. Rev. 1258 (1990); Sundby, *A Return to Fourth Amendment Basics: Undoing the Mischief of Camara and Terry*, 72 Minn. L. Rev. 383 (1988).

[2] Amsterdam, at 388.

[3] 387 U.S. 523 (1967). *See* § 47 *supra*.

[4] 392 U.S. 1 (1968).

[5] 389 U.S. 347 (1967).

[6] *See, e.g.,* § 107 *infra*.

Third, although *Terry* does not require such a holding, the Supreme Court has applied the "reasonableness" balancing test that stems from it and *Camara* to hold that some seizures and searches of persons may be conducted without individualized suspicion of any kind.[7]

§ 94 *Terry v. Ohio*: The Opinion

[A] Majority Opinion

O, a police officer with more than 30 years of experience, became "thoroughly suspicious" when he observed two, and later three, men walking back and forth repeatedly in front of a store, peering in. *O* suspected that the men were "casing a job," *i.e.*, planning to commit an armed robbery.

O approached the suspects, asked for their names, and when he received only a mumbled reply, patted down ("frisked") the outside of the men's clothing. *O* felt a pistol in the breast pocket of *D*'s overcoat, pulled it out, and arrested him. *D* was prosecuted for carrying a concealed weapon.

At a pre-trial hearing to determine the admissibility of the weapon, *O* testified that he frisked the suspects only to see whether they were armed, and that he put his hands in *D*'s clothing only after he felt the weapon. At the time of the pat-down, *O* lacked probable cause to arrest the suspects or to search them.

The Supreme Court, per Chief Justice Warren, upheld the officer's action, although it rejected the government's claim that the "stop and frisk" procedure fell outside the purview of the Fourth Amendment. The Court stated that persons can be "seized" short of being arrested: a "seizure" occurs "whenever a police officer accosts an individual and restrains his freedom to walk away."[8] It held that *O* seized *D* at least as soon as he initiated physical contact with *D* in order to search him. Likewise, the pat-down was a "serious intrusion" — therefore, a "search" — albeit "something less than a 'full' " one.

Although the stop-and-frisk conducted by *O* involved Fourth Amendment activity, the Court concluded that the warrant clause does not apply to this type of police practice. The Chief Justice stated that the Court would "not retreat" from the ordinary rule that the police must, whenever practicable, secure a search warrant, but, he said, "we deal here with an entire rubric of police conduct — necessarily swift action predicated upon the on-the-spot observations of a police officer on the beat — which historically has not been, and as a practical matter could not be, subjected to the warrant procedure."

Because the warrant clause was deemed inapplicable to this "entire rubric of police conduct," the Court held that the "probable cause" standard, which is textually tied to the warrant requirement in the Fourth Amendment,[9] also does not apply.[10] Instead, the Court stated, the "central inquiry" is "the reasonableness

---

[7] *See* §§ 102, 106[B], and 108 *infra*.

[8] Since *Terry*, the Court has refined the definition of "seizure." *See* § 40 *supra*.

[9] "[N]o Warrants shall issue, but upon probable cause. . . ." (U.S. Const. amend. IV).

[10] This conclusion need not follow. When an exigency justifies an exception to the warrant requirement, the Court ordinarily retains the probable-cause standard, as it has done, for example, in the case of searches of cars stopped on the highway. *See generally* chapter 14 *supra*.

in all the circumstances of the particular governmental invasion of a citizen's personal security." Quoting *Camara*, the Chief Justice observed that "there is 'no ready test for determining reasonableness other than by balancing the need to search [or seize] against the invasion which the search [or seizure] entails.' "[11]

The Court balanced the competing interests in the case. From *D*'s perspective, the pat-down, because it was less than a full-blown search, intruded on his security, but less so than a full search. On the government's side of the scale were two interests: the general interest in "effective crime prevention and detection" that would be impaired if the police could not confront suspects for investigative purposes on less than probable cause; and the immediate interest of *O* in assuring himself that *D* was "not armed with a weapon that could unexpectedly and fatally be used against him."

The Chief Justice concluded that when an officer has what has come to be known as "reasonable suspicion" that "the individual whose suspicious behavior he is investigating at close range is armed and presently dangerous to the officer or others," the officer has the constitutional authority to ascertain whether the person in fact is armed and, if he is, to disarm him. The procedure used by the officer to protect himself, however, must be "strictly circumscribed [in manner] by the exigencies which justify its initiation."

The purpose of the *Terry* search is limited: to determine whether the suspect is armed. Unlike a search incident to an arrest, a *Terry*-type search "is not justified by any need to prevent the disappearance or destruction of evidence of crime."

The appropriate manner of the protective search depends on the facts of the case, but the Court approved the technique used here: a pat-down of the outside of the suspect's clothing that is reasonably designed to discover "guns, knives, clubs, or other hidden instruments for the assault of the police officer"; and, when a hard object that feels like a weapon is discovered during the pat-down, a full search under the clothing to remove it.

[B] Justice Harlan's Concurring Opinion

Justice Harlan, while "unreservedly agree[ing]" with the Court's holding, sought "to fill in a few gaps" in the Chief Justice's opinion. In doing so, he provided two important insights into the stop-and-frisk process.

First, the majority opinion focused on the protective search — the pat-down — of *D*. But, as Justice Harlan observed, the right to frisk ought to depend on whether the officer had authority to insist on the encounter that placed his safety in jeopardy. Just as an officer may ask a citizen a question, the "person addressed [ordinarily] has an equal right to ignore his interrogator and walk away."

Therefore, the first issue in any stop-and-frisk situation should be whether the officer had a right to "forcibly stop" — *i.e.*, "seize" — the suspect. In *Terry*, Justice Harlan believed that *O* had such a right because he "observed circumstances that would reasonably lead an experienced, prudent policeman to suspect that [*D*] was about to engage in burglary or robbery."

---

[11] The *Camara-Terry* "reasonableness" test is now often stated in the form of a three-prong test. *See* n. 82 and accompanying text *infra*.

Second, Justice Harlan concluded that when a forcible stop is justified, "the right to frisk must be immediate and automatic if the reason for the stop is, as here, an articulable suspicion of a crime of violence." This comment is significant because of language in the majority opinion that appears to require the officer, after seizing a suspect, to investigate further before conducting a pat-down.[12] As discussed in § 98, Justice Harlan has the better side of this controversy, as the Supreme Court has implicitly acknowledged.

§ 95 "Reasonable Suspicion"[13]

[A] Quantum of Information

Terry did not indicate what quantum of evidence is required to justify a less-than-ordinarily-intrusive seizure of a person or to conduct a less-than-ordinarily-intrusive search of a suspect, although Chief Justice Warren did make the rather obvious point in the context of a pat-down that the officer need not be "absolutely certain" that the suspect is armed.

Subsequently, the Court has stated that the reasonable-suspicion standard of *Terry* is "obviously less demanding than that for probable cause."[14] The latter standard does not require proof by even a preponderance of the evidence,[15] and "reasonable suspicion" requires "considerably less"[16] proof of wrongdoing than this. Therefore, all that is required to justify a *Terry*-level search or seizure is "some minimal level of objective justification."[17]

[B] Types of Information

[1] Personal Police Observation

The Supreme Court has stated that the "reasonable suspicion" standard cannot be "readily, or even usefully, reduced to a neat set of legal rules."[18] Instead, the justifiability of a *Terry*-type seizure or search, like a seizure or search based on probable cause, must be evaluated on "the totality of the circumstances — the whole picture."[19]

Typically, as occurred in *Terry*, a forcible stop of a suspect will be based on the officer's personal observations of the suspect and the surrounding circumstances. According to *Terry*, a "police officer must be able to point to specific and articulable facts which, taken together with rational inferences from those facts, reasonably warrant [the] intrusion."

---

[12] *See* n. 58 and accompanying text *infra*.
[13] *See generally* 3 W. LaFave, at §§ 9.3, 9.5(a)-(b).
[14] United States v. Sokolow, 109 S.Ct. 1581, 1585 (1989).
[15] *See* § 43 *supra*.
[16] *Sokolow*, 109 S.Ct at 1585.
[17] I.N.S. v. Delgado, 466 U.S. 210, 217 (1984).
[18] *Sokolow*, 109 S.Ct. at 1585 (*quoting* Illinois v. Gates, 462 U.S. 213, 232 (1983)).
[19] United States v. Cortez, 449 U.S. 411, 417 (1981), *reh'g denied*, 455 U.S. 1008 (1982).

Although a police officer is entitled to make "common-sense conclusions about human behavior,"[20] including those based on his law enforcement expertise, "reasonable suspicion" cannot be based on what *Terry* called an "inchoate and unparticularized suspicion or 'hunch'."

[2] Drug-Courier Profiles

An officer's observations may properly be supplemented by "consideration of the modes or patterns of operation of certain kinds of lawbreakers."[21] Particularly in the drug-trafficking field, an officer's suspicions will often be buttressed by his awareness that the suspect's conduct or appearance conforms to a so-called "drug-courier profile," which is a set of characteristics often associated with drug traffickers compiled by law enforcement agencies, such as the Drug Enforcement Administration.

Many litigated drug-courier-profile cases occur in the following factual context: officers observe *D* embarking on, or disembarking from, an airplane; *D*'s conduct is lawful in all respects, but it and *D*'s appearance fit a drug-courier profile; therefore, the officers detain *D* in order to question him. If the investigation constitutes or develops into a *Terry*-level seizure, the issue that must be determined is whether the seizure was based on "reasonable suspicion."[22]

The fact that a suspect's behavior and appearance conforms to a drug-courier profile does not by itself constitute "reasonable suspicion."[23] However, the mere fact that conduct is lawful does not prohibit a finding of "reasonable suspicion," and the fact that the suspect's conduct conforms to a drug-courier profile "does not somehow detract from [the] evidentiary significance [of the factors] as seen by a trained agent."[24]

Each drug-courier-profile case must be decided on its own merits, and it is difficult to draw any broad principles from the cases the Court has decided. However, as a descriptive matter, the Court now seems more willing than in the past to validate seizures based on drug-courier profiles.

The Supreme Court took a comparatively strict view of the subject in *Reid v. Georgia*,[25] one of the first drug-courier-profile cases to reach the Court. In *Reid*, it held that an officer lacked reasonable suspicion to detain a suspect in an airport who fit a drug profile in that he: (1) arrived from a "drug source" city; (2) arrived early in the morning, a time when law enforcement activity is reduced; (3) appeared to conceal the fact that he was travelling with another person; and (4) had no luggage except for shoulder bags.

Notwithstanding the profile, the Court believed that, except for the third point, the factors "describe[d] a very large category of presumably innocent travelers,

---

[20] *Id.* at 418.

[21] *Id.*

[22] The action might not constitute a "seizure" at all, *see* § 40 *supra*, and therefore not require any level of suspicion. On the other hand, the seizure could be tantamount to an arrest, *i.e.*, a full-scale seizure, and therefore require probable cause. *See* § 96 *infra*.

[23] *See* Reid v. Georgia, 448 U.S. 438 (1980) (*per curiam*).

[24] *Sokolow*, 109 S.Ct. at 1587.

[25] 448 U.S. 438 (1980) (*per curiam*).

who would be subject to virtually random seizures were the Court to conclude that as little foundation as there was in this case could justify a seizure."

The Court disposed of the furtive conduct on the ground that the officer's suspicion that the suspect was concealing something was no more than an inchoate and unparticularized hunch. The Court did warn, however, that "there could . . . be circumstances in which wholly lawful conduct might justify the suspicion that criminal activity was afoot."

The Court was presented with a case of lawful, but reasonably suspicious, conduct in *Florida v. Royer*.[26] In *Royer*, D, a suspect about to embark on an airplane, fit a drug-courier profile in that he: (1) was travelling from a major drug source city; (2) paid for his ticket in cash with a large sum of small bills; (3) travelled under an assumed name; and (4) appeared to be nervous. In a plurality opinion, Justice White stated that when the police learned that D was travelling under an assumed name, "this fact, and the facts already known to the officers" justified a temporary detention.

In *United States v. Sokolow*,[27] a case that the dissent argued was factually "strikingly similar" to *Reid*, the conduct of D, a passenger disembarking from an airplane, was consistent with a drug-courier profile in that: (1) he paid for airplane tickets totalling $2,100 with a roll of $20 bills; (2) he travelled under a name different than that listed for his telephone number; (3) his original destination was Miami, a major drug source city; (4) he stayed in the city, in July, for only two days, although his round-trip flight from Hawaii lasted 20 hours; (5) he appeared nervous; and (6) he checked in none of his luggage.

The Court conceded that each of these factors was "quite consistent with innocent travel." On the other hand, it found factors (1) and (4) "out of the ordinary"; and it thought that the existence of factor (2) gave the police reasonable grounds for believing that D was travelling under an alias. Taken together, the Court concluded that these three factors amounted to reasonable suspicion of drug trafficking.

[3] Hearsay Information

"Reasonable suspicion," like "probable cause," may be based in whole or in part on hearsay. Furthermore, because "reasonable suspicion" is a less demanding standard than "probable cause," it may be satisfied not only on the basis of a lesser quantum of evidence, but also on the basis of "information that is less reliable than required to show probable cause."[28] The same factors that apply to information supplied by an informant in the probable-cause context — his basis of knowledge and veracity — apply in the *Terry* context, "although allowance must be made in applying them for the lesser showing required to meet that standard."[29]

For example, in *Adams v. Williams*,[30] the Supreme Court sustained a *Terry* stop and frisk based in part on an informant's personal tip that would not have justified

---

[26] 460 U.S. 491 (1983).
[27] 109 S.Ct. 1581 (1989).
[28] Alabama v. White, 110 S.Ct. 2412, 2416 (1990).
[29] *Id.* at 2415.
[30] 407 U.S. 143 (1972).

an arrest or a search based on probable cause. In *Williams*, an informant known personally to the officer told him late at night that *D* was seated in a nearby car with narcotics in his possession and a gun concealed at his waist. The informant did not indicate the basis of his knowledge. As a result of the tip the officer proceeded to *D*'s car. He ordered *D* to open the door; instead, *D* opened his window, at which point the officer reached in and removed a revolver from *D*'s waistband.

The Supreme Court, per Justice Rehnquist, conceded that the unverified tip might not have been sufficient to justify any action that required probable cause. Nonetheless, it held that the tip "carried enough indicia of reliability" to justify the *Terry*-level forcible stop.

The Court considered the tipster's information sufficiently reliable because he had provided the police with information about a crime on a prior occasion, and because he personally came to the officer with the present information, rather than making an anonymous report. As a result, the informant subjected himself to the risk of arrest for making a false complaint, if the information he provided had proved to be false. The Court was not dissuaded by the fact, pointed out by the dissenters, that the informant's prior track record consisted of a single tip, pertaining to a different type of conduct (alleged homosexual behavior in a railroad station), which did not even result in an arrest.

The Court in *Williams* warned that "[s]ome tips, completely lacking in indicia of reliability, would either warrant no police response or require further investigation before a forcible stop of a suspect would be authorized." *Alabama v. White*[31] provides a good example of such an unsatisfactory tip, but one that was made satisfactory by further investigation.

In *White*, the police received a telephone call from an anonymous informant who stated that *D* (a woman she named) would be leaving a specified apartment at a specified time in a "brown Plymouth station wagon with the right taillight broken," and that she would drive to a specified motel, in possession of an ounce of cocaine in a brown attache case.

The officers proceeded to the apartment, where they observed an automobile fitting the tipster's description parked in a lot in front of the apartment building. They spotted a woman, empty handed, enter the car and drive in the direction of the motel. Before the car reached the predicted location, police officers stopped the vehicle and ordered *D* out. A subsequent search based on consent resulted in seizure of marijuana found in an attache case.

The Court held, 6-3, that the anonymous tip in this case, by itself, was insufficient to justify a forcible stop of *D*. It pointed out that the caller provided "absolutely no indication of the basis for the . . . predictions regarding [*D*'s] criminal activities"; furthermore, the call "provide[d] virtually nothing from which one might conclude that [the tipster] . . . [was] either honest or his information reliable."

Nonetheless, the Supreme Court upheld the forcible stop in this case because the police corroborated various aspects of the anonymous tip. The corroboration

---

[31] 110 S.Ct. 2412 (1990).

was far from complete: it was not clear prior to the stop that the woman getting into the vehicle was *D* or that she had exited the correct apartment at the specified address; because the person entering the car did not have an attache case in her possession, the police could not know if one was in the vehicle; and the car was stopped before it reached its destination, so the police could not say with certainty that it would have stopped at the predicted address. Nonetheless, for purposes of "reasonable suspicion," as distinguished from "probable cause," the Court believed that there was sufficient corroboration to justify the stop.

[4] Information from Another Police Department

In the highly mobile society in which we live, the police often are asked to detain a suspect in their jurisdiction because there is an arrest warrant for him in another community. The question arises whether a detention based exclusively on a "wanted flyer" issued by another jurisdiction is constitutionally permissible. That is, is a seizure permitted although the detaining jurisdiction lacks independent knowledge of the underlying facts that allegedly support it?

In *United States v. Hensley*,[32] the Supreme Court held that the police in one jurisdiction may briefly detain a person who is the subject of a felony[33] "wanted flyer" from a police department in another community in order to determine whether there is an arrest warrant issued for the detainee. The temporary seizure is permissible although the detaining jurisdiction is unaware of the facts supporting it.[34]

However, the detention is justifiable only if two conditions are met: (1) the department issuing the flyer in fact had reasonable suspicion to order the person to be detained; and (2) the actual detention was not "significantly more intrusive" than would have been permitted if it had occurred in the issuing jurisdiction. If the issuing jurisdiction lacked an adequate basis to detain the suspect, any evidence seized from him by the detaining jurisdiction is inadmissible.[35]

§ 96 Distinguishing a *"Terry Stop"* From an Arrest[36]

An encounter between a police officer and a private person can be so non-intrusive — for example, if an officer asks a person for the time of day — that it does not constitute a "seizure" and, therefore, does not trigger Fourth Amendment

---

[32] 469 U.S. 221 (1985).

[33] The Court expressly left open the issue of whether the police may similarly seize persons wanted for misdemeanor violations.

[34] If the jurisdiction issuing the flyer has probable cause to arrest the suspect, the detaining jurisdiction may arrest him, even though they are unaware of the supporting evidence. *See* Whiteley v. Warden, 401 U.S. 560 (1971).

[35] Unfortunately, according to projections of the Federal Bureau of Investigation, as many as 12,000 invalid or inaccurate reports on suspects wanted for arrest are transmitted daily to federal, state, and local law enforcement agencies. Burnham, *F.B.I. Says 12,000 Faulty Reports on Suspects Are Issued Each Day*, New York Times, Aug. 25, 1985, at 1, col. 4.

[36] *See generally* 3 W. LaFave, at §§ 9.2(f)-(g), 9.6(b)-(c); LaFave, n. 1 *supra*, at 426-38; Maclin, n.1 *supra*.

scrutiny. On the other hand, a forcible stop can be so intrusive that it constitutes a *de facto* arrest and, therefore, requires probable cause. The line between a *Terry*-level seizure and a *de facto* arrest is not bright, but various factors deserve note.

[A] Extended Duration of the Detention

Terry involved a very brief detention of persons suspected of criminal activity. More than once the Supreme Court has stated that the justifiability of a seizure on less than probable cause is predicated in substantial part on the brevity of the detention.[37]

Nonetheless, there is no bright-line time limitation to a *Terry*-type seizure. A seizure based on reasonable suspicion may be permitted although it lasts longer than the ones that occurred in *Terry*. For example, in *United States v. Sharpe*[38] the Court upheld a twenty-minute detention of a suspect, stopped in his automobile on a public highway, in order to investigate criminal activity.

Although the Court upheld the seizure, its legitimacy was based on the presence of three critical temporal factors: (1) the officer "pursued his investigation in a diligent and reasonable manner"; (2) the method of investigation "was likely to confirm or dispel [the officers'] suspicions quickly"; and (3) the detention lasted no longer than was necessary to effectuate the purpose of the stop. Furthermore, the *Sharpe* Court warned, even if these conditions are met, a detention that "continues indefinitely at some point . . . can no longer be justified" as a *Terry* stop.

[B] Forcible Movement of the Suspect

A seizure is not tantamount to an arrest merely because the police move the suspect against his will from one location to another for reasons of safety or security during an investigatory detention. For example, in *Pennsylvania v. Mimms*,[39] an officer lawfully stopped *D* for a traffic violation. As a matter of routine self-protection, he ordered *D* out of the vehicle. The Court upheld the latter seizure as a "*de minimis*" intrusion.

On the other hand, if a suspect is transported against his will from his home or some other place in which he has a right to be to another site for interrogation, particularly if the interrogation could have taken place where the detention arose, the Court is inclined to treat the seizure as a *de facto* arrest, which requires probable cause.

For example, in *Florida v. Royer*[40] the police moved *D*, originally encountered in an airport concourse, to a small room 40 feet away, where the investigation continued. Among the reasons given by the Court for treating this act as tantamount to an arrest was that there was no finding of a legitimate law enforcement purpose for moving the suspect.

---

[37] *See, e.g.*, Dunaway v. New York, 442 U.S. 200 (1979); Florida v. Royer, 460 U.S. 491 (1983); United States v. Place, 462 U.S. 696 (1983).

[38] 470 U.S. 675 (1985).

[39] 434 U.S. 106 (1977).

[40] 460 U.S. 491 (1983).

One line is rather bright. If an officer removes a suspect from his home or other place in which he is entitled to be and transports him against his will to the police station for interrogation,[41] the detention is treated as tantamount to an arrest.[42]

[C] Existence of "Less Intrusive Means"[43]

In *Florida v. Royer*,[44] Justice White, author of the four-justice plurality opinion, but probably with the support of a fifth justice, asserted that when a suspect is seized under the *Terry* principle, "the investigative methods employed should be the least intrusive means reasonably available to verify or dispel the officer's suspicions in a short period of time."[45]

In *Royer*, this principle was violated when the police moved *D*, an embarking airplane passenger suspected of drug smuggling, from the public concourse to a small room nearby so that the police could retrieve his luggage and search it, a process that took 15 minutes.

According to Justice White, the government did not "touch[] on the question whether it would have been feasible to investigate the contents of [*D*'s] bag in a more expeditious way." In particular, he noted that "[t]he courts are not strangers to the use of trained dogs to detect the presence of controlled substances in luggage." Because there was no indication in this case that the latter investigatory technique "was not feasible and available," the officers' conduct was considered more intrusive than necessary.

The Court's post-*Royer* opinions demonstrate that the least-intrusive-means doctrine applies, if at all, only in the *Royer* context, namely, when the issue is whether the length of an investigatory seizure was excessive. For example, in *United States v. Sokolow*,[46] *D* claimed that the police were constitutionally required, if they could, to verify their suspicions that he was smuggling narcotics before they seized him. The Court quickly disposed of this argument by stating that Justice White's "statement" in *Royer* "was directed at the length of the investigative stop, not at whether the police had a less intrusive means to verify their suspicions before stopping [*D*]." According to *Sokolow*, "the reasonableness of the officer's decision to stop a suspect does not turn on the availability of less intrusive investigatory techniques."[47]

Even in length-of-detention cases, the Court has limited its use of the least-intrusive-means doctrine. In *United States v. Sharpe*,[48] *D* was detained for twenty

[41] But if he is brought to the stationhouse to be fingerprinted, *see* § 97[C] *infra*.

[42] *See* Dunaway v. New York, 442 U.S. 200 (1979).

[43] *See generally* Strossen, *The Fourth Amendment in the Balance: Accurately Setting the Scales Through the Least Intrusive Alternative Means*, 63 N.Y.U. L. Rev. 1173 (1988).

[44] 460 U.S. 491 (1983).

[45] Justice Brennan concurred in the judgment. He believed that a *Terry* seizure must be so short in duration that it would be "difficult to conceive of a less intrusive means that would be effective to accomplish the purpose of the stop."

[46] 109 S.Ct. 1581 (1989).

[47] *See also* Michigan v. Long, 463 U.S. 1032, 1052 (1983) (a *Terry*-type weapons-search of an automobile is valid even if the police could have "adopt[ed] alternative means to ensure their safety in order to avoid the intrusion involved in a *Terry* encounter.").

[48] 470 U.S. 675 (1985).

minutes while the police sought to determine whether he was involved in transporting drugs in his pickup truck. The Court stated that in assessing whether this detention was too long to constitute a *Terry* stop, "[t]he question is not simply whether some other alternative was available, *but whether the police acted unreasonably in failing to recognize it or to pursue it.*" And, in answering the latter question, the Court warned reviewing courts "not [to] indulge in unrealistic second-guessing."

§ 97 Grounds for "*Terry* Stops"[49]

[A] Crime Prevention versus Crime Detection

Terry involved the brief seizure and limited search of a person suspected of imminent criminal activity. The officer's actions were considered reasonable in view of the government's interest in crime prevention.

The Supreme Court unanimously held in *United States v. Hensley*[50] that a *Terry*-level seizure is also permitted in order to investigate a crime already committed. However, a seizure that is reasonable in the crime-prevention context will not necessarily be permissible in the crime-investigation setting.

As the Court explained in *Hensley*, the factors that go into the *Terry* "reasonableness" balancing inquiry are not same in the two contexts. For example, the exigent circumstances that justify a brief detention when an officer reasonably suspects that serious crime is afoot are often missing in the crime-detection framework. Furthermore, in crime-detection cases officers often can choose a time and place for the stop that is more convenient to the suspect than is possible when crime is afoot.

[B] Nature of the Crime

Most *Terry*-type seizures involve the detention of persons suspected of involvement in violent crimes. The principles of *Terry* extend, however, to the investigation of drug trafficking "or of any other serious crime."[51] The Supreme Court has not determined whether, for purposes of either crime prevention or detection, the police may detain a person suspected of involvement in a very minor offense.[52]

Assuming that seizures of persons are permitted in the prevention and investigation of very minor crimes, it is reasonable to argue that in view of the less serious nature of such crimes, a seizure to investigate or prevent a minor offense should be less intrusive, *e.g.*, shorter in duration, than an ordinary *Terry* stop.

[C] Fingerprinting

The Court considers fingerprinting a less serious intrusion on a person's security than other police practices. For example, fingerprinting does not probe a person's

---

[49] *See generally* 3 W. LaFave, at §§ 9.2(a)-(c), 9.6(a)-(b) Maclin, n. 1 *supra*.
[50] 469 U.S. 221 (1985).
[51] Florida v. Royer, 460 U.S. at 498-99.
[52] The issue, at least for investigatory purposes, was explicitly left open by the Court in United States v. Hensley, 469 U.S. at 229.

private life and thoughts as an interrogation or a search can do. The process is more reliable than lineups and confessions, and "is not subject to such abuses as the improper [suggestive] line-up and the 'third degree' [interrogation]."[53] Furthermore, unlike many other police procedures, fingerprinting can be conducted at a time convenient to the suspect and need not be repeated.

Because of these differences, the transportation of a suspect to the police station for fingerprinting, if he is detained there only briefly, is permissible on the basis of probable cause or, the Court has hinted in dictum, "on less than probable cause" if it is "under judicial supervision."[54] The implication — it currently is only that — is that legislatures or courts are permitted to develop procedures for special "fingerprint search warrants," grounded on reasonable suspicion. Some courts have approved such warrants, even without legislation.[55]

Also, the Court has indicated that there is support in its prior cases for the view that a brief detention of a suspect "in the field" for fingerprinting is permissible if: (1) the belief that the suspect has committed a crime meets the reasonable-suspicion standard; (2) there is a reasonable basis for believing that fingerprinting will establish or negate the suspect's connection with that crime; and (3), the fingerprinting is conducted "with dispatch."[56]

§ 98 Weapons Searches: Of Persons[57]

[A] Permissibility

At the conclusion of the majority opinion in *Terry*, Chief Justice Warren stated the conditions under which a protective weapons-search is permissible:

> where a police officer observes unusual conduct which leads him reasonably to conclude that . . . criminal activity may be afoot and that the persons with whom he is dealing may be armed and presently dangerous, *where in the course of investigating this behavior he . . . makes reasonable inquiries,* and where nothing in the initial stages of the encounter serves to dispel his reasonable fear for his own or others' safety. . . .[58]

The implication of this remark, in particular the italicized words, is that an officer must use the least intrusive means to protect himself when he detains a suspect: he must investigate first, and search only if necessary.

In contrast, Justice Harlan argued in his concurrence that the right to conduct a weapons-search of a detained suspect is immediate and automatic if the reason for the seizure is that the officer believes that a violent crime is afoot, as was the case in *Terry*. In other words, assuming that the officer was justified in seizing the suspect for investigation of a violent crime, the officer should not be required to jeopardize himself further by questioning the suspect before he conducts a weapons-search.

---

[53] Davis v. Mississippi, 394 U.S. 721, 727 (1969).

[54] Hayes v. Florida, 470 U.S. at 816-17.

[55] *E.g.*, In re Fingerprinting of M.B., 125 N.J.Super. 115, 309 A.2d 3 (1973).

[56] Hayes v. Florida, 470 U.S. at 817.

[57] *See generally* 3 W. Lafave, at § 9.4(a)-(d).

[58] Emphasis added.

Justice Harlan's approach makes sense. *Terry* properly rejects any bright-line rule that would permit the police to frisk all persons lawfully seized, even those suspected of non-violent crimes.[59] But, where there exists reasonable, individualized suspicion that the suspect is armed and presently dangerous, which will exist if the basis for the seizure was that a violent crime is afoot, the police should not be obligated to give the suspect a chance to dissuade them of the need to conduct the weapons-search.

The Court's treatment of the facts in *Adams v. Williams*[60] suggests that Justice Harlan's view of the subject is now accepted. In *Williams*, an officer received information that *D* was sitting in a parked car, carrying narcotics, with a handgun concealed at his waist. The officer confronted *D*, after which he seized the gun, without asking the suspect any questions that might have dispelled his concern. The Court upheld the officer's actions.

[B] Method

[1] Pat-Down ("Frisk")

Terry did not mandate a particular weapons-search procedure, although it approved the one conducted in that case, which consisted of a careful pat-down of the exterior of the suspect's clothing, and a subsequent search of the area in which the weapon was felt. In contrast, in *Sibron v. New York*,[61] a companion case to *Terry*, the Court disapproved a search in which the officer thrust his hand into the suspect's pocket without first frisking him.

Notwithstanding *Sibron*, a pat-down is not always a prerequisite to a valid weapons-search. Rather obviously, if a suspect whom the officer has reason to believe is armed and presently dangerous suddenly moves his hand into a pocket or under a piece of clothing that might contain a weapon, the officer need not jeopardize himself by conducting a pat-down.[62]

The facts in *Adams v. Williams*[63] provide another example of a valid weapons-search that was not preceded by a pat-down. In *Williams*, an officer who had been informed that *D* was in his parked car with a weapon concealed at his waist, asked *D* to open his car door; when *D* opened his window instead, the officer reached into the car and, without frisking *D*, seized the gun. The Court, without discussion of the procedure, approved the officer's conduct.

Although an explanation by the Court would have been helpful, the officer's no-frisk approach can be justified on the ground that a pat-down would have been

---

[59] A suspect lawfully seized for investigation of a non-violent crime may not be searched for weapons unless circumstances exist in the particular case to justify the officer's belief that the suspect might be armed and presently dangerous. For example, a search might be justified if the suspect, without explanation, made a sudden movement toward a pocket large enough to contain a weapon, or if the officer observed a bulge in the suspect's clothing that is characteristic of a weapon. *E.g.*, Pennsylvania v. Mimms, 434 U.S. 106 (1977) (the observation by an officer of a bulge in a jacket worn by a motorist stopped for an expired license plate justified a weapons-search).

[60] 407 U.S. 143 (1972).

[61] 392 U.S. 40 (1968).

[62] 3 W.LaFave, § 9.4(b) at 518.

[63] 407 U.S. 143 (1972).

difficult, even dangerous, under the circumstances: *D* was seated in the car; the door was shut, notwithstanding the officer's request that he open it; if the officer had sought to frisk *D*, he would have been in a physically awkward and, therefore, vulnerable position. As the officer reached only to the spot in which he had been told that the gun was concealed, his actions were reasonable.

[2] After the Pat-Down

If the pat-down dispels the officer's suspicion that the suspect is armed, no further search is justifiable under the *Terry* principle.

If the officer feels an object during the pat-down, no further search is justified unless he has reason to believe that the object is a weapon. The Supreme Court has not stated how certain the officer must be that the object is a weapon, but the reasonable-suspicion standard would seem to be appropriate. Thus, it would rarely be justifiable for an officer to conduct a further search if he feels only soft objects during the frisk.

If the officer feels a hard object that he reasonably believes is a weapon, the officer may put his hand under the clothing where the object was felt. If the object he pulls out is a container, he may feel the container to see if it might contain a weapon inside.

If his fears regarding the container are not reasonably dispelled by its size, weight, and from touching it, the officer may, at a minimum, retain possession of the container so as to separate the suspect from any weapon that might be inside. Probably, he may open the container and look inside, on the ground "that this is simply a continuation, in a sense, of the frisk of the person and thus may be carried out on the same terms." [64]

If evidence of a crime is found during a lawful weapons-search, the officer may seize the evidence pursuant to the plain-view doctrine, and it is admissible against the suspect in any criminal trial.

§ 99 Weapons Searches: Of Automobiles [65]

In a controversial [66] extension of the *Terry* principle, the Supreme Court ruled in *Michigan v. Long* [67] that, in some circumstances, the police may conduct a weapons-search of the passenger compartment of an automobile stopped during a lawful investigation of its driver. That is, as the Court has subsequently explained the case, "[i]n a sense, *Long* authorize[s] a 'frisk' of [portions of] an automobile for weapons." [68]

In *Long*, police officers in a rural area of Michigan observed *D*, at night, drive his car erratically, at an excessive rate of speed, and swerve into a ditch. The

---

[64] 3 W. LaFave, § 9.4(d) at 526.

[65] *See generally* 3 W. LaFave, at § 9.4(e).

[66] *See, e.g., id*; People v. Torres, 74 N.Y.2d 224, 543 N.E.2d 61, 544 N.Y.S.2d 796 (1989) (rejecting *Long* on the basis of the state constitution).

[67] 463 U.S. 1032 (1983).

[68] Maryland v. Buie, 110 S.Ct. 1093, 1097 (1990).

officers stopped to investigate. As they did, *D* got out of his car and, leaving the door open, met the officers at the rear of the automobile. *D* appeared to be intoxicated.

The officers requested to see *D*'s vehicle registration. After repeated requests, and no response, *D* began to walk towards the open door of the car. The officers followed him, and observed a hunting knife on the floor of the driver's side of the car. At that point, the officers frisked *D*, but they felt no weapon.

The officers then shone a light inside the car to look for other weapons. They noticed something, although they could not identify it, protruding from under the armrest on the front seat. One officer entered the car, lifted the armrest, and found an open pouch containing marijuana. *D* was arrested for possession of the contraband.

The Court upheld the officers' actions. It observed that investigative detentions of persons in cars "are especially fraught with danger to police officers," and that the passenger compartment of a car is within the immediate control of a suspect. Therefore, it reasoned, if a weapon is inside a car, it represents a danger to the police.

Although this reasoning might suggest that the police, after *Long*, may conduct a weapons-search of the passenger compartment of any automobile they lawfully stop, the holding of *Long* is narrower than this. The Court stated that "the search of the passenger compartment of an automobile, limited to those areas in which a weapon may be placed or hidden, is permissible if the police officer possesses a reasonable belief . . . that the suspect is dangerous and the suspect may gain immediate control of weapons."

The Court further stressed that its "decision does not mean that the police may conduct automobile searches whenever they conduct an investigative stop." Instead, it pointed to specific, articulable facts that it believed justified the officers in this case to enter the car to search for weapons.

Unfortunately, the facts to which the Court pointed were remarkably weak. If they are used as a mode of comparison to cases that arise in the future, a court inclined to permit a weapons-search of the passenger compartment of a car could easily justify one. The facts to which the Court pointed were: (1) it was late at night; (2) the area was rural; (3) *D* appeared to be intoxicated; (4) the officers observed a hunting knife in the vehicle; and (5) *D* intended to re-enter the vehicle.

The Court did not explain why the hour of the night was relevant, nor why the rural nature of the area was an aggravating, rather than an ordinary or even mitigating, feature. Furthermore, *D* was suspected of drunk driving, not of an armed crime; as Justice Brennan pointed out in dissent, "a drunk driver is indeed dangerous while driving, but not while stopped on the roadside by the police."

The fact that a knife was observed in the automobile, the strongest point in favor of the search, does not demonstrate that *D* was "presently dangerous," in light of the fact that the area in which the investigation occurred was one commonly frequented by lawful hunters.[69] As for the fact that D appeared to be re-entering

---

[69] In so far as the knife was concerned, *D* was probably more dangerous to wildlife than to the police.

the vehicle, the police could have ordered him to move away from the car, a less intrusive procedure than to search the entire passenger compartment of the automobile.[70]

§ 100   Protective Sweeps of Residences

The Supreme Court ruled in *Maryland v. Buie*[71] that as an incident to an arrest of a person in a residence, the police may automatically — *i.e.*, without probable cause or reasonable suspicion — conduct a protective sweep of "spaces immediately adjoining the place of arrest."[72] As explained by the Court, a "protective sweep" of a residence "is a quick and limited search of a premises, incident to an arrest and conducted to protect the safety of police officers or others. It is narrowly confined to a cursory visual inspection of those places in which a person might be hiding."

Beyond the automatic search of the "spaces immediately adjoining the place of arrest," the *Buie* Court held that the police may conduct a warrantless protective sweep of other parts of the premises in which the arrest occurs, but only if there exists *Terry*-level reasonable suspicion "that the area [to be] swept harbor[s] an individual posing a danger to the officer or others."

For example, in *Buie*, six or seven officers entered *D*'s house with a warrant to arrest him for a crime allegedly committed by *D* and *X*. When they entered, they discovered a basement; standing on the first floor, an officer ordered anyone in the basement to come out. Eventually, *D* emerged and was arrested and hand-cuffed on the first floor. Thereafter, an officer went into the basement to see if anyone else was present. Although he found no one, he discovered evidence related to the crime, which he seized. The Court stated that the officer acted properly in entering the basement if there were facts that warranted him in suspecting that a person posing a danger to him or others was downstairs.[73]

The Court did not determine what procedures the police may or must follow if they discover a person during a lawful protective sweep, *i.e.*, whether they may frisk such a person automatically or may do so only if they have reasonable grounds to believe that he is armed and presently dangerous. Language in *Buie* strongly suggests, however, that a pat-down is not permitted unless the officers have reasonable suspicion to justify the frisk.

---

[70] Of course, if *D* had not been arrested, he eventually would have returned to the car to leave the scene, and thus could have reached the knife and any other weapon in the car. However, if he were not under arrest and no longer in temporary custody, there would have been little incentive for *D* to use a weapon against the officers.

[71] 110 S.Ct. 1093 (1990).

[72] *See* § 67[A] *supra.*

[73] The Court remanded the case to the state court to determine whether reasonable suspicion existed in this case. In a concurrence, Justice Stevens doubted that the police could justify the protective sweep. He argued that the police may only conduct a sweep if it will reduce the risk of harm to themselves or others: "in short, the search must be protective." He described the officer's decision to enter the basement after *D* was arrested as "a surprising choice for an officer, worried about safety." On remand, however, the Maryland court ruled that the officers had reasonable suspicion to conduct the sweep. *Buie v. State*, 320 Md. 696, 580 A.2d 167 (1990).

Buie noted that *Terry* "did not adopt a bright-line rule authorizing frisks for weapons in all confrontational encounters," but instead required "reasonable, individualized suspicion before a frisk for weapons can be conducted." It also described *Ybarra v. Illinois*[74] as an "analogous case." In *Ybarra*, the Court held that police officers, armed with a warrant to search commercial premises for drugs, were not permitted to frisk customers on the scene without individualized suspicion that those being frisked were armed and presently dangerous.

§ 101   *Terry*-Level Seizures of Property

In *United States v. Place*,[75] federal officers had advance information that *D* would disembark from an airplane with luggage that might contain narcotics. When *D* arrived, the officers seized his luggage and, ninety minutes later, subjected it to a "non-search"[76] sniff by a trained narcotics-detection dog. The dog's response confirmed the officers' suspicions, after which they applied for and received a warrant to search the suitcase.

The Supreme Court held that police officers may temporarily detain luggage on the basis of reasonable suspicion that it contains narcotics, in order to investigate the circumstances that aroused their suspicion. In short, *Terry* principles apply to seizures of property, and not simply of persons. However, the Court concluded that the hour-and-a-half detention in this case was excessive, and therefore disapproved the police action.

In reaching its conclusion, the Court applied the *Terry-Camara* balancing test. It determined that the government's interest in seizing the personal property was substantial, but it found that it was outweighed by *D*'s Fourth Amendment interests. Nonetheless, the Court's reasoning in rejecting the seizure in this case was narrow.

A critical aspect of the case was that *D*'s property was seized from his "immediate custody and control," rather than after possession had been voluntarily relinquished to another.[77] Therefore, the seizure not only intruded upon *D*'s possessory interest in his property but also on his "liberty interest in proceeding with his itinerary," since a person will ordinarily not feel free to leave an airport without his personal belongings. Consequently, the Court treated the seizure of the property as if it included a seizure of *D* himself.

Under these circumstances, the Court concluded that the ninety-minute detention was excessive. The justices noted the importance of brevity in *Terry* cases, and the fact that the police did not diligently pursue their investigation in this case. With their prior knowledge that *D* would be arriving with suspicious luggage, the

---

[74] 444 U.S. 85 (1979). *See* § 54[C][1] *supra.*

[75] 462 U.S. 696 (1983).

[76] *See* § 36[A] *supra.*

[77] *E.g.,* United States v. Van Leeuwen, 397 U.S. 249 (1970) (29-hour investigatory seizure of packages by postal authorities, based on reasonable suspicion, was upheld; the case involved no significant privacy intrusion because *D* had placed the packages in the mail, they were not opened, and a warrant was secured before they were due to reach their destination).

Court felt that the officers should have brought the trained dog to the scene in advance of *D*'s arrival.

§ 102 Suspicionless *Terry*-Level Seizures[78]

Terry approved a temporary detention of a suspect, based on reasonable suspicion that he was about to commit a serious crime. The Court justified the seizure on less than probable cause by applying a "reasonableness" test, in which it balanced the government's interest in crime prevention against the suspect's interest in personal security.

A question not posed in *Terry*, but which follows from it, is this: Are there circumstances in which a brief *Terry*-level seizure is reasonable, even in the absence of reasonable suspicion, in view of the government's interest in law enforcement?

The Supreme Court has considered the question several times. In *United States v. Martinez-Fuerte*,[79] *D* was stopped at a permanent Border Patrol checkpoint, 66 miles north of the Mexican border, as part of the government's effort to prevent the entry into the country of illegal aliens. The patrol agents had no basis for believing that *D* or his passengers were involved in any criminal activities.

As discussed in the next chapter,[80] the Supreme Court upheld the suspicionless seizure. The decision, however, was based in great part on the special features of the case: the right of a sovereign to protect its borders; the large number of persons seeking illegal entry into the United States; and the "formidable" law enforcement problems in interdicting the flow of illegal entrants from Mexico. For these reasons, the case was originally interpreted by many observers as having little significance outside the "special need" circumstances of the case.

In *Delaware v. Prouse*,[81] the Supreme Court disallowed a random, suspicionless seizure of a motorist who was stopped by a highway patrol officer as part of a license and car-registration check. According to the Court, the officer "was not acting pursuant to any standards, guidelines, or procedures pertaining to document spot checks, promulgated either by his department [or the state]." In rejecting the seizure, the Court held that:

> except in those situations in which there is at least articulable and reasonable suspicion that a motorist is unlicensed or that an automobile is not registered, or that either the vehicle or the occupant is otherwise subject to seizure for violation of the law, stopping an automobile and detaining the driver in order to check his driver's license and the registration of the automobile are unreasonable under the Fourth Amendment.

However, the Court did not rule out the possibility that suspicionless license and vehicle inspections might be allowed. In dictum, it stated that "[t]his holding does not preclude [a state] . . . from developing methods for spot checks that are

---

[78] *See generally* 3 W.LaFave, at § 9.5(b), and 4 W. LaFave, at § 10.8(d).
[79] 428 U.S. 543 (1976).
[80] *See* § 106[B] *infra.*
[81] 440 U.S. 648 (1979).

less intrusive or that do not involve the unconstrained exercise of discretion." It inferred that routine checks might be permitted if safeguards were set up to assure that "persons in automobiles on public roadways [do] not for that reason alone have their travel and privacy interfered with at the unbridled discretion of police officers." According to *Prouse*, "[q]uestioning of all oncoming traffic at roadblock-type stops is one possible alternative."

Shortly after *Prouse* was decided, the Court again hinted that suspicionless seizures of persons might be permissible under limited circumstances. In *Brown v. Texas*,[82] the police stopped *D* in an alley and requested identification because he "looked suspicious" and had not been seen in the area before. The Court disapproved of the seizure because it was not based on reasonable suspicion.

In an opinion authored by Chief Justice Burger, the Court articulated a three-prong test for determining whether a *Terry*-level seizure of a person is reasonable: "Consideration of the constitutionality of such seizures involves a weighing of [1] the gravity of the public concerns served by the seizure, [2] the degree to which the seizure advances the public interest, and [3] the severity of the interference with individual liberty."

The Court stated that a "central concern in balancing these competing considerations" is "to assure that an individual's reasonable expectations of privacy is not subject to arbitrary invasions solely at the unfettered discretion of officers in the field." In order to prevent such discretion, the Court stated that a seizure of a person must be based on individualized reasonable suspicion "or . . . be carried out pursuant to a plan embodying explicit, neutral limitations on the conduct of individual officers."

The dictum in *Prouse* and *Brown* bore fruit more than a decade later in *Michigan Dept. of State Police v. Sitz*.[83] In *Sitz*, state police devised guidelines for setting up and conducting highway sobriety checkpoints. In the one implementation of the state's procedures, 126 vehicles were stopped at the checkpoint, and the drivers were briefly examined for signs of intoxication. On average, this detention took 25 seconds. Two drivers who appeared to be intoxicated were required to move out of the traffic flow, to another point where a second officer could check their licenses and conduct sobriety tests. One of these drivers was arrested. Another motorist, who attempted to break through the checkpoint, was also arrested.

The state courts ruled that the sobriety checkpoint was unconstitutional. Applying the three-prong test articulated in *Brown v. Texas*, they held that although the state's interest in curbing drunken driving was "grave and legitimate," the checkpoint program was "ineffective" and, therefore, did not significantly further the state's interest. The state courts also determined that, although the objective intrusion on individual liberty was minimal, the "subjective intrusion" was substantial, because the checkpoints generated fear and surprise among motorists.

The Supreme Court disagreed with the lower courts' analysis. In an opinion authored by Chief Justice Rehnquist, it held, 6-3, that the state's use of the

---

[82] 443 U.S. 47 (1979).
[83] 110 S.Ct. 2481 (1990).

highway sobriety checkpoint did not violate the Fourth Amendment, insofar as it pertained to the initial stop and associated preliminary questioning and observation of all motorists. The Court did not address the constitutionality of the detention of motorists for more extensive field sobriety tests, which it stated "may require satisfaction of an individualized suspicion standard."

As the state courts did, the Supreme Court applied the *Brown* three-prong test. It stated that "[n]o one can seriously dispute the magnitude of the drunken driving problem or the States' interest in eradicating it." On the other scale, the Court described the intrusion on motorists' security as "slight." The majority analogized the sobriety checkpoint to the fixed interior-border checkpoints set up to detect illegal aliens approved in *Martinez-Fuerte*. It stated that it saw "virtually no difference between the levels of intrusion on law-abiding motorists from brief stops necessary to the effectuation of these two types of checkpoints. . . ."

The majority also discounted the state court's finding that the checkpoint was an ineffective way to combat drunken driving. It explained that this prong of the *Brown* test "was not meant to transfer from politically accountable officials to the courts the decision as to which among reasonable alternative law enforcement techniques should be employed to deal with a serious public danger." In any case, the Court was satisfied that the approximately one-percent arrest rate arising from the procedure demonstrated its effectiveness.

In dissent, Justice Stevens, who was joined by Justices Brennan and Marshall, contended that:

> [t]he Court overvalues the law enforcement interest in using sobriety checkpoints, undervalues the citizen's interest in freedom from random, unannounced investigatory seizures, and mistakenly assumes that there is "virtually no difference" between a routine stop at a permanent, fixed checkpoint and a surprise stop at a sobriety checkpoint.

Justice Stevens stated that the element of surprise, and thus the subjective intrusion on the security of motorists, is the "most obvious distinction" between a highway sobriety checkpoint and the suspicionless interior-border stops approved in *Martinez-Fuerte*. In the latter case, the checkpoint site was known to all drivers because of its fixed nature, whereas the procedures implemented in the present case called for roving checkpoints.[84] Furthermore, in *Martinez-Fuerte*, many of the stops occurred during the daytime; in contrast, sobriety checkpoints are usually set up at nighttime, when fear is more easily generated.

The dissent also criticized the majority's treatment of the public-interest factor. Justice Stevens accused the majority of "tampering with the scales of justice" by "plac[ing] a heavy thumb on the law enforcement interest by looking only at gross receipts instead of net benefits." He pointed out that the evidence in the case indicated that the checkpoint resulted in an arrest rate of less than one percent of the motorists detained, and that "there is absolutely no evidence that this figure represents an increase over the number of arrests that would have been made by using the same law enforcement resources in conventional patrols."

---

[84] In the border-search context, the Supreme Court had previously drawn this distinction, permitting suspicionless seizures at fixed checkpoints, but disapproving of them as part of roving border patrols. *See* § 106 *infra*.

Justice Stevens concluded that the case was "driven by nothing more than symbolic state action — an insufficient justification for an otherwise unreasonable program of random seizures." He accused the majority of being "transfixed by the wrong symbol — the illusory prospect of punishing countless intoxicated motorists — when it should keep its eyes on the road plainly marked by the Constitution."

"SPECIAL GOVERNMENTAL NEED" (FORMERLY, "ADMINISTRATIVE") SEARCHES

§ 103 "Special Governmental Needs" Exception: In General[1]

An increasingly significant exception to the Fourth Amendment rule that searches and seizures are unreasonable if they are not authorized by a warrant, supported by probable cause, is the so–called "special governmental needs" — or, formerly, "administrative search" — exception.

In general, a search or seizure falls within this category when "special needs, beyond the normal need for law enforcement, make the warrant and[/or] probable–cause requirement[s] impracticable."[2] In reality, this category consists of various independent special–need exceptions, some of which are considered below.[3]

The distinguishing feature of this exception, as the quoted statement above would suggest, is that it applies to a search (or, as it is sometimes termed, "inspection") or seizure conducted primarily for reasons unrelated to the investigation and prosecution of criminal activity. As a consequence, those who conduct the search often are not police officers, and those subjected to the search often are not criminal suspects.

A corollary of this feature is that in resolving Fourth Amendment cases in this field "the Court [has] one of its rare opportunities to hear face–to–face, as Fourth Amendment claimants, those law–abiding citizens for whose ultimate benefits the constitutional restraints on public power were primarily intended."[4] The remarkable irony in this is that, as seen in this chapter, the Court has been inclined to require ordinary, law–abiding persons to open up their homes, businesses, papers, effects, and bodies to greater scrutiny than is required of criminal suspects.[5]

As will be seen, however, the line between a "special need" search and an ordinary one is thin and getting thinner. Furthermore, because evidence of a crime, if discovered during a lawful special–need search, is admissible in a

---

[1] *See generally* Schulhofer, *On the Fourth Amendment Rights of the Law–Abiding Public*, 1989 Sup. Ct. Rev. 87.

[2] Griffin v. Wisconsin, 483 U.S. 868, 872 (1987) (*quoting* New Jersey v. T.L.O., 469 U.S. 325, 351 (1985) (Blackmun, J., concurring)).

[3] *See also* chapter 16 (inventory searches) *supra*. For discussion of "special governmental needs" not covered in this treatise, *see* 3–4 W. LaFave, at §§ 10.3 (searches of: homes of welfare recipients; government workplaces; mail; soldiers); 10.6 (airport searches); 10.7 (searches of: courthouses; jails; prisons; military installations); 10.9 (searches of prisoners); 10.10 (searches of: parolees; probationers).

[4] Schulhofer, n. 1 *supra*, at 88.

[5] *Id.* at 89.

criminal trial, a significant risk exists that a special–governmental–need search will "give rise to an inference of pretext, or otherwise impugn the administrative nature of the . . . program."[6] To date the Court has not seriously wrestled with the pretext issue.[7]

§ 104 Administrative-Code Searches[8]

Modern "special governmental needs" law begins with the Supreme Court's decisions in *Camara v. Superior Court*[9] and *See v. City of Seattle*,[10] the so–called "administrative search" cases.

Camara involved the attempt of a municipal employee of the Department of Public Health to enter *D*'s apartment without a warrant or consent in order to conduct a routine inspection of the building for possible violations of the city's housing code. *See* involved a Fire Department employee's warrantless entry of a warehouse under a city ordinance that authorized entries into non–dwellings in order to inspect for fire code violations. In neither *Camara* nor *See* did the public employee who entered the building without a warrant possess probable cause to believe that code violations (much less, evidence of a crime) would be found in the inspected area.

Camara and *See* are important cases for two reasons. First, as discussed elsewhere in this text,[11] the Court in *Camara* developed a non–traditional version of "probable cause," applicable to administrative searches, that does not require individualized suspicion of criminal activity, and that requires only that the searches be "reasonable." To determine "reasonableness," *Camara* approved the use of a balancing test, in which "the need to search [is weighed] against the invasion which the search entails." This balancing test has come to be used generally in special–needs cases, and even in some traditional criminal investigations.[12]

Second, *Camara* and *See* considered the question of whether the Fourth Amendment warrant requirement applies to health and safety inspections of homes and commercial buildings. The Court held in both cases that, except in the event of emergency or consent, the right of entry to conduct an administrative inspection requires a search warrant, albeit one based on the administrative version of "probable cause." The Court noted that in the cases under consideration

---

[6] Skinner v. Railway Labor Executives Ass'n, 109 S.Ct. 1402, 1415 n.5 (1989).

[7] Regarding the issue of pretext generally, *see* § 74, *supra*.

[8] *See generally* 3 W. LaFave, at §§ 10.1–.2; Bacigal, *The Fourth Amendment in Flux: The Rise and Fall of Probable Cause*, 1979 U. Ill. L. Forum 763; LaFave, *Administrative Searches and the Fourth Amendment: The Camara and See Cases*, 1967 Sup. Ct. Rev. 1; Sundby, *A Return to Fourth Amendment Basics: Undoing the Mischief of Camara and Terry*, 72 Minn. L. Rev. 383 (1988); Note, *Administrative Search Warrants*, 58 Minn. L. Rev. 607 (1974).

[9] 387 U.S. 523 (1967).

[10] 387 U.S. 541 (1967).

[11] *See* § 47 *supra*.

[12] *See* § 94 *supra*.

the "burden of obtaining a warrant [was not] likely to frustrate the government purpose behind the search."

Post–*See* cases demonstrate that under certain circumstances, warrantless, non–exigent, non–consensual administrative inspections of commercial premises are permitted. As explained by the Court in *New York v. Burger*,[13] a "closely regulated" business[14] may be inspected without a warrant if three conditions are met. First, the regulatory scheme must advance a "substantial interest," such as to protect the health and safety of workers.[15]

Second, warrantless inspections must be necessary to further the regulatory scheme. This element is met if there is a serious possibility that a routine warrant requirement would allow the subjects of the regulations to conceal their violations of the rules, and thereby frustrate the administrative system.

Third, the ordinance or statute that permits warrantless inspections must, by its terms, provide an adequate substitute for the warrant, such as rules that limit the discretion of the inspectors, regarding the time, place, and scope of the search.

The line between administrative inspections and traditional criminal searches can be thin, as is evidenced by the facts, and the Court's treatment of them, in *Burger*. In that case, police officers entered *D*'s automobile junkyard, a closely regulated business, without a warrant or probable cause. Pursuant to an administrative statute that authorized them to do so, they requested to see *D*'s business license and "police book," *i.e.*, a record of automobiles and vehicle parts on the premises. *D* conceded that he had neither document, whereupon the officers searched the junkyard, found evidence of stolen vehicle parts, and arrested him for possession of stolen property.

The Court upheld the search. It did not consider it fatal to the scheme that police officers, rather than administrative inspectors, conducted the search. The justices observed that many communities lack the resources to hire inspectors to enforce non–penal regulations.

More troublingly, the Court considered it irrelevant to the Fourth Amendment aspects of the case that the regulations had the same ultimate purpose as criminal larceny laws, namely, to deter car thefts. The saving feature of the regulations was that they had "different subsidiary purposes and prescribe[d] different methods of addressing the problems." In this case, the Court concluded, the regulations established the conditions under which vehicle–dismantling businesses could be operated, including the institution of a requirement that the businesses be licensed and maintain certain records.

---

[13] 482 U.S. 691 (1987).

[14] A business is "closely regulated" if there is "a long tradition of close government supervision" of the business, Marshall v. Barlow's Inc. 436 U.S. 307 (1978), or, in the case of new and emerging industries, there is a "pervasiveness and regularity" of regulation. Donovan v. Dewey, 452 U.S. 594 (1981).

Examples of "closely regulated businesses" are: liquor dealers, Colonnade Catering Corp. v. United States, 397 U.S. 72 (1970); gun dealers, United States v. Biswell, 406 U.S. 311 (1972); mining companies, Donovan v. Dewey, *supra*; and automobile junkyards, New York v. Burger, 482 U.S. 691 (1987).

[15] Donovan v. Dewey, 452 U.S. 594 (1981) (mine workers).

Burger is also troubling because *D* admitted to the police officers when they arrived that he was in violation of the regulations. Therefore, there was no administrative reason to inspect the premises: the ensuing search was probably intended to uncover evidence of criminal activity.

§ 105 Fire-Scene Inspections[16]

When fire–fighters enter a home to extinguish a fire, they necessarily act without a search warrant. Typically, they remain in the building, and sometimes re–enter it later, in order to search for the causes of the fire. Sometimes these searches result in the discovery of evidence of arson or of other crimes.

The Fourth Amendment issue arising from these activities is this: Under what circumstances is an entry and inspection of a fire–damaged structure to determine the cause of the fire constitutional in the absence of a warrant supported by probable cause? Two cases, *Michigan v. Tyler*[17] and *Michigan v. Clifford*,[18] provide the Supreme Court's answer to this question in relation to private homes.

First, a person maintains a reasonable expectation of privacy in her fire–damaged home, unless the fire is "so devastating that no reasonable privacy interests remain in the ash and ruins."[19]

Second, a fire–fighter may enter a structure to put out the fire and remain there "for a reasonable time" to investigate its cause without a warrant.[20] The warrant-less entry, of course, is justified on the basis of the exigency of the situation. It is constitutionally reasonable for the fire–fighter to remain inside, in order to fulfill her related duty to find the cause of the fire.[21]

Third, a re–entry of a home by a member of the fire department ordinarily requires a warrant. The nature of the warrant depends on the purpose of the entry. If the "primary object" is to gather evidence of criminal conduct, a traditional search warrant, supported by traditional probable cause, is required. If the purpose is to determine the origin of the fire, an administrative search warrant suffices.[22]

Fourth, and notwithstanding the last point, a majority of the members of the Court apparently would allow an administrative inspection without a warrant,

---

[16] *See generally*, 3 W. LaFave, at § 10.4.

[17] 436 U.S. 499 (1978).

[18] 464 U.S. 287, *reh'g denied*, 465 U.S. 1084 (1984).

[19] *Id.* at 292.

[20] *Tyler*, 436 U.S. at 511.

[21] The fact that a fire–fighter leaves the building does not in itself preclude a finding that a subsequent warrantless re–entry falls within the remain-inside rule. In *Tyler*, for example, after the fire was put out at approximately 4:00 a.m., the fire–fighters left the premises because of poor visibility, and returned four hours later in order to search for the cause of the fire. The Court treated the latter investigation as a continuation of the original entry, as if the fire–fighters had stayed in the house until daylight arrived.

[22] *Clifford*, 464 U.S. at 294. To secure such a warrant, fire investigators need only show that a fire of undetermined origin occurred, that the scope of the proposed inspection is reasonable, that they "will not intrude unnecessarily on the fire victim's privacy, and that the search will be executed at a reasonable and convenient time."

even in the absence of consent, if reasonable efforts are made to give the fire victim notice of the planned entry.[23]

§ 106   International Border Searches and Seizures[24]

[A]   At the Border

People may be stopped (seized) at the international border or its functional equivalent (*e.g.*, at an airport where an international flight arrives), and they and their belongings may be searched, without a warrant and in the absence of any suspicion of wrongdoing, "pursuant to the long–standing right of the sovereign to protect itself"[25] from the entry of persons or objects dangerous to the nation. In short, such warrantless, suspicionless searches and seizures are "reasonable simply by virtue of the fact that they occur at the border."[26]

Furthermore, a person lawfully stopped at the border may be detained further, beyond the scope of a routine customs search, if the officers have reasonable suspicion of criminal activity. For example, in *United States v. Montoya de Hernandez*,[27] in an opinion described by one scholar as "at best, a most distressing one,"[28] the Court approved a 24–hour detention of *D*, a woman who officers reasonably suspected of having swallowed balloons containing heroin in order to avoid detection. After *D* refused to undergo an x–ray, she was compelled to remain in a small room furnished only with hard chairs and a table, until she defecated.

The Court concluded that the seizure was reasonable, although it conceded that *D* underwent a "long, uncomfortable, indeed humiliating" detention. It found that *D*'s interest in personal freedom was outweighed by the substantial national interest in preventing the importation of illegal drugs.

[B]   Near the Border

Border officers frequently stop cars near, but not at the functional equivalent of, the international border with Mexico, in order to question occupants regarding their citizenship, and/or to search the vehicles for contraband or aliens being smuggled into the country. The reasonableness of these seizures and searches depends in part on whether they arise at a fixed interior checkpoint or as the result of a "roving" border patrol.

Roving border patrols present significant Fourth Amendment concerns. First, the patrols occur without notice, often at night on seldom–traveled roads, and their approach is apt to frighten motorists. Therefore, the subjective intrusion,

---

[23] This conclusion is drawn from the fact that in *Clifford* only four justices would have required an administrative warrant, absent consent. Justice Stevens concurred in the judgment, but he stated that he would allow a non–consensual warrantless entry if constructive notice were given to the fire victim. The four dissenters favored warrantless entry even without such notice.

[24] *See generally* 3 W. LaFave, at § 10.05.

[25] United States v. Ramsey, 431 U.S. 606, 616 (1977).

[26] *Id.*

[27] 473 U.S. 531 (1985).

[28] 3 W. LaFave, § 10.5(b) at 720.

measured by the surprise and fear of lawful travelers, is significant. Second, roving border patrol agents have substantial discretion regarding whom to stop.

As a consequence, the Supreme Court has applied traditional Fourth Amendment standards to searches and seizures conducted by roving border–patrol agents. Specifically, the agents may not detain a person in a vehicle even briefly for questioning, *i.e.*, conduct a *Terry*-level investigatory seizure, in the absence of reasonable suspicion of illegal presence in the country;[29] nor may a vehicle be searched by officers in the absence of traditional probable cause.[30]

As with roving border patrols, warrantless vehicle searches at fixed interior checkpoints require probable cause or consent.[31] However, the Supreme Court held in *United States v. Martinez–Fuerte*[32] that vehicle occupants may be stopped at fixed checkpoints, and briefly detained in order to be questioned, without individualized suspicion of wrongdoing.

The Court in *Martinez–Fuerte* distinguished fixed checkpoints from roving border patrols on two grounds. First, the subjective intrusion on the security of lawful travelers "is appreciably less in the case of a [fixed] checkpoint stop." In the latter circumstance, "the motorist can see that other vehicles are being stopped, he can see visible signs of the officers' authority, and he is much less likely to be frightened or annoyed by the intrusion."[33]

Second, fixed checkpoints involve less discretionary enforcement activity than roving patrols. The location of the fixed checkpoint is not determined by the patrol officers, and they may only stop cars that pass through it.

The Court approved suspicionless seizures at the fixed checkpoints because it determined that the objective intrusion was minimal, in that travelers were stopped only momentarily, and that the subjective intrusion was less than in the case of roving border patrols. Balanced against these minimal intrusions was the "substantiality of the public interest" in preventing the entry of illegal aliens. Furthermore, evidence was presented that a reasonable-suspicion requirement was impractical and would "eliminate any deterrent to the conduct of well–disguised smuggling operations."

§ 107 Searches of Public School Students[34]

The Supreme Court held in *New Jersey v. T.L.O.*[35] that public school teachers and administrators may search students without a warrant if two conditions are

---

[29] United States v. Brignoni–Ponce, 422 U.S. 873 (1975). The Court indicated some of the factors that may justify a *Terry* seizure: information about recent illegal border crossings in the area; furtive behavior by the occupants of the vehicle; and evidence that the car has an "extraordinary number" of occupants. "Reasonable suspicion" may not be based solely on the fact that occupants of the vehicle appear to be of foreign ancestry.

[30] Almeida–Sanchez v. United States, 413 U.S. 266 (1973).

[31] United States v. Ortiz, 422 U.S. 891 (1975).

[32] 428 U.S. 543 (1976).

[33] *Martinez–Fuerte, quoting* United States v. Ortiz, 422 U.S. 891, 894–95 (1975).

[34] *See generally* 4 W. LaFave, at § 10.11.

[35] 469 U.S. 325 (1985).

met: (1) they possess reasonable suspicion that the search will result in evidence that "the student has violated or is violating either the law or the rules of the school"; and (2) once initiated, the search is "not . . . excessively intrusive in light of the age and sex of the student and the nature of the infraction."

In *T.L.O.*, two female students were caught smoking in a school lavatory, in violation of school rules. The students were brought to the vice–principal. When one of them, *D*, denied that she had been smoking, the administrator demanded her purse, opened it, and observed a package of cigarettes. He removed the cigarettes from the purse, and in doing so discovered cigarette paper, which is often used to make marijuana cigarettes. Based on that observation, he conducted a full search of *D*'s purse, during which he found other evidence that implicated her in the sale of marijuana. The evidence was handed over to the police and used in a juvenile court proceeding against her.

The Supreme Court held that the introduction of the evidence in the juvenile court proceeding was constitutional, even assuming, but without deciding, that the Fourth Amendment exclusionary rule applies to such proceedings.

In reaching this conclusion, the Court rejected the state's initial claim that the Fourth Amendment does not apply to the actions of school officials. This argument was based on the premise that teachers and administrators, because they act *in loco parentis*, are mere agents of the parents and, thus, are private parties whose actions fall outside the scope of the Fourth Amendment. The Court declared that this argument was "in tension with contemporary reality," and inconsistent with its prior rulings that school officials are subject to the commands of the Constitution.

The Court also ruled that public–school students retain a legitimate expectation of privacy in the private property that they bring to school. Conditions in public schools are not so dire, the Court observed, that it is ready to equate schools with prison cells, in which inmates retain no legitimate expectation of privacy in their surroundings.[36]

Nonetheless, the Court concluded that neither the warrant requirement nor probable cause applies to public–school searches. The Court disposed of the warrant requirement summarily. It stated that it is "unsuited to the school environment," as it would "unduly interfere with the maintenance of the swift and informal disciplinary proceedings needed in the schools."

Regarding probable cause, the Court observed that "[w]here a careful balancing of governmental and public interests suggests that the public interest is best served by a Fourth Amendment standard of reasonableness that stops short of probable cause, we have not hesitated to adopt such a standard." The Court found that this was such a case, and substituted for it the standard of "reasonable suspicion."[37]

---

[36] *See* Hudson v. Palmer, 468 U.S. 517 (1984).

[37] The Court rejected *D*'s additional claim that, even if the vice–principal had the right to open her purse, once he observed the cigarettes, and thus had an adequate basis to conclude that she was in violation of school rules, he had no justification for pulling the cigarettes out of the purse. Had the vice–principal not done so, *D* pointed out, he would not have discovered the cigarette paper, which, in turn, led him to the evidence of the marijuana sale. The Court stated that "[s]uch hairsplitting argumentation has no place in an inquiry addressed to the issue of reasonableness."

Justices Brennan and Marshall dissented. They agreed with the majority that school officials should not be required to obtain warrants to conduct searches, because "[a] teacher or principal could neither carry out essential teaching functions nor adequately protect students' safety if required to wait for a warrant before conducting a necessary search."

However, as the search in this case was full–scale in nature, they "emphatically" rejected the majority's decision to "cast aside" the probable–cause standard. They criticized the majority for "jettison[ing]" the latter standard, "the only standard that finds support in the text of the Fourth Amendment," and replacing it with the "Rohrschach [*sic*]–like 'balancing test.' "

Justice Stevens also dissented. In an opinion that the other two dissenters joined, he contended that a search by a school official should not be permitted at all if it is intended to "reveal evidence of . . . the most trivial school regulation." He complained that under the majority rule, "a search for curlers and sunglasses in order to enforce the school dress code is . . . just as important as a search for evidence of heroin addiction or violent gang activity."

§ 108 Drug and Alcohol Testing of Public Employees[38]

[A] Overview

In 1989, in *Skinner v. Railway Labor Executives' Association*[39] and *National Treasury Employees Union v. Von Raab*,[40] the Supreme Court upheld warrantless, suspicionless, blood, breath, and urine testing of some public employees, conducted pursuant to administrative regulations, in order to detect drug or alcohol usage.[41] The opinions in these cases do not suggest, however, that routine testing of any public employee for drug or alcohol use will inevitably be upheld.

Based on *Skinner* and *Von Raab*, various factors are important in determining whether such testing will be permitted. First, testing is likely to be more favorably treated by the courts if the employees are working in a job already pervasively regulated by the government.

Second, there should be a significant relationship between the employee's job responsibilities and the employer's concern about drug or alcohol use. In these cases, for example, the employees tested were in "safety–sensitive" occupations (railroad employees, in *Skinner*; Customs Service employees required to carry firearms, in *Von Raab*), or in other "sensitive" jobs (Customs Service employees applying for promotions to positions involving drug interdiction or the handling of classified materials, in *Von Raab*).

---

[38] *See generally* 3 W. LaFave, at §§ 10.2(f–1), 10.3(e); Schulhofer, n. 1 *supra*.

[39] 109 S.Ct. 1402 (1989).

[40] 489 U.S. 646 (1989).

[41] Ordinarily, evidence secured lawfully in a regulatory search may be introduced at trial in a criminal prosecution. However, in an intriguing footnote, the Court left "for another day" the issue of whether the "routine use" of the evidence of drug and alcohol tests in criminal prosecutions "would give rise to an inference of pretext, or otherwise impugn the administrative nature of the . . . program." *Skinner*, 109 S.Ct. at 1415 n.5.

Third, testing is more likely to be upheld if the regulations authorizing it remove most or all of the discretion of the employer in determining who will be tested and under what circumstances the testing will occur.

Fourth, it is preferable, although apparently not necessary, for the employer to provide empirical evidence of a substantial need for the particular testing program in question.

Fifth, scrupulous care must be taken to ensure that the dignity of employees is respected in the specimen collection process. This is particularly a matter of concern with urine testing.

[B] *Skinner* and *Von Raab*: Analysis

The Court in *Skinner* stated that blood, breath, and urine tests intrude on Fourth Amendment interests. Blood tests, because they involve intrusions beneath the skin, constitute a "search";[42] the subsequent chemical testing of the blood to obtain "physiological data" invades an individual's privacy interests still further. In cursory fashion, the Court also held that a breath test "implicates . . . concerns about bodily integrity" similar to blood testing. Urine collection, "which may in some cases involve visual or aural monitoring of the act of urination," is a "search" and, perhaps, also a "seizure."[43]

Notwithstanding the fact that the testing in *Skinner* and *Von Raab* constituted Fourth Amendment activity, the Court held that the tests in these cases fell within the special–governmental–needs exception to the warrant and probable–cause requirements of the Fourth Amendment.

In *Skinner*, the Court upheld regulations that in some cases required and in other cases merely permitted railroad companies to administer warrantless breath, urine, and blood tests to employees involved in railroad accidents or who had violated safety rules. The regulations were adopted as a response to detailed findings of the Federal Railroad Administration (F.R.A.), to the effect that drug or alcohol use by railroad employees was a causal factor in a significant number of accidents that had resulted in death or property damage, and that railroad companies are unable to detect on–the–job drug or alcohol use on the basis of visual observation.

The *Skinner* Court disposed of the warrant requirement on various grounds. First, it concluded that a warrant was not needed because the circumstances under which the testing was permitted were specifically set out in the regulations authorizing the tests: "[i]ndeed, in light of the standardized nature of the tests and the minimal discretion vested in those charged with administering the program, there [we]re virtually no facts for a neutral magistrate to evaluate."

Second, because evidence of ingestion of alcohol and drugs is eliminated from the body quickly, imposing a warrant requirement would have "significantly hinder[ed], and in many cases frustrat[ed], the objectives of the Government

---

[42] *See* Schmerber v. California, 384 U.S. 757 (1966).
[43] *Skinner* observed that a urine test "might also be characterized as a . . . seizure, since it may be viewed as a meaningful interference with the employee's possessory interest in his bodily fluids."

testing program." Finally, the Court considered it unreasonable to impose "unwieldy warrant procedures" on the railroads, who are unfamiliar with the intricacies of the system.

The Court disposed of the probable–cause requirement on the ground that the privacy interests implicated by the testing were minimal. It characterized as "not significant" the bodily intrusion occasioned by blood testing;[44] breath testing was treated as less intrusive still, because it does not involve physical penetration of the skin.

The Court was more troubled by the specter of urine testing. It conceded that the excretory function "traditionally [is] shielded by great privacy." Nevertheless, the Court was satisfied that the employees' privacy needs were satisfied in this case, because the regulations did not require the employees to be observed while they urinated, and the urine was collected "in a medical environment" by non–employer personnel.

Furthermore, and "more importantly" to the privacy issue, the Court found that the railroad employees' expectations of privacy regarding the testing were "diminished by reason of their participation in an industry that is regulated pervasively to ensure safety."

Weighed against the employees' "minimal" privacy interest in this case, was the government's "compelling" interest in suspicionless testing. In support of this proposition, the Court pointed to the accident findings and the conclusions of the F.R.A. that impaired employees generally are able to escape visual detection. Furthermore, the Court concluded that the suspicionless testing in this case was an effective way to deter violations of safety regulations, because the employees were aware that testing would take place "upon the occurrence of a triggering event, the timing of which no employee [could] predict with certainty" — a railroad accident.

Justices Marshall and Skinner dissented in *Skinner*. They agreed with the majority that the railroad had a right to take the blood and urine without a warrant. They argued, however, that a warrant, supported by probable cause, was needed to conduct the *subsequent* testing of the samples taken, because any drug or alcohol metabolites that might have been in the samples would not have been lost as the result of the delay. The dissenters also rejected the majority's contention that these "full–scale personal searches" were anything less than "highly intrusive."

The Court applied very similar reasoning in *Von Raab* to justify the routine, warrantless, suspicionless urine testing of United States Customs Service employees who were seeking transfer or promotion to positions directly involved in the interdiction of illegal drugs, the handling of classified materials, or which required the possession of a firearm.

---

[44] As the dissent observed, the Court reached this conclusion by wrenching prior language of the Court out of context. The majority cited Schmerber v. California, 384 U.S. 757 (1966), which *did* hold that blood testing, conducted in a reasonable manner, can be performed with "virtually no risk, trauma, or pain." However, prior to *Skinner*, the Court had stated that "[t]he intrusion [in *Schmerber*] implicated [the] most personal and deep–rooted expectations of privacy. . . ." Winston v. Lee, 470 U.S. 753, 760 (1985).

The Court justified the regulations on various grounds, including the need to reduce the risk of bribe–taking, mishandling of weapons, use of drugs by employees with ready access to contraband, and "unsympathetic" enforcement of the narcotics laws by persons whose mission it would be to interdict narcotics.

It is noteworthy, however, that the testing in this case was supported by only five members of the Court. Justice Scalia, who joined the majority opinion in *Skinner*, and Justice Stevens, who concurred in *Skinner*, dissented in *Von Raab*. Justice Scalia stated their reason for dissenting here: the Court in *Von Raab* failed to present "real evidence of a real problem that [would] be solved by urine testing of Customs Service employees." As he put it:

> [W]hat is absent in the Government's justifications — notably absent, revealingly absent, and as far as I am concerned dispositively absent — is the recitation of *even a single instance* in which any of the speculated horribles [of bribe–taking, poor aim, or unsympathetic law enforcement as the result of drug–usage] actually occurred.

The dissenters, per Justice Scalia, warned that "the impairment of individual liberties cannot be the means of making a point; that symbolism, even symbolism for so worthy a cause as the abolition of unlawful drugs, cannot validate an otherwise unreasonable search."

CHAPTER 20

FOURTH AMENDMENT: "STANDING"

§ 109 The Role of "Standing" in Fourth Amendment Law[1]

The Fourth Amendment guarantees "[t]he right of the people to be secure in their persons, houses, papers, and effects against unreasonable searches and seizures." This substantive right is enforced in part by the exclusionary rule,[2] which states that, in general, evidence secured in violation of the Fourth Amendment may not be admitted in a criminal trial.

It has long been the case, however, that nearly all claims to enforce constitutional rights may be raised only by those who have "standing" to assert them.[3] The Fourth Amendment is no exception: a claim of a Fourth Amendment violation and, therefore, a motion to exclude evidence seized as the result of the alleged violation,[4] may be raised only by "a victim of the search or seizure . . . as distinguished from one who claims prejudice only through the use of evidence gathered as a consequence of a search or seizure directed at someone else."[5]

In short, Fourth Amendment rights are personal. They may not be vicariously asserted.[6] The fact that *X* was the victim of an unreasonable search or seizure, during which evidence was seized that incriminates *D*, does not give *D* a right to have the evidence excluded at his criminal trial — even though the same evidence would be inadmissible against *X* — unless he can show that *his* Fourth Amendment rights were violated by the police action, *i.e.*, that he was a victim of the unconstitutional activity.

---

[1] *See generally* Coombs, *Shared Privacy and the Fourth Amendment, or The Rights of Relationships*, 75 Calif. L. Rev. 1593 (1987); Gutterman, *Fourth Amendment Privacy and Standing: "Wherever the Twain Shall Meet"*, 60 N.C. L. Rev. 1 (1981); Kuhns, *The Concept of Personal Aggrievement in Fourth Amendment Standing Cases*, 65 Iowa L. Rev. 493 (1980).

[2] *See generally* chapter 21 *infra*.

[3] However, "standing" is not required in some First Amendment cases. N.A.A.C.P. v. Button, 371 U.S. 415 (1963) (statute declared overly broad, although the overbreadth did not affect plaintiff's rights).

[4] A "person aggrieved" by a Fourth Amendment violation may make a pre–trial motion to have the seized property returned to him as well to exclude the evidence at his trial. *E.g.*, FRCP 41(e).

[5] Jones v. United States, 362 U.S. 257, 261 (1960), *overruled on other grounds*, United States v. Salvucci, 448 U.S. 83 (1980).

[6] Alderman v. United States, 394 U.S. 165, 174, *reh'g denied*, 394 U.S. 939 (1969).

§ 110 Rationale of the Standing Requirement

Professor Anthony Amsterdam once noted that there are two competing perspectives on the Fourth Amendment. One view, the "atomistic" perspective, is that the Fourth Amendment is "a collection of protections of atomistic spheres of interest of individual citizens."[7] That is, the Fourth Amendment protects isolated individuals ("atoms") from unreasonable searches and seizures.

The second view, the "regulatory" perspective, is that the Fourth Amendment functions "as a regulation of governmental conduct." In other words, the amendment is intended to safeguard the collective "people," as in "we, the people," from governmental overreaching.

As Fourth Amendment jurisprudence has developed, "standing" — based as it is on the premise that a person may only raise a Fourth Amendment challenge if he personally was a victim of unreasonable police activity — is based on the atomistic philosophy. In contrast, the exclusionary rule is regulatory in nature, in that its purpose is to deter police misconduct, so as to safeguard society as a whole.

Understood in this way, the standing requirement and the exclusionary rule act, at least in part, in opposition to each other. This is because evidence seized in violation of the Fourth Amendment is excluded at trial in order to deter police misconduct; but, the requirement of standing to raise a Fourth Amendment claim often undercuts this deterrence goal, as it limits the number of people ("atoms") who can bring the misconduct to the attention of the courts so that the exclusionary rule can be applied.

For example, consider *United States v. Payner.*[8] In *Payner*, Internal Revenue Service (I.R.S.) agents launched an investigation into the financial activities of United States citizens living in the Bahamas. As part of "Operation Trade Winds," the I.R.S. approved a plan in which a private investigator it hired illegally photographed the contents of a bank official's briefcase, which resulted in incriminating evidence against *D*, a target of the I.R.S. investigation. A district court found that the I.R.S. "affirmatively counsel[ed] its agents that the Fourth Amendment standing limitation permits them to purposefully conduct an unconstitutional search and seizure of one individual in order to obtain evidence against third parties."

Payner points up this problem: government agents purposely flaunted Fourth Amendment values by securing evidence against the suspects by invading the privacy of innocent people, knowing that the targets of their investigation would lack standing to object to the misconduct. From a regulatory perspective, this was a nearly perfect case for application of the exclusionary rule. But, the atomistic standing requirement frustrated that effort; indeed, it functioned as an incentive to the government to act unlawfully.

The Fourth Amendment standing requirement makes sense only if it is treated as a purposeful limitation on the goals of the exclusionary rule.[9] As explained more fully in the next chapter, the exclusionary rule is an expensive doctrine. In

---

[7] Amsterdam, at 367.

[8] 447 U.S. 727, *reh'g denied*, 448 U.S. 911 (1980).

[9] Kuhns, n. 1 *supra*, at 509–13.

the law's efforts to deter unreasonable searches and seizures, courts suppress reliable evidence — the fruits of the police misconduct — at criminal trials. The consequence of this is that guilty people are convicted less often than they would be if society were willing to use the wrongfully seized evidence.

The standing requirement constitutes the point at which society is no longer willing to bear the cost of the exclusionary rule: that is, it is unwilling to let guilty people go free unless they were the victims of the unreasonable conduct. The incremental deterrence value of extending standing to non–victims is arguably outweighed by the costs of such an approach.[10]

Even if the law of standing is justified on this ground, however, the question remains how narrowly or broadly courts ought to define the concept of a "victim" in the context of the standing requirement, because the term is not self–defining. In turn, the answer to this question depends on the resolution of two empirical questions: how expensive *really* is the exclusionary rule?; and to what extent does the standing requirement undermine the purposes of the exclusionary rule?

As discussed in the next chapter, the Supreme Court has become increasingly concerned about the costs of the exclusionary rule. At the same time, it does not believe that a narrow interpretation of the standing requirement appreciably undermines the justifiable goals of the exclusionary rule. Therefore, it is more difficult now to obtain standing to raise a Fourth Amendment claim than it was a few decades ago.

§ 111   Target Standing

Does a person have standing to raise a Fourth Amendment claim simply because he was the target of the search that resulted in the seizure of evidence against him? For example, suppose that the police enter X's house without a search warrant for the express purpose of seizing evidence belonging to D. May D — the target of the search — contest the police action, although it was X's privacy that was invaded?

A plausible regulatory argument might be made that D should have standing. Presumably, there would be a beneficial deterrent effect in a rule that informs the police that the target of their search will always have standing to challenge their conduct if they skirt the Fourth Amendment, even if the direct victim of their activity is another person.

Notwithstanding this argument, as well as language in some cases that appeared to make a point of the fact that the defendant was the target of the contested search,[11] the Supreme Court explicitly — and unanimously — rejected the doctrine of target standing in *Rakas v. Illinois.*[12]

---

[10] *See* Alderman v. United States, 394 U.S. at 174–75.

[11] *E.g.*, United States v. Jeffers, 342 U.S. 48, 52 (1951) (the search and seizure were "bound together by one sole purpose — to locate and seize the narcotics of the [defendant]"); Jones v. United States, 362 U.S. at 261 (describing a person with standing as one who is "a victim of a search or seizure, *one against whom the search was directed*") (emphasis added).

[12] 439 U.S. 128 (1978), *reh'g denied*, 439 U.S. 1122 (1979). Although there were four dissenters in *Rakas*, they agreed "[f]or the most part" with the majority's rejection of target standing.

The Court concluded that standing need not be granted to the target of a search, if he is not the immediate victim of the unreasonable conduct, in order to obtain the beneficial deterrent effect of the exclusionary rule. According to *Rakas*, an officer will be deterred from improperly intruding on *X*'s (the non–target's) privacy, even without target standing by *D*, because *X* will have ample motivation to raise his own Fourth Amendment claim; and, where *X* is not a party to a criminal prosecution, the officer still will be deterred because *X* may recover damages in a civil suit for violation of his privacy.

§ 112   Derivative Standing

In *McDonald v. United States*,[13] the Supreme Court reversed *D*'s conviction because evidence used against him had been seized in violation of the Fourth Amendment rights of *X*, his co–defendant. The Court reasoned that *X* had the right to have his property returned to him prior to trial as the result of the Fourth Amendment violation; therefore, the evidence would not have been in the government's hands to use against *D*.

Although *McDonald* did not speak in terms of "standing," lower courts interpreted the case to mean that so–called "derivative standing" exists: that is, a defendant has the right to raise a Fourth Amendment claim if the rights of any co–defendant or co–conspirator were violated.

The doctrine of derivative standing, if it ever existed at the Supreme Court level, was overruled *sub silentio* in *Wong Sun v. United States*,[14] when the Court held that evidence unconstitutionally seized from one defendant, James Toy, was nonetheless admissible against another defendant, Wong Sun, because the action against Toy invaded no Fourth Amendment right of Wong Sun.

The Court made the point explicit in *Alderman v. United States*,[15] when it stated that "[c]oconspirators and codefendants [are] . . . accorded no special standing." The Court concluded that the potential deterrent benefit of applying the exclusionary rule to co–defendants who did not otherwise have standing was outweighed by the costs of such a rule.

The Court's deterrence argument is compelling. Although it is difficult to prove such claims empirically, it is unlikely that police officers would act differently if they knew that the fruits of their unconstitutional conduct would be excluded in two cases rather than in only one.

§ 113   Automatic Standing

For a little more than a decade, the Supreme Court recognized the doctrine of "automatic standing." First announced in a unanimous opinion by Justice Felix Frankfurter in *Jones v. United States*,[16] the rule was that a defendant did not have

---

[13] 335 U.S. 451 (1948).

[14] 371 U.S. 471 (1963).

[15] 394 U.S. 165, *reh'g denied*, 394 U.S. 939 (1969).

[16] 362 U.S. 257 (1960), *overruled in* United States v. Salvucci, 448 U.S. 83 (1980).

to prove standing to raise a Fourth Amendment claim if possession of the evidence seized was a necessary element of the crime for which he was prosecuted.

For example, in *Jones*, federal agents seized narcotics belonging to *D* in a search of *X*'s apartment. *D* was prosecuted for possession of the narcotics. Under the automatic–standing rule announced in the case, *D* was allowed to contest the legality of the search of *X*'s apartment. In practical terms, this meant that *D* did not have to prove that the narcotics belonged to him, which would have been the usual basis for securing standing in such circumstances.[17]

Automatic standing was permitted for two reasons. First, in what was subsequently described as the "cornerstone" rationale of the *Jones* opinion,[18] the Court expressed concern about the dilemma confronting a defendant charged with a crime of possession who wished to contest a search: to prove standing to raise a Fourth Amendment claim he might have to testify in a pre–trial hearing that he owned or possessed the seized evidence, the very "facts the proof of which would tend, if indeed not be sufficient to convict him"; at the same time, lower courts had held that such incriminating testimony could lawfully be used against the defendant at his trial. The automatic–standing rule freed the defendant from that dilemma.

Second, the Court believed that a prosecutor should not "have the advantage of contradictory positions": namely, that *D* possessed the contraband in violation of the law, and yet that he lacked standing to contest the search because he did not have a possessory interest in the seized materials.

The Court abandoned the automatic–standing rule in *United States v. Salvucci*.[19] In *Salvucci*, the Court observed that the self–incrimination dilemma described in *Jones* was eliminated by the Court in *Simmons v. United States*.[20] In *Simmons*, the Court held that the testimony of a defendant in support of a Fourth Amendment motion to suppress evidence may not be used against him at trial, over his objection, on the issue of guilt.[21]

Salvucci disposed of the remaining justification for the automatic–standing rule — that prosecutors should not be permitted the advantage of contradictory claims — by stating that post–*Jones* "standing" decisions, in particular the Court's watershed opinion in *Rakas v. Illinois*,[22] demonstrated that there is nothing inherently self–contradictory about a prosecutor charging a defendant with possession of contraband and simultaneously maintaining that he was not the victim of an unconstitutional search.

This conclusion stems from the fact that, as discussed below, under *Rakas*, standing to contest a search requires that the person asserting the claim have had a reasonable expectation of privacy in the area searched at the time of the police

---

[17] *See* § 114 *infra.*

[18] Brown v. United States, 411 U.S. 223, 228 (1973).

[19] 448 U.S. 83 (1980).

[20] Simmons v. United States, 390 U.S. 377 (1968).

[21] *Salvucci* expressly left open the issue of whether the *Simmons* rule prevents the prosecutor from using the defendant's testimony at the suppression hearing to impeach his trial testimony.

[22] 439 U.S. 128, *reh'g denied*, 439 U.S. 1122 (1979). *See* § 115 *infra.*

action. Therefore, in light of *Rakas*, it is possible for a person to possess contraband and yet lack standing to object to the search that turned it up, if the contraband was seized from a place in which *D* lacked a legitimate privacy expectation.

§ 114 General Principles of Standing: Pre-*Rakas*

The substantive nature of the Fourth Amendment underwent substantial change in 1967 with the Supreme Court's landmark *Katz*[23] opinion. The doctrine of standing took a similarly significant turn in 1978 when the Court decided *Rakas v. Illinois*.[24] The implications of *Rakas* are discussed in the subsequent sections of this chapter.

Prior to *Rakas*, the Supreme Court handed down only twelve opinions that dealt with the scope of the doctrine of standing.[25] However, based on the Court's few opinions and lower court jurisprudence, the following summary of the pre-*Rakas* law is possible.

A defendant had standing to raise a Fourth Amendment claim if he: (1) owned or had a possessory interest in the premises searched;[26] (2) was legitimately on the premises at the time of the search;[27] (3) owned the property seized;[28] or (4) had lawful possession of the property seized, such as in the status of a bailee.[29] Automatic standing existed in limited circumstances.[30]

§ 115 General Principles of Standing: *Rakas v. Illinois*

Rakas v. Illinois[31] is the leading Supreme Court case in modern "standing" jurisprudence. It brought a new language and a different approach to the doctrine of standing. Under *Rakas*, the test for standing to contest a search — or what the Court described as the "capacity to claim the protection of the Fourth Amendment" — is "whether the person who claims the protection of the Amendment has a legitimate expectation of privacy in the invaded place."

In *Rakas*, police officers stopped an automobile on the road because it met the description of the vehicle used in a robbery that had occurred moments earlier. The three occupants of the automobile, including its owner who had been driving, were ordered out, after which the police searched the passenger compartment. Rifle shells were found in the locked glove compartment, and a sawed-off rifle was

---

[23] Katz v. United States, 389 U.S. 347 (1967).

[24] 439 U.S. 128 (1978), *reh'g denied*, 439 U.S. 1122 (1979).

[25] Kuhns, n. 1 *supra*, at 514 & n.143 (listing the cases, some of which did not use the term "standing," and some of which dealt only peripherally with the question).

[26] *See* Brown v. United States, 411 U.S. at 229.

[27] Jones v. United States, 362 U.S. 257 (1960), *overruled on other grounds in* United States v. Salvucci, 448 U.S. 83 (1980).

[28] *See* United States v. Jeffers, 342 U.S. 48 (1951).

[29] 4 W. LaFave, § 11.3(f) at 344.

[30] *See* § 113 *supra*.

[31] 439 U.S. 128 (1978), *reh'g denied*, 439 U.S. 1122 (1979).

found under the front passenger seat. After the search, the occupants were arrested.

D, a passenger, moved to suppress the rifle and the shells found in the car on the basis that the search was unlawful. As the Court pointed out various times in the opinion, *D* did not base his claim for standing on the ground that he had an ownership interest in the vehicle or in the property seized. Instead, his key[32] claim was that he was "legitimately on the premises" at the time of the search, a basis for standing previously authorized by the Court in *Jones v. United States*.[33]

By a 5–4 vote, the Court, per Justice Rehnquist, held that *D*'s motion to suppress the evidence on the basis of his status as a legitimate passenger in the car was properly denied by the trial court. In reaching this conclusion, the Court reaffirmed the basic principle that Fourth Amendment rights are personal in nature and that the amendment may be enforced only by those whose own rights were infringed. Furthermore, according to the Court:

> [It does not] serve[] any useful analytical purpose to consider this principle a matter of standing, distinct from the merits of a defendant's Fourth Amendment claim. . . . [T]he type of standing requirement discussed in [prior cases] . . . is more properly subsumed under substantive Fourth Amendment doctrine. . . . The inquiry under either approach is the same. But we think the better analysis forthrightly focuses on the extent of a particular defendant's rights under the Fourth Amendment rather than on any theoretically separate, but invariably intertwined concept of standing.[34]

In other words, the Court in *Rakas* believes that "standing," although conceptually a threshold issue, should be treated as merely a reiteration of the basic point that a person may not successfully challenge a search unless his own rights were violated. Therefore, instead of asking whether *D* has "standing" to challenge a search, it is now sufficient (indeed preferable) to ask the question: Were *D*'s Fourth Amendment rights (as distinguished from someone else's) violated by the police action?

The Court turned to the issue raised by the latter question. It concluded that *D* failed to prove that he had any legitimate expectation of privacy in the areas searched, namely, in the locked glove compartment and the area under the front passenger seat. According to the Court, "[l]ike the trunk of an automobile, these are areas in which a passenger *qua* passenger simply would not normally have a legitimate expectation of privacy." Therefore, *D* could not successfully claim the protections of the Fourth Amendment in this case.

Rakas abandoned the phrase "legitimately on the premises," coined in *Jones*, stating that it provided "too broad a gauge for measurement of Fourth Amendment rights." Under the language in *Jones*, Justice Rehnquist pointed out, a casual visitor to a house, who had never seen or been permitted to enter the basement, would have standing to contest a search that occurred there if the visitor happened

---

[32] *D* also alleged standing on the ground that he was the target of the search, a theory rejected by the Court. *See* § 111 *supra*.

[33] 362 U.S. 257 (1960), *overruled on other grounds in* United States v. Salvucci, 448 U.S. 83 (1980).

[34] *Rakas*, 439 U.S. at 138–39.

to be in the kitchen at the time. Yet, the Court said, such a person has no legitimate privacy expectation in the basement.

Likewise, a guest who enters the premises one minute before a search begins and leaves one minute after it ends would have standing to contest the search, yet such a person has no legitimate expectation of privacy in the house at all.**35** The Court pointed out, however, that "[t]his is not to say that such visitors could not contest the lawfulness of the seizure of evidence or the search if their own property were seized. . . ."**36**

Although the Court rejected *Jones*'s language, it did not reject the holding in that case. Instead, it sought to place the latter decision within the new, legitimate–expectation–of–privacy terms announced in *Rakas*. In *Rakas*, *D* was a mere passenger in the car driven by its owner. In contrast, the defendant in *Jones* was the sole occupant of his friend's apartment when the contested search occurred. He had a key to the premises, used it to admit himself to the apartment, had clothing in it, had slept on the premises "maybe a night," and had "complete dominion and control" (*Rakas*'s words) over the apartment, except *vis a vis* the absent host.

As *Rakas* analyzed *Jones*, the latter case stood "for the unremarkable proposition that a person can have a legally sufficient interest in a place other than his own home so that the Fourth Amendment protects him from unreasonable governmental intrusion into that place." As *Rakas* explained, "the holding in *Jones* can best be explained by the fact that Jones had a legitimate expectation of privacy in the premises he was using and therefore could claim the protection of the Fourth Amendment with respect to a governmental invasion of those premises. . . ."

Justice White wrote the dissenting opinion in *Rakas*. He warned that the Court had "declare[d] 'open season' on automobiles." Specifically, he interpreted the case to stand for the proposition that "a legitimate occupant of an automobile may not invoke the exclusionary rule and challenge a search of that vehicle unless he happens to own or have a possessory interest in it."

The dissent argued that the holding in *Rakas* would undercut the regulatory purpose of the exclusionary rule, as it would serve as an invitation to the police to search any automobile containing more than one person, on the ground that any evidence unlawfully found in it would probably be admissible against at least some of the occupants.

---

35 The Court's conclusion in this regard is unpersuasive. Why does the fortuity of the guest's recent arrival and imminent departure inevitably undermine his privacy expectation at the time of his presence? While a guest is legitimately inside a host's home, he should have as much of a right to expect that the police will not break in unlawfully as one whose presence is longer lasting. The key point is that the guest was on the premises with the host's approval, and that he was there — and, thus, suffered the invasion — at the time of the unlawful conduct.

36 However, the implication of this statement — that a casual visitor in a house may challenge a search or seizure on the premises if he asserts an interest in the property seized — apparently was rejected, at least in part, in Rawlings v. Kentucky, 448 U.S. 98 (1980). *See* § 116[D] *infra*.

The dissent objected to the Court's opinion on two other grounds. First, it criticized the majority for rejecting *Jones*'s legitimately–on–the–premises rule, which was relatively easy to apply by police and courts, and substituting for it a non–bright–line test ("legitimate expectation of privacy in the area searched"), which it predicted would present greater difficulties of application.[37]

Second, the dissent accused the Court of returning to pre–*Katz* property–rights distinctions, even as it denied that it was doing so. As the dissent viewed the facts in *Rakas*, D was in a private place (an automobile) with the permission of the owner of that place, yet this did not entitle him under the Court's analysis to a legitimate expectation of privacy. "But," the dissent asked rhetorically, "if that is not sufficient, what would be?" Its answer was that "it is hard to imagine anything short of a property interest [in the car] that would satisfy the majority."

As a matter of privacy rights, Justice White believed that the holding of the Court was not only contrary to precedent, "but also to the everyday expectations of privacy that we all share." He pointed out that if the owner of the car in *Rakas* had invited D to be a passenger and had said, "I give you a temporary possessory interest in my vehicle so that you will share the right of privacy that the Supreme Court says that I own," then the majority "apparently" would have reached a different conclusion. "But," he said, "people seldom say such things, though they may mean their invitation to encompass [the passengers] if only they had thought of the problem."

§ 116   What Has *Rakas* Wrought?: An Analysis[38]

[A]   "Standing" as a Separate Concept

After *Rakas*, "standing" is no longer considered a distinct issue in Fourth Amendment litigation.[39] Instead, the issue is subsumed within substantive Fourth Amendment analysis. Justice Blackmun has contended,[40] however, that it is not improper for lower courts to treat "standing" and the issue of whether a substantive Fourth Amendment violation has occurred as distinct inquiries. It remains possible, he pointed out, for a claimant to have standing to raise a Fourth Amendment challenge but to lose on the merits, and vice–versa. To lose sight of this fact, Justice Blackmun warned, is to invite confusion.

Justice Blackmun's point is this: the *Katz* reasonable–expectation–of–privacy test asks a slightly different question than does *Rakas*. Under *Katz*, and thus under substantive Fourth Amendment "search" jurisprudence, the issue is whether *someone* had a reasonable expectation of privacy under specific circumstances. If so, there was a "search." In contrast, *Rakas* asks whether the *defendant* in particular had such an expectation.

---

[37] The majority replied that the *Jones* rule had only "superficial clarity" and concealed "underneath that thin veneer all of the problems of line drawing which must be faced in any conscientious effort to apply the Fourth Amendment."

[38] *See generally* 4 W. LaFave, at § 11.3(a)–(f).

[39] *See* n. 34 and accompanying text *supra*.

[40] Rawlings v. Kentucky, 448 U.S. at 112 (concurring opinion).

For example, someone — certainly the owner — had a reasonable expectation of privacy in the automobile stopped by the police, even if *D* did not. Therefore, the automobile was "searched," perhaps unreasonably, although *D* did not possess a privacy expectation that was violated by it.

On the other hand, a person might have standing to raise a Fourth Amendment claim but ultimately lose on the merits. For example, *D* might have a reasonable expectation of privacy in the contents of a diary, and thus have "standing" to challenge the police search of it, but if he left the diary open, in plain view of an officer invited into *D*'s house, *D* would lose on the merits because of the plain–view doctrine.

It is often helpful, therefore, to treat "standing" as a separate inquiry, notwithstanding *Rakas*.

[B] Contesting a Search of Another Person's Home

After *Rakas*, a person may not challenge a search of another person's home merely on the ground that he was legitimately on the premises at the time of the search. Although such a basis was satisfactory in *Jones*,[41] it is now necessary to determine whether the guest had a reasonable expectation of privacy in the premises.

According to *Rakas*, the defendant in *Jones* had a reasonable expectation of privacy in his friend's apartment when it was searched. Among the facts the Court noted in support of this conclusion were that the defendant had a key to the premises, he used it to admit himself to the apartment, he had clothing in it, he had slept on the premises "maybe a night," and he was its sole occupant at the time of the search. Based on these facts, *D* had "complete dominion and control" over the premises, except as against the absent host.

In contrast, in dictum, the Court in *Rakas* suggested, perhaps wrongly,[42] that a person does not have a reasonable expectation of privacy in another person's home if he lawfully enters the premises moments before a search begins and leaves moments after it ends. Apparently, the visitor's connection to the premises in such a case is too insubstantial to justify an expectation of privacy in it.

This leaves a lot of room between the visitor in *Jones* and the momentary guest in the *Rakas* hypothetical. For example, does an overnight guest have a reasonable expectation of privacy in another person's home if (unlike *Jones*) the host is present at the time of the search?

The Court answered this question affirmatively in *Minnesota v. Olson*.[43] In *Olson*, *D*, an overnight guest, was arrested without a warrant in *X*'s home, in violation of the rule announced in *Payton v. New York*[44] that an in–home arrest requires a warrant. By a 7–2 vote, the Court rejected the state's claim that *D* lacked standing to object to the *Payton* violation because he was never alone in the home, did not have a key, and lacked dominion and control over the premises.

---

[41] Jones v. United States, 362 U.S. 257 (1960), *overruled on other grounds in* United States v. Salvucci, 448 U.S. 83 (1980).

[42] *See* n. 35 and accompanying text *supra*.

[43] 110 S.Ct. 1684 (1990).

[44] 445 U.S. 573 (1980). *See* § 59 *supra*.

Speaking for the Court, Justice White (the author of the *Rakas* dissent) stated that "[w]e do not understand *Rakas*. . . to hold that an overnight guest can never have a legitimate expectation of privacy except when his host is away and he has a key. . . ." Instead, *Olson* holds, any overnight guest, even one who lacks "untrammeled power to admit and exclude" others because the host is present at all times, can challenge a search in his host's home.

According to the Court, this holding "merely recognizes the everyday expectations of privacy that we all share." If a guest were required to have complete dominion and control in order to have standing, Justice White pointed out, "an adult daughter living temporarily in the home of her parents would have no legitimate expectation of privacy because her right to admit or exclude would be subject to her parents' veto."

[C] Contesting a Search of Another Person's Automobile

[1] When the Owner is Absent

After *Rakas*, a person has standing to contest a search of an automobile in which he is an occupant, although he is not its owner, if he has a reasonable expectation of privacy in the area of the automobile searched.

An expectation of privacy would exist if *D*, the occupant, has a possessory interest comparable to that of the defendant in *Jones*. For example, if *X*, the owner of an automobile, lends his car to *D* for a few days, *D* would have standing to contest a search of those portions of the vehicle that he has authority to use, if he is stopped while he is driving it in *X*'s absence. At the time of the search, *D* would have exclusive dominion and control over the automobile, and thus would have a legitimate expectation of privacy in it.

On the other hand, if the key that *X* gives *D* does not open the trunk, it is likely that *D* would not have standing to contest a search of that particular part of the car. It must be remembered that *Rakas* found that *D* lacked a reasonable expectation of privacy in the particular areas searched; similarly, regarding the right of a guest in a house to contest a search, the Court distinguished between a search of the kitchen, where the hypothetical guest was invited to be, and the basement, to which the guest was not invited.[45]

[2] When the Owner is Present

In his dissent in *Rakas*, Justice White suggested that a passenger *qua* passenger no longer has standing to contest a search of a car in which he was an invited occupant. However, the majority in *Rakas* denied that this was the holding of the case. Certainly, as a conceptual matter, a "mere" passenger may have a reasonable expectation of privacy in an automobile, or at least in portions of it.[46]

For example, if *X*, the owner–driver of a vehicle, gives *D* a second key to the car with the explicit understanding that *D* may place his property in the glove

---

[45] *See* the text preceding n. 35 *supra*.

[46] Of course, a special relationship between the passenger and the car owner, such as by marriage, would differentiate it from the "mere" passenger situation. In such a case, the spouse–passenger should have standing to object, as lower courts have consistently held. 4 W. LaFave, § 11.3(e) at 335–36.

compartment or trunk any time he wishes, X's presence in the car should not preclude a finding that D has a protectible privacy interest in the glove compartment and trunk.

Indeed, in view of the Court's holding in *Olson*,[47] namely, that an overnight guest in a home may have a reasonable expectation of privacy in that dwelling even if the host is present at all times, it should be possible for D to prove that he has standing to object to a search of some portions of a car in which he is a "mere" passenger, at least if his connection to the automobile is significant.

For example, if D were allowed to hitch a ride in X's car for a week–long cross–country trip, D ought to have standing to object to a search of those portions of the car in which X allows D to place his valuables, even if X never gives D a key to the car. The fact that X would have the right to admit or exclude the police from those portions of the car in which D's belongings are placed, does not necessarily demonstrate that D does not have a legitimate expectation of privacy in those areas. As the Court said in *Olson*, "hosts will more likely than not respect the privacy interests of their guests, who are entitled to a legitimate expectation of privacy despite the fact they have no legal interest in the premises and do not have the legal authority to determine who may or may not enter."

[D] Contesting a Search Resulting in the Seizure of One's Own Property

Prior to *Rakas*, a person had standing to contest a search if he claimed an ownership or possessory interest in the property seized as a result of a search.

Rakas did not expressly overrule this doctrine. Indeed, the Court noted various times in the case that D, the passenger in the car, had not claimed that either the rifle or ammunition seized in the search were his, the implication being that had either been his property, D would have had standing to object to the car search. The Court also implied in *Rakas* that a casual visitor to a house, even one who lacks a reasonable expectation of privacy in it, could contest a search that culminated in the seizure of his own property on the premises.[48]

Nonetheless, the holding of *Rawlings v. Kentucky*[49] belies the implications of *Rakas*. *Rawlings* holds that a person may not successfully challenge a search of an area in which he has no reasonable expectation of privacy, even if he has a legitimate interest in the property seized during the search.

In *Rawlings*, D placed a vial containing a controlled substance in X's purse shortly before the police ordered X, apparently unconstitutionally, to empty her purse. When she did, they discovered the vial. D, who was sitting next to her on a couch when these events occurred, admitted ownership of the vial.

The Court held that under the principles of *Rakas*, D could not contest the search of X's purse on the basis that he had an ownership interest in the property seized. The Court, per Justice Rehnquist, stated that *Rakas* rejected the view that "arcane" concepts of property law controlled the issue; therefore, the question that had to be considered was whether D had a reasonable expectation of privacy in

---

[47] Minnesota v. Olson, 110 S.Ct. 1684 (1990).
[48] *See* n. 36 and accompanying text *supra*.
[49] 448 U.S. 98 (1980).

X's purse, of which *D*'s ownership of the drug vial was only one factor in the determination.

The Court held that *D* did not have a reasonable expectation of privacy in *X*'s purse. Among the reasons given by the Court were: (1) at the time of the "sudden bailment" *D* had known *X* for only a few days; (2) *D* had never before sought or received access to *X*'s purse; (3) *D* did not have a right to exclude others from the purse; (4) *Y*, a "longtime acquaintance and frequent companion" of *X*, had "free access" to her purse and, in fact, had rummaged through it for a hairbrush that morning; and (5) the "precipitous nature of the transaction hardly supports a reasonable inference that [*D*] took normal precautions to maintain his privacy." The Court contrasted *D*'s behavior here with that of Katz,[50] who closed the door on the booth when he made his telephone call, and that of Chadwick,[51] who placed his belongings in a double–locked footlocker.

As Professor LaFave has written, "[n]o one of the several points made by Justice Rehnquist can withstand close scrutiny. . . ."[52] There is no reason why a bailor — here, *D* — should not be able to expect privacy in the area in which his goods are kept by the bailee. Indeed, the selection of a bailee is made in large part on the basis that the bailor believes that his goods will be protected and his privacy in them respected. In any case, any expectation of privacy that would otherwise exist is not diminished merely because the bailor recently met the bailee (point 1), or was using that person for the first time (point 2).

Nor should it be fatal to the bailor's claim that he cannot exclude others from the bailee's "premises" (here, the purse) (point 3). Such a conclusion is inconsistent with the Court's later reasoning in *Olson*,[53] in which it held that the mere fact that a homeowner has the right to admit persons into a house in which he has an overnight guest, does not deprive the guest of a legitimate expectation of privacy in the premises. It follows from *Olson* that *X*'s right to allow others to look in her purse, even over *D*'s objection, should not render *D*'s expectation of privacy in the purse illegitimate.[54]

As for *Y*'s access to the purse (point 4), this point should add very little. The right to privacy is not lost merely because it is shared, as long as it is not shared with the public at large.

The Court's fifth point, that *D* did not take reasonable precautions to protect his privacy, is also unpersuasive. *D* did not leave the drug vial on a table; he put it in *X*'s purse. A person ordinarily has a reasonable expectation of privacy in a container as long as it is closed.[55] *X*'s purse was such a container.

---

[50] Katz v. United States, 389 U.S. 347 (1967).

[51] United States v. Chadwick, 433 U.S. 1 (1977). *See* § 79[C][2] *supra*.

[52] 4 W. LaFave, § 11.3(c) at 308. Professor LaFave went on to say that "it is to be hoped that the decision will have a short life." *Id.* at 311. His wish has not been fulfilled.

[53] Minnesota v. Olson, 110 S.Ct. 1684 (1990).

[54] Furthermore, as Professor LaFave has pointed out, 4 W. LaFave, § 11.3(c) at 309, the Court's conclusion leads to a poor policy result: the police can search the bailee's premises not only with the latter's consent, but even without it, because the bailor will lack standing to object.

[55] *See* United States v. Ross, 456 U.S. 798, 822 (1982).

Unless the Court narrows the apparent holding of *Rawlings*, the case has broad implications. For example, if *D* were to place his suitcase in *X*'s, a friend's, house, with the latter's express permission, he would not have standing to object to a search of *X*'s house for *D*'s property, unless *D* had some independent privacy interest in the area in *X*'s house in which the search occurred.[56]

[E] Contesting a Seizure or Subsequent Search of One's Own Property

In *Rakas* and other subsequent "standing" cases, the defendant sought to challenge the constitutionality of a search of another person's private property, in which the property seized as a result of the search might, or might not, have belonged to the defendant. For example, in *Rakas*, *D* sought to challenge the search of *X*'s car, in which property apparently not belonging to *D* was seized and used against him at his trial. In *Rawlings*, *D* sought to challenge the search of *X*'s purse, in which a drug vial belonging to *D* was discovered.

A conceptually different question is raised if a defendant seeks to challenge the seizure of an article that he claims belongs to him or its subsequent search, although it was found in a search of another person's premises. In this case, the focus of the challenge is not on the search that resulted in the discovery of the claimant's property, but rather is on the police action after it was discovered: did they search or seize the defendant's property unreasonably?

For example, suppose that in *Rawlings*, *D* had conceded that he could not object to the search of *X*'s purse because he had no legitimate expectation of privacy in it. However, assuming appropriate supporting facts, he might have sought to challenge the officers' seizure of his drug vial, or the search of its contents, on the ground that they lacked probable cause and/or a warrant to do so. Could *D* have challenged *these* actions on the ground that he had a property interest in the vial and its contents?

Or, consider the facts in *Paulino v. United States*.[57] As was the case in *Rakas*, *D* was a passenger in another person's car. When the police stopped the automobile in which he was riding, *D* placed an object under a rear floor mat. Fearing the presence of a weapon, an officer lifted the mat, and found a packet of currency. He picked it up, removed a rubber band, and examined the bills carefully. He observed that they all had the same serial number, so he concluded that they were counterfeit, whereupon *D* was arrested for a counterfeiting offense.

---

[56] In United States v. Jeffers, 342 U.S. 48 (1951), the police seized contraband belonging to *D* in a hotel room registered to *X*. *D* had a key to the room (with *X*'s permission) and had the right to enter at will, although he was not present when the search occurred. The Court held that *D* had standing to contest the police conduct, noting that the search and seizure were "bound together by one sole purpose — to locate and seize the narcotics" of *D*.

Jeffers is hard to justify in the post–*Rakas*, and especially post–*Rawlings*, era. It is now interpreted to stand for the proposition that *D*'s right to contest the police action in that case was based on the fact that he maintained an interest "in *both* the premises searched and the property seized." United States v. Salvucci, 448 U.S. 83, 90 n.5 (1980) (*quoting Rakas*, 439 U.S. at 136) (emphasis supplied in *Salvucci*).

[57] 109 S.Ct. 1967 (1989) (denial of certiorari).

Based on *Rakas*, *D* probably lacked standing to challenge the search that turned up the money. But, his objection to the police action was not that they improperly searched the car, but was "that the officer, upon determining that the item beneath the floor mat was neither a weapon nor plainly contraband, 'had no basis to take any further action.' "[58] In short, he wished to challenge the search and seizure of his own property, although it was found in an area in which he did not have a reasonable expectation of privacy.

The Court did not grant certiorari in *Paulino*, so the issue raised in that case remains unresolved. It is submitted here, however, as it was by Justices White and Brennan who dissented from the denial of certiorari in the case, that a defendant should have standing to challenge a search or seizure of his own property, whether or not the property is discovered in a public place or in any other place in which he has no legitimate expectation of privacy.

As the dissenters pointed out, if a person is not permitted to challenge a search or seizure of his own property, anomalous results will follow: for example, the police, without a warrant, and based on no suspicion whatsoever, could seize and search a person's briefcase if it were checked in a public checkroom, or could open and rummage through a person's locked suitcase if it were temporarily left sitting in an airport concourse.

---

[58] *Id.* at 1967–68 (*quoting* in part the Second Circuit opinion in the case).

CHAPTER **21**

FOURTH AMENDMENT: EXCLUSIONARY RULE

The Fourth Amendment exclusionary rule provides, in general, that evidence secured in violation of the Fourth Amendment is inadmissible in a criminal trial of the person whose rights were violated. This chapter considers the history of the rule, its scope, and the controversies surrounding it.[1]

§ 117 Development of the Exclusionary Rule[2]

[A] *Weeks v. United States*

The Supreme Court adopted the Fourth Amendment exclusionary rule for the first time in 1914 in *Weeks v. United States.*[3] In *Weeks*, the justices held that in federal trials the Fourth Amendment bars the use of evidence unconstitutionally seized by federal law enforcement officers. Without such a rule, the Court subsequently explained, the Fourth Amendment would be reduced to a mere "form of words."[4]

[B] *Wolf v. Colorado*

At the time of *Weeks*, the guarantees of the Fourth Amendment did not apply to the states pursuant to the Fourteenth Amendment due process clause. Therefore, the Court in *Weeks* did not have reason to consider whether the exclusionary rule applied in state criminal trials.

In 1949, however, in *Wolf v. Colorado*,[5] the Court, per Justice Felix Frankfurter, held that "security of one's privacy against arbitrary intrusion by the police — which is at the core of the Fourth Amendment — is basic to a free society." As a consequence of *Wolf*, therefore, states are now subject to the substantive provisions of the Fourth Amendment.

On the other hand, the Court indicated in *Wolf* that "the ways of enforcing such a basic right raise questions of a different order." According to *Wolf*, the

---

[1] Other constitutional rights have exclusionary rules, which are discussed in conjunction with the rights in question. Various nonconstitutional rules have exclusionary rules. As to them, *see* Dix, *Nonconstitutional Exclusionary Rules in Criminal Procedure*, 27 Am. Crim. L. Rev. 53 (1989).

[2] *See generally* Allen, *Federalism and the Fourth Amendment: A Requiem for Wolf*, 1961 Sup. Ct. Rev. 1; Kamisar, *Wolf and Lustig Ten Years Later: Illegal State Evidence in State and Federal Courts*, 43 Minn. L. Rev. 1083 (1959); Stewart, *The Road to Mapp v. Ohio and Beyond: The Origins, Development and Future of the Exclusionary Rule in Search-and-Seizure Cases*, 83 Colum. L. Rev. 1365 (1983).

[3] 232 U.S. 383 (1914).

[4] Silverthorne Lumber Co. v. United States, 251 U.S. 385, 392 (1920).

[5] 338 U.S. 25 (1949), *overruled on other grounds in* Mapp v. Ohio, 367 U.S. 643 (1961).

exclusionary rule adopted in *Weeks* "was not derived from the explicit requirements of the Fourth Amendment. . . . The decision was a matter of judicial
implication."

The Court hinted that the federal exclusionary rule of *Weeks* was not constitutionally required. It stated that "a different question [than was raised in *Weeks*]
would be presented if Congress . . . were to pass a statute purporting to negate
the *Weeks* doctrine." In "default of that judgment," the Court indicated, it would
"stoutly adhere" to *Weeks*.

Although the Court was unwilling to back down from its holding in *Weeks*, it
refused to extend the exclusionary rule to the states. The Court concluded that
the states were not compelled to exclude "logically relevant evidence" from their
trials, even if such evidence was obtained as a result of an unreasonable search
or seizure. Justice Frankfurter took note of the fact that none of the ten jurisdictions within the United Kingdom and the British Commonwealth excluded
evidence obtained by illegal search and seizure, and that a majority of the states
in this country, left to their own devices, had rejected the *Weeks* doctrine.

[C]   *Rochin v. California* and Its Progeny

Although *Wolf* held that evidence was not inadmissible in a state trial merely
because it was secured in violation of the principles of the Fourth Amendment,
the Court demonstrated in *Rochin v. California*[6] that it was prepared to require
the adoption of an exclusionary rule in state trials, albeit not by the route of the
Fourth (via the Fourteenth) Amendment.

In *Rochin*, police officers, without a search warrant and perhaps without
probable cause, entered *D*'s home at night, forcibly opened his second-floor
bedroom door, and found *D* and his wife on the bed. When *D* swallowed capsules
that had been on a night stand, three officers "jumped" on him and unsuccessfully
tried to extract them from his mouth. When they failed, they took *D*, handcuffed,
to a hospital where they directed physicians to force an emetic solution through
a tube into his stomach in order to cause him to expel the capsules, which he did.
The capsules contained morphine. *D* was prosecuted for the possession of the
morphine.

The Court, per Justice Frankfurter (the author of *Wolf*), held that the police
conduct in this case — specifically, "[i]llegally breaking into the privacy of the
petitioner, the struggle to open his mouth and remove what was there, the forcible
extraction of his stomach's contents" — "shock[ed] the conscience." It said that
the police conduct was "bound to offend even hardened sensibilities," and was
"too close to the rack and screw to permit."

The Court concluded that the Fourteenth Amendment due process clause
prohibits the use at trial of evidence, even of a reliable nature, that was secured
in a manner that violates "certain decencies of civilized conduct." To hold
otherwise, *Rochin* concluded, "would be to afford brutality the cloak of law.
Nothing would be more calculated to discredit law and thereby to brutalize the
temper of society."

---

[6] 342 U.S. 165 (1952).

In subsequent cases, the Court has interpreted *Rochin* narrowly. In *Irvine v. California*,[7] the Court ruled, 5-4, over Justice Frankfurter's dissent, that the government was within its rights to introduce at trial statements that the police had obtained illegally by entering *D*'s home to install and then later move a hidden microphone. *Rochin* was distinguished on the ground that it, unlike the present case, involved "coercion, violence, or brutality to the person."

Rochin was again distinguished in *Breithaupt v Abram*.[8] In *Breithaupt*, the police took a blood sample from *D* while he was unconscious. Because the blood was extracted nonviolently by a physician in a hospital, the Court concluded that the "sense of justice of which we spoke in *Rochin*" was not offended.

The shock-the-conscience test of *Rochin* remains good law. However, in light of its narrow scope, and the Supreme Court's post-*Rochin* Fourth Amendment exclusionary-rule jurisprudence, the doctrine is only infrequently applied today to exclude real evidence secured from a person in a violent manner.[9] The *Rochin* doctrine retains somewhat greater relevance in other contexts.[10]

[D] *Mapp v. Ohio*

In *Mapp v. Ohio*,[11] officers conducting an investigation of a bombing sought to enter *D*'s house in order to find and question a suspect they believed was hiding there. When they demanded entrance, *D* telephoned her attorney and, on his advice, refused to admit them without a search warrant.

After keeping the house under surveillance for three hours, and apparently[12] still without a warrant, the officers returned to the house. When *D* did not come to the door immediately, they forcibly entered, damaging the door in the process. Once inside, the officers displayed a piece of paper that they claimed was a search warrant. *D* grabbed it and "placed it in her bosom." A struggle ensued, in which *D*'s hand was twisted, after which the police removed the "warrant" from her clothing.

D was forcibly taken upstairs to her bedroom, where the officers searched her belongings. Later, the rest of the house, including her child's bedroom, the living room, the kitchen, and the basement were thoroughly searched. Nobody, nor any evidence regarding the bombing, was found. However, "obscene materials"[13] were found and seized. *D* was prosecuted for their possession, and convicted.

---

[7] 347 U.S. 128, *reh'g denied*, 347 U.S. 931 (1954).

[8] 352 U.S. 432 (1957).

[9] Real evidence obtained as the result of a blood test might be excluded, for example, "if the police initiated . . . violence, refused to respect a reasonable request to undergo a different form of testing, or responded to resistance with inappropriate force." Schmerber v. California, 384 U.S. 757, 760 n.4 (1966).

[10] A confession obtained with such brutality that it shocks the conscience would doubtlessly be inadmissible under the due process clause. Indeed, *Rochin* cited Brown v. Mississippi, 297 U.S. 278 (1936), a coerced confession case, in support of its holding. *See* § 129 *infra*. The shock-the-conscience doctrine might also serve as a basis to prohibit a prosecution on the basis of entrapment. *See* § 174 *infra*.

[11] 367 U.S. 643, *reh'g denied*, 368 U.S. 871 (1961).

[12] No warrant was produced by the prosecutor, nor was this failure ever explained.

[13] The materials consisted of four books — *Affairs of a Troubadour, Little Darlings, London Stage Affairs*, and *Memories of a Hotel Man* — and a hand-drawn picture "of a very obscene nature." Stewart, n. 2 *supra*, at 1367.

Although the Fourth Amendment aspects of the case were not briefed, argued, or discussed in the state courts, nor raised by D's attorney,[14] the Supreme Court granted hearing in the case, and used it as its vehicle to overrule *Wolf.*

Mapp holds that the Fourth Amendment exclusionary rule applies in state trials, just as it does in the federal system via *Weeks*. In an opinion written by Justice Tom Clark, the Court stated that it was "logically and constitutionally necessary that the exclusion doctrine . . . be also insisted upon as an essential ingredient of the right . . . recognized by the *Wolf* case." In short, the exclusionary rule is of constitutional origin. To hold otherwise, *Mapp* said, would be "to grant the right [to be free from unreasonable searches and seizures] but in reality to withhold its privilege and enjoyment."

§ 118 Rationale of the Exclusionary Rule

Mapp v. Ohio[15] provides two justifications for the exclusionary rule. First, and primarily, the "purpose of the exclusionary rule 'is to deter — to compel respect for the constitutional guaranty in the only effectively available way — by removing the incentive to disregard it.' "[16]

A second justification for the exclusionary rule is "the imperative of judicial integrity."[17] This rationale was first identified by the Court (although not in "integrity" terms) in *Weeks v. United States*.[18] In *Weeks*, the Court stated that the judiciary is "charged at all times with support of the Constitution" and that "people . . . have a right to appeal [to the courts] for the maintenance of . . . fundamental rights." To permit prosecutors to use unconstitutionally seized evidence, *Weeks* reasoned, would be to "affirm by judicial decision a manifest neglect if not an open defiance of the prohibitions of the Constitution." In such circumstances, judges would be acting as "accomplices in the willful disobedience of a Constitution they are sworn to uphold."[19]

Since *Mapp* was decided, the Supreme Court has de-emphasized the judicial-integrity justification of the rule to the point of near extinction.[20] "[W]hile it is quite true," Justice Rehnquist has observed, "that courts are not to be participants in 'dirty business,' neither are they to be ethereal vestal virgins of another world."[21] The Court now states that the judicial–integrity theory has only a

---

[14] D's attorney argued that the police conduct shocked the conscience, in violation of *Rochin*, and that the conviction for possession of obscene materials violated First Amendment principles. An *amicus* brief included one paragraph calling on the Court to overrule *Wolf*. When D's attorney was questioned about this in oral argument, he indicated that he had never heard of *Wolf*. *Id.*

[15] 367 U.S. 643, *reh'g denied*, 368 U.S. 871 (1961).

[16] *Id.* at 656 (*quoting* Elkins v. United States, 364 U.S. 206, 217 (1960)).

[17] *Id.* at 659 (*quoting* Elkins v. United States, 364 U.S. at 222).

[18] 232 U.S. 383 (1914).

[19] Elkins v. United States, 364 U.S. at 223.

[20] For arguments in favor of retention of the doctrine, *see* Note, *Judicial Integrity and Judicial Review: An Argument for Expanding the Scope of the Exclusionary Rule*, 20 UCLA L. Rev. 1129 (1973).

[21] California v. Minjares, 443 U.S. 916, 924 (1979) (Rehnquist, J., dissenting); *see also* McGuigan, *An Interview with Judge Robert H. Bork*, Judicial Notice, June, 1986, at 1, 6

"limited role [to play] . . . in the determination whether to apply the rule in a particular context."[22] In short, deterrence is the " 'prime purpose' of the rule, if not the sole one."[23]

The subordination of "judicial integrity" to "deterrence" in exclusionary-rule jurisprudence has a pragmatic explanation. The concept of judicial integrity potentially functions as a moral imperative: "Thou shalt not be an accessory to an illegal act." As the Court has pointed out,[24] if this view of judicial integrity were taken seriously, the exclusionary rule would require the suppression of evidence in all judicial proceedings, not merely, as is now the case, in criminal trials, and it would require abandonment of the "standing" requirement. These are consequences that the Court, even during the Warren Court era, was unwilling to accept.

§ 119 Is the Exclusionary Rule Constitutionally Required?[25]

Weeks[26] implicitly, and *Mapp*[27] explicitly, determined that the exclusionary rule is an essential component — "part and parcel" according to *Mapp* — of the Fourth Amendment.

Under the holding of *Mapp*, the Fourth Amendment not only safeguards people against unreasonable searches and seizures, but it guarantees that evidence obtained in violation of their Fourth Amendment rights will not be used against them in criminal trials. Although Justice Harlan, who dissented, did not believe that the exclusionary rule was constitutionally required, he had no doubt that this was the holding of the Court. As he observed:

> Essential to the majority's argument against *Wolf* is the proposition that the [exclusionary] rule . . . derives not from the "supervisory power" of this Court over the federal judiciary system, but from Constitutional requirement. This is so because no one, I suppose, would suggest that this Court possesses any supervisory power over the state courts.

Notwithstanding *Mapp*, the Supreme Court apparently de-constitutionalized the exclusionary rule in *United States v. Calandra*.[28] In *Calandra*, Justice Powell, speaking for six members of the Court, described the rule as "a judicially created remedy designed to safeguard Fourth Amendment rights through its deterrence effect, rather than a personal constitutional right of the party aggrieved."

(in which Judge Bork observed that "I have never been convinced by that [judicial integrity] argument because it seems the conscience of the court ought to be at least equally shaken by the idea of turning a criminal loose upon society.").

[22] Stone v. Powell, 428 U.S. 465, 485, *reh'g denied*, 429 U.S. 874 (1976) (footnote deleted).

[23] United States v. Janis, 428 U.S. 433, 446 (1976).

[24] Stone v. Powell, 428 U.S. at 485.

[25] *See generally* Schrock & Welsh, *Up From Calandra: The Exclusionary Rule as a Constitutional Requirement*, 59 Minn. L. Rev. 251 (1974).

[26] Weeks v. United States, 232 U.S. 383 (1914). *See* § 117[A] *supra*.

[27] Mapp v. Ohio, 367 U.S. 643, *reh'g denied*, 368 U.S. 871 (1961). *See* § 117[D] *supra*.

[28] 414 U.S. 338 (1974).

In other words, the exclusionary rule is not an essential component of the Fourth Amendment, but is merely a remedy devised by the Supreme Court to deter governmental conduct in violation of the Fourth Amendment. The implication of *Calandra* is that if the Supreme Court were to determine that another remedy would better safeguard Fourth Amendment rights, it could — and might — abolish the exclusionary rule.

Calandra is controversial. In support of the proposition that the suppression doctrine is not constitutionally required is the Constitution's silence regarding an exclusionary rule. As a judge once observed, "[t]his rule of evidence did not come from on high. It's man-made, not God-given. . . . It's not even in the Constitution."[29] Further, the "time lag" between the adoption of the Fourth Amendment and the Court's first acceptance of the exclusionary rule "is some indication that it is hardly basic to the constitutional purpose."[30]

Those who believe that the exclusionary rule is an essential ingredient of the Fourth Amendment respond by saying that the fact that the rule is not explicit does not distinguish it from countless other rights that are thought — in some cases relatively uncontroversially — to exist by implication.[31] As for the time lag, they point out that virtually all constitutional rights pertaining to the states were late arrivals. For example, the right of indigents to the assistance of counsel at trial in state courts was not recognized until 1963,[32] two years after *Mapp* was decided, yet few people question the fundamental nature of the right to counsel.

The apparent de-constitutionalization of the exclusionary rule is significant. It removes much of the underlying force of *Mapp*'s reasoning. And, if the rule is not constitutionally compelled, the Supreme Court has authority to abolish it or narrow its scope, as it sees fit. Furthermore, as Justice Harlan pointed out, the Court does not have authority to require states to apply a rule not derived from the Constitution. Therefore, the legitimacy of federal cases that enforce the exclusionary rule against the states is in question.

---

[29] *Quoted in* Mathias, *The Exclusionary Rule Revisited*, 28 Loyola. L. Rev. 1, 7 (1982) (comment of Judge Malcolm Wilkey in testimony before the Attorney General's Task Force on Violent Crime).

[30] Kaplan, *The Limits of the Exclusionary Rule*, 26 Stan. L. Rev. 1027, 1031 (1974).

[31] Kamisar, *Does (Did) (Should) the Exclusionary Rule Rest on a "Principled Basis" Rather than an "Empirical Proposition"?*, 16 Creighton L. Rev. 565, 581-89 (1983).

[32] Gideon v. Wainwright, 372 U.S. 335 (1963).

§ 120   Exclusionary Rule: Is It a Good Idea?[33]

[A]   General Observations

Justice William Douglas predicted that *Mapp v. Ohio* would end the "storm of constitutional controversy" evoked by *Wolf*.[34] It did nothing of the sort. Debate regarding *Mapp* and the exclusionary rule began almost as soon as the decision was announced. It has not ceased.

Generally speaking, the policy debate revolves around three questions: (1) To what degree does the exclusionary rule deter unreasonable searches and seizures?; (2) Even if the rule deters police misconduct, do the costs of the rule outweigh its benefits?; and (3) Is there a better way to safeguard Fourth Amendment rights? These questions are discussed below.

[B]   Does the Rule Deter?

The exclusionary rule "is calculated to prevent, not to repair."[35] It applies after the victim's privacy has been invaded. The privacy lost "cannot be restored. Reparation comes too late."[36] Therefore, the first question to be asked is: Does the exclusionary rule serve its purpose of preventing unlawful searches and seizures?

Critics: Empirical studies[37] suggest, and common sense tells us, that the exclusionary rule does not, and probably cannot, function as a meaningful deterrent. Most violations of the Fourth Amendment occur at its edges: an officer in good faith misunderstands a complex Fourth Amendment rule or interprets the facts regarding a search or seizure differently than a court does subsequently. These errors cannot be prevented; by definition they are inadvertent. In any case, we would not want to deter good-faith police activity: all we can ask of the police is that they make reasonable, good-faith efforts to obey the Constitution.

---

[33] *See generally* Blumberg, *The Case Against the Exclusionary Rule*, 14 Human Rights 41 (Winter 1987); Goodpaster, *An Essay on Ending the Exclusionary Rule*, 33 Hastings L.J. 1065 (1982); Joseph, *The Case for the Exclusionary Rule*, 14 Human Rights 38 (Winter 1987); Kamisar, n. 31 *supra*; Kamisar, *The Exclusionary Rule in Historical Perspective*, 62 Judicature 337 (1979); Kaplan, n. 30 *supra*; Mertens & Wasserstrom, *Foreword: The Good Faith Exception to the Exclusionary Rule: Deregulating the Police and Derailing the Law*, 70 Geo. L.J. 365 (1981); Oakes, *Studying the Exclusionary Rule in Search and Seizure*, 37 U. Chi. L. Rev. 665 (1970); Posner, *Rethinking the Fourth Amendment*, 1981 Sup. Ct. Rev. 49; Morris, *The Exclusionary Rule, Deterrence, and Posner's Economic Analysis of Law*, 57 Wash. L. Rev. 647 (1982); Stewart, n. 2 *supra*; Sunderland, *Liberals, Conservatives, and the Exclusionary Rule*, 71 J. Crim. L. & Crimin. 343 (1980); Uviller, *The Acquisition of Evidence for Criminal Prosecution: Some Constitutional Premises and Practices in Transition*, 35 Vand. L. Rev. 501 (1982); Wilkey, *The Exclusionary Rule: Why Suppress Valid Evidence?*, 62 Judicature 214 (1978); Note, *The Exclusionary Rule and Deterrence: An Empirical Study of Chicago Narcotics Officers*, 54 U. Chi. L. Rev. 1016 (1987).

[34] *Mapp*, 367 U.S. at 670 (concurring opinion).

[35] Elkins v. United States, 364 U.S. at 217.

[36] Linkletter v. Walker, 381 U.S. 618, 637 (1965).

[37] *E.g.*, Oaks, n. 33 *supra*; Spiotto, *Search and Seizure: An Empirical Study of the Exclusionary Rule and its Alternatives*, 2 J. Legal Studies 243 (1973).

In contrast, those who knowingly violate the Fourth Amendment can be deterred, but the exclusionary rule is too indirect and attenuated a form of punishment to do the job. Doubtlessly, bad-faith police officers would prefer that those whom they arrest are convicted, but the possibility that the evidence that they seize will be excluded at trial is unlikely to have an appreciable effect on their behavior: officers acting in bad faith will be satisfied that they have put the arrestee to the expense, trouble, and anxiety of a criminal prosecution. They may even believe, perhaps with reason,[38] that by committing perjury regarding the circumstances of their conduct, they can avoid suppression of the evidence.[39]

Moreover, studies indicate that police institutional norms have more influence on individual officers (good-faith and bad-faith included) than court decisions.[40] Police officers "on the beat" are more interested in the views of their peers and supervisors than in the opinions of judges. A search that a court might later consider unreasonable is apt to be viewed with sympathy within the police milieu, so that the loss of the evidence will not deter the average officer.

Response: As with all arguments regarding deterrence, it is easier to prove that a penalty has *not* had its deterrent effect than that it is to show that it has succeeded.

Scientifically reliable evidence regarding deterrence may never be available. As one commentator has stated, "there is virtually no likelihood that the Court is going to receive any 'relevant statistics' which objectively measure the 'practical efficacy' of the exclusionary rule."[41] That is why deterrence is always "partly a matter of logic and psychology, [but] largely a matter of faith."[42]

Fair-minded critics of the exclusionary rule admit that the evidence is not that the rule does not deter, but rather that, as Judge Posner has written, "[n]o one actually knows how effective the exclusionary rule is as a deterrent."[43] Indeed, Professor Dallin Oaks, the author of the study most commonly cited by the rule's critics, candidly warns that his study "obviously falls short of an empirical substantiation or refutation of the deterrent effect of the exclusionary rule."[44] His harshest comments about the exclusionary rule are found in the postscript to the study, in which he presents his self-described "polemic on the rule," one which "brushes past the uncertainties identified in the discussion of the data."[45]

Furthermore, many of the no-deterrence criticisms are misdirected. They seek to show that the rule does not directly deter specific police officers. But, systemic

---

[38] Kaplan, n. 30 *supra*, at 1032 & n.40.

[39] Police perjury "disturbingly [is] a well-documented aspect of criminal justice administration." R. Van Duizend, *et al.*, at 108.

[40] *See* J. Skolnick, Justice Without Trial: Law Enforcement in Democratic Society 219-25 (Univ. of California 1966).

[41] Comment, *On the Limitations of Empirical Evaluations of the Exclusionary Rule: A Critique of the Spiotto Research and United States v. Calandra*, 69 Nw.U.L.Rev. 740, 763-64 (1974).

[42] Dworkin, *Fact Style Adjudication and the Fourth Amendment: The Limits of Lawyering*, 48 Ind. L.J. 329, 333 (1973).

[43] Posner, n. 33 *supra*, at 54 (footnote deleted).

[44] Oaks, n. 33 *supra*, at 709.

[45] *Id.* at 755.

deterrence, not specific deterrence, is the primary goal of the exclusionary rule.[46] That is, as Justice Brennan has observed, "the chief deterrent function of the rule is its tendency to promote institutional compliance with Fourth Amendment requirements on the part of law enforcement agencies generally."[47]

Mapp seeks to deter unconstitutional police conduct by promoting professionalism within the ranks, specifically by creating an incentive for police departments to hire persons sensitive to civil liberties, to better train police officers, to keep them updated on constitutional law, and to develop internal guidelines regarding arrests and searches.

There is anecdotal evidence that *Mapp* has had these effects in large urban police departments. As Justice Stewart said after he left the Court, "the world has changed since the *Mapp* decision was announced."[48] Various observers of police practices, including Professor Oaks, report that *Mapp* has promoted professionalism.[49] Oaks found that police adherence to constitutional doctrine increased after *Mapp* was decided, and that the rule "contributed to an increased awareness of constitutional requirements by the police."[50]

Furthermore, search warrants are sought more often now than before *Mapp*.[51] Police departments that once paid no attention to the Fourth Amendment now "at least . . . consider the parameters of an unconstitutional search and seizure."[52] And, although there is no way to prove it, flagrant cases of police misconduct — such as occurred in *Mapp* — appear to be less common today than they were before the exclusionary rule was adopted.

[C] Is the Rule (Even If It Deters) Worth Its Cost?

[1] Should This Question Even Be Asked?

Exclusionary rule critics often provide a list of the alleged costs of the rule to society, the sum of which, they argue, is greater than the rule's supposed benefits in terms of deterrence. Advocates of the exclusionary rule believe that the costs have been exaggerated, just as its deterrent benefits have been undervalued. A brief discussion of some of the alleged costs of the rule follows.

However, it is worth noting at the outset that such cost-benefit analysis is not without its critics. According to Justice Brennan, "the language of deterrence and of cost/balance analysis . . . can have a narcotic effect. It creates an illusion of technical precision and ineluctability."[53]

Critics of cost-benefit analysis of the exclusionary rule maintain that it is nearly impossible to analyze objectively the costs and benefits of the rule, because the

---

[46] Mertens & Wasserstrom, n. 33 *supra*, at 394.

[47] United States v. Leon, 468 U.S. 897, 953, *reh'g denied*, 468 U.S. 1250 (1984) (Brennan, J., dissenting) (footnote deleted).

[48] Stewart, n. 2 *supra*, at 1386.

[49] American Bar Association, Criminal Justice in Crisis 8 (A.B.A. 1988).

[50] Oaks, n. 33 *supra*, at 708.

[51] *See* Note, n. 33 *supra*, at 1017-18.

[52] Kaplan, n. 30 *supra*, at 1034.

[53] United States v. Leon, 468 U.S. at 929 (dissenting opinion).

process involves "measuring imponderables and comparing incommensurables."[54] For example, how much does "privacy" weigh in the cost-benefit balance? Is one unreasonable search that is deterred equal to one guilty person going free?

These critics believe that it would be better if we were to place weight on the principled grounds for the exclusionary rule, including the fact that it promotes judicial integrity, rather than on cost-benefit analysis.

[2] The "Costs"

[a] The Rule Protects the Wrong People

Critics: Consider the effects of the exclusionary rule. First, the purpose of a criminal trial is to learn the truth regarding a defendant's innocence or guilt. Yet, the Fourth Amendment exclusionary rule "deflects the truthfinding process"[55] by excluding reliable evidence.

Second, as a result of the suppression of the truth, the rule "often frees the guilty."[56] Third, while the guilty go free, innocent people receive no benefit from the rule. An innocent person has nothing that can be seized from her, for which she can be prosecuted. Therefore, she must turn to a civil remedy to obtain redress if her privacy is invaded unconstitutionally.

Response: First, the preceding argument is misdirected. If the criminal justice system is an obstacle course, it is the Fourth Amendment itself, and not the exclusionary rule *per se*, that constructs the barriers that make it harder to convict guilty persons.[57] The values implicit in the requirements of probable cause, search warrants, and reasonableness are what "get in the way."

Second, the cost of guilty people going free is overstated by the rule's critics. The most that the Supreme Court has been willing to say on the matter is that "some guilty defendants may go free or receive reduced sentences" as a consequence of the rule. It has conceded that "[m]any of [the] researchers have concluded that the impact of the exclusionary rule is insubstantial."[58]

In fact, one study of the impact of the exclusionary rule in seven communities found that in cases in which warrants had been issued, evidence was found in more than 90 percent of the resulting searches, yet motions to suppress evidence seized during the searches were filed in only 39 percent of the prosecutions, and were granted in only 12 percent of the cases, for an overall suppression rate of a mere 5 percent of the total number of warrant-related cases.[59]

Another study indicates that the rule results in nonprosecution or nonconviction of only between 0.6 and 2.35 percent of felony arrestees, although the figure is higher for some offenses.[60] Furthermore, a 1979 study by the General

---

[54] Kamisar, *Gates, "Probable Cause," "Good Faith," and Beyond*, 69 Iowa L. Rev. 551, 613 (1984).

[55] Stone v. Powell, 428 U.S. at 490.

[56] *Id.*

[57] Stewart, n. 2 *supra*, at 1393.

[58] United States v. Leon, 468 U.S. at 907 & n.6.

[59] R. Van Duizend, *et al.*, at 48-56.

[60] *Leon*, 468 U.S. at 907 n.6 (*citing* Davies, *A Hard Look at What We Know (and Still Need to Learn) About the "Costs" of the Exclusionary Rule: The NIJ Study and Other Studies of "Lost" Arrests*, 1983 A.B.F. Res.J. 611, 621).

Accounting Office found that of cases declined for federal prosecution, Fourth Amendment problems explained only 0.4 percent of the total.[61]

Third, it is inaccurate to say that innocent people do not benefit from the rule. If the exclusionary rule serves its deterrent purpose, there will be fewer intrusions on the security of innocent persons. There is no way to know how many innocent people have had their privacy safeguarded as a result of *Mapp*. In any case, even if it were true that only the guilty derive benefit from the rule, this would not demonstrate "that the rule is not a necessary remedy, only that it is not a sufficient one."[62]

[b] The Rule Promotes Public Cynicism

Critics: "The solid majority of Americans," one critic has stated, "rejects the idea that [t]he criminal is to go free because the constable has blundered.' "[63] "[T]he public is revulsed [*sic*]"[64] by the sight of guilty people going free because reliable evidence that could convict them is suppressed by judges on the basis of a "technicality." The legal system pays a high cost in lost public respect when it violates natural feelings of justice.

Response: If the public is outraged, it should not be. First, as noted above, fewer guilty people go free than is believed. Second, although the rule does obstruct the truth by suppressing reliable evidence, responsibility for this should be placed at the door of the government, whose officers violated the Fourth Amendment. As Justice Harlan has explained, judges "do not release a criminal from jail because we like to do so, or because we think it is wise to do so, but only because the government has offended constitutional principle in the conduct of [the defendant's] case."[65]

[c] The Rule Has a Disproportionate Effect

Critics: Even if the exclusionary rule should not be abandoned entirely, the *Mapp* version of the doctrine goes too far because the "penalty" for violation of the Fourth Amendment is often disproportionate to the "crime" committed by the police.

First, *Mapp* applies to the inadvertent mistake of the good-faith police officer in the same way that it does to the malicious conduct of the bad-faith officer.[66] Although "[f]reeing either a tiger or a mouse in a schoolroom is an illegal act, . . .

---

[61] Comptroller General, U.S. General Accounting Office, Impact of the Exclusionary Rule on Federal Criminal Prosecutions 14 (1979) (Rep. No. GGD-79-45).

[62] Stewart, n. 2 *supra*, at 1396.

[63] Kaplan, n. 30 *supra*, at 1035 (*quoting* Justice Cardozo in People v. Defore, 242 N.Y. 13, 21, 150 N.E. 585, 587 (1926)).

[64] Statement of the Co-Chairman of the Attorney-General's Task Force on Violent crime, *quoted in* The New York Times, Aug. 18, 1981, at 10, col. 6, *as reported in* LaFave, *The Fourth Amendment in an Imperfect World: On Drawing "Bright Lines" and "Good Faith",* 43 U. Pitt. L. Rev. 307, 336 (1982).

[65] Desist v. United States, 394 U.S. 244, 258, *reh'g denied,* 395 U.S. 931 (1969) (dissenting opinion).

[66] This is no longer completely so. *See* § 122 *infra.*

no rational person would suggest that these two acts should be punished in the same way."[67]

Second, the rule does not distinguish between a trial for a serious crime and one for a minor offense. Therefore, a potentially dangerous offender may escape incarceration, even if the wrong committed by the officer was trivial in nature.

Response: This argument assumes that the exclusionary rule is meant to compensate the victim of the Fourth Amendment violation. In fact, its purpose is to create an incentive for police departments to become more professional. Therefore, just as we do not precisely calibrate the severity of the punishment of a criminal to the facts of the particular case if we seek general deterrence, it is wrong to measure the effect of the exclusionary rule in an individual case.

[D] Are There Better Remedies?

Critics: Even if the exclusionary rule deters, and even if its benefits slightly outweigh its costs, there are other remedies that would provide greater net benefits. Furthermore, as long as the exclusionary rule exists, there is no incentive for police departments, legislatures, and courts to develop or use existing alternative remedies.

Among the options available to the victims of police misconduct — guilty and innocent alike — are: state civil tort actions against wrongdoing police officers; federal civil rights suits[68] ; federal criminal prosecutions[69] ; and injunctions against police departments that violate the Fourth Amendment. Furthermore, through use of civilian police-review boards or by internal police supervision, individual officers can be disciplined or fired for wrongdoing.

Response: None of these remedies works. Juries are disinclined to issue monetary judgments against police officers, except "in those unusual cases where the violation has been flagrant."[70] Even if the suit if successful, the ordinary officer lacks the resources to pay the judgment. For these reasons, and because they do not want to gain a reputation for being "anti-police," lawyers willing to bring such law suits are difficult to find.[71]

There are also various legal obstacles to a successful law suit against a police department or municipality. A police department is not liable under federal law unless its policies give rise to the constitutional violation;[72] it is not enough to show that an individual officer on her own violated the plaintiff's rights. Nor does inadequacy of police training serve as a basis for a federal civil suit unless the

[67] Bivens v. Six Unknown Named Agents, 403 U.S. 388, 419 (1971) (Burger, C.J. dissenting).
[68] *E.g.*, 42 U.S.C. § 1983 (making it an offense for any person "under color of any statute, ordinance, custom, or usage, of any State" to subject any person to "the deprivation of any rights, privileges, or immunities secured by the Constitution"); 28 U.S.C. § 2680(h) (permitting a civil suit against federal officers for constitutional violations).
[69] *E.g.*, 18 U.S.C. § 242 (making it a federal crime for anyone acting under color of law to deprive a person of her constitutional rights).
[70] Bivens v. Six Unknown Named Agents, 403 U.S. at 421 (Burger, C.J., dissenting).
[71] Stewart, n. 2 *supra*, at 1387-88.
[72] *See* Monell v. Department of Social Serv., 436 U.S. 658 (1978).

plaintiff can prove that the department's failure to train its officers amounts to deliberate or conscious indifference to the rights of the persons with whom the police come into contact.[73] Similarly, injunctive relief is permitted only if a departmental policy violates the Fourth Amendment,[74] and only if the victim can show that she is likely to be injured in the future by that policy.[75]

Policing the police doubtlessly is a good idea. However, it is unrealistic to believe that alone it can prevent police abuses or that such a review board would punish officers whose misconduct was not flagrant.

§ 121   Limitations On The Scope of the Exclusionary Rule

[A]   Non-Criminal Proceedings

The Supreme Court has stated that, "as with any remedial device, the application of the [exclusionary] rule [should be] restricted to those areas where its remedial objectives are thought most efficaciously served."[76] That is, in determining whether the rule should be applied to a particular proceeding, the issue is whether the cost of its use in the particular context is likely to outweigh the incremental deterrent benefit of extending the doctrine to the new situation.

The Court has held that the exclusionary rule applies in some quasi-criminal contexts, such as in proceedings in which property will be forfeited because of criminal wrongdoing.[77] On the other hand, the rule does not apply in civil tax proceedings[78] or deportation hearings.[79]

Many state courts apply the suppression rule in juvenile court proceedings.[80] Some courts have also applied the rule in civil suits to suppress evidence seized by the police from one of the parties to the suit. However, these applications of the exclusionary rule are not likely to withstand Supreme Court scrutiny if the issues should ever arise.

[B]   Criminal Proceedings

[1]   Non-Trial Proceedings

Evidence seized unconstitutionally may be introduced in grand jury proceedings without violation of the Fourth Amendment.[81] Presumably, such evidence may also be used in preliminary hearings,[82] in proceedings to determine bail,[83] and

---

[73] City of Canton, Ohio v. Harris, 489 U.S. 378 (1989).

[74] Rizzo v. Goode, 423 U.S. 362 (1976).

[75] City of Los Angeles v. Lyons, 461 U.S. 95 (1983).

[76] United States v. Calandra, 414 U.S. at 348.

[77] One 1958 Plymouth Sedan v. Pennsylvania, 380 U.S. 693 (1965).

[78] United States v. Janis, 428 U.S. 433 (1976).

[79] I.N.S. v. Lopez-Mendoza, 468 U.S. 1032 (1984).

[80] 1 W. LaFave, at § 1.7(b).

[81] United States v. Calandra, 414 U.S. 338 (1974).

[82] *See* Giordenello v. United States, 357 U.S. 480 (1958) (magistrates lack authority to adjudicate the admissibility of evidence); FRCP 5.1(a) (stating that "[o]bjections to evidence based on the ground that it was acquired by unlawful means are not properly made at the preliminary examination.").

[83] *E.g.*, 18 U.S.C. § 3142(f).

in sentencing hearings and proceedings to revoke probation or parole.[84]

Furthermore, although the exclusionary rule applies to state criminal trials, it has limited applicability in federal habeas corpus proceedings brought to overturn state criminal convictions. The Supreme Court ruled in *Stone v. Powell*[85] that a person incarcerated in a state prison is not entitled to federal habeas corpus relief on the ground that evidence obtained in violation of the Fourth Amendment was improperly introduced at her criminal trial, as long as the state provided her with "an opportunity for full and fair litigation of [the] Fourth Amendment claim."

[2] At a Criminal Trial

[a] Good-Faith Exception

The Supreme Court has ruled that, in specified circumstances, the Fourth Amendment does not bar the use at a criminal trial of evidence obtained by a police officer acting in reasonable reliance on a search warrant that subsequently is determined to be invalid.[86] Because of the complexity of this so-called "good faith" exception to the exclusionary rule, it is considered below in § 122.

[b] Impeachment Exception

As the result of a string of complicated and seemingly conflicting Supreme Court opinions,[87] the government may introduce evidence obtained from the defendant in violation of her Fourth Amendment rights for the limited purpose of impeaching her: (1) direct testimony; or (2) answers to legitimate questions put to her during cross-examination. However, the government may not use evidence obtained in violation of the defendant's Fourth Amendment rights to impeach all defense witnesses.

For example, if *D* testifies in a drug prosecution that she has never seen narcotics,[88] or denies in cross-examination that she previously possessed particular evidence of a crime,[89] the prosecutor may introduce evidence that contradicts these claims in order to impeach her credibility, even though the impeachment evidence was secured in violation of *D*'s Fourth Amendment rights. On the other hand, the prosecutor may not use a statement obtained from *D* in violation of the Fourth Amendment to impeach defense witnesses who provide testimony in conflict with that statement.[90]

The Supreme Court has determined that the use of Fourth Amendment tainted evidence to impeach a defendant's false testimony significantly furthers the truth-seeking process by deterring perjury; at the same time, the use of such evidence creates only a speculative possibility that the police will be encouraged to violate the Fourth Amendment.

---

[84] *See* 1 W. LaFave, at § 1.6(f).

[85] 428 U.S. 465, *reh'g denied*, 429 U.S. 874 (1976).

[86] United States v. Leon, 468 U.S. 897, *reh'g denied*, 468 U.S. 1250 (1984).

[87] For a thorough discussion of the cases, *see* 4 W. LaFave, at § 11.6(a).

[88] Walder v. United States, 347 U.S. 62 (1954).

[89] United States v. Havens, 446 U.S. 620, *reh'g denied*, 448 U.S. 911 (1980).

[90] James v. Illinois, 110 S.Ct. 648 (1990).

In contrast, in *James v. Illinois*,[91] the Court refused, 5-4, to extend the impeachment exception to all defense witness' testimony. Speaking for the majority, Justice Brennan stated that such a rule would not further the truth-seeking process to the same degree, because it might deter defendants from calling witnesses who would otherwise provide truthful and probative evidence, out of fear that the truthful witnesses might unexpectedly make a statement "in sufficient tension with the tainted evidence" to allow impeachment. The majority also felt that expansion of the exception to all defense witnesses would significantly weaken the exclusionary rule's deterrent effect, as it would greatly increase the number of times such evidence could be used during a trial.

§ 122   The *Leon* "Good Faith" Exception: General Principles[92]

[A]   Rule

[1]   In General

In *United States v. Leon*,[93] police officers executed a warrant later determined to be invalid because it was not supported by probable cause. In *Massachusetts v. Sheppard*,[94] a companion case, the police seized evidence under a warrant that was invalid because of a technical error by the magistrate.[95]

Under *Mapp*, the evidence obtained in these cases would not have been admissible at the defendants' criminal trials, except for impeachment purposes, because the warrants supporting the searches were invalid. Nonetheless, the Court permitted the evidence to be introduced at the trials.

As a result of these two cases, there now exists a so-called "good faith" (or *Leon*) exception to the Fourth Amendment exclusionary rule. In general, this exception provides that evidence obtained from the defendant pursuant to a search warrant

---

[91] *Id.*

[92] *See generally* 1 W. LaFave, at § 1.3; Bacigal, *The Road to Exclusion Is Paved With Bad Intentions: A Bad Faith Corollary to the Good Faith Exception*, 87 W. Va. L. Rev. 747 (1985); Bradley, *The "Good Faith Exception" Cases: Reasonable Exercises in Futility*, 60 Ind. L.J. 287 (1985); Dripps, *Living With Leon*, 95 Yale L.J. 906 (1986); Duke, *Making Leon Worse*, 95 Yale L.J. 1405 (1986); Goldstein, *The Search Warrant, the Magistrate, and Judicial Review*, 62 N.Y.U. L. Rev. 1173 (1987); Hanson, *The Aftermath of Illinois v. Gates and United States v. Leon: A Comprehensive Evaluation of Their Impact Upon the Litigation of Search Warrant Validity*, 15 Western State U. L. Rev. 393 (1988); Kamisar, n. 54 *supra*; LaFave, *The Fourth Amendment in an Imperfect World: On Drawing "Bright Lines" and "Good Faith"*, 43 U. Pitt. L. Rev. 307 (1982); Marsh, *On Rollercoasters, Submarines, and Judicial Shipwrecks: Acoustic Separation and the Good Faith Exception to the Fourth Amendment Exclusionary Rule*, 1989 U. Ill. L. Rev. 941; Note, *The Supreme Court, 1983 Term*, 98 Harv. L. Rev. 87, 108 (1984).

[93] 468 U.S. 897, *reh'g denied*, 468 U.S. 1250 (1984).

[94] 468 U.S. 981 (1984).

[95] The issuing magistrate failed to cross out inappropriate words in the warrant form; therefore, the warrant as signed unintentionally authorized the seizure of controlled substances, although the search was for evidence connected to a murder. The officer who executed the warrant apparently did not look at it after the magistrate signed it, because he was assured by the judge that all of the incorrect words in the form had been excised.

issued by a neutral and detached magistrate, but which warrant is subsequently determined to be invalid, may be introduced at the defendant's criminal trial in the prosecutor's case-in-chief, if a reasonably well-trained officer would have believed that the warrant was valid.

[2] "Good Faith"

Notwithstanding the "good faith" appellation, mere good faith by a police officer is an insufficient, and perhaps not even a necessary, element of the *Leon* rule.

Leon states that the inquiry into "good faith" is limited "to the objectively ascertainable question whether a reasonably well trained officer would have known the search was illegal despite the magistrate's authorization." Thus, even if the officer executes an invalid warrant in subjective good faith, the exclusionary rule applies — *i.e.*, *Leon* does not authorize an exception to *Mapp* — unless the officer's actions meet the objective standard of a "reasonably well trained officer."

On the other hand, under a literal reading of this test, evidence apparently would be admissible in a criminal trial, even if the officer executing the warrant subjectively knew that it was invalid, as long as the "reasonably well trained officer" would have believed that the warrant was good. In that sense, "good faith" is a misnomer.

However, even if it is possible for a bad-faith officer sometimes to take advantage of the "good-faith" rule, *Leon* does not hold that *all* information actually known by the officers involved in the warrant process is irrelevant to the question of what a "reasonably well trained officer" would believe.

Specifically, the Court stated that "all of the circumstances — including whether the warrant application had previously been rejected by a different magistrate — may be considered." In other words, the "reasonably well trained officer" is assumed to have knowledge of the actual officer's experiences with previous magistrates in the present case. It also ought to mean that the Court will incorporate into the "reasonably well trained officer" the knowledge of the actual officer in regards to other cases with facts similar to the present one.

[3] "Exceptions" to *Leon*

In dictum, *Leon* noted four situations in which an officer's reliance on a magistrate's probable-cause determination and on the technical sufficiency of the warrant would not be considered objectively reasonable. These four situations are sometimes described as "exceptions" to the *Leon* rule. In fact, however, they represent four examples of circumstances in which "objective good faith" does not exist as a matter of law.

First, the non-suppression rule of *Leon* does not apply if the magistrate who issued the warrant relied on information in the affidavit supplied by an affiant who knew that the statements therein were false or who recklessly disregarded the truth, in violation of the principles of *Franks v. Delaware.*[96]

Second, evidence is properly excluded if, in the language of *Leon*, the "issuing magistrate wholly abandoned his judicial role in the manner condemned in *Lo-Ji*

---

[96] 438 U.S. 154 (1978). *See* § 52 *supra*.

Sales, Inc. v. New York."[97] In other words, the *Leon* rule does not apply if the magistrate's behavior in the particular case was so lacking in judicial neutrality that the reasonable officer would have realized that the magistrate was not functioning in a judicial fashion. Because of the Court's specification of *Lo-Ji*, some courts have ruled that this "exception" to *Leon* does not apply if the magistrate "merely" lacked legal authority to issue the warrant.[98]

Third, the officer may not rely "on a warrant based on an affidavit 'so lacking in indicia of probable cause as to render official belief in its existence entirely unreasonable.' "[99] Although the thrust of this remark is not self-evident,[100] it probably means that an officer may not rely on a warrant issued by a magistrate based on a wholly conclusory — "bare bones" — affidavit, in gross violation of the "totality-of-the-circumstances" test enunciated in *Illinois v. Gates.*[101]

Notice, however, that *Leon* focuses on the *officer's* reliance on the magistrate's determination of probable cause, whereas *Gates* focuses directly on the *magistrate's* decision. Therefore, it is likely that there will be cases in which the magistrate errs in her probable-cause analysis (in violation of *Gates*), but in which the officer's reliance on that analysis could be objectively reasonable.

Fourth, evidence must be excluded if an officer relies on a warrant "so facially deficient — *i.e.*, in failing to particularize the place to be searched or the things to be seized — that the executing officers cannot reasonably presume it is valid." For example, the benefits of *Leon* are unavailable to the prosecutor if the warrant authorizes her to search "a house" but does not identify it, or if it states without further particularity that the officer should seize "all stolen jewelry" in a specific house. In each of these cases, unrelated to any question of probable cause, the warrant is facially deficient because it fails to meet the particularity clause of the Fourth Amendment.[102]

[B] Rationale of the *Leon* Exception

Much of the Court's opinion in *Leon*, written by Justice White, reads like a well-reasoned, but not out-of-the-ordinary, general criticism of the exclusionary rule. These aspects of *Leon* could be used to defend a broader exception to *Mapp* or

---

[97] 442 U.S. 319 (1979) (magistrate accompanied police to an "adult bookstore" and selected the materials to be seized). *See* § 51 *supra*.

[98] *E.g.*, People v. Dantzler, 206 Cal.App.3d 289, 253 Cal.Rptr. 526 (1988) (the warrant was invalid because the issuing magistrate lacked jurisdiction to grant a search in another county; however, because out-of-county warrants are permitted by state law under some circumstances, and the officer had no basis for knowing that the magistrate in this case lacked legal authority, the *Leon* good-faith rule applies).

[99] *Leon*, 468 U.S. at 923 (*quoting* Brown v. Illinois, 442 U.S. 590, 610-11 (1975)).

[100] For more complete analysis, *see* 1 W. LaFave, at § 1.3(f), at 71-77.

[101] 462 U.S. 213, *reh'g denied*, 463 U.S. 1237 (1983). *See* § 46 *supra*.

[102] In *Sheppard*, the Court left open the question of "[w]hether an officer who is . . . [un]familiar with the warrant application or who has unalleviated concerns about the proper scope of the search would be justified in failing to notice a defect [in the warrant]." In *Sheppard*, the officer executing the warrant also applied for it, and he had been assured by the magistrate that it was in proper form, so the Court held that it was reasonable for the officer to believe the magistrate without looking at the warrant.

even its abandonment. Other features of *Leon* are directed to the narrower question before it, namely, whether the deterrent benefits of the exclusionary rule outweigh its costs in the context of the officers' reasonable reliance on the warrants that had been authorized in these cases.

Justice White's general criticism of the exclusionary rule is that it is too costly: it impedes the truth-finding process, and the rule may result in the release of some guilty persons and reduced sentences for others. Furthermore, "[p]articularly when law enforcement officers have acted in objective good faith or their transgressions have been minor, the magnitude of the benefit conferred on such guilty defendants offends basic concepts of the criminal justice system." In short, the penalty inflicted for a violation of the Fourth Amendment often is grossly disproportional to the "crime" of the violation.

As for the benefits of the exclusionary rule, the Court first considered the rule's influence on the magistrates who issue search warrants. According to the Court, no evidence was presented to it to suggest that magistrates "are inclined to subvert the Fourth Amendment or that lawlessness among these actors requires application of the extreme sanction of exclusion."[103]

Even "more important" to the Court's analysis was that it did not discern a basis "for believing that exclusion of evidence seized pursuant to a warrant will have a significant deterrent effect on the issuing judge or magistrate." As neutral and detached officers of the court, Justice White reasoned, judges have no stake in the outcome of the particular prosecution. Therefore, the exclusionary rule threat does not affect their conduct, and removal of that threat would not alter their behavior.

The Court also doubted that the change in the rule announced in *Leon* would have a counter-deterrent effect on police officers. It treated as "speculative" the fear that the rule would result in "magistrate shopping," *i.e.*, officers seeking out more lenient judges to issue warrants.

Furthermore, in language that could be used to extend the *Leon* exception to good-faith *warrantless* searches, Justice White stated that "even assuming that the [exclusionary] rule effectively deters some police misconduct . . . it cannot be expected, and should not be applied, to deter objectively reasonable law enforcement activity." In such circumstances, exclusion of the evidence "will not further the ends of the exclusionary rule in any appreciable way; for it is painfully apparent that . . . the officer is acting as a reasonable officer would and should act in similar circumstances."

§ 123   Criticism of the *Leon* "Good Faith" Exception

Leon has been criticized on various counts. Some believe that the exclusionary rule as formulated in *Weeks* and *Mapp* is constitutionally compelled; therefore, the Court lacked the authority to narrow it. However, that argument was rejected by the Court well before *Leon* was decided.[104]

---

[103] In a footnote, the Court acknowledged the claim that magistrates sometimes act as "rubber stamps" for the police, but it stated that "we are not convinced that this is a problem of major proportions."

[104] *See* § 119 *supra*.

Other persons criticize *Leon* because they do not believe that the legitimacy of the exclusionary rule should be determined by cost-benefit analysis.[105] Others object to *Leon* because they disagree with one or more of the Court's general criticisms of the exclusionary rule.

Various criticisms of *Leon*, and the "good-faith" exception in particular, merit mention here. First, criticism has been levelled at the Court's calculation of the costs and benefits involved in good-faith warrant cases. In dissent, Justice Brennan asserted that the Court has created a "curious world where the 'costs' of excluding illegally obtained evidence loom to exaggerated heights and where the 'benefits' . . . are made to disappear with a mere wave of the hand." In particular, the Court included on the scale all of the costs of the exclusionary rule — not simply those that might be avoided by the good-faith principle — while it considered only those benefits of the exclusionary rule that arise in good-faith cases.

For example, the Court cited the existing data on prosecutions lost as a result of the exclusionary rule. Those figures are not especially high in percentage terms,[106] but in any case the only data that should have been considered are those costs — lost prosecutions — that will be avoided by the *Leon* rule.

Some lost prosecutions are the result of bad-faith police conduct or objectively unreasonable conduct by officers armed with search warrants, while some prosecutions are lost due to errors by police in non-warrant cases. These losses will continue after *Leon* and, therefore, should not have been placed on the scales.

Second, some critics believe that the Court understated the value of the exclusionary rule in inducing magistrates to act more carefully. Current data suggest that many magistrates already provide little oversight of the warrant process.[107] Perhaps in some cases, therefore, judges already function as adjunct law officers; if so, the message of *Leon* is not a good one, as it allows those magistrates to "protect" the prosecution from the exclusion of evidence.

Furthermore, one factor in the minds of some magistrates is that they do not want their decisions to be overturned by a higher court. If so, *Leon* might undercut their incentive to scrutinize warrant applications with care, because appellate courts will have less reason after *Leon* to decide whether a warrant was invalid: they can skip directly to the good-faith issue and rule in favor of the government.

Third, as discussed earlier,[108] the objective test of *Leon* might permit evidence to be used in a criminal trial even if the officer acted in bad faith, as long as the "reasonably well trained" officer would have believed that the warrant was good. If this is so, significant loss of deterrence is possible as a result of the "good faith" exception.

Fourth, the objective test of *Leon* is hard to understand, and even harder to utilize meaningfully. As Justice Stevens pointed out in dissent, the exclusion issue conceptually arises only if the Fourth Amendment was violated, *i.e.*, the police conducted an unreasonable search or seizure. Under *Leon*, evidence may be

---

[105] *See* § 120[C][1] *supra.*
[106] *See* nn. 59-61 and accompanying text *supra.*
[107] *See* § 50 *supra.*
[108] *See* § 122[A][2] *supra.*

introduced if the "reasonable" officer would have believed that the "unreasonable" search or seizure was lawful, but what does that mean?

In particular, how does one apply *Leon* in light of *Gates*? *Gates*' totality-of-the-circumstances test is flexible to begin with. "Probable cause" exists if there is a "fair probability" or a "substantial chance" that the search will result in the discovery of criminal evidence. In turn, the magistrate's determination of probable cause is entitled to substantial deference by the appellate court, *i.e.*, as long as there is a "substantial basis" for the magistrate's ruling.

Now, after *Leon*, the matter is taken a step further: to a "double dilution"[109] or even, perhaps, triple dilution, of "probable cause," which is all the more incomprehensible. What one is left with is "the mind-boggling concept of objectively reasonable reliance upon an objectively unreasonable warrant."[110] Or, put even more incomprehensibly, the rule now seems to be that evidence is admissible even if police officers "lacked a 'substantial basis' for a 'substantial chance' of criminal activity as long as they had a reasonable belief that they had a 'substantial basis' for a 'substantial chance'."[111]

§ 124   The Long-Term Implications of *Leon*

[A]   Warrant Cases

Leon's effect on Fourth Amendment litigation and on police procedures is only beginning to be measured. Obviously, *Leon* should result in the admission of evidence that, prior to the decision, would have been excluded. Lower court data support this prediction.[112] It is not yet clear, however, whether *Leon* results in more convictions, fewer plea bargains, and/or less lenient sentences than previously existed.

Some critics of *Leon* have expressed concern that in states that choose to apply the decision,[113] and in the federal courts that must apply it, there will be an increase in speculative search warrants, as police officers become emboldened to request warrants on less than probable cause, in the hope that if the warrants are granted, and criminal evidence is found, they will be able to avoid its suppression on the basis of *Leon*.

There is insufficient evidence to determine whether this fear is well–founded. However, for differing reasons, some commentators believe that *Leon* poses little risk of such a result. One view[114] is that the pre-*Leon* search-warrant process was reliable — *i.e.*, evidence was almost always found in warranted searches[115] —

---

[109] Kamisar, n. 54 *supra*, at 589.

[110] *Leon*, 468 U.S. at 958-59 (Brennan, J., dissenting).

[111] Kamisar, n. 54 *supra*, at 589 (emphasis deleted).

[112] *See* Hanson, n. 92 *supra*, at 542-46.

[113] Connecticut, Michigan, New Jersey, New York, and Oregon have rejected the *Leon* doctrine or have indicated in dictum that they might not, based on independent state grounds. *See generally* Hanson, n. 92 *supra*, at 515-22; State v. Marsala, 216 Conn. 150 (1990).

[114] Dripps, n. 92 *supra*, at 923.

[115] See n. 59 and accompanying text *supra*.

because the warrant-application procedure was too "expensive" in terms of police resources to justify fishing expeditions. The same costs will ensure that after *Leon* the police will continue to seek warrants only when they have good reason to believe that they will find the evidence that they are seeking.

Another view,[116] more cynical, is that "[e]ven before *Leon*, there were so many incentives to conduct unconstitutional searches and so few disincentives to do so, that little was left to the exclusionary sanction."

Some commentators also predicted that the good-faith doctrine would "freeze" Fourth Amendment case law,[117] that is, that substantive search-and-seizure law would remain static after *Leon* was decided, because lower courts would no longer need to address the question of whether the officer's actions were constitutional. Instead, courts would assume *arguendo* that the warrant was invalid, and then determine that the officer acted in objective good faith.

Although it is too soon to reach a definitive conclusion, at least one survey of post-*Leon* published appellate decisions does not support this prediction.[118] In general, courts have not skirted the substantive Fourth Amendment questions when they have ruled for the government, although they sometimes use the *Leon* exception as a backup theory to defend their holding.

[B] Non-Warrant Cases

The good-faith exception of *Leon* does not apply to non-warrant cases, but will it be extended to them?[119] There is reasoning in *Leon* to support both an affirmative and a negative answer.

On the negative side, *Leon* focused on the non-deterrability of magistrates and on the justifiability of officers relying on the magistrates' determinations. This reasoning does not support an extension of *Leon* to non-warrant cases. Moreover, such a change would run counter to the Court's overall policy of providing incentives to the police to seek warrants rather than to act on their own.

On the other hand, much of Justice White's reasoning applies with equal force to "objective good faith" conduct by officers acting without search warrants. Many of the no-deterrence assertions in *Leon* regarding police conduct could be repeated in non-warrant cases. Moreover, the costs of the suppression doctrine are at least as substantial in non-warrant cases as they were in *Leon*.

In view of the Court's personnel changes since *Leon* was decided in 1984,[120] which have moved the Court further away from the Warren Court principles that

---

[116] Duke, n. 92 *supra*, at 1422.

[117] Stewart, n. 2 *supra*, at 1400.

[118] Hanson, n. 92 *supra*, at 533-42; *see also* Bradley, *Are State Courts Enforcing the Fourth Amendment? A Preliminary Study*, 77 Geo. L.J. 251 (1988) (in a study of published Fourth Amendment opinions of several state courts in 1986, some cases of which involved search warrants, the opinions summarized in the study reached the substantive Fourth Amendment issues and did not rely on *Leon*).

[119] In general, prosecutors have not been successful in convincing state courts to extend *Leon* to non-warrant cases. One survey reports that appellate courts in nine states (Alabama, California, Florida, Georgia, Idaho, Illinois, Kentucky, Ohio and Virginia) have expressly refused the invitation. Hanson, n. 92 *supra*, at 546-48.

[120] *See* § 4[E] *supra*.

inspired the *Mapp* doctrine, extension of the *Leon* good-faith exception to non-warrant cases is an increasing possibility.

§ 125 "Fruit of the Poisonous Tree" Doctrine [121]

[A] General Principles

In general, the Fourth Amendment exclusionary rule extends not only to the direct products of the governmental illegality, but also to secondary evidence that is the so-called "fruit of the poisonous tree." [122]

For example, suppose that a police officer, on a sheer hunch, unconstitutionally searches *D*'s house for evidence of her suspected connection to a murder. During the search, the officer seizes a diary. The diary provides the police with a name of a witness to the murder, who agrees to testify against *D* at her trial.

The unlawful search constitutes the Fourth Amendment "poisonous tree." Under ordinary exclusionary rule principles, of course, the diary is inadmissible at *D*'s trial because it was the direct product of the unlawful search.

However, the trial testimony of the witness named in the diary is "secondary" or "derivative" evidence, in that it was secured as the result of the information found in the diary. It is the fruit of the poisonous tree. Under the fruit-of-the-poisonous-tree doctrine, this evidence is also inadmissible.

The fruit-of-the-poisonous-tree doctrine, however, is subject to three limitations: (1) the independent-source doctrine; (2) the inevitable-discovery rule; and (3) the attenuated-connection principle. These three limitations are discussed in subsections [C]-[E] below.

[B] Identifying the Nature of the Poisonous Tree

The fruit-of-the-poisonous-tree doctrine applies to other constitutional provisions — *i.e.*, there are Fifth Amendment and Sixth Amendment poisonous trees, as well as the Fourth Amendment variety.[123] On the other hand, there is either no *Miranda*[124] poisonous tree or it is substantially more limited.[125] Therefore, it is important to be able to identify the nature of the poisonous tree.

Sometimes the identification is tricky. For example, if *D* is arrested for murder without probable cause, informed of her *Miranda* rights, voluntarily waives those rights, and confesses, the confession will be admissible (as is discussed in other parts of this text) under Fifth Amendment, Sixth Amendment, and *Miranda* principles. Nonetheless, the confession might be inadmissible as a fruit of the Fourth Amendment poisonous tree (the unlawful arrest).

On the other hand, if *D* is lawfully arrested for murder, not informed of her *Miranda* rights, and subjected to custodial interrogation, during which she

---

[121] *See generally* 4 W. Lafave, at § 11.4.
[122] Nardone v. United States, 308 U.S. 338, 341 (1939).
[123] *See* §§ 135[B] (Fifth Amendment); 155[E] (Sixth Amendment) *infra*.
[124] Miranda v. Arizona, 384 U.S. 436, *reh'g denied*, 385 U.S. 890 (1966).
[125] *See* § 147[C] *infra*.

informs the police where she hid the gun used in the crime, the gun is a fruit of a *Miranda*, not a Fourth Amendment, poisonous tree. Its admissibility, therefore, is a matter of *Miranda* jurisprudence, and not of Fourth Amendment law.

[C] Independent-Source Doctrine

[1] General Rule

The threshold issue in any fruit-of-the-poisonous-tree claim is whether "the challenged evidence is in some sense the product of illegal governmental activity."[126] Evidence that is not causally connected to police illegality is admissible pursuant to the "independent source doctrine."[127] Quite simply, such evidence is a fruit of a *non*-poisonous tree.

The rationale of the independent-source doctrine has been described this way:

> [T]he interest of society in deterring unlawful police conduct and the public interest in having juries receive all probative evidence are properly balanced by putting the police in the same, not a *worse* position, that they would have been if no police error or misconduct had occurred. . . . When the challenged evidence has an independent source, exclusion of such evidence would put the police in a worse position than they would have been in absent any error or violation.[128]

[2] Evidence Initially Discovered Lawfully

In its simplest case, the independent-source doctrine applies if the challenged evidence is discovered for the first time during lawful police activity.

For example, suppose that the police lawfully seize *D*'s diary in a murder investigation. The diary identifies *W*, an eye-witness to *D*'s conduct. The police contact *W*, who agrees to testify against *D*. Later, the police search *D*'s premises a second time, but this time unlawfully. In the second search, the police discover *W*'s name again in another seized document. Under the independent-source doctrine, *D* may not successfully challenge *W*'s trial testimony as a fruit of the poisonous tree, because the police originally obtained *W*'s testimony lawfully, *i.e.*, in the first search.

[3] Evidence Initially Discovered Unlawfully

The independent-source doctrine also applies if evidence is initially discovered unlawfully, but is *seized* in a manner independent of the original discovery.

For example, in *Murray v. United States*[129] police officers unconstitutionally entered a warehouse and observed burlap-wrapped bales, which they suspected contained marijuana. The officers left the premises without seizing the bales. While they kept the area under surveillance, other officers obtained a warrant to search the building based on an untainted affidavit, *i.e.*, nothing learned from the

---

[126] United States v. Crews, 445 U.S. 463, 471 (1980).

[127] *See* Silverthorne Lumber Co. v. United States, 251 U.S. 385 (1920).

[128] Nix v. Williams, 467 U.S. 431, 443 (1984).

[129] 487 U.S. 533 (1988).

unlawful entry was used to secure the search warrant. The officers then returned and seized the bales.

According to the Court, the evidence potentially was admissible under the independent-source doctrine: it was seized as the result of the untainted warrant rather than as the result of the initial entry and search.

One controversial feature of the independent-source doctrine, in view of the Court's holding in *Murray*, is that it could provide an incentive to police to conduct unlawful "confirmatory searches" — *i.e.*, warrantless searches "to make sure that what they expect to be on the premises is in fact there."[130] The fear is that because the warrant-application process is inconvenient, police officers will want to confirm their suspicions before they seek a warrant. If they search and find nothing, they save the time of applying for a warrant. If they find criminal evidence, they may request a warrant and, as long as they leave out their observations from the unlawful search, seize the evidence.

Justice Scalia, speaking for the four-justice majority[131] in *Murray*, discounted this concern. He reasoned that if the police have probable cause before the confirmatory search, they would be "foolish" to conduct it, because they will later have to prove that all of the information in the warrant affidavit was obtained lawfully, an "onerous" burden. On the other hand, if they lack probable cause before the confirmatory search, nothing learned during the search may be used to strengthen their case.

Furthermore, the Court in *Murray* held that, just as the independent-source doctrine does not apply if the warrant would not have been *issued* but for the information secured from the original unlawful search, the doctrine is also inapplicable if the officers' *decision* to request the warrant was "prompted by what they had seen during the initial entry."

For example, suppose that the police suspect *D* of drug activities in her home, but they doubt that they have enough evidence to secure a search warrant. They search *D*'s premises without a warrant and confirm their suspicions. As a result, the police now apply for a search warrant, despite their continuing doubts that they have sufficient lawfully-obtained information to obtain a warrant. To their surprise, a search warrant, in no way based on the information from the confirmatory search, is issued. Under *Murray*, the independent-source doctrine does not apply: the evidence obtained *is* a fruit of the poisonous tree, because the police would not have sought the warrant but for the unlawful confirmatory search.[132]

[4] A Statement Obtained After an Unlawful Arrest

A confession obtained from a suspect arrested without probable cause is inadmissible unless the taint from the illegal arrest is dissipated. For example, a statement obtained from a person arrested on less than probable cause is not free

---

[130] *Id.* at 539.

[131] The vote was 4-3. Justices Brennan and Kennedy did not participate in the case.

[132] Justice Scalia stated that the officer's assurance on the point — "I would have requested this warrant anyway" — is not dispositive: "Where the facts render those assurances implausible, the independent source doctrine will not apply."

of taint solely because *Miranda* warnings were given and waived before the confession was received.[133]

However, a different rule applies if the police arrest a suspect in her house *with* probable cause, but without an arrest warrant in violation of *Payton v. New York*.[134] According to the Supreme Court in *New York v. Harris*,[135] a confession obtained outside the arrestee's home is admissible under the independent-source doctrine, even though the arrest was unconstitutional for want of a warrant.

In *Harris*, D was arrested in his apartment without the required arrest warrant. He was taken to the police station and read his *Miranda* rights, after which he waived his Fifth and Sixth Amendment constitutional rights, and made a statement that the police sought to introduce at D's trial. The Court, 5-4, held that the statement was admissible, because it was not the product of that aspect of the arrest that made it illegal.

The Court reasoned that the purpose of the *Payton* rule is to prohibit unwarranted entries into peoples' homes; the rule is not based on the conclusion that "an arrest in a home without a warrant but with probable cause somehow renders unlawful continued custody of the suspect once he is removed from the house." As the Court has consistently held, a person is not immune from prosecution merely because her presence in court is the fruit of an illegal arrest.[136]

Consequently, although D should not have been arrested as he was, he could lawfully have been arrested in his apartment later with a warrant, or outside his apartment without a warrant. Therefore, his continued custody at the police station was not unlawful. His confession, concededly a product of the arrest and of being in police custody, was not a product "of the fact that the arrest was made in the house rather than someplace else."[137]

[D] Inevitable-Discovery Rule

The independent-source doctrine described above provides that evidence is admissible, despite a prior illegality, if the prosecutor proves that the evidence seized was not in fact causally linked to the prior wrongdoing. Suppose, however, that the prosecutor concedes that the evidence is causally tied to the initial illegality, but she asserts that the police inevitably would have discovered the evidence lawfully, even in the absence of the unconstitutional conduct. If the court accepts the prosecutor's factual claim, is the derivative evidence admissible?

The Supreme Court held in *Nix v. Williams*[138] that evidence linked to an earlier illegality is admissible in a criminal trial if the prosecutor proves by a preponderance of the evidence that the challenged evidence "ultimately or inevitably would

---

[133] *See* § 125[E][2][c] *infra.*

[134] 445 U.S. 573 (1980). *See* § 59 *supra.*

[135] 110 S.Ct. 1640 (1990).

[136] *See* § 57[B] *supra.*

[137] Therefore, as a practical matter, the only evidentiary implications of a *Payton* violation is that physical evidence seized in a home, as an incident of the unlawful arrest, is inadmissible as the direct product of the *Payton* illegality; and a confession obtained *in the house* is subject to suppression under ordinary fruit-of-the-poisonous-tree principles.

[138] 467 U.S. 431 (1984).

have been discovered by lawful means." This is the so-called "inevitable discovery" rule. Although *Nix* involved a Sixth Amendment right-to-counsel fruit-of-the-poisonous-tree question, the rule applies in the same manner in Fourth Amendment cases.

In *Nix*, police officers, in violation of *D*'s Sixth Amendment right to counsel, deliberately elicited incriminating information from him and induced him to lead them to the body of the murder victim. At the time that *D* agreed to show the police where the body would be found, a search team was within a few miles of the victim's corpse; however, the search had been temporarily called off.

The Court held that the evidence secured from the victim's body was admissible, notwithstanding the Sixth Amendment illegality, on the basis of the inevitable-discovery doctrine. The trial court found that the body would have been discovered "within a short time" in "essentially the same condition" even if the police had not violated *D*'s Sixth Amendment rights. Consequently, the police should not be punished for the officer's illegality by placing them in a worse position than they would have been had they acted lawfully.

Justices Brennan and Marshall dissented. They agreed that evidence that would ultimately be discovered lawfully should be admissible, but they would have required the prosecutor to prove such inevitability by the higher standard of "clear and convincing evidence."

The dissenters reasoned that the doctrine, although akin to the independent-source doctrine, differs from it in the key respect that there is *not* an independent source, only a hypothetically independent one. The higher burden of proof is needed in order to confine the inevitable-discovery rule to circumstances that closely resemble the independent-source doctrine.

[E] Attenuated-Connection Principle (The *Wong Sun* Rule)[139]

[1] General Rule

In *Nardone v. United States*[140] the Supreme Court held that evidence secured as the result of police illegality is admissible if the connection between the illegality and the challenged evidence has "become so attenuated as to dissipate the taint."

The Supreme Court explained the attenuated-connection principle further in *Wong Sun v. United States*.[141] In *Wong Sun*, the Court stated that not all evidence "is 'fruit of the poisonous tree' simply because it would not have come to light but for the illegal actions of the police." Instead, the correct question is "whether, granting establishment of the primary illegality, the evidence to which instant objection is made has been come at by exploitation of that illegality or instead by means sufficiently distinguishable to be purged of the primary taint."[142]

There is no bright-line test for determining whether derivative evidence is free of the original taint. As the Court explained in *Brown v. Illinois*,[143] each case must

---

[139] *See generally* Note, *The Attenuation Exception to the Exclusionary Rule: A Study in Attenuated Principle and Dissipated Logic*, 75 J. Crim. L. & Crimin. 139 (1984).

[140] 308 U.S. 338 (1939).

[141] 371 U.S. 471 (1963).

[142] *Wong Sun, quoting* J. Maguire, Evidence of Guilt 221 (Little, Brown 1959).

[143] 422 U.S. 590 (1975).

be determined on its own facts, and no single fact is dispositive. Ultimately, the attenuation doctrine requires consideration of the admissibility of the evidence in light of the distinct policies and interests of the constitutional right in question.

[2] "Attenuation" Factors

[a] Temporal Proximity

The shorter the time lapse between the initial illegality and the acquisition of the challenged evidence, the more likely a court will conclude that the evidence is poisoned. For example, in *Wong Sun*, the police secured a statement from *D* in his bedroom immediately after his unlawful arrest. The Court suppressed this evidence, "which derive[d] so immediately from the unlawful entry."

[b] Length of the Causal Chain

The more factors that intervene between the initial illegality and the seizure of the challenged evidence, the more likely the evidence will be admitted. As the causal chain of events lengthens, the less likely it is that the police "foresaw the challenged evidence as a probable product of their illegality."[144] Consequently, the deterrent value of the exclusionary rule is reduced.

[c] The Existence of an Act of Free Will

An intervening act of free will is especially likely to remove the taint. For example, in *Wong Sun*, *D* was released from jail after his unlawful arrest. Subsequently, he voluntarily returned to the police station and provided them with a written statement. The Court found that the voluntary nature of *D*'s conduct rendered his statement sufficiently free of taint to be admissible.

On the other hand, the Court has consistently held that "Miranda warnings, *alone* and per se, cannot always make the act [of confessing] a product of free will to break, for Fourth Amendment purposes, the causal connection between the illegality and the confession."[145] Therefore, if the police arrest a suspect on less than probable cause, read her the *Miranda* warnings, obtain a waiver, and thereafter secure a confession, the question of whether the subsequent statement is the product of the suspect's free will must be determined on the facts of the individual case.

[d] Flagrancy of the Violation

Derivative evidence is less likely to be free of taint if the initial illegality was flagrant rather than accidental.[146] Metaphorically, a flagrant violation results in greater poison, and thus takes longer to dissipate. In terms of the deterrence principle, it is justifiable to apply the Fourth Amendment exclusionary rule more extensively if the secondary evidence is causally linked to egregious police misconduct.

---

[144] Comment, *Fruit of the Poisonous Tree - A Plea for Relevant Criteria*, 115 U. Pa. L. Rev. 1136, 1148-49 (1967).

[145] Brown v. Illinois, 422 U.S. at 603; *e.g.,* Dunaway v. New York, 442 U.S. 200 (1979); Taylor v. Alabama, 457 U.S. 687 (1982).

[146] *See* Brown v. Illinois, 422 U.S. at 604.

[e] Nature of the Derivative Evidence

By its nature, some contested evidence is more susceptible to dissipation of taint than other evidence. In particular, verbal evidence is more likely to be admissible than physical evidence.

For example, in *United States v. Ceccolini*,[147] the police unlawfully obtained the name of *X*, a witness to a crime. When contacted by the police, *X* cooperated fully with them and offered to provide important testimony against *D*. *D* sought to exclude *X*'s testimony as a fruit of the unlawful search.

The Court rejected the prosecutor's claim that the testimony of a witness should never "be excluded at trial no matter how close and proximate the connection between it and a violation of the Fourth Amendment." But, the Court also rejected language from *Wong Sun*, which stated that "the policies underlying the exclusionary rule [do not] invite any logical distinction between physical and verbal evidence."

Instead, the Court held that a witness' testimony is more likely than physical evidence to be free of taint. It offered two reasons in support of the special treatment of live testimony. First, witnesses often come forward of their own volition, whereas inanimate objects must be discovered by others. Therefore, there is a greater likelihood that the police will discover a witness by lawful means; consequently, the police have less incentive to violate the Constitution in order to obtain their testimony.

But, this argument is unpersuasive. Essentially, the majority's reasoning adds up to this: live testimony will often be admissible under the independent-source or inevitable-discovery doctrine, because witnesses (unlike inanimate objects) can and often do come forward voluntarily. But, even if a witness does not come forward in a particular case, the possibility that she might do so makes her testimony more susceptible to dissipation. This reasoning, however, amounts to nothing more than, as the dissent put it, "judicial double counting" of the free-will factor.

The second reason for the Court's belief that the testimony of witnesses should be more easily purged of taint than physical evidence is that if this were not the case, the relevant and material testimony of witnesses would be "permanently disabled." However, as the dissent in *Ceccolini* observed, physical evidence is also susceptible to permanent disability; and witness testimony is more apt to be unreliable than physical evidence.

---

[147] 435 U.S. 268 (1978).

CHAPTER 22

INTERROGATION LAW: OVERVIEW

§ 126 Historical Overview

Police interrogation law has come a long way since "the stone age"[1] — or "the good old days," depending on one's views of the trends in the law — of American criminal procedure. Although the Supreme Court in 1884 adopted the common law rule of evidence that a suspect's statements to the police are inadmissible at trial if they were obtained involuntarily,[2] this rule did not become a part of constitutional law until 1897 in the federal courts,[3] and 1936 in the state courts.[4]

In the past half century, interrogation law has undergone revolutionary change. A suspect has a far greater legal opportunity now than in the distant past to avoid police interrogation altogether or, at least, to bring a lawyer into the interrogation room with him. And, more so than in the early years, the fruits of custodial interrogations — confessions — are subject to exclusion at trial.

Most of the changes occurred during the Warren Court era, particularly in the 1960s and early 1970s. In large part the expansion ended when the balance of power on the Supreme Court shifted,[5] as justices with "due process model" values were replaced by advocates of the "crime control model" of criminal justice.[6]

The leading Warren Court interrogation cases have not been overruled. However, the "new" Court has, on the whole, applied existing interrogation law narrowly and has announced new exceptions to the old rules. The effect is an uneasy amalgam of old and new law; the rules and the exceptions to them sit uncomfortably next to each other.

§ 127 Relevant Constitutional Provisions

[A] Due Process Clauses

The Fifth Amendment, which applies to the actions of the federal government, provides that "[n]o person shall . . . be deprived of life, liberty, or property, without due process of law." The Fourteenth Amendment, which applies to the actions of state and local government, has a similar due process clause.

---

[1] Kamisar, *Kauper's "Judicial Examination of the Accused" Forty Years Later — Some Comments on a Remarkable Article*, 73 Mich. L. Rev. 15, 16 (1974).

[2] Hopt v. Utah, 110 U.S. 574 (1884).

[3] Bram v. United States, 168 U.S. 532 (1897).

[4] Brown v. Mississippi, 297 U.S. 278 (1936).

[5] *See generally* § 4[E] *supra.*

[6] For discussion of the competing models of the criminal justice system, *see* § 5 *supra.*

As discussed in the next chapter, a person is denied due process of law if a statement obtained from him involuntarily is used against him at a criminal trial.

[B] Self-Incrimination Clause

[1] Traditional "Voluntariness" Analysis

The Fifth Amendment provides that "[n]o person . . . shall be compelled in any criminal case to be a witness against himself." This right has come to be known as the "privilege against self-incrimination," but more accurately is the "privilege against *compelled* self-incrimination."

The general principles of the Fifth Amendment privilege are discussed in Chapter 26. In the interrogation context, however, the Supreme Court has drawn upon due process concepts of "voluntariness" to define "compulsion."

In 1964, the Supreme Court held that the privilege against compelled self-incrimination is a fundamental right, applicable to the states pursuant to the Fourteenth Amendment due process clause.[7] Consequently, the admissibility of a confession in a state criminal prosecution is now tested by the same voluntariness standard as is applied in federal prosecutions.

[2] *Miranda* "Voluntariness" Analysis

In *Miranda v. Arizona*,[8] the Supreme Court devised a set of warnings that the police must give a suspect in their custody before they may interrogate him, in order to protect his privilege against self-incrimination. The Court stated that in the absence of the procedural safeguards set out in the case, "no statement obtained from the defendant [during custodial interrogation] can truly be the product of his free choice."

Although the original understanding of *Miranda* was that a violation of the rules set out in the case constituted a breach of the Fifth Amendment privilege against self-incrimination, subsequent opinions of the Court have held that the *Miranda* safeguards are "prophylactic" in nature, *i.e.*, they are non-constitutional rules intended to prevent violations of the Fifth Amendment.[9] Consequently, although *Miranda* is a branch of Fifth Amendment law, it is necessary for analytical purposes to treat *Miranda* jurisprudence separately from "pure" self-incrimination law.

[C] Assistance of Counsel

[1] Sixth Amendment

Whether or not a statement was secured by the police in a coercive manner, it is inadmissible at trial if it was obtained in violation of the accused's constitutional right to counsel. The Sixth Amendment provides that "[i]n all criminal prosecutions, the accused shall enjoy the right to . . . the Assistance of Counsel

---

[7] Malloy v. Hogan, 378 U.S. 1 (1964).

[8] 384 U.S. 436, *reh'g denied*, 385 U.S. 890 (1966).

[9] The concept of "prophylactic rules" is discussed at § 15 *supra*.

for his defence." This right applies to the states through the Fourteenth Amendment due process clause.[10]

As developed in Chapter 25, the Sixth Amendment right to counsel is violated if the government deliberately elicits statements from a suspect in the absence of his counsel or waiver of the right. However, the right to counsel does not attach until adversary judicial criminal proceedings commence, which usually does not occur until a suspect is arrested and appears before a magistrate or is indicted.

[2] Fifth Amendment

There is no express Fifth Amendment right to counsel. However, as a result of *Miranda*, a suspect is entitled to what has come to be known as the "Fifth Amendment (more accurately, *Miranda*) right to counsel," a right that attaches when a suspect is subjected to custodial interrogation. The purpose of this right to counsel is to protect the suspect's privilege against compulsory self-incrimination.

It is necessary to treat the Fifth Amendment and Sixth Amendment versions of the right to counsel separately. They attach at different times (the Fifth Amendment right usually comes into play earlier), under different circumstances, and for somewhat different reasons.[11]

§ 128   Interrogation Law: The Policy Debate[12]

[A]   The "Uneasy Conflict of Worthy Interests"

Interrogation law is controversial. In large part this is because there is an "uneasy conflict of worthy interests [that] produces a curious ambivalence of attitudes toward the confession of crime by one taken into police custody."[13]

The "uneasy conflict of worthy interests" is considered in detail in subsequent chapters, but students should be sensitive to the debate at the outset. As will be seen, various overarching issues of criminal procedure come into sharp focus in the field of interrogation law. In particular, students of interrogation law must consider (or reconsider) their commitment to the sometimes-conflicting values of truth in the trial process and of a non-inquisitorial system of criminal justice.[14]

[B]   Society's Ambivalence Toward Confessions

Interrogation law is partially the product of contradictory attitudes held by the public regarding confessions.[15]

---

[10] Gideon v. Wainwright, 372 U.S. 335 (1963).

[11] *See* § 156 *infra*.

[12] *See generally* J. Grano, Police Interrogation and Confessions: A Rebuttal to Misconceived Objections (Occasional Papers from the Center for Research in Crime and Justice, New York University School of Law, No. 1, 1987); Y. Kamisar, Police Interrogation and Confessions (U. Michigan Press 1980); Grano, *Selling the Idea to Tell the Truth: The Professional Interrogator and Modern Confession Law*, 84 Mich. L. Rev. 662 (1986); Sutherland, *Crime and Confession*, 79 Harv. L. Rev. 21 (1965).

[13] Sutherland, n. 12 *supra*, at 22.

[14] *See* §§ 6-7 *supra*.

[1] Why the Public Favors Confessions

Supposedly, confessions are desirable because it is good for wrongdoers to confess their guilt: when a person feels remorse for his wrongdoing and accepts responsibility for his actions, he has taken a significant step toward paying his debt to society. The admission of responsibility may also be the first step in the criminal's rehabilitation.

From a law enforcement perspective, society wants people to confess because a confession may be the only or best evidence of a person's guilt; a conviction may be impossible without it. And, confessions relieve us of our fear that we might be prosecuting innocent people.

People also consider confessions reliable. As Justice Jackson once observed, "[i]t probably is the normal instinct to deny and conceal any shameful or guilty act." [16] Therefore, when an accused person takes the "unnatural" step of admitting his guilt we assume that the admission is true. Why else would a person confess?

[2] Why the Public Disfavors Confessions

As much as society values confessions, it also worries about them. The answer to the question ending the last subsection — "Why would a person confess if he were not guilty?" — might be: "Because he was coerced to do so." That is, it is precisely because the confessional act runs contrary to ordinary behavior that we are suspicious that it might be the result of police overreaching. If it were, the confession might not be reliable: the truth-seeking process could be jeopardized rather than advanced.

Many people also worry that if the police are too free to obtain confessions from suspects, they are apt to turn to inquisitorial techniques that not only create an undue risk of false confessions but also violate "the law's ethical or moral responsibility to treat criminal suspects and defendants in a manner consistent with their dignity as autonomous human beings." [17] Even if the law is unwilling "to grant each citizen indefeasible control over his or her own personal preserves of mind," [18] many people believe that the government's use of a person's thoughts as an instrument of self-destruction is disquieting.

[C] Has the Law Gone Too Far To Disfavor Confessions?

In view of society's conflicting attitudes regarding confessions, the question that arises is whether the Supreme Court's efforts, particularly in the Warren Court era, to place greater restrictions on the police in the interrogation process were wise.

Persons who favor restrictions believe, as Justice Goldberg observed in *Escobedo v. Illinois*,[19] an interrogation case:

> We have . . . learned the . . . lesson of history that no system of criminal justice can, or should, survive if it comes to depend for its continued

---

[15] See Dix, *Federal Constitutional Confession Law: The 1986 and 1987 Supreme Court Terms*, 67 Tex. L. Rev. 231, 254 (1988).

[16] Ashcraft v. Tennessee, 322 U.S. 143, 160 (1944) (Jackson, J., dissenting).

[17] Dix, n. 15 *supra*, at 261.

[18] Uviller, at 1146.

[19] 378 U.S. 478 (1964).

effectiveness on the citizens' abdication through unawareness of their constitutional rights. No system worth preserving should have to *fear* that if an accused is permitted to consult with a lawyer [before interrogation], he will become aware of, and exercise these rights. If the exercise of constitutional rights will thwart the effectiveness of a system of law enforcement, then there is something very wrong with that system.

People who are suspicious of police interrogations have argued that there should be as much justice "in the gatehouses" of American criminal procedure as in its "mansions."[20] That is, just as the defendant in the courtroom (the mansion) is regaled with adversarial protections, which are provided in large part to ensure that he can tell his side of the story effectively, the suspect in the police station (the gatehouse) should receive comparable safeguards.

In contrast, many persons believe that "a civilized, decent society need not be embarrassed by police interrogation and confessions."[21] They argue that courts have created an "equality in the police station [that] thwarts rather than serves the goal of truth."[22] They contend that the Supreme Court has devised a system of criminal justice reminiscent of a fox hunt, in which rules are written to give the fox (the criminal) a fair chance to escape.

Critics of the "pro-defendant" interrogation cases believe that this "sporting view of justice"[23] is irrational. As long as police procedures do not create an undue risk of false confessions, the system *should* be unequal, because it is desirable to give the police the upper hand in their battle to find and convict the guilty. Put simply, the foxes are not supposed to succeed.[24]

[D] Questions To Think About

In studying interrogation law, the key policy question to think about is the one raised in the last sub-section: Has the law gone too far in protecting suspects? But, there are a number of sub-issues and independent questions that also should be considered.

1. *To what extent were confessions unreliable before the Supreme Court became involved?* The implicit point raised by this question is, "If it ain't broke, don't fix it." Was the system broken before the Supreme Court "fixed" it in the 1960s and 1970s?

---

[20] Kamisar, *Equal Justice in the Gatehouses and Mansions of American Criminal Procedure*, in Criminal Justice in Our Time (A. Howard ed.) (U. Virginia Press 1965), *reprinted in* Y. Kamisar, n. 12 *supra*, at 27.

[21] J. Grano, n. 12 *supra*, at 1.

[22] *Id.* at 4.

[23] Pound, *The Causes of Popular Dissatisfaction With the Administration of Justice*, 40 Am. Law Rev. 729, 738 (1906).

[24] As Justice Scalia has put it, "even if I were to concede that an honest confession is a foolish mistake [by a suspect], I would welcome, rather than reject it; a rule that foolish mistakes do not count would leave most offenders . . . unconvicted. More fundamentally, it is wrong, and subtly corrosive of our criminal justice system, to regard an honest confession as a 'mistake,' " Minnick v. Mississippi, 111 S. Ct. 486 (1990) (dissenting opinion).

2. *How important are confessions in the prosecution of crime?* Is police interrogation "an indispensable instrumentality of justice."[25] Or, are there other reliable methods to prove a person's guilt, so that a reduction in the number of confessions would not be a matter of legitimate societal concern?

3. *To what extent has the Supreme Court made it more difficult for the police to obtain reliable confessions?* The empirical questions here are various. First, have the constitutional obstacles significantly reduced the number of confessions obtained by the police? If the answer is "no," is police efficiency undermined in other ways?

On the other hand, if there has been a reduction in confessions attributable to the Court's decisions, does this mean that the truth-seeking process has been hurt, or are the police primarily losing the unreliable confessions? Is it also possible that the stringent rules have provided an incentive for the police to seek more reliable methods to prove guilt?

4. *Have the constitutional rules created equality in the interrogation room; if they have, is that a good or bad outcome?* The empirical question is whether the Supreme Court has devised "fox hunt" rules of interrogation that have placed suspects on an equal footing with the police in the interrogation room? The normative question is: Is equality in this context irrational, as some contend, or does it further a valid concern for human dignity and fair play?

5. *Regardless of the answers to the preceding questions, is the Supreme Court the proper institution to develop interrogation rules?* This question has two components. First, has the Supreme Court gone beyond its legitimate constitutional authority to develop the confession rules? This issue is especially pertinent in the context of *Miranda* jurisprudence.

Second, even if the Supreme Court has not exceeded its lawful authority, is the federal judiciary the best institution to develop the law, or should it defer more often to others, such as to state courts and legislatures?

---

[25] Ashcraft v. Tennessee, 322 U.S. at 160 (dissenting opinion).

CHAPTER **23**

COERCED ("INVOLUNTARY") CONFESSIONS

As clarified in this chapter, a statement of a suspect obtained by the police by coercive measures is inadmissible in that person's criminal trial under the due process clause and the Fifth Amendment privilege against compulsory self–incrimination.[1]

§ 129   Coerced-Confession Law: Historical Development

[A]   Common Law

In early English common law, all statements of a suspect, even those obtained by torture, were admissible at trial. By the end of the eighteenth century, however, the rule had changed, and it was determined that "no credit" was to be given to "a confession forced from the mind by the flattery of hope, or by the torture of fear."[2]

The purpose of this exclusionary rule was to exclude from consideration by the factfinder any statement obtained in a manner that rendered it untrustworthy and thus that might result in the conviction of an innocent person. With that goal in mind, most English courts phrased the issue to be whether the confession was made voluntarily. If it were not, it was considered unreliable and inadmissible.

English courts applied the exclusionary rule strictly. Confessions secured by brutality or threat of force were inadmissible, but so also were statements induced by promises not to prosecute or to provide lenient treatment in sentencing.

American federal courts, including the Supreme Court, followed the English lead, although they were less inclined than the English courts to invalidate confessions. In *Hopt v. Utah*,[3] for example, the Supreme Court remarked that "the

---

[1] *See generally* Benner, *Requiem for Miranda: The Rehnquist Court's Voluntariness Doctrine in Historical Perspective*, 67 Wash. U.L.Q. 59 (1989); Dix, *Federal Constitutional Confession Law: The 1986 and 1987 Supreme Court Terms*, 67 Texas L. Rev. 231 (1988); Dix, *Mistake, Ignorance, Expectation of Benefit, and the Modern Law of Confessions*, 1975 Wash. U.L.Q. 275; Grano, *Voluntariness, Free Will, and the Law of Confessions*, 65 Va. L. Rev. 859 (1979); Kamisar, *What is an Involuntary Confession? Some Comments on Inbau and Reid's Criminal Interrogation and Confessions*, 17 Rutgers L. Rev. 728 (1963); Schulhofer, *Confessions and the Court*, 79 Mich. L. Rev. 865 (1981); White, *Police Trickery in Inducing Confessions*, 127 U. Pa. L. Rev. 581 (1979); Comment, *The Coerced Confession Cases in Search of a Rationale*, 31 U. Chi. L. Rev. 313 (1964); Note,, *Guarding the Guardians: Police Trickery and Confessions*, 40 Stan. L. Rev. 1593 (1988); *Developments in the Law — Confessions*, 79 Harv. L. Rev. 935 (1966).

[2] The King v. Warickshall, 1 Leach C.L. 263, 264, 168 Eng. Rep. 234, 235 (K.B. 1783).

[3] 110 U.S. 574 (1884).

rule against . . . admissibility [of coerced confessions] has been sometimes carried too far, and in its application justice and common sense have too frequently been sacrificed at the shrine of mercy."

[B] Constitutionalization of the Common Law

In 1897 in *Bram v. United States*,[4] the Supreme Court stated that the Fifth Amendment privilege against compelled self–incrimination "was but a crystallization of the [common law] doctrine relative to confessions." The effect of *Bram* was to bring the common law voluntariness rule under the umbrella of the Fifth Amendment: thereafter, statements obtained by the police by coercive measures were inadmissible in federal criminal trials as a matter of constitutional law.

Because the privilege against compelled self–incrimination was not then considered a fundamental right,[5] *Bram* did not apply to the states. However, in 1936, in *Brown v. Mississippi*,[6] the Supreme Court invoked the Fourteenth Amendment due process clause to invalidate murder convictions obtained solely on the basis of confessions "shown to have been extorted by officers of the State by brutality and violence."

In *Brown*, three defendants, "all ignorant negroes" who denied involvement in a murder, were brutalized by sheriff deputies, and in one case by a mob of white vigilantes with a deputy's participation. One suspect was hanged by a rope to the limb of a tree three times and whipped; two others were stripped, laid over chairs in the jail, and whipped with a leather strap so severely that their backs were "cut to pieces."

The Court stated that "[i]t would be difficult to conceive of methods more revolting to the sense of justice than those taken to procure the confessions of the [defendants]." It compared the actions of the state officials to "[t]he rack and torture chamber," and concluded that a conviction secured in this manner "was a clear denial of due process."

Although *Brown* did not speak in terms of "voluntariness," subsequent opinions of the high court have confirmed that, as with the Fifth Amendment privilege against self–incrimination, a confession's inadmissibility under the due process clause is based on a finding of "involuntariness."[7]

In 1964, the Fifth Amendment privilege against self–incrimination was made applicable to the states through the Fourteenth Amendment.[8] Consequently, a defendant in a state trial who wishes to have his confession excluded may now allege general "due process" or more specific "self–incrimination" grounds. Primarily for historical reasons, most defendants in state prosecutions allege a violation of the due process clause. In either case, the issue is whether the confession was acquired involuntarily.

---

[4] 168 U.S. 532 (1897).

[5] *See* Twining v. New Jersey, 211 U.S. 78 (1908).

[6] 297 U.S. 278 (1936).

[7] *See, e.g.*, Spano v. New York, 360 U.S. 315 (1959).

[8] Malloy v. Hogan, 378 U.S. 1 (1964).

[C] *McNabb–Mallory* Federal Rule

There is no litmus test for determining the voluntariness of a confession.[9] Each case must be decided on its own merits, a judicially inefficient way to filter out coerced confessions. Consequently, beginning in the 1940s, the Supreme Court developed a bright–line *per se* rule, applicable only in federal courts, intended to exclude a class of confessions that might have been coerced. The rule came be known as the *McNabb–Mallory*[10] rule.

By federal statute then, and by federal rule now,[11] an arrestee must be brought before a magistrate "without unnecessary delay" following her arrest.[12] In *McNabb* and *Mallory* (and some intervening cases), the Supreme Court used its supervisory power over the federal courts to define the phrase "unnecessary delay" and to provide a remedy for violations of the so–called "prompt arraignment rule."

The essence of the *McNabb–Mallory* rule was that although the police could properly delay a suspect's first appearance before a magistrate in order to "book" her, they could not delay the appearance in order to interrogate her. The Court's remedy for a violation of the prompt–arraignment rule was to exclude from federal trials any statement obtained during the unnecessary delay, whether or not the confession was "involuntary" under traditional principles.

The *McNabb–Mallory* rule was not applied enthusiastically by federal courts and was criticized in Congress.[13] In 1968, Congress purported to overrule the doctrine when it enacted the Omnibus Crime Control and Safe Streets Act, which provides in part that any confession secured in the first six hours after arrest is admissible notwithstanding any delay, and that a confession obtained thereafter may also be admissible, depending on the totality of the circumstances.[14]

Because the *McNabb–Mallory* rule is not of constitutional origin, it does not apply to the states and Congress very likely had authority to override it by the 1968 legislation. In any case, the rule is no longer of practical significance in view of the *Miranda*[15] ruling.

---

[9] *See* § 133 *infra.*

[10] McNabb v. United States, 318 U.S. 332, *reh'g denied*, 319 U.S. 784 (1943); Mallory v. United States, 354 U.S. 449 (1957); *see generally* Hogan & Snee, *The McNabb–Mallory Rule: Its Rise, Rationale and Rescue*, 47 Geo.L.J. 1 (1958); Kamisar, *Illegal Searches or Seizures and Contemporaneous Incriminating Statements: A Dialogue on a Neglected Area of Criminal Procedure*, 1961 U. Ill.L.F. 78; Keene, *The Ill–Advised State Court Revival of the McNabb–Mallory Rule*, 72 J. Crim. L. & Crimin. 204 (1981).

[11] FRCP 5(a).

[12] The "first appearance" before the magistrate is discussed at § 3[C][3] *supra.*

[13] *See* 1 C. Wright, at § 72.

[14] 18 U.S.C. § 3501.

[15] Miranda v. Arizona, 348 U.S. 436, *reh'g denied*, 385 U.S. 890 (1966). *See* chapter 24 *infra.*

§ 130 "Involuntariness": General Constitutional Rule

A statement obtained from a suspect as a result of police coercion is inadmissible in her state or federal criminal trial under the due process clauses of the Constitution and the Fifth Amendment privilege against compulsory self–incrimination.[16] Although the Fifth Amendment notion of "compulsion" could be defined differently than the due process concept of "involuntariness" — indeed, some scholars believe that it should be [17] — the Supreme Court has relied on the latter doctrine to define "compulsion."

If a defendant's coerced confession is introduced into evidence at her trial over her objection,[18] and she is subsequently convicted, the judgment must be reversed even if there is overwhelming independent evidence of the defendant's guilt.[19]

§ 131 Rationale of the "Voluntariness" Requirement

According to the Supreme Court, a "complex of values"[20] underlie the "voluntariness" requirement. First, a coerced confession is potentially untrustworthy.[21] Second, even if a coerced confession is reliable (i.e., there is corroborating evidence), it should be excluded because the police should "obey the law while enforcing the law."[22] Third, coerced confessions are inadmissible because their use is "so offensive to a civilized system of justice that they must be condemned."[23]

Fourth, "ours is an accusatorial and not an inquisitorial system."[24] One principle of an accusatorial system is that "the mind, as the center of the self, may

---

[16] E.g., Spano v. New York, 360 U.S. 515 (1959) (due process); Ziang Sun Wan v. United States, 266 U.S. 1 (1924) (privilege against self–incrimination).

[17] See n. 34 infra.

[18] Typically, a defendant must make a timely pre–trial motion to suppress a confession. See, e.g., FRCP 12(b)(3). Failure to do so results in the forfeiture of the claim. FRCP 12(f). In the pre–trial hearing the judge must suppress the evidence unless she finds by a preponderance of the evidence that the confession was not coerced by the police. Lego v. Twomey, 404 U.S. 477 (1972). In most jurisdictions, the judge's determination of the matter is final pending appeal.

Some states follow the so–called "Massachusetts procedure": the judge makes the initial voluntariness determination, which is final if she rules that the confession was coerced; if she finds that it was not, the jury is allowed to hear the confession and the circumstances surrounding its acquisition, and is instructed that it may consider the confession only if it first determines that it was voluntarily given.

[19] Payne v. Arkansas, 356 U.S. 560 (1958). This per se prejudicial-error rule was recently called into question. See Arizona v. Fulminante, 161 Ariz. 237, 778 P.2d 602 (1989), cert. granted, 110 S. Ct. 1522 (1990) (89-939). An issue raised in Fulminante is: "Can [an] erroneous admission of [an] involuntary confession be subjected to harmless error analysis in [a] case in which there is overwhelming evidence of guilt . . . ." 58 U.S.L.W. 3614 (Mar. 26. 1990).

[20] Blackburn v. Alabama, 361 U.S. 199, 207 (1960).

[21] See Spano v. New York, 360 U.S. 315 (1959).

[22] Id. at 320.

[23] Miller v. Fenton, 474 U.S. 104, 109 (1985).

[24] Rogers v. Richmond, 365 U.S. 534, 541 (1961).

not be pressed by the government into an instrument of its own destruction."[25] Indeed, the use of coercion to obtain a confession "was the chief iniquity, the crowning infamy of . . . the Inquisition. . . ."[26]

Fifth, values of personal autonomy and mental freedom support the premise that a person should not be convicted on the basis of a confession unless it is the "untrammeled exercise of personal determination."[27] Finally, the exclusion of a coerced confession deters police misconduct, and thus serves to prevent the harms described above.[28]

Although all of these concerns probably retain force in current litigation, the unreliability of a coerced confession, which was the common law rationale for the coerced–confession exclusionary rule, no longer is a necessary or sufficient basis for its exclusion. That is, a confession coerced by the police, although trustworthy in the particular case, is still inadmissible because its use is fundamentally unfair;[29] and, as explained in the next chapter section, a coerced confession, no matter how untrustworthy, is constitutionally admissible if it was obtained in the absence of government misconduct.[30]

§ 132   "State Action" Requirement

The Supreme Court held in *Colorado v. Connelly*[31] that coercive police activity, as distinguished from private compulsion, is a prerequisite to a finding that a confession is "involuntary" within the meaning of the due process clause. As the Court put it, "the most outrageous behavior by a private party seeking to secure evidence against a defendant does not make that evidence inadmissible under the Due Process Clause."

In view of the state–action requirement in the context of other constitutional rights, this rule is not surprising. However, in light of the traditional desire of the courts to prevent the introduction at trial of unreliable confessions, the requirement of state coercion is noteworthy.

In *Connelly, D*, a mentally disturbed man suffering from "command hallucinations" — *i.e.*, he was hearing "the voice of God" order him to confess or to commit suicide — approached a police officer on the street and confessed to a murder. The perplexed officer ascertained that the speaker was not drunk or on drugs, but was

[25] Uviller, at 1146.

[26] Brown v. Mississippi, 297 U.S. at 287 (*quoting* Fisher v. State, 145 Miss. 116, 134, 110 So. 361, 365 (1926)).

[27] Uviller, at 1146; *see also* Miranda v. Arizona, 384 U.S. at 460 ("[T]he constitutional foundation underlying the privilege [against compulsory self–incrimination] is the respect a government . . . must accord to the dignity and integrity of its citizens. . . . [It must] respect the inviolability of the human personality. . . .").

[28] Colorado v. Connelly, 479 U.S. 157, 165–66 (1986).

[29] Lisenba v. California, 314 U.S. 219, 236 (1941), *reh'g denied*, 315 U.S. 826 (1942). ("The aim of the [voluntariness] requirement . . . is not to exclude presumptively false evidence, but to prevent fundamental unfairness in the use of evidence whether true or false.").

[30] Colorado v. Connelly, 479 U.S. 157 (1986).

[31] *Id.*

told by *D* that he had been a patient in several mental hospitals. After the officer informed him of his constitutional rights, *D* answered questions about the crime.

Due to his mental disease, *D* probably lacked the capacity to confess voluntarily. Furthermore, his confession was no less untrustworthy than if it had been wrung from him by the police rather than by "God."

Nonetheless, despite language in two cases that seemed to some to support *D*'s claim that an involuntary confession is inadmissible even if it were secured in the absence of police overreaching,[32] the Court concluded in *Connelly* that the " 'involuntary confession' jurisprudence is entirely consistent with the settled law requiring some sort of 'state action' to support a [due process clause] violation."

The Court justified its holding on the ground that the purpose of the co-erced–confession exclusionary rule is "to substantially deter future violations of the Constitution." In the absence of police misconduct there is no constitutional wrongdoing to deter.

The Court explained that the potential unreliability of a confession is a matter that "the Constitution rightly leaves . . . to be resolved by state laws governing the admission of evidence." As Justice Stevens stated in his partial concurrence, "[t]he fact that the statements [made by D] were involuntary — just as the product of Lady Macbeth's nightmare was involuntary — does not mean that their use for whatever evidentiary value they may have is fundamentally unfair or a denial of due process."

§ 133   "Voluntariness": Totality-of-the-Circumstances Test

[A]   Critical Overview

In *Bram v. United States*,[33] the Supreme Court's first effort to define "compul-sion" in a constitutional context, the justices stated that a confession "must not be extracted by any sorts of threat or violence, nor obtained by any direct or implied promises, however slight, nor by the exertion of any improper influence."

---

[32] In Blackburn v. Alabama, 361 U.S. 199 (1960), the Court excluded as involuntary a confession obtained from a mentally ill person after a nine–hour interrogation. In the opinion, the Court noted that "[s]urely in the present stage of our civilization a most basic sense of justice is affronted by the spectacle of incarcerating a human being upon the basis of a statement he made while insane. . . ."

In Townsend v. Sain, 372 U.S. 293 (1963), a police physician administered medication, which had "truth–serum" qualities to it, to *D* in order to reduce his severe stomach pains caused by heroin withdrawal. The resulting confession was declared to be involuntary. The Court noted that it was irrelevant to its holding whether the police were aware of the medication's truth–serum qualities.

The Court in Connelly contended that both of these cases involved police overreaching: in Blackburn, the police were aware of *D*'s psychiatric history, and they "exploited this weakness" by conducting the long interrogation in a small room, in the presence of many officers, and in the absence of friends or relatives of *D*; in Townsend, the drug was administered by a state agent, and the police knew that it had been administered to the suspect (although they may not have known of its truth–serum qualities).

[33] 168 U.S. 532 (1897).

The Court warned that because "the law cannot measure the force of the influence used or decide upon its effect upon the mind of the prisoner," it would hold a confession inadmissible "if any degree of influence" was exerted.

This virtual bright–line rule has not prevailed. As discussed more fully in subsection [B], the voluntariness of a confession is now assessed from a totality of the circumstances.[34] The Court has described the issue of voluntariness this way:

> Is the confession the product of an essentially free and unconstrained choice by its maker? If it is, if he has willed to confess, it may be used against him. If it is not, if his will has been overborne and his capacity for self–determination critically impaired, the . . . confession [is inadmissible].[35]

This notion of voluntariness is not entirely accurate. First, no matter how unfree the speaker's choice, a confession is admissible if it was the result of private, rather than government, misconduct.[36]

Second, the implication of the statement is that "voluntariness" is an empirical issue: Was the defendant "free" to choose or was her will "overborne" by the police? In fact, however, the issue of voluntariness, like that of duress in the criminal law,[37] raises as well a normative question: How much, and what kind of, pressure placed on a person is morally permissible?

Ultimately, a normative analysis is inevitable. No statement is involuntary, except metaphorically.[38] That is, all confessions, even those obtained by torture, are "free" in the sense that the speaker preferred confessing to the continuation of the pressures. On the other hand, nearly all confessions are "unfree" in the sense that they are caused by the police–induced pressure, *i.e.*, but for the police action the defendant would not have confessed. Therefore, the issue becomes, how "free" is "free?"

The Supreme Court has conceded that "voluntariness" is "an amphibian"[39] notion. Although the determination of voluntariness requires a finding of the "crude historical facts"[40] regarding the acquisition of the suspect's confession, the ultimate issue is a legal one.[41]

---

[34] Why did the bright line of *Bram* give way to the totality–of–the–circumstances test? As various scholars have pointed out, the issue in *Bram* was the meaning of "compulsion" in the Fifth Amendment self–incrimination context; in contrast, the great majority of pre–*Miranda* confession cases, in which the totality–of–the–circumstances–test was developed, were decided on due process "voluntariness" grounds. *See* Schulhofer, *Reconsidering Miranda*, 54 U. Chi. L. Rev. 435, 444–45 (1987); Benner, n. 1 *supra*, at 113–17. Once the due process clause entered center stage, however, the justices "drew on voluntariness concepts to explain 'compulsion.'" Schulhofer, *supra*, at 440. As a result, the Court may have lost sight of the bright–line rule of *Bram*.

[35] Culombe v. Connecticut, 367 U.S. 568, 602 (1961) (opinion of Frankfurter, J.).

[36] Colorado v. Connelly, 479 U.S. 157 (1986). *See* § 132 *supra*.

[37] *See* Dressler, *Exegesis of the Law of Duress: Justifying the Excuse and Searching for Its Proper Limits*, 62 So. Cal. L. Rev. 1331 (1989).

[38] *See* Kadish, *Excusing Crime*, 75 Calif. L. Rev. 257, 266–66 (1987).

[39] Culombe v. Connecticut, 367 U.S. at 605.

[40] *Id.* at 603.

[41] Miller v. Fenton, 474 U.S. at 110.

In resolving the legal issue, the "Court's decisions reflect a frank recognition that the Constitution requires the sacrifice of neither security nor liberty."[42] That is, the Court has balanced the society's perceived need for police interrogation against the importance of ensuring that the process does not become "so offensive [as to violate] a civilized system of justice."[43]

The result of this balancing process, not surprisingly, has been a collection of Supreme Court cases in which conflicting value judgments are expressed. In its "pro–liberty" cases, the Court has stated that the police should not "take advantage"[44] of suspects, and that there should be a "fair state–individual balance"[45] in the interrogation process. In the "pro–security" cases, however, the Court has suggested that confessions should be admissible unless the interrogation process is "so offensive to a civilized system of justice that [it] must be condemned."[46]

[B] "Voluntariness": Factors

The totality–of–the–circumstances test makes "everything relevant but nothing determinative."[47] As one critic of the rule has observed, the typical co-erced–confession case is one "in which the court[] provide[s] a lengthy factual description followed by a conclusion . . . , without anything to connect the two."[48] Nonetheless, case law suggests the following relevant points in determining voluntariness.

First, a confession obtained by the threatened or actual use of violence, probably even by "one truncheon blow on the head,"[49] is inadmissible.[50] Even a lawful threat to inflict pain on a suspect may render a subsequent confession inadmissible. For example, an officer's remarks to a rape suspect during interrogation that he might have to submit to a penile swab for a semen sample if he did not admit to having intercourse with the complainant, coupled with his remarks regarding the painful nature of the test, rendered a subsequent confession legally involuntary.[51]

Second, the use of psychological pressures to extract a confession may render a statement inadmissible.[52] Among the relevant factors in this regard are: the

---

[42] See Schneckloth v. Bustamonte, 412 U.S. 218, 226 (1973).

[43] Miller v. Fenton, 474 U.S. at 109.

[44] Blackburn v. Alabama, 361 U.S. at 207.

[45] Miranda v. Arizona, 384 U.S. at 460 (quoting 8 Wigmore, Evidence 317 (McNaughton rev. 1961)).

[46] See Miller v. Fenton, 474 U.S. at 109.

[47] Grano, Miranda v. Arizona and the Legal Mind: Formalism's Triumph Over Substance and Reason, 24 Am. Crim. L. Rev. 243, 243 (1986).

[48] See Weinreb, Generalities of the Fourth Amendment, 42 U. Chi. L. Rev. 47, 57 (1974).

[49] Fikes v. Alabama, 353 U.S. 191, 198, reh'g denied, 352 U.S. 1019 (1957) (Frankfurter and Brennan, JJ. concurring) (assuming that "[i]t is common ground" that a confession obtained in such a manner violates due process).

[50] E.g., Brown v. Mississippi, 297 U.S. 278 (1936).

[51] State v. Phelps, 235 Neb. 569, 456 N.W.2d 290 (1990) (in which the court also stated that "pain, to render a defendant's statement involuntary, need not be of such a nature or degree that would have resulted in recoil by Tomas de Torquemada of the Spanish Inquisition.").

length of the interrogation; the physical conditions under which the questioning took place; whether the suspect was deprived of food, clothing, or sleep; and the personal characteristics of the suspect (*e.g.*, age, character, level of education, psychological makeup, prior experience with the police).

Third, promises of leniency could render a confession involuntary. For example, in *Lynumn v. Illinois*,[53] the police informed *D* of the potential implications of a criminal conviction: ten years of imprisonment, loss of custody of her children, and loss of welfare payments. However, they indicated that if she cooperated, "it would be easier on her." Although there was no evidence that the police breached their promise to recommend leniency or that their statements of law were inaccurate, the Court unanimously held that the confession was coerced. Whether such promises of leniency would invalidate a confession today, at least in the Supreme Court, is questionable.

Fourth, police deception sometimes will invalidate a confession, although less often today than in the past. For example, the Court once held that the police violated due process when they masqueraded a police psychiatrist as a physician called in to treat the suspect's sinus condition, who interrogated him.[54] More recently, however, they approved the ruse of placing an undercover officer in a jail cell masquerading as a burglar, who purposely elicited incriminating statements.[55] And, when the police falsely informed a suspect that the case against him was strong because his cousin had already confessed, the Court held that this lie alone did not render the confession inadmissible.[56]

In general, deception by concealment of facts, as distinguished from their misrepresentation, does not render a confession involuntary, even if the undisclosed information would have affected the suspect's decision to talk. For example, a confession is not involuntary simply because a suspect is unaware of the fact that the person to whom she is speaking is an undercover agent rather than an apparent friend,[57] or if the interrogating officer does not inform the suspect that she will be questioned about a crime other than the one about which she agreed to talk.[58]

---

[52] *E.g.*, Spano v. New York, 360 U.S. 315 (1959); Ashcraft v. Tennessee, 322 U.S. 143 (1944).

[53] 372 U.S. 528 (1963).

[54] Leyra v. Denno, 347 U.S. 556, *reh'g denied*, 348 U.S. 851 (1954).

[55] Illinois v. Perkins, 110 S.Ct. 2394 (1990).

[56] Frazier v. Cupp, 394 U.S. 731 (1969). In this regard, consider the following ruse by *O*, a New York homicide investigator. In an effort to obtain a confession from *D*, a suspect in a murder investigation, *O* told *D* that "when a person is murdered the last thing a person sees is the person who killed them. And this image remains on the lens of their eyes after they die." *O* went on to say that modern medical technology made it possible to remove the eyes during autopsy and have them "developed" like film in a lab, and thereby learn who the killer was. Based on this "information," *D* confessed. *See* Rosenbaum, *Crack Murder*, New York Times Magazine, Feb. 15, 1987, at 24, 30. Should this trickery render the confession involuntary, or is this simply good, creative police work?

[57] Hoffa v. United States, 385 U.S. 293, 304 (1966).

[58] Colorado v. Spring, 479 U.S. 564, 574 (1987).

§ 134   Standing to Raise an "Involuntariness" Claim

If the police coerce X into making a statement in which she incriminates D, is X's statement inadmissible at D's criminal trial, or is the direct victim of the coercion the only person with standing to raise a coercion claim?

Some of the reasons for suppressing coerced confessions, such as their inherent untrustworthiness, would argue in favor of permitting a defendant to raise a coercion claim of another. Other justifications for the exclusionary rule, such as the principle that coercion abridges the mental freedom of the individual, favor the usual rule that constitutional rights are personal.

The Supreme Court has not ruled directly on the standing issue in the context of a coerced–confession claim, but there is virtually no doubt that standing is a requirement. In a different context, the Court has stated that the Fifth Amendment privilege against compulsory self–incrimination is "intimate and personal,"[59] and that it "adheres basically to the person, not to information that may incriminate him."[60] It has also expressed concern in the coerced–confession context "that the exclusionary rule imposes a substantial cost on the societal interest in law enforcement."[61]

§ 135   Scope of the Coerced-Confession Exclusionary Rule

[A]   In General

A coerced confession is inadmissible at the defendant's criminal trial for all purposes: it may not be introduced in the prosecutor's case–in–chief to prove the defendant's guilt, and it is also inadmissible for impeachment purposes.[62] As such, this exclusionary rule is broader than the exclusionary rules related to the Fourth Amendment, *Miranda*, and to at least certain aspects of the Sixth Amendment right to counsel.[63]

[B]   Fruit-of-the-Poisonous-Tree Doctrine

The Supreme Court has not expressly stated that the fruit–of–the–poisonous–tree doctrine[64] applies to coerced confessions, but it is assumed that it does.

The Court has applied the attenuated–connection principle of the doctrine in a related context. In *Harrison v. United States*,[65] the prosecutor was improperly

---

[59] Couch v. United States, 409 U.S. 322, 327 (1973) (summons served on X, D's accountant, requiring X to hand over D's personal business records in his possession, does not violate D's Fifth Amendment privilege).

[60] *Id.* at 328.

[61] Colorado v. Connelly, 479 U.S. at 166 (*quoting* United States v. Janis, 428 U.S. 433, 448–49 (1976)).

[62] Mincey v. Arizona, 437 U.S. 385 (1978); *see also* New Jersey v. Portash, 440 U.S. 450 (1979).

[63] *See* § 121[B][2][b] (Fourth Amendment) *supra*; §§ 147[A] (*Miranda*) and 155[D] (Sixth Amendment) *infra*.

[64] *See* § 125 *supra*.

[65] 392 U.S. 219 (1968).

permitted to introduce three confessions by D that the police obtained in violation of the *McNabb–Mallory* rule.[66] As a result, D changed his trial strategy, and testified in his own behalf. Ultimately, D's conviction was overturned because of the *McNabb–Mallory* violations. At D's second trial, at which the confessions were properly excluded, the prosecutor sought to introduce D's testimony from the first trial. However, the Court held that the testimony was inadmissible, because the prosecutor had not adequately proved that it "was obtained 'by means sufficiently distinguishable' from the underlying illegality 'to be purged of the primary taint.' "

Since the "poisonous tree" in *Harrison* was a non–constitutional supervisory–authority rule, it should follow that a violation of the Constitution itself requires implementation of the poisonous–tree doctrine in all of its features.

---

[66] The *McNabb–Mallory* rule is discussed at § 129[C] *supra*.

CHAPTER 24

MIRANDA v. ARIZONA

§ 136 Introductory Observations

Miranda v. Arizona[1] is among the most famous Supreme Court decisions in American history. It may be the case most recognized by name. If Justice Rehnquist is correct that "virtually every schoolboy is familiar with the concept"[2] of the privilege against self-incrimination, it is probably also true that nearly every American, adult or "schoolboy," has heard of *Miranda*. Among lawyers, it is the most memorable Supreme Court criminal case in American jurisprudence.[3]

The holding of *Miranda* has proved to be extraordinarily controversial. The majority opinion mustered only five votes. Although there was substantial support for the ruling in various quarters, the decision also "evoked much anger and spread much sorrow"[4] among the police and legislatures. Congress has sought to "overrule" it by legislation,[5] one recent United States Attorney General described it as "infamous,"[6] and one office of his Department of Justice recommended that the Supreme Court be urged to overrule it.[7]

Miranda's influence has stretched well beyond the police interrogation room. The decision, the values underlying it, and the public's perception of it were factors in preventing Justice Abe Fortas, a member of the *Miranda* majority, from being confirmed by the United States Senate as Chief Justice of the Supreme Court, and it may have helped elect Richard Nixon to the presidency.[8]

Miranda — the legal doctrine — is alive, but not very well.[9] None of the justices who formed the slim majority in the case are on the Court today. Most of the new members of the Court have expressed different degrees of criticism of the case.

Nonetheless, although one former member of the Court has stated that the doctrine is "twisting slowly in the wind,"[10] there is a good possibility that the basic

---

[1] 384 U.S. 436, *reh'g denied*, 385 U.S. 890 (1966).

[2] Michigan v. Tucker, 417 U.S. 433, 439 (1974).

[3] J. Lieberman, Milestones! vii (West 1976).

[4] Kamisar, *A Dissent From the Miranda Dissents: Some Comments on the "New" Fifth Amendment and the Old "Voluntariness" Test*, 65 Mich. L. Rev. 59, 59 (1966).

[5] 18 U.S.C. § 3501.

[6] Washington Post, Aug. 26, 1985, § A, at 6, col. 1 (statement of Attorney General Edwin Meese).

[7] *See* Office of Legal Policy, U.S. Dep't of Justice, Report to the Attorney General on the Law of Pre-Trial Interrogation (Feb. 12, 1986).

[8] *See generally* L. Baker, Miranda: Crime, Law and Politics (Atheneum 1983).

[9] That is more than can be said for Ernesto Miranda. He was killed in a barroom brawl ten years after the case was decided. His suspected killer was given *Miranda* warnings. *Id.* at 408.

[10] Goldberg, *Escobedo and Miranda Revisited*, 18 Akron L. Rev. 177, 182 (1984).

holding of *Miranda* will not be overruled in the foreseeable future. A factor in favor of its retention is that a great deal of jurisprudence has developed around it; to overrule *Miranda* would have significant implications in related areas of the law.

Furthermore, as will be seen in this chapter, *Miranda* has been, in large part, narrowly interpreted in recent years, and exceptions to the doctrine have been created, so that much of the case's potential impact — for good or for ill, depending on one's view of the matter — has been muted.

§ 137 *Miranda*: Placing It In Legal Context

In the pre-*Miranda* era, the police usually interrogated suspects in private. Lawyers were not entitled to be in the interrogation room with their clients. Perhaps because of the incommunicado nature of the process, police brutality was common into the 1930s.[11] Violence only lessened after the Supreme Court applied the due process clause of the Constitution to exclude confessions obtained by coercion.[12]

In the place of the "third degree," many police officers were taught by their departments to use psychological ploys to secure confessions from unwilling suspects. The techniques were sophisticated, and consistent with the social psychology literature of the time.[13] Among other things, the police manuals instructed officers on the proper arrangement of interrogation rooms,[14] on the characteristics of the ideal interrogator,[15] and on the most effective means to manipulate suspects to confess.[16]

The new procedures troubled some observers who believed that they differed only in degree rather than in kind from those used in totalitarian societies.[17] On the other side, the authors of the manuals defended the use of tricks to secure confessions on the ground that "[o]f necessity, criminal interrogators must deal

---

[11] *See* National Commission on Law Observance and Enforcement, Report on Lawlessness in Law Enforcement (1931); Hall, *Police and Law in a Democratic Society*, 28 Ind. L.J. 133, 140 (1953) ("[T]here is hardly a single physical brutality inflicted by the Gestapo . . . which American policemen have not at some time perpetrated.").

[12] *E.g.*, Brown v. Mississippi, 297 U.S. 278 (1936).

[13] *See* Driver, *Confessions and the Social Psychology of Coercion*, 82 Harv. L. Rev. 42 (1968).

[14] *E.g.*, they should give the suspect the "illusion that the environment . . . is withdrawing." A. Aubry & R. Caputo, Criminal Interrogation 38 (C.C. Thomas 1965).

[15] *E.g.*, the interrogator should be male, tall, deep voiced, and dressed in a business suit.

[16] *E.g.*, interrogators should falsely tell suspects that there is sufficient evidence to convict them, minimize the moral significance of the charges against them, and/or employ the "Mutt and Jeff" routine, in which one officer acts hostile to the suspect while his partner is conciliatory.

[17] *E.g.*, Sterling, *Police Interrogation and the Psychology of Confession*, 14 J. Public L. 25, 37 (1965) ("Moreover, if the American police manuals are examined, there is a striking similarity between their recommendations and Russian and Chinese interrogation techniques.").

with criminal offenders on a somewhat lower moral plane than that upon which ethical law-abiding citizens are expected to conduct their every day affairs."[18]

As the police became more sophisticated in their interrogation techniques, the Supreme Court increasingly treated confessions "darkly as the product of police coercion."[19] The justices came to believe that encounters in the interrogation room should be more evenly balanced between the suspects and the police.

Moreover, by the early 1960s the Court had become dissatisfied with the due process "voluntariness" test[20] as a mechanism for dealing with the new interrogation techniques. Based upon thirty years of struggle with the doctrine — with a test in which "almost everything was relevant, but almost nothing was decisive"[21] — the Court concluded that the test resulted in "intolerable uncertainty,"[22] and that a brighter-line rule was needed.

In 1964, interrogation law took a dramatic turn. First, the Court held that the Fifth Amendment privilege against compulsory self-incrimination is a fundamental right applicable to the states through the Fourteenth Amendment due process clause.[23]

Second, in *Massiah v. United States*,[24] the Court turned its sights to the Sixth Amendment, and held that the government may not deliberately elicit statements from a person under indictment in the absence of counsel. Shortly thereafter in *Escobedo v. Illinois*,[25] it extended the right to counsel to a pre-indictment interrogation.

Massiah and *Escobedo* generated confusion and controversy among legal observers.[26] When the Court granted a hearing in *Miranda*, lawyers expected it to clarify *Escobedo*. Instead, the justices shifted gears again, this time moving from the Sixth Amendment right to counsel to the Fifth Amendment privilege against compulsory self-incrimination.

§ 138 The Road to *Miranda*: *Escobedo v. Illinois*

In *Escobedo*,[27] *D*, who was under arrest for murder, was taken into custody late in the evening and interrogated at the police station. During the questioning, he was handcuffed and kept standing.

---

[18] F. Inbau & J. Reid, Criminal Interrogation and Confessions 208 (Williams & Wilkins Co. 1962).

[19] Caplan, *Questioning Miranda*, 38 Vand. L. Rev. 1417, 1425 (1985).

[20] *See* § 133 *supra*.

[21] Kamisar, *Gates, Probable Cause, "Good Faith," and Beyond*, 69 Iowa L. Rev. 551, 570 (1984).

[22] Grano, *Voluntariness, Free Will, and the Law of Confessions*, 65 Va. L. Rev. 859, 863 (1979).

[23] Malloy v. Hogan, 378 U.S. 1 (1964).

[24] 377 U.S. 201 (1964).

[25] 378 U.S. 478 (1964).

[26] *See* Stone, *The Miranda Doctrine in the Burger Court*, 1977 Sup. Ct. Rev. 99, 103.

[27] 378 U.S. 478 (1964).

At various times during the interrogation, *D* asked to consult with his lawyer, but his requests were refused on the false ground that his lawyer "didn't want to see" him. The truth was that shortly after the questioning began, *D*'s counsel arrived at the station in order to talk to him, but he was not permitted to do so because, as one officer put it, "they hadn't completed questioning."

Later in the night, the police suggested to *D* that he confront *X*, an accomplice who had implicated him as the triggerman, in their presence. *D* agreed. During the encounter, he made statements to *X* that, for the first time, indicated his knowledge of the crime, *i.e.*, "I didn't shoot [*V*], you did it." Subsequently, *D* made additional statements to the police implicating himself as an accomplice. At no time was *D* informed of his privilege against self-incrimination.

D sought to exclude his statements on the basis that they were coerced, in violation of the due process clause, but the trial court found that they were voluntarily given. *D* was convicted. On appeal, however, the Supreme Court held that the confession was inadmissible because it was obtained in violation of *D*'s Sixth Amendment right to counsel.

Escobedo was path-breaking. Never before had the Court held that the Sixth Amendment right to counsel applied to a person against whom criminal proceedings had not yet formally begun, such as by indictment. Speaking for the Court, Justice Goldberg stated that the fact that *D* had not been indicted when the statements were obtained was irrelevant because, "[w]hen [*D*] requested, and was denied, an opportunity to consult with his lawyer, the investigation had ceased to be a general investigation. . . ." By that time, the investigation had "focused" on *D*; for all practical purposes he had become the accused.

The Court observed that *D*, who had no prior criminal record, "undoubtedly" was unaware that his admissions of complicity were legally as damaging as an admission that he had fired the fatal shot. Therefore, he needed the "guiding hand of counsel" to advise him "in this delicate situation." According to *Escobedo*, it would have "exalt[ed] form over substance to make the right to counsel . . . depend on whether at the time of the interrogation, the authorities had secured a formal indictment."

Despite broad language in the opinion, the Court's ultimate holding was narrow. It held only that a suspect's Sixth Amendment right to counsel is violated when, "as here": (1) the investigation focuses on him; (2) he is in custody; (3) the police interrogate him; (4) he requests and is denied an opportunity to consult with his lawyer; and (5) the police have not informed him of his privilege against self-incrimination.

Escobedo was controversial. Some criticized it for "opening the door" of some interrogation rooms to defense attorneys, while others criticized it for not going far enough in that direction.[28] However, the cross-criticisms of *Escobedo* were soon over-shadowed by *Miranda*.

Escobedo's long-term impact as a Sixth Amendment case was undercut shortly after the decision. The Court "in retrospect" concluded that the underlying

---

[28] Critics of the latter variety pointed out that under *Escobedo* a person who did not ask to see his attorney was not protected. Effectively, this left out lawyer-less indigents and those too timid or naive to ask for counsel during interrogation.

rationale of the case was "not to vindicate the right to counsel as such, but, like *Miranda*, 'to guarantee full effectuation of the privilege against self-incrimination. . . .' "[29] In short, *Escobedo*, although nominally a right-to-counsel case, became a self-incrimination opinion.

The Supreme Court also limited the holding of *Escobedo* to its own facts.[30] Consequently, it is the only high court opinion to hold that the Sixth Amendment right to counsel attaches before formal adversary criminal proceedings have begun.

Escobedo's long-term significance, therefore, is not found in its holding, but rather in the majority's expressed attitudes toward interrogations and confessions.[31] Justice Goldberg's opinion provides a classic — and controversial — defense of the accusatorial system of criminal justice, in which the government must shoulder the entire load of proving the defendant's guilt, and in which confessions are disfavored.

In this context, the essence of the Court's opinion was that *D* needed the guiding hand of a lawyer in his encounter with the police. But, had he been given that right, his lawyer almost certainly would have advised him not to talk. The Court's reaction to this outcome was to state that this demonstrated why custodial interrogation is a critical stage in the criminal justice process. "The right to counsel would indeed be hollow," it stated, "if it began at a period when few confessions were obtained." Justice Goldberg also observed that:

> [T]he lesson of history, ancient and modern, [is] that a system of criminal law enforcement which comes to depend on the "confession" will, in the long run, be less reliable and more subject to abuses than a system which depends on extrinsic evidence independently secured through skillful investigation. As Dean Wigmore so wisely stated: *"[A]ny system of administration which permits the prosecution to trust habitually to compulsory self-disclosure as a source of proof must itself suffer morally thereby."*

It was with this attitude toward confessions that the Warren Court turned to *Miranda*.

§ 139 *Miranda*: The Case

[A] The Facts

Miranda v. Arizona involved four cases consolidated for a single appeal. In view of the *per se* holding of the case, the facts relating to the prosecutions received little attention by the Court. Although the cases involved police practices in four jurisdictions, there were significant common facts: (1) each of the suspects had been taken into custody (in three, by arrest; in one, before arrest); (2) they were

---

[29] Kirby v. Illinois, 406 U.S. 682, 689 (1972) (*quoting* Johnson v. New Jersey, 384 U.S. 719, 729 (1966)).

[30] Johnson v. New Jersey, 384 U.S. 719, *reh'g denied*, 385 U.S. 890 (1966).

[31] *See* Grano, *Selling the Idea to Tell the Truth: The Professional Interrogator and Modern Confessions Law*, 84 Mich. L. Rev. 662, 666 (1986).

questioned in an interrogation room; (3) the questioning occurred in a police-dominated environment, in which each suspect was alone with the questioners; (4) the suspects were not informed of their privilege against compulsory self-incrimination; and (5) statements were obtained.

[B] The Holding

[1] General Rule

[a] Self-Incrimination

Any statement, whether exculpatory or inculpatory, obtained as the result of custodial interrogation may not be used against the speaker in a criminal trial unless the prosecutor proves that the police provided procedural safeguards effective to secure the speaker's privilege against compulsory self-incrimination.[32]

"Custodial interrogation" — the triggering mechanism of *Miranda* — is defined as "questioning initiated by law enforcement officers after a person has been taken into custody or otherwise deprived of his freedom of action in any significant way." The Court said that "[t]his is what we meant in *Escobedo* when we spoke of an investigation which had focused on the suspect."

[b] Right to Counsel

According to the Court, "[t]he circumstances surrounding in-custody interrogation can operate very quickly to overbear the will of one merely made aware of his privilege" against compulsory self-incrimination. Therefore, it held that an in-custody suspect has a right to consult counsel prior to questioning and to have counsel present during any interrogation that occurs.

Under *Miranda*, the primary purpose of defense counsel during custodial interrogation is to assure that the suspect's ability to choose whether to speak or to remain silent is unfettered. The lawyer serves other "significant subsidiary functions": his presence during interrogation reduces the likelihood that the police will act coercively; he can testify at trial regarding any coercion; and he can make sure that any statement given by his client is accurate and that it is reported correctly at trial.

The right to counsel discussed in *Miranda* has come to be known as the Fifth Amendment, or *Miranda*, right to counsel. It should not be confused with the Sixth Amendment right to counsel discussed in the next chapter, which differs in various respects.[33]

[2] Procedural Safeguards

According to *Miranda*, Congress and the states are free to develop procedural safeguards for protecting a suspect's Fifth Amendment rights during custodial interrogation. However, unless they are "fully as effective" as those described in the opinion, the following warnings must be provided by the police prior to custodial questioning.

---

[32] Exceptions to this rule now exist. *See* § 146 *infra.*
[33] *See* § 156 *infra.*

First, the police must "in clear and unequivocal terms" indicate that the suspect has a right to remain silent.

Second, the consequence of foregoing the preceding right must be explained to the suspect. Specifically, the first warning "must be accompanied by the explanation that anything said can and will be used against the individual in court."

Third, a suspect held for interrogation must "clearly" be informed that "he has a right to consult with a lawyer and to have the lawyer with him during the interrogation."

Fourth, because the financial ability of the suspect has no relation to the scope of the right to counsel or its importance, the police must inform him that "if he is indigent a lawyer will be appointed to represent him."

[3] Waiver

[a] In General

The suspect may waive his privilege against self-incrimination and his Fifth Amendment right to the assistance of counsel before or during interrogation. A "heavy burden" rests on the prosecutor, however, to demonstrate that the alleged waiver meets the *Zerbst*[34] waiver test, *i.e.*, that the defendant "voluntarily, knowingly, and intelligently" waived his rights.

[b] Voluntariness of the Waiver

The Court stated that the mere "fact of lengthy interrogation or incommunicado incarceration before a statement is made is strong evidence" of involuntary relinquishment of the Fifth Amendment privilege. Furthermore, evidence that the suspect was "threatened, tricked, or cajoled into a waiver will . . . show that [he] . . . did not voluntarily waive his privilege."

[c] Intelligence of the Waiver

A waiver is not "knowing and intelligent" unless the *Miranda* warnings are given. The Court stated that because the rights are fundamental, it "will not pause to inquire in individual cases whether the defendant was aware of his rights without a warning being given"; and "[n]o amount of circumstantial evidence that the person may have been aware of [his] right[s] will suffice to stand in its stead."

[4] Enforcing the Rights

[a] Right to Silence

After the warnings are given, if the suspect "indicates in any manner, at any time prior to or during questioning, that he wishes to remain silent, the interrogation must cease." The Court indicated that any statement obtained after the suspect invokes his privilege "cannot be other than the product of compulsion, subtle or otherwise."

However, if an individual asserts his privilege in his attorney's presence, the Court stated that "there may be circumstances in which further questioning would be permissible," particularly "[i]n the absence of evidence of overbearing."

---

[34] Johnson v. Zerbst, 304 U.S. 458 (1938). *See* § 12 *supra.*

[b] Right to Counsel

An "express statement" by a suspect that he is willing to make a statement, and that he does not want an attorney present "followed closely by a statement could constitute a waiver." A waiver "will not be presumed simply from the silence of the accused after warnings are given."

If a suspect at any time prior to or during the questioning states that he wants to consult with an attorney, "the interrogation must cease until an attorney is present." When the lawyer is furnished, "the individual must have an opportunity to confer with the attorney and to have him present during any subsequent questioning."

[C] Reasoning of the Court

[1] Custodial Interrogation As "Compulsion"

The Court was critical of police interrogation techniques, as evidenced by the manuals in publication at the time. It stated that custodial interrogation "exacts a heavy toll on individual liberty and trades on the weakness of individuals." Suspects are "thrust into an unfamiliar atmosphere and run through menacing police interrogation procedures." And, they are "surrounded by antagonistic forces," kept "incommunicado" in a "police-dominated atmosphere," and "deprived of every psychological advantage."

Although later cases suggest a different interpretation of *Miranda*,[35] the most common understanding of the case at the time was that it stands for the proposition that "compulsion *inheres* in custodial interrogations to such an extent that *any* confession, in *any* case of custodial interrogation, is compelled."[36] That is, in the absence of procedural safeguards (*i.e.*, the "*Miranda* warnings" or their equivalent) custodial interrogation necessarily *will* — not simply *can* — result in unconstitutional compulsion.[37] In short, the Court appeared to replace the old totality-of-the-circumstances "voluntariness" test with a *per se* definition of "compulsion."

Support for this reading of *Miranda* is evident in the Court's statements that custodial interrogation "carries its own badge of intimidation," and that persons "subjected to the techniques of persuasion described above cannot be otherwise than under compulsion to speak." The Court also stated that in the absence of warnings or their equivalent, which are "employed to dispel the compulsion inherent in custodial surroundings, no statements obtained from the defendant can truly be the product of his free choice."[38]

---

[35] *See* § 141 *infra.*

[36] *See* Herman, *The Supreme Court, the Attorney General, and the Good Old Days of Police Interrogation*, 48 Ohio St.L.J. 733, 735 (1987).

[37] Schulhofer, *Reconsidering Miranda*, 54 U. Chi. L. Rev. 435, 447 (1987).

[38] Not all of the language in *Miranda* supports the thesis that custodial interrogation is inherently coercive. For example, the opinion states that "we might not find the defendants' statements [in these cases] to have been involuntary in traditional terms. . . . [However,] [t]he *potentiality* for compulsion is forcefully apparent. . . ." (Emphasis added.)

[2] The Limited Importance of Confessions in Law Enforcement

The Court stated that it was "not unmindful of the burden which law enforcement officials must bear, often under trying circumstances" to obtain evidence to convict guilty persons. But it was not persuaded by the "recurrent argument . . . that society's need for interrogation outweighs the privilege."

Although the Court conceded that "confessions may play an important role in some convictions," it considered the cases at hand "graphic examples of the overstatement of the 'need' for confessions." It pointed out that in each case before it, the police possessed considerable incriminating evidence against the suspects that was secured through standard non-interrogation investigatory practices.

[3] The Importance of the Adversarial System

The Court described the Fifth Amendment privilege against compulsory self-incrimination as a "noble principle," based on the "individual's substantive right, a 'right to a private enclave where he may lead a private life. That right is the hallmark of our democracy.' " It described the privilege as "the essential mainstay of our adversary system." According to *Miranda*, the principles underlying it add up "to one overriding thought, namely":

> the respect a government . . . must accord to the dignity and integrity of its citizens. To maintain a "fair state-individual balance," to require the government "to shoulder the entire load," . . . to respect the inviolability of the human personality, our accusatory system of justice demands that the government seeking to punish an individual produce the evidence against him by its own independent labors, rather than by the cruel, simple expedient of compelling it from his own mouth.

Consequently, *Miranda* suggested, it "is not for the authorities to decide" when a suspect should speak: rather, it is the right of the individual, with such assistance as he may wish to obtain from an attorney, to decide whether and when to talk to the police. When an attorney recommends to his client that he remain silent, he "is merely carrying out what he is sworn to do under his oath — to protect to the extent of his ability the rights of his client." As such, the defense attorney "plays a vital role in the administration of criminal justice under our Constitution."

§ 140   Criticisms of *Miranda*[39]

[A]   "*Miranda* Lacks Historical and Textual Support"

Criticism: Justice White stated in his dissent in *Miranda* that the holding of the Court has "no significant support in the history of the privilege or in the language of the Fifth Amendment." As he pointed out, in England the privilege against compulsory self-incrimination applied only to judicial interrogations. Furthermore, the most sensible reading of the text of the Fifth Amendment — "No person . . . shall be compelled to be a *witness* against himself" — is that the privilege was intended only to prevent the compulsion of testimony during a criminal trial.

Reply: The original understanding of the privilege may never be fully known. But, it would be odd to think that the constitutional framers would have allowed police coercion while they barred judicial compulsion.[40] Even the Office of Legal Policy in the Department of Justice, which called for the Court to overrule *Miranda*, conceded that the applicability of the Fifth Amendment to custodial police interrogations is consistent with the historical understanding of the privilege.[41]

[B]   "The Rule Is Unnecessary and Irrational"

Criticism: The *per se* rule of *Miranda* is unnecessary. The criticism of the traditional totality-of-the-circumstances voluntariness test is unwarranted.[42] According to Justice Harlan in his dissent, the old test was — and is — workable, effective, sophisticated, and sensitive. Under the voluntariness test, and the case law applying it, the police receive adequate guidance: they know that if they engage in certain types of acts (*e.g.*, physical abuse of any kind, prolonged detention, food or sleep deprivation), they do so at their risk.

In contrast, the *Miranda* rule is formalistic.[43] The premise that *every* custodial interrogation is coercive is counter-intuitive and empirically incorrect. In his dissent, Justice White pointed out the fallacy of *Miranda*: if a suspect in custody

---

[39] *See generally* Caplan, n. 19 *supra*; Grano, *Miranda's Constitutional Difficulties: A Reply to Professor Schulhofer*, 55 U. Chi. L. Rev. 174 (1988) (hereafter, Grano, *Constitutional Difficulties*); Grano, *Miranda v. Arizona and the Legal Mind: Formalism's Triumph Over Substance and Reason*, 24 Am. Crim. L. Rev. 243 (1986) (hereafter Grano, *Legal Mind*); Grano, n. 31 *supra*; Inbau & Manak, *Miranda v. Arizona — Is It Worth the Cost? (A Sample Survey, with Commentary, of the Expenditure of Court Time and Effort)*, 24 Cal. West. L. Rev. 185 (1988); Kamisar, n. 4 *supra*; Lippman, *A Commentary on Inbau and Manak's "Miranda v. Arizona — Is It Worth the Cost? (A Sample Survey, with Commentary, of the Expenditure of Court Time and Effort)"*, 25 Cal. West. L. Rev. 87 (1988); Office of Legal Policy, n. 7 *supra*; Ogletree, *Are Confessions Really Good for the Soul?: A Proposal to Mirandize Miranda*, 100 Harv. L. Rev. 1826 (1987); Rosenberg & Rosenberg, *A Modest Proposal for the Abolition of Custodial Confessions*, 68 N.C. L. Rev. 69 (1989); Schulhofer, n. 37 *supra*; White, *Defending Miranda: A Reply to Professor Caplan*, 39 Vand. L. Rev. 1 (1986).

[40] *See* Kamisar, n. 4 *supra*, at 68-76.

[41] Office of Legal Policy, n. 7 *supra*, at 42.

[42] Caplan, n. 19 *supra*, at 1432.

[43] *See* Grano, *Legal Mind*, n. 39 *supra*, at 246.

blurts out a confession, it is admissible despite the "compulsion" inherent in the custody. But, a single question — "Did you commit the crime?" — asked of the suspect in the absence of warnings and waiver supposedly renders the process coercive. Yet, Justice White claims, "common sense informs us to the contrary." It cannot be the case that *any* question of *any* person, regardless of the latter's fortitude, overbears the will.

Reply: Only a person with "an extravagant faith" in the voluntariness test "could fail to see that the safeguards provided by [it] . . . were largely 'illusory.' "[44] Even a critic of *Miranda* has stated that the old test resulted in "intolerable uncertainty."[45] As with other bright-line rules, *Miranda* sends a clearer message to the police than the totality-of-the-circumstances test did or ever will do.

Moreover, criticism of the *per se* nature of the rule is historically misguided:[46] *Miranda* merely returned the law to the point at which it began. In *Bram v. United States*,[47] the Supreme Court applied a virtual bright-line definition of Fifth Amendment "compulsion." Although the Court used the term "involuntary" in its analysis, it did not mean by this that the suspect's will had to be overborne in order for there to be a violation. Only later did the Court conflate the concepts of "involuntariness" (a term that is appropriate in the context of the due process clause) and "compulsion" (the Fifth Amendment term).

In self-incrimination analysis, the amount of pressure required to invalidate a confession should be less than is required in the due process context because the Fifth Amendment is linked to the anti-inquisitorial values of the privilege's framers. The critical question should be, as in *Miranda*, whether the pressure was "imposed for the *purpose* of discouraging the silence of a criminal suspect."[48]

[C] *"Miranda* is Against Confessions and In Favor of 'Fox Hunts' "

Criticism: According to Justice White, the "obvious underpinning [of *Miranda*] . . . is a deep-seated distrust of all confessions." He described "the not so subtle" thesis of the opinion as follows: "[I]t is inherently wrong for the police to gather evidence from the accused himself."

Miranda all but tells lawyers to advise their clients to remain silent. In fact, however, there is nothing wrong with confessions, as long as they are not obtained in an objectionable manner, which the traditional voluntariness test guards against.

Miranda's advocates want a pure adversarial system, but the American system of justice is and should be one mixed with inquisitorial procedures. As Justice White observed, the Court ignored the fact that "[t]he most basic function of any government is to provide for the security of the individual and of his property." Respect for the inviolability of the suspect is not all that is valued by the Constitution: "the human personality of others in the society must also be preserved."

---

[44] Kamisar, n. 4 *supra*, at 62.
[45] Grano, n. 22 *supra*, at 863.
[46] *See* Schulhofer, n. 37 *supra*, at 440-46.
[47] 168 U.S. 532 (1897).
[48] Schulhofer, n. 37 *supra*, at 445.

Miranda values only the interests of the suspect. The majority opinion treats suspects as if they were underdogs,[49] who need lawyers to match wits with the police and to protect them against the pressures generated by custodial interrogation.[50] *Miranda* tries to place the suspect on an even playing field with the police.[51] It gives the "underdogs" a sporting chance to be acquitted, even when they are factually guilty, just as people give the fox a chance to survive the hunt.

But, this sporting view of justice is senseless. Nobody who believes in the basic legitimacy of a society should "endorse the view that a guilty suspect, like a fox during a hunt, must be given a sporting chance to escape conviction and punishment."[52] We should want guilty people to confess.

Reply: The critics' real objection is less to *Miranda* than it is to the Fifth Amendment privilege against self-incrimination, and the accusatorial system of justice that underlies it. It is the Constitution, not the Supreme Court, that prohibits compulsory self-incrimination.

Furthermore, *Miranda* is not based on a "fox hunt" or "sporting" approach to justice. It is based on the premise that it is "unseemly" for the police "systematically to . . . take advantage of the psychological vulnerability of a citizen."[53] The weak — and that is what the suspect is when dealing alone with the police while in custody — should not be exploited. Values of human autonomy and dignity require no less than what *Miranda* seeks to safeguard.[54]

[D] *"Miranda* Is Injurious to Law Enforcement"

Criticism: Confessions are an important, often indispensable, part of criminal investigations.[55] The logical implication of *Miranda* is that once the suspect is informed of his privilege against compulsory self-incrimination and of his right to talk to a lawyer before any interrogation occurs, he *will* talk to his lawyer, and any lawyer worth his salt will tell his client to remain silent. *Miranda's* effect, therefore, is to make it more difficult for the police to secure confessions. As a consequence, more guilty people will escape justice.

There is empirical support for the claim that *Miranda* has taken its toll.[56] Researchers in Pittsburgh found that the police secured confessions in 54 percent of all pre-*Miranda* cases, but immediately after *Miranda* the confession rate

---

[49] *See* Caplan, n. 19 *supra*, at 1441.

[50] Grano, n. 31 *supra*, at 665.

[51] It may do more: "[I]t gives the suspect too great an advantage. If the police are too formidable for the average offender, a lawyer will be too formidable for the average investigator." Caplan, n. 19 *supra*, at 1443.

[52] Grano, n. 31 *supra*, at 677.

[53] Schulhofer, *Confessions and the Court*, 79 Mich. L. Rev. 865, 871 (1981).

[54] *See* Greenawalt, *Silence as a Moral and Constitutional Right*, 24 Wm. & Mary L. Rev. 15, 40-41 (1981).

[55] Inbau & Manak, n. 39 *supra*, at 195; Ashcraft v. Tennessee, 322 U.S. 143, 160 (1944) ("[W]e cannot read an undiscriminating hostility to mere interrogation into the Constitution without unduly fettering the States in protecting society from the criminal.") (Jackson, J., dissenting).

[56] Caplan, n. 19 *supra*, at 1464.

dropped to 37 percent.[57] Another study found that the police were losing the "collateral" benefits of confessions, such as the names of accomplices.[58]

Reply: Miranda's impact on police practices has been minimal. Many people who originally feared its effect now agree that the decision has not handcuffed the police.[59]

Among the studies of *Miranda's* effects, only the Pittsburgh one concluded that the decision resulted in a significant decrease in the confession rate.[60] Yet, even in that city the Chief of Police told the researchers that *Miranda* had been good for his department, as it "provided an opportunity to professionalize the police."[61] Other studies have found that *Miranda* had little negative influence on criminal prosecutions.[62]

One reason why *Miranda* has had so little impact on the confession rate is that, as one critic of *Miranda* has conceded, "[a]ll the studies suggest that suspects frequently waive their [*Miranda*] rights."[63] Police almost always read suspects the warnings, the suspects frequently waive their rights without consulting with an attorney, and the interrogations proceed. As a result, *Miranda* "liberates the police,"[64] because the warnings reduce the chances that a court will subsequently find that the interrogation process was coercive.

Furthermore, the high waiver rate was predictable. *Miranda* is a compromise: the Court did not take its own reasoning to its logical conclusion. As Justice White accurately pointed out in his dissent, the same coercion that requires that warnings be given logically should invalidate the suspect's lawyer-less waiver of his rights.

It is no wonder, therefore, that an American Bar Association study of police attitudes concluded that "[p]olice do not complain that *Miranda* prevents them from obtaining confessions from suspects. Prosecutors report that *Miranda* is not a significant factor which impedes the prosecution of cases."[65]

---

[57] Seeburger & Wettick, *Miranda in Pittsburgh — A Statistical Study*, 29 U. Pitt. L. Rev. 1, 11 (1967).

[58] Witt, *Non-Coercive Interrogation and the Administration of Criminal Justice: The Impact of Miranda on Police Effectuality*, 64 J. Crim. L. & Criminology 320, 332 (1973).

[59] Schulhofer, n. 37 *supra*, at 456 (citing the post-*Miranda* views of Los Angeles District Attorney (later State Attorney General) Evelle Younger, Kansas City Chief of Police (later FBI Director) Clarence Kelly, and Supreme Court Justice Tom Clark (a dissenter in *Miranda*), all of whom concluded that *Miranda* does not pose a significant obstacle to the police).

[60] White, n. 39 *supra*, at 18-19.

[61] *See* Kamisar, "Landmark Rulings Had No Detrimental Effect," *Boston Globe*, Feb. 1, 1987, at A27, *as quoted in* Schulhofer, n. 37 *supra*, at 458 n.59.

[62] *See* the studies summarized in White, n. 39 *supra*, at 19 n.99.

[63] Caplan, n. 19 *supra*, at 1466.

[64] Schulhofer, n. 37 *supra*, at 454.

[65] American Bar Association, Criminal Justice in Crisis 27 (A.B.A. Criminal Justice Section, Nov. 1988).

§ 141   *Michigan v. Tucker*: Deconstitutionalizing *Miranda*

The constitutional underpinnings of *Miranda* were cut out from under it by the Supreme Court in *Michigan v. Tucker*.[66] In *Tucker*, *D* was not fully informed of his constitutional rights as mandated by *Miranda*. Consequently, the statement obtained by the police in violation of *Miranda* was excluded from *D's* trial. At issue, however, was whether the fruits of the confession — the testimony of a witness whose name was mentioned in the *Miranda*-less statement — was also inadmissible.[67]

In order to determine whether and how the fruit-of-the-poisonous-tree doctrine should apply, the Court, per Justice Rehnquist, asked a foundational question: "[W]hether the police conduct complained of directly infringed upon [*D's*] right against compulsory self-incrimination or whether it instead violated only the prophylactic rules developed to protect that right." The Court's answer was that *D's* Fifth Amendment rights had not been violated, because a violation of *Miranda* is not in itself a violation of the Fifth Amendment.

Justice Rehnquist reasoned that the Fifth Amendment privilege against compulsory self-incrimination requires the exclusion of statements obtained involuntarily, but that in *Miranda* the Court held "that a defendant's statements might be excluded at trial despite their voluntary character under traditional principles."

According to the Court, the failure of the police to provide proper warnings to a suspect prior to custodial interrogation does not render a confession involuntary; it only violates the procedural safeguards devised by the Court in *Miranda*, safeguards that the *Miranda* Court itself stated were not constitutionally required.

Thus, *Tucker* deconstitutionalized *Miranda*. As the Court has subsequently explained *Miranda*: "[T]he *Miranda* exclusionary rule . . . serves the Fifth Amendment and sweeps more broadly than the Fifth Amendment itself. It may be triggered even in the absence of a Fifth Amendment violation."[68]

This interpretation of *Miranda* has been criticized as "an outright rejection of [its] core premises,"[69] and inconsistent with language in *Miranda* and in other pre-*Tucker* Supreme Court explanations of the case.[70] Although the Court in *Miranda* stated that the specific procedural safeguards laid out in the opinion were not constitutionally required, it also indicated that in the absence of the warnings or their equivalent, any custodial interrogation was inherently coercive. Whether one agrees with *Miranda* or not, it is probably fair to say that its authors considered it to be a constitutionally-based decision.

The effect of *Tucker* on *Miranda* jurisprudence is considerable. First, because a *Miranda* violation is a violation of a "prophylactic" rule and not of the Constitution itself, the scope of the *Miranda* exclusionary rule and of other rules

---

[66] 417 U.S. 433 (1974).

[67] This "fruit of the poisonous tree" issue is discussed at § 147[C] *infra*.

[68] Oregon v. Elstad, 470 U.S. 298, 306 (1985).

[69] Stone, n. 26 *supra*, at 118.

[70] *E.g.*, Orozco v. Texas, 394 U.S. 324, 326 (1969) ("[T]he use of these admissions obtained in the absence of the required warnings was a *flat violation of the Self-Incrimination Clause of the Fifth Amendment.* . . .") (emphasis added).

stemming from *Miranda*, are narrower than the Fifth Amendment coerced-confession exclusionary rule.[71]

Second, if *Miranda* is not a constitutionally-based decision, as *Tucker* suggests, Congress arguably has the authority to overrule *Miranda*, as it sought to do in the Omnibus Crime Control and Safe Streets Act of 1968,[72] a law that has been largely ignored by federal prosecutors and courts.

Third, although the Court has not so held, it is also arguable in light of *Tucker* that the holding of *Miranda* does not apply in state prosecutions. Inasmuch as a *Miranda* violation is not a violation of the Constitution, and as the Supreme Court has no supervisory authority over the states' criminal justice systems, the Court might lack the authority to compel states to exclude evidence that "merely" violates a "prophylactic" non-constitutional rule.[73]

§ 142 Meaning of *Miranda*: "Custody"

[A] Definition: In General

The police are required to give *Miranda* warnings prior to questioning "only where there has been such a restriction on a person's freedom as to render him 'in custody.' "[74]

According to *Miranda*, "custody" arises when a person is "taken into custody or otherwise deprived of his freedom of action in any significant way." As the Court has subsequently explained that phrase, a person is "in custody" for purposes of receiving *Miranda* warnings if "there is a 'formal arrest or restraint on freedom of movement' of the degree associated with a formal arrest."[75]

Furthermore, in determining whether a person not under formal arrest is in custody, an officer's "unarticulated plan has no bearing on the question. . . . [T]he only relevant inquiry is how a reasonable man in the suspect's position would have understood his situation."[76]

For example, suppose that a police officer, with an arrest warrant hidden in his back pocket, comes to *D*'s house and requests permission to "ask a few questions"; the officer promises to leave after the interrogation. In fact, after the questioning, the officer arrests *D* pursuant to the warrant. Under these circumstances, *Miranda*

---

[71] *Compare* § 135 *supra* (coerced-confession exclusionary rule) *with* §§ 147 (*Miranda* exclusionary rule) and 155[D] (right-to-counsel rule stemming from *Miranda*) *infra*.

[72] 18 U.S.C. § 3501(a)-(b) (reinstating the totality-of-the-circumstances "voluntariness" test).

[73] *See especially* Grano, *Constitutional Difficulties*, n. 39 *supra*; and Grano, *Prophylactic Rules in Criminal Procedure: A Question of Article III Legitimacy*, 80 Nw. U. L. Rev. 100 (1985). Even a supporter of *Miranda* has noted this potential effect of *Tucker*. *See* Stone, n. 26 *supra*, at 119-20 ("[T]he Rehnquist analysis, if taken seriously, would seem in practical effect to overrule *Miranda* [in state prosecutions].").

[74] Oregon v. Mathiason, 429 U.S. 492, 495 (1977) (*per curiam*).

[75] California v. Beheler, 463 U.S. 1121, 1125 (1983) (*per curiam*) (*quoting* Oregon v. Mathiason, 429 U.S. at 495)).

[76] Berkemer v. McCarty, 468 U.S. 420, 442 (1984).

warnings probably were not required prior to the questioning, because a reasonable person in *D*'s situation would not have believed that he was in custody at the time of the interrogation (although he doubtlessly was, in view of the warrant).

[B] Specific Issues

[1] "Custody" versus "Focus"

The Court in *Miranda* said that "custody" and "focus," as the latter term was used in *Escobedo*,[77] were synonyms. In fact, however, as the Court has since conceded, "focus" can exist in the absence of "custody," in which case *Miranda* warnings are not required.

For example, in *Beckwith v. United States*,[78] *D* was questioned by Internal Revenue Service agents at his home. At the time of the questioning, *D* was the focus of a criminal tax investigation. Nonetheless, because *D* was not in custody at the time of the questioning — he was free to leave or to ask the agents to go — *Miranda* warnings were not required.

[2] Site of the Interrogation

A person can be "in custody" in his house, and yet not be "in custody" at the police station, depending on whether his freedom of movement is significantly curtailed.

For example, in *Orozco v. Texas*,[79] the Court held that *D* was in custody when four police officers entered his bedroom and questioned him there at 4:00 A.M. One of the officers subsequently testified that *D* was under arrest at the time of the questioning, although *D* had not been informed of this fact. Presumably, however, in light of the timing of the interrogation, the pointed nature of the questions, and the fact that four officers were present, a reasonable person in *D*'s situation would have believed that he was in custody.

In contrast, in *Oregon v. Mathiason*,[80] *D* was a parolee suspected of a burglary. At the request of the police, he agreed to come to the police station, where he was questioned (in the absence of *Miranda* warnings) in an office with the door closed. Prior to the interrogation, *D* was told that he was not under arrest, and he was permitted to leave after he confessed to the crime.

Although a reviewing court found that the questioning took place in a coercive environment, and *D* was even falsely told that they had evidence implicating him in the crime, the Supreme Court held that *Miranda* warnings were not required, because *D* was free to go.

[3] Nature of the Crime

The nature of the offense for which a suspect is in custody does not affect the applicability of the *Miranda* rule. A person under formal arrest for a minor traffic offense is as entitled to warnings prior to questioning as is a murder suspect.[81]

---

[77] Escobedo v. Illinois, 378 U.S. 478 (1964).

[78] 425 U.S. 341 (1976).

[79] 394 U.S. 324 (1969).

[80] 429 U.S. 492 (1977) (*per curiam*).

[81] Berkemer v. McCarty, 468 U.S. 420 (1984).

Assuming that a suspect is in custody for an offense, warnings are required even if the interrogation pertains to a crime for which the suspect is not in custody.[82]

[4] Duration of the Detention

Under *Miranda*, warnings are required if a person is deprived of his freedom of action "in any significant way." The key word here is "significant." A person is not "in custody" for purposes of *Miranda* merely because his freedom of movement has been curtailed by the police, i.e., that he has been "seized" in a Fourth Amendment sense.

Thus, the Supreme Court held in *Berkemer v. McCarty*[83] that a motorist is not "in custody" if he is subjected to roadside questioning during a routine traffic stop. Traffic stops are brief, occur in public, and usually involve only one or two officers; consequently, the motorist does not feel "completely at the mercy of the police." In the absence of coercive conditions, therefore, the short detention involved in a traffic stop falls outside the scope of *Miranda's* "custody" definition.

§ 143   Meaning of *Miranda*: "Interrogation"[84]

[A]   Definition: *Rhode Island v. Innis*

In *Rhode Island v. Innis*,[85] D was arrested for a murder in which the weapon used in the crime had not yet been discovered. *D* was placed in a police car with three officers. En route to the station, one of the officers initiated a conversation with his colleague, in which he mentioned that a school for handicapped children was in the vicinity, and that "God forbid one of [the children] might find a weapon with shells and they might hurt themselves." After the officer added that "it would be too bad if a little girl would pick up the gun, maybe kill herself," *D* interrupted and offered to show the police where he had abandoned the gun.

These events occurred after *Miranda* warnings had been given. However, because *D* had previously requested to see a lawyer, the police were under an obligation to cease interrogation until *D* talked to his attorney.[86] The precise issue

---

[82] Mathis v. United States, 391 U.S. 1 (1968) (a person serving a prison sentence for one crime is "in custody" when he is under interrogation for another, unrelated crime).

Although the general proposition stated in the text may be good law, some courts have resisted *Mathis* by holding that a prison inmate is not "in custody" for purposes of *Miranda* unless his freedom of movement is restricted more than is normal in a prison environment. *E.g.*, United States v. Cooper, 800 F.2d 412, 414-15 (4th Cir. 1986).

In an unexplained aside in Illinois v. Perkins, 110 S.Ct. 2394, 2398 (1990), the Supreme Court cited and distinguished *Mathis*, and then, perhaps presaging reconsideration of the case, wrote: "(The bare fact of custody may not in every instance require a warning even when the suspect is aware that he is speaking to an official, but we do not have occasion to explore that issue here.)."

[83] 468 U.S. 420 (1984).

[84] *See generally* Note, *Confusing the Fifth Amendment with the Sixth: Lower Court Misapplication of the Innis Definition of Interrogation*, 87 Mich. L. Rev. 1073 (1989).

[85] 446 U.S. 291 (1980); *see generally* White, *Interrogation Without Questions: Rhode Island v. Innis and United States v. Henry*, 78 Mich. L. Rev. 1209 (1980).

[86] Edwards v. Arizona, 451 U.S. 477, *reh'g denied*, 452 U.S. 973 (1981). *See* § 145[D][2][a] *infra*.

in the case, therefore, was whether the handicapped-children statement by the officer constituted "interrogation," so as to violate the "cease interrogation" rule.

The *Innis* Court announced that for purposes of *Miranda*, "interrogation" refers not only to "express questioning," but also to its "functional equivalent." It defined the "functional equivalent" of express questioning as "any words or actions on the part of the police (other than those normally attendant to arrest and custody) that the police should know are reasonably likely to elicit an incriminating response from the suspect."[87]

As the Court did in *Miranda*, the *Innis* Court stated that the phrase "incriminating response" in the preceding definition "refer[s] to any response — whether inculpatory or exculpatory — that the prosecution may seek to introduce at trial."

[B] A Closer Look at the *Innis* Definition

The Court in *Innis* explained that its definition of the "functional equivalent" of "interrogation" "focuses primarily upon the perceptions of the suspect, rather than the intent of the police."

In other words, the officer's subjective intent to elicit an incriminating response by his words or actions is not the key to the *Innis* definition. Instead, the definition of "interrogation" (in the "functional equivalent" sense) for *Miranda* purposes is primarily an objective test: *Should* the officer have realized that his acts or words were *reasonably likely* to result in an incriminating response?

However, the mental state of the police officer, although not the primary focus of the *Innis* test, can be relevant in determining whether an "interrogation" has occurred, as the Court acknowledged in a footnote:

> Any knowledge the police may have had concerning the susceptibility of a defendant to a particular form of persuasion might be an important factor in determining whether the police should have known that their words or actions were reasonably likely to elicit an incriminating response.[88]

---

[87] Dissenting Justices Marshall and Brennan would have held that conduct "intended or likely to produce a response from a suspect in custody" is the functional equivalent of "interrogation." Dissenting Justice Stevens defined "interrogation" as "any police statement . . . that appears to call for a response, as well as those that are designed to do so."

[88] The intent of the police officer may be relevant for another reason: in another footnote, the Court stated that "[t]his is not to say that the intent of the police is irrelevant, for it may well have a bearing on whether the police should have known that their words or actions were reasonably likely to evoke an incriminating response."

This remark, by itself, is perplexing. The mere fact that an officer intends to elicit an incriminating response does not make it more likely that the response will be elicited. Therefore, there is no additional reason why such an officer "should know" that a response is "reasonably likely."

One scholar, White, n. 85 *supra*, at 1232, has sought to make sense of the footnote in light of the overall test. He has suggested that the Court may have meant that an officer should know that his words or actions are reasonably likely to result in an incriminating response when he "should realize that the . . . conduct will probably be viewed by the suspect as designed to achieve that purpose." That is, if an objective observer would "infer that the remarks were designed to elicit an incriminating response [even if they were not], then the remarks should constitute 'interrogation.' "

Brewer v. Williams,[89] a Sixth Amendment case,[90] provides an example of what the Court probably had in mind by the footnote. In *Williams*, the police subjected *D*, a highly religious man and a recent escapee from a mental hospital who had been formally charged with the murder of a small child, to a so-called "Christian burial speech." The speech was designed to convince *D* to tell the officers where he had left the body, so that the parents could give the victim a "Christian burial." Although *D* did not respond immediately — indeed, not as quickly as did the suspect in *Innis* — he eventually made incriminating remarks and led them to the body.

The Court in *Williams* did not consider the implications of the police conduct in light of *Miranda*, instead choosing to decide the case on Sixth Amendment grounds. However, under the definition of "interrogation" it subsequently developed in *Innis*, and in light of the officers' knowledge of *D*'s susceptibility to religious arguments and to his mental instability, the "Christian burial speech" very plausibly would have satisfied the *Innis* test.

As a consequence of the "knowledge of susceptibilities" footnote, the Court in a four-justice plurality opinion in *Pennsylvania v. Muniz*[91] has re-stated the *Innis* definition of "interrogation" this way:

> Thus, custodial interrogation for purposes of *Miranda* includes both express questioning, and also words or actions [other than those normally attendant to arrest and custody] that, given the officer's knowledge of any special susceptibilities of the suspect, the officer knows or reasonably should know are likely to "have . . . the force of a question on the accused," . . . and therefore be reasonably likely to elicit an incriminating response.

The plurality did not purport to affect the substance of the definition of "interrogation" by this new phraseology.

[C]   Supreme Court Application of the *Innis* Test

[1]   *Innis*

Although the three dissenters in *Innis* would have defined "interrogation" slightly differently than did the majority,[92] the primary dispute in the case pertained to the application of the Court's definition to the facts.

The majority concluded that the handicapped-children statement did not amount to the functional equivalent of "interrogation," *i.e.*, the Court did not believe that the officers should have known that their conversation — what it described as "a few off hand remarks" — was reasonably likely to elicit an incriminating response from *D*.

---

[89] 430 U.S. 387 (1977).

[90] *Innis* expressly states that the definition of "interrogation" for *Miranda* purposes is *not* informed by the Court's Sixth Amendment right-to-counsel jurisprudence. Under the latter provision, the government may not "deliberately elicit" an incriminating response from a person formally charged with a crime in the absence of the accused's lawyer. Thus, the latter test is subjective, not objective. *See* § 152[B] *infra*.

[91] 110 S.Ct. 2638 (1990).

[92] *See* n. 87 *supra*.

Without alluding to *Brewer v. Williams*, the Court implicitly distinguished the present case from it: it noted that the police conversation here was brief (it was not "a lengthy harangue in the presence of the suspect"); the comments were not especially "evocative"; and there was no evidence that the officers knew that D was "peculiarly susceptible to an appeal to conscience," or that he was disoriented or upset when the remarks were made.

This conclusion is dubious. As Justice Marshall pointed out in dissent, an appeal to a suspect's conscience (as was used in *Williams* as well as here) is a classic interrogation technique recommended in the police manuals that the *Miranda* Court criticized. An officer's call-to-conscience will often succeed, even in the absence of "peculiar susceptibilities" to such techniques, in circumstances in which a direct, accusatorial question will not.

[2] *Arizona v. Mauro*

An irony stemming from *Innis* is that the Court defined "interrogation" broadly, but then applied its definition very narrowly. Therefore, to the extent that the facts in *Innis* and the Court's "no interrogation" conclusion are used as a benchmark for comparison to other police tactics that fall short of express questioning, there should be relatively few findings of "interrogation."

At the Supreme Court level, this has proved to be the case. For example, in *Arizona v. Mauro*,[93] the Court held that no interrogation occurred when the police allowed the wife of a man suspected of killing his son to talk to her husband in their presence. The justices stated that the decision by the police to permit the spousal conversation was not "the kind of psychological ploy that properly could be treated as the functional equivalent of interrogation." Using *Innis* as its benchmark, the Court concluded that the police conduct in the case was "far less questionable than the 'subtle compulsion' that we held *not* to be interrogation in *Innis*."

[3] *Pennsylvania v. Muniz*

In *Pennsylvania v Muniz*,[94] D was arrested for driving his automobile under the influence of alcohol. At the police station, in preparation for giving D various physical sobriety tests, an officer read the suspect "carefully scripted" instructions on how the tests should be performed. In the process of attempting to understand the instructions and to perform the tests, D made several incriminating statements to the officer.

Eight members of the *Muniz* Court ruled that the instructions given to D "were not likely to be perceived as calling for any verbal response and therefore were not 'words or actions' constituting custodial interrogation." Therefore, D's incriminating utterances were held to be voluntary admissions rather than responses to custodial interrogation.[95]

---

[93] 481 U.S. 520, *reh'g denied*, 483 U.S. 1034 (1987).

[94] 110 S.Ct. 2638 (1990).

[95] However, the officer also asked D to count aloud while performing two of the physical sobriety tests. The Court acknowledged that the "counting at the officer's request qualifies as a response to custodial interrogation."

Only Justice Marshall dissented in *Muniz*. He argued that instructions that might not result in verbal responses from sober persons are reasonably likely to lead to incriminating responses from intoxicated ones. Furthermore, in this case, the officer had first given *D* the sobriety tests on the road, during which *D* sought to explain his inability to pass the tests by stating that he had been drinking. The officer arguably knew, therefore, that *D* was reasonably likely to utter incriminating responses at the stationhouse during the same tests.

§ 144 Adequacy of the *Miranda* Warnings

Because the specific warnings promulgated in *Miranda* are not constitutionally required, the Supreme Court has ruled that no "talismanic incantation" of the warnings is required, as long as the officer's explanation of the suspect's constitutional rights is a "fully effective equivalent" of the *Miranda* warnings.[96]

Although this rule is not in conflict with *Miranda*, the Court's application of it in *Duckworth v. Eagan*[97] may have "dealt *Miranda* a heavy blow."[98] In *Duckworth*, the police provided ordinary *Miranda* warnings, including the statements that "you have the right to a lawyer for advice before we ask you any questions, and to have him with you during questioning," and that a lawyer would be hired for him if he could not afford one. However, the officer also stated that "we have no way of giving you a lawyer, but one will be appointed for you, if you wish, *if and when you go to court.*"

In light of the italicized remark, a federal court concluded that the warnings were defective because the suspect could have reasonably interpreted the words to mean that a lawyer would not be available to him as an indigent until formal charges were brought, even if the questioning proceeded at that time.

Nonetheless, the Supreme Court held, 5-4, that the warnings in their totality were adequate, in that as a whole they made clear to the suspect that questioning would not occur until he had a lawyer or waived the right. According to Chief Justice Rehnquist, the warnings "touched all of the bases required by *Miranda*," and the officer's additional comment was accurate in terms of state law and under *Miranda*.[99]

As Professor Yale Kamisar has observed, however, the difficulty with this reasoning is that "if [*D*] were a smart, sophisticated fellow, he might have dissected the . . . police warning the way [the Court] did. . . . But the *Miranda* warnings weren't designed for smart, sophisticated people."[100]

---

[96] California v. Prysock, 453 U.S. 355 (1981) (*per curiam*).

[97] 109 S.Ct. 2875 (1989).

[98] Kamisar, *Duckworth v. Eagan: A Little-Noticed Miranda Case That May Cause Much Mischief*, 25 Crim. L. Bull. 550, 552 (1989).

[99] That is, *Miranda* does not require the presence of a "stationhouse lawyer." Waiver issues aside, *Miranda* only requires that the police not interrogate a suspect who cannot be furnished immediate legal assistance until counsel can be obtained.

[100] Kamisar, n. 98 *supra*, at 554.

§ 145 Waiver of *Miranda* Rights

[A] Burden of Proof

The *Miranda* opinion states that a suspect's waiver is not valid unless the prosecutor overcomes an undefined "heavy burden" of proof that the waiver was voluntary, knowing, and intelligent.

In *Colorado v. Connelly*[101] the Court held that this "heavy burden" is met if the prosecutor proves the validity of the waiver by a preponderance of the evidence. This is the same burden that applies to proof of the voluntariness of a confession under the due process clause.

[B] Types of Waiver: Express versus Implied

Miranda states that "a valid waiver will not be presumed simply from the silence of the accused after warnings are given or simply from the fact that a confession was in fact actually obtained." Nonetheless, the Court held in *North Carolina v. Butler*[102] that a custodial suspect's express waiver of his *Miranda* rights is neither sufficient nor necessary to be valid.

An express waiver is invalid, of course, if it was coerced. On the other hand, "an explicit statement of waiver is not invariably necessary to support a finding that the defendant waived the right to remain silent or the right to counsel guaranteed by the *Miranda* case." According to *Butler*, although the burden of proof is on the government to prove that the custodial suspect validly waived his *Miranda* rights, "in at least some cases waiver can be clearly inferred from the actions and words of the person interrogated," after *Miranda* warnings are given.

The Supreme Court has not indicated what actions or words short of an express waiver are sufficient to overcome the presumption against waiver. However, the prosecutor's burden of proof is not met solely on the basis of the testimony of a police officer that he read the *Miranda* warnings and that the suspect then answered questions. At a minimum, the officer must believe, and be able to testify as to the basis of his belief, that the suspect understood his rights as read to him.[103]

[C] Elements of a Valid Waiver

[1] Voluntariness of the Waiver

To be valid, a waiver must be "the product of a free and deliberate choice rather than intimidation, coercion or deception."[104]

In determining voluntariness, the Court has stated that "[t]here is obviously no reason to require more in the way of a 'voluntariness' inquiry in the *Miranda* waiver context than in the Fourteenth Amendment confession context."[105] In short, due process "voluntariness" jurisprudence applies to *Miranda* waiver law, and the troublesome factual questions of the former test return.

---

[101] 479 U.S. 157 (1986).

[102] 441 U.S. 369 (1979).

[103] *See* Tague v. Louisiana, 444 U.S. 469 (1980) (*per curiam*).

[104] Moran v. Burbine, 475 U.S. 412, 421 (1986).

[105] Colorado v. Connelly, 479 U.S. at 169-70.

As with the due process clause, a waiver of *Miranda* rights is not involuntary if the "moral and psychological pressures to confess emanat[e] from sources other than official coercion."[106] For example, a suspect's waiver of his *Miranda* rights is valid if he was coerced to do so by his belief that God commanded him to confess or commit suicide.[107] Furthermore, the Court has held that the psychological pressures that arise from having a "guilty secret" do not invalidate a subsequent decision to confess.[108]

[2] "Knowing and Intelligent" Nature of the Waiver

[a] In General

The Supreme Court has warned that to be valid a "waiver must have been made with a full awareness of both the nature of the right being abandoned and the consequences of the decision to abandon it."[109]

The Court has not enforced this rule strictly. For example, the Court has held that a waiver is not invalid merely because the suspect was unaware of the full consequences of his decision to relinquish his rights. Thus, in *Oregon v. Elstad*,[110] *D* confessed to a crime unaware that his statement would be inadmissible at trial because it was obtained in violation of *Miranda*. The police then read *D* the *Miranda* warnings, after which *D* waived his rights and provided more incriminating statements. The Court held that the fact that the suspect incorrectly believed that "the cat was out of the bag" — that he had nothing to lose in confessing a second time because of the first confession — did not render his waiver uninformed.

Similarly, a waiver is valid even if the suspect is not aware of the possible topics of the interrogation. In *Colorado v. Spring*,[111] *D* was arrested for interstate transportation of stolen firearms. Based on prior information that linked him to a murder, the after-waiver interrogation turned quickly from the firearms charge to the uncharged murder. *D* ultimately confessed to the latter crime. The Court held that the suspect's waiver was knowing and intelligent: he knew what his rights were, including the right to cut off the questioning at any time; and he knew that *any* statement he might make could be used against him.

[b] *Moran v. Burbine*

In one of its most controversial interpretations of *Miranda*, the Supreme Court held in *Moran v. Burbine*[112] that *D*'s waiver of his *Miranda* rights was not invalid, although the police did not tell him that his attorney had sought to contact him during the questioning, and although the police falsely told his counsel that *D* was not being interrogated. Although *Burbine* is not inconsistent with some of the

---

[106] Oregon v. Elstad, 470 U.S. 298, 305 (1985).

[107] Colorado v. Connelly, 479 U.S. 157 (1986).

[108] Oregon v. Elstad, 470 U.S. 298 (1985).

[109] Moran v. Burbine, 475 U.S. at 421.

[110] 470 U.S. 298 (1985).

[111] 479 U.S. 564 (1987).

[112] 475 U.S. 412 (1986); *contra* Bryan v. State, 571 A.2d 170 (Del. Sup. Ct. 1990) (rejecting *Moran v. Burbine*, and adopting a more stringent waiver rule on the basis of the state constitution).

Court's post-*Miranda* waiver decisions, its underlying rationale demonstrates how far the Court has moved philosophically since *Miranda* was decided.

On the matter of waiver, the Court discounted the police officers' culpability in failing to inform *D* of his attorney's efforts to contact him. It stated that the state of mind of the police, even if they acted with "deliberate or reckless irresponsibility," was irrelevant to the issue of the intelligence or voluntariness of *D*'s waiver.

The Court conceded that the information withheld by the police "would have been useful to [*D*]; perhaps even it might have affected his decision to confess." But, the Court said, "we have never read the Constitution to require that the police supply a suspect with a flow of information to help him calibrate his self-interest in deciding whether to speak or stand by his rights."

The Court also granted that the police conduct was "objectionable as a matter of ethics," but this fact was irrelevant to the waiver issue because the undisclosed information did not deprive the suspect of the "knowledge essential to his ability to understand the nature of his rights and the consequences of abandoning them." According to *Burbine*, once the prosecutor shows that a suspect was fully informed of his *Miranda* rights and that he was not coerced to waive them, "the analysis is complete and the waiver is valid as a matter of law."

However, as the dissent correctly observed, the majority opinion "represents a startling departure from the basic insight" that was at the core of *Miranda*, namely, that a pure accusatorial system of criminal justice should be maintained.

For example, the Court in *Burbine* stated that it "shared [*D*'s] distaste for the deliberate misleading of an officer of the court," but it concluded that it lacked "the authority to mandate a code of behavior for state officials wholly unconnected to any federal right or privilege." To rule for *D*, the Court said, "would work a substantial and . . . inappropriate shift in the subtle balance struck" in *Miranda* between society's "compelling" need for police questioning, and the competing need to prevent police from "inadvertently travers[ing] the fine line between legitimate efforts to elicit admissions and constitutionally impermissible compulsion."

Contrast these remarks to *Miranda*. Whereas *Burbine* speaks of the importance of confessions and the need to balance that "compelling" interest against the need to prevent police from "inadvertently" coercing suspects, *Miranda* was founded (as the dissent in that case rightly observed) on the anti-confession, anti-inquisitorial premise that the dignity and autonomy of suspects is inviolable, and that the importance of confessions in law enforcement is often exaggerated.

Furthermore, in *Miranda*, the justices expressed the belief that defense lawyers play a critical and positive role in the adversary system, by neutralizing some of the coercive influences in the interrogation process and by assisting the suspect in deciding whether to invoke his constitutional rights. But, in *Burbine* the officers' efforts to keep defense counsel away from his client was permitted on the ground that any rule to the contrary would be "wholly unconnected to any federal right or privilege."

[D] Waiver After the Suspect Asserts His Rights

[1] Assertion of the Right to Remain Silent

According to *Miranda*, once warnings are given, if the suspect "indicates in any manner, at any time prior to or during questioning, that he wishes to remain silent, the interrogation must cease."

In *Michigan v. Mosley*,[113] the Court held that the quoted language in *Miranda* does not mean that the police may never resume interrogation after a suspect asserts his right to silence. Instead, the Court held, the suspect's right to cut off questioning is satisfied if the police "scrupulously honor" his right to silence after he asserts the privilege.

In *Mosley*, D was arrested and read his *Miranda* rights, at which time he invoked his Fifth Amendment right to remain silent. The police ceased interrogation and placed D in a jail cell. Two hours later, a different officer, who wanted to interrogate D about a different crime (one for which D was not under arrest), went to the cell and re-read D the *Miranda* warnings, whereupon D agreed to answer questions. The Court found that on these facts the police scrupulously honored the suspect's Fifth Amendment rights.

[2] Assertion of the Right to Consult With Counsel

[a] General Rule: *Edwards v. Arizona*

The Supreme Court held in *Edwards v. Arizona*[114] that when a suspect invokes his right under *Miranda* to consult with an attorney prior to interrogation, the suspect "is not subject to further interrogation by the authorities until counsel has been made available to him, unless the accused himself initiates further communication, exchanges, or conversations with the police." This bright-line rule also bars police-initiated interrogation about an offense that is unrelated to the subject of the initial interrogation.[115]

If a suspect asserts his *Miranda-Edwards* right to consult with a lawyer but subsequently initiates conversations with the police before he consults with counsel, the police may interrogate the suspect, but the burden remains on the prosecutor to show that any statement subsequently obtained was founded on a valid waiver.[116]

As the Court has subsequently explained the *Edwards* rule, its purpose is "to prevent police from badgering a defendant into waiving his previously asserted *Miranda* rights."[117] In view of this purpose, the Supreme Court held, 6-2, in *Minnick v. Mississippi*[118] that once a suspect in custody invokes his *Miranda-Edwards* right to have counsel made available to him, thereby requiring cessation of questioning, the police may not re-initiate interrogation in the absence of

---

[113] 423 U.S. 96 (1975).

[114] 451 U.S. 477, *reh'g denied*, 452 U.S. 973 (1981).

[115] Arizona v. Roberson, 486 U.S. 675 (1988).

[116] Oregon v. Bradshaw, 462 U.S. 1039 (1983).

[117] Michigan v. Harvey, 110 S.Ct. 1176, 1180 (1990).

[118] 111 S. Ct. 486 (1990). Justice Scalia, with whom Chief Justice Rehnquist joined, dissented. Justice Souter did not participate in the case.

counsel, even if the suspect consults with his lawyer outside the interrogation room in the meantime.[119]

Because *Miranda* is a "prophylactic" rule, and *Edwards* is a "second layer of protection"[120] to *Miranda*, the *Edwards* rule is also prophylactic in nature, as is any other rule stemming from it.[121]

[b] Ambiguous Request

Lower courts have split on the issue of whether the *Edwards* rule applies when a suspect ambiguously or equivocally asserts his desire to consult with a lawyer. Some courts apply the *Edwards* test in such circumstances, others permit the police to ask only threshold questions to clarify the suspect's intentions, while still others believe that an interrogation need not cease unless the suspect clearly invokes his right to consult with a lawyer.[122] The Supreme Court has not resolved the division among the courts.

If the initial request to consult with an attorney is clear, however, the *Edwards* rule strictly applies and all interrogation must cease. Therefore, the *per se* rule is violated if the police ask the suspect to clarify his unambiguous request, and thereby receive a more equivocal response.[123]

[c] Incomplete Request

The *Edwards* rule is satisfied if the police honor a suspect's incomplete assertion of his right to counsel to the extent that it is asserted. For example, if *D* states that he will not give a written statement without seeing a lawyer, but that he will make an oral confession without one, the police may continue to interrogate *D* orally without counsel present.[124]

[d] Definition of "Initiation"

In *Oregon v. Bradshaw*,[125] a four-justice plurality ruled that communications, exchanges or conversations are "initiated" for purposes of the *Edwards* rule by any comment or inquiry that can "fairly be said to represent a desire . . . to open up a . . . generalized discussion relating directly or indirectly to the investigation." In contrast, comments or inquiries "relating to routine incidents of the

---

[119] In his dissent, Justice Scalia sharply criticized the majority holding. He warned that "[o]ne should not underestimate the extent to which the [*Minnick*] Court's expansion of *Edwards* constricts law enforcement." The practical result of the decision, he said, is that a "permanent prohibition" on police questioning of a counsel-less suspect attaches once an *Edwards* request is made: the police may not resume questioning of the suspect, even many years later, unless a defense lawyer is present. The effect of *Minnick*, he argues, is to wrongfully protect the suspect from his own voluntary and honest, but "foolish 'mistakes.'" Instead, Scalia said, "we shold rejoice at an honest confession, rather than pity the 'poor fool' who has made it . . . ."

[120] Michigan v. Harvey, 110 S. Ct. 1176, 1180 (1990).

[121] *See* § 153[C][1] *infra*.

[122] *See* Smith v. Illinois, 469 U.S. 91 (1984) (*per curiam*) (summarizing the lower court split of authority).

[123] *Id.*

[124] Connecticut v. Barrett, 479 U.S. 523 (1987).

[125] 462 U.S. 1039 (1983).

custodial relationship," such as requests for water or to use a telephone, fall outside the scope of this definition.

The latter exclusion is a narrow one. Thus, in *Bradshaw*, the plurality determined that D "initiated" communications when he asked the police, "Well, what is going to happen to me now?" Although this statement apparently was intended only to find out where the police were going to take him at that time, the question was indirectly related to the general investigation. Therefore, the plurality held that the police did not act improperly by resuming their interrogation of D.

Four justices dissented. They defined "initiation" more narrowly, as a statement by a suspect involving "communication or dialogue about the subject matter of the criminal investigation." As D's question in this case did not go to the subject matter of the offense under investigation, the dissent would have held that the police could not resume questioning.

The *Bradshaw* justices agreed, however, that even if the suspect, rather than the police, "re-initates" conversations about the crime, the prosecution must still demonstrate that, after the re-initiation, the suspect validly waived his right to silence and to counsel.

§ 146 *Miranda*: Exceptions to the Rule

Since *Miranda* was decided, the Supreme Court has recognized various exceptions to the rule, *i.e.*, circumstances in which *Miranda* warnings need not be given prior to custodial interrogation.

[A] Public-Safety Exception

In *New York v. Quarles*,[126] the Supreme Court recognized a "public safety" exception to *Miranda*. In *Quarles*, a woman informed two officers shortly after midnight that she had been raped, that her assailant was armed, and that he had fled into a nearby all-night grocery store with a weapon. One of the officers entered the store and spotted a man, D, fitting the woman's description of her assailant.

D fled to the rear of the store, with the officer in pursuit. The officer, now accompanied by three other officers, frisked D and handcuffed him. When he discovered that D had an empty shoulder holster, the officer (without giving *Miranda* warnings) asked him where the gun was. D nodded in the direction of some empty cartons and said "the gun is over there." The officers retrieved the weapon.

The lower courts suppressed D's statement about the gun. However, the Supreme Court reversed on the ground that the custodial interrogation occurred in a situation posing a threat to the public safety and, therefore, fit within the newly recognized exception to *Miranda*.

The Court justified the new exception on the ground that the interest in public safety outweighed D's right to his *Miranda* warnings. According to Justice Rehnquist, the officers were "confronted with the immediate necessity" of finding

---

[126] 467 U.S. 649 (1984).

the weapon. If the police had not found the gun, the majority reasoned, an accomplice might have made use of it, or a customer or employee might have gained access to it.

The Court considered it irrelevant that there was no evidence that the interrogating officer was motivated by a concern for public safety. It stated that the public-safety exception "should not be made to depend on *post hoc* findings at a suppression hearing concerning the subjective motivation of the . . . officer." Indeed, the Court admitted that in emergency circumstances most officers act for a "host of different, instinctive, and largely unverifiable motives . . . [including] the desire to obtain incriminating evidence from the suspect."

The precise boundaries of the exception are difficult to ascertain, except that there must be an "objectively reasonable need to protect the police or the public from [an] immediate danger"; there must exist an "exigency requiring immediate action beyond the normal need expeditiously to solve a serious crime."

The Court conceded that its recognition of the public-safety exception reduced the "desirable clarity" of *Miranda*. But it said that "the exception will not be difficult for police officers to apply because in each case it is circumscribed by the exigencies which justify it." The Court expressed confidence that the police "can and will distinguish almost instinctively between questions necessary to secure their own safety or the safety of the public and questions designed solely to elicit testimonial evidence from a suspect."

The holding in *Quarles* is dubious on its facts. Where was the exigency? The events occurred in the middle of the night in a nearly deserted market. There were no customers in the store, and the clerks were at the checkout station. At the time of the questioning, *D* was handcuffed and surrounded by four officers. Despite the Court's allusion to accomplices, the police had no reason to believe that any existed. By cordoning off the area, the gun could easily have been found without questioning *D*.

Quarles is also hard to justify in light of *Miranda*. First, *Quarles* expressly balanced the costs and benefits of the rule it was implementing; the *Miranda* Court was less inclined to balance interests, talking instead about the "respect a government . . . must accord to the dignity and integrity of its citizens," and of the requirement that the government "shoulder the entire load" and "respect the inviolability of the human personality."

Second, the Court dealt with unknowable facts in the two cases very differently. In *Miranda*, the Court did not know precisely what occurred in interrogation rooms. Therefore, it conclusively presumed the worst of the police and of the circumstances — *i.e.*, that custodial interrogations are coercive. In *Quarles*, the Court conceded that it could not know what goes on in the minds of officers during emergencies; therefore, it presumed the best of the police, *i.e.*, that public safety motivates their actions.

Third, *Miranda* envisioned an underdog suspect in need of warnings and the police in need of restraint; *Quarles* treated the police as public guardians who should not be restrained, absent evidence of coercion.

[B] Covert Custodial Interrogation

Despite dictum to the contrary in one Supreme Court opinion,[127] the Court held in *Illinois v. Perkins*[128] that "*Miranda* warnings are not required when the suspect is unaware that he is speaking to a law enforcement officer and gives a voluntary statement."

In *Perkins*, the police obtained information from *I*, an informant, that *D*, a fellow jail inmate, had made statements to *I* that implicated *D* in a murder then under investigation. The police placed *X*, an undercover police agent, in the cellblock with *D* and *I*. *X*, posing as a burglar, was instructed to engage *D* in "casual conversation and report anything he said about the . . . murder." As part of the ruse, *X* directed a conversation with *D* to the subject of murder, and asked *D* whether he had ever killed anybody. In response, *D* admitted that he had, and then proceeded to provide details of the crime.

With only Justice Marshall dissenting, the Court held that *D*'s statements to *X*, although the result of interrogation while he was in custody, and in the absence of *Miranda* warnings, were admissible at *D*'s trial. It reasoned that "[c]onversations between suspects and undercover agents do not implicate the concerns underlying *Miranda*."

Miranda was founded on the premise that the interplay between police custody and police interrogation triggers the need to provide protections against coercion. Coercion, however, is determined from the suspect's perspective;[129] therefore, the requisite coercion is lacking when a custodial suspect encounters a person he believes is a cellmate rather than a law enforcement officer. Quoting Professor Yale Kamisar, the Court observed that "when the agent carries neither badge nor gun and wears not 'police blue but the same prison gray' as the suspect, there is no '*interplay* between police interrogation and police custody.' "[130]

[C] Routine-Booking-Questions Exception

In *Pennsylvania v. Muniz*,[131] a four-justice plurality announced a " 'routine booking question' exception which exempts from *Miranda's* coverage express questions to secure the 'biographical data necessary to complete booking or pretrial services.' "

In *Muniz*, *D* was arrested for driving his car under the influence of alcohol. At the police station, an officer asked *D* questions regarding his name, address, weight, eye color, date of birth, and age, as part of a "routine practice for receiving persons suspected of driving while intoxicated." These questions, and his answers,

---

[127] *See* Patterson v. Illinois, 487 U.S. 285 n.9 (1988) ("[A] surreptitious conversation between an undercover police officer and an unindicted suspect would not give rise to any violation as long as the 'interrogation' was not in a custodial setting. . . .").

[128] 110 S.Ct. 2394 (1990).

[129] *See* Rhode Island v. Innis, 446 U.S. 291 (1980); Berkemer v. McCarty, 468 U.S. 420 (1984).

[130] *Perkins, quoting* Kamisar, *Brewer v. Williams, Massiah, and Miranda: What Is Interrogation? When Does It Matter?*, 67 Geo. L.J. 1, 67, 63 (1978).

[131] 110 S.Ct. 2638 (1990).

were videotaped with his knowledge, but before *D* was informed of his *Miranda* rights. *D*'s slurred performance was introduced at his trial.

The plurality held that these questions did not need to be preceded by *Miranda* warnings: the questions were routine, requested for record-keeping purposes only, "and therefore . . . reasonably related to the police's administrative concerns."

The plurality warned, however, that the mere fact that a question is asked during the booking process does not necessarily immunize it. According to the plurality, "[w]ithout obtaining a waiver of the suspect's *Miranda* rights, the police may not ask questions, even during booking, that are designed to elicit incriminating admissions."

Therefore, assuming that this exception musters a majority vote, as it doubtlessly will,[132] various new questions will arise in the context of express questioning, such as: Were the questions asked during the booking process "routine"?; and, Were the questions reasonably related to the police department's administrative concerns, or were they instead designed to elicit incriminating responses?

§ 147 Scope of the *Miranda* Exclusionary Rule

[A] Impeachment Exception

The Supreme Court held in *Harris v. New York*[133] that a prosecutor may use a statement obtained in violation of *Miranda* to impeach a defendant if the latter testifies at trial in a fashion inconsistent with the custodial statement.

The Court concluded that the privilege to testify in one's defense "cannot be construed to include the right to commit perjury." Once a witness agrees to take the stand he must testify truthfully. If he does not, the prosecutor is entitled to use "the traditional truth-testing devices of the adversary process." According to the Court, the value of the information to the jury in assessing the defendant's credibility outweighs the "speculative possibility that impermissible police conduct [would] be encouraged" by the prophylactic *Miranda* rule.[134]

[B] Use of Post-*Miranda* Silence at Trial

In *Doyle v. Ohio*,[135] *D* was prosecuted for sale of marijuana. At trial he testified in his own defense and claimed that he was framed. In cross-examination, the prosecutor asked him why he had failed to tell the same story to the police after he was arrested and received his *Miranda* warnings.

---

[132] Justice Marshall dissented from the adoption of a new *Miranda* exception. Four members of the Court (Chief Justice Rehnquist, and Justices Blackmun, Stevens, and White) did not reach the issue.

[133] 401 U.S. 222 (1971).

[134] The Fourth Amendment has a similar impeachment rule, *see* 121[B][2][b] *supra*. No such impeachment exception applies to traditional, coerced confessions, however. *See* 135[A] *supra*.

[135] 426 U.S. 610 (1976); *see generally* Snyder, *A Due Process Analysis of the Impeachment Use of Silence in Criminal Trials*, 29 Wm. & Mary L. Rev. 285 (1988).

The Supreme Court held that the prosecutor's use of *D*'s post-*Miranda* silence to impeach his trial testimony violated the due process clause. It concluded that a suspect's silence after *Miranda* warnings are given is "insolubly ambiguous." Furthermore, the implication of the *Miranda* warning that "anything you say will be used against you" is that silence will *not* be used against the suspect. Therefore, use of the silence under such circumstances is "fundamentally unfair."

The due process clause is also violated by the prosecutor's use of post-*Miranda* silence as substantive evidence against the defendant. For example, in *Wainwright v. Greenfield*,[136] the Court held that the prosecutor was not permitted to use *D*'s assertion of his Fifth Amendment privilege as evidence of his sanity in order to rebut *D*'s insanity claim.

The *Doyle* principle is not violated, however, by the use of pre-*Miranda* silence to impeach a defendant. In the absence of *Miranda* warnings, and thus in the absence of an implicit promise that silence will not be used against the suspect, there is no fundamental unfairness in using silence against the accused.[137]

[C] Fruit-of-the-Poisonous-Tree Doctrine

[1] In General

The *Miranda* rule apparently supports no fruit-of-the-poisonous-tree doctrine or, if it does, the doctrine is exceedingly limited. That is, although a statement obtained from *D* in violation of *Miranda* is inadmissible at *D*'s trial in the prosecutor's case-in-chief, verbal fruits of the *Miranda* violation, and probably even physical fruits thereof, are admissible at *D*'s trial, without regard to whether the connection between the challenged evidence and the *Miranda* violation is so attenuated as to dissipate the taint.

Two cases explain the Court's approach to the fruit-of-the-poisonous-tree doctrine when the "poisonous tree" is a *Miranda* violation.

[2] *Michigan v. Tucker*

In *Tucker*,[138] the police provided incomplete warnings to *D* prior to custodial interrogation. Although the questioning occurred before the Court's holding in *Miranda*, *D*'s trial took place after *Miranda* was decided; therefore, its safeguards applied retroactively to the interrogation.[139] As a consequence, *D*'s statements obtained in violation of *Miranda* were inadmissible at his trial.

In *D*'s inadmissible statement, the police obtained the name of a witness, *X*, who was later called as a prosecution witness at *D*'s trial. *Tucker* raised the question of whether *X*'s testimony was inadmissible on the basis of the *Wong Sun*[140] fruit-of-the-poisonous-tree doctrine.

---

[136] 474 U.S. 284 (1986).
[137] Fletcher v. Weir, 455 U.S. 603 (1982) (*per curiam*) (involving post-arrest pre-*Miranda* silence); Jenkins v. Anderson, 447 U.S. 231 (1980) (involving the pre-arrest pre-*Miranda* failure of the defendant to come forward to report his involvement in a homicide).
[138] 417 U.S. 433 (1974).
[139] Johnson v. New Jersey, 384 U.S. 719, *reh'g denied*, 385 U.S. 890 (1966).
[140] Wong Sun v. United States, 371 U.S. 471 (1963). *See* § 125 *supra*.

The Court distinguished *Wong Sun* on the ground that the latter case involved the admissibility of a fruit of a constitutional violation (*i.e.*, a violation of the Fourth Amendment), whereas *X*'s testimony in the present case was a fruit of a violation of a non-constitutional prophylactic rule (*i.e.*, *Miranda*). Consequently, the Court believed that it was not compelled to apply the *Wong Sun* holding in the *Miranda* context.

Analyzing the issue as one of principle rather than precedent, the Court concluded that *X*'s testimony was admissible. First, it observed that the fruit in this case, *X*'s testimony, was not untrustworthy, because *X* was subject to cross-examination at trial by *D*. Second, the deterrence rationale of the exclusionary rule lost "much of its force" in the pre-*Miranda* context of the case, because the police had acted in good faith when they provided the incomplete warnings. Third, the Court rejected "judicial integrity" as an independent basis for excluding the challenged evidence.

[3] *Oregon v. Elstad*

In *Oregon v. Elstad*,[141] the police obtained an incriminating statement from *D* in violation of *Miranda*. Subsequently, *D* was arrested and given his *Miranda* warnings. *D* waived his rights and made a second, more damaging, statement. The first statement was clearly inadmissible under *Miranda*. The issue on appeal was whether the second confession was also inadmissible as a fruit of the earlier *Miranda* violation.

The Court in *Elstad* concluded that the reasoning of *Tucker* "applies with equal force when the alleged 'fruit' of a noncoercive *Miranda* violation is neither a witness nor an article of evidence but the accused's own voluntary testimony."

The Court stated that in the absence of compulsion "or improper tactics," the "twin rationales" of the *Miranda* exclusionary rule — trustworthiness and deterrence — did not call for the exclusion of *D*'s testimony, although it was a fruit of the original violation. Somewhat oddly, the original *Miranda* violation was not considered an "improper tactic" that merited a different conclusion.

It should be noted that in both *Tucker* and *Elstad*, the admissible fruits were volitional statements by human beings. Even in the Fourth Amendment context, the Court has treated such fruits more leniently than physical evidence, which cannot come forward on its own.[142] A plausible case might be made, therefore, for the proposition that physical evidence, such as a gun, should still constitute an inadmissible fruit of a *Miranda* violation, subject to ordinary fruit-of-the-poisonous-tree principles. The expansive language and reasoning of *Elstad*, however, appears to defeat such a claim.

---

[141] 470 U.S. 298 (1985).
[142] *See* § 125[E][2][e] *supra*.

CHAPTER 25

INTERROGATION LAW: SIXTH AMENDMENT RIGHT TO COUNSEL

§ 148   Sixth Amendment Right to Counsel: In General[1]

The Sixth Amendment guarantees that "[i]n all criminal prosecutions, the accused shall enjoy the right . . . to have the Assistance of Counsel for his defence." This right is fundamental and applies to the states through the Fourteenth Amendment due process clause.[2]

The right only applies if two conditions are met. First, with one exception, "adversary judicial criminal proceedings"[3] must have commenced against the individual.[4] According to the Court, "the possibility that [an] encounter [between the government and a suspect] may have important consequences at trial, standing alone, is insufficient to trigger the Sixth Amendment right to counsel."[5]

Second, despite the prefatory phrase, "in all criminal prosecutions," the right to counsel only applies to "critical" stages of the prosecution.[6] The Court once implied that a stage is critical if "[w]hat happens there may effect the whole trial."[7] However, because the latter language appears to encompass virtually every pre-trial stage of the prosecution, the Court has become more circumspect. It now states that it takes a "pragmatic approach" by "asking what purposes a lawyer can serve at the particular stage of the proceedings in question, and what assistance he could provide to an accused at that stage."[8]

---

[1] This chapter focuses on the Sixth Amendment right to counsel in the context of police interrogations. The *Miranda*, or Fifth Amendment, version of the right to counsel is considered in Chapter 24, although comparisons between the two versions of the rights are set out in this chapter. For discussion of the right to counsel in other procedural contexts, *see* §§ 166-67 (eyewitness identification procedures) and chapter 29 (trial and on appeal) *infra*.

[2] Gideon v. Wainwright, 372 U.S. 335 (1963).

[3] This phrase is defined at § 151 *infra*.

[4] In Escobedo v. Illinois, 378 U.S. 478 (1964), the Supreme Court applied the Sixth Amendment to a post-arrest custodial interrogation that occurred prior to the initiation of adversary judicial criminal proceedings. However, the holding of *Escobedo* has been limited to its facts. See § 138 *supra*.

Some state courts have adopted a broader right to counsel under their own constitutions. *E.g.*, State v. Spencer, 305 Or. 59, 750 P.2d 147 (1988) (holding that a drunk-driving suspect has a limited right to counsel prior to making a decision relative to a breathalyzer test); Forte v. State, 759 S.W.2d 128 (Tex.Cr.App. 1988) (applying a flexible right-to-counsel standard).

[5] Moran v. Burbine, 475 U.S. 412, 432 (1986).

[6] United States v. Wade, 388 U.S. 218 (1967).

[7] Hamilton v. Alabama, 368 U.S. 52, 55 (1961).

[8] Patterson v. Illinois, 487 U.S. 285, 298 (1988).

§ 149 *Massiah v. United States*[9]

[A] Historical Overview

When the Supreme Court announced its holding in *Massiah v. United States*[10] it took "a giant step in a wholly new direction"[11] in police interrogation law.

Massiah brought the Sixth Amendment guarantee of the assistance of counsel "out of the courtroom . . . [and] into new precincts."[12] The Court held for the first time that the Constitution is violated when government agents, in the absence of defense counsel, deliberately elicit incriminating information from a person against whom adversary judicial criminal proceedings have commenced.

Although controversial, the *Massiah* rule is alive and well. The case was temporarily eclipsed by *Miranda*,[13] but it moved out of *Miranda's* shadows in 1977 when the Court applied the rule in controversial circumstances in *Brewer v. Williams*.[14] Since then, *Massiah* has not only survived but has "had the audacity to expand"[15] in a time of rare criminal defense successes in the Supreme Court.

[B] *Massiah*: The Facts

D was indicted for a narcotics offense. He retained a lawyer, pleaded not guilty, and was released from custody on bail. In the meantime, *I*, who was charged in the same indictment, agreed to cooperate with the government in its continuing investigation of *D*. *I* permitted federal agents to install a listening device in his car so that they could listen while *D* (unaware of *I*'s informant status) had lengthy conversations with him.

During the intercepted conversations, which occurred in the absence of *D*'s counsel, *D* made incriminating statements that were introduced at trial over his objection.

[C] The Holding

D argued that the admission at trial of the statements he made in *I*'s automobile violated his Sixth Amendment right to counsel. The Supreme Court, per Justice

---

[9] *See generally* Enker & Elsen, *Counsel for the Suspect: Massiah v. United States and Escobedo v. Illinois*, 49 Minn. L. Rev. 47 (1964); Kamisar, *Brewer v. Williams, Massiah, and Miranda: What is Interrogation? When Does it Matter?*, 67 Geo. L.J. 1 (1978); Tomkovicz, *An Adversary System Defense of the Right to Counsel Against Informants: Truth, Fair Play, and the Massiah Doctrine*, 22 U.C. Davis L. Rev. 1 (1988) (hereafter Tomkovicz, *Adversary System*); Tomkovicz, *The Massiah Right to Exclusion: Constitutional Premises and Doctrinal Implications*, 67 N.C. L. Rev. 751 (1989) (hereafter Tomkovicz, *The Massiah Right*); Uviller, *see* Frequently Cited Sources; White, *Interrogation Without Questions: Rhode Island v. Innis and United States v. Henry*, 78 Mich. L. Rev. 1209 (1981).

[10] 377 U.S. 201 (1964).

[11] Uviller, at 1155.

[12] *Id.* at 1159.

[13] Miranda v. Arizona, 384 U.S. 436, *reh'g denied*, 385 U.S. 890 (1966).

[14] 430 U.S. 387, *reh'g denied*, 431 U.S. 925 (1977).

[15] Tomkovicz, *Adversary System*, n. 9 *supra*, at 5.

Stewart, agreed. It held that the Sixth Amendment was violated "when there was used against [D] at his trial evidence of his own incriminating words, which federal agents had deliberately elicited from him after he had been indicted and in the absence of his counsel."

[D] The Rationale

Justice Stewart reasoned that the Sixth Amendment applied in D's circumstances because the period after a suspect is formally charged with an offense and before trial is "the most critical period of the proceedings." It is during this time that "consultation, thoroughgoing investigation and preparation" occur. To deny the accused counsel during this period would deny him "effective representation by counsel at the only stage when legal aid and advice would help him."

The Court accepted the government's claim that the agents in the present case had a right to continue their post-indictment investigation of D. But, it concluded that to be effective, the right to counsel had to apply to the surreptitious conduct that occurred here. Indeed, D was "more seriously imposed upon" than in traditional interrogation circumstances because he was unaware that he was "under interrogation by a government agent."

[E] Making Sense of *Massiah*: The Role of Counsel

Despite Justice Stewart's assurance that the government had the right to continue its investigation of D, the practical effect of the *Massiah* rule is that in the instance of surreptitious deliberate elicitation of incriminating statements, "the government [must] either reveal its presence [to the accused] and afford the opportunity to consult with counsel, or suffer [at his trial] the exclusion of the product of its adversarial encounter with the accused."[16]

Can such a rule be defended? In his dissent, Justice White criticized the majority because it barred the use by the government of "relevant, reliable, and highly probative evidence" obtained in a non-coercive environment. More recently, Justice Rehnquist has stated that *Massiah*'s "doctrinal underpinnings . . . have been largely left unexplained, and the result . . . is difficult to reconcile with the traditional notions of the role of an attorney."[17] Even a supporter of *Massiah* has conceded that "[t]he original . . . opinion provides a good example of . . . analytical shallowness."[18]

Indeed, how was D's Sixth Amendment right to counsel violated in *Massiah*? His lawyer was not barred from I's automobile during the conversations. Furthermore, in light of the surreptitious nature of the police activity, it would not have served any meaningful purpose if D's lawyer coincidentally had been present; there was little way that he could have used his expertise to protect D.[19] In fact, the lawyer's presence in the car could have represented a more serious risk to D's

---

[16] *Id.* at 91.

[17] United States v. Henry, 447 U.S. 264, 290 (1980) (Rehnquist, J., dissenting).

[18] Tomkovicz, *Adversary System*, n. 9 *supra*, at 22.

[19] The lawyer could have told D not to talk to I on the general principle that the co-defendants' legal interests might eventually conflict, but he could have given this advice before the meeting in the automobile.

Sixth Amendment rights than his absence, because the government could have overheard lawyer-client confidences.[20]

According to two commentators, "[t]he real issue presented in *Massiah* was not one of the right to counsel but rather the permissible extent of governmental deceit inherent in undercover work and the use of informers."[21] If this observation is accurate, *Massiah* should have rested its holding on the Fourth Amendment, or on the Fifth Amendment due process clause. Such an approach, however, would have been inconsistent with existing and subsequent constitutional doctrine in those fields.[22]

Is there a way to find a Sixth Amendment interest implicated in *Massiah*? The answer depends on what is meant by the "assistance of counsel." In other words, what is the pre-trial role of a defense attorney and how could that role have been filled by *D*'s attorney in this case?

One scholar has identified three roles a lawyer can play in the pre-trial phase of a criminal prosecution.[23] First, she can provide assistance in those encounters with the government in which her innocent client's "weakness, ignorance, or inertia"[24] threatens to result in an unjust conviction. The Court could not have had this role in mind in *Massiah*, however, because there was no serious reason to fear that an innocent person would make incriminating statements in the non-coercive environment of *I*'s automobile.

Second, a lawyer can provide "preventive assistance." The thesis here is that "[t]he accused, alone and friendless, faces the immense forces of the state arrayed against [her]."[25] Counsel's purpose here is to make an uneven match more even, not so much in order to insure that the State's "immense forces" do not crush an innocent person, but instead to give the accused, even if she is guilty, a fair chance to win.

This so-called "fox hunt" or "sporting" view of justice has been criticized in many quarters.[26] In his dissent in *Massiah*, Justice White warned that the majority was "guarantee[ing] sporting treatment for sporting peddlers of narcotics." However, even if this defense role is justifiable, there was no practical way

---

[20] In Weatherford v. Bursey, 429 U.S. 545 (1977), *D* and *X*, an undercover agent, participated in the vandalization of private property. In order to protect *X*'s undercover status, the police charged *X* along with *D* with the offense. Prior to trial, *D* invited *X* to sit in while he discussed trial strategy with his attorney. At no time did *X* pass on any of the lawyer-client conversations to the government. The Court held that under the circumstances of the case (*i.e.*, there was "no tainted evidence in this case, no communication of defense strategy to the prosecution, and no purposeful intrusion by [*X*]"), no Sixth Amendment violation resulted.

[21] Enker & Elsen, n. 9 *supra*, at 57.

[22] Only two years after *Massiah*, Justice Stewart wrote the opinion of the Court in Hoffa v. United States, 385 U.S. 293 (1966), *reh'g denied*, 386 U.S. 940 (1967), which reaffirmed the Fourth Amendment principle that one who talks to another person assumes the risk that the listener will betray her. *See* § 32 *supra*. *Hoffa* also rejected the claim that the use of secret government informers is a *per se* violation of the due process clause.

[23] Uviller, at 1168-83.

[24] *Id.* at 1169.

[25] *Id.* at 1173.

[26] *See* §§ 128[C], 140[C] *supra*.

for *D*'s counsel in this case to assist him in the "fox hunt" that was occurring in *I*'s car, as neither *D* nor counsel realized that the "hunt" was underway.

The third role of counsel is to provide "adversarial assistance." The premise is that once the government commits itself to a prosecution — once the investigation turns "into a hardened adversarial alignment"[27] — a form of "cloture," or limitation on access to the accused, should occur.

Once the adversarial system begins, the lawyer serves as the "guardian of the fortress."[28] She "is the essential medium through which the demands and commitments of the sovereign are communicated to the citizen."[29] Once adversarial proceedings have commenced, the prosecutor and the police "have an affirmative obligation not to act in a manner that circumvents and thereby dilutes the protection afforded by the right to counsel."[30] In particular, it is no longer appropriate for agents of the government to enter the fortress in order to obtain verbal evidence from the accused, at least in the absence of counsel or a valid waiver of the right.

Although *Massiah* has been criticized by many commentators,[31] the holding can be justified on the latter basis. The government violated the cloture concept: it deliberately elicited incriminating information from *D* after he was indicted and in his counsel's absence; and, in view of the surreptitious approach used to obtain the evidence, *D* had no meaningful way to waive his right to counsel.

It should be observed again, however, that the *Massiah* Court never offered this (or any other) significant policy justification for the new rule it announced in the case.

§ 150   The *Massiah* Doctrine: In General

The majority opinion in *Massiah* was short and the holding was narrow. The rule announced in the case was that the Sixth Amendment was violated "when there was used against [*D*] at his trial evidence of his own incriminating words, which federal agents had deliberately elicited from him after he had been indicted and in the absence of his counsel."

The right to counsel that has evolved is somewhat broader than that which was announced in *Massiah*. First, the right applies not only to conduct by federal agents, but also to the states, through the Fourteenth Amendment due process clause.[32] Second, although the Court in *Massiah* noted the aggravating circumstance that the defendant in the case was subjected to surreptitious "interrogation" techniques, the right to counsel applies as well to traditional interrogations.

---

[27] Uviller, at 1176.

[28] *Id.* at 1161.

[29] Maine v. Moulton, 474 U.S. 159, 170 n.7 (1985) (*quoting* Brewer v. Williams, 430 U.S. at 415 (Stevens, J., concurring)).

[30] *Id.* at 171.

[31] *See* Uviller, at 1147; Enker & Elsen, n. 9 *supra*, at 57-58; Dix, *Undercover Investigations and Police Rulemaking*, 53 Tex. L. Rev. 203, 226 (1975).

[32] *See* Brewer v. Williams, 430 U.S. 387, *reh'g denied*, 431 U.S. 925 (1977).

Subject to clarification in the chapter sections that follow, the *Massiah* rule can be summarized as follows. First, in the context of ordinary interrogations, the Sixth Amendment renders inadmissible in the prosecution's case-in-chief any statement deliberately elicited from the defendant after adversary judicial criminal proceedings have begun, in the absence of the accused's counsel or a knowing and voluntary waiver of the right.

In the case of covert police activity as occurred in *Massiah*, the rule is the same except that, because of the surreptitious nature of the police conduct, the "concept of a knowing and voluntary waiver of Sixth Amendment rights does not apply,"[33] or, more accurately, there can never be a valid waiver of the Sixth Amendment if the accused does not know that the person with whom she is speaking is an agent of the state.

§ 151 "Adversary Judicial Criminal Proceedings"

The accused's Sixth Amendment right to the assistance of counsel does not attach until adversary judicial criminal proceedings have commenced. The Court explained in *Brewer v. Williams*[34] that:

> Whatever else it may mean, the right to counsel granted by the Sixth and Fourteenth Amendments means at least that a person is entitled to the help of a lawyer at or after the time that judicial proceedings have been initiated against him — "whether by way of formal charge, preliminary hearing, indictment, information, or arraignment."[35]

Despite the open-ended language in the quotation — "whatever else it may mean" and "the right . . . means at least" — the Court, with one exception,[36] has shut the door on the possibility that the right-to-counsel provision might apply before judicial proceedings begin.[37]

The Court has justified this threshold requirement on the basis of the language of the Sixth Amendment, which provides that the right to counsel applies "in all criminal *prosecutions*" and is guaranteed to "the *accused*." Only when the formalities occur — when the "suspect" becomes the "accused" — does the "prosecution" commence.

The Court has asserted[38] that this interpretation of the Sixth Amendment "is far from a mere formalism. It is the starting point of our whole system of adversary criminal justice." It is at this time that the accused is "faced with the prosecutorial forces of organized society, and immersed in the intricacies of substantive and procedural criminal law."

---

[33] United States v. Henry, 447 U.S. at 273.

[34] 430 U.S. 387, *reh'g denied*, 431 U.S. 925 (1977).

[35] For definition of the terms "indictment" and "information," *see* § 3[C][4]-[5] *supra.* The Court has not explained what it means in this quotation by "formal charge" and "arraignment," but the Sixth Amendment attaches at least as soon as the accused appears before a magistrate immediately after arrest. *See* Brewer v. Williams, 430 U.S. 387, *reh'g denied*, 431 U.S. 925 (1977); Moore v. Illinois, 434 U.S. 220 (1977).

[36] *See* n. 4 *supra.*

[37] *See* United States v. Gouveia, 467 U.S. 180 (1984).

[38] Kirby v. Illinois, 406 U.S. 682, 689 (1972).

However, as Professor Richard Uviller has pointed out,[39] "[n]either semantics nor reason obstructs the designation of an arrest as the point of accusation in the constitutional sense." Indeed, under the Sixth Amendment, the "accused" in all "criminal prosecutions" is entitled to a speedy trial, yet this right has been interpreted to attach at the time of arrest or the filing of an indictment or information, whichever comes first.[40]

§ 152 "Deliberate Elicitation"[41]

[A] "Deliberate Elicitation" versus "Interrogation"

Although *Massiah* prohibits "deliberate elicitation" — those were the words in its holding — Justice Stewart stated at one point in the opinion that *D* had been "under interrogation" by *I*. The use of the word "interrogation" in the opinion was misleading as there was no evidence presented that *I* questioned *D*; instead, they had "lengthy conversations."

The Court confused matters more in *Brewer v. Williams*.[42] In *Williams*, *D* was arrested and arraigned for the murder of a small girl. While being transported in a police car from one part of the state to another, *D* was subjected to what has been characterized as the "Christian burial speech" by a police officer.

In the speech, the officer prefaced his comments to *D* by saying, "I want to give you something to think about. . . ." He concluded his remarks by indicating, "I do not want you to answer me. I don't want to discuss it any further. Just think about it. . . ." In between, the officer, playing on *D*'s religious beliefs and psychological vulnerability as an escaped mental patient, expressed concern regarding the possibility that the little girl's body, which had not been discovered, would soon be buried under the winter's snow, thus depriving her parents of a chance to give her "a Christian burial."

At no time during the "speech" did the officer question *D*. Nonetheless, the Court described "the clear rule of *Massiah*" to be that, once judicial criminal proceedings commence, the accused "has a right to legal representation when the government interrogates him." It also stated that "no such constitutional protection would have come into play if there had been no interrogation." And, it described the burial speech as "tantamount to interrogation." Yet, in language reminiscent of *Massiah*, the Court remarked that the officer "deliberately and designedly set out to elicit information . . . just as surely as — and perhaps more effectively than — if he had formally interrogated him."

This language in *Williams* suggested the possibility that the terms "deliberate elicitation" and "interrogation" were constitutional synonyms. If they were, it could have meant that anything that constitutes "deliberate elicitation" in the Sixth Amendment context is an "interrogation" for purposes of *Miranda* law, and vice-versa.

---

[39] Uviller, at 1167.
[40] United States v. Marion, 404 U.S. 307 (1971).
[41] *See generally* Kamisar, n. 9 *supra*; White, n. 9 *supra*.
[42] 430 U.S. 387, *reh'g denied*, 431 U.S. 925 (1977).

However, in *Rhode Island v. Innis*,[43] the first Supreme Court case to define "interrogation" in the *Miranda* context, the justices indicated that it was erroneous to suggest that "the definition of 'interrogation' under *Miranda* is informed by this Court's [Sixth Amendment] decision[s]. . . . The definitions of 'interrogation' under the Fifth and Sixth Amendments, if indeed the term 'interrogation' is even apt in the Sixth Amendment context, are not necessarily interchangeable. . . .'"

The meaning of "deliberate elicitation" in the Sixth Amendment context is described more fully below. However, in view of the warning in *Innis*, it is important to treat the Sixth Amendment and Fifth Amendment versions of the right to counsel separately.

[B] What Does "Deliberate" Mean?

[1] "Deliberate" as "Purposeful"

In the most obvious situation, "deliberate elicitation" occurs when a government agent purposely elicits the incriminating statements from the accused, *i.e.*, when it is her conscious object to obtain statements from the defendant.

For example, purposeful (and, therefore, deliberate) elicitation occurs when an officer formally interrogates the accused person. Or, as in *Massiah*, it occurs when an undercover agent engages the accused in a conversation in order to obtain incriminating comments. Or, as in *Williams*, the Sixth Amendment is triggered when an officer makes statements that are designed to play on the conscience of the accused, in order to induce incriminating remarks.

To this extent, *Massiah*'s "deliberate elicitation" differs from the *Miranda-Innis* concept of "interrogation"[44] in that the former test centers on the subjective motivation of the officer, whereas the latter one focuses on the suspect and is based on an objective finding that the process will likely result in incriminating information.

[2] "Deliberate" As Less Than "Purposeful"

[a] United States v. Henry

In *United States v. Henry*,[45] the Supreme Court further examined the concept of "deliberate elicitation." Unfortunately, the language of the opinion is imprecise and the facts pertaining to the case are unclear. However, it appears that "deliberate elicitation" can occur even if the elicitation is not purposeful.

In *Henry*, *I*, a paid informant for the Federal Bureau of Investigation (F.B.I.), was placed in a jail cell with *D* after the latter had been indicted. The F.B.I. agent told *I* "to be alert to any statement" made by *D*, "but not to initiate any conversation with or question" him. In fact, however, *I* "engaged in conversation" with *D* various times, during which *D* made statements that the government sought to introduce at his trial.

In an opinion written by Chief Justice Burger, the Court held that the government "deliberately elicited" the statements "within the meaning of *Massiah*." In

---

[43] 446 U.S. 291 (1980).
[44] *See* § 143 *supra*.
[45] 447 U.S. 264 (1980).

reaching this conclusion, it pointed to three factors: (1) *I* was paid on a contingent-fee basis, and thus had an incentive to obtain information from *D*; (2) *I* pretended to be a fellow inmate, which made it possible for him to engage in conversations with *D* without arousing his suspicion; and (3) *D* was in custody, which "bring[s] into play subtle influences that . . . make [an inmate] particularly susceptible to the ploys of undercover Government agents."

Based on these factors, the Court concluded that the government "must have known" that *I*'s proximity to *D* "likely would lead" to the incriminating statements. And, in the critical language of the opinion, the Court stated that "[b]y intentionally creating a situation likely to induce [*D*] to make incriminating statements without the assistance of counsel, the Government violated [*D*'s] Sixth Amendment right to counsel." This conclusion followed, it said, regardless of who — *I* or *D* — raised the subject of the accused's criminal activities, and whether or not *I* expressly questioned *D* about the crime or merely "engaged in general conversation about it."

A careful reading of the language of *Henry* raises questions about the meaning of "deliberate elicitation." If *Massiah* and *Williams* involved "purposeful" elicitation, *Henry* involved no more than "knowledge" by the F.B.I. agent that *I* would attempt to secure incriminating information.

In fact, in view of the Court's statement that the F.B.I. "must have known" that *I*'s conduct "likely" would result in information, the agent's state of mind might more accurately be described as "reckless." This conclusion would also be consistent with the Court's statement that the government "intentionally" created a situation "likely to induce" the statements. That is, the "intent" here relates not to the elicitation but to the creation of the circumstances in which the elicitation was likely to occur.

[b] *Maine v. Moulton*

Henry was reinforced and the *Massiah* doctrine extended further in *Maine v. Moulton*,[46] a case remarkably similar to *Massiah*. In *Moulton*, *D* and *I* were indicted for theft and were released from custody pending trial. Unbeknownst to *D*, *I* agreed to cooperate with the prosecution and to testify against *D*.

I informed the police that *D* had suggested to him that a witness in the case ought to be killed. In order to obtain information regarding this proposed crime, the police received permission from *I* to install a recording device on his telephone. Thereafter, *D* telephoned *I* three times, during which conversations he commented on the pending theft charges.

In the last conversation, *D* asked *I* to meet with him to plan their defense in the theft case. *I* agreed and went to the meeting with a transmitter hidden on his body. During the meeting, some of the discussion concerned *D*'s thoughts, by now discarded, about "eliminating" the witness, but most of the conversation "encouraged" by *I* involved the pending charges. Specifically, during the meeting *I* professed a bad memory and repeatedly asked *D* to "remind him" about the details of the theft. As a consequence, *D* made various incriminating statements about the crime.

---

[46] 474 U.S. 159 (1985).

The government sought to introduce statements made by *D* on the telephone as well as during his meeting with *I*. It argued that *Massiah* and *Henry* were distinguishable on the ground that, in those cases, the police set up the encounters with the defendants, whereas here it was *D* who initiated the telephone calls and meeting.[47]

The Supreme Court disagreed. It stated that the Sixth Amendment right to counsel did not depend on the identity of the instigating party. Rather, the Sixth Amendment "guarantees the accused . . . the right to rely on counsel as a 'medium' between him and the State. . . . [T]his guarantee includes the State's affirmative obligation not to act in a manner that circumvents the protections accorded the accused by invoking this right."

The Court agreed that the Sixth Amendment is not violated if the government obtains incriminating information from the accused "by luck or happenstance." But, it warned, "knowing exploitation by the State of an opportunity to confront the accused without counsel being present is as much a breach of the State's obligation . . . as is the intentional creation of such an opportunity."

In short, there is no constitutionally significant difference between, on the one hand, a case in which the government *purposely* sets up an encounter between a government agent and the defendant in which it is likely that the accused will make incriminating remarks about the pending charges, and, on the other hand, one in which the government *knowingly* takes advantage of a meeting already set up by the defendant in which incriminating statements are likely.

[3] Summary

"Deliberate elicitation" arises when the government through its agent: (1) acts with the purpose of eliciting incriminating information from the accused regarding the pending charges, regardless of the likelihood that the elicitation will be successful (*Massiah*, *Williams*); (2) purposely sets up a situation in which incriminating information is likely to be elicited (*Henry*); or (3) exploits an encounter set up by the accused with the agent that it knows is likely to result in incriminating information (*Moulton*).

[C] What Is "Elicitation"?

[1] Why the Question Matters

Massiah, *Henry*, and *Moulton* involved conversations by an informant with the accused. Williams involved a speech by a known police officer. What else might constitute "deliberate elicitation"?

For example, is it permissible for the police to put an informant in the accused's cell and instruct her as follows: "Act like a deaf mute. Pretend you hear nothing and can say nothing. *D* is a blabbermouth, so just report anything that *D* says to you or others." If the agent follows these instruction — if she is a mere passive listener or "listening post" — is the Sixth Amendment violated, on the theory that the government "must have known" that "blabbermouth *D*" would talk?

---

[47] The state also argued that the statements were admissible because they were obtained during a legitimate investigation of the proposed murder. This issue is considered at § 155[C] *infra*.

Alternatively, Fourth Amendment issues aside, would it be permissible for the police to install a listening device in a jail cell instead of the "deaf mute," in order to hear *D*'s conversations with her non-informant cellmate?

Henry and *Moulton* explicitly left open the questions raised by these hypotheticals.

[2] The Court's Answer: *Kuhlmann v. Wilson*

In *Kuhlmann v. Wilson*,[48] an informant was placed in a jail cell with the instruction to "keep his ears open," to avoid asking *D* any questions, and to report to the police any statements made by *D*. The trial court found that the informant followed these instructions. Subsequently, the prosecutor sought to introduce statements made by *D* to the undercover agent in the jail.

The Supreme Court held that the Sixth Amendment is not violated by the placement of a covert police agent in a jail cell with a person against whom formal charges have been brought, unless the government conducts "investigatory techniques that are the equivalent of direct police interrogation."

According to the justices, in order to prove a violation of the Sixth Amendment, "the defendant must demonstrate that the police and their informant took some action, beyond mere listening, that was designed deliberately to elicit incriminating remarks." The present case was distinguished from *Henry*, in which the informant "stimulated" conversations with the accused, and from *Moulton*, in which the informant asked the defendant questions to "refresh his memory."

§ 153 Waiver of the Right to Counsel

[A] General Principles

The concept of waiver does not apply in the context of "secret interrogations," *i.e.*, the use of an undercover agent to deliberately elicit incriminating statements. There is no way for a person to waive a right to be free from police-initiated "interrogation" that she does not know is occurring.[49]

In all other circumstances, the *Zerbst*[50] test of waiver applies to the Sixth Amendment right to counsel: that is, the Constitution is not violated if the prosecution overcomes the presumption against waiver by proving that the accused intentionally relinquished a known right or privilege.[51]

[B] Relinquishment of the Right

In *Brewer v. Williams*,[52] *D* was arrested and arraigned in Davenport, Iowa, for a murder that occurred in Des Moines. *D* received *Miranda* warnings after he was arrested and again after his arraignment. At the arraignment, *D* spoke briefly to

---

[48] 477 U.S. 436 (1986).
[49] United States v. Henry, 447 U.S. at 273.
[50] Johnson v. Zerbst, 304 U.S. 458 (1938). *See* § 12 *supra*.
[51] Brewer v. Williams, 430 U.S. 387, *reh'g denied*, 431 U.S. 925 (1977).
[52] *Id.*

an attorney, who advised him to remain silent until he saw his lawyer in Des Moines. *D* also spoke by telephone to his Des Moines counsel, who gave him the same advice. The police agreed not to question *D* while they transported him to Des Moines.

On the trip, *D* told the officers in the car that he would talk to them after he arrived at his destination and spoke to his lawyer. Nonetheless, an officer deliberately sought to elicit incriminating information from *D* by giving a "Christian burial speech."[53] Later, apparently as the result of the speech, *D* showed the police where he had hidden the body of the victim.[54]

The Supreme Court, per Justice Stewart, held that *D*'s incriminating statements to the police during the trip were obtained in violation of the Sixth Amendment. Adversary judicial criminal proceedings had commenced against *D*, so his Sixth Amendment right to counsel had attached. The statements obtained from *D* were the result of deliberate elicitation. And, although *D* could have waived his right to counsel, a valid waiver was not secured in this case.

But, why was there no valid waiver here? *D* had been read his *Miranda* rights twice, so he knew that he had a right to counsel, and the Court agreed that he appeared to understand the warnings. And, the Court assumed that *D*'s disclosures were voluntarily made, so there is no basis to argue that he was coerced to waive his right to counsel and talk.

The Court's simple answer to the question — "Why was there no valid waiver?" — was that there had been no waiver at all, valid or otherwise: "[W]aiver requires nor merely comprehension but relinquishment, and [*D*'s] consistent reliance upon the advice of counsel in dealing with the authorities refutes any suggestion that he waived that right."

If there was no waiver in *Williams* does this mean, as Chief Justice Burger claimed in dissent, that the Court "conclusively presumes a suspect is legally incompetent to change his mind and tell the truth until an attorney is present"?

The Court's opinion does not go that far. It criticized the officers because, despite *D*'s "express and implicit assertions of his right to counsel," they sought to elicit incriminating statements "without prefacing this effort by telling [*D*] that he had a right to the presence of a lawyer, and made no effort at all to ascertain whether [*D*] wished to relinquish that right." In other words, the opinion suggests that once the accused asserts his right to counsel, a valid waiver is possible, but only if the officer re-informs the suspect of his right to counsel and secures an express waiver.

Concurring Justice Powell offered another solution: a waiver could be found if the prosecutor had proved that "police officers refrained from coercion and interrogation . . . and that [*D*] freely on his own initiative . . . confessed the

---

[53] *See* § 152[A] *supra*.

[54] For a fascinating account of the facts regarding the crime, the Christian burial speech, and defense counsel's trial strategy, much of which is not evident in the Supreme Court opinion, *see* Johnson, *The Return of the Christian Burial Speech Case*, 32 Emory L.J. 349 (1983) (which discusses but discounts information that suggests that *D* might not have been the murderer); Kamisar, *Brewer v. Williams — A Hard Look at a Discomfiting Record*, 66 Geo. L.J. 209 (1977).

crime." In short, once the defendant indicates a desire to talk to an attorney, police-initiated conversation should cease. As discussed in the next sub-section, Justice Powell's "solution" has prevailed.

[C] When May a Waiver Be Secured?

[1] After *D* Requests Counsel: The *Jackson* Rule

In *Williams*, the Court held that *D* did not relinquish his Sixth Amendment right to counsel. The Court implied that a valid waiver could have been secured if, after *D* had expressed a wish to talk to his attorney, the police had not deliberately elicited statements from him until they had re-informed him of his rights and obtained an express waiver.

This solution apparently will no longer do. In *Michigan v. Jackson*,[55] the Court held that once the Sixth Amendment right to counsel attaches and the accused requests the assistance of a lawyer, the government may no longer deliberately elicit information from her until she has talked to her counsel, unless she initiates further communications, exchanges, or conversations with the government. In effect, the Court extended the protections announced in *Edwards v. Arizona*,[56] a Fifth Amendment *Miranda* waiver case, to the Sixth Amendment.

In *Jackson*, *D* was arraigned for murder. At the hearing, the judge informed *D* of his right to the appointment of counsel. *D* expressly invoked the right. A notice of appointment of counsel was promptly mailed to a law firm. Before the firm received the notice, however, the police contacted *D*, read him his *Miranda* rights, and questioned him. Although *D* asked several times about his lawyer, he answered their questions.

The Supreme Court, per Justice Stevens, held that the waiver was invalid because the police initiated the conversation — or "private interview,"[57] as Stevens has since described it — after *D* had requested counsel.

Although the Court applied the Fifth Amendment *Edwards* rule in the Sixth Amendment context, Justice Stevens stated that the "reasons for prohibiting the interrogation of an uncounseled prisoner who has asked for the help of a lawyer are even stronger after he has been formally charged with an offense than before." Once formal charges are brought — "and a person who had previously been just a 'suspect' has become an 'accused' " — a defendant is entitled to "rely on counsel as a 'medium' between him and the State."[58] In these circumstances, the Court concluded in *Jackson*, "the reasoning of . . . [*Edwards*] applies with even greater force. . . ."

Notwithstanding the *Jackson* Court's emphasis on the Sixth Amendment aspects of the case, the Supreme Court has subsequently said that the holding in *Jackson*, although "based on the Sixth Amendment, . . . [has] its roots . . . in [the] Court's decisions in *Miranda* . . ., and succeeding cases."[59] Since *Edwards*

---

[55] 475 U.S. 625 (1986).

[56] 451 U.S. 477, *reh'g denied*, 452 U.S. 973 (1981). *See* § 145[D][2][a] *supra*.

[57] Patterson v. Illinois, 487 U.S. 285, 261 (1988) (dissenting opinion); Michigan v. Harvey, 110 S.Ct. 1176, 1182 (1990) (dissenting opinion).

[58] *Jackson, quoting* Maine v. Moulton, 474 U.S. at 176.

[59] Michigan v. Harvey, 110 S.Ct. at 1180.

is a prophylactic rule designed to enforce the prophylactic *Miranda* doctrine, *Jackson* is now also characterized as a prophylactic rule, albeit one attached to the Sixth Amendment.[60]

[2] If *D* Does Not Request Counsel

[a] Before Counsel is Appointed or Hired

In *Jackson*, *D* was interrogated after he requested the assistance of a lawyer, and a lawyer had been assigned to him. However, suppose that the police in *Jackson* had sought a waiver from *D* before counsel had been hired or assigned, and in the absence of any express request by *D* for counsel. Would the waiver have been valid in such circumstances?

This was the issue raised in *Patterson v. Illinois*.[61] In *Patterson*, *D* was arrested and jailed. He was read his *Miranda* rights, after which he volunteered to answer questions. Subsequently, he was indicted, thus triggering his Sixth Amendment right to counsel.

When the police informed D of the indictment, he asked the officers various questions about the charges and then began to talk about the crime. The police interrupted him, repeated the *Miranda* warnings, and secured a waiver of his rights. The Court noted "as a matter of some significance" that at the time of the post-indictment questioning, *D* had not yet "retained, or accepted by appointment, a lawyer to represent him."

The Court, per Justice White, upheld the admissibility of the post-indictment statements. It held, 5-4, that *Jackson* did not bar all counsel-less interrogation after the Sixth Amendment attaches, but only such questioning that occurs after the accused asks for the help of a lawyer. In effect, in the absence of such a request, the police are not prohibited from attempting to secure a waiver of the defendant's Sixth Amendment rights.

Justice White contended that there is no practical difference between a person who is formally accused of a crime, and thus whose Sixth Amendment right to counsel has come into play, and a pre-indicted custodial suspect about to undergo questioning. In both cases, the interrogatee has the right to the assistance of counsel; in both cases, that right must be honored if it is asserted; but, in the absence of the exercise of the right, the government is not barred from questioning her after obtaining a valid waiver.

Justice Stevens, the author of *Jackson*, dissented. He sharply rejected the majority's assertion that the Fifth Amendment and Sixth Amendment rights to counsel are fundamentally the same. Quoting from *Jackson* and other Sixth Amendment cases, Justice Stevens concluded that "our prior decisions have . . . made clear that the return of a formal charge fundamentally alters the relationship between the state and the accused, conferring increased protections upon defendants in their interactions with state authorities."

---

[60] This characterization of *Jackson* has practical significance in relation to the *Massiah* exclusionary rule. *See* § 155[D] *infra.*

[61] 487 U.S. 285 (1988).

He and the three other dissenting justices would have held that the police may not conduct a "private interview," *i.e.*, an interrogation of the accused in the absence of counsel, once formal adversary proceedings have commenced, with or without an assertion of the right to counsel by the defendant.

[b] After Counsel is Appointed or Hired

In *Jackson*, the accused requested the appointment of counsel; therefore, interrogation had to cease. In *Patterson*, a lawyer had not yet been retained or appointed, nor had *D* affirmatively requested a lawyer; therefore, the police were permitted to seek a waiver of his right to counsel and interrogate him.

In a footnote in *Patterson*, however, the Court stated that it was "a matter of some significance" that *D* had not yet retained or accepted by appointment a lawyer to represent him. When an accused person is represented by counsel at the time that the police seek to question her, it said, "a distinct set of constitutional safeguards aimed at preserving the sanctity of the attorney-client relationship takes effect."

Although *Patterson* did not amplify on this statement, the Court cited *Maine v. Moulton*,[62] a case in which it held that once adversary proceedings commence, the government is required to rely on defense counsel as a "medium" between it and the accused. Perhaps, therefore, once the Sixth Amendment attaches and the accused has a lawyer, the government may not directly initiate communications with the accused, but must deal with her through counsel, even if she does not expressly request the assistance of her lawyer.[63]

[D] Elements of a Valid Waiver

[1] "Voluntary"

The Supreme Court has not considered the issue of what constitutes a voluntary waiver of the Sixth Amendment right to counsel, but it will probably look to its *Miranda* jurisprudence, which in turn is based on general due process concepts of voluntariness.[64]

[2] "Knowing and Intelligent"

The elements of a "knowing and intelligent" waiver for purposes of the Sixth Amendment appear to be the same as for a waiver of a suspect's *Miranda* rights. Therefore, according to *Patterson v. Illinois*,[65] if a person against whom formal adversary proceedings have commenced is read her *Miranda* rights, the information in those warnings adequately informs her not only of her Fifth Amendment rights but also of her Sixth Amendment right to counsel.

According to *Patterson*, *Miranda* warnings convey "the sum and substance" of the Sixth Amendment right to counsel. The warnings inform the accused that she has the right to have a lawyer appointed prior to questioning and to have counsel

---

[62] 474 U.S. 159 (1985). *See* § 152[B][2][b] *supra*.
[63] *E.g.*, Dew v. United States, 558 A.2d 1112 (D.C. 1989).
[64] *See* §§ 145[C][1] (*Miranda*), 133 (due process) *supra*.
[65] 487 U.S. 285 (1988).

present during questioning. The warnings also inform her of the "ultimate adverse consequence" of foregoing the right to counsel, namely that any statement she makes can be used against her. And, the warnings tell her what a lawyer can do for her, "namely, advise [the accused] to refrain from making any such statements."[66]

§ 154   Standing to Raise a Sixth Amendment Claim

Little doubt exists, although the Supreme Court has not yet so ruled, that the Sixth Amendment right to counsel is a personal right, which therefore may only be raised in a criminal trial by the individual whose right was infringed.

This assumption is supported by language in *Massiah*, in which the Court held that the Sixth Amendment is violated when the accused's own incriminating statement is "used by the prosecution as evidence against *him* at his trial." The emphasis on "him" is found in Justice Stewart's opinion for the Court.

§ 155   Scope of the Sixth Amendment Exclusionary Rule[67]

[A]   General Observations

Most of the Supreme Court's Sixth Amendment right-to-counsel opinions have considered the nature of the right or its waiver, but few have discussed the scope of the Sixth Amendment exclusionary rule.

At times, the Court has implied that the Sixth Amendment right is not a right to counsel *per se*, but rather a right to have deliberately elicited evidence obtained in the absence of counsel excluded at trial. Under this view, the exclusionary rule is the right itself, and not merely a remedy.

For example, *Massiah* stated that *D* "was denied the basic protections of that [Sixth Amendment] guarantee when there was used against him at his trial evidence of his own incriminating words." The Court, it will be remembered, implied that it was not inappropriate for the government to continue its investigation of *D* after the indictment, presumably including the surreptitious questioning that took place. It was the use of *D*'s statements at trial that troubled the Court.

At other times, however, the Court has treated the Sixth Amendment right as if it were violated as soon as the elicitation of the statements occurred. For

---

[66] Justice Stevens, with whom Justices Brennan and Marshall, joined, dissented. He argued that the defense lawyer's role after adversary proceedings have begun is more significant than the majority suggested. *Miranda* warnings, therefore, do not adequately inform the accused of the implication of giving up the Sixth Amendment right to counsel. For example, the dissent argued, *Miranda* warnings do not convey the fact "that a lawyer might examine the indictment for legal sufficiency before submitting . . . her client to interrogation or that a lawyer is likely to be more skillful in negotiating a plea bargain and that such negotiations may be most fruitful if initiated prior to any interrogation."

[67] *See generally* Loewy, *Police-Obtained Evidence and the Constitution: Distinguishing Unconstitutionally Obtained Evidence from Unconstitutionally Used Evidence*, 87 Mich. L. Rev. 907 (1989); Tomkovicz, *The Massiah Right*, n. 9 *supra*; Note, *The Impeachment Exception to the Sixth Amendment Exclusionary Rule*, 87 Colum. L. Rev. 176 (1987).

example, in *Maine v Moulton*,[68] the justices stated that "[t]he Sixth Amendment protects the right of the accused not to be confronted by an agent of the State. . . . This right [is] violated as soon as the State's agent engage[s] [*D*] in conversation about the charges pending against him." Under this view, exclusion of the evidence at trial is a remedy for the violation of the right, which occurred prior to trial.

A possible implication of the latter analysis is that the Sixth Amendment exclusionary rule might meet the same fate as the Fourth Amendment exclusionary rule. That is, if the exclusion of the evidence is merely a remedy, and not a constitutional right *per se*, then the Supreme Court might determine that the remedy should only be applied in those circumstances in which the exclusion of the evidence constitutes a meaningful deterrent to police misconduct. In turn, this analysis would leave the Sixth Amendment exclusionary rule subject to a narrowing process, much as has occurred in the search-and-seizure context.

These observations should be kept in mind as the reader considers the Court's decisions to date on the scope of the Sixth Amendment exclusionary rule.

[B] Good Motive: No Exception to the Exclusionary Rule

There is no "good motive" exception to the Sixth Amendment exclusionary rule. That is, the exclusionary rule applies even if, as occurred in *Massiah*, the government deliberately elicits statements in order to obtain additional information about the crime and the defendant's confederates; it also applies even if the reason for the police action is to prevent a serious crime from occurring, as was the case in *Maine v. Moulton*,[69] in which the police elicited information from D, who was under indictment for a theft, because he had indicated that he might kill a witness.

The Court stated in *Moulton* that to allow evidence obtained in violation of a defendant's right to counsel to be used against her at trial, on the ground that the police had a legitimate reason for the investigation, "invites abuse by law enforcement personnel in the form of fabricated investigations and risks the evisceration of the Sixth Amendment right recognized in *Massiah*."

[C] Different-Crime Evidence

Although the right to counsel attaches as soon as adversary judicial criminal proceedings commence, the exclusionary rule does not apply to evidence introduced at a trial of a crime for which the prosecution had not yet commenced at the time the statements were elicited.

That is, although *D*'s right to counsel has attached regarding Crime 1, if the police deliberately elicit incriminating information from *D* regarding not-yet-prosecuted Crime 2, the latter evidence is admissible in a subsequent prosecution of Crime 2. To hold otherwise, the Court has said, "would unnecessarily frustrate the public's interest in the investigation of criminal activities."[70]

---

[68] 474 U.S. 159 (1985).

[69] *Id.*

[70] *Id.* at 180.

[D] Use of Evidence for Impeachment Purposes

The Court has not yet determined whether statements obtained in violation of the Sixth Amendment right to counsel, although inadmissible in the prosecutor's case-in-chief, may be used by the prosecutor to impeach the defendant's false or inconsistent trial testimony.

In *Michigan v. Harvey*,[71] however, the Supreme Court held that statements secured in violation of the rule announced in *Michigan v. Jackson*,[72] a rule designed (according to *Harvey*) "to ensure voluntary, knowing, and intelligent waivers of the Sixth Amendment right to counsel," may be introduced at trial for impeachment purposes, if the subsequent waiver is valid.

In *Harvey*, D was arraigned on rape charges, and counsel was appointed to represent him. D told an officer that he wanted to make a statement, but that he did not know whether he should first talk to his lawyer. After the officer convinced him that he did not need to talk to his lawyer because the "lawyer was going to get a copy of the statement anyway," D signed a waiver form and subsequently made incriminating statements about the crime.

The prosecution conceded that these statements were taken in violation of the *Jackson* rule, which prohibits police questioning of an accused who requests to see a lawyer, and, therefore, were inadmissible in the prosecutor's case-in-chief. The prosecutor used the statements, however, in cross-examination, after D testified in his own defense and provided an account of the events that conflicted with his pre-trial statements to the police.

The Supreme Court characterized the Sixth Amendment *Jackson* rule as prophylactic in nature, because it was founded on a Fifth Amendment case[73] adopted as a "second layer of protection" to the *Miranda* rules, which are themselves prophylactic in character. Therefore, just as a statement obtained in violation of *Miranda* is admissible for impeachment purposes,[74] a statement secured in violation of the *Jackson* rule may be used to impeach a defendant. The *Harvey* Court concluded that "the 'search for truth in a criminal case' outweighs the 'speculative possibility' that exclusion of evidence might deter future violations of rules not compelled directly by the Constitution in the first place."

[E] Fruit-of-the-Poisonous-Tree Doctrine

The fruit-of-the-poisonous-tree doctrine[75] applies to violations of the Sixth Amendment right to counsel, which means that the limitations on the poisonous-tree rule — the independent-source doctrine, the inevitable-discovery rule, and the attenuated-connection principle — also apply, although the Supreme Court has had little occasion to discuss the basic doctrine or its limitations in this context.

The inevitable-discovery rule was expressly recognized in the Sixth Amendment context in *Nix v. Williams*,[76] a follow-up case to *Brewer v. Williams*.[77] In

---

[71] 110 S.Ct. 1176 (1990).

[72] 475 U.S. 625 (1986). *See* § 153[C][1] *supra*.

[73] Edwards v. Arizona, 451 U.S. 477 (1981). *See* § 145[D][2][a] *supra*.

[74] *See* § 147[A] *supra*.

[75] *See* § 125 *supra*.

Williams II, the issue was whether the body of the victim found by the police as the result of their use of the Christian burial speech was inadmissible as a fruit of the initial Sixth Amendment violation. The Court held that evidence relating to the condition of the victim's body could be used in *D*'s trial because the prosecutor proved by a preponderance of the evidence "that the information ultimately or inevitably would have been discovered by lawful means."[78]

On another matter, the Supreme Court has not determined whether "taint" is dissipated differently in Sixth Amendment cases than in Fourth Amendment circumstances. In *Hoffa v. United States*,[79] the Court applied the Fourth Amendment *Wong Sun* attenuation doctrine[80] in a Sixth Amendment context. Even as it did so, however, it expressly left open the issue of whether the "same strict standard of excludability" applicable in search-and-seizure cases applies to Sixth Amendment cases.

In view of the fact that the current members of the Supreme Court are more sympathetic to the Sixth Amendment right to counsel than they are to the Fourth Amendment exclusionary rule, it is likely that the principles of *Wong Sun* will be applied no less strictly in the former case than in the latter.

§ 156 Right-to-Counsel Summary: Sixth Amendment versus *Miranda*

Supreme Court winds have blown hot and cold over the Sixth Amendment right to counsel. It has observed that "the policies underlying the constitutional protections are quite distinct,"[81] and it has had occasion to warn that *Miranda* jurisprudence is not always informed by the Court's Sixth Amendment case law.[82] Indeed, the Supreme Court has conceded[83] that the clear impression of many courts and commentators has been that the Sixth Amendment version of the right to counsel is stronger, *i.e.*, that it is a broader right and one more difficult to relinquish, than its *Miranda* cousin.

Particularly in recent years, however, the Court has denied the latter assertion. It has stated that it "never suggested that one right is 'superior' or 'greater' than the other,"[84] and it has begun to merge its discussion of the two rights. In some circumstances, *Miranda* law is applied in the Sixth Amendment context.[85]

Nonetheless, differences remain between the two rights. The following is a checklist of those key areas in which, at least now, the Court has recognized a

---

[76] 467 U.S. 431 (1984).

[77] 430 U.S. 387, *reh'g denied*, 431 U.S. 925 (1977). *See* § 152[A] *supra*.

[78] The inevitable-discovery rule is discussed more fully at § 125[D] *supra*.

[79] 385 U.S. 293 (1966).

[80] Wong Sun v. United States, 371 U.S. 471 (1963). *See* § 125[E] *supra*.

[81] Rhode Island v. Innis, 446 U.S. 291, 300 n.4 (1980).

[82] *Id.*

[83] Patterson v. Illinois, 487 U.S. at 297.

[84] *Id.*

[85] *E.g.*, Michigan v. Jackson, 475 U.S. 625 (1986) (*Edwards v. Arizona* rule relating to waiver of *Miranda* applies to the Sixth Amendment); Patterson v. Illinois, 487 U.S. 285 (1988) (knowing and intelligent waiver of *Miranda* rights serves as a waiver of the Sixth Amendment); Michigan v. Harvey, 110 S.Ct. 1176 (1990) (impeachment rule, applicable to *Miranda*, applies to violations of the *Michigan v. Jackson* "prophylactic" rule).

difference between the Sixth Amendment right to counsel and the *Miranda* version.

1. The Sixth Amendment right applies only after adversary judicial criminal proceedings have been initiated against the accused; the Fifth Amendment right is not limited in this manner.

2. The Fifth Amendment right does not attach unless the suspect is in custody; the Sixth Amendment is not so limited.

3. The Fifth Amendment applies if the suspect is "interrogated," whereas the Sixth Amendment prohibits "deliberate elicitation." The terms are not equivalent.

4. The Sixth Amendment applies to deliberate elicitation by undercover agents, which is not the case under *Miranda*.

5. Fruit-of-the poisonous-tree principles apply to Sixth Amendment violations; the doctrine does not apply or is more limited in the *Miranda* context.

CHAPTER 26

PRIVILEGE AGAINST SELF-INCRIMINATION: GENERAL PRINCIPLES

§ 157 Fifth Amendment Self-Incrimination Clause: Overview

The Fifth Amendment to the United States Constitution provides that "[n]o person . . . shall be compelled in any criminal case to be a witness against himself. . . ." The privilege applies to the states through the Fourteenth Amendment due process clause.[1]

Generally speaking, the privilege may be raised in any proceeding, civil or criminal, formal or informal, if the testimonial evidence that would be produced there might incriminate the speaker in a future criminal proceeding.[2] Consequently, legal issues regarding the Fifth Amendment privilege arise throughout the legal system.

There is an enormous body of law and scholarly literature in the field. Unfortunately, as one writer observed, "[t]he privilege against self-incrimination is much discussed but little understood."[3] Also unfortunately, it is "unlikely that anyone could argue persuasively that . . . the elements of fifth amendment law . . . fit[] neatly into an internally consistent, sensible whole."[4] Furthermore, even if the law were not confusing and inconsistent, the privilege itself would still be controversial.

This chapter focuses on the history of the privilege, the policies underlying it, and the general contours of the privilege. On the whole, except in the police interrogation context, which is discussed in a separate chapter, the privilege is interpreted narrowly by the Supreme Court, even as other constitutional rights "have been allowed to blossom."[5]

---

[1] Malloy v. Hogan, 378 U.S. 1 (1964).

[2] Lefkowitz v. Turley, 414 U.S. 70 (1973).

[3] McKay, *Self-Incrimination and the New Privacy*, 1967 Sup. Ct. Rev. 193, 193.

[4] Stuntz, *Self-Incrimination and Excuse*, 88 Colum. L. Rev. 1227, 1228 (1988).

[5] Saltzburg, *The Required Records Doctrine: Its Lessons for the Privilege Against Self-Incrimination*, 53 U. Chi. L. Rev. 6, 8 (1986).

§ 158 History of the Privilege Against Self-Incrimination[6]

The origins of the Fifth Amendment self-incrimination clause lie in a "tangled web of obscure historical events."[7] According to Wigmore, its roots lie in a twelfth century power struggle between the Crown and the Church.[8] Other scholars believe that this reading of history is too narrow, and that the privilege is also the result of religious, political, constitutional, and human-rights debates that racked England during the sixteenth and seventeenth centuries.[9]

One factor in the development of the privilege was opposition in England to the sixteenth and seventeenth century process by which the ecclesiastical courts and the Court of Star Chamber investigated claims of heresy. Under the then-existing law, persons suspected of heresy were administered an "oath *ex officio*," which required them to answer truthfully all questions put to them by the court, even before they were informed of the nature of the charges against them.

The oath was abolished in 1641. However, courts were still permitted to pressure witnesses to testify and to use their silence against them. Gradually, opposition to the oath turned into a general rejection of the perceived "unjust, unnatural, and immoral"[10] inquisitorial requirement that persons furnish evidence to convict themselves of crimes.

The English opposition to compulsory self-incrimination was brought to this side of the ocean by colonists who were ardent critics of the ecclesiastical oaths. Over time, the colonies enacted laws that prohibited the oath *ex officio* as well as the use of torture to obtain confessions. According to a leading scholar of the Fifth Amendment, by the time of the Revolution the "colonies and mother country differed little, if at all, on the right against self-incrimination"; the privilege was viewed by the Constitution's framers as "a self-evident truth."[11]

---

[6] *See generally* L. Levy, The Origins of the Fifth Amendment (Oxford 1968); Benner, *Requiem for Miranda: The Rehnquist Court's Voluntariness Doctrine in Historical Perspective*, 67 Wash. U.L.Q. 59 (1989); Helmholz, *Origins of the Privilege Against Self-Incrimination: The Role of the European Ius Commune*, 65 N.Y.U.L. Rev. 962 (1990) (providing a historical account contrary to "current orthodoxy "); Morgan, *The Privilege Against Self-Incrimination*, 34 Minn. L. Rev. 1 (1949).

[7] Benner, n. 6 *supra*, at 68.

[8] 8 J. Wigmore, Evidence, § 2251, at 317 (McNaughton rev.) (Little, Brown 1961).

[9] L. Levy, n. 6 *supra*, at 42; *see* C. McCormick, McCormick on Evidence § 114 (Cleary rev. 1984) (stating that the privilege was, in part, the result of "important policies of individual freedom and dignity").

[10] L. Levy, n. 6 *supra*, at 330.

[11] *Id.* at 404, 430. For a much narrower view of the framers' intent, *see* L. Mayers, Shall We Amend the Fifth Amendment? 178-91 (Harper & Brothers 1959).

§ 159   Is the Privilege a Good Idea?: The Controversy [12]

[A]   In General

The Fifth Amendment self-incrimination clause is controversial. During the Warren Court era the Supreme Court "waxed eloquent" [13] about the privilege, stating that it "reflects many of our fundamental values and most noble aspirations," [14] and that it "registers an important advance in the development of our liberty — one of the great landmarks in man's struggle to make him[self] civilized.' " [15]

But, the Supreme Court has not always thought so highly of the privilege. At one time, Justice Cardozo stated that "[j]ustice . . . would not perish if the accused were subject to a duty to respond to orderly inquiry." [16]

Scholars, too, have been critical of the privilege. Wigmore described it as a "mark of traditional sentimentality." [17] Bentham said it was based on "the old woman's reason" that "tis hard upon a man to be obliged to criminate himself." [18] A recent scholar observed that "the leading contemporary efforts to justify the privilege as more than a historical relic are uniformly unsatisfactory." [19]

In view of these disparate observations, the question must be asked: Is the privilege against compelled self-incrimination defensible, or should it be abolished? [20] What follows is a brief survey of the arguments in defense of the privilege and the responses of its critics.

---

[12] *See generally* E. Griswold, The Fifth Amendment Today (Harvard 1955); Dolinko, *Is There a Rationale for the Privilege Against Self-Incrimination?*, 33 UCLA L. Rev. 1063 (1986); Dripps, *Against Police Interrogation — And the Privilege Against Self-Incrimination*, 78 J. Crim. L. & Criminology 699 (1988); Friendly, *The Fifth Amendment Tomorrow: The Case for Constitutional Change*, 37 U. Cin. L. Rev. 671 (1968); Gerstein, *The Demise of Boyd: Self-Incrimination and Private Papers in the Burger Court*, 27 UCLA L. Rev. 343 (1979); Greenawalt, *Silence as a Moral and Constitutional Right*, 23 Wm. & Mary L. Rev. 15 (1981); McNaughton, *The Privilege Against Self-Incrimination: Its Constitutional Affectation, Raison d'Etre and Miscellaneous Implications*, 51 J. Crim. L. Criminology & Police Sci. 138 (1960); Menlowe, *Bentham, Self-Incrimination and the Law of Evidence*, 104 L.Q.Rev. 286 (1988); Rosenberg & Rosenberg, *In the Beginning: The Talmudic Rule Against Self-Incrimination*, 63 N.Y.U. L. Rev. 955 (1988); Seidman, *Rubashov's Question: Self-Incrimination and the Problem of Coerced Preferences*, 2 Yale J. Law & Humanities 149 (1990); Stuntz, n. 4 *supra*; Tague, *The Fifth Amendment: If An Aid to the Guilty Defendant, An Impediment to the Innocent One*, 78 Geo. L.J. 1 (1989).

[13] Saltzburg, n. 5 *supra*, at 6.

[14] Murphy v. Waterfront Commission, 378 U.S. 52, 55 (1964).

[15] Ullmann v. United States, 350 U.S. 422, 426 (1956) (*quoting* E. Griswold, n. 12 *supra*, at 7).

[16] Palko v. Connecticut, 302 U.S. 319, 326 (1937).

[17] 8 J. Wigmore, n. 8 *supra*, at § 2251, at 317.

[18] 7 J. Bentham, Rationale of Judicial Evidence 452 (Bowring ed. Simpkin, Marshall 1843).

[19] Dolinko, n. 12 *supra*, at 1064.

[20] The answer might be "neither." That is, even if the privilege is indefensible, it might be better now to keep it rather than abolish it, particularly if one considers its relationship to other aspects of the Constitution. As one critic of the rule has pointed out, "one does

[B] The Purposes of the Privilege: The Debate

[1] Compelled Self-Accusation As a Moral Wrong

Defenders: Society rightly "hesitate[s] to say that someone has a moral duty to bring conviction and imprisonment upon himself."[21] Even if an admission of guilt is in the wrongdoer's best interests, the decision to admit culpability should be his own: "an individual ought to be autonomous in his efforts to come to terms in his own conscience with accusations of wrongdoing against him."[22] In this context, our society properly has "respect for the inviolability of the human personality and of the right of each individual to a private enclave where he may lead a private life."[23]

Critics: Those who claim that it is wrong to require persons to confess their own guilt "give no reasons for this judgment save for an appeal to intuition."[24] This is an intuition not shared by all people. Indeed, the privilege is morally counter-intuitive: "No parent would teach such a doctrine to his children; the lesson parents teach is that while a misdeed . . . will generally be forgiven, a failure to make a clean breast of it will not be."[25]

[2] The "Cruel Trilemma" Thesis

Defenders: The Fifth Amendment privilege "[a]t its core, . . . reflects our fierce unwillingness to subject those suspected of crime to the cruel trilemma of self-accusation, perjury or contempt.' "[26] That is, if there were no privilege against self-incrimination, a person could be forced (as he was in the ecclesiastical courts and the Star Chamber) to testify under oath and either admit the truth, which could result in his punishment, lie under oath (and thus be subjected to punish-ment for perjury), or be held in contempt of court for failing to answer the questions (and thus be jailed on the latter charge).

Critics: Although superficially satisfying, the "cruel trilemma" argument goes too far. First, it is not self-evident that it is cruel to require a guilty person to admit his own guilt or else accept the consequences of his refusal to testify truthfully. In any case, this "cruelty" — if it is such — is less so than many other "cruelties" the law justifiably permits: "[i]t is not 'plain' or 'obvious' . . . why it is more cruel to require a man to admit commission of a misdemeanor than to testify to his mother's immorality or his partner's peculations."[27] To require a parent to testify

---

not, when he performs the surgery on one part of the body, do it without regard for the impact on other parts of the body." McNaughton, n. 12 *supra*, at 153. Professor Dolinko has observed that "[a] rule whose existence lacks any principled justification may neverthe-less come to serve important functions in the legal system as a whole, so that its repeal would do violence to the entire system." Dolinko, n. 12 *supra*, at 1064.

[21] Greenawalt, n. 12 *supra*, at 36.

[22] Gerstein, n. 12 *supra*, at 347.

[23] Murphy v. Waterfront Commission 378 U.S. at 55 (*quoting* United States v. Grunewald, 233 F.2d 556, 581-82 (2d Cir. 1956)).

[24] Dolinko, n. 12 *supra*, at 1092.

[25] Friendly, n. 12 *supra*, at 680.

[26] Pennsylvania v. Muniz, 110 S.Ct. 2638, 2647 (1990) (*quoting* Murphy v. Waterfront Commission, 378 U.S. at 55).

[27] Friendly, n. 12 *supra*, at 683.

against his child in a death penalty case is "an infinitely greater cruelty than requiring an ordinary witness to disclose some . . . minor infraction of a penal regulation!"[28]

[3] The Privilege as Part of the Adversary System

Defenders: The privilege is defensible on systemic grounds. It is based in part on "our preference for an accusatorial rather than an inquisitorial system of criminal justice."[29] Without the privilege, we "fear that self-incriminating statements will be elicited by inhumane treatment and abuses."[30] With the privilege, we promote a "sense of fair play which dictates 'a fair state-individual balance by requiring the government . . . in its contest with the individual to shoulder the entire load.' "[31]

Critics: The anti-inquisitorial arguments for the privilege do not apply in the American constitutional system. We do not have Star Chambers or heresy trials. Nor would the abolition of the privilege result in inhumane treatment of suspects: if the police used torture to obtain incriminating statements, the due process clause would safeguard the victim. Once one ensures against such abuses, there is no basis — other than shibboleths about the adversary system[32] — to deny the government the right to compel testimony from the defendant.

[4] Protection of the Innocent

Defenders: The privilege against compulsory self-incrimination, although "sometimes a 'shelter to the guilty,' is often 'a protection to the innocent.' "[33] It protects the innocent in two ways. First, compelled confessions are inherently unreliable: even innocent persons can be forced to confess. Second, an innocent person forced to testify at trial might convict himself by a bad performance on the witness stand.

Critics: Neither of these arguments is persuasive. First, in most cases, confessions serve only to corroborate other reliable evidence of the defendant's guilt. Second, innocent persons rarely hurt themselves on the witness stand: "[t]he truth is consistent with itself, and everyone who is speaking the truth can tell in the main a straight story."[34]

---

[28] L. Mayers, n. 11 *supra*, at 168-69.

[29] Murphy v. Waterfront Commission 378 U.S. at 55.

[30] *Id.*

[31] *Id.* (*quoting* 8 J. Wigmore, n. 8 *supra*, at § 2251, at 317).

[32] *See* McKay, n. 3 *supra*, at 208-09 (the arguments for the privilege are "largely ritualistic"; "no matter how often repeated, no matter not eloquently intoned, [these arguments are] . . . merely a restatement of the privilege itself.").

[33] Murphy v. Waterfront Commission 378 U.S. at 55 (*quoting* Quinn v. United States, 349 U.S. 155, 162 (1955)).

[34] Terry, *Constitutional Provisions Against Forcing Self-Incrimination*, 17 Yale L.J. 127, 127 (1906).

§ 160 The Fifth Amendment Privilege: Who Is Protected?

[A] Collective-Entity Doctrine

The Fifth Amendment begins with the words "no person." As a consequence, the Supreme Court has declared under the so-called "collective entity" doctrine that artificial entities, such as corporations,[35] labor unions,[36] and partnerships,[37] may not assert the privilege against self-incrimination, although a sole proprietor may.[38]

Furthermore, under this rule a custodian of an entity's records may not oppose a subpoena *duces tecum* by invoking his personal privilege against self-incrimination in order to protect the entity.[39] Nor is he entitled to assert the privilege if his claim is that production of the entity's documents will incriminate him personally.[40] In short, the collective-entity doctrine "trumps"[41] the personal privilege.

[B] Required-Records Doctrine[42]

Even when a person in a business retains his Fifth Amendment privilege generally, in some circumstances he may not assert the privilege regarding business records.

In a series of cases decided over the past half decade, the Supreme Court has developed the "required records" doctrine. A leading case in the development of the law was *Shapiro v. United States*.[43] In *Shapiro*, the Court upheld the constitutionality of federal regulations issued under the Emergency Price Control Act, which required certain licensed businesses to maintain records of their activities and to make them available for inspection by the government upon request.

Quoting language from a 1911 case,[44] *Shapiro* held that the Fifth Amendment privilege does not attach to the production of records which the defendant is "required to keep, not for his private uses, but for the benefit of the public, and for public inspection." Although the Court warned that "there are limits which the Government cannot constitutionally exceed in requiring the keeping of records which may be inspected by an administrative agency," it did not indicate what those limits might be.

Subsequent opinions suggest that the required-records doctrine applies if: (1) the regulatory scheme is imposed in an "essentially noncriminal and regulatory area of inquiry" rather than in an "area permeated with criminal statutes;"[45] (2)

---

[35] Hale v. Henkel, 201 U.S. 43 (1906).

[36] United States v. White, 322 U.S. 694 (1944).

[37] Bellis v. United States, 417 U.S. 85 (1974).

[38] United States v. Doe, 465 U.S. 605 (1984).

[39] Wilson v. United States, 221 U.S. 361 (1911).

[40] Braswell v. United States, 487 U.S. 99 (1988); *contra*, Commonwealth v. Doe, 405 Mass. 676, 544 N.E.2d 860 (1989) (*Braswell* rule rejected under the state constitution).

[41] *The Supreme Court — Leading Cases*, 102 Harv. L. Rev. 143, 170 (1988).

[42] *See generally* Saltzburg, n.5.

[43] 335 U.S. 1 (1948).

[44] Wilson v. United States, 221 U.S. 361 (1911).

[45] Albertson v. Subversive Activities Control Board, 382 U.S. 70, 79 (1965).

the requirements are "directed at the public at large" and not at a "selective group inherently suspect of criminal activities;"[46] and (3) the records requirement is rationally related to the regulatory purpose.[47]

The required-records doctrine applies even when the information that must be disclosed could be a link in the chain of evidence leading to a criminal prosecution. For example, in *California v. Byers*,[48] the Court upheld against attack a state hit-and-run statute, which required the driver of any motor vehicle involved in an accident to stop at the scene and report his name and address. In part, the holding was based on the four-justice plurality's conclusion that the statute was regulatory in character in that it "was not intended to facilitate criminal convictions but to promote the satisfaction of civil liability," the statute was directed at the public at large, and "self-reporting [was] indispensable to . . . fulfillment" of the legislative purpose.

Similarly, in *Baltimore City Department of Social Services v. Bouknight*,[49] the Supreme Court ruled, 7-2, that a mother, who had previously lost custody of her child because of suspected child abuse, but who had been permitted temporary custody of the youth subject to various Juvenile Court conditions, could not assert the privilege against self-incrimination, to resist compliance with a subsequent Juvenile Court order that she produce the child or otherwise reveal its whereabouts.

Primarily citing required-records cases, but also invoking language from cases applying the collective-entity doctrine, the Court stated that "[w]hen a person assumes control over items that are the legitimate object of the government's non-criminal regulatory powers, the ability to invoke the privilege is reduced."

The Court concluded that once the child was adjudicated in need of assistance, "his care and safety became the particular object of the State's regulatory interests." By accepting temporary custody of the child, the mother thereby "submitted to the routine operation of the regulatory system and agreed to hold [the child] in a manner consonant with the State's regulatory interests and subject to inspection [by the juvenile court]."[50]

§ 161   The Privilege: At What Proceedings May It Be Asserted?

Although the language of the Fifth Amendment — "No person . . . shall be compelled *in any criminal case* to be a witness against himself. . . ." — suggests that the privilege against compulsory self-incrimination may only be asserted

---

[46] *Id.*

[47] *See* Saltzburg, n. 5 *supra*, at 24-25.

[48] 402 U.S. 424 (1971).

[49] 110 S.Ct. 900 (1990).

[50] Although the mother could not properly assert the Fifth Amendment privilege, and thus she could be held in civil contempt if she refused to produce the child or indicate its whereabouts, the Supreme Court did not decide whether any incriminating evidence that might arise from her compliance with the order could be used against her in a criminal proceeding. It noted that, "[i]n a broad range of contexts, the Fifth Amendment limits prosecutors' ability to use testimony that has been compelled." *See generally* § 164 *infra*.

during a "criminal case," the Court has interpreted the clause to mean that the right may be asserted in any proceeding, "civil or criminal, formal or informal, where the answers might incriminate him in future criminal proceedings."[51]

As a consequence, a person who is compelled to answer questions may invoke the Fifth Amendment privilege, among other places, in grand jury proceedings, civil trials, legislative and administrative hearings, and police stations, if the testimony he would give might be used against him in a criminal proceeding.

For purposes of the self-incrimination clause, a proceeding is "criminal" in nature if it is identified as such. However, a civil label on a proceeding is not dispositive of its character: a proceeding is "criminal" if "a defendant has provided 'the clearest proof' that 'the statutory scheme [is] so punitive either in purpose or effect as to negate [the State's] intention' that the proceeding be civil."[52]

§ 162 Procedures Relating to the Invocation of the Privilege[53]

The Fifth Amendment does not forbid the *asking* of incriminating questions or the *demanding* of the production of incriminating documents.[54] Nor does it prohibit a person from voluntarily *answering* the questions propounded or producing the documents subpoenaed.[55] Therefore, if a witness under compulsion to testify wishes the protection of the privilege because he fears incrimination, he must assert it, or else he forfeits his self-incrimination claim.[56]

If a person subpoenaed or otherwise compelled to testify in any formal proceeding asserts his privilege against self-incrimination, the interrogator must honor the privilege or seek a judicial determination "as to the bona fides of the witness' Fifth Amendment claim,"[57] *i.e.*, that the threat of incrimination is real.[58]

If the judge determines that the privilege has been legitimately asserted, the government must permit the witness to stand on the privilege or apply for an immunity order. An immunity order requires the witness to testify, but it also protects him at least as broadly as the constitutional privilege itself.

The most common immunity order provides "use" and "derivative use" immunity to the witness. For example, the federal immunity statute provides that "[n]o testimony or other information compelled under the order (or any

---

[51] Lefkowitz v. Turley, 414 U.S. 70, 77 (1973).

[52] Allen v. Illinois, 478 U.S. 364, 369 (1986) (*quoting* United States v. Ward, 448 U.S. 242, 248-49 (1980)).

[53] *See generally* Lushing, *Testimonial Immunity and the Privilege Against Self-Incrimination: A Study in Isomorphism*, 73 J. Crim. L. & Criminology 1690 (1983).

[54] *See* United States v. Mandujano, 425 U.S. 564, 574 (1976).

[55] *See* United States v. Monia, 317 U.S. 424, 427 (1943).

[56] *See* Garner v. United States, 424 U.S. 648, 654 n.9 (1976) (except in the case of police custodial interrogation, "he may lose the benefit of the privilege without making a knowing and intelligent waiver.").

[57] United States v. Mandujano, 425 U.S. at 575.

[58] *See* § 163[B] *infra*.

information directly or indirectly derived from such testimony or other information) may be used against the witness in any criminal case. . . ."[59]

If the immunity is granted, the individual must answer all questions truthfully. If he testifies falsely, his statements may be used against him in a perjury prosecution.[60] If he refuses to testify, he may be held in contempt of court and jailed as a consequence.

§ 163 Elements of the Privilege: What Must Be Proved

[A] The Evidence Is "Testimonial or Communicative"

[1] Nature of the Requirement

The Fifth Amendment provides that a person may not be compelled "to be a witness against himself." In *Schmerber v. California*,[61] the Supreme Court held that a person is not an involuntary "witness" against himself unless "he is compelled to testify . . . or otherwise provide the State with evidence of a testimonial or communicative nature." As the Court explained, "[t]he distinction which has emerged, often expressed in different ways, is that the privilege is a bar against compelling 'communications' or 'testimony,' but that compulsion which makes a suspect or accused the source of 'real or physical evidence' does not violate it."

In *Doe v. United States*,[62] the Supreme Court explored the "testimony or communications" requirement further. It stated that "in order to be testimonial an accused's communication must itself, explicitly or implicitly, relate a factual assertion or disclose information." *Doe* explained that "[t]he privilege is [intended] to spare the accused from having to reveal, directly or indirectly, his knowledge of facts relating him to the offense or from having to share his thoughts and beliefs with the Government."

According to *Doe*, this definition of "testimony" — and, thus, the meaning of the "witness" requirement in the Fifth Amendment — stems from the historical fact that "the privilege was intended to prevent the use of legal compulsion to extract from the accused a sworn communication of facts which would incriminate him," as occurred in the ecclesiastical courts and the Star Chamber.

The outer boundaries of the "testimony or communications" requirement remain unexplored. However, the Court stated in *Pennsylvania v. Muniz*[63] that, at its core, a person is compelled to be a "witness" against himself "at least

---

[59] 18 U.S.C. § 6002. In some states, prosecutors who wish to compel testimony from a witness must give "transactional" immunity, wherein the witness is guaranteed that he will not be prosecuted for any offense that is the subject of the questioning. *E.g.*, N.Y. Crim. Proc. Law § 50.10(1). Transactional immunity is broader than the Fifth Amendment privilege itself. Kastigar v. United States, 406 U.S. 441, *reh'g denied*, 408 U.S. 931 (1972).

[60] United States v. Mandujano, 425 U.S. 564 (1976).

[61] 384 U.S. 757 (1966); *see generally* Arenella, *Schmerber and the Privilege Against Self-Incrimination: A Reappraisal*, 20 Am. Crim. L. Rev. 31 (1982).

[62] 487 U.S. 201 (1988).

[63] 110 S.Ct. 2638 (1990).

whenever he must face the modern-day analog" of the "cruel trilemma" of self-accusation, perjury or contempt that confronted sixteenth century Star Chamber witnesses.[64]

[2] Identifying "Testimony or Communications"

[a] In General

According to *Schmerber*, "the protection of the privilege reaches an accused's communications, whatever form they might take. . . ." Thus, the privilege "applies to both verbal and nonverbal conduct,"[65] and thus the line between "testimony or communications," on the one hand, and "real or physical evidence," on the other hand, is not always easy to draw.

[b] Verbal Conduct

According to the Supreme Court, "[t]here are very few instances in which a verbal statement, either oral or written, will not convey information or assert facts [*i.e.*, be 'testimonial or communicative' in nature]."[66]

Most obviously, trial testimony, confessions to the police, and statements expressed in personal documents, constitute protectible "testimony or communications." Indeed, in view of the history of the self-incrimination clause, "[w]hatever else it may include, . . . the definition of 'testimonial' evidence . . . must encompass all responses to questions that, if asked of a sworn suspect during a criminal trial, could place the suspect in the 'cruel trilemma'."[67]

Nonetheless, not all uses of the human voice or written words are protected. For example, a person may lawfully be compelled at a lineup to utter the words allegedly expressed by the malefactor if the purpose is to require the suspect "to use his voice as an identifying physical characteristic, not to speak his guilt."[68] Likewise, a person may be required to put words down on paper if the purpose of the demand is to exhibit the suspect's handwriting, another physical characteristic, for identification purposes.[69] In neither of these cases is the person confronted with the "cruel trilemma" that is at the core of the Fifth Amendment privilege.

[c] Non-verbal Conduct

Non-verbal conduct falls within the scope of the Fifth Amendment privilege if it "reflects the actor's communication of his thoughts to another,"[70] such as when he nods or shakes his head.

On the other hand, the actor does not communicate his thoughts to another, and therefore the privilege does not apply, when the government compels him to

---

[64] For discussion of the "cruel trilemma," *see* § 159[B][2] *supra*. The history of the Fifth Amendment is discussed at § 158 *supra*.

[65] *Muniz*, 110 S.Ct. at 2647 n.9.

[66] Doe v. United States, 487 U.S. at 213.

[67] *Muniz*, 110 S.Ct. at 2647.

[68] United States v. Wade, 388 U.S. 218, 222-23 (1967).

[69] United States v. Dionisio, 410 U.S. 1 (1973); Gilbert v. California, 388 U.S. 263 (1976).

[70] *Muniz*, 110 S.Ct. at 2647 n.9.

put on clothing to see if it fits,[71] to stand in a lineup,[72] to move his eyes or walk on a straight line as part of a sobriety test,[73] or to give blood after being arrested for driving under the influence of alcohol,[74] although in each of these cases the product of the compulsion might be incriminating.

[3]   A Closer Look: *Pennsylvania v. Muniz*

The difficulty in drawing the line between testimonial communications and real or physical evidence is apparent in the Court's treatment of the facts in *Pennsylvania v. Muniz*.[75]

In *Muniz*, *D*, under arrest for driving under the influence of alcohol, was compelled to give his name, address, height, weight, date of birth, current age, and the date of his sixth birthday, as part of a sobriety test. *D*'s slurred answers to these questions were videotaped and introduced at his subsequent trial.

Eight justices agreed that *D*'s compelled answers to the questions were not inadmissible merely because the slurred nature of his speech incriminated him. As the Court explained, "[t]he physical inability to articulate words in a clear manner due to 'the lack of muscular coordination in his tongue and mouth,' . . . is not itself a testimonial component of [*D*'s] responses to [the] . . . questions." The words expressed by *D* were physical evidence of his intoxication; *D* was not compelled "to share his thoughts and beliefs with the Government" or to relate a factual assertion.

On the other hand, the Court, per Justice Brennan, held, although only 5-4, that *D*'s answer "No, I don't," to the question, "Do you know what the date was of your sixth birthday?" was testimonial in nature. The majority was unpersuaded by the government's claim that *D*'s answer did not implicate the Fifth Amendment because (the government argued) the police did not have an investigative interest in the actual date of *D*'s sixth birthday, nor even in *D*'s "assertion of belief that was communicated by his answer to the question." According to the government, the incriminating aspect of *D*'s answer — that his mental state was confused — concerned the physiological function of *D*'s brain, a matter "every bit as 'real or physical' as the physiological makeup up of his blood and the timbre of his voice."

The majority reasoned, however, that even if the fact to be inferred from *D*'s words was the physical status of his brain, "[t]he correct question . . . [was] whether the incriminating inference of mental confusion [was] drawn from a testimonial act or from physical evidence." The majority concluded that *D*'s answer to the sixth-birthday question was a testimonial act because the question confronted *D* with the "cruel trilemma" that the Fifth Amendment seeks to prevent.

Because the question arose during custodial interrogation, "the inherently coercive environment . . . precluded the option of remaining silent." *D* was left,

---

[71] Holt v. United States, 218 U.S. 245 (1910).

[72] United States v. Wade, 388 U.S. 218 (1967).

[73] Pennsylvania v. Muniz, 110 S.Ct. 2638 (1990).

[74] Schmerber v. California, 384 U.S. 757 (1966).

[75] 110 S.Ct. 2638 (1990).

therefore, with just two choices: admitting that he could not answer the question, an incriminating admission under the circumstances, "or answering untruthfully by reporting a date that he did not then believe to be accurate."[76] Thus, the incriminating inferences from *D*'s admission that he could not answer the question "stemmed not just from the fact that [*D*] slurred the response, but also from a testimonial aspect of that response."

The dissenters, led by Chief Justice Rehnquist, equated the sixth-birthday question to other non-testimonial physical sobriety tests: "If the police may require [*D*] to use his body in order to demonstrate the level of his physical coordination, there is no reason why they should not be able to require him to speak or write in order to determine his mental coordination."

[B]   The Possibility of Incrimination Is Real

The Fifth Amendment privilege does not apply if the only concern of the person asserting the claim is that the statements he will be forced to make will result in personal disgrace,[77] loss of employment,[78] or civil confinement.[79] His claim must be that the evidence he is required to produce will incriminate him in a criminal proceeding.

The privilege against compulsory self-incrimination does not apply unless the personal threat of incrimination is "real and appreciable" and "not merely a remote possibility,"[80] or non-existent.[81] Although the privilege-holder must have "reasonable cause to apprehend danger"[82] of incrimination from answering a question or producing the testimonial evidence, the privilege is to "be accorded liberal construction in favor of the right it was intended to secure."[83]

[C]   The Privilege-Holder is Being Compelled to Testify

[1]   Nature of "Compulsion"

Voluntary self-incrimination does not violate the Fifth Amendment. The Fifth Amendment is violated only by compulsion, more specifically, by "the use of 'physical or moral compulsion' exerted on the person asserting the privilege."[84]

---

[76] As *Muniz* explained, the "cruel trilemma" must be analyzed somewhat differently in the context of a custodial interrogation. First, the pressure to talk does not stem from the threat of contempt sanctions, but rather from the inherently coercive atmosphere of a custodial interrogation. Nor does an untruthful answer during custodial interrogation directly result in a sanction, because the suspect's answers are not given under oath, but it does result in indirect sanction: "either because it links (albeit falsely) the suspect to the crime or because the prosecution might later prove . . . that the suspect lied to the police, giving rise to an inference of guilty conscience."

[77] *See* Brown v. Walker, 161 U.S. 591 (1896).

[78] Ullmann v. United States, 350 U.S. 422 (1956).

[79] Allen v. Illinois, 478 U.S. 364 (1986).

[80] Heike v. United States, 227 U.S. 131, 144 (1913).

[81] For example, if the witness cannot be prosecuted because of the statute of limitations or the Fifth Amendment double jeopardy clause, the privilege does not apply. *See* Brown v. Walker, 161 U.S. at 598-99.

[82] Hoffman v. United States, 341 U.S. 479, 486 (1951).

[83] *Id.*

[84] Fisher v. United States, 425 U.S. 391, 397 (1976).

The required compulsion occurs if the holder of the privilege is forced by subpoena to testify at trial or to produce incriminating documents. In the police interrogation field, the use of physical force, psychological pressures, or deception may render a confession involuntary.[85]

A witness's free choice is also foreclosed by a threat of discharge from state employment for refusal to testify. Thus, a police officer is subjected to Fifth Amendment "compulsion" if he is warned that he is subject to dismissal if he refuses to answer questions that might incriminate him in a subsequent criminal trial.[86]

The Fifth Amendment is probably violated as well if a person provides testimonial evidence against himself as an alternative to submitting "to a test so painful, dangerous, or severe, or so violative of religious beliefs, that almost inevitably a person would prefer 'confession.' "[87]

On the other hand, not all difficult choices are "compelled." For example, Fifth Amendment values are not violated if the government requires a driver stopped on suspicion of driving under the influence of alcohol to choose between submitting to a comparatively painless blood test, or have the refusal used against him in a criminal trial and his driving privileges revoked for up to one year.[88]

[2] Connecting the Privilege-Holder to the Compulsion

The impermissible compulsion must be directed at the person asserting the privilege. That is, the Fifth Amendment privilege is "intimate and personal,"[89] and "adheres basically to the person, not to information that may incriminate him."[90] As Justice Holmes once put it, "[a] party is privileged from producing the evidence [that incriminates him] but not from its production."[91]

For example, D may not successfully assert the privilege against compulsory self-incrimination if a judge issues a subpoena directing X, D's accountant, to produce tax records that will incriminate D.[92] In such a case, the incriminating documents are testimonial or communicative, and by being subpoenaed their disclosure is compelled. However, the compulsion here is directed at X, who is not the person incriminated by the records. Put slightly differently, there is no

---

[85] See § 133 supra.

[86] Garrity v. New Jersey, 385 U.S. 493 (1967).

[87] South Dakota v. Neville, 459 U.S. 553, 563 (1983) (dictum); see State v. Phelps, 235 Neb. 569, 456 N.W.2d 290 (1990) (lawful threat to compel a rape suspect to submit to a painful penile swab for a semen sample if he did not admit having sexual intercourse with the victim rendered a subsequent statement involuntary).

[88] South Dakota v. Neville, 459 U.S. 553 (1983); for a critique of Neville, and an analysis of the general issue of whether a suspect's refusal to submit to a search should be admissible under the Fifth Amendment, see Uviller, Self-Incrimination by Inference: Constitutional Restrictions on the Evidentiary Use of a Suspect's Refusal to Submit to a Search, 81 J. Crim. L. & Crimin. 37 (1990).

[89] Couch v. United States, 409 U.S. 322, 327 (1973).

[90] Id. at 328.

[91] Johnson v. United States, 228 U.S. 457, 458 (1913).

[92] See Couch v. United States, 409 U.S. 322 (1973).

compelled *self*-incrimination: in the words of the Fifth Amendment, *X* is not being compelled to be a "witness against himself," as he is incriminating *D*.[93]

Nor is the Fifth Amendment violated if, as in *Andresen v. Maryland*,[94] the police seize *D*'s business records from his home or office pursuant to a search warrant, as long as *D* is not required to participate in the seizure, *i.e.*, he is not required to aid in the discovery, production, or authentication of the seized evidence.

In such circumstances, although *D*'s documents might incriminate him, he is not a compelled witness against himself: the papers were prepared voluntarily (so, in this regard, *D* is a *non*-compelled witness against himself); and the police, per the warrant, took possession of the documents without his assistance (so, in regard to the production of the evidence, he was not a participant in his own incrimination).

On the other hand, even if a business record or personal[95] paper is voluntarily prepared by *D*, the act of producing it in response to a subpoena "has communicative aspects of it own, wholly aside from the contents of the paper produced."[96] By handing over the document, *D* concedes that the article produced exists, that he was in possession of it, and that he believes that the item he is handing over is that described in the subpoena. If such an act of production is incriminating, *D* may assert the privilege in that regard.[97]

§ 164 Privilege Against Self-Incrimination: Exclusionary Rule

The Fifth Amendment privilege against compelled self-incrimination contains its own exclusionary rule. That is, the constitutional right and the remedy for its violation commingle: by its own terms, the privilege "excludes" the witness' compelled testimony against himself. And, as the result of judicial interpretation, the privilege also prohibits the use at trial of incriminating testimonial or communicative evidence compelled from the witness *prior* to his criminal trial.

---

[93] The result would be the same if the incriminating documents seized from *X* had earlier been prepared by *D*. The compulsion in the case pertains to the *production* of the papers, and not to their earlier non-compelled *preparation*. *See* Fisher v. United States, 425 U.S. 391 (1976); Wilson v. United States, 221 U.S. 361 (1911).

[94] 427 U.S. 463 (1976).

[95] The Supreme Court once held that a subpoena of private papers violates the Fourth and Fifth Amendments. Boyd v. United States, 116 U.S. 616 (1886). The Fourth Amendment aspect of the *Boyd* holding no longer applies. *See* § 42[E] *supra*. And, as is evident from the discussion in this section, private papers apparently no longer retain special Fifth Amendment protection. Although the Court in *Andresen* repeatedly described the papers seized in that case as "business records," as if that distinction mattered, the reasoning of the case applies to personal papers.

[96] Fisher v. United States, 425 U.S. at 410.

[97] Doe v. United States, 465 U.S. 605 (1984); *see also* Baltimore City Department of Social Services v. Bouknight, 110 S.Ct. 900 (1990) (in which the Court assumed that a court order, requiring a mother suspected of child abuse to produce her child, might incriminate her, because the act of production could constitute "implicit communication of control" over the child at the moment of production, which might aid the state in criminal prosecution of *D* for child abuse).

In *New Jersey v. Portash*,[98] the Supreme Court held that testimony given by a witness before a grand jury, who was compelled to testify under an immunity statute, could not be used against him at trial, even for impeachment purposes.

The no-impeachment rule announced in *Portash* undermines the state's valid interest in deterring perjury at trial. Nonetheless, the Court reasoned that because immunized testimony is "the essence of coerced testimony," the privilege against self-incrimination is implicated "in its most pristine form. Balancing [of interests], therefore, is not simply unnecessary. It is impermissible."

---

[98] 440 U.S. 450 (1979).

CHAPTER 27

EYEWITNESS IDENTIFICATION PROCEDURES

§ 165 Eyewitness Identification: The Problem[1]

"The vagaries of eyewitness identification are well known. . . ."[2] Erroneous eyewitness identification of suspects has long been recognized as a serious problem in the administration of justice.

Some misidentifications result from the intentional use of suggestive techniques by police officers, such as by displaying a suspect in a lineup with persons who do not look like her or fit the description of the criminal given by the witness.

Most misidentifications, however, are attributable to conditions beyond the control of the police, namely, the "inherent unreliability of human perception and memory and . . . human susceptibility to unintentional, and often quite subtle, suggestive influences."[3] As two observers have summarized the research data, "people quite often do not see or hear things which are presented clearly to their senses, see or hear things which are not there, do not remember things which have happened to them, and remember things which did not happen."[4]

Studies indicate that a person can simultaneously perceive only a limited number of stimuli from her environment, even if her attention level is high.[5] As a consequence, it is difficult for a witness to observe the height, weight, age, and other features of a suspect at the time of the crime. Reliability is reduced further by the fact that the encounter between the witness or victim and the criminal is often brief, frequently in poorly lit conditions, and often in stressful circumstances.

Beyond the difficulties that arise from the original observation, human memory decays over time. Worse still, "memory . . . is an active, constructive process,"[6] in which a person tends to fill in memory gaps with new "information." People have a psychological need to reduce uncertainty and to make consistent that which

---

[1] *See generally* Eyewitness Testimony (G. Wells & E. Loftus eds.) (Cambridge U. Press 1984); Ellis, Davies & Shepherd, *Experimental Studies of Face Identification*, 3 J. Crim. Def. 219 (1977); Gross, *Loss of Innocence: Eyewitness Identification and Proof of Guilt*, 16 J. Legal Studies 395 (1987); Levine & Tapp, *The Psychology of Criminal Identification: The Gap from Wade to Kirby*, 121 U. Pa. L. Rev. 1079 (1973); Note, *Did Your Eyes Deceive You? Expert Psychological Testimony on the Unreliability of Eyewitness Identification*, 29 Stan. L. Rev. 969 (1977).

[2] United States v. Wade, 388 U.S. 218, 228 (1967).

[3] Note, n. 1 *supra*, at 970.

[4] Levine and Tapp, n. 1 *supra*, at 1087-88.

[5] *See id.* at 1087-1118; Note, n. 1 *supra*, at 974-89.

[6] Note, n. 1 *supra*, at 983.

is not; therefore, witnesses often unconsciously fill in memory holes with details that are inaccurate.

The police identification process itself can aggravate the situation. By its nature, a lineup "is a multiple-choice recognition test"[7] in which the eyewitness-participant often believes (or is led to believe) that there is no "none of the above" option. The effect of this can be that the witness picks the "most correct answer," *i.e.*, the person who most resembles the culprit. Then, once the identification is made, the witness often substitutes in her mind the accused's image as it appeared at the lineup for the prior image of the criminal at the time of the offense.

Witnesses are also subject to socio-psychological pressures that can render identifications untrustworthy. For example, a comment or action by a police officer — the authority figure — that inadvertently or deliberately suggests the "right" choice in a lineup may cause the witness to select that person.

Small-group pressures also influence the process. If witnesses are in each other's presence during the identification process,[8] there is a significant risk that once a person is identified as the perpetrator by some witnesses, others will feel an unconscious pressure to select the same person. In turn, the uniformity in the identification strengthens the resolve of each witness to stand by her identification.

Finally, all of these concerns are aggravated by the fact that, although eyewitness identifications are untrustworthy, juries often place a high value on eyewitness testimony.

§ 166 Corporeal Identification Procedures: Right to Counsel[9]

[A] Rule

Pursuant to the so-called *Wade-Kirby*[10] doctrine, a person has a Sixth Amendment constitutional right to counsel at any corporeal identification procedure[11] conducted after, but not before, adversary judicial criminal proceedings have commenced against her.[12]

Unless the accused's counsel is present at the post-formal-charges corporeal identification procedure, or her presence is waived by the accused, the prosecutor

---

[7] *Id.* at 986.

[8] *E.g.*, Gilbert v. California, 388 U.S. 263 (1967) (*D* was identified in an auditorium containing about 100 witnesses).

[9] *See generally* J. Grano, *A Legal Response to the Inherent Dangers of Eyewitness Identification Testimony*, in Eyewitness Testimony, n. 1 *supra*, at 315; Grano, *Kirby, Biggers and Ash: Do Any Constitutional Safeguards Remain Against the Danger of Convicting the Innocent?*, 72 Mich. L. Rev. 719 (1974); Read, *Lawyers at Lineups: Constitutional Necessity or Avoidable Extravagance?*, 17 UCLA L. Rev. 339 (1969); Note, *Lawyers and Lineups*, 77 Yale L.J. 390 (1967).

[10] United States v. Wade, 388 U.S. 218 (1967); Kirby v. Illinois, 406 U.S. 682 (1972).

[11] A "corporeal" identification procedure in one in which a suspect is physically presented to an eyewitness for identification. Typically, this is done by displaying the suspect in a lineup or by bringing her to the victim or eyewitness for a one-on-one confrontation.

[12] For a definition of "adversary judicial criminal proceedings," *see* § 151 *supra*.

is not permitted to present evidence at trial of the results of the identification procedure. For example, if *W* identifies *D* at a post-indictment lineup at which *D* was denied the assistance of counsel, neither *W* nor anyone else may testify at trial regarding the results of the lineup.

Furthermore, if the accused is denied her right to counsel at the lineup or other corporeal identification procedure, the prosecutor is prohibited from obtaining an in-court identification of the accused by the witness, unless the prosecutor proves by clear and convincing evidence that the in-court identification is not a fruit of the tainted out-of-court identification procedure.[13] Among the factors that a trial court may consider in determining whether the prosecutor has met her burden of proof in this regard are those listed as examples by the Supreme Court:

> [The trial court may consider] the prior opportunity [of the witness] to observe the alleged criminal act, the existence of any discrepancy between any pre-lineup description and the defendant's actual description, any identification prior to lineup of another person, the identification by picture of the defendant prior to the lineup, failure to identify the defendant on a prior occasion, and the lapse of time between the alleged act and the lineup identification.[14]

[B] How and Why the Rule Developed

[1] *United States v. Wade*

A person is entitled to the assistance of counsel at all critical stages of a criminal prosecution. Justice Brennan, author of the majority opinion in *United States v. Wade*,[15] defined "critical stage" as "any stage of the prosecution, formal or informal, in court or out, where counsel's absence might derogate from the accused's right to a fair trial."

The Court determined that absent legislative or police reform of eyewitness-identification procedures, the pretrial exhibition of a suspect to a witness for identification purposes is a critical stage of the prosecution because the process is "peculiarly riddled with innumerable dangers and variable factors which might seriously, even crucially, derogate from a fair trial."

The Court expressed concern regarding the inherent unreliability of eyewitness identifications and the fact that it is seldom possible for defense counsel, if she is absent when the identification is made, to reconstruct the procedure in order to demonstrate at trial why the witness' identification should be discounted.[16] As a result, counsel cannot conduct effective cross-examination of the eyewitness at trial. In passing, the Court also noted that "presence of counsel itself can often avert prejudice and assure a meaningful confrontation at trial."

---

[13] *Wade*, 388 U.S. at 241.

[14] *Id.*

[15] 388 U.S. 218 (1967).

[16] Justice Brennan pointed out that the identity of the other persons in a lineup may not be known or divulged to defense counsel, and it is unlikely that either the eyewitness or the defendant will have been sufficiently alert to the potential deficiencies to be able to testify to any suggestive features of the procedure.

Justice White dissented from the Court's right-to-counsel holding. He criticized the majority for its "pervasive distrust of all official investigations," and its "treacherous and unsupported assumptions" that lineups are unreliable and that police misconduct is undiscoverable if counsel is absent. He accused the majority of basing its rule on the premise that "improper police procedures are so widespread that a broad prophylactic rule must be laid down."[17]

Justice White also worried that the introduction of lawyers into the lineup process would undermine the investigative procedure. His remarks in this regard are considered in subsection [C] below.

[2] *Kirby v. Illinois*

Although *Wade* involved a post-indictment lineup, the Court in that case stated that a court must "scrutinize *any* pretrial confrontation of the accused to determine whether the presence of his counsel is necessary to preserve the defendant's basic right to a fair trial. . . ."

In *Kirby v. Illinois*,[18] the Supreme Court considered the applicability of the *Wade* right-to-counsel rule to a one-on-one confrontation between the victim and D conducted before formal judicial criminal proceedings had begun. In doing so, it refused to apply — or, as the Court put it, to "extend" — the *Wade* rule to this identification on the ground that the Sixth Amendment right to counsel does not apply to police conduct that occurs prior to the initiation of formal judicial proceedings. As most identification procedures occur before formal charges are brought, the *Wade* right-to-counsel rule is now largely ineffectual.

Today, in view of a long line of "critical stage" case law in other contexts,[19] *Kirby's* formalistic line-drawing analysis is not surprising, but it was at the time. Most pre-*Kirby* commentators and lower courts assumed that *Wade* applied to pre-charge identification procedures.[20] Indeed, this was Justice White's view, as expressed in his dissents in *Wade*[21] and *Kirby*, which he believed was controlled by *Wade*.

From a policy perspective, *Kirby* is unjustifiable. The risks inherent in lineups and other identification procedures are as substantial before formal charges are brought as they are after. If defense counsel is needed at a post-indictment lineup, she is also needed at a pre-indictment identification procedure.

[C] The Role of Counsel In the Identification Process

In Justice White's dissent in *Wade*, he expressed concern that the introduction of defense lawyers into the witness-identification process would undermine the

---

[17] The majority denied this accusation. It stated that it did "not assume that these risks [of unreliability] are the result of police procedures intentionally designed to prejudice an accused. Rather we assume they drive from the dangers inherent in eyewitness identification. . . ."

[18] 406 U.S. 682 (1972).

[19] *See especially* § 151 *supra*.

[20] *See* J. Grano, n. 6 *supra*, at 321.

[21] In *Wade*, Justice White warned that the counsel rule announced in that case "applies . . . regardless of when the identification occurs, . . . and whether before or after indictment or information."

state's legitimate interest in conducting prompt and efficient investigations and would even make the process less trustworthy.

His prediction was based on the assumption that defense lawyers would play an active role at lineups and other corporeal identification procedures. Because of *Wade*, he expected the process to become adversarial: attorneys would "hover over witnesses and begin their cross-examination then, menacing truthful fact-finding as thoroughly as the Court fears the police now do."

Furthermore, because the role of defense counsel in the adversary system is to represent her client faithfully,[22] Justice White expected that lawyers would advise their clients how to behave at lineups, *e.g.*, not to move or talk when requested, or even to recommend that they not appear in them. He predicted that defense lawyers would "suggest rules for the lineup[s] and . . . manage and produce [them] as best [they] can."

Justice White's reading of the majority opinion in *Wade* is overblown. The role of the defense attorney at the lineup, at least as it is described in the majority opinion, is more passive: primarily, she is present so that she can later reconstruct the events and cross-examine the eyewitness at trial. She is an observer of the events, not a catalyst for change.

The majority in *Wade* did state, without explaining, that the "presence of counsel itself can often avert prejudice." Presumably, this means only that if a lawyer is present, the police have an additional incentive to make sure that the procedure is fair to the defendant. Although there is nothing in *Wade* that suggests that a lawyer cannot make suggestions to the police to improve the procedure, there is also nothing in it that suggests that counsel has a right to be heard on such matters, much less that her suggestions must be taken.[23]

---

[22] *See* § 181[A] *infra.*

[23] In Moore v. Illinois, 434 U.S. 220 (1977), the Court shed a little more light on the lawyer's possible role in the identification process, albeit in unusual circumstances. In *Moore*, D was prosecuted for the rape of V. The police brought V to D's joint arraignment/ preliminary hearing, at which D was not represented by counsel, so that she could view him and determine if he were the assailant. V was in the courtroom while the judge informed D of the charges against him. The judge then called V to the bench, at which point the prosecutor asked her if she saw her assailant in the courtroom. She identified D.

The Court held, 8-1, that this identification, coming as it did after judicial proceedings had commenced against D, was unconstitutional because defense counsel was absent. It mentioned various ways in which counsel, if present, could have assisted D: the lawyer might have requested postponement of the hearing until a lineup could be conducted; he could have requested that V be excused from the courtroom until she was needed for the identification; or the attorney might have suggested to the court that D be seated in the audience among onlookers during the identification process.

These comments suggest a more active role by defense counsel than was described in *Wade*. However, the circumstances in *Moore* were atypical, as the events occurred in a courtroom rather than in a police station. And, even at that, the Court said that because "[s]uch requests ordinarily are addressed to the sound discretion of the court . . . we express no opinion as to whether the . . . court would have been required to grant such requests."

§ 167 Non-Corporeal Identification Procedures: Right to Counsel

In *United States v. Ash*,[24] the Supreme Court held that, notwithstanding *Wade*, a person against whom adversary judicial proceedings have been initiated is not entitled to the presence of counsel when the police display one or more photographs, including one of the accused, to an eyewitness to see if she can identify the culprit. According to *Ash*, such a display is not a critical stage of the prosecution.

The Court, per Justice Blackmun, concluded that the purpose of the Sixth Amendment right to counsel is to furnish the accused with a lawyer to cope with the intricacies of the law, and to lessen the inequality inherent in trial-like adversarial confrontations. However, the accused has no right to be present during the photographic display, and thus there is no "trial-like" confrontation at which the defendant might be misled by her lack of familiarity with the law or overpowered by an opposing attorney.

The Court also rejected the assertion that the lawyer's presence at a photographic display is necessary to protect the accused's trial rights. It concluded that the risks inherent in this type of procedure are not so great that special safeguards are required. Furthermore, because of the tangible nature of photographs, an absent defense attorney can adequately reconstruct the display in order to determine if it was suggestive.[25]

§ 168 Identification Procedures: Due Process of Law[26]

The due process clause requires the exclusion at trial of evidence of a pretrial identification of the defendant if, based on the totality of the circumstances: (1) the procedure used to obtain the identification was unnecessarily suggestive; and (2) there is a very substantial likelihood of misidentification.[27] This rule applies regardless of whether the identification was corporeal or non-corporeal, occurred before or after formal charges were initiated, and whether or not counsel was present.

It should be noticed that under this rule the identification procedure does not offend due process, and thus the evidence of the out-of-court identification is not inadmissible at trial, merely because the procedure used was suggestive. As a threshold matter, it must have been *unnecessarily* suggestive.

For example, in *Stovall v. Denno*,[28] D, a black man, was taken to the hospital the day after V, an eyewitness to the stabbing murder of her husband and also a

---

[24] 413 U.S. 300 (1973).

[25] However, as the dissenters pointed out, unless counsel or her representative is present, there will be no way to know if the officer's or prosecutor's "inflection, facial expression, physical motions, and myriad other almost imperceptible means of communication . . . intentionally or unintentionally . . . compromise[d] the witness' objectivity."

[26] *See generally* Grano, n. 9 *supra*; Pulaski, *Neil v. Biggers: The Supreme Court Dismantles the Wade Trilogy's Due Process Protection*, 26 Stan. L. Rev. 1097 (1974).

[27] Neil v. Biggers, 409 U.S. 188 (1972).

[28] 388 U.S. 293 (1967).

victim of a stabbing, had undergone life-saving surgery. *D* was handcuffed to one of five police officers, all of whom were white. *V* identified *D* as the assailant. Although the Court agreed that the procedure was highly suggestive, it also found — ignoring the possibility of using one or more black officers — that its use was "imperative," as the police were not sure that *V* would survive the surgery.

However, even if an identification procedure is unnecessarily suggestive, the reliability of the identification is the due process "linchpin in determining the admissibility of identification testimony."[29] Therefore, the ultimate issue to be determined is the likelihood that a misidentification has occurred. The relevant factors in determining reliability include those noted by the Court in the right-to-counsel context.[30]

If the out-of-court identification offends due process under this test, it must be excluded at trial. In such circumstances, no in-court identification by the witness is permitted unless the government proves that the out-of-court procedure did not create "a very substantial likelihood of irreparable misidentification."[31] In effect, this brings into play fruit-of-the-poisonous-tree analysis: it requires the trial court to determine whether, based on the totality of the circumstances, the in-court identification is sufficiently purged of the taint of the out-of-court, inadmissible identification.

§ 169   Identification Procedures: Other Constitutional Issues

[A]   Fourth Amendment

The non-consensual placement of a suspect in a lineup or other eyewitness-identification procedure raises potential Fourth Amendment issues. First, may the police forcibly take a suspect who is not under arrest from her home (or from some other place where she has a right to be) to the police station or to the scene of the crime in order to be part of an identification procedure?

As discussed earlier in the treatise in the context of interrogations,[32] such a seizure is ordinarily tantamount to an arrest and requires probable cause. However, a seizure for eyewitness-identification purposes might be permissible on the basis of reasonable suspicion, if the police were to obtain prior judicial authorization.[33]

Second, if a person is arrested on probable cause and the administrative procedures pertaining to the booking process are completed, may the police delay the suspect's appearance in court until she is placed in a lineup involving a different offense, or would this act constitute a violation of the Fourth Amendment?

There is little law on this point. Occasionally, however, federal courts have dealt with the issue on non-constitutional grounds, holding that the delay in placing the

---

[29] Manson v. Brathwaite, 432 U.S. 98, 114 (1977).

[30] See n. 14 and the accompanying text *supra.*

[31] Simmons v. United States, 390 U.S. 377, 384 (1968).

[32] *See* § 96[B] *supra.*

[33] The Court has hinted that such an approach might be permissible in the context of fingerprinting. *See* § 97[C] *supra.*

suspect in a lineup violates the federal rule that requires that the police "shall take the arrested person without unnecessarily delay before the nearest available federal magistrate."[34]

It is doubtful that the Fourth Amendment is violated by such a delay. A validly arrested person has a substantially reduced legally-protected interest in freedom of movement. Therefore, it is probably not an unreasonable seizure to put her in a lineup, rather than to take her immediately to the magistrate.

[B] Fifth Amendment (Self-Incrimination)

A person is not a "witness" against himself in violation of the Fifth Amendment privilege against compulsory self-incrimination unless he is "compelled to testify against himself, or otherwise provide the State with evidence of a testimonial or communicative nature."[35]

Compulsory display of a suspect's physical characteristics in a lineup is not "testimonial" or "communicative" evidence because it does not require the accused "to disclose any knowledge he might have."[36] The same principle applies to the requirement that the suspect utter words allegedly spoken by the perpetrator of the crime, as this constitutes no more than the use of the voice to identify the suspect.

---

[34] FRCP 5(a); *see generally* 3 W. LaFave, at § 9.6(d).
[35] Schmerber v. California, 384 U.S. 757, 761 (1966). *See* § 163[A] *supra*.
[36] *Wade*, 388 U.S. at 222.

CHAPTER **28**

ENTRAPMENT

§ 170   Entrapment: In General[1]

Entrapment is a criminal law defense. That is, like such defenses as insanity, duress, and self–defense, entrapment is pleaded by the defendant, evidence of it is presented at trial, and if the claim is believed the defendant is acquitted. In short, a finding of entrapment does more than result in the exclusion of evidence at trial: it bars the successful prosecution of the defendant.

Entrapment is not a constitutional doctrine. That is, when the police entrap a person they do not thereby violate the Constitution. As a consequence, no jurisdiction is required to recognize the defense, although all of the states and the federal courts presently do allow the claim;[2] and the definition of the defense and the procedural rules relating to it may and do vary by jurisdiction.

In general, there are two divergent approaches to the defense, frequently termed the "subjective" and "objective" tests of entrapment. Although the definition of "entrapment" depends on which test is used, both versions usually require proof that: (1) the defendant was induced to commit the crime by a government agent (typically, an undercover police officer); (2) the defendant or, at least, a hypothetically average person, would not have committed the offense but for the inducement; and (3) the government agent acted as he did in order to obtain evidence to prosecute the defendant.

§ 171   Entrapment: The Subjective Test

[A]   Rule

The Supreme Court recognized a federal defense of entrapment for the first time in 1932 in *Sorrells v. United States*,[3] when Chief Justice Hughes, speaking for five

---

[1] *See generally* Carlson, *The Act Requirement and the Foundations of the Entrapment Defense*, 73 Va. L. Rev. 1011 (1987); Dworkin, *The Serpent Beguiled Me and I Did Eat: Entrapment and the Creation of Crime*, 4 Law & Philos. 17 (1985); Park, *The Entrapment Controversy*, 60 Minn. L. Rev. 163 (1976); Seidman, *The Supreme Court, Entrapment, and Our Criminal Justice Dilemma*, 1981 Sup. Ct. Rev. 111; Whelan, *Lead Us Not Into (Unwarranted) Temptation: A Proposal to Replace the Entrapment Defense With a Reasonable–Suspicion Standard*, 133 U. Pa. L. Rev. 1193 (1985); Comment, *Causation and Intention in the Entrapment Defense*, 28 UCLA L. Rev. 859 (1981); Note, *Entrapment Reconsidered: A Nonexculpatory Defense Based on the Need for Reciprocity Between the Government and the Governed*, 35 Wayne L. Rev. 99 (1988).

[2] Carlson, n. 1 *supra*, at 1013.

[3] 287 U.S. 435 (1932).

members of the Court, allowed the defense based on what has come to be called the "subjective" test of entrapment. The Court reaffirmed its support for the subjective version of the defense in *Sherman v. United States*[4] and *United States v. Russell.*[5]

As the Court has explained the subjective test, "artifice and stratagem may be employed to catch" criminals,[6] but "a different question is presented when the criminal design originates with the officials of the Government, and they implant in the mind of an innocent person the disposition to commit the alleged offense and induce its commission in order that they may prosecute."[7] In short, the Supreme Court distinguishes between the trap set for the "unwary criminal" and for the "unwary innocent."[8]

Under the subjective test, entrapment is proved if a government agent induces an "innocent" person — that is, a person not predisposed to commit the type of offense charged — to violate the law so that he can be prosecuted. A person is "predisposed" to commit the offense if he is "ready and willing"[9] to commit the type of crime charged if presented with a favorable opportunity to do so.[10]

Examples of nondisposed persons are found in *Sorrells* and *Sherman*. In *Sorrells*, D was prosecuted for violation of the National Prohibition Act after he sold a one–half gallon jug of whiskey to a government agent who posed as a tourist. D sold him the liquor only after three requests by the agent, who had befriended him by claiming to be a former member of the World War I military division in which D had served. The Court stated that D "had no previous disposition to commit [the criminal act] but was an industrious, law–abiding citizen . . . lured [by the agent] . . . to its commission by repeated and persistent solicitation. . . ."

In *Sherman*, a government informer met D at a doctor's office where both men were being treated for narcotics addiction. After befriending D, the informer asked him if he knew of a good source of narcotics, and pleaded with D to supply him with the drugs. D turned him down various times before ultimately obtaining narcotics for the informer, apparently as a favor to him.

The Court in *Sherman* concluded that D was entrapped as a matter of law. It rejected the government's argument that D "evinced a 'ready complaisance' to accede" to the informant's request. Although D had previously been convicted of drug–related offenses, the Court considered him to be nondisposed: no evidence was presented that he was still in the drug trade; no narcotics were found in a search of his apartment; he did not seek profit from the sales; and his initial hesitancy to sell the drugs did not appear to be "the natural wariness of the criminal."

On the other hand, entrapment was proved in *Russell*. In *Russell*, a covert federal agent met D, who was manufacturing illegal narcotics, and stated that he

[4] 356 U.S. 369 (1958).
[5] 411 U.S. 423 (1973).
[6] *Sorrells*, 287 U.S. at 441.
[7] *Sherman*, 356 U.S. at 372.
[8] *Id.* at 372–73.
[9] *See Russell*, 411 U.S. at 426 n.4 (quoting the "standard entrapment instructions" given in federal courts).
[10] *See* Park, n. 1 *supra*, at 176.

represented an organization interested in controlling the manufacture and distri-
bution of the drugs in the Pacific Northwest. The agent offered to supply *D* with
a difficult–to–obtain chemical that was necessary in the production of the drug.
D agreed to the arrangement. The Court held that entrapment was not proved in
view of *D*'s predisposition to commit drug offenses of the sort for which he was
prosecuted.

[B] Rationale of the Rule

The acquittal of persons induced to commit crimes by government agents is
justified on the ground that "Congress could not have intended criminal punishment for a defendant who has committed all the elements of a prescribed offense
but was induced to commit them by the government."[11]

According to the Court, convictions in circumstances such as those in *Sorrells*
and *Sherman* can stand only if a court rests its interpretation of the applicable
criminal statute "entirely upon the letter of the statute."[12] However, such a
"[l]iteral interpretation of statutes at the expense of the reason of the law" results
in "absurd consequences or flagrant injustice."[13]

[C] Procedural Features of the Rule

[1] Role of the Judge and Jury

Entrapment is an issue of fact that is raised by the defendant at trial and resolved
by the trier of fact, ordinarily the jury. The defendant is entitled to have the jury
instructed on the defense as long as he presents some evidence that government
agents induced him to commit the offense.[14]

The judge may refuse to submit the issue to the jury and acquit the defendant
if there are no factual issues in dispute and entrapment exists as a matter of law,
i.e., no reasonable juror could conclude other than that the defendant was
entrapped. However, studies of federal appellate decisions support the conclusion
that the defense is "easy to raise and supremely difficult to establish as a matter
of law."[15]

[2] Proof of Predisposition

The key issue in subjective entrapment cases is whether the defendant was
predisposed at the time of the crime to commit an offense of the type charged in
the indictment. The issue is not whether the defendant was predisposed at an
earlier time in his life. For example, in *Sherman*, *D*'s drug addiction and prior
drug activities did not bar the Court from concluding that at the time of the offense
he was an innocent person.

Predisposition may be proved in various ways. First, the facts of the incident
itself may demonstrate the defendant's "ready complaisance" to commit the

---

[11] *Russell*, 411 U.S. at 435.
[12] *Sorrells*, 287 U.S. at 446.
[13] *Id.*
[14] Sagansky v. United States, 358 F.2d 195, 202–03 (1st Cir.), *cert. denied*, 385 U.S.
816 (1966).
[15] Park, n. 1 *supra*, at 178 (footnotes deleted).

crime. For example, the prosecutor may point to the defendant's non–hesitancy to commit the offense, his ready knowledge of how to commit it, or his comments leading up to the offense that demonstrate his propensity to commit the crime.

Second, predisposition may be proved by reference to the defendant's character in the community. This is done by introducing evidence, in most other circumstances inadmissible, of the defendant's reputation in the community and/or his prior criminal record, including arrests and convictions for related offenses.[16]

[3] Burden of Proof

The defendant has the burden of producing evidence that he was induced by a government agent to commit the crime. However, the prosecutor typically carries the burden of persuasion regarding the defense.[17] In the federal courts and in many states, he must disprove entrapment beyond a reasonable doubt.

§ 172 Entrapment: The Objective Test

[A] Rule

For more than a half–century, the so–called "objective" version of the entrapment defense has been defended by a minority of the members of the Supreme Court. In *Sorrells*, Justice Roberts, speaking also for Justices Brandeis and Stone, favored an objective test. In *Sherman*, Justice Frankfurter wrote a four–justice concurrence in favor of the test. In *Russell*, four justices dissented from the Court's application of the subjective test.

Whereas the subjective test primarily centers on the defendant — was he predisposed to commit the crime? — the objective standard focuses more on police conduct. According to Justice Frankfurter in *Sherman*, entrapment occurs when "the police conduct falls below standards, to which common feelings respond for the proper use of government power." As the Justice explained the objective approach:

> [The police] should act in such a manner as is likely to induce only those persons [ready and willing to commit further crime should the occasion arise] and not others who would normally avoid crime and through self–struggle resist ordinary temptations. This test . . . [focuses on] the likelihood, objectively considered, that [the police conduct] would entrap only those ready and willing to commit crime.

Coined by one scholar as the "hypothetical–person"[18] test, police inducements constitute entrapment if they "might have seduced a hypothetical individual who was not . . . predisposed,"[19] or would be "likely to cause normally law–abiding persons to commit the offense."[20]

---

[16] *See id.* at 200–01, 211–16.

[17] United States v. Sherman, 200 F.2d 880, 882–83 (2d Cir. 1952), *revs'd on other grounds*, 356 U.S. 369 (1958).

[18] Park, n. 1 *supra*, at 165–66.

[19] *Russell*, 411 U.S. at 434.

[20] National Commission on Reform of Federal Laws, A Proposed New Federal Code § 702(2) (1971).

Although advocates of the objective test of entrapment are rarely explicit on this issue, the hypothetical person that it measures is analogous to the "reasonable person" in tort law,[21] except that the issue is whether the police conduct would induce a person of ordinary moral fortitude or self–control to violate the law in question.

The "hypothetical person" is infused with some of the characteristics of the defendant. For example, it is hard to justify the view of the concurring justices in *Sherman* that the defendant in that case was entrapped as a matter of law unless the objective test is understood to be whether the police conduct in the case would have caused the average addict–seeking–cure, rather than the average law–abiding non–addict, to supply illegal drugs.[22]

[B] Rationale of the Rule

The objective standard is justified on grounds of judicial integrity and deterrence. The theme of judicial integrity was first expressed in the entrapment context by Justice Roberts in *Sorrells*, when he stated that courts were obligated to enforce the defense in order to protect "the purity of its own temple." In the same vein, Justice Frankfurter expressed the view in *Sherman* that the "transcending value at stake" was "public confidence in the fair and honorable administration of justice." As a consequence, "courts have an obligation to set their face against enforcement of the law by lawless means. . . ."

Advocates of the objective approach also justify the test on grounds of deterrence. Justice Stewart condemned the police conduct in *Russell* on the ground that it was "precisely the type of governmental conduct that the entrapment defense is meant to prevent." Similarly, the drafters of the Model Penal Code justified their adoption of an objective standard of entrapment on the basis that "the attempt to deter wrongful conduct on the part of the government . . . provides the justification for the defense. . . ."[23]

[C] Procedural Features of the Rule

Most states that apply the objective standard follow the lead of the Model Penal Code, which allocates the burden of proof to the defendant in entrapment cases.[24] The Model Penal Code requires the defendant to prove entrapment by a preponderance of the evidence.

Advocates of the objective test, including the drafters of the Model Penal Code, also contend that the defense should be submitted to a judge rather than to the jury. They reason that courts, not jurors, should protect "the temple's purity," and that only through judicial opinions can appropriate police standards be developed.

---

[21] Whelan, n. 1 *supra*, at 1210; Park, n. 1 *supra*, at 204.

[22] Park, n. 1 *supra*, at 174.

[23] Model Penal Code § 2.13, Comment at 406–07 (1985).

[24] Model Penal Code § 2.13(2) (1985); *see* Park, n. 1 *supra*, at 264–65.

§ 173 Entrapment: The Debate

[A] Overview

Controversy swirls around the defense of entrapment. Most of it relates to the question of whether the subjective or the objective standard is preferable. Although most courts follow the Supreme Court's lead and apply the subjective test, most scholars favor the objective version.[25]

The underlying issue in the debate is whether, on the one hand, the entrapped defendant should be excused because he is morally blameless for the commission of the offense or, on the other hand, he should be exculpated, despite his blameworthiness, because of the wrongdoing of the police.

Most of the entrapment debate is of a negative nature. That is, most advocates of each standard point to the weaknesses in the opposing position rather than to provide support for their own version of the defense. Many of the criticisms on both sides are powerful, so much so that one scholar has observed that "no member of the [Supreme] Court — and none of the numerous commentators on its work — has advanced a defense of the doctrine that is satisfactory."[26]

If this judgment is correct, what one is left with is the conclusion that a more satisfactory entrapment defense than either existing version is needed, or the defense in any form should be abandoned.

[B] Criticisms of the Subjective Test

[1] "The Legislative-Intent Rationale is Fictional"

"It is painfully obvious," one scholar has observed, that the rationale of the subjective test, namely that Congress did not intend for its statutes to be enforced by tempting innocent persons into violations, is "wholly fictional."[27] There is nothing in the legislative history to suggest that Congress intended for non-disposed persons who violate its laws as the result of police inducements to be acquitted, while predisposed persons, subjected to the same blandishments, are convicted.

The Supreme Court in *Russell* virtually conceded the fictional nature of the legislative–intent argument when it stated that criticism of the rationale was "not devoid of appeal." Nonetheless, it reaffirmed the subjective standard on the basis of *stare decisis*, the fact that the arguments raised against the objective test were "at least equally cogent," and because Congress, if the legislative–intent rationale is unacceptable to it, can "address itself to the question and adopt any substantive definition of the defense that it may find desirable."

This is hardly a spirited defense of the theoretical underpinnings of the subjective test.

---

[25] Seidman, n. 1 *supra*, at 115 n.4 ("The commentators have overwhelmingly favored an objective approach. . . .").

[26] *Id.* at 112.

[27] *Id.* at 129–30; *see also Sherman*, 356 U.S. at 379 (Frankfurter J., dissenting) (describing the legislative–intent theory as "sheer fiction").

[2] "The Subjective Test Acquits Culpable Persons"

The subjective test conflicts with existing criminal law concepts of culpability. An entrapped person knowingly and without compulsion violates the law. The same criminal acts, committed by the same person, as the result of the same inducements, would result in a conviction if the inducing party were another private person rather than a police officer.

In the non–entrapment context, the criminal law does not excuse people who commit crimes because of tempting offers or who accede to minor threats. The reason for this rule is that society believes that people who are tempted by others to commit crimes have sufficient free choice to be held accountable for their actions.[28] A person who responds to similar inducements by the government is no less culpable — no less morally accountable for his actions — than a victim of private temptation.[29]

Critics of the subjective test suggest that the reason why we acquit the entrapped defendant while we convict one who gives in to non–coercive privately–induced pressures, is that (as the objective standard suggests) non–coercive pressures are unacceptable if, but only if, it is the government that plays an ignoble part in producing them.

[3] "The Subjective Test Is Unfair"

Because the subjective test focuses on the criminal disposition of the defendant, the standard is unfair. It permits the prosecution to introduce evidence of the defendant's bad character, in the form of rumors, reputation evidence, and information on his criminal history. Yet, evidence of this sort ordinarily is inadmissible because it is of only slight probative value and may be prejudicial to the rights of the defendant.[30]

Even an advocate of the subjective test has conceded that courts have, "despite the lack of any pressing need, . . . permitted otherwise inadmissible evidence to be introduced. Some of it has been shockingly unreliable."[31]

[C] Criticisms of the Objective Test

[1] "The Test Leads to Inappropriate Results"

Because the objective standard focuses on the conduct of the police, critics of the test argue that it can lead to inappropriate results.

First, a hardened criminal can avoid conviction if the police behave improperly. This result is not only dangerous but anomalous: when the police violate the Fourth Amendment or another constitutional provision, evidence obtained as the result of the illegal police conduct is excluded, but the prosecution of the defendant

---

[28] *See generally* Dressler, *Exegesis of the Law of Duress: Justifying the Excuse and Searching for Its Proper Limits*, 62 So. Cal. L. Rev. 1331 (1989).

[29] Model Penal Code § 2.13, Comment at 406 (1985).

[30] The introduction of evidence of prior convictions appears to have a powerful impact on jurors in subjective–test entrapment trials. *See* Borgida & Park, *The Entrapment Defense*, 12 Law & Human Behavior 19 (1988) (report of a simulated–jury study).

[31] Park, n. 1 *supra*, at 248.

may proceed. In the case of entrapment, however, police conduct of which we do not approve, but which is not unconstitutional, prevents society from bringing the defendant to justice.

At the same time, under the objective standard, it is possible for a nondangerous, ordinarily nondisposed, person to be convicted, if he is led astray at a weak moment by police conduct that would not have tempted the hypothetical person to commit the crime.

[2] "The Test's Stated Rationales are Indefensible"

Critics maintain that the "purity of the temple" judicial–integrity argument is unpersuasive. They argue that society does not want judges to protect their temples' purity by releasing criminals to the streets. Furthermore, as with similar claims in the Fourth Amendment context,[32] "judicial integrity" is said to constitute little more than a rephrased argument based on deterrence.

The deterrence argument also fails, critics contend.[33] First, advocates of the objective standard fail to explain why courts should deter police conduct that is not in itself unconstitutional or otherwise illegal.

Second, the hypothetical–person test is too ambiguous to result in clear guidelines to the police. A general verdict of acquittal does not tell the police what conduct is unacceptable: they must guess as to where the line is being drawn.

Third, by its own standards, the objective test does not focus entirely on the police conduct. Only police conduct that would cause the average person to violate the law constitutes entrapment, a principle that undercuts the deterrence goal. For example, suppose that undercover officers nab prostitutes by standing in alleys exposing their penises, or catch thieves by urinating in streets with $20 bills visibly hanging from their coat pockets.[34] Under the objective test, the police have not entrapped their "victims," because ordinary people do not commit prostitution or theft when induced by such obnoxious conduct.

§ 174 Entrapment: Due Process

Entrapment–like police conduct, if sufficiently outrageous, may violate the due process clause of the Constitution. Nonetheless, the Court has yet to hold that the police have crossed the constitutional line.

[A] *United States v. Russell*

In *Russell*,[35] D was convicted of the illegal manufacture of amphetamines after federal undercover agents furnished him with a difficult–to–obtain legal chemical necessary in the production of the narcotics. Because D was predisposed to commit the crime, an entrapment defense did not lie. He argued, however, that

---

[32] *See* § 118 *supra*.

[33] *See* Seidman, n. 1 *supra*, at 136–46; Park, n. 1 *supra*, at 225–39.

[34] These police actions are not fanciful. *See* Rybak, *Officer Nabs Prostitute Suspect with "Unbecoming" Technique*, Minneapolis Tribune, August 30, 1980, at 3A, col 1.

[35] 411 U.S. 423 (1973).

the police violated the due process clause by supplying him with the chemical and by becoming "enmeshed in the criminal activity."

In an opinion for five justices, Justice Rehnquist stated that "we may some day be presented with a situation in which the conduct of law enforcement agents is so outrageous that due process principles would absolutely bar the government from invoking judicial process to obtain a conviction, *cf. Rochin v. California.* . . . ." Nonetheless, the Court held that the case at hand was not of that nature, as the chemical that the government furnished was lawful, harmless in itself, and not unobtainable elsewhere.

The Court's citation to *Rochin*[36] suggests that it would find a due process violation if the police conduct is "shocking to the conscience." If so, and if the Court applies the *Rochin* test as it has in other contexts, this is a narrow limitation on police conduct. In the past, only police violence against an individual has "shocked the conscience."

[B] *Hampton v. United States*

In *Hampton*,[37] undercover police officers were involved in "[t]he beginning and the end of [the] crime": an undercover agent supplied heroin to *D* so that he could sell it to another government agent.

Justice Rehnquist, this time speaking only for himself, Chief Justice Burger, and Justice White, backed off from his earlier due–process remarks in *Russell.* He conceded that the present case differed from the prior one in that the police here furnished *D* with an illegal substance, and played a much more significant role in the crime.

Nonetheless, Justice Rehnquist stated that the due process clause "comes into play only when the Government activity in question violates some protected right of the *defendant*," which does not occur, he reasoned, if the police act in concert with a defendant to commit a crime. If the police act illegally, "the remedy lies, not in freeing the equally culpable defendant, but in prosecuting the police under the applicable provisions of state or federal law."

Despite the plurality's comments, a majority of the members of the *Hampton* Court expressed the belief that due process violations are possible in the entrapment context. Justices Powell and Blackmun, who concurred in the judgment in the case, stated that they were "unwilling to join the plurality in concluding that, no matter what the circumstances, . . . due process principles . . . could [not] support a bar to conviction."[38] The three dissenters — Justices Brennan, Stewart, and Marshall — agreed with these remarks.[39]

---

[36] Rochin v. California, 342 U.S. 165 (1952). *See* § 117[C] *supra.*

[37] 425 U.S. 484 (1976).

[38] They also contended that in a proper case the Supreme Court should apply its supervisory power over the federal courts to bar a conviction.

[39] Justice Stevens, who joined the Court after oral arguments were heard in the case, did not participate.

CHAPTER **29**

THE RIGHT TO COUNSEL: AT TRIAL AND ON APPEAL

§ 175 The Importance of Defense Lawyers in the Adversary System

Defense lawyers "are necessities, not luxuries"[1] in an adversarial system of criminal justice. Potentially, they serve as equalizers in the confrontation between the government, which hires a lawyer to prosecute, and the person charged with an offense.[2] Although defense lawyers sometimes can be "a nettlesome obstacle to the pursuit of wrongdoers,"[3] they also play a vital role in reducing the risk that the innocent will be convicted of crimes and in ensuring that the guilty receive due process.

Defense lawyers serve as "an antidote to the fear, ignorance, and bewilderment of the . . . defendant, not only in the courtroom but throughout the criminal process."[4] It is not an exaggeration to state, therefore, that the legitimacy of the American criminal justice system depends in great part on the participation of competent, ethical defense lawyers who diligently represent their clients' interests.

This chapter considers the extent to which the Sixth Amendment right-to-counsel provision[5] guarantees a person accused of a crime the assistance of competent, ethical representation at trial and in post-conviction proceedings.

§ 176 The Right to Counsel: At Trial

[A] The Right to Employ Counsel

It has always been clear that, at a minimum, the Sixth Amendment entitles the accused in a federal prosecution to employ a lawyer to assist in her defense at trial.[6] Because the right to counsel is fundamental,[7] the accused in a state prosecution has a similar Fourteenth Amendment right to retain an attorney to represent her during trial.

---

[1] Gideon v. Wainwright, 372 U.S. 335, 344 (1963).

[2] *See* Wright, *The New Role of Defense Counsel Under Escobedo and Miranda*, 52 A.B.A.J. 1117, 1120 (1966).

[3] Moran v. Burbine, 475 U.S. 412, 468 (1986) (Stevens, J., dissenting).

[4] Alschuler, *The Defense Attorney's Role in Plea Bargaining*, 84 Yale L.J. 1179, 1179 (1975).

[5] "In all criminal prosecutions, the accused shall enjoy the right . . . to have the Assistance of Counsel for his defence." U.S. Const. amend. vi.

[6] *See* Scott v. Illinois, 440 U.S. 367, 370 (1979).

[7] Gideon v. Wainwright, 372 U.S. 335 (1963).

[B] Indigents: The Right to Appointed Counsel

[1] Overview

In 1986, lawyers were appointed to represent indigents in 4.4 million state prosecutions.[8] In the majority of these cases, private attorneys were assigned by judges on a case-by-case basis or contracted with the county to represent all indigent defendants. In about one-third of the counties, indigents were represented by public-defender programs.[9]

It was not always this way. Although the Supreme Court ruled in 1938 in *Johnson v. Zerbst*[10] that the Sixth Amendment "withholds from federal courts, in all criminal proceedings, . . . the power and authority to deprive an accused of his life or liberty unless he has or waives the assistance of counsel," the justices did not construe the Constitution to require the states to appoint counsel for indigents until their 1963 landmark decision in *Gideon v. Wainwright*.[11] Until *Gideon*, legal representation of indigents in state courts was sporadic and often ineffective.[12]

[2] The Road to *Gideon*

[a] *Powell v. Alabama*

In *Powell*,[13] nine teenage black youths were prosecuted for the alleged rape of two white girls in an Alabama community "explosive with rage and vengeance."[14] The youths, described by the Court as "ignorant and illiterate," and residents of another state, were indicted, arraigned, and brought to trial in less than two weeks after the capital offenses supposedly occurred.

The youths were not represented by counsel until the day of trial, when two lawyers, one of whom was from out of state and unfamiliar with local law, offered to represent them. They were appointed by the trial court, but were denied a continuance so that they could adequately prepare their defense. Eight of the defendants were convicted in the one-day trial that followed and were sentenced to death.

The Supreme Court, per Justice Sutherland, overturned the convictions. Treating the youths as constructively unrepresented by counsel at trial because the lawyers had not been given time to prepare, Justice Sutherland wrote:

> The right to be heard would be, in many case, of little avail if it did not comprehend the right to be heard by counsel. Even the intelligent and educated layman has small and sometimes no skill in the science of law. . . .

---

[8] *See* U.S. Department of Justice, *Criminal Defense for the Poor, 1986* 1 (Bureau of Justice Statistics, NCJ 112919, Sept. 1988).

[9] *Id.*

[10] 304 U.S. 458 (1938).

[11] 372 U.S. 335 (1963).

[12] *See generally* W. Beaney, The Right to Counsel in American Courts (U. of Michigan 1955); Willcox & Bloustein, *Account of a Field Study in a Rural Area of the Representation of Indigents Accused of Crime*, 59 Colum. L. Rev. 551 (1959).

[13] 287 U.S. 45 (1932).

[14] Willcox & Bloustein, n. 12 *supra*, at 551.

Left without the aid of counsel he may be put on trial without a proper charge, and convicted upon incompetent evidence, or evidence irrelevant to the issue. . . . He lacks both the skill and knowledge adequately to prepare his defense, even though he has a perfect one. He requires the guiding hand of counsel at every step in the proceedings against him. Without it, though he not be guilty, he faces the danger of conviction because he does not know how to establish his innocence.

Despite this broad language, the Court's holding was narrow. It held only that under the special circumstances of the case, including the fact that the defendants had been charged with a capital crime and were incapable of making their own defense because of their age, ignorance, and illiteracy, the youths were entitled by the due process clause to effective assistance of counsel.

[b] *Betts v. Brady*

In *Betts v. Brady*,[15] the Court was invited to announce that indigents have a *per se* constitutional right to free counsel. It did not take the step.

In *Betts*, D, an indigent, was indicted for robbery. He requested, but was denied, the assistance of counsel at trial. He was convicted of robbery and sentenced to prison. D appealed his conviction on the ground that he was entitled to free assistance of counsel at trial.

The Supreme Court rejected the principle that "due process of law demands that in every criminal case, whatever the circumstances, a State must furnish counsel to an indigent defendant." Based on its reading of constitutional history and contemporary state practices, the Court concluded that the right to counsel was not essential to a fair trial in light of the "common understanding of those who lived under Anglo-American system of law."

The Court applied the *Powell* special-circumstances standard and concluded that no circumstances existed in the present case to justify the appointment of counsel. Unlike the facts in *Powell*, D was prosecuted for a non-capital crime, and the case presented only the "simple issue" of whether D's alibi claim should be believed. The Court concluded that D, "not helpless,. . . a man forty-three years old, [and] of ordinary intelligence," could handle his defense satisfactorily by himself.

[3] *Gideon v. Wainwright*[16]

The Supreme Court overruled *Betts* in *Gideon v. Wainwright*. In *Gideon*, D was prosecuted for the felony of breaking and entering a poolroom. D requested, but was denied, the assistance of counsel. According to the Court, he conducted his own defense "about as well as could be expected from a layman." Nonetheless, the jury convicted him and he was sentenced to five years imprisonment.

---

[15] 316 U.S. 455 (1942).

[16] 372 U.S. 335 (1963). *See generally* A. Lewis, Gideon's Trumpet (Random House 1964); Israel, *Gideon v. Wainwright: The "Art" of Overruling*, 1963 Sup. Ct. Rev. 211; Kamisar, *Betts v. Brady Twenty Years Later: The Right to Counsel and Due Process Values*, 61 Mich. L. Rev. 219 (1962); Kamisar, *The Right to Counsel and the Fourteenth Amendment: A Dialogue on "The Most Pervasive Right" of an Accused*, 30 U. Chi. L. Rev. 1 (1962).

The Court, per Justice Black, overturned the conviction. It stated that the Court in *Betts* had "made an abrupt break with its own well-considered precedents," especially that of *Powell*. It described as an "obvious truth" the fact that "in our adversary system of criminal justice, any person haled into court, who is too poor to hire a lawyer, cannot be assured a fair trial unless counsel is provided for him." The Court observed:

> Governments . . . quite properly spend vast sums of money to establish machinery to try defendants accused of crime. Lawyers to prosecute are everywhere deemed essential to protect the public's interest in an orderly society. Similarly, there are few defendants charged with crime, few indeed, who fail to hire the best lawyers they can get to prepare and present their defenses. [The implication of this is] that lawyers in criminal courts are necessities, not luxuries. The right of one charged with crime to counsel may not be deemed fundamental in some countries, but it is in ours.

On retrial, but now with the assistance of counsel, *D* was acquitted of the offense.

[4] Post-*Gideon* Law: The Misdemeanor Cases

[a] *Argersinger v. Hamlin*[17]

In *Argersinger*, the Supreme Court considered for the first time the applicability of *Gideon* to misdemeanor trials. In the case, *D*, an indigent, was charged with carrying a concealed weapon, a misdemeanor carrying a potential penalty of six-months imprisonment, a $1000 fine, or both. *D* requested, but was denied, the appointment of counsel. Consequently, he represented himself, was convicted, and was sentenced to 90 days in jail.

The state supreme court upheld the trial court's decision not to appoint counsel. It followed the line drawn by the Supreme Court in its Sixth Amendment trial-by-jury jurisprudence: it reasoned that the Sixth Amendment right to the assistance of counsel, like the right to trial by jury,[18] extends only to the trial of "non-petty" offenses, *i.e.*, offenses punishable by more than six-months imprisonment. Because *D*'s trial involved a "petty" offense (the maximum potential punishment for the offense was six-months imprisonment), *D* was not entitled to appointed counsel.

The Supreme Court, per Justice Douglas, overturned the conviction. It stated that the right to counsel "has a different genealogy" than the trial-by-jury right: "While there is historical support for limiting the . . . trial by jury to 'serious criminal cases,' there is no such support for a similar limitation on the right to assistance of counsel."

The Court indicated that although both *Gideon* and *Powell* involved felony trials, "their rationale has relevance to any criminal trial, where an accused is deprived of his liberty." It concluded that "the problems associated with misdemeanor and petty offenses" — legal complexities and the danger of "assembly-line

---

[17] 407 U.S. 25 (1972). *See generally* L. Herman, The Right to Counsel in Misdemeanor Court (Ohio State U. 1974); Duke, *The Right to Appointed Counsel: Argersinger and Beyond*, 12 Am. Crim. L. Rev. 601 (1975).

[18] Duncan v. Louisiana, 391 U.S. 145 (1968).

justice" that "looms large" in such cases — "often require the presence of counsel to insure the accused a fair trial."

Although the reasoning of *Argersinger* could apply to all misdemeanor cases, the Court's holding was limited: "[A]bsent a knowing and intelligent waiver, no person may be imprisoned for any offense, whether classified as petty, misdemeanor, or felony, unless he was represented by counsel at his trial." In other words, an indigent is entitled to the appointment of counsel if she actually, not merely potentially, will be jailed if she is convicted.

Justice Powell, with whom Justice Rehnquist joined, concurred in the result. He rejected the imprisonment/no-imprisonment line drawn by the majority, describing it as "illogical" and "without discernible support" in the Constitution.

Justice Powell argued that not all misdemeanor cases are complex, and the line between the difficult and simple ones is not drawn on the basis of whether the defendant is sentenced to imprisonment. Although he agreed that the right to a lawyer "does not mysteriously evaporate" when an indigent is charged with a misdemeanor, he would have applied the *Powell-Betts* special-circumstances rule in all petty-offense cases.

The concurring justices also criticized the majority for being "disquietingly barren of details" as to how the new rule would be implemented. Under *Argersinger*, the trial judge is faced with an "awkward dilemma." She must decide before trial — before evidence is presented — whether to appoint counsel in misdemeanor cases. If she does not appoint counsel, she cannot jail a convicted defendant, even for a day, no matter how justifiable such punishment might be. If the judge wishes to retain her option to incarcerate the defendant, she must provide counsel. The concurrence predicted that the effect of the Court's decision would be to overburden local courts, exacerbate delays, and increase court congestion.

[b] *Scott v. Illinois*[19]

In *Scott*, D, an indigent, was charged with theft, a misdemeanor that carried a potential penalty of one-year imprisonment, a $500 fine, or both. Denied the assistance of counsel, D was convicted and fined $50.

On appeal, D argued that although he was not imprisoned he should have been provided counsel at his trial. For various reasons, his contention was plausible. First, the Court's reasoning in *Argersinger* could apply with nearly equal force in non-jail cases.

Second, a *per se* rule — either that a lawyer is required in all petty offenses or, at least, in those in which imprisonment is authorized — would have resolved the "awkward dilemma" noted by the concurring justices in *Argersinger*.

Third, and perhaps most significantly, the crime for which D was prosecuted, although denominated as a misdemeanor, was not a petty offense. Because the potential penalty was one-year imprisonment, D was entitled to a jury trial. *Argersinger* had apparently concluded that the right to counsel is more encompassing than the jury-trial right; therefore, D's request for appointment of counsel should have been granted.

---

[19] 440 U.S. 367 (1979). *See generally* Herman & Thompson, *Scott v. Illinois and the Right to Counsel: A Decision in Search of a Doctrine*, 17 Am. Crim. L. Rev. 71 (1979).

Nonetheless, by a 5-4 vote, the Supreme Court left the counsel/no-counsel line where it had been drawn in *Argersinger*. It held that the Constitution requires "only that no indigent criminal defendant be sentenced to a term of imprisonment unless the State has afforded him the right to assistance of appointed counsel in his defense."

[c] *Baldasar v. Illinois*

The "awkward dilemma" facing judges as the result of *Argersinger* and *Scott* was complicated further by the Court's *per curiam* decision in *Baldasar v. Illinois*.[20]

In *Baldasar*, D was convicted of misdemeanor theft without the assistance of counsel at trial. Although he was subject to a potential punishment of one-year imprisonment, D was fined and sentenced to one-year probation. Because D was not jailed, the conviction was valid under *Scott*.

However, less than a year later D was prosecuted for another theft. Under state law at the time, a misdemeanor theft was elevated to a felony, with a potential prison term of three years, if a prior theft conviction were proved at trial. At the second trial, D was represented by counsel. His lawyer unsuccessfully argued that the first conviction could not be used to elevate the crime to a felony because he had not been represented by counsel at the prior trial. D was convicted by a jury and sentenced to enhanced imprisonment based on the prior conviction.

The Court, 5-4, reversed his conviction "for the reasons stated in the [various] concurring opinions" in the case. Although this leaves the reasoning of *Baldasar* somewhat obscure, apparently the Court concluded that, as explained by Justice Marshall in a three-justice concurrence, D's "prior conviction was not valid for all purposes. Specifically, under the rule of *Scott* and *Argersinger*, it was invalid for the purpose of depriving [D] of his liberty." In other words, because D could not have obtained the increased term of imprisonment at the second trial but for the conviction at his counsel-less first trial, his Sixth Amendment right to counsel was violated.

The dissenters understandably stated that the holding "undermines the rationale of *Scott* and *Argersinger* and leaves no coherent rationale in its place." It is illogical, they argued, to suggest that a misdemeanor conviction is valid, and therefore presumptively reliable, and yet hold that it cannot be used to enhance a defendant's sentence in a subsequent trial at which he is represented by counsel.

[5] Summary of the Law

The Supreme Court ruled in *Scott* that counsel does not have to be furnished to an indigent prosecuted for a serious, albeit misdemeanor, offense if he is not jailed upon conviction. It is plausible to reason that *Scott* narrows *Gideon sub silentio*: that is, that an indigent's right to the appointment of counsel, *even in felony cases*, is limited to those trials in which she receives a jail sentence as the result of the conviction.

This does not seem to be the rule. In *Baldasar*, the Court described the rule of *Scott* to be that "an uncounseled *misdemeanor* conviction is constitutionally valid

---

[20] 446 U.S. 222 (1980).

if the defendant is not incarcerated." As well, the four *Baldasar* dissenters stated that whereas *Gideon* "established the right to counsel in felony cases . . . misdemeanor convictions . . . have been treated differently."

Apparently, therefore, a felony/misdemeanor distinction has been drawn. That is, the cases discussed above can be summarized as follows. An indigent is constitutionally entitled to the appointment of counsel for: (1) all felony trials (*Gideon*); and (2) any misdemeanor trial in which the conviction for that misdemeanor results in incarceration, either for that offense (*Argersinger-Scott*) or as enhanced punishment in a subsequent prosecution (*Baldasar*).

If a defendant is actually (as in *Gideon*) or constructively (as in *Powell*) denied her constitutional right to the assistance of counsel at trial, any conviction that results must be reversed, *i.e.*, the error is never harmless.[21]

§ 177   The Right to Counsel: On Appeal

[A]   Overview

[1]   Inapplicability of the Sixth Amendment

By its language, the Sixth Amendment does not apply to criminal appeals. The amendment entitles a person to the assistance of counsel "for his *defence*" in "criminal *prosecutions*." When the trial is completed, the "prosecution" ends; on appeal, it is the defendant/appellant who seeks to upset the status quo, and it is the prosecutor who seeks to "defend" the conviction.

Despite the inapplicability of the Sixth Amendment to criminal appeals, state appellate procedures are subject to the standards of the Fourteenth Amendment equal protection and due process clauses.

[2]   The *Griffin* Equality Principle

In *Griffin v. Illinois*,[22] the Supreme Court held that a state that requires a defendant to furnish a trial transcript to the appellate court as a condition of hearing her appeal must provide the transcript at state expense for indigents.

Applying both due process and equal protection standards to reach this conclusion, Justice Black stated in his four-justice plurality opinion that:

> a State can no more discriminate on account of poverty than on account of religion, race, or color. . . . There can be no equal justice where the kind of trial a man gets depend on the amount of money he has. Destitute defendants must be afforded as adequate appellate review as defendants who have money enough to buy transcripts.

The *Griffin* equality principle has been applied in various contexts to ensure that indigent defendants at trial and on appeal obtain meaningful access to procedures

---

[21] See Strickland v. Washington, 466 U.S. 668, 692 (1984).
[22] 351 U.S. 12 (1956).

available to nonindigent persons.[23] It serves as the point of departure for consideration of the indigent's right to the assistance of counsel on appeal.

[B] First Appeal of Right

[1] Recognition of the Right to Assistance of Counsel

In *Douglas v. California*[24] the Supreme Court, per Justice Douglas, held that the Fourteenth Amendment requires a state to provide counsel for an indigent on her first statutory appeal of right.[25] In doing so, the Court invalidated a California rule that permitted appellate courts, on the request of an indigent for the assistance of appellate counsel, to look at the trial record to determine "whether it would be of advantage to the defendant or helpful to the appellate court to have counsel appointed."

Justice Douglas stated that although states do not have to provide absolute equality to the rich and the poor in their procedures, "where the merits of *the one and only appeal* an indigent has as of right are decided without the benefit of counsel, we think an unconstitutional line has been drawn between the rich and poor."

Without distinguishing between due process and equal protection principles, the Court concluded that it is impermissible to require an indigent appellant to "run the gantlet of a preliminary showing of merit," if persons wealthy enough to hire a lawyer do not have to face the same obstacle.

As Justice Douglas explained, the discrimination in the case was not between "possibly good and obviously bad cases," but between people rich enough to hire lawyers and those who were not. In this, the Court said, "[t]here is lacking that equality demanded by the Fourteenth Amendment. . . . The indigent . . . has only a right to a meaningless ritual, while the rich man has a meaningful appeal."

[2] Special Problem: Frivolous Appeals[26]

A component of the right to counsel on appeal is the right to "an active advocate, rather than a mere friend of the court assisting in a detached evaluation

---

[23] E.g., Ake v. Oklahoma, 470 U.S. 68 (1985) (due process requires that the state provide access to a psychiatrist to an indigent defendant who makes a preliminary showing that his sanity will be an issue at trial); Draper v. Washington, 372 U.S. 487 (1963) (a state rule providing for a free transcript only if the defendant can convince the trial judge that the appeal is non-frivolous violates the Fourteenth Amendment); Burns v. Ohio, 360 U.S. 252 (1959) (a state rule that requires indigent defendants to pay a fee before filing a notice of appeal violates *Griffin*).

[24] 372 U.S. 353 (1963).

[25] Although a convicted defendant has no constitutional right to appeal, every state permits at least one appeal of right after conviction. Thereafter, courts have discretion not to hear appeals of criminal convictions.

[26] *See generally* Comment, *The Right to Counsel in "Frivolous" Criminal Appeals: A Reevaluation of the Guarantees of Anders v. California*, 67 Texas L. Rev. 181 (1988).

of the appellant's claim."[27] However, the defendant has no constitutional right to demand that her attorney act unethically by prosecuting a frivolous appeal.[28]

Beginning with *Anders v. California*,[29] the Supreme Court has dealt with these potentially conflicting principles by holding that a state appellate court may not refuse to provide counsel to brief and argue an indigent's first appeal of right merely on the basis of a conclusory statement by the appointed counsel that the appeal is frivolous and that she wishes to be removed from the case.[30]

Under *Anders*, an indigent is entitled to have her appointed lawyer conduct "the same diligent and thorough evaluation of the case as a retained lawyer before concluding that an appeal is frivolous."[31] When appointed counsel determines that an appeal is nonmeritorious, however, she may so advise the court and request permission to withdraw. However, the request must be accompanied by what has come to be known as an *Anders* brief, *i.e.*, a "brief referring to anything in the record that might arguably support the appeal."[32] The purpose of the brief is to ensure the court that counsel has fully performed her duty to support her client's appeal to the best of her ability, as well as to assist it to determine whether the appeal is frivolous.

The brief must then be furnished to the indigent appellant, who may raise any additional points that she chooses. Then, the appellate court, after a full examination of the materials, decides whether the case is "wholly frivolous." If it is not wholly frivolous, new counsel must be appointed to represent the appellant. If it determines that the appeal is frivolous, it may proceed to consider the case on the merits without the assistance of counsel or a traditional brief.

If the appellate court's decision is later found to be erroneous — that is, if it should have appointed counsel to file a traditional brief in the case — the error is prejudicial *per se,* and the defendant is entitled to a new appeal, this time with the assistance of appointed counsel.[33]

[C] Discretionary Appeals

In *Ross v. Moffitt*,[34] the Supreme Court held that the Fourteenth Amendment does not require the appointment of counsel to assist indigent appellants in their second, discretionary state appeals and for applications for review in the United

---

[27] Evitts v. Lucey, 469 U.S. 387, 394 (1985).

[28] McCoy v. Court of Appeals of Wisconsin, Dist. 1, 486 U.S. 429, 436 (1988) (*citing* American Bar Association, Standards for Criminal Justice, Commentary to 4-3.9 (2d ed. 1980).

[29] 386 U.S. 738 (1967).

[30] The rules laid down in *Anders*, and described in the text *infra*, do not apply if the appellant has no constitutional right to the assistance of counsel, *i.e.*, on appeals that do not fall within the *Douglas* rule. Pennsylvania v. Finley, 481 U.S. 551 (1987).

[31] McCoy v. Court of Appeals of Wisconsin, Dist. 1, 486 U.S. at 438 (explaining the *Anders* rule).

[32] A state may also require that counsel include citations to case or statutory authority supporting her conclusion that the appeal is frivolous. McCoy v. Court of Appeals of Wisconsin, Dist. 1, 486 U.S. 429 (1988).

[33] Penson v. Ohio, 488 U.S. 75 (1988).

[34] 417 U.S. 600 (1974).

States Supreme Court. Since *Ross* was decided, the Court has extended the no-right-to-counsel principle to state *habeas corpus* proceedings.[35]

In *Ross*, the Court discussed separately the issues of due process (which "emphasizes fairness between the State and the individual dealing with the State") and equal protection (which "emphasizes disparity in treatment by a State between classes of individuals whose situations are arguably indistinguishable"), although there was little difference in the ultimate analysis.

In its due process discussion, the Court focused on the difference between trials and appeals: whereas states cannot dispense with trials, they do not have to permit appeals. Therefore, when appeals are permitted, it "does not automatically mean that a State then acts unfairly by refusing to provide counsel to indigent defendants at every stage of the way." According to *Ross*, the due process clause requires only that indigents not be singled out "and denied meaningful access [to appellate courts] . . . because of their poverty."

In the Court's equal protection discussion, it gave lip service to the *Griffin* equality principle, but it emphasized language in both *Griffin* and *Douglas* that stated that absolute equality between the rich and poor is not constitutionally required. According to *Ross*, the equal protection clause does not require a state "to duplicate the legal arsenal that may be privately retained by a criminal defendant." All that the constitutional provision demands, the Court said, is that the indigent have "an adequate opportunity to present his claims fairly in the context of the . . . appellate process."

The Court conceded that "a skilled lawyer, particularly one trained in the somewhat arcane art of preparing petitions for discretionary review, would . . . prove helpful to any litigant able to employ" the lawyer. Nonetheless, it concluded that indigents on discretionary appeals have an "adequate opportunity" to present their claims (or, in due process terms, have "meaningful access" to appellate review) without the assistance of counsel.

The Court pointed out that with discretionary appeals, the appellate court will have various documents to consider: a transcript or other record of the trial proceedings; a brief on the appellant's behalf filed by her attorney during the first (*Douglas*) appeal of right; often an opinion of the lower court disposing of the case; and any submission by the indigent herself. The Supreme Court concluded that with these materials the appellate court has "an adequate basis on which to base its decision to grant or deny review."

---

[35] Pennsylvania v. Finley, 481 U.S. 551 (1987); Murray v. Giarratano, 109 S.Ct. 2765 (1989) (death penalty appeal) (plurality opinion).

§ 178   The Right of Self-Representation[36]

[A]   *Faretta v. California*

[1]   Recognition of the Right

In *Faretta*,[37] the Supreme Court held that a defendant has a constitutional right voluntarily and knowingly to waive her right to the assistance of counsel and to represent herself at trial. In essence, the Sixth Amendment right-to-counsel provision includes two rights: the right of a criminal defendant to the assistance of counsel and an independent right of self-representation.

In *Faretta*, *D*, charged with theft, requested permission to represent himself at trial. The judge originally agreed to the request, but later changed his mind when *D* failed adequately to answer various questions intended to determine his knowledge of applicable procedural and evidentiary law. Represented at his trial by a public defender, *D* was convicted.

The Supreme Court, per Justice Stewart, reversed the conviction, concluding that *D* had a constitutional right to represent himself. According to Justice Stewart, the Sixth Amendment "does not provide merely that a defense shall be made for the accused; it grants to the accused personally the right to make the defense."

According to *Faretta*, the personal nature of the right is evident from the fact that it is the defendant, and not counsel, who must be informed of the nature of the charges, who has the right to confront accusers, and who must be accorded compulsory process for obtaining witnesses. According to the Court, "the right to defend is given directly to the accused; for it is he who suffers the consequences if the defense fails."

The Court also found support for the right of self-representation in the language of the Sixth Amendment itself, which speaks of the right of the defendant to the "assistance" of counsel. Thus, the lawyer is the assistant; the defendant is the master.[38]

Justice Blackmun, joined by Chief Justice Burger and Justice Rehnquist, dissented. They argued that the fact that Sixth Amendment rights are personal does not "guarantee[] any particular procedural method of asserting those rights." According to the dissenters, the Sixth Amendment does not require "the States to subordinate the solemn business of conducting a criminal prosecution to the

---

[36] *See generally* Chused, *Faretta and the Personal Defense: The Role of a Represented Defendant in Trial Tactics*, 65 Calif. L. Rev. 636 (1977).

[37] 422 U.S. 806 (1975).

[38] The majority also found support for the right of self-representation in English law and in the even "more fervent" attitude of American colonists, who believed that they possessed a "natural right" of self-representation.

The dissent questioned the Court's historical analysis. It pointed out that at the time of the framing of the Sixth Amendment, criminal defendants had a statutory right of self-representation and the right to the assistance of counsel. The fact that the framers expressly provided a constitutional right to the assistance of counsel but were silent regarding self—representation supports the view, the dissenters claimed, that the framers intended to dispense with the latter right.

whimsical — albeit voluntary — caprice of every accused who wishes to use his trial as a vehicle for personal or political self-gratification."

[2] Reflections Regarding the Right

Justice Stewart conceded in *Faretta* that "[t]here can be no blinking the fact that the right of an accused to conduct his own defense seems to cut against the grain of this Court's [prior right-to-counsel] decisions."

There is irony in this. Among the justices forming the majority in *Faretta* — an opinion that says, in essence, that a defendant has the right to forego the "necessity, not luxury"[39] of the assistance of counsel — were those who had argued most strenuously for the expansion of the right to counsel. Meanwhile, it was the dissenters — members of the Court not generally sympathetic to the extension of the Sixth Amendment right — who were called on to point out that "representation by counsel is essential to ensure a fair trial."

The essence of *Faretta* is that a defendant has a protectible right of autonomy. As it is the defendant, not the lawyer, who will suffer the consequences of a conviction, it is the accused's personal right to decide whether counsel is a benefit or a detriment. As Justice Stewart explained, "whatever else may be said of those who wrote the Bill of Rights, surely there can be no doubt that they understood the inestimable worth of free choice." Even if the defendant's freely-willed decision is "ultimately to his detriment, [the] choice must be honored out of 'that respect for the individual which is the lifeblood of the law.' "[40]

In dissent, Justice Blackmun quoted the proverb that "one who is his own lawyer has a fool for a client." He needled the majority by stating that the Court "now bestows a *constitutional* right on one to make a fool of himself." The essence of the Court's holding, as he put it, is that "so long as the accused is willing to the pay the consequences of his folly, there is no reason for not allowing a defendant the right. . . ."

Justice Stewart's answer to the dissenters was that "[p]ersonal liberties are not rooted in the law of averages." As he pointed out, "it is not inconceivable that in some rare instances, the defendant might in fact present his case more effectively by conducting his own defense."

He is correct, of course, but it is also the case, as the majority conceded, that "in most criminal prosecutions defendants could better defend with counsel's guidance than by their own unskilled efforts." And, as important as the right of autonomy is, it is not the only value at stake in criminal trials.

The majority opinion runs counter to "the established principle that the interest of the State in a criminal prosecution 'is not that it shall win a case, but that justice shall be done.' "[41] Moreover, as the Court has subsequently pointed out, "courts have an independent interest in ensuring that . . . legal proceedings appear fair to all who observe them."[42] *Faretta* threatens these interests.

---

[39] *See* § 175 *supra.*

[40] *Faretta*, 422 U.S. at 834 (*quoting* Illinois v. Allen, 397 U.S. 337, 350-51 (1970)).

[41] *Id.* at 849 (Blackmun, J., dissenting) (*quoting* Berger v. United States, 295 U.S. 78, 88 (1935)).

[42] Wheat v. United States, 486 U.S. 153, 160 (1988).

[B] Procedural Issues

[1] Informing the Accused of the Right

Under *Faretta*, the right of self-representation is independent of the right to the assistance of counsel. Therefore, courts are confronted with a dilemma: must the accused be informed of both rights and then waive one of them?

In general, the lower courts have held that a defendant does not need to be informed of her right of self-representation,[43] although she must be informed of her right to the assistance of counsel.[44] However, because self-representation is an independent right, and not simply a waiver of the right to counsel, a defendant who expresses the wish to represent herself must be permitted to do so as long she is mentally competent to understand the basic nature of the right that she is foregoing.

Specifically, the Court stated in *Faretta* that a defendant "should be made aware of the dangers and disadvantages of self-representation, so that the record will establish that 'he knows what he is doing and his choice is made with eyes open.' "[45]

[2] Timeliness of the Request

A defendant must assert her right of self-representation in timely fashion. In *Faretta*, the Court pointed out that *D*'s request was made "well before" the trial began. The implication is that a defendant must not only make the request before the trial begins, but she must make it sufficiently early that her request does not unduly delay orderly processes.

[3] Hybrid Representation

It might seem that a defendant should be entitled to assert simultaneously both of her Sixth Amendment rights, *i.e.*, her right to the assistance of counsel and to represent herself. Nonetheless, the nearly-universal view of the lower courts is that there is no constitutional right to "hybrid" representation,[46] although trial courts may permit it in their discretion and do so on occasion.

The hybrid arrangement arguably allows the defendant the "best of both worlds." She has the opportunity to display herself to the jury in a favorable fashion, while simultaneously obtaining the benefits of the lawyer's expertise.

[4] Standby Counsel

Faretta permits a trial court to appoint standby counsel in self-representation cases. The purpose of standby counsel is to assist the defendant if and when she seeks help, and to take over the case if self-representation must be terminated during trial. However, in *McKaskle v. Wiggins*,[47] the Court's first post-*Faretta*

---

[43] *See* 2 W. LaFave & J. Israel, Criminal Procedure § 11.5(b) (West 1986).

[44] *E.g.*, FRCP 5(c).

[45] *Faretta*, 422 U.S. at 835 (*quoting* Adams v. United States ex. rel. McCann, 317 U.S. 269, 279 (1942)).

[46] 2 W. LaFave & J. Israel, n. 43 *supra*, at § 11(f).

[47] 465 U.S. 168 (1984).

discussion of the role of standby counsel, the justices upheld a conviction in which standby counsel provided unsolicited, at times unwanted, "assistance."

In *Wiggins*, the Court, per Justice O'Connor, stated that the right of self-representation "exists to affirm the dignity and autonomy of the accused and to allow the presentation of what may, at least occasionally, be the accused's best possible defense." Therefore, in evaluating whether a defendant's self-representation rights have been vindicated, "the primary focus must be on whether the defendant had a fair chance to present the case in his own way."

Under *Wiggins*, the right of self-representation is not violated unless standby counsel substantially interferes with "significant tactical decisions" of the defendant, "control[s] the questioning of witnesses," speaks in defendant's place against her wishes "on . . . matter[s] of importance," or in some other way "destroy[s] the jury's perception that the defendant is representing" herself.

In the case, the Court concluded that *D*'s standby counsel did not violate his right of self-representation, although the lawyer intervened without *D*'s permission, and sometimes over his vocal objection, more than 50 times during the three-day trial. In part, the Court refused to disapprove of counsel's actions because some of the intrusions occurred outside the presence of the jury, and therefore did not destroy its perception that *D* was representing himself, and also because *D* wavered during the trial, sometimes vehemently objecting to standby counsel's participation but other times inviting it.

[5] Legal Significance of Poor Self-Representation

A defendant has a constitutional right to effective assistance of counsel.[48] However, a defendant who chooses to represent himself "cannot thereafter complain that the quality of his defense amounted to a denial of 'effective assistance of counsel.' "[49]

[6] Legal Effect of an Erroneous Denial of the Right

If a court wrongfully refuses to permit the defendant to represent herself at trial or if the right is violated by standby counsel, any subsequent conviction must be reversed.

The Supreme Court has reasoned that because the right of self-representation serves to affirm a defendant's freedom of choice, denial of the right "is not amenable to 'harmless error' analysis. The right is either respected or denied; its deprivation cannot [ever] be harmless."[50]

---

[48] *See* § 181 *infra*.

[49] *Faretta*, 422 U.S. at 835 n.46; McKaskle v. Wiggins, 465 U.S. at 177 n.8.

[50] McKaskle, 465 U.S. at 177 n.8.

§ 179   The Right to Representation by One's Preferred Attorney[51]

[A]   In General

The Sixth Amendment comprehends the right of a nonindigent defendant "to select and be represented by one's preferred attorney."[52] With few exceptions, courts have not granted indigents a similar right to choose their appointed counsel.[53]

The right of a defendant to hire and be represented by the attorney of her choice is not unqualified. First, although defense counsel "should seek to establish a relationship of trust and confidence with the accused,"[54] a defendant has no Sixth Amendment right to a "meaningful" attorney-client relationship.[55]

Second, a defendant is not permitted to be represented by a non-attorney, except herself.[56] Third, a defendant may not be represented by an attorney who has a conflict of interest, even if the defendant is willing to accept the risks inherent in such representation.[57]

Fourth, a defendant "may not insist on representation by an attorney he cannot afford."[58] This latter limitation is of particular significance in view of the comparatively recent enactment of statutes that permit the government to seize assets, including money that would be used to pay for an attorney, that allegedly were obtained illegally. This issue is discussed immediately below.

[B]   Special Problem: Seizing Lawyers' Fees

[1]   The Law

In two cases, *Caplin & Drysdale, Chartered v. United States*[59] and *United States v. Monsanto,*[60] the Supreme Court held, 5-4, that the right to counsel is not violated if a court, pursuant to statute,[61] grants an *ex parte* motion by the government to freeze the defendant's assets, including assets that would be used to pay for legal representation, on the ground that they were obtained as a result of illegal drug activities; nor is the Sixth Amendment violated by an order that any monies paid to defense counsel be recaptured if the client is convicted of such drug activities.

---

[51] *See generally* Green, *"Through a Glass Darkly": How the Court Sees Motions to Disqualify Criminal Defense Lawyers,* 89 Colum. L. Rev. 1201 (1989); Tague, *An Indigent's Right to the Attorney of His Choice,* 27 Stan. L. Rev. 73 (1974).

[52] Wheat v. United States, 486 U.S. at 159.

[53] Tague, n. 51 *supra,* at 79-80.

[54] American Bar Association, Standards for Criminal Justice 4-3.1 (Little Brown 2d. ed. 1980).

[55] Morris v. Slappy, 461 U.S. 1 (1983).

[56] *See* Wheat v. United States, 486 U.S. at 159.

[57] *See* § 182[D] *infra.*

[58] *Wheat,* 486 U.S. at 159.

[59] 109 S.Ct. 2646 (1989).

[60] 109 S.Ct. 2657 (1989).

[61] 21 U.S.C. § 831.

The Court reasoned that forfeiture statutes of the sort involved in these two cases do not impinge on a defendant's constitutional right to counsel of choice, because they do not prevent the defendant from hiring any attorney whom she can afford or who is willing to represent her without assurances that she will have adequate funds. Furthermore, even if such statutes prevent her from hiring an attorney, the right to the counsel of one's choice encompasses only the right to spend one's own money, and not to spend another person's money, to hire a lawyer.

[2] The Objection: The Value of Private Counsel

Justice Blackmun, joined by Justices Brennan, Marshall, and Stevens, dissented in *Caplin & Drysdale* and *Monsanto*. They argued "that it is unseemly and unjust for the Government to beggar those it prosecutes in order to disable their defense at trial." Perhaps the most interesting feature of the dissent is its examination of the reasons why the four dissenters believe that a defendant wealthy enough to hire an attorney is usually better served than one who must accept appointed counsel.

First, to be an effective advocate, an attorney needs her client's trust. Trust is fostered when a defendant can choose her own attorney. It is undermined, the dissenters stated, "[w]hen the Government insists upon the right to choose the defendant's counsel" for her.

Second, the right to hire private counsel "serves to assure some modicum of equality between the government and those it chooses to prosecute." The government expends considerable resources to prosecute persons accused of crime, "[b]ut when the Government provides for appointed counsel, there is no guarantee that levels of compensation and staffing will be even average."[62]

Third, according to the dissent, the "socialization" of criminal-defense representation too easily excludes "the maverick and risk-taker, [whose approach] might not fit into the structured environment of a public defender's office, or that might displease a judge whose preference for non-confrontational styles of advocacy might influence the judge's appointment decisions."[63]

Finally, private attorneys can more easily specialize in complex areas of the criminal law than can public defenders, who must have a broader — but necessarily thinner — range of skills.

---

[62] For example, in 1985, public expenditures on the defense of indigents was only 26% of that spent on their prosecution. *See* Sourcebook of Criminal Justice Statistics — 1986, Table 1.1 (U.S. Dept. of Justice 1987). *See also* U.S. Dept. of Justice, Office of Justice Programs, Bureau of Justice Statistics, *Justice Expenditure and Employment, 1988* 10 (reporting that expenditures at the state and local level for "prosecution and legal services" outpaced "public defense" expenditures, by approximately a three to one margin in 1988).

[63] For a contrary view, *see* L. McIntyre, The Public Defender: The Practice of Law in the Shadows of Repute (U. Chicago Press 1987).

§ 180   Interference With The Right to Counsel

The right to counsel includes the right "that there be no restrictions upon the functions of counsel in defending a criminal prosecution in accord with the traditions of the adversary [system] . . . that has been constitutionalized in the Sixth and Fourteenth Amendments."[64]

This means, among other things, that the government may not restrict defense counsel's decision on whether and when in the course of the presentation of the defendant's case the accused will testify,[65] may not prevent counsel from eliciting testimony from her client through direct examination,[66] and may not deny counsel the opportunity to make a summation to the jury.[67]

The Constitution is also violated if a trial judge prohibits a defendant from consulting with her attorney during an overnight recess, even if the recess is called while the defendant is on the witness stand and is about to be cross-examined by the prosecutor.[68] However, a judge may prohibit consultation between the defendant and her counsel during a brief same-day recess, while the accused is testifying.[69]

Any direct interference by the government with the defendant's right to the assistance of counsel constitutes *per se* prejudicial error.[70]

§ 181   Effective Assistance of Counsel: General Principles[71]

[A]   Nature of the Issue

The Supreme Court has observed that the fact "[t]hat a person who happens to be a lawyer is present at trial alongside the accused . . . is not enough to satisfy" the Sixth Amendment.[72] If the Sixth Amendment "is to serve its purpose, defendants cannot be left to the mercies of incompetent counsel. . . ."[73] The

---

[64] Herring v. New York, 422 U.S. 853, 857 (1975).

[65] Brooks v. Tennessee, 406 U.S. 605 (1972) (applying the Fifth Amendment self-incrimination and due process clauses).

[66] Ferguson v. Georgia, 365 U.S. 570 (1961).

[67] Herring v. New York, 422 U.S. 853 (1975).

[68] Geders v. United States, 425 U.S. 80 (1976).

[69] Perry v. Leeke, 488 U.S. 272 (1989).

[70] Strickland v. Washington, 466 U.S. 668, 686 (1984).

[71] *See generally* L. McIntyre, n. 63 *supra*; D. Wasserman, The Appellate Defender as Monitor, Watchdog, and Gadfly (Occasional Papers from The Center for Research in Crime and Justice, New York University School of Law, VII, 1989); Bazelon, *The Realities of Gideon and Argersinger*, 64 Geo.L.J. 811 (1976); Berger, *The Supreme Court and Defense Counsel: Old Roads, New Paths — A Dead End?*, 86 Colum. L. Rev. 9 (1986); Genego, *The Future of Effective Assistance of Counsel: Performance Standards and Competent Representation*, 22 Am. Crim. L. Rev. 181 (1984); McConville & Mirsky, *Criminal Defense of the Poor in New York City*, 15 N.Y.U. Law & Soc. Change 581 (1987); Willcox & Bloustein, n. 12 *supra*.

[72] Strickland v. Washington, 466 U.S. at 685.

[73] McMann v. Richardson, 397 U.S. 759, 771 (1970).

Constitution requries lawyers, whether retained or appointed, to provide effective assistance to their clients at trial and on the first appeal of right.[74]

Effective representation entails various duties, among them the following. First, the lawyer owes her client "a duty of loyalty, a duty to avoid conflicts of interest."[75] Second, she must consult with her client on important decisions and keep her informed on critical developments in the pre-trial process.[76] Third, counsel must "bring to bear such skill and knowledge as will render the trial a reliable adversarial process."[77]

Issues regarding the effectiveness of the assistance of counsel are especially acute in the representation of indigents, who must rely on often-harried lawyers in understaffed and underfinanced public-defender offices or on private attorneys who by contract or judicial appointment represent them, often with less than complete vigor.

For example, some studies report that private attorneys who are assigned to represent indigents at trial frequently fail to perform such basic responsibilities as interviewing their clients, investigating the facts underlying the charges, and filing written motions to suppress evidence or to discover evidence from the prosecutor.[78]

[B] "Ineffective Assistance": The *Strickland* Test

[1] General Principles

The Supreme Court defined "ineffective assistance of counsel" for the first time in *Strickland v. Washington*.[79] The standard announced in the case applies in the context of criminal trials and capital sentencing hearings.[80]

---

[74] The due process clause, rather than the Sixth Amendment, entitles a convicted defendant to the effective assistance of counsel on her first appeal of right. Evitts v. Lucey, 469 U.S. 387 (1985). On discretionary appeals, for which there is no constitutional right to the assistance of counsel, *see* § 177[C] *supra*, there is also no constitutional right to effective assistance. *Evitts* at 396 n.7.

[75] Strickland v. Washington, 466 U.S. at 688; *see* American Bar Association, Model Rules of Professional Conduct, Rule 1.7, Comment at 9 (1983) (hereafter, Model Rules). This right is discussed in § 182 *infra*.

[76] *See* Model Rules, n. 75 *supra*, Rules 1.2(a) and 1.4.

[77] *Id.*, Rule 1.1.

[78] McConville & Mirsky, n. 71 *supra*, at 746-47. The authors' study of New York County during the mid-1980s indicates that assigned counsel interviewed their clients in only 26 percent of homicide cases and 18 percent of all other felonies; they conducted investigations in 27 percent of homicide cases and 12 percent of other felony cases; and they filed written motions in only a quarter of the homicide cases, and in 20 percent of other cases.

[79] 466 U.S. 668 (1984). Until *Strickland*, lower courts generally applied one of two "ineffectiveness" tests. Some courts held that assistance was constitutionally inadequate if it was "such a kind as to shock the conscience of the court and make the proceedings a farce and mockery of justice." *E.g.*, United States v. Wright, 176 F.2d 376, 379 (2d Cir. 1949), *cert. denied*, 338 U.S. 950 (1950). Other courts interpreted the Sixth Amendment to require "reasonably competent assistance of an attorney acting as a diligent and conscientious advocate" of her client. *E.g.*, United States v. DeCoster, 487 F.2d 1197, 1202 (D.C. Cir. 1973).

According to the Court, the "benchmark" for evaluating a claim of ineffective assistance of counsel is "whether counsel's conduct so undermined the proper functioning of the adversarial process that the trial [or capital sentencing hearing] cannot be relied on as having produced a just result." According to *Strickland*, the purpose of the Sixth Amendment right-to-counsel provision "is simply to ensure that criminal defendants receive a fair trial."

Under *Strickland*, the claim of a convicted defendant that her lawyer's representation was constitutionally ineffective has two prongs. Both elements must be proved if the defendant is to show that her conviction or resulting death sentence "resulted from a breakdown in the adversary process that renders the result unreliable."

[2]   The First Prong: The Deficiency of Representation

[a]   The Standard

The defendant must prove that her counsel's performance was constitutionally deficient, that is, that the "errors [were] so serious that counsel was not functioning as the 'counsel' guaranteed the defendant by the Sixth Amendment."

Strickland eschewed explicit guidelines for effective representation. The inquiry is simply "whether counsel's assistance was reasonable considering all the circumstances." Prevailing norms of practice, as manifested in ethical canons and other guidelines,[81] "are guides to determining what is reasonable, but they are only guides." Thus, under *Strickland*, the breach of an ethical canon or divergence from other detailed rules does not by itself prove ineffectiveness of representation.[82]

The *Strickland* "deficiency" test is not easy to satisfy. The defendant must identify with precision the acts or omissions that she claims were constitutionally unreasonable. Further, the court evaluating the claim must consider the issue from the lawyer's perspective at the time of the act or omission, rather than "second-guess" counsel's performance with the "distorting effects of hindsight." The court's scrutiny "must be highly deferential": it "must indulge a strong presumption that counsel's conduct falls within the wide range of reasonable professional assistance."

Strategic decisions made by the lawyer are "virtually unchallengeable" if they were made after thorough investigation of the law and facts relevant to the case. Strategic choices made after "less than complete investigations are reasonable precisely to the extent that reasonable professional judgments support the limitations on investigation."

---

[80] A slightly different version of the *Strickland* test is used for the evaluation of the effectiveness of counsel during the negotiations that result in a guilty plea. *See* § 195[C][4] *infra*.

[81] *E.g.*, American Bar Association, Standard for Criminal Justice 4-1.1 to 4-8.6 (Little, Brown 2d ed. 1980) ("The Defense Function").

[82] On the other hand, *conformity* with applicable ethical canons may immunize defense counsel from a successful claim of ineffectiveness. *See* § 183 *infra*.

[b] Application of the Standard: Case Law

It is difficult for a defendant to prove that her counsel performed inadequately. The difficulty is evident in *Strickland* itself. Over his lawyer's objection, *D* pleaded guilty to three counts of capital murder. *D* told the judge at the time that he had no significant prior criminal record, that he had acted under extreme stress due to economic problems in his family, but that he accepted responsibility for the crimes. The judge stated that he had "a great deal of respect" for persons who admit their responsibility, but that he was not prejudging the sentencing issue.

D's objection to his lawyer's conduct related to counsel's post-plea preparation for, and conduct at, the capital sentencing hearing. *D* alleged various omissions on his lawyer's part, including his failure to request a psychiatric report, to investigate and present character witnesses at the hearing, to seek a presentence investigation report, and to present "meaningful" arguments for leniency to the sentencing judge.

The Court found all of these claims unpersuasive. It was satisfied that counsel, after talking to his client and *D*'s wife and mother, made a strategic decision that the best approach was to argue that *D*'s emotional stress mitigated his blameworthiness for the murders, and to rely on his client's acceptance of responsibility for the crimes. Counsel did not request a presentence report because he learned from his investigation that D had a somewhat more serious criminal history than he had disclosed to the judge.

The Court stated that "although counsel understandably felt hopeless about [*D*'s] prospects, . . . nothing in the record indicates . . . that counsel's sense of hopelessness distorted his personal judgment." It concluded that the lawyer's behavior "was well within the range of professionally reasonable judgments."

The Court demonstrated even greater deference to defense counsel's judgment in *Burger v. Kemp*.[83] In *Burger*, *D*'s counsel offered no mitigating evidence whatsoever during two capital-sentencing hearings, although he could have presented evidence that his client, a minor, had no adult criminal record, that his I.Q. was only 82, and that he "had an exceptionally unhappy and unstable childhood."

D's lawyer was aware of some, but not all, of his client's background. Prior to the hearing, he had talked to *D*'s mother several times, to an out-of-state lawyer who had served as his client's "big brother" and who offered to come to the hearing to testify, and to a psychiatrist who had conducted a pre-trial examination of his client. Counsel had also reviewed various psychologists' reports based on meetings with *D* before the crime was committed.

The Supreme Court held, 5-4, that the lawyer's conduct was not deficient. It conceded that he "could well have made a more thorough investigation than he did." However, the Court stated that counsel's decision not to conduct an "all-out investigation" into his client's background was supported by reasonable professional judgment, in that his interviews and studies of the reports indicated that "an explanation of [*D*'s] history would not have minimized the risk of the death penalty."

---

[83] 483 U.S. 776 (1987).

Strickland and *Burger* involved strategic decisions by defense counsel. On the other hand, when counsel's alleged ineffectiveness is linked to ignorance of applicable law, proof that the performance was deficient is less difficult.

For example, in *Kimmelman v. Morrison*[84] defense counsel failed to file a timely motion to suppress evidence obtained in violation of the Fourth Amendment. The lawyer did not make the motion because he was unaware of the search that resulted in the seizure of highly incriminating evidence; his lack of knowledge of the search was the result of his failure to request discovery, which in turn was based on his mistaken belief that the prosecutor was required on his own initiative to turn over to the defense all of the incriminating evidence in his possession.

The Court, by a 6-3 vote, reversed the conviction, holding that, although counsel's representation of his client at trial was "creditable," his failure to conduct the pre-trial discovery in this case, which would have put him on notice of the incriminating evidence that might have been suppressed, was contrary to prevailing professional norms.

[3] The Second Prong: Prejudice

[a] The Standard

To successfully prove inadequacy of counsel, the defendant must show that her counsel's deficiencies prejudiced her, in that, as *Strickland* put it, the "errors were so serious as to deprive the defendant of a fair trial, a trial whose result is reliable."

To prove prejudice, "[t]he defendant must show that there is a reasonable probability that, but for counsel's unprofessional errors, the result of the proceeding would have been different." Under this test, "reasonable probability is a probability sufficient to undermine confidence in the outcome."

Although the *Strickland* Court rejected any mathematical formula to measure "reasonable probability," it stated that the defendant must prove more than simply that the error "had some conceivable effect on the outcome of the proceeding"; on the other hand, she does not need to show that it is more likely than not that counsel's deficient conduct affected the outcome.

Generally speaking, in measuring prejudice, a reviewing court "should proceed on the assumption that the decisionmaker is reasonably, conscientiously, and impartially applying the standards that govern the decision." That is, it is irrelevant to the defendant's prejudice claim that the particular judge might have had an idiosyncratic approach to the law or to sentencing decisions; what matters is whether counsel's errors would have effected the outcome of a reasonable decisionmaker.

[b] Application of the Standard; Case Law

The Court in *Strickland* stated that a defendant is not prejudiced unless her counsel's deficiencies rendered the trial unreliable. This does not mean, however, that factually guilty defendants cannot be prejudiced by ineffective representation. It does mean, however, that the defendant must show that there is a reasonable probability that, but for the deficient conduct, a more favorable *legal* result would have occurred.

---

[84] 477 U.S. 365 (1986).

For example, consider *Kimmelman v. Morrison*,[85] in which *D*'s lawyer unreasonably failed to raise a Fourth Amendment claim that arguably would have resulted in the exclusion of reliable, but unconstitutionally seized, evidence of *D*'s guilt.

The *Kimmelman* Court did not determine whether counsel's deficient conduct prejudiced his client. Instead, it remanded the case to a lower court to conduct a hearing on the matter. However, it stated that to win his Sixth Amendment claim *D* would have to prove that it was reasonably probable that he would have won his Fourth Amendment claim if it had been properly made and, further, that in the absence of the incriminating evidence "there is a reasonable probability that the [the factfinder] . . . would have had a reasonable doubt as to [*D*'s] guilt."

Justice Powell, joined by Chief Justice Burger and Justice Rehnquist, disagreed with this analysis. Justice Powell argued that the alleged prejudice suffered by *D* was "the absence of a windfall." The fact that *D*'s lawyer failed to make a motion that arguably would have resulted in the exclusion of reliable incriminating evidence did not affect "the fundamental fairness of the trial. . . . [O]ur reasoning in *Strickland* strongly suggests that such harm does not amount to prejudicial ineffective assistance of counsel under the Sixth Amendment."

§ 182 Effective Assistance of Counsel: Conflicts of Interest[86]

[A] Nature of the Issue

A defendant is entitled to the undivided loyalty of her attorney. However, when one attorney or law firm[87] represents multiple clients, especially if they are co-defendants, a risk is created that the interests of the clients will clash, and that the attorney (or firm) will be unable to represent all of the clients effectively. For this reason, joint representation is ordinarily unethical if the representation of one client will materially limit counsel's ability to represent another client.[88]

A breach of ethical standards, however, does not in itself constitute a violation of the Sixth Amendment. The subsections that follow relate to the constitutional right to conflict-free legal representation.

---

[85] *Id.*

[86] *See generally* Geer, *Representation of Multiple Criminal Defendants: Conflicts of Interest and the Professional Responsibility of the Defense Attorney*, 62 Minn. L. Rev. 119 (1978); Green, n. 51 *supra*; Moore, *Conflicts of Interest in the Simultaneous Representation of Multiple Clients*, 61 Texas L. Rev. 211 (1985); Tague, *Multiple Representation and Conflicts of Interest in Criminal Cases*, 67 Geo.L.J. 1075 (1979).

[87] Although the Supreme Court has acknowledged that "[t]here is certainly much substance to [the] argument that the appointment of two partners to represent coindictees . . . creates a possible conflict of interest," it has only assumed without deciding that law partners should be treated as if they were one attorney for purposes of conflict-of-interest analysis. Burger v. Kemp, 483 U.S. at 783.

[88] Model Rules, n. 75 *supra*, Rule 1.7(a)-(b).

[B]　Pre-Trial Procedures to Avoid Conflicts

The Supreme Court ruled in *Holloway v. Arkansas*[89] that when an attorney representing co-defendants makes a timely pretrial motion for appointment of separate counsel, based on her assertion of a potential conflict of interest, a trial judge is required either to grant the motion or "to take adequate steps to ascertain whether the risk [is] too remote to warrant separate counsel." Failure of the judge to grant the motion or, at least, to conduct a hearing on the matter constitutes *per se* prejudicial error.

According to *Holloway*, joint representation is constitutionally suspect. Because a defense lawyer is in a better position than a court to know prior to trial whether a conflict exists or may develop — *i.e.*, she is more familiar with the facts of the case, and may become aware of a conflict as the result of confidential communications with a client — the Supreme Court generally favors the granting of motions for separate counsel.

However, to protect the authority of the trial court and to avoid the possibility of abuse by unscrupulous attorneys, the Court stated in *Holloway* that it does not "preclude a trial court from exploring the adequacy of the basis of defense counsel's representation," as long as it can do so without requiring counsel to disclose confidential communications.

On the other hand, the Sixth Amendment does not require a trial court on its own motion to inquire into joint-representation arrangements. Unless the trial court knows or reasonably should know that a conflict exists, it "may assume [absent a motion] either that multiple representation entails no conflict or that the lawyer and his clients knowingly accept such risk of conflict as may exist."[90]

[C]　Post-Trial Proof of a Conflict

A conviction will not be overturned on the basis of an after-trial allegation of a conflict of interest unless the defendant demonstrates that: (1) an actual conflict of interest existed; and (2) the conflict adversely affected her lawyer's performance.[91]

As the second element stated immediately above suggests, it is not necessary for the defendant to meet the prejudice standard applied in ordinary ineffective-assistance-of-counsel cases. A conviction must be overturned if the conflict "adversely affected" the lawyer's performance, even if it cannot be shown that there is a reasonable probability that the trial was unreliable.

---

[89] 435 U.S. 475 (1978).

[90] Cuyler v. Sullivan, 446 U.S. 335, 346-47 (1980). This constitutional rule is less demanding than the Federal Rules of Criminal Procedure, which provide that when persons jointly charged with an offense are represented by the same attorney or by different attorneys from the same law firm, "the court shall promptly inquire with respect to such joint representation and shall personally advise each defendant of the right to the effective assistance of counsel, including separate representation." FRCP 44(c). Unless there is good cause to believe that no conflict is likely to arise, the federal rules provide that the trial court must "take such measures as may be appropriate to protect each defendant's right to counsel."

[91] Cuyler v. Sullivan, 446 U.S. 335 (1980).

[D] Waiver of the Right to Conflict-Free Representation

Although representation of co-defendants by a single attorney or law firm often leads to a conflict of interest, co-defendants may nonetheless wish to be represented by the same attorney or law firm. For example, by pooling their resources, co-defendants may be able to afford a respected attorney whose services would otherwise be unavailable to them; or the defendants may commit themselves in advance to a united sink-or-swim strategy that reduces or eliminates the risk of a conflict.

Nonetheless, the Supreme Court ruled in *Wheat v. United States*[92] that a trial court has the authority, over the defendant's objection, to disqualify defense counsel over her client's objection if it concludes that there is a serious possibility that a conflict of interest exists. Put somewhat differently, a defendant does not have unlimited authority to waive her right to conflict-free representation in order to be represented by the attorney of her choice.

In *Wheat*, D was indicted for participation in an alleged drug conspiracy. C, an attorney, represented X and Y, co-conspirators of D. Prior to D's trial, C secured X's acquittal on some of the conspiracy charges and helped him to negotiate a guilty plea on lesser charges. C also assisted Y to negotiate a guilty plea. A few days prior to his own trial, D made a timely request to substitute or add C as his own attorney.

The prosecutor objected to the substitution. He raised two possible conflicts of interest. First, the trial court had not yet accepted X's guilty plea; if the plea were rejected, and thus if X ultimately had to go to trial, the prosecutor warned that he might need to call D as a witness at X's trial. In such circumstances, C would be faced with a conflict, because he could not effectively cross-examine D without disclosing confidences. Second, the prosecutor indicated that he was likely to call Y as a witness at D's trial, which would again result in a conflict.

Based on these representation, the trial court refused to grant D's request to substitute or add C as his counsel. In doing so, the trial judge conceded that "[w]ere I in [D's] position, I'm sure I would want [C] representing me, too. He did a fantastic job in . . . [X's] trial."

The Supreme Court, 5-4, upheld the trial court's decision. In doing so, it came close to creating a *per se* rule prohibiting waiver of the right to conflict-free counsel,[93] and it undermined *sub silentio* the principle expressed in *Faretta v. California*[94] that a defendant has a constitutional right to retain effective control over the conduct of her own defense.

The majority in *Wheat* stated that although the right to "be represented by one's preferred attorney is comprehended by the Sixth Amendment, the essential aim of the amendment is to guarantee an effective advocate for each criminal defendant. . . ." Furthermore, courts "have an independent interest in ensuring that

---

[92] 486 U.S. 153 (1988); *see generally* Comment, *The Supreme Court, Leading Cases*, 102 Harv. L. Rev. 143 (1988) (hereafter, Comment, *The Supreme Court*); Comment, *Paternalistic Override of Waiver of Right to Conflict-Free Counsel at Expense of Right to Counsel of One's Choice*, 79 J. Crim. L. & Criminology 735 (1988).

[93] Comment, *The Supreme Court*, n. 92 *supra*, at 184.

[94] 422 U.S. 806 (1975). *See* § 178[A] *supra*.

criminal trials are conducted within the ethical standards of the profession and that legal proceedings appear fair to all who observe them."

The majority stated that when a court finds an actual conflict of interest, "there can be no doubt that it may decline a proffer of waiver, and insist that defendants be separately represented." Furthermore, it held that, as in the present case, trial courts "must be allowed substantial latitude" to refuse waivers of conflict of interest "where a [serious] potential for conflict exists which may or may not burgeon into an actual conflict as the trial progresses."

The Court conceded that prosecutors might manufacture conflicts in order to prevent a defendant from being represented by a particularly able attorney. However, it stated that "trial courts are undoubtedly aware of this possibility, and must take it into consideration with all of the other factors which inform this sort of a decision."

§ 183 Effective Assistance: How Far Must Defense Counsel Go?[95]

In *Nix v. Whiteside*,[96] the Supreme Court held that a defendant's right to effective representation, including the right to zealous advocacy of her cause, is not violated when an attorney refuses to cooperate with the client's desire to testify falsely at trial.

In *Whiteside*, D was prosecuted for stabbing V to death. In conversations with C, his lawyer, D claimed that he killed V in self-defense because he believed that V was pulling a gun out from under a bed. No weapon was found on or around V, and witnesses observed no gun. Furthermore, D admitted to C that he had not actually seen the weapon. C explained that this was not fatal to D's self-defense claim, as long as he reasonably believed that the victim was armed. A week before trial, however, D told C for the first time that he saw something metallic at the time of the incident. He explained: "There was a gun. If I don't say I saw a gun, I'm dead."

C explained to D that such testimony would constitute perjury. He warned his client that if he persisted in his wish to testify in this manner, it was C's duty to advise the court of D's plan, that he "would probably be allowed to attempt to impeach that particular testimony," and that he would seek to withdraw from the case. C's warnings apparently worked: although D testified at trial, he did not make the false claim.

Whiteside involves "one of the easier client perjury scenarios."[97] First, C knew, based on D's prior admissions, that D's testimony would be perjurious. The case

---

[95] *See generally* J. Kunen, "How Can You Defend Those People?": The Making of a Criminal Lawyer (Random House 1983); Appel, *The Limited Impact of Nix v. Whiteside on Attorney-Client Relations*, 136 U. Pa. L. Rev. 1913 (1988); Freedman, *Client Confidences and Client Perjury: Some Unanswered Questions*, 136 U. Pa. L. Rev. 1939 (1988); Freedman, *Professional Responsibility of the Criminal Defense Lawyer: The Three Hardest Questions*, 64 Mich. L. Rev. 1469 (1966); Noonan, *The Purposes of Advocacy and the Limits of Confidentiality*, 64 Mich. L. Rev. 1485 (1966); Pye, *The Role of Counsel in the Suppression of Truth*, 1978 Duke L.J. 921; Note, *Nix v. Whiteside: Is a Client's Intended Perjury a Real Dilemma?*, 22 Tulsa L.J. 399 (1987).

[96] 475 U.S. 157 (1986).

[97] Note, n. 95 *supra*, at 422.

does not answer the question of whether *C*'s actions would have been constitution-ally justified if he had merely suspected perjury.

Second, *C* knew of the planned perjury before trial; the case does not raise the issue of "what a lawyer must, should, or may do after his client has given testimony that the lawyer does not believe."[98] Third, *D* testified truthfully. The case does not dispose of the problem of whether a lawyer acts properly if she convinces her client not to testify at all.

The Court unanimously agreed that *D* failed to make out a case of ineffective representation by *C*. Chief Justice Burger, for five justices, held that neither prong of the *Strickland*[99] ineffective-representation-of-counsel test was proved in the case. The four concurring justices relied solely on the prejudice prong of *Strickland* to reach their conclusion.

Regarding the first prong, the Chief Justice ruled that the lawyer's conduct "fell within the wide range of professional responses to threatened client perjury acceptable under the Sixth Amendment." He stated that the ethical and constitu-tional duty of a lawyer to be loyal to her client "is limited to legitimate, lawful conduct compatible with the very nature of a trial as a search for truth."

The majority emphasized the fact that *C*'s conduct in the case was ethically appropriate. Indeed, according to the Chief Justice, although a breach of an ethical canon does not by itself make out a violation of the Sixth Amendment, where "there has been no breach of any recognized professional duty, it follows that there can be no deprivation of the right to assistance of counsel under the *Strickland* standard."

Second, the Court held that as a matter of law, *C*'s conduct could not establish the prejudice required for relief under *Strickland*. As the benchmark of the inquiry under *Strickland* is the fairness of the adversary proceeding, *D* "had no valid claim that confidence in the result of his trial has been diminished by his desisting from the contemplated perjury."

---

[98] *Whiteside*, 475 U.S. at 191 (Stevens J., concurring).

[99] Strickland v. Washington, 466 U.S. 668 (1984). *See* § 181[B] *supra*.

CHAPTER 30

PRETRIAL RELEASE OF THE DEFENDANT

§ 184 Pretrial Release: Procedural Context

After a suspect is arrested and booked at the police station, he is ordinarily taken to jail. Except for minor offenses, his first opportunity to be released pending trial arises at his first appearance[1] before a judicial officer (or "magistrate").[2] This appearance should occur "without unnecessary delay,"[3] usually within one day after arrest, except on weekends.

At the hearing, the magistrate determines whether to release the arrestee "on recognizance," *i.e.*, on the promise that he will appear as required at criminal proceedings, or to attach conditions to his release. A common condition is that the accused deposit cash or property with the court or, more often, post a bond provided by a commercial surety (a "bondsman") in an amount determined by the magistrate, which is subject to forfeiture if he fails to appear as required. The money deposited or the bond posted is called "bail."

In some states, and in the federal courts, the magistrate also has the authority to order the continued confinement of the accused pending trial ("preventive detention"), on the ground that no conditions will reasonably assure his appearance as required, or that his release will jeopardize the safety of another person (*e.g.*, a witness to the crime) or the community as a whole.

In the federal courts, the defendant is entitled to representation by counsel, appointed by the court if he is indigent, at the bail hearing.[4] In state systems, however, indigents often are unrepresented at this stage.[5]

§ 185 Pretrial Release: Interests at Stake

[A] The Community's Interest

Although the Supreme Court has stated that an accused person has a "traditional right to freedom before conviction,"[6] the community has a long recognized interest in protecting the integrity of the judicial process. Therefore, it is entitled

---

[1] The proceeding serves multiple purposes. *See* § 3[C][2]–[3] *supra*.

[2] In some jurisdictions, a person arrested for a minor offense is released if he posts bail at the police station or jail in an amount set on a fixed bail schedule.

[3] FRCP 5(a).

[4] FRCP 44(a) (right to representation at the initial appearance, at which bail is set).

[5] *See* P. Wice, Freedom for Sale 48 (Lexington 1974) (lawyers are present at bail hearings in only 25 percent of the cases surveyed).

[6] Stack v. Boyle, 342 U.S. 1, 4 (1951).

to adequate assurance that if the defendant is released he will attend trial and sentencing if convicted,[7] and that he will not intimidate witnesses and others involved in his prosecution.[8]

The community also has an interest in making sure that persons charged with crimes who are released pending trial do not commit other offenses while they are free. Although the issue was once in doubt,[9] the Court now recognizes pretrial crime prevention as a constitutionally justifiable interest in regulating pretrial release.[10]

[B] The Arrestee's Interest

An arrestee's interest in liberty — and, therefore, in release pending trial — is substantial and fundamental.[11] Although the presumption of innocence implied by the Constitution's due process clause[12] does not come into play until the trial,[13] the Supreme Court has observed that "unless this right to bail before trial is preserved, the presumption of innocence, secured only after centuries of struggle, would lose its meaning."[14]

Second, confinement can hamper the defendant's or his counsel's preparation of the trial defense.[15] For example, it may be necessary for the defendant to assist his lawyer to identify and convince alibi witnesses to testify, or to search the accused's home for relevant evidence.

Third, confinement is emotionally and financially disruptive to the accused and his family. He may lose his job if he is incarcerated pending trial; in turn, he may be unable to support his family or earn the money necessary to pay for the attorney he wishes to retain.

---

[7] *See* Bell v. Wolfish, 441 U.S. 520, 534 (1979).

[8] *See* United States v. Salerno, 481 U.S. 739, 753 (1987).

[9] *See* Bell v. Wolfish, 441 U.S. at 534 n.15 (expressly leaving open the issue of whether government objectives other than ensuring the defendant's presence at trial may justify pretrial detention).

[10] United States v. Salerno, 481 U.S. 739 (1987).

[11] *Id.* at 751.

[12] *See* In Re Winship, 397 U.S. 358 (1970); J. Dressler, at § 7.03.

[13] *See* Bell v. Wolfish, 441 U.S. at 523.

[14] Stack v. Boyle, 342 U.S. at 4.

[15] *Id.* Data suggest that "some defendants unable to make bail are, for that reason alone, more likely to be convicted and, if convicted, more likely to be sentenced to jail." Zeisel, *Bail Revisited*, 1979 Am. Bar. Found. Res. J. 769, 779.

§ 186 Pretrial Release: Eighth Amendment[16]

Traditionally, persons charged with non–capital offenses have had an absolute statutory or state constitutional right to be admitted to bail.[17] As one commentator put it, "a person arrested for a [non–capital] criminal offense [has] the right to purchase his release pending trial."[18]

How expensive may the key to the jail be? The Eighth Amendment to the United States Constitution provides in part that "[e]xcessive bail shall not be required." Although the Supreme Court has not decided whether this provision applies to the states through the Fourteenth Amendment due process clause, all states, by constitution or statute, similarly prohibit excessive bail.

In *Stack v. Boyle*,[19] the Court stated that although pretrial release is a traditional right, it is permissible for a judge to condition freedom on "adequate assurance that [the accused] will stand trial and submit to sentence if found guilty." In that context, it held that "[b]ail set at a figure higher than an amount reasonably calculated to fulfill this purpose is 'excessive' under the Eighth Amendment."[20]

The fixing of bail must be based upon standards relevant to the purpose of assuring the presence of the defendant. In *Stack*, the justices listed the "traditional standards" as: the nature and circumstances of the offense charged; the weight of the evidence against the accused; the accused's character; and the financial ability of the defendant to meet the bail requirements.

A former member of the Court once argued that "to demand a substantial bond which the defendant is unable to secure raises considerable problems for the equal administration of the law."[21] Nonetheless, the Supreme Court has never ruled that the Constitution entitles an indigent to be released without bail if he cannot afford to meet any financial conditions.

---

[16] *See generally* E. De Hass, The Antiquities of Bail (Columbia U. Press 1940); Foote, *The Coming Constitutional Crisis in Bail: I*, 113 U. Pa. L. Rev. 959 (1965); Meyer, *Constitutionality of Pretrial Detention (pt. 1)*, 60 Geo.L.J. 1140 (1972); Tribe, *An Ounce of Detention: Preventive Justice in the World of John Mitchell*, 56 Va. L. Rev. 371 (1970); Note, *The Eighth Amendment and the Right to Bail: Historical Perspectives*, 82 Colum. L. Rev. 328 (1982).

[17] In most states, bail may be denied in capital offenses "where the proof is evident, or the presumption great" that the defendant is guilty of the crime. The high risk that such a person will flee if released is thought to justify this exception.

[18] W. Thomas, Bail Reform in America 11 (U. California 1976).

[19] 342 U.S. 1 (1951).

[20] The possible implication of this statement is that bail is "excessive" if it is used for any purpose other than to assure the defendant's appearance. The Supreme Court has rejected this interpretation of *Stack*. *See* § 188[C] *infra*.

[21] Bandy v. United States, 81 S.Ct. 197, 197 (1960) (opinion of Justice Douglas, in chambers).

§ 187 Pretrial Release: Statutory Law

[A] Pre-Reform[22]

Until statutory reform occurred in the 1960s, magistrates typically conditioned pretrial release on deposit of cash with the court. In the majority of cases, the defendant, lacking sufficient resources to make the payment, contacted a bail bondsman who, if he was satisfied that the accused was a good risk, furnished security to the court for the defendant's appearance. In exchange for this service, the bondsman usually received a nonrefundable fee in the amount of ten percent of the bond.

For example, if the magistrate set bail at $10,000, the defendant would pay the bondsman $1,000, who would then guarantee the full sum to the court. If the defendant failed to appear as required at criminal proceedings, the bond was subject to remission; unless the bondsman had obtained collateral from the arrestee, which he often did, he lost the money.[23] If the defendant appeared at all proceedings, the bondsman was released from his obligations. The accused, however, would not receive his ten percent share, as this was the bondsman's fee for taking the risk.

If the defendant lacked sufficient resources to pay the bondsman's fee (the ten percent share) or if the bondsman refused for any other reason to serve as his surety (*e.g.*, insufficient collateral), he remained in jail through the trial.

[B] Federal Bail Reform Act of 1966

Growing disenchantment with the pretrial release system resulted in state and federal reform during the 1960s. Beginning with the Illinois Ten Percent Deposit Plan,[24] some states put commercial bondsman out of business by permitting release of a defendant who deposited ten percent of the required bond directly with the court. The defendant remained liable for the remainder of the bond if he fled. Unlike the private bondsman, the court returned the deposited money (less a nominal administrative fee) to the defendant on completion of the case if he did not flee.

At the federal level, Congress enacted the Federal Bail Reform Act of 1966.[25] The Act created a presumption in favor of the release of arrestees on their own recognizance. Further, it provided that conditions for release could be imposed only if the magistrate determined that they were necessary to reasonably assure the appearance of the defendant at criminal proceedings. When conditions were deemed necessary, the law required the magistrate to attach the least restrictive condition or combination of conditions.

Non–financial conditions were preferred to bail. For example, the statutory preference was that the magistrate place the defendant in the custody of a

---

[22] *See generally* W. Thomas, n. 18 *supra*.

[23] For this reason, bondsmen occasionally tracked down fugitives and returned them to court, sometimes by violent means, in order to avoid the forfeiture.

[24] Ill. Ann. Stats ch. 38, § 110.7.

[25] 18 U.S.C. §§ 3146–3152, *repealed in part* by the Bail Reform Act of 1984, discussed in the next subsection.

designated individual, such as an employer or clergyman who agreed to supervise him, rather than that he set bail. If the magistrate determined that financial conditions were necessary, the preferred condition was that he permit the defendant to deposit up to ten percent of the bond directly with the court rather than that he be compelled to execute a full bond, presumably with a commercial bondsman.

[C] Federal Bail Reform Act of 1984

Congress amended the federal bail law in 1984.[26] The new law differs in two key respects from the Bail Reform Act of 1966. First, for the first time it authorizes the magistrate in setting conditions for release of the defendant to consider the extent to which the release "will endanger the safety of any other person or the community."[27] Second, under specified circumstances discussed in the next chapter section, the magistrate may order the detention of a defendant prior to trial.

Notwithstanding the preventive–detention provision, the new statute, as the old one, follows a "no or least restrictive condition" approach. The judicial officer is required to release the defendant on his own recognizance "or upon execution of an unsecured appearance bond in an amount specified by the court,"[28] unless he concludes that more restrictive conditions are necessary to reasonably assure that the defendant will not flee or endanger others while free.

For the first time, federal law explicitly provides that "[t]he judicial officer may not impose a financial condition that results in the pretrial detention of the person."[29] Although this provision does not require a magistrate to reduce bail merely because it is hard for the defendant to pay,[30] Congress' apparent intention is to prohibit the use of bail as a form of *sub rosa* preventive detention. If a judge believes that the accused should be detained pending trial, he must follow the detention provisions set out in the Act.

---

[26] 18 U.S.C. §§ 3141–3150.

[27] § 3142(b).

[28] § 3142(b). An "unsecured appearance bond" is one in which the defendant promises that if he does not appear as required he will pay in full the bond set by the court. However, he is not compelled to secure the bond with any collateral.

[29] § 3142(c)(2).

[30] *See* United States v. Szott, 768 F.2d 159 (7th Cir. 1985) (holding that bail may properly be set at a figure high enough to cause severe hardship to the accused if he were to forfeit it).

§ 188   Preventive Detention[31]

[A]   Federal Bail Reform Act of 1984

Preventive detention of persons charged with non–capital offenses was rarely authorized by statute until the 1980s. However, the Federal Bail Reform Act of 1984 permits the detention of arrestees in specific circumstances if, after a hearing, the magistrate determines that "no condition or combination of conditions will reasonably assure the appearance of the person as required and the safety of any other person and the community. . . ."[32]

According to a 1987 Department of Justice study of the effects of the statute, the percentage of persons able to post a bond increased in the first year after the new law was implemented from the year immediately preceding it (63 percent compared to 50 percent). On the other hand, the percentage of persons detained pending trial rose from two percent under the old statute to 19 percent after. According to the Justice Department, "pretrial detention has largely been substituted for bail as a means of detaining defendants."[33]

Under the new Act, the magistrate must hold a detention hearing on the motion of the prosecutor if the defendant is charged with a crime of violence, any offense for which the maximum sentence is life imprisonment or death, a drug offense for which the maximum term of imprisonment is ten years or more, or any other felony committed by a person previously convicted of two or more of the above offenses.[34]

A hearing is also required on a motion of the prosecutor or on the judge's own motion in cases that involve an allegation of "a serious risk" of flight, obstruction of justice, or intimidation of a prospective witness or juror.

At the detention hearing, which ordinarily must be held at the defendant's first appearance before the magistrate,[35] the accused is entitled by statute to be

---

[31] *See generally* Alschuler, *Preventive Pretrial Detention and the Failure of Interest–Balancing Approaches to Due Process,* 85 Mich. L. Rev. 510 (1986); Richards, *The Jurisprudence of Prevention: The Right of Societal Self–Defense Against Dangerous Individuals,* 16 Hastings Const. L.Q. 329 (1989); Scott, *Pretrial Detention Under Bail Reform Act of 1984: An Empirical Analysis,* 27 Am. Crim. L. Rev. 1 (1989); Comment, *When Preventive Detention Is (Still) Unconstitutional: The Invalidity of the Presumption in the 1984 Federal Bail Statute,* 61 So. Cal. L. Rev. 1091 (1988); Comment, *Preventive Detention and Presuming Dangerousness Under the Bail Reform Act of 1984,* 134 U. Pa. L. Rev. 225 (1985); Note, *Preventive Detention: An Empirical Analysis,* 6 Harv. C.R.– C.L. L. Rev. 300 (1971).

[32] 18 U.S.C. § 3142(e).

[33] U.S. Department of Justice, Pretrial Release and Detention: The Bail Reform Act of 1984 1 (Bureau of Justice Statistics: Special Report, Feb. 1988).

[34] § 3142(f)(1).

[35] Under § 3142(f), except for good cause, a continuance on the defendant's motion may not exceed five days, and a continuance on the motion of the prosecutor may not exceed three days. However, the failure to comply with these provisions does not require the release of a person who should otherwise be detained. The error is considered harmless, unless a court concludes from the record as a whole that it had a substantial influence on the outcome of the proceeding. United States v. Montalvo–Murillo, 110 S.Ct. 2072 (1990).

represented by counsel, to testify in his own behalf, to present witnesses, and to cross–examine witnesses called by the prosecutor. Rules concerning the admissibility of evidence at criminal trials do not apply at the hearing. For example, hearsay and evidence obtained in violation of the Constitution, although ordinarily inadmissible at trial, may be introduced at the hearing.

In order to determine whether any condition or combination of conditions will reasonably assure the appearance of the defendant and the safety of others, the magistrate must take into account various factors, including the nature of the offense charged, the weight of the evidence against the defendant, and "the history and characteristics of the person," including his physical and mental condition, his ties to family and the community, and whether, at the time of the current arrest, he was already on probation or parole or on pretrial release from another offense.[36]

The Act provides that the facts the judicial officer uses to support a determination that no condition or combination of conditions will reasonable assure the safety of any person and the community, must be supported by clear and convincing evidence.[37] However, the Act creates two rebuttable presumptions.[38]

First, the accused is presumed to be too dangerous to be released if the prosecutor proves that the defendant has previously been convicted of one of the enumerated offenses that justifies a detention hearing,[39] that the offense for which he was convicted was committed while he was on release pending trial for another crime, and that five years have not elapsed since the date of conviction or of release from imprisonment (whichever is later) of the prior conviction.

Second, it is presumed that no conditions of release will reasonably assure that the defendant will not flee or commit a crime if the magistrate determines that there is probable cause to believe that, on the present occasion, he committed a specified drug offense or an offense involving the use or possession of firearms.

If the judge orders the defendant to be detained, he must include written findings of fact, stating the reasons for his decision.[40] The defendant may immediately appeal the detention order, as the government may appeal a decision to release the accused person.[41]

[B] The Policy Debate

It is difficult to disagree with the proposition that the government should have the power to detain persons prior to trial in some circumstances. For example, suppose that an extremely wealthy defendant, one who could pay any bail imposed and who is charged with a very serious crime, tells the magistrate, "If you release me, I will be on my private jet within the day to a country that will not extradite me." Or, worse, suppose that he says, "If you release me, I will walk out the door

---

[36] § 3142(g).
[37] § 3142(f).
[38] § 3142(e).
[39] See n. 34 and accompanying text supra.
[40] § 3142(i).
[41] § 3145.

and kill every police officer I observe from now until I am stopped." Are we to say that the defendant in these extreme circumstances *must* be released?

Real cases rarely are this clear–cut. But, if one concedes that preventive detention is permissible in these or similar extreme cases, then the issue no longer is whether the government should have the right to detain some persons, but instead is under what circumstances it should use its legitimate power.

Questions abound. Suppose that the accused is suspected of being a serial rapist–murderer. If he is guilty of the offenses charged there is reason to worry that he will continue to rape and kill other people pending trial. How strong should the evidence be of his guilt before he is detained? As discussed above, the presumption under the Federal Bail Reform Act is that the alleged serial rapist–murderer (at least if he used or possessed a firearm during one of the crimes) is too dangerous to be released if there is probable cause to believe — which is less than a fifty percent possibility[42] — that he is guilty of one of the charged offenses. Is that an adequate basis to detain him?

To complicate matters further, suppose that the evidence of the defendant's guilt, although strong, is legally inadmissible at trial. Is it appropriate for the judge to incarcerate a person who, he knows, cannot be convicted? Again, under the federal law, inadmissible evidence may be considered. Does this smack of using preventive detention as a subterfuge for punishment that cannot otherwise be inflicted?

Critics of preventive detention argue that even if detention is theoretically justifiable, it is improper in today's society because experts lack the capacity accurately to predict future dangerousness. According to one scholar, "statistical predictions of criminal behavior in general, and violent behavior in particular, are much more likely to be wrong than right."[43]

If experts are unsuccessful in predicting dangerousness, critics maintain, there is no reason to be optimistic that judges can do a better job. Indeed, the conclusion of two studies[44] of a Washington D.C. preventive–detention statute was that the law resulted in a high number of "false positive" detentions: in order to incarcerate two to four genuinely dangerous persons, ten persons (thus, six to eight persons "innocent" of dangerousness) had to be jailed.

Another criticism of preventive detention is that it is wrong to jail persons on the basis of what society fears they will do, rather than for what they have already done. Professor Alschuler has argued,[45] for example, that cost–benefit analysis of preventive detention leaves out a key issue: society's historical belief in human free will, *i.e.*, in the belief that a person has a right to his liberty until he has chosen to abuse it. As Alschuler puts it, "even funnel clouds sometimes turn around, and

---

[42] *See* § 43 *supra*.

[43] Ewing, *Schall v. Martin: Preventive Detention and Dangerousness Through the Looking Glass*, 34 Buff. L. Rev. 173, 196 (1985). Ewing concludes that the accuracy rate is "no more than one out of three clinical predictions. . . ." *Id.* at 185–86.

[44] *See* J. Locke, R. Penn, J. Rick, E. Bunten, & G. Hare, Compilation and Use of Criminal Court Data in Relation to Pre–Trial Release of Defendants: Pilot Study (Nat'l Bureau of Standards Technical Note # 535) (1970); Note, n. 31 *supra*.

[45] Alschuler, n. 31 *supra*, at 556–57.

human beings sometimes defy predictions." Thus, although "sensible people usually do not allow murderers and highwayman to roam among them," people are entitled not to be treated as if they were murderers or highwayman unless there is strong evidence that they are.

Professor Alschuler argues that any form of preventive detention based solely on predictions of future dangerousness — no matter how reliable — is impermissible. Detention should be allowed only if there is a "predicate of past conduct": that is, the accused should not be detained in the absence of "substantial preliminary proof of guilt" of a serious crime. However, the Federal Bail Reform Act of 1984 permits a presumption in favor of detention on as little as probable cause of prior criminality.

[C] The Constitutional Debate: *U.S. v. Salerno*[46]

In *United States v. Salerno*, the Supreme Court upheld, 6–3, the constitutionality of the preventive–detention provisions of the Federal Bail Reform Act of 1984, against a facial challenge[47] that the Act violated the Fifth Amendment due process clause and the Eighth Amendment no–excessive bail provision.

[1] Substantive Due Process

The Court, per Chief Justice Rehnquist, rejected the defendant's claim that the preventive–detention provisions of the statute violate the due process clause by imposing punishment prior to trial. It stated that although pretrial punishment is unconstitutional,[48] "the mere fact that a person is detained does not inexorably lead to the conclusion that the government has imposed punishment."

The majority stated that absent an expressed intention by Congress to punish pretrial detainees, the constitutionality of preventive detention depends on "whether an alternative purpose to which [the restriction] may rationally be connected is assignable for it, and whether [the restriction] appears excessive in relation to the alternative purpose assigned."[49]

The Court concluded that the detention imposed by the Bail Reform Act "falls on the regulatory side of the [regulatory–penal] dichotomy." It explained:

> The legislative history of the [Act] clearly indicates that Congress did not formulate the . . . provisions as punishment for dangerous persons. . . . Congress instead perceived pretrial detention as a potential solution to a pressing societal problem. . . . There is no doubt that preventing danger to the community is a legitimate regulatory goal.

---

[46] 481 U.S. 739 (1987). *See generally* Note, *The Trial of Pretrial Dangerousness: Preventive Detention After United States v. Salerno*, 75 Va. L. Rev. 639 (1989); Note, *Pretrial Detention: What Will Become of the Innocent?*, 78 J. Crim. L. & Crimin. 1048 (1988).

[47] A "facial" challenge is one that asserts that the law is void on its face. As the Court observed, this is "the most difficult challenge to mount successfully, since the challenger must establish that no set of circumstances exists under which the Act would be valid."

[48] *See* Bell v. Wolfish, 441 U.S. 520 (1979).

[49] *Salerno*, *quoting* Kennedy v. Mendoza–Martinez, 372 U.S. 144, 168–69 (1963).

The Court proceeded to balance the government's "legitimate and compelling" regulatory interest in protecting the community against the individual's liberty interest. It noted that the provisions of the Act operate only against persons arrested for a "specific category of extremely serious offenses," and who Congress has found "are far more likely [than others] to be responsible for dangerous acts in the community after arrest." Consequently, it concluded, the law "narrowly focuses on a particularly acute problem in which the government's interests are overwhelming."

Weighed against this "overwhelming" and "narrowly focused" interest "is the individual's strong interest in liberty," which the Court described as "important" and "fundamental." The majority said no more about this interest, however, except that "this right may, in circumstances where the government's interest is sufficiently weighty, be subordinated to the greater needs of society."

The Court concluded thatwhen the government must prove by clear and convincing evidence, as required by the Act, "that an arrestee presents an identified and articulable threat to an individual or the community, . . . consistent with the Due Process Clause, a court may disable the arrestee from executing the threat."

[2] Procedural Due Process

The Court disposed quickly of the procedural due process claim. It concluded that the procedures authorized by the Act are constitutionally adequate, "whether or not they might be insufficient in some particular circumstances." Concluding that "there is nothing inherently unattainable about a prediction of future criminal conduct," the majority found that the safeguards in the statute are "specifically designed to further the accuracy of that determination."

[3] Eighth Amendment

The majority concluded that the detention provisions of the Act do not violate the Eighth Amendment prohibition of excessive bail.[50] As Chief Justice Rehnquist explained, the Amendment prohibits excessive bail, but it "says nothing about whether bail should be available at all."

The majority agreed that the primary purpose of bail is to ensure that the defendant does not flee or intimidate witnesses. But, the Eighth Amendment does not prohibit "the government from pursuing other admittedly compelling interests through regulation of pretrial release." The bail clause requires only that the magistrate's "conditions of release or detention not be 'excessive' in light of the perceived evil."

---

[50] The Court raised the question, which it did not answer, "whether the Excessive Bail Clause speaks at all to Congress' power to define the classes of criminal arrestees who shall be admitted to bail." The implication of this remark is that the bail clause might apply only to judicial action. In dissent, Justice Marshall responded that "[t]he majority is correct that this question need not be decided today; it was decided long ago." He reasoned that because the other clauses of the Eighth Amendment, such as the prohibition on cruel and unusual punishment, apply to legislative action, the bail clause also pertains to legislation.

[4] Dissenting Opinions

Justice Marshall, with whom Justice Brennan joined, dissented. He criticized the majority for what he described as the "sterile formalism" of "divid[ing] a unitary argument into two independent parts [the due process and excessive–bail arguments] and then profess[ing] to demonstrate that the parts are individually inadequate."

According to Justice Marshall, the majority's "cramped" substantive due process analysis allows Congress to characterize as regulatory, and thereby save from constitutional attack, virtually any form of preconviction detention imposed for crime–prevention purposes. For example, he posited, suppose that Congress were to determine that most serious crimes are committed by unemployed persons at night. Under the majority's approach, as long as Congress stated that its reasons were non–penal in nature, it could constitutionally create a dusk–to–dawn curfew on all unemployed people.

Justice Marshall also criticized the majority's Eighth Amendment analysis, which he described as "sophistry," because it results in the conclusion that a judge cannot set bail at an excessive amount, such as $1 billion, the effect of which is the pretrial detention of the defendant, but that he can reach the same outcome by denying bail altogether.

According to Justice Marshall, the preventive–detention provisions of the Federal Bail Reform Act are unconstitutional because they rob the constitutional presumption of innocence of its meaning. As he explained, if a person indicted for a crime is detained because a magistrate determines by clear and convincing evidence that he is dangerous and he is later acquitted, he must be released even if the evidence of his future dangerousness remains unchallenged. If he were not released, "that would allow the government to imprison someone for uncommitted offenses upon 'proof' not beyond a reasonable doubt."

But, Justice Marshall argued, "our fundamental principles of justice declare that the defendant is as innocent on the day before his trial as he is on the morning after his acquittal." The indictment merely indicates that there is probable cause to believe that he has committed a crime, and that the government intends to bring him to trial for that offense. It does not demonstrate beyond a reasonable doubt that the defendant is guilty of the offense or that he is dangerous.

Justice Marshall argued that the purpose of bail, as limited by the Eighth Amendment, is to ensure the defendant's appearance at trial and to prevent him from destroying evidence or intimidating witnesses. Detention is permissible if bail cannot guarantee that he will not be a fugitive. Use of the pretrial release decision for other purposes, however, is impermissible.

Justice Stevens filed a separate dissent. He agreed with Justice Marshall that an indictment is not entitled to any weight in determining whether an individual poses a risk to the community. However, he left open the possibility that the government may have the authority to detain a person it considers dangerous if, for example, "it is a virtual certainty that he or she would otherwise kill a group of innocent persons in the immediate future."

CHAPTER **31**

PLEA BARGAINING AND GUILTY PLEAS

§ 189 Guilty Pleas: Procedural Context

After the accused has been indicted by a grand jury or an information is filed by the prosecutor, she must be arraigned on the indictment or information. Although procedures vary by jurisdiction, at a federal arraignment, the defendant is read the charges, a copy of the indictment or information is provided to her or her counsel, and she is asked to enter a plea to each of the charges.[1]

The defendant may plead not guilty, *nolo contendere*,[2] or guilty.[3] In some jurisdictions, she may also plead not guilty by reason of insanity, a prerequisite in those states to presenting evidence of insanity at the trial. In some states and in the federal courts,[4] a defendant may enter a conditional plea of guilty or *nolo contendere*, if she has the approval of the court and the consent of the prosecutor.

§ 190 Guilty Pleas: Constitutional and Policy Context

Although results vary by locality, by crime, and by year, guilty pleas are secured in a very high number of criminal prosecutions. Some studies suggest that 90 percent or more of the convictions for felonies are the result of guilty pleas.[5] The guilty plea process, therefore, is a matter of considerable practical significance and the subject of a number of significant constitutional and policy controversies.

From a constitutional perspective, a person who pleads guilty relinquishes various rights, including her Fifth Amendment privilege against self-incrimination, and her Sixth Amendment rights to a speedy and public trial by an impartial jury, to be confronted with the witnesses against her, and to call witnesses in her own

---

[1] FRCP 10.

[2] *"Nolo contendere"* literally means "I will not contest it [the charges]." Although it is not an admission of guilt, it has the same effect in the criminal proceeding as a guilty plea. 1 C. Wright, at § 177. The primary benefit to the defendant of a *nolo* plea is that — unlike a guilty plea — it may not be used as an admission of guilt in a civil action based on the same conduct.

Under the federal rules, a defendant may plead *nolo contendere* only with the consent of the court, which is to be granted "only after due consideration of the views of the parties and the interest of the public in the effective administration of justice." FRCP 11(b).

[3] *E.g.*, FRCP 11(a)(1).

[4] FRCP 11(a)(2).

[5] H. Miller, W. McDonald, & J. Cramer, Plea Bargaining in the United States 21-23 (Law Enforcement Assistance Administration, National Institute of Law Enforcement and Criminal Justice 1978); *see* Alschuler, *The Changing Plea Bargaining Debate*, 69 Calif. L. Rev. 652, 652 n.1 (1981).

behalf. It is important, therefore, to determine whether the procedures used to obtain guilty pleas adequately ensure that defendants waive their constitutional rights voluntarily and knowingly, rather than as the result of coercion or ignorance.

Furthermore, a defendant usually must rely on her lawyer to represent her in any plea negotiations and to advise her regarding whether to plead guilty. It is essential, therefore, that she receive her constitutional right to the effective assistance of counsel in the plea process.

Constitutional issues aside, the overriding policy question is whether the law should encourage, merely tolerate, or actively discourage guilty pleas. A risk of unknown magnitude exists that in a system that encourages or condones self-conviction, innocent persons or, at least, persons against whom there is insufficient evidence to convict, will plead guilty. Because most guilty pleas are the product of plea bargaining, most of the policy debate pertaining to guilty pleas centers on that process.

§ 191 Plea Bargaining: General Principles

[A] Overview

Plea bargaining is the process by which a defendant in a criminal prosecution agrees, in exchange for some official concession, to an act of self-conviction, *i.e.*, to plead guilty to one or more criminal charges.[6]

At least since the beginning of the twentieth century, the great majority of guilty pleas have been the result of plea negotiations between prosecutors and defendants or their counsel. However, because of the controversial nature of plea bargaining and related doubts about its constitutionality, the process was usually conducted *sub rosa*[7] until the Supreme Court made clear in 1970 that plea bargaining is not unconstitutional *per se*.[8]

[B] Types of Plea Agreements

Plea negotiations involve "charge bargaining," "sentencing bargaining," or both. In charge bargaining, in exchange for a guilty plea to one or more charges, the prosecutor agrees to the dismissal of other charges in the indictment or information (a "dismissal agreement"), or to accept the guilty plea to a lesser degree of the charge (a "charge-reduction agreement").

Sentencing bargaining is also of two kinds. In some cases, the prosecutor agrees that, in exchange for a guilty plea, she will recommend to the judge that the latter

---

[6] Alschuler, *Plea Bargaining And Its History*, 79 Colum. L. Rev. 1, 3 (1979).

[7] The judge at arraignment would ask the defendant whether her proposed guilty plea was the result of any promises by the prosecutor; the defendant, on the advice of her counsel and with the prosecutor's knowledge, would state that it was not. In nearly all cases, the judge knew that this statement was false. The result was that plea bargaining was legally unreviewable, and the defendant was required to participate in a cynical charade.

[8] *See* Brady v. United States, 397 U.S. 742 (1970); McMann v. Richardson, 397 U.S. 759 (1970); Parker v. North Carolina, 397 U.S. 790 (1970).

impose the sentence agreed upon by the defendant or, less favorably to the defendant, not oppose the defendant's request for a particular sentence (a "sentencing-recommendation agreement"). Alternatively, the prosecutor may agree to a specified sentence (a "sentencing agreement").

[C] Federal Plea Agreement Procedures[9]

The Federal Rules of Criminal Procedure permit the prosecutor and the defendant's attorney, or the defendant herself if she has waived her right to counsel, to engage in plea negotiations. The existence and nature of the plea agreement must be disclosed by the parties at the arraignment.

The judge is not required to accept a dismissal, charge-reduction, or sentencing plea agreement, although the rules are silent regarding the factors she should consider in determining whether to accept the agreement.[10] The judge may accept the agreement at the arraignment, reject it at that time, or defer a decision until she receives a presentence report.[11] If the judge rejects the plea agreement, the defendant must be given the opportunity to withdraw her plea, and she must be informed that if she does not withdraw it "the disposition of the case may be less favorable to the defendant than that contemplated by the plea agreement."[12]

A guilty plea based on a sentencing-recommendation agreement is treated differently. Such an agreement does not require the judge to commit herself to anything; therefore, in order to assure that the defendant realizes this fact, the judge must inform the defendant that if she does not accept the recommendation, the defendant will not be permitted to withdraw the plea.

§ 192 Plea Bargaining: Policy Debate

[A] Is Plea Bargaining Inevitable?[13]

Most commentators and participants in the criminal justice system believe that plea bargaining is inevitable. The thesis is that if the process were abolished, the guilty-plea rate would be substantially reduced, and society would be unable to provide the personnel and facilities necessary to handle the newly-needed trials without creating unacceptable and, perhaps, unconstitutional,[14] delays.

---

[9] FRCP 11. *See generally* 1 C. Wright, at § 175.1; Purdy & Lawrence, Plea Agreements Under the Federal Sentencing Guidelines, 26 Crim. L. Bull. 483 (1990).

[10] The United States Sentencing Commission recommends that no agreement be accepted unless, in the case of a sentencing agreement, the recommended sentence falls within applicable sentencing guidelines or there are "justifiable reasons" to depart from them; a dismissal agreement should not be accepted unless "the remaining charges adequately reflect the seriousness of the actual offense behavior and . . . accepting the agreement will not undermine the statutory purposes of sentencing." 18 U.S.C. App. § 6B1.2.

[11] The United States Sentencing Commission recommends deferral. 18 U.S.C. App. § 6B1.1(c).

[12] FRCP 11(e)(4).

[13] *See generally* Schulhofer, *Is Plea Bargaining Inevitable?*, 97 Harv. L. Rev. 1037 (1984).

[14] "In all criminal prosecutions, the accused shall enjoy the right to a speedy . . . trial. . . ." U.S. Const. amend VI.

Consequently, plea bargaining would either be reinstituted or participants in the system would subvert the no-bargaining policy in an underhanded, and therefore undesirable,[15] manner.

Some studies support the inevitability thesis, particularly the claim that plea bargaining will be forced underground where it is not expressly permitted.[16] A study of a ban on prosecutorial bargaining in Alaska, which purports to reach the opposite conclusion,[17] is inconclusive because the study focused on a period in which judges were permitted to initiate plea bargaining. Furthermore, it is unclear whether Alaska's experiences can be applied in urban, high-crime areas.

On the other hand, two studies[18] of the Philadelphia criminal justice system, in which guilty pleas were obtained in considerably fewer cases than is the national norm, suggest that an urban criminal justice system can make trials available in most cases without causing insurmountable difficulties. According to the author of these studies, the results "throw into question" the assumption of plea bargaining inevitability.[19]

[B] Is Plea Bargaining Good in Principle?[20]

[1] In Support of Plea Bargaining

The Supreme Court has described plea bargaining as "not only an essential part of the process but a highly desirable part."[21] Advocates emphasize the "mutuality of advantages" that the process offers to the participants. First, from the defendant's perspective, plea bargaining permits the accused to make the rational

---

[15] *See* n. 7 *supra*.

[16] *E.g.*, Church, *Plea Bargains, Concessions and the Courts: Analysis of a Quasi-Experiment*, 10 Law & Soc'y Rev. 377 (1976); Heumann & Loftin, *Mandatory Sentencing and the Abolition of Plea Bargaining: The Michigan Felony Firearm Statute*, 13 Law & Soc'y Rev. 393 (1979).

[17] Rubinstein & White, *Alaska's Ban on Plea Bargaining*, 13 Law & Soc'y Rev. 367 (1979).

[18] Schulhofer, *No Job Too Small: Justice Without Bargaining in the Lower Criminal Courts*, 1985 Am. B. Found. Res. J. 519; Schulhofer, n. 13 *supra*.

[19] However, more recent reports in the national media indicate that the Philadelphia criminal justice system is, in the words of a District Attorney, "on the verge of collapse." A report commissioned by the state supreme court indicated that at the end of 1989 a backlog of 12,199 criminal cases existed, and that the average case took 245 days from arrest to final disposition. One — but only one — reason given for the alleged crisis was the plea-bargaining policy in that city. Hinds, *Philadelphia System Overwhelmed*, New York Times, Aug. 15, 1990, A1, col. 2.

[20] *See generally* Alschuler, *Personal Failure, Institutional Failure, and the Sixth Amendment*, 14 N.Y.U. Rev. L. & Soc. Change 149 (1986) (hereafter, Alschuler, *Failure*); Alschuler, *The Defense Attorney's Role in Plea Bargaining*, 84 Yale L.J. 1179 (1975) (hereafter, Alschuler, *Defense Attorney's Role*); Alschuler, *The Prosecutor's Role in Plea Bargaining*, 36 U. Chi. L. Rev. 50 (1968) (hereafter, Alschuler, *Prosecutor's Role*); Alschuler, n. 5 *supra*; Hughes, *Pleas Without Bargains*, 33 Rutgers L. Rev. 753 (1981); Uviller, *Pleading Guilty: A Critique of Four Models*, 41 Law & Contemp. Probs. 102 (1977); White, *A Proposal for Reform of the Plea Bargaining Process*, 119 U. Pa. L. Rev. 439 (1971).

[21] Santobello v. New York, 404 U.S. 257, 261 (1971).

determination that the risk of conviction and substantial punishment justifies the acceptance of the bargain, which is apt to result in less punishment, fewer legal expenses, and considerably less anxiety.[22]

Second, the prosecutor can use the process to "fit the crime to the punishment," *i.e.*, to determine what punishment is in the best interests of all concerned, and to shape the agreement so that the defendant pleads guilty to the offense that permits the appropriate sentencing disposition.

Third, the state more efficiently attains the objectives of criminal punishment by ensuring that it is more promptly imposed, and that it is imposed on persons who by pleading guilty demonstrate their willingness to participate in the correctional process.

Fourth, by "the avoidance of trial, scarce judicial and prosecutorial resources are conserved for those cases in which there is a substantial issue of the defendant's guilt or in which there is substantial doubt that the State can sustain its burden of proof."[23] In short, those whose guilt is clearest are bargained out of the trial process, allowing time and energy to go to the more troubling cases.

[2] In Opposition to Plea Bargaining

[a] Overview

Critics maintain that principled support for plea bargaining adds up to little more than the "jurisprudence of joy,"[24] *i.e.*, bargaining is good because the system pleases the participants. Critics reject the implicit premise that a system is inevitably good if it makes everyone (except the commentators) happy.[25]

Opponents of plea bargaining come from divergent political-philosophical camps. The "hawks" oppose the process because they believe that it prejudices the crime-control interests of the community. The "doves" are concerned with the effect of plea bargaining on the accused's ability to retain her constitutional right to a trial.[26]

[b] Sentencing Differential

The hawks oppose plea bargaining because, in their view, it results in undue leniency to criminals. The evidence of leniency is overwhelming in this regard: according to the United States Sentencing Commission, those who plead guilty

---

[22] *See* Brady v. United States, 397 U.S. at 752.

[23] *Id.*

[24] Alschuler, n. 5 *supra*, at 683 n.83.

[25] One party traditionally not considered in the plea bargaining calculus is the victim or her family. Whether justified or not, many victims are distressed when they learn that a bargain has been arranged. Recent concern about "victims' rights" has resulted in statutory and state constitutional reforms that often require the parties to consider the wishes of the victim in the resolution of criminal cases. *See generally* Lamborn, *Victim Participation in the Criminal Justice Process: The Proposals for a Constitutional Amendment*, 34 Wayne L. Rev.125 (1987); Murphy, *Getting Even: The Role of the Victim*, 7 Soc. Phil. & Policy 209 (1990); Welling, *Victim Participation in Plea Bargains*, 65 Wash. U.L.Q. 301 (1987).

[26] Church, *In Defense of "Bargain Justice"*, 13 Law & Soc'y Rev. 509, 510 (1979).

are likely to receive a sentence from 30 to 40 percent below that which they would have received had they pleaded not guilty and been convicted at trial of the same offense.[27] Other studies support this conclusion.[28]

Whether such leniency is "undue," as the hawks claim, is more problematic. Advocates of plea bargaining suggest that leniency is appropriate, on the ground that a defendant who pleads guilty shows remorse by her plea (and therefore deserves mitigation of punishment) or, at least, makes herself more susceptible to the benefits of the punishment.

Critics maintain that the ordinary guilty pleader is not remorseful. The plea is motivated by the defendant's rational desire to "save her skin," and not as the result of a guilty conscience. Moreover, the purpose of punishment is deterrence. Assuming that the person is no less dangerous after the guilty plea than she was before, she needs to be punished just as much; also, reduced penalties weaken the general deterrent value of punishment. Therefore, the leniency is undue.

Dovish critics of plea bargaining also attack the leniency shown defendants, but their sympathies lie with those who do not plead guilty. As they view it, plea bargaining burdens the defendant who chooses to assert her constitutional right to a trial. In essence, the rare defendant who forces the state to prove its case against her is penalized for her actions.

[c] Prosecutorial Overcharging

Some critics maintain that prosecutors overcharge defendants. As a result, the deal that the defendant receives through plea negotiations is illusory.

Defense attorneys allege that prosecutors treat the charging process "like horse trading," in which "both sides start out asking for more than they expect to get."[29] They claim that most prosecutors either divide a criminal transaction into as many offenses as they can and charge them all ("horizontal overcharging"), or charge the highest degree of an offense that the evidence could remotely permit ("vertical overcharging"), or both.

If the evidence does not support the charges filed, it is genuine overcharging. But even if there is sufficient evidence to support the charges, critics of plea bargaining reason that the purpose of the extra charges is to compel the defendant to participate in the "horse trading." Ultimately, if the prosecutor succeeds, she gets the defendant to plead guilty to the crime for which, in the absence of bargaining, she would have originally sought to bring the accused to trial. Thus, the bargain is illusory: the prosecutor ends up where she should have started, but the defendant waives her trial rights.

[d] Inadequate Representation

Defense lawyers are supposed to be equalizers. They zealously and loyally defend their clients against the state, serving as "an antidote to the fear, ignorance, and bewilderment of the impoverished and uneducated defendant, . . . throughout the criminal process."[30] Therefore, whatever "chicanery" the prosecutor

---

[27] United States Sentencing Commission, Supplemental Report on the Initial Sentencing Guidelines and Policy Statements 48 (Govt. Printing Office 1987).

[28] *See* Alschuler, n. 5 *supra*, at 652-56.

[29] Alschuler, *Prosecutor's Role*, n. 20 *supra*, at 85.

[30] Alschuler, *Defense Attorney's Role*, n. 20 *supra*, at 1179.

might seek to commit in the plea bargaining process, the defense lawyer is present to stop it.

Some critics of plea bargaining question whether the quality of representation of defendants in the bargaining process merits this optimistic, even romantic, view.[31]

Critics of plea bargaining argue that defense attorneys, like other people, desire money. For the private defense attorney, there are two ways to become financially successful: develop a reputation as a high-quality trial attorney; or do a high-volume business. The latter approach is the path of least resistance. But, to handle large quantities of cases, a defense lawyer must go to trial in few of them. In short, private defense attorneys too often become "pleaders." The result is that defendants receive misleading advice, or they are unduly influenced to plead guilty by their own attorneys.

Second, fatigue and a desire to minimize one's workload brought on by overwhelmingly large caseloads, can cause even the most ethical public defender to rely too heavily on plea bargaining.

Third, public defenders have an incentive to cooperate with the prosecutors with whom they deal on a daily basis; the result is that bargaining is not always in the best interests of an individual client.

Fourth, lawyers, like other people, do not like to be wrong, and the decision to plead guilty is never "wrong," in the sense that there is no way to know whether a trial would have resulted in a better outcome than the deal secured for the client. On the other hand, the lawyer's recommendation *not* to plead guilty can prove to be wrong, if the defendant is convicted and receives a more severe sentence than that which was previously offered.

[e] Conviction of the Innocent

Critics worry that lawful plea bargaining, *i.e.*, bargaining that courts do not consider coercive, often places too much pressure on defendants, even those who are represented by competent counsel.

For example, in one reported case,[32] *D* was charged with kidnapping and forcible rape, punishable by life imprisonment. *D* continually asserted his innocence to his lawyer, and the case against him was so weak that his counsel was confident of acquittal at trial. However, the prosecutor (doubtlessly aware of the weakness of the case) offered *D* a deal: he would drop the rape and kidnapping charges in exchange for a guilty plea to simple battery, a thirty-day misdemeanor. Over the lawyer's objections, the defendant pleaded guilty, saying "I can't take the chance." Thus, a possibly factually innocent defendant (or, at least, one unlikely to have been proved guilty) was lawfully pressured to plead guilty.

Advocates of plea bargaining have defended the events in the latter case on the ground that innocent people are not necessarily exonerated at trial and, therefore, it is appropriate to give the defendant the opportunity to choose whether to take

---

[31] *See especially id.* at 1181-1270; Alschuler, *Failure*, n. 20. The ideas expressed in this subsection come largely from these two articles.

[32] Alschuler, *Prosecutor's Role*, n. 20 *supra*, at 61.

the risk.[33] Critics respond that in the absence of plea bargaining, the prosecutor would have requested a dismissal of the charges. Thus, again, the bargain was illusory.

§ 193 Plea Bargaining: Judicial Participation[34]

Judicial participation in the plea bargaining process is possible in various ways, in varying degrees, and at various times. For example, a judge might initiate bargaining between the prosecution and the defense, much as a judge in a civil suit seeks to bring the parties together to negotiate. She might ask the defense attorney what the prosecutor would need to do to convince her client to plead guilty, and then she might try to convince the prosecutor to accept the "offer" or to make a counter-offer. Alternatively, the judge might participate as an information provider, by answering the parties questions about her sentencing philosophy if the defendant stands trial.

Participation by judges in plea bargaining is not uncommon. A 1977 national study found that approximately one-third of criminal trial judges attended plea discussions, most of whom reported that their attendance was not as a mere spectator.[35] Another study of ten cities found that judicial participation was common in nine of them.[36] Recent surveys suggest that judicial involvement remains extensive in some jurisdictions.[37] On the other hand, the Federal Rules of Criminal Procedure prohibit judicial participation in plea agreement discussions.[38]

Judicial participation in plea bargaining is controversial. Advocates contend that it is unwise to ban judges from the process. In the final analysis they will have to approve or reject the plea agreement; therefore, it is sensible to include them early enough in the process that negotiations can take a fruitful path.

Furthermore, when negotiations focus on a sentencing-recommendation agreement, the defense cannot easily measure the value of the prosecutor's offer unless it knows whether the judge is likely to accept the recommendation. Judicial participation, therefore, informs the process. It also reduces the anxiety of the defendant, who can get her "first authoritative statement" of her likely sentence prior to trial, rather than having to wait until trial, which one public defender has described as "a plunge from an unknown height."[39] Indeed, advocates of judicial

---

[33] Church, n. 26 *supra*, at 516.

[34] *See generally* Alschuler, *The Trial Judge's Role in Plea Bargaining, Part I*, 76 Colum. L. Rev. 1059 (1976); Gallagher, *Judicial Participation in Plea Bargaining: A Search for New Standards*, 9 Harv. Civ.R.-Civ.Lib. L. Rev. 29 (1974); Hoffman, *Plea Bargaining and the Role of the Judge*, 53 F.R.D. 499 (1971).

[35] Ryan & Alfini, *Trial Judges' Participation in Plea Bargaining: An Empirical Perspective*, 13 Law & Soc'y Rev. 479, 487 (1979).

[36] Alschuler, n. 34 *supra*, at 1061-62.

[37] *E.g.*, Anderson, *Judicial Participation in the Plea Negotiation Process: Some Frequencies and Disposing Factors*, 10 Hamline J. Pub. L. & Policy 39 (1990).

[38] FRCP 11(e)(1).

[39] Alschuler, n. 34 *supra*, at 1081.

participation ask, if the judge knows what sentence she would give if the defendant elects to go to trial, "what interests of the defendant are protected by prohibiting the judge from communicating this information to him?"[40]

Critics of judicial participation believe that they have an answer to the latter question: a bar on participation would serve the defendant's interest in not being coerced into a guilty plea. They maintain that a judge is like a stick of dynamite placed in the negotiation room: she is apt to blast out a guilty plea that might not otherwise have been obtained. In short, judicial participation is efficient precisely because it compels defendants, already fearful, to plead guilty rather than to stand trial. What is the defendant expected to do, critics ask, if the judge is present and "suggests" that a particular offer is a good one?

Experienced participants in plea bargaining frequently report cases of "judicial blasting" aimed at either the defense attorney or the prosecutor. For example, in one case[41] a judge told an inexperienced attorney who was hesitant to recommend that his client accept a particular offer that "I'm not going to tell you what to do, young man, but I can tell you what *I'll* do." He then explained his sentencing philosophy, which was to double the prison sentence of anyone who stood trial (in this case, it meant a minimum twenty, rather than a ten, year prison sentence). As the judge explained, "He takes some of my time — I take some of his." The defendant immediately accepted the plea offer. One moral of this story is that the judge's participation rendered the defendant's decision more informed. The opposing interpretation of the story is that, although knowledge sometimes empowers, it can also coerce.

Critics of judicial participation also fear that a judge whose suggestions are rejected by the defendant will be unable to conduct a fair trial. Even if she can, they find it unseemly for a judge, the neutral trial arbiter, to participate in the "horse trading," the aim of which is to avoid a trial and convict a defendant.

Advocates of judicial participation do not discount some of these concerns. Some of them would set limits on, but not ban, participation by judges. For example, the judge might be permitted to moderate negotiations but to do no more. Or, her participation might be limited to stating what charges she would be willing to dismiss or what sentencing concessions she might be prepared to accept. Or, a "cooling off period" after a deal is reached in the judge's presence might be required. Finally, if the defendant rejected an agreement hammered out with the judge, the latter might be prohibited from trying the case.

§ 194 Plea Bargaining: Broken Deals

In *Santobello v. New York*,[42] the Supreme Court announced that when a guilty plea rests in significant part "on a promise or agreement by a prosecutor, so that it can be said to be part of the inducement or consideration, such promise must be fulfilled."

---

[40] Uviller, n. 20 *supra*, at 117.
[41] Alschuler, n. 34 *supra*, at 1089.
[42] 404 U.S. 257 (1971).

In *Santobello*, the prosecutor, in exchange for a guilty plea by *D*, agreed to make no sentencing recommendation, but the promise was breached when another prosecutor sought the maximum sentence, which the judge imposed. *D* unsuccessfully sought to vacate his plea.

The justices unanimously agreed that the prosecutor wronged the defendant. However, the opinion of the Court by Chief Justice Burger failed to state what constitutional right was violated by the prosecutor's actions. Nor did the Court indicate what remedy ought to be granted in cases of breach.

The Chief Justice stated only that in "the interests of justice" the case should be remanded to the state court to determine what relief should be granted. He suggested two possibilities: the trial court could require specific performance of the agreement, or it could grant the relief sought by *D*, namely, to vacate the plea and permit him to plead anew to the original charge.[43]

The Supreme Court attached a constitutional justification to the *Santobello* rule in *Mabry v. Johnson*,[44] when it stated that the holding in *Santobello* was based on the proposition that a plea may be challenged under the due process clause "when it develops that the defendant was not fairly apprised of its consequences." In other words, when a defendant pleads guilty on the basis of a promise subsequently broken,[45] the effect of the unfulfilled promise is to render the plea invalid because it was based on "a false premise," and thus was not intelligently made.

For example, in *Mabry* the prosecutor offered, in exchange for a guilty plea, to recommend a sentence of 21 years, to be served concurrently with other sentences already being served by *D*. After *D* accepted the offer, the prosecutor told *D*'s counsel that he had misspoken, and that he had intended to recommend a sentence of 21 years to be served *consecutively* with the other sentences. *D* rejected this new offer and elected to stand trial, but later changed his mind and pleaded guilty on the basis of the prosecutor's second offer.

The Court held that, unlike the circumstances in *Santobello*, the guilty plea here was intelligently made, as *D* knew the conditions of the bargain (*i.e.*, that the prosecutor would recommend consecutive, not concurrent, sentences) when he pleaded guilty. Therefore, no constitutional violation occurred.

---

[43] Justices Marshall, Brennan and Stewart concurred in part and dissented in part. They would have required the trial court to permit *D* to withdraw his guilty plea, since that was his motion. Justice Douglas, who concurred, stated that "a court ought to accord a defendant's preference considerable, if not controlling weight" when the prosecutor breaches a deal.

[44] 467 U.S. 504 (1984).

[45] As is evident by the Court's *per curiam* holding in United States v. Benchimol, 471 U.S. 453 (1985), defense counsel should seek to have all aspects of a deal expressed if she wishes to have a remedy under *Santobello*. In *Benchimol*, the prosecutor agreed to recommend probation. At the sentencing hearing, defense counsel told the judge that the prosecutor agreed to recommend probation. The prosecutor said only, "That is an accurate representation [of the arrangement.]" The Court held that the "[g]overnment did not commit itself to enthusiastically make a particular recommendation." In short, the defendant got what he bargained for.

§ 195   Validity of a Guilty Plea: Constitutional Principles[46]

[A] In General

By pleading guilty, a defendant waives various constitutional rights.[47] Yet, the plea may be the result of "[i]gnorance, incomprehension, coercion, terror, induce-ments, subtle or blatant threats."[48] Therefore, the guilty plea of a counseled[49] defendant is invalid unless: (1) it is voluntarily and knowingly made;[50] and (2) at least in some cases, a factual basis for the plea exists.[51] A conviction based on a plea that does not meet these conditions violates the due process clause and must be set aside.

[B] Voluntariness of the Plea

The Supreme Court has not fully defined the standard of voluntariness in the guilty plea context. It has stated that a plea is invalid if it is the result of actual or threatened physical harm or of mental coercion overbearing the defendant's will.[52] However, the Court does not apply as strict a standard of coercion in the guilty plea context as it does in police interrogation cases.

Perhaps the most complete statement of the voluntariness principle was expressed by the Court in *Brady v. United States,* in which it stated that a guilty plea is valid, if intelligently made, unless it was "induced by threats (or promises to discontinue improper harrassment), misrepresentation . . ., or perhaps by promises that are by their nature improper as having no proper relationship to the prosecutor's business (*e.g.,* bribes)."[53]

The Supreme Court is hesitant to invalidate guilty pleas of counseled defendants on the grounds of involuntariness, short of physical threats or extreme mental coercion. For example, in *Brady, D* pleaded guilty to kidnapping under a federal statute that authorized the death penalty if, but only if, a jury recommended the sentence. *D* pleaded guilty, thus avoiding the death penalty, after he learned that a co-defendant would testify against him at trial.

Subsequently in another case,[54] the Supreme Court held that the death penalty portion of the kidnapping statute was unconstitutional because it placed an impermissible burden on the defendant's right to a jury trial. As a result of that

---

[46] *See generally* Alschuler, *The Supreme Court, the Defense Attorney, and the Guilty Plea,* 47 U. Colo. L. Rev. 1 (1975); Becker, *Plea Bargaining and the Supreme Court,* 21 Loy. L.A. L. Rev. 757 (1988); Note, *The Alford Plea: A Necessary But Unpredictable Tool for the Criminal Defendant,* 72 Iowa L. Rev. 1063 (1987).

[47] *See* § 190 *supra.*

[48] Boykin v. Alabama, 395 U.S. 238, 242-43 (1969).

[49] The defendant must be represented by counsel or waive the right. Moore v. Michigan, 355 U.S. 155 (1957).

[50] McCarthy v. United States, 394 U.S. 459 (1969).

[51] North Carolina v. Alford, 400 U.S. 25 (1970).

[52] Brady v. United States, 397 U.S. at 750.

[53] *Id.* at 755 (*quoting* Shelton v. United States, 242 F.2d 101, 115 (dissenting opinion) (5th Cir. 1957), *reversed on other grounds,* 356 U.S. 26 (1958)).

[54] United States v. Jackson, 390 U.S. 570 (1968).

decision, *D* sought to vacate his plea, claiming that he would not have pled guilty but for the improper statutory threat of death.

The *Brady* Court rejected the argument, largely because it did not want to discourage guilty pleas and the plea bargaining process that usually precedes them. It stated that there was no evidence that *D* was so "gripped by fear" that, with the assistance of competent counsel, he could not "rationally weigh" the advantages of trial against the benefits of pleading guilty. It saw little difference between *D*'s situation and that of a defendant who is informed by her lawyer that a judge will very likely be more lenient than a jury, or of a defendant who pleads guilty on the basis of an understanding that more serious charges will be dismissed.

[C] Intelligent Nature of the Plea

[1] In General

A guilty plea is invalid, even if evidence of the defendant's guilt is overwhelming, unless the record shows that she was aware of: (1) the nature of the charges to which she is pleading; and (2) the consequences of the plea.[55] However, a plea may not successfully be attacked merely on the basis that the defendant or her counsel incorrectly assessed the legal or factual circumstances surrounding the case.

[2] Nature of the Charges

In *Henderson v. Morgan*,[56] *D* pleaded guilty to second-degree intent-to-kill murder, even as he told the court that he "meant no harm" to the victim. The Supreme Court held that, despite what it assumed to be "overwhelming evidence of guilt," *D*'s plea was constitutionally invalid because the trial judge found that neither *D*'s defense attorney nor the prosecutor explained to him that intent was a "critical element" of the crime,[57] nor did the record disclose that the trial judge remedied the omission.

However, in the absence of a factual finding to the contrary, the Court stated that "it may be appropriate to presume that in most cases defense counsel routinely explain the nature of the offense in sufficient detail to give the accused notice of what he is being asked to admit."[58]

[3] Consequences of the Plea

The Supreme Court announced in *Boykin v. Alabama*[59] that it will not presume from a silent record that a defendant was aware of the constitutional rights that

---

[55] McCarthy v. United States, 394 U.S. 459 (1969).

[56] 426 U.S. 637 (1976).

[57] The Court assumed without deciding that a defendant need be informed only of the "critical elements" of the charge to which she is pleading guilty. It did not define "critical element."

[58] *See also* Marshall v. Lonberger, 459 U.S. 422 (1983) (in which the Court concluded that there was "fair support" in the record to conclude that *D*'s plea met the *Morgan* standard, on the ground that the lower court assumed that *D*'s counsel explained to him the nature of the offense).

[59] 395 U.S. 238 (1969).

she abandoned by pleading guilty. However, a plea is not invalid merely because the trial judge did not expressly inform the defendant of the rights that are being waived. It is sufficient if, from the record supplemented by a post-conviction hearing, it is clear that the defendant was aware of the consequences of the plea.[60]

The "conventional wisdom"[61] is that a defendant must also be informed of the "direct," as distinguished from "collateral," consequences of her guilty plea. At a minimum this means that she should be informed of the maximum possible sentence for the crime to which she is pleading guilty.

[4] "Bad" Legal Advice[62]

The Supreme Court observed in *Brady v. United States* that a decision whether to plead guilty "is heavily influenced by the defendant's appraisal of the prosecution's case against him and by the apparent likelihood of securing leniency should a guilty plea be offered and accepted. Considerations like these frequently present imponderable questions for which there are no certain answers."[63]

Consequently, the Court held that a plea is not vulnerable to later attack if it turns out that the defendant, or more accurately her counsel, "did not correctly assess every relevant factor entering into [her] decision." Thus, in *Brady, D* was not permitted to attack his guilty plea on the ground that the death penalty provision in the statute to which he was pleading guilty was later declared unconstitutional. The Court stated that the plea was intelligently made because "the defendant's lawyer correctly advised him with respect to the then existing law as to possible penalties. . . ."

Similarly, in *McMann v. Richardson*,[64] the Court considered three cases in which the defendants alleged that their bargained pleas were the result of unconstitutionally coerced confessions. In each case, the defendant pleaded guilty on the basis of advice by his lawyer that the confessions could not be kept from the jury. This advice was correct under then-existing New York law, but incorrect on the basis of later case law.

The justices ruled that it "is not a requirement that all advice offered by the defendant's lawyer withstand retrospective examination in a post-conviction hearing." When the intelligence of a guilty plea is at issue, the question is merely "whether that advice was within the range of competence demanded of attorneys in criminal cases."

Even if it is determined that a lawyer's advice was incompetent, the guilty plea may not be vacated unless the defendant also proves that she was prejudiced by her lawyer's deficient conduct, *i.e.*, that "there is a reasonable probability that, but for counsel's errors, [s]he would not have pleaded guilty and would have insisted on going to trial."[65]

---

[60] Wilkins v. Erickson, 505 F.2d 761, 764 (9th Cir. 1974).
[61] 2 W. LaFave & J. Israel, Criminal Procedure, § 20.4(d) at 645 (West 1984).
[62] *See also* § 197 *infra*.
[63] 397 U.S. at 756.
[64] 397 U.S. 759 (1970).
[65] Hill v. Lockhart, 474 U.S. 52, 59 (1985).

[D] Factual Basis of the Plea

In *North Carolina v. Alford*,[66] the Supreme Court ruled that a personal admission of guilt by the defendant is not constitutionally required to validate a guilty plea. Furthermore, the plea is not constitutionally infirm if the defendant, while pleading guilty, expressly asserts her innocence, as long as the record before the judge "contains strong evidence of actual guilt."

In *Alford*, D pleaded guilty to second-degree murder, although he testified to the judge that he did not commit the crime. D asserted that he was pleading guilty on the advice of his counsel in order to avoid the possibility of receiving the death penalty.

The Supreme Court concluded that there is no meaningful difference between, on the one hand, a defendant who pleads guilty but who is psychologically unable to admit his guilt and, on the other hand, a defendant who claims innocence, but against whom there is strong evidence of guilt. The Court did not define "strong evidence," but it did state that there was "overwhelming evidence" of D's guilt.

§ 196 Obtaining a Guilty Plea: Federal Procedures[67]

[A] Ensuring Voluntariness

Rule 11(d) of the Federal Rules of Criminal Procedure requires that the trial court withhold acceptance of a guilty plea until it determines that the plea is voluntary. The rule does not define "voluntary," except to state that it must not be the "result of force or threats or of promises apart from a plea agreement."

The rule requires that the judge make the determination of voluntariness "by addressing the defendant personally in open court." Although the Supreme Court once held that a guilty plea must be set aside if the trial court failed to follow this procedure,[68] the rule has since been amended to provide that "[a]ny variance from the procedures required by this rule which does not affect substantial rights shall be disregarded."[69]

[B] Ensuring An Intelligent Plea

Rule 11(c) requires the trial court to "address the defendant personally in open court and inform the defendant of, and determine that the defendant understands" a variety of matters that pertain to the nature and consequences of her plea.

The defendant must be informed of the rights that she waives by her plea, the nature of the charge to which she is pleading guilty, the maximum penalty for the offense, and any mandatory minimum penalty provided by law. She must also be warned that the court "intends to question the defendant under oath [in order to determine the factual basis of the plea], . . . [and] that the defendant's answers may later be used against the defendant in a prosecution for perjury or false statement."

---

[66] 400 U.S. 25 (1970).
[67] 1 C. Wright, at §§ 172-174.
[68] McCarthy v. United States, 394 U.S. 59 (1969).
[69] FRCP 11(h).

[C]　Determining the Factual Basis

Rule 11(f) provides that "the court should not enter a judgment upon such [guilty] plea without making such inquiry as shall satisfy it that there is a factual basis for the plea." This requirement does not apply to pleas of *nolo contendere.*

§ 197　Effect of a Guilty Plea on Prior Constitutional Claims[70]

[A]　General Rule

A state defendant who pleads guilty ordinarily is barred from raising a claim in federal court of a constitutional violation that allegedly occurred prior to the guilty plea, even if the claim might have served as a bar to conviction had she chosen to go to trial in the state court. The defendant is not barred, however, from proving that there was a procedural defect in the guilty plea procedure, or that the plea was not voluntarily or intelligently made.

For example, in *McMann v. Richardson*[71] three defendants in New York state court pleaded guilty to their crimes, based on their lawyers' advice that under state law there was no way to keep the jury from hearing their confessions, even though they were arguably coerced. When the New York procedure was later declared unconstitutional, and the new rule was applied retroactively, the defendants filed a *habeas corpus* petition on the ground that their guilty pleas were motivated by the coerced confessions.

The Court in *McMann* was unimpressed. It treated the defendants' guilty pleas as a break in the chain of events that preceded them in the criminal process.[72] As the *McMann* Court explained, a defendant who pleads guilty "is convicted on his counseled admission in open court that he committed the crime charged against him. The prior confession [or other constitutional claim] is not the basis for the judgment. . . ." The Court declared: "It is no denigration of the right to trial to hold that when the defendant waives his state court remedies and admits his guilt, he does so under the law then existing; further, he assumes the risk of ordinary error in either his or his attorney's assessment of the law and facts."

Although *McMann* used the word "waiver" in its explanation of the rule, this term is a misnomer, as the Supreme Court later recognized.[73] A waiver involves an intelligent relinquishment of a known right, which may not be involved if a defendant acts on the basis of faulty legal advice. Therefore, it is more accurate to say that the defendant who pleads guilty *forfeits* the right to assert constitutional claims pertaining to actions that occurred prior to the plea.[74]

---

[70] *See generally* Westen, *Away From Waiver: A Rationale for the Forfeiture of Constitutional Rights in Criminal Procedure*, 75 Mich. L. Rev. 1214 (1977); Note, *The Guilty Plea as a Waiver of "Present But Unknowable" Constitutional Rights: The Aftermath of the Brady Trilogy*, 74 Colum. L. Rev. 1435 (1974).

[71] 397 U.S. 759 (1970).

[72] *See* Tollett v. Henderson, 411 U.S. 258, 267 (1973) (explaining *McMann*).

[73] *Id.* at 266.

[74] Westen, n. 70 *supra*, at 1215.

[B] Exceptions to the General Rule

A defendant who pleads guilty is not barred in all circumstances from raising antecedent constitutional claims in federal court. First, although a defendant assumes the risk of "ordinary error" by her attorney, she does not assume the risk that her lawyer is incompetent. If her attorney's conduct does not fall within the range of competence demanded of attorneys in criminal cases and she was prejudiced as a result, she may attack her guilty plea.

Second, the Supreme Court has admitted a few exceptions to its forfeiture rule, although it has struggled to explain the basis for the exceptions. In *Blackledge v. Perry*,[75] it permitted a defendant who pleaded guilty to raise a due process claim that he was the victim of prosecutorial vindictiveness in the charging process. And, in *Menna v. New York*,[76] it permitted a defendant to raise an antecedent double jeopardy claim, even as it warned that "[w]e do not hold that a double jeopardy claim may never be waived."

On the other hand, the Court ruled in *Tollett v. Henderson*[77] that a person who pleads guilty is barred from raising a claim of racial discrimination in the selection of the grand jurors who indicted him. And, in *United States v. Broce*,[78] the Court confirmed its warning in *Menna* by holding that the defendant in *Broce* was barred from raising a double jeopardy claim.

How are these exceptions and non-exceptions justified? The *Menna* Court sought to explain the distinction on the basis of "factual" versus "legal" guilt: a plea of guilty is an admission of factual guilt and therefore removes that issue from the case; it does not remove claims that the defendant, although factually guilty, may not legally be subjected to conviction and punishment.

That distinction does not adequately explain the Court's decisions.[79] First, one reason for the double jeopardy clause is to prevent factually innocent persons from being wrongly convicted as the result of successive prosecutions.[80] Thus, a double jeopardy claim arguably falls on the "factual guilt" side of the line, which would mean that the defendant's claim in *Menna* should have been barred. One the other hand, the racial discrimination claim in *Tollett* can be treated as a "legal guilt" defense, since discrimination in the selection of a grand jury is constitutionally wrong even if the people its indicts are guilty. Therefore, the claim in *Tollett* arguably should not have been barred.

Beyond this, as a matter of policy, it is hard to defend a proposition that legal rights relating to factual innocence may be lost through inadvertence, whereas claims that have nothing to do with factual innocence are not barred.[81]

The Supreme Court in *Blackledge* provided a different explanation for the rules: the defendant is not barred from raising antecedent constitutional claims that go

---

[75] 417 U.S. 21 (1974).

[76] 423 U.S. 61 (1975).

[77] 411 U.S. 258 (1973).

[78] 488 U.S. 563 (1989).

[79] Westen, n. 70 *supra*, at 1223.

[80] *See* § 199[D] *infra*.

[81] Seidman, *Factual Guilt and the Burger Court: An Examination of Continuity and Change in Criminal Procedure*, 80 Colum. L. Rev. 436, 475 (1980).

"to the very power of the State to bring the defendant into court to answer the charge brought against him." Thus, the prosecutorial vindictiveness alleged in *Blackledge*, if proved, would have barred the government from haling the defendant into court at all on the felony charge for which he pleaded guilty. Similarly, a double jeopardy claim, if upheld, bars future prosecution of that offense. On the other hand, in *Tollett*, the government could have cured the problem of the tainted indictment by securing a new indictment from a properly selected tribunal.

This explanation comes closer to explaining the Court's treatment of antecedent constitutional claims. However, the justices added a wrinkle to the rule in *Broce*. In that case, *D* pleaded guilty to two separate charges of conspiracy. Thereafter, his co-defendants, who did not plead guilty, convinced the trial court that the two conspiracies were actually only one. In effect, this meant that *D* had been convicted and punished twice for a single conspiracy offense, in violation of the double jeopardy clause. *D* argued that this claim was not barred in light of *Menna*.

The Supreme Court disagreed. It noted that in *Menna* and *Blackledge*, in which the Court held that the antecedent claims were not barred, the defendants did not "seek further proceedings at which to expand the record with new evidence." In those cases, the defendants' claims were capable of determination on the basis of the indictment and the original record before the court that accepted the guilty plea.

In *Broce*, however, the legitimacy of *D*'s double jeopardy claim could not be proved without adding to the original record, since there was nothing in the indictments that suggested that the two conspiracies were actually one. Therefore, the Court was unwilling to permit the antecedent claim to be raised.

[C] Conditional Pleas

The rule that a guilty plea bars most antecedent constitutional claims creates practical difficulties for the defense and can result in wasteful allocation of judicial resources at the trial level.

Ordinarily, a defendant whose pretrial motion to suppress evidence is denied cannot seek interlocutory relief, *i.e.*, she cannot appeal the denial of her motion before the trial. Therefore, if the defendant wishes to preserve her constitutional claim, she must plead not guilty and go to trial, so that she can later appeal the trial court's denial of her constitutional motion, if she is convicted.

In order to avoid a trial that neither side wants, some jurisdictions, now including the federal courts,[82] permit conditional pleas of guilty. Under the federal rules, if the court and the prosecutor consent, the defendant may enter a conditional plea of guilty or *nolo contendere*, reserving the right, "on appeal from the judgment, to review of the adverse determination of any specified pretrial motion." If the defendant prevails on appeal, she may withdraw the plea. If she does not prevail, the plea stands.

---

[82] FRCP 11(a)(2).

§ 198 Prosecutorial (and Judicial) Vindictiveness

[A] Explanation of the Issue

Consider the facts in *State v. Halling*:[83] The prosecutor made a plea offer to D through his counsel. D's lawyer informed the prosecutor that his client wished to go to trial rather than to plead guilty, and he informed her to expect "three or four days of [pre-trial] motions." The prosecutor then told counsel, "I have a brilliant idea. I have just thought of a way to cause further evil to [your client]." She explained that she intended to charge D with additional crimes. Assuming that she did so, did the prosecutor act improperly?

The facts demonstrate a tension in the law. On the one hand, the law affords prosecutors substantial discretion in determining whether to prosecute and what charges to bring.[84] The law also tolerates, and even encourages, plea bargaining. Arguably, the prosecutor's actions in this case constituted hard, but lawful, bargaining.

On the other hand, with substantial discretion comes the power to abuse. A prosecutor might be lenient or severe for inappropriate reasons. In the *Halling* case, for example, the prosecutor's decision to "up the ante" might have been a vindictive response on her part to D's unwillingness to accept her plea offer. She may have been punishing him for his insistence on his constitutional right to go to trial.

This section deals with the extent to which a due process clause "vindictiveness defense" is recognized in circumstances such as those in *Halling*. However, to understand the law on this subject, one must consider prosecutorial vindictiveness more generally, *i.e.*, outside the plea-bargaining context.

Furthermore, the law regarding prosecutorial vindictiveness is an off-shoot of a separate line of Supreme Court cases pertaining to judicial vindictiveness. These two lines of cases are only partially independent of each other; therefore, the issue of judicial vindictiveness is also considered here.

As will be seen, the early holdings of the Supreme Court in the vindictiveness area were broad and seemed to be sweeping in nature; however, the Court has backed off and narrowed the scope of the rules in both lines of cases. Therefore, the reader must consider the narrower version of the rules (subsection [C]) in light of the original ones (subsection [B]).

[B] The Original Vindictiveness Rules

[1] Judicial Vindictiveness

In *North Carolina v. Pearce*,[85] D successfully appealed his conviction for assault with intent to rape on the ground that his confession was improperly admitted

---

[83] 66 Or. App. 180, 672 P.2d 1386 (1983).

[84] *See generally* Frase, *The Decision to File Federal Criminal Charges: A Quantitative Study of Prosecutorial Discretion*, 47 U. Chi. L. Rev. 246 (1980); Kaplan, *The Prosecutorial Discretion — A Comment*, 60 Nw. U. L. Rev. 174 (1965); LaFave, *The Prosecutor's Discretion in the United States*, 18 Am. J. Comp. L. 532 (1970).

[85] 395 U.S. 711 (1969).

against him at trial. On retrial, *D* was convicted again, but the prison sentence imposed was more severe than that handed out after the first trial.

The Supreme Court held that a judge may not punish a defendant for successfully appealing a conviction by imposing a more severe sentence after a second trial and conviction. According to *Pearce*, due process "requires that vindictiveness against a defendant for having successfully attacked his first conviction must play no part in the sentence he received after a new trial." Moreover, since fear of vindictiveness may deter a defendant from exercising his right to appeal, "due process also requires that a defendant be freed of apprehension of such a retaliatory motivation on the part of the sentencing judge."

In order to insure the absence of judicial vindictiveness, the Court held in *Pearce* that a judge may not impose a more severe sentence upon a defendant after a new trial unless the reasons for doing so appear on the record and are "based upon objective information concerning identifiable conduct on the part of the defendant occurring after the time of the original sentencing proceeding."

For example, under *Pearce*, a court may impose a more severe penalty after a second trial if, after the first sentencing hearing, the defendant committed another crime and thereby demonstrated her heightened dangerousness. But the trial court may not impose a more severe penalty on the basis of new evidence introduced at the second trial regarding the defendant's involvement in the original crime.

[2] Prosecutorial Vindictiveness

In *Blackledge v. Perry*,[86] the Court applied the principles of *Pearce* to a case involving alleged prosecutorial vindictiveness. In *Blackledge*, *D* was convicted of assault with a deadly weapon, a misdemeanor, in a court with jurisdiction over misdemeanor prosecutions only. *D* exercised his right under state law to a trial *de novo* in a superior court. Before the new trial began, however, the prosecutor sought and obtained a new indictment charging *D* with assault with a deadly weapon with the intent to kill, a felony.

D did not produce evidence that the prosecutor's motivation for seeking the higher charge was to punish him for exercising his statutory right to a new trial. Nonetheless, the Supreme Court concluded that the *Pearce* rationale — that a defendant should be free from the apprehension of retaliation for exercising a constitutional or statutory right — applied to the case, and that the prosecutor was barred from bringing the more serious charge.

In a footnote, the Court observed that "[t]his would clearly be a different case if the State had shown that it was impossible to proceed on the more serious charge at the outset." It gave an example of such a case: if the defendant were originally charged with battery, but prior to the second trial the victim died from his wounds and the prosecutor therefore charged the defendant with criminal homicide.

---

[86] 417 U.S. 21 (1974).

[C] Narrowing the Vindictiveness Rules

[1] *Pearce-Blackledge* as a Rebuttable Presumption

The Supreme Court no longer treats the *Pearce-Blackledge* rules as constitutional doctrine applicable in all cases of enhanced sentences or charges. Instead, the rules of these cases are considered prophylactic rules[87] intended to prevent due process violations.

That is, as the Court now explains the *Pearce-Blackledge* doctrine,[88] the Constitution is violated only by enhanced sentences or charges motivated by *actual* vindictiveness toward the defendant for having exercised a constitutional or statutory right.

Pearce and *Blackledge* only create a rebuttable presumption of vindictiveness. This presumption is applied in those circumstances in which its objectives are "most efficaciously served,"[89] namely in those cases in which "there is a 'reasonable likelihood' . . . that the increase in sentence [or charge] is the product of actual vindictiveness. . . . Where there is no such reasonable likelihood, the burden remains upon the defendant to prove actual vindictiveness."[90]

In other words, in *all* circumstances the due process clause prohibits vindictiveness in sentencing and charging. If a defendant can prove that she was the victim of such vindictiveness, perhaps as in the *Halling* case,[91] due process requires that the enhanced penalty or charge be voided. However, only in *some* circumstances will the Supreme Court now presume such vindictiveness and require the state to rebut the presumption.

Thus, it is now necessary to determine two matters in any alleged vindictiveness case: (1) Does the *Pearce-Blackledge* presumption apply?; and (2) If it does, did the state overcome the presumption? Those issues are discussed immediately below.

[2] Applicability of the Presumption

[a] Judicial Vindictiveness

The presumption of judicial vindictiveness applies in those circumstances in which there is a reasonable likelihood that an increase in sentence was the result of vindictiveness.

According to the Supreme Court, no such reasonable likelihood exists and, therefore, the presumption of judicial vindictiveness does not apply, if the second sentence is imposed by a different sentencer: that is, the second sentence was imposed by a different-level court than the original one;[92] the first sentencer was

---

[87] For discussion of the significance of identifying a rule as "prophylactic," *see* § 15 *supra*.

[88] *See especially* United States v. Goodwin, 457 U.S. 368 (1982); Texas v. McCullough, 475 U.S. 134 (1986); Alabama v. Smith, 109 S.Ct. 2201 (1989).

[89] Texas v. McCullough, 475 U.S. at 138.

[90] Alabama v. Smith, 109 S.Ct. at 2205.

[91] *See* § 198[A] *supra*.

[92] Colten v. Kentucky, 407 U.S. 104 (1972) (first trial was held in a minor county court; *D* was retried in a superior court of general criminal jurisdiction).

a jury and the second one was a judge;[93] two different juries imposed the sentences;[94] or, probably, if the sentencers were different trial judges.[95]

Nor does the presumption now automatically apply even if the same judge is involved in both trials. For example, in *Alabama v. Smith*,[96] D pleaded guilty to charges of burglary and rape, was sentenced, but later succeeded in vacating his plea. Thereafter he pleaded not guilty, was convicted, and received a more severe sentence from the same judge.

The Court held that the presumption of vindictiveness does not apply when the first (and lesser) penalty was imposed after a guilty plea, and the second (and more severe) punishment was imposed after a trial. The *Smith* Court stated that in such circumstances the increase in sentence is "not more likely than not attributable to vindictiveness." The Court concluded that the more likely reason for any increase in sentence is that "the relevant sentencing information available to a judge after the plea will usually be considerably less than that available after a trial."

Likewise, in *Texas v. McCullough*,[97] the Court refused to apply the presumption in a case in which, after D's first conviction, the trial judge granted D's motion for a new trial based on his claim of prosecutorial misconduct. In view of the judge's favorable ruling on the motion, which indicated that he was not hostile to D's wishes for a second trial, the Court concluded that the possibility of vindictiveness was too speculative to require the operation of the presumption. This conclusion was reinforced by the fact that D chose to be sentenced by the judge in the second trial, rather than to invoke his statutory right to be sentenced by the jury.

[b] Prosecutorial Vindictiveness

Just as the scope of the *Pearce* doctrine has been narrowed, the Supreme Court has reduced the scope of the *Blackledge* prosecutorial vindictiveness rule.

In *Bordenkircher v. Hayes*,[98] the Court refused to apply the presumption of vindictiveness in the context of pretrial plea bargaining. In *Bordenkircher*, the prosecutor obtained an indictment of D for uttering a forged instrument, a felony carrying a two-to-ten year prison sentence. In plea negotiations, the prosecutor offered to recommend a five-year prison sentence if D would plead guilty, but he also told D's counsel that if his client did not plead guilty, he would return to the grand jury and seek an indictment of D, a prior two-time felon, under the state's

---

[93] Texas v. McCullough, 475 U.S. 134 (1986).

[94] Chaffin v. Stynchcombe, 412 U.S. 17 (1973).

[95] *See McCullough*, 475 U.S. at 140 n.3. *Pearce* involved two different judges, but *McCullough* suggested that this fact "may not have been drawn to the [*Pearce*] Court's attention. . . ." Therefore, it stated, "[w]e . . . decline to read *Pearce* as governing this issue." One state court has held that, notwithstanding *McCullough*, a presumption of vindictiveness is required under the state due process clause when the second, and more severe, sentence is imposed by a different trial judge. People v. Van Pelt, 76 N.Y.2d 156, 556 N.Y.S.2d 984, 556 N.E.2d 423 (1990).

[96] 109 S.Ct. 2201 (1989).

[97] 475 U.S. 134 (1986).

[98] 434 U.S. 357, *reh'g denied*, 435 U.S. 918 (1977).

habitual offender law, thereby subjecting him to a maximum sentence of life imprisonment for the present offense.

D refused to plead guilty, whereupon the prosecutor went through with his threat and secured a new indictment charging *D* with violation of the state's recidivist law. After a jury found *D* guilty, he was sentenced to life imprisonment on the basis of his two prior felonies.

The Supreme Court distinguished *Blackledge*, which the justices described as involving a "unilateral imposition of a penalty upon a defendant who had chosen to exercise a legal right to attack his original conviction," from the present situation, which it described as the "give-and-take negotiation common in plea bargaining." In short, whereas the defendant in *Blackledge* was arguably punished for seeking a trial *de novo*, the defendant in *Bordenkircher* was merely the "victim" of hard pretrial plea bargaining.

The Court took the *Bordenkircher* exception a step further in *United States v. Goodwin*,[99] when it placed the entire pretrial setting outside the scope of the *Blackledge* presumption. *Goodwin* did not involve the give-and-take of plea bargaining. Instead, *D* was charged with misdemeanor assault, after which he advised the prosecutor that he desired a trial by jury, which necessitated transferring the case to a higher court and to a different prosecutor.[100] The new prosecutor obtained a new indictment based on the same incident, charging *D* with the more serious offense of assault on a federal officer, a felony.

The Court distinguished *Blackledge* from the pretrial setting of the present case on the ground that *Blackledge* involved the defendant's exercise of a right that "caused a complete retrial after he had been once tried and convicted." The Court reasoned that the "deep-seated bias" against retrial of issues creates "institutional pressures" that support a presumption of prosecutorial vindictiveness; such pressures are absent, the Court concluded, in the pretrial context. Therefore, after *Goodwin*, the *Blackledge* presumption of prosecutorial vindictiveness does not apply in any purely pretrial setting.

[3] Rebutting the Presumption

[a] Judicial Vindictiveness

The Supreme Court stated in dictum in *Texas v. McCullough*[101] that, notwithstanding the language of *Pearce*, the presumption of judicial vindictiveness may be overcome on the basis of *any* objective information justifying the increased sentence, including information relating to the defendant's conduct *before* the time of the original sentencing proceeding. For example, new, more damaging evidence

---

[99] 457 U.S. 368 (1982).

[100] Does the fact that a second prosecutor was involved take the case outside the *Blackledge* presumption, just as the *Pearce* presumption is now inapplicable in the case of different sentencers? *Goodwin* did not so state or hint. However, in Thigpen v. Roberts, 468 U.S. 27 (1984), the Court held that the presumption is not inapplicable merely because of a change in the prosecutorial team (*i.e.*, two attorneys working for the same office). The Court left open "the correct rule when two independent prosecutors are involved."

[101] 475 U.S. 134 (1986).

of the defendant's involvement in the crime, presented at the second trial, may now be used to justify enhanced punishment.

The effect of *McCullough* is to eviscerate the *Pearce* rule because, as the Court conceded, "a defendant may be more reluctant to appeal if there is a risk that new, probative evidence supporting a longer sentence may be revealed on retrial." The Court stated, however, that this "chilling effect" is not "sufficient reason to create a constitutional prohibition against considering relevant information in assessing sentences."

[b] Prosecutorial Vindictiveness

In *Blackledge*, the Court left open only a narrow window of possibility for rebuttal of the presumption of prosecutorial vindictiveness, namely in circumstances in which the government can show that "it was impossible to proceed on the more serious charge at the outset."

In *United States v. Goodwin*,[102] however, the Court described more broadly the method by which the presumption may be rebutted, stating that it "could be overcome by objective evidence [in the record] justifying the prosecutor's action." Ambiguously, though, it then quoted the original, narrower language from *Blackledge*, thus implying that it was not intending any change in the rule.

The Supreme Court has not decided a prosecutorial-vindictiveness case in which the prosecutor sought to overcome the presumption of vindictiveness. However, in view of the *McCullough* Court's apparent expansion of *Pearce* in this context, it is likely that the justices will permit prosecutorial rebuttal on the basis of any objective information of non-vindictiveness.

---

[102] 457 U.S. at 376 n.8.

CHAPTER 32

DOUBLE JEOPARDY

§ 199   Double Jeopardy Clause: General Principles[1]

[A]   Constitutional Text

[1]   In General

The Fifth Amendment provides that no person shall "be subject for the same offence to be twice put in jeopardy of life or limb." This provision, the so–called "double jeopardy clause," has roots in Greek and Roman law, as well as in English canon and common law.[2] It is a fundamental right applicable to the states through the Fourteenth Amendment due process clause.[3]

[2]   "In Jeopardy"

A person is not "in jeopardy" of life or limb until the jury is empaneled and sworn[4] or, in a bench trial, until the first witness is sworn.[5] As a result, the prosecutor is not constitutionally barred from appealing a pretrial dismissal of the criminal charges against a defendant, or from refiling charges against him, even if the judge's ruling was based on the evidence that would have been introduced at trial.[6]

[3]   "Of Life or Limb"

The Fifth Amendment provides that a defendant may not be twice placed in jeopardy "of life or limb" for the "same offence."[7] Notwithstanding this constitutional language, the Court long ago held that the double jeopardy clause applies to all crimes, regardless of the form of punishment imposed, including fines.[8]

The double jeopardy clause does not apply to civil proceedings, *i.e.*, to trials in which life or limb are not in jeopardy. Therefore, *D* may be subjected to a civil

---

[1] *See generally* M. Friedland, Double Jeopardy (Clarendon Press 1969); Thomas, *An Elegant Theory of Double Jeopardy*, 1988 U. Ill. L. Rev. 827; Westen, *The Three Faces of Double Jeopardy: Reflections on Government Appeals of Criminal Sentences*, 78 Mich. L. Rev. 1001 (1980); Westen & Drubel, *Toward a General Theory of Double Jeopardy*, 1978 Sup. Ct. Rev. 81; Comment, *Twice in Jeopardy*, 75 Yale L.J. 262 (1965).

[2] *See* M. Friedland, n. 1 *supra*, at 5–15.

[3] Benton v. Maryland, 395 U.S. 784 (1969), *overruling* Palko v. Connecticut, 302 U.S. 319 (1937).

[4] Crist v. Bretz, 437 U.S. 28 (1978).

[5] Serfass v. United States, 420 U.S. 377 (1975).

[6] *See id.*

[7] For the definition of "same offence," *see* § 205[B]–[C] *infra*.

[8] *See* Ex parte Lange, 85 U.S. (18 Wall.) 163 (1873).

suit, and a civil sanction imposed on him, even if he was previously criminally prosecuted and punished for the same conduct, or vice–versa.[9]

However, the government may not escape the dictates of the Fifth Amendment merely by denominating a proceeding as "civil." For example, D may not be prosecuted in a criminal court for conduct that was the basis of a previous juvenile court "civil" proceeding, because the potential negative outcome of a juvenile court hearing — loss of liberty and stigmatization — is analogous to a criminal conviction.[10]

Similarly, a sanction labelled as civil constitutes criminal punishment if its imposition serves the goal of punishment. For example, a government–imposed fine is criminal in nature if it does not roughly approximate the government's actual damages, and thus appears to be serving a deterrent or retributive penal goal.[11]

[B] "Dual Sovereignty" Doctrine

A single act may simultaneously constitute a violation of federal and state law. For example, the unprovoked act of D striking V, a federal officer, constitutes the federal offense of assault upon a federal officer,[12] and a state offense, such as simple assault or battery.

Likewise, a single act may constitute a violation of the criminal statutes of two states. For example, if D, while standing in state X, shoots and kills V, who is standing across the border in state Y, both states have sufficient connection to the homicide to claim jurisdiction.

Moreover, the same conduct may simultaneously violate a state law and a local ordinance. For example, if D steals a painting attached to a wall in a city building, this act might constitute theft under state law as well as larceny of city property under a city ordinance.

In *United States v. Lanza*,[13] the Supreme Court announced the dual sovereignty doctrine, which provides that "an act denounced by both national and state sovereignties is an offense against the peace and dignity of both and may be [prosecuted and] punished by each." In effect, prosecutions under laws of separate sovereigns are prosecutions of "different offenses," not reprosecutions of the "same offense." Therefore, it is permissible under the dual sovereignty doctrine for the federal government to prosecute a defendant after a state prosecution of the same conduct,[14] or vice–versa,[15] regardless of the outcome of the first prosecution.

The doctrine also applies to dual state prosecutions. For example, D may be prosecuted for a single homicide in states X and Y, assuming that both states have adequate ties to the conduct to claim jurisdiction over it. The Fifth Amendment

---

[9] *See* Helvering v. Mitchell, 303 U.S. 391 (1938).
[10] Breed v. Jones, 421 U.S. 519 (1975).
[11] United States v. Halper, 109 S.Ct. 1892 (1989).
[12] 18 U.S.C. § 111.
[13] 260 U.S. 377 (1922).
[14] Abbate v. United States, 359 U.S. 187 (1959).
[15] Bartkus v. Illinois, 359 U.S. 121, *reh'g denied*, 360 U.S. 907 (1959).

is not violated in such circumstances, even if the purpose of the second prosecution is to secure the death penalty after the defendant received a lesser penalty for the murder at the first trial.[16]

A city is a subordinate instrumentality of the state in which it is located, and thus it is not an independent sovereign for purposes of the double jeopardy clause. Consequently, successive municipality and state prosecutions for the same offense ordinarily are barred.

[C] Guarantees of the Double Jeopardy Clause

The Supreme Court's "favorite saying"[17] about the double jeopardy clause, adopted from a law review article,[18] and repeated frequently in its opinions, is the following:

> [T]he Fifth Amendment guarantee against double jeopardy . . . consists[s] of three separate constitutional protections. [1] It protects against a second prosecution for the same offense after acquittal. [2] It protects against a second prosecution for the same offense after conviction. [3] And it protects against multiple punishments for the same offense.[19]

This statement, technically correct as far as it goes, fails to mention three other "protections." First, the double jeopardy clause protects against reprosecution for the same offense after a mistrial. Second, it protects against reprosecution for the same offense after a dismissal. Third, embodied in the prohibition of double jeopardy is the doctrine of collateral estoppel.

Even with these additions to the list of guarantees, the Court's statement is potentially misleading in at least two respects.[20] First, it implies that the Fifth Amendment protections are absolute. However, only the rule against reprosecution for the same offense following an acquittal is absolute.

Second, the simplicity of the Court's explanation of the double jeopardy clause belies the remarkable complexity of its jurisprudence. Most of the guarantees are riddled with exceptions, and many of the key terms in double jeopardy jurisprudence — e.g., "same offense" and "acquittal" — are not self-defining.

The Court has conceded that "the decisional law in the area is a veritable Sargasso Sea which could not fail to challenge the most intrepid judicial navigator,"[21] and that its holdings "can hardly be characterized as models of consistency and clarity."[22] The result is that the double jeopardy clause is "the embodiment of technical . . . rules that require the Government to turn square corners."[23]

---

[16] Heath v. Alabama, 474 U.S. 82 (1985); see generally Allen & Ratnaswamy, Heath v. Alabama: A Case Study of Doctrine and Rationality in the Supreme Court, 76 J. Crim. L. & Crimin. 801 (1985).

[17] Westen, n. 1 supra, at 1062.

[18] Comment, n. 1 supra, at 265–66.

[19] North Carolina v. Pearce, 395 U.S. 711 (1969) (footnotes omitted) (numbers in brackets are added).

[20] See Westen, n. 1 supra, at 1062; Thomas, n. 1 supra, at 830.

[21] Albernaz v. United States, 450 U.S. 333, 343 (1981).

[22] Burks v. United States, 437 U.S. 1, 9 (1978).

[23] Jones v. Thomas, 109 S.Ct. 2522, 2533, reh'g denied, 110 S.Ct. 12 (1989) (Scalia, J., dissenting).

[D] Values Underlying the Double Jeopardy Clause

The Supreme Court has advanced various justifications for, or values of, the double jeopardy clause. First, reprosecution for the same offense subjects the individual "to embarrassment, expense and ordeal." It "compel[s] him to live in a continuing state of anxiety and insecurity."[24]

Second, reprosecution for the same offense presents an unacceptably high risk that the government will convict an innocent person, either because the prosecutor will use "the first trial as . . . a dry run for the second prosecution"[25] — using the first prosecution to discover the strengths of the defendant's case and the weaknesses of his own — or simply by wearing down the defendant with the State's superior resources.[26]

Third, in the context of mistrials, the Fifth Amendment protects the defendant's "valued right to have his trial completed by a particular tribunal."[27] Once a trial begins the defendant has a "weighty"[28] interest in "being able, once and for all, to conclude his confrontation with society through the verdict of a tribunal he might believe to be favorably disposed to his fate."[29]

Fourth, the Court has stated that "a" or "the" primary purpose of the double jeopardy clause is "to preserve the finality of judgments."[30] One scholar believes that verdict finality is the "core" interest of the double jeopardy clause;[31] others believe that it "is a relatively soft [interest that] . . . can be overridden by a strong and justifiable societal interest to the contrary."[32]

Overall, the Court has stated frequently in recent years that the aim of the double jeopardy clause is to bar reprosecution that results in "government oppression."[33] In other words, at least if society's interest in permitting reprosecution is substantial, the Fifth Amendment is not violated by reprosecution for the same offense unless the government action is unreasonably burdensome.

§ 200 Reprosecution After a Mistrial[34]

[A] Overview of the Issue

The "most often litigated and most puzzling aspect"[35] of double jeopardy law concerns reprosecutions following mistrials. A "mistrial" is a judicial termination

---

[24] Green v. United States, 355 U.S. 184, 187 (1957).

[25] Ashe v. Swenson, 397 U.S. 436, 447 (1970).

[26] United States v. Scott, 437 U.S. 82, 91, *reh'g denied*, 439 U.S. 883 (1985).

[27] Wade v. Hunter, 336 U.S. 684, 689, *reh'g denied*, 337 U.S. 921 (1949).

[28] Illinois v. Somerville, 410 U.S. 458, 471 (1973).

[29] United States v. Jorn, 400 U.S. 470, 486 (1971).

[30] Crist v. Bretz, 437 U.S. at 33.

[31] Thomas, n. 1 *supra*, at 828–29.

[32] Westen & Drubel, n. 1 *supra*, at 161.

[33] *See, e.g.*, Lockhart v. Nelson, 488 U.S. 33, 42 (1988); United States v. Scott, 437 U.S. at 91.

[34] Schulhofer, *Jeopardy and Mistrials*, 125 U. Pa. L. Rev. 449 (1977); Westen & Drubel, n. 1 *supra*, at 85–106.

[35] Thomas, n. 1 *supra*, at 831.

of a trial before a verdict is reached, granted on the motion of either party or on the judge's own motion. The intention of a judge in granting a mistrial is "that the prosecutor will be permitted to proceed anew notwithstanding the defendant's plea of double jeopardy."[36]

The declaration of a mistrial especially brings into play the defendant's valued interest in having his fate decided at the first trial. The Supreme Court has explained the double jeopardy concerns this way:

> Even if the first trial is not completed, a second prosecution may be grossly unfair. It increases the financial and emotional burden on the accused, prolongs the period in which he is stigmatized by an unresolved accusation of wrongdoing, and may even enhance the risk that an innocent defendant may be convicted. The danger of such unfairness to the defendant exists whenever a trial is aborted before it is completed. Consequently, as a general rule, the prosecutor is entitled to one, and only one, opportunity to require an accused to stand trial.[37]

The "general rule" stated in the preceding sentence is only partially accurate. The rule against reprosecution following a mistrial applies only if the mistrial was granted over the defendant's objection. Moreover, as discussed in the next subsection, an exception to this rule exists, one that is so broadly interpreted that it is invoked more often than the general rule itself.

[B] Mistrials Over the Defendant's Objection

[1] The "Manifest Necessity" Standard

In *United States v. Perez*,[38] the seminal Supreme Court case in the field, a mistrial was declared over *D*'s objection because the jury could not reach a verdict. The Court upheld the right of the government to reprosecute *D*, holding for the first time that the double jeopardy clause is not an absolute bar to reprosecution after a mistrial.

According to *Perez*, reprosecution following a defendant–opposed mistrial is permitted if a "manifest necessity" existed for terminating the trial, or, in other words, if "the ends of public justice would otherwise [have] be[en] defeated."

Perez stated that judges may exercise "sound discretion on the subject." However, the Court warned that in view of the defendant's weighty double jeopardy interests, the power to declare a mistrial "ought to be used [only] with the greatest caution, under urgent circumstances, and for very plain and obvious causes."

[2] "Manifest Necessity": The Case Law

[a] The Early Cases

Although *Perez* appeared to state only a limited exception to the general rule, post–*Perez* Supreme Court jurisprudence has belied that appearance. Indeed, until

---

[36] United States v. Scott, 437 U.S. at 92.
[37] Arizona v. Washington, 434 U.S. 497, 503–05 (1978) (footnotes deleted).
[38] 22 U.S. (9 Wheat) 579 (1824).

1963, the Court upheld every retrial after the grant of a defense–opposed mistrial that it considered.[39]

The Court justified mistrials for a variety of reasons, including the following circumstances that occurred or were discovered after jeopardy attached: the jury was unable to reach a verdict;[40] the defendant failed to plead to the indictment;[41] a juror served on the grand jury that had indicted the defendant;[42] a *petit* juror knew the defendant personally;[43] and two co–defendants, previously tried and convicted but not yet sentenced, and who were called as witnesses by the prosecutor, asserted their constitutional privilege not to testify until their sentences were imposed.[44]

In perhaps the most questionable decision in this period, *Gori v. United States*,[45] the trial judge abruptly declared a mistrial over *D*'s objection during the prosecutor's examination of a witness, because the judge feared that the questioning would ultimately lead to testimony prejudicial to *D*'s rights. As no improper question had yet been asked, much less answered, an appellate court found that the judge acted "overassiduous[ly]," "premature[ly]," "too hastily," and "overzealously."

The Supreme Court, 5–4, upheld the trial judge's actions under the manifest–necessity standard. The majority observed that the mistrial "order was the product of the trial judge's extreme solicitude — an overeager solicitude, it may be — in favor of the accused." Describing the judge's actions as "neither apparently justified nor clearly erroneous," the Court stated that it was "unwilling, where it clearly appears that a mistrial has been granted in the sole interest of the defendant, to hold that its necessary consequence is to bar all retrial."

[b] The "Radical Transformation"

Two years after *Gori* was decided, but after a personnel change on the Court,[46] the Supreme Court "radically transformed the jurisprudence of mistrials"[47] — or, at least, so it appeared — in *Downum v. United States*.[48]

In *Downum*, immediately after the jury was impaneled and sworn, the prosecutor requested a mistrial because his key witness had not yet been subpoenaed. The motion was granted over *D*'s objection.

The Supreme Court held that the Fifth Amendment barred reprosecution. In language reminiscent of *Perez*, it declared that mistrials should be granted only "in very extraordinary and striking circumstances,"[49] which it concluded were

---

[39] Schulhofer, n. 34 *supra*, at 459.

[40] Besides *Perez*, *see* Dreyer v. Illinois, 187 U.S. 71 (1902).

[41] Lovato v. New Mexico, 242 U.S. 199 (1916).

[42] Thompson v. United States, 155 U.S. 271 (1894).

[43] Simmons v. United States, 142 U.S. 148 (1891).

[44] Brock v. North Carolina, 344 U.S. 424 (1953).

[45] 367 U.S. 364, *reh'g denied*, 368 U.S. 870 (1961).

[46] Justice Frankfurter, author of *Gori*, was replaced by Arthur Goldberg, who voted with the new majority in *Downum*.

[47] Schulhofer, n. 34 *supra*, at 463.

[48] 372 U.S. 734 (1963).

[49] *Downum*, *quoting* United States v. Coolidge, 25 Fed. Cas. 622, 623 (1815).

absent in the present case because the prosecutor had been aware of the problem prior to the attachment of jeopardy. Furthermore, the *Downum* Court announced that it would "resolve any doubt 'in favor of the liberty of the citizen, rather than exercise what would be an unlimited, uncertain, and arbitrary judicial discretion.' "[50]

The Supreme Court followed this stricter approach in *Jorn v. United States*.[51] In *Jorn*, the judge expressed concern during the trial that various government witnesses had not been adequately informed of their constitutional privilege against self–incrimination. Therefore, he declared a mistrial so that they could consult with attorneys. The Supreme Court held that the trial judge abused his discretion because he did not conduct a "scrupulous" search for alternative remedies to the perceived problem.

[c] *Illinois v. Somerville*

Two years after *Jorn*, the Court turned directions again in *Illinois v. Somerville*.[52] In *Somerville*, the day after the jury was sworn in *D*'s theft trial, the prosecutor discovered that the indictment was defective, because it failed to allege *D*'s specific intent to steal. Under Illinois law, this defect could not be cured by an amendment to the indictment. Therefore, over *D*'s objection, the judge granted the prosecutor's motion for a mistrial, so that a new indictment could be issued. A few weeks later, after a new indictment was handed down, *D* was retried and convicted.

The Supreme Court, while conceding that no "mechanical formula" exists for determining the propriety of declaring a mistrial, stated that it was "possible to distill from [the prior cases] . . . a general approach" to the problem, which was:

> A trial judge properly exercises his discretion to declare a mistrial if an impartial verdict cannot be reached, or if a verdict of conviction could be reached but would have to be reversed on appeal due to an obvious procedural error in the trial.

For example, under this approach, "manifest necessity" for a mistrial exists when an impartial verdict is impossible because the jury is hopelessly deadlocked or because of juror bias. Likewise, a mistrial is proper if a subsequent conviction "would automatically" be overturned by an appellate court, such as when it is discovered during trial that the defendant failed to plead to the indictment or, as in *Somerville*, because he was tried on the basis of a fatally deficient indictment.

Not all of the prior cases "distilled" by the Court are explainable on the basis of this "general approach."[53] Also, as one scholar has observed, *Somerville* is "exceedingly difficult to reconcile with . . . *Downum* and *Jorn*,"[54] two cases that placed a very high value on the defendant's interest in having his fate settled at the first trial.

The Court in *Somerville* distinguished *Downum* on the ground that the latter case, in which a mistrial was declared so that the prosecutor could subpoena his

---

50 *Downum, quoting* United States v. Watson, 28 Fed. Cas. 499, 501 (1868).

51 400 U.S. 470 (1971).

52 410 U.S. 458 (1973).

53 For example, *see* n. 44 and accompanying text *supra*.

54 Schulhofer, n. 34 *supra*, at 468.

key witness, involved a situation "that lent itself to prosecutorial manipulation," in that the mistrial "operated . . . to allow the prosecution an opportunity to strengthen its case." In *Somerville*, however, there was no suggestion that the "legitimate state policy" against the amendment of indictments "could be manipulated so as to prejudice the defendant."

The *Somerville* Court distinguished *Jorn*, in which a mistrial was granted so that the government witnesses could consult with attorneys before they testified, on the basis that the judge in that case failed to consider alternatives to a mistrial, such as a continuance. In *Somerville*, however, the Court concluded that a mistrial was the only way to cure the problem.[55]

Although the retrial following the mistrial was upheld in *Somerville*, the Court did state that a defendant's interest in having his fate determined at the first trial is a "weighty one," and that the determination to abort a proceeding "is not be to be lightly undertaken." It also indicated that the fact that a defendant cannot prove prejudice beyond that which would ordinarily occur from any reprosecution does not "preclude . . . invocation of the double jeopardy bar in the absence of some important countervailing interest of proper judicial administration."

[d] *Arizona v. Washington*

In *Arizona v. Washington*,[56] *D*'s attorney made improper remarks in his opening statement to the jury. As a consequence, the judge declared a mistrial over *D*'s objection, although in doing so he did not expressly state that was there was a manifest necessity for his order, nor did he indicate whether he had considered other remedies, such as a cautionary jury instruction. Nonetheless, the Supreme Court held that the double jeopardy clause did not bar reprosecution.

The holding can be justified on the basis of the *Somerville* "general approach": due to the attorney's improper remarks, an impartial verdict was, perhaps, impossible. But, in view of the "weighty" interests at stake, the Court might have held that the decision to abort the proceeding was, in *Somerville's* words, too "lightly undertaken," particularly in view of the *Downum* Court's warning that it would "resolve any doubt in favor of the liberty of the citizen."

The Supreme Court's reasoning in this case provides clues to its current view of the proper role of appellate courts in scrutinizing mistrials. First, it stated that the burden of proof is on the government to prove the existence of a manifest necessity. However, as is now obvious, the word "necessity" is not to be taken literally. According to the Court, "we assume that there are degrees of necessity and we require a 'high degree' before concluding that a mistrial is appropriate."

Second, the extent to which an appellate court should oversee a judge's mistrial ruling depends on the problem that allegedly necessitated the mistrial. According to *Washington*:

> [T]he strictest scrutiny is appropriate when the basis for the mistrial is the unavailability of critical prosecution evidence, or when there is reason to

---

[55] Not so, said the dissenters. In view of *D*'s valued right to have the case decided on the present occasion, they argued that the trial judge should have allowed the case to be completed, as there was the possibility that *D* would be acquitted.

[56] 434 U.S. 497 (1978).

believe that the prosecutor is using the superior resources of the State to harass or to achieve a tactical advantage over the accused.

Thus, strict scrutiny was appropriate in *Downum*. Moreover, this language justifies the Court's comparative lack of scrutiny in *Gori*, because the mistrial in that case was declared "in the sole interest of the defendant."

On the other end of the scrutiny spectrum is a mistrial granted because of a hung jury, "long considered the classic basis for a proper mistrial." Virtually no scrutiny is required in such cases because of "society's [compelling] interest in giving the prosecution one complete opportunity to convict those who have violated its laws."

Between these extremes, but falling much closer to the latter end of the continuum, the Court concluded, was the case before it, one involving the possibility of juror bias. Because a trial judge is more conversant with the subjective factors relating to bias, his "determination is entitled to special respect."

In *Washington*, the Court concluded that the judge acted "responsibly and deliberately," rather than "irrationally," "irresponsibly," or "precipitately." Although he did not expressly state that the mistrial was necessary, nor that he had considered alternatives to his order, the Court held that the record as a whole demonstrated that the trial judge "accorded careful consideration to [*D*'s] interest in having the trial concluded in a single proceeding."

The Court noted that a factor in support of its conclusion, although not determinative, was that *D* did "not attempt to demonstrate specific prejudice from the mistrial ruling, other than the harm which always accompanies retrial."

[3] Making Sense of the Case Law

The manifest–necessity standard cannot be applied mechanistically or without regard to the particular facts of the case. Nonetheless, four factors are of particular importance in the resolution of mistrial cases:[57] (1) whether the government was responsible for the difficulty that gave rise to the motion for the mistrial; (2) whether the motivation of the party associated with the "difficulty" was improper, *e.g.*, the prosecutor acted with the intent to provoke the mistrial or, at least, the case is one in which there was a potential for manipulation; (3) whether the defendant suffered special prejudice as the result of the mistrial; and (4) whether meaningful alternatives to the mistrial existed.

A mistrial is probably improper (and, thus, double jeopardy will bar reprosecution) if there is a conjunction of factors (1) and (2) (as in *Downum*) or of (1) and (4) (as in *Jorn*), but not if (1) exists alone (as in *Somerville*).

Based on *Washington*, a mistrial might be improper in some circumstances even if (1) does not exist, *i.e.*, even if the defense, rather than the government, is responsible for the difficulty resulting in the mistrial. Specifically, if it can be shown that the defendant suffered extraordinary prejudice as the result of the mistrial (factor 3), and other suitable alternatives to the mistrial existed (factor 4), reprosecution might be inappropriate, at least if bad faith by the defense (factor

---

57 *See* Schulhofer, n. 34 *supra*, at 468–69.

2) is absent. For example, in *Washington*, if a key defense witness had died during the delay (factor 3), and a jury instruction could have cured the prejudice (factor 4), a valid double jeopardy claim might have been proved.

[C] Mistrials With the Defendant's Consent

[1] General Rule

As explained in *United States v. Dinitz*,[58] subject to one exception discussed in the next subsection, a defendant who requests a mistrial or who consents to one may not object on double jeopardy grounds to the institution of a second trial. His decision to request or consent to a termination of the proceedings serves as a deliberate relinquishment of his constitutional interest in obtaining a verdict at the first trial.

Is this rule fair when the request for a mistrial is the result of prosecutorial or judicial error that seriously prejudiced the defendant's capacity to obtain an acquittal at the first trial? Can it fairly be said in such circumstances that the defendant voluntarily waived his double jeopardy rights?

The Court's answer to these questions in *Dinitz* was that "traditional waiver concepts have little relevance where the defendant must determine whether or not to request or consent to a mistrial in response to judicial or prosecutorial error." According to the Court, "[t]he important consideration [for double jeopardy purposes] . . . is that the defendant retain primary control over the course to be followed in the event of such error."

That is, if the defendant decides that because of prejudicial error an acquittal is no longer realistic, he may prefer to have the proceedings terminated immediately, rather than to complete the trial, almost certainly be convicted, and then face the anxiety, expense, and delay of an appeal, which if successful would result in a retrial.[59] As long as the decision whether to continue the trial primarily rests with the defendant, his rights are adequately protected.

[2] Exception: Intent to Provoke a Mistrial Motion

In *Dinitz*, the Court noted the following exception to the general rule:

> The Double Jeopardy Clause . . . protect[s] a defendant against governmental actions intended to provoke mistrial requests. . . . It bars retrials where "bad faith conduct by judge or prosecutor" . . . threatens the "[h]arassment of an accused by successive prosecutions or declaration of a mistrial. . . ."[60]

The Supreme Court clarified this language in *Oregon v. Kennedy*.[61] In *Kennedy*, the trial judge granted *D*'s motion for a mistrial after the prosecutor improperly asked a witness whether the reason he did not do business with *D* was "because

---

[58] 424 U.S. 600 (1976).

[59] The ordinary rule is that reprosecution is permitted after a defendant successfully appeals his conviction. *See* § 203[A] *infra.*

[60] *Dinitz*, 424 U.S. at 611 (*quoting* United States v. Jorn, 400 U.S. at 485).

[61] 456 U.S. 667 (1982); *see generally* Ponsoldt, *When Guilt Should Be Irrelevant: Government Overreaching As a Bar to Reprosecution Under the Double Jeopardy Clause After Oregon v. Kennedy*, 69 Cornell L. Rev. 76 (1983).

[*D*] is a crook?" The trial judge subsequently ruled that the prosecutor had not intended to provoke a mistrial by his question. Therefore, he denied *D*'s motion to bar reprosecution on the basis of double jeopardy. However, an appellate court, relying on the full *Dinitz* statement quoted above, ruled in *D*'s favor because it found that the prosecutor's question was motivated by bad faith or was undertaken to harass or prejudice *D*.

The Supreme Court disagreed with the appellate court. In an opinion authored by Justice Rehnquist, and joined by four other members of the Court, the majority held that, as *Dinitz* suggested, reprosecution is barred when a mistrial is declared at the defendant's request, if the prosecutor or the judge intended to provoke or goad the mistrial motion. However, it rejected the implication in *Dinitz* that reprosecution is also barred upon the "more generalized standard of 'bad faith conduct' or 'harassment' on the part of the judge or prosecutor."

The Court rejected the "bad faith" and "harassment" tests because, in its opinion, they "offer virtually no standards for their application." The majority reasoned that "[e]very act on the part of a rational prosecutor during a trial is designed to 'prejudice' the defendant by placing before the judge or jury evidence leading to a finding of his guilt."

The Court also expressed concern that if these more general standards were used, a trial judge might be hesitant to grant a mistrial motion, because he would know that by doing so he would "all but inevitably bring with it an attempt to bar a second trial." As a result, fewer mistrial motions would be granted, and more defendants would be compelled to complete their tainted trials.

Justice Stevens, also speaking for Justices Brennan, Marshall, and Blackmun criticized the majority's narrow reading of *Dinitz*. He argued that under the Court's test, reprosecution would not be barred if it were determined that a prosecutor intended to inject prejudice into a trial in order to obtain a conviction, rather than to cause a mistrial. Likewise, the Fifth Amendment would not bar reprosecution if the prosecutor intended to harass the defendant, but was indifferent regarding whether a mistrial was declared. According to Stevens, a defendant's double jeopardy rights should outweigh the society's interest in obtaining a judgment on the merits in cases of such prosecutorial overreaching or harassment.

§ 201　Reprosecution After an Acquittal[62]

[A]　General Rule

Acquittals are accorded "special weight" in double jeopardy jurisprudence.[63] It has been the unequivocal rule since *Ball v. United States*[64] that a defendant who is acquitted of an offense may not be reprosecuted for that crime.

The bar on reprosecution after an acquittal is absolute. The prohibition applies whether the acquittal is the result of a "not guilty" verdict by the jury or a judge

---

[62] Westen, n. 1 *supra*, at 1004–23; Westen & Drubel, n. 1 *supra*, at 122–55.
[63] United States v. DiFrancesco, 449 U.S. 117, 129 (1980).
[64] 163 U.S. 662 (1896).

in a bench trial, an "implied" acquittal by the judge or jury,[65] or a ruling by the judge, whatever label he attaches to it, that "represents a resolution [in the defendant's favor], . . . of some or all of the factual elements of the offense charged."[66] An example of the latter variety of acquittal is a ruling (however denominated) by a judge in a jury trial that the State's evidence is insufficient to establish the defendant's guilt.[67]

The bar on reprosecution after an acquittal applies even if the verdict or ruling is "based upon an egregiously erroneous foundation,"[68] such as when a judge, who lacks the authority to do so, directs a verdict of acquittal before the prosecution has rested its case.

Similarly, an acquitted defendant may not be retried, "even if the legal rulings underlying the acquittal were erroneous."[69] For example, reprosecution is barred if a judge acquits a defendant of criminal recklessness, even if the basis of his verdict was the judge's legally erroneous understanding of the definition of "recklessness."[70]

Reprosecution is also prohibited if the verdict was the result of the judge's erroneous exclusion of evidence favorable to the prosecution at trial.[71] As the Supreme Court has stated, "the fact that 'the acquittal may result from erroneous evidentiary rulings or erroneous interpretations of governing legal principles,' . . . affects the accuracy of that determination, but it does not alter its essential character."[72]

Although retrial after an acquittal is always barred, the double jeopardy clause does not prohibit the government from appealing an acquittal if the defendant would not be exposed to a second trial if the appeal were successful.

For example, if a jury returns a guilty verdict, after which the judge grants D's motion for judgment of acquittal notwithstanding the verdict, the government may appeal the judicial acquittal.[73] If the appeal is successful, no new trial is required, as the original conviction may be reinstated. On the other hand, the government may not appeal a judgment of acquittal granted by the trial court following the declaration of a mistrial due to a deadlocked jury, because a new trial would be required if the appeal of the acquittal were successful.[74]

---

[65] See § 203[C] infra.

[66] United States v. Martin Linen Supply, 430 U.S. 564, 571 (1977).

[67] See Smalis v. Pennsylvania, 476 U.S. 140, 144 (1986).

[68] Fong Foo v. United States, 369 U.S. 141, 143 (1962).

[69] Sanabria v. United States, 437 U.S. 54, 64 (1978).

[70] Smalis v. Pennsylvania, 476 U.S. at 144–45 n.7.

[71] See Sanabria v. United States, 437 U.S. 54 (1978).

[72] United States v. Scott, 437 U.S. at 98 (quoting Brennan, J., dissenting in Scott).

[73] See United States v. Wilson, 420 U.S. 332 (1975); United States v. Scott, 437 U.S. at 91 n.7.

[74] United States v. Martin Linen Supply, 430 U.S. 564 (1977). However, a motion for judgment of acquittal must be made in timely fashion after the mistrial is declared, or else the acquittal rules do not apply.
For example, in United States v. Sanford, 429 U.S. 14 (1976), D did not make a timely motion for a judgment of acquittal after a mistrial was declared due to a deadlocked jury. Under the federal rules, the motion should have been made within seven days after the

[B] Rationale of the Rule

In *United States v. Scott*, the Supreme Court explained the prohibition on reprosecution following an acquittal this way:

> To permit a second trial after an acquittal, however mistaken the acquittal may have been, would present an unacceptably high risk that the Government, with its vastly superior resources, might wear down the defendant so that "even though innocent he may be found guilty."[75]

However, as has been forcefully argued,[76] this rationale is questionable in light of the contrasting rule that a defendant who successfully appeals a wrongful *conviction* ordinarily may be reprosecuted.[77] There is no reason to believe that a defendant who has been wrongly convicted as the result of prejudicial trial error is more likely to be guilty than one who is wrongly acquitted as the result of a ruling prejudicial to the government.

Nor can the rule adequately be justified as the dissenters in *Scott* sought to do, by claiming "that the second trial would present all the untoward consequences the Clause was designed to prevent," such as allowing the prosecutor to strengthen his case, and "to subject the defendant to the expense and anxiety of a second trial." This argument fails because in other double jeopardy contexts, such as after a mistrial, these concerns are not ordinarily considered sufficiently substantial to outweigh society's interest in bringing potentially guilty persons to justice.

Two commentators have argued that the most persuasive rationale for the rule against reprosecution following a jury acquittal is that it "may be a product of the jury's legitimate authority to acquit against the evidence."[78] That is, no verdict of acquittal by a jury is "wrong" as long as its power to acquit is not limited to simple fact–finding, which it is not, in view of the doctrine of "jury nullification."[79]

---

jury was discharged without having reached a verdict. FRCP 29(c). Instead, *D* waited until immediately prior to the second trial, at which time he successfully sought dismissal of the indictment on the basis of the evidence developed at the original trial.

Although the trial court's dismissal could have been interpreted as an "acquittal," the Supreme Court treated the case as one involving a mistrial in which manifest necessity justified the second trial (hung jury); it then treated the subsequent dismissal as a *pretrial* dismissal, which, like any other pretrial action, is not subject to the double jeopardy clause. *See* § 199[A][2] *supra*.

[75] 437 U.S. at 91 (*quoting* Green v. United States, 355 U.S. 184, 188 (1957)).

[76] Westen & Drubel, n. 1 *supra*, at 124–29.

[77] *See* § 203[A] *infra*.

[78] Westen & Drubel, n. 1 *supra*, at 129.

[79] The "jury nullification" doctrine provides that a jury may exercise its prerogative to disregard uncontradicted evidence and the legal instructions of the judge in order to acquit a defendant. Historically, juries have used their nullification power to acquit defendants charged with controversial offenses, such as the Fugitive Slave Act, which made it an offense to assist slaves to escape. But, the jury can use its nullification power for any reason, including as an act of compassion toward a factually guilty defendant. *See generally* Scheflin & Van Dyke, *Jury Nullification: The Contours of a Controversy*, 43 Law & Contemp. Prob. 51 (1980); Scott, *Jury Nullification: An Historical Perspective on a Modern Debate*, 91 W. Va. L. Rev. 389 (1989); Comment, *Jury Nullification and Jury-Control Procedures*, 65 N.Y.U. L. Rev. 825 (1990).

However, this rationale, one which the Court now acknowledges,[80] cannot justify the bar on reprosecution after an erroneous acquittal by a judge, who is not entitled to acquit against the evidence. Nonetheless, the no–reprosecution rule is one to which the Court has "clung tenaciously."[81]

§ 202 Reprosecution After a Dismissal

[A] Nature of a "Dismissal"

A dismissal often takes on the appearances of a mistrial or an acquittal. Furthermore, the trial court's characterization of its action does not control its classification.[82] Because a correct characterization is necessary in order to determine which double jeopardy rules apply — *i.e.*, "mistrial," "acquittal" or "dismissal" rules — it is important to understand the differences between these three procedural events.

Like a mistrial, a dismissal involves a judicial termination of the trial before a verdict is reached. However, unlike a mistrial, the granting of a dismissal "contemplates that the proceedings will terminate then and there in favor of the defendant,"[83] such as when a prosecution is dismissed due to government misconduct.

Like an acquittal, a dismissal involves a termination of a trial in favor of the defendant under circumstances in which it is assumed by the trial court that no further prosecution of the defendant for the offense will occur. The difference lies in the fact that a dismissal, but not an acquittal, involves a termination of the trial in the defendant's favor "on a basis unrelated to factual guilt or innocence."[84] For example, a ruling during the trial that the proceedings must be terminated because of preindictment delay[85] constitutes a dismissal and not an acquittal.[86]

[B] General Rules

[1] Dismissal on the Defendant's Motion

In *United States v. Jenkins*,[87] the Supreme Court held that the government is barred from appealing a dismissal. The Court concluded that an appeal would violate the double jeopardy clause because if it were successful the defendant

---

[80] *See* United States v. DiFrancesco, 449 U.S. at 130 n.11 (*quoting* Westen, n. 1 *supra*, at 1012, 1063).

[81] Thomas, n. 1 *supra*, at 852.

[82] United States v. Jorn, 400 U.S. at 478 n.7.

[83] United States v. Scott, 437 U.S. at 94.

[84] *Id.* at 99.

[85] *See* United States v. Wilson, 420 U.S. 332 (1975).

[86] Usually, dismissal motions must be made prior to trial, *e.g.*, FRCP 12(b), and thus before jeopardy attaches. However, some motions to dismiss may be raised for the first time during trial, *e.g., id.* 12(b)(2) (the indictment fails to show jurisdiction in the court). Furthermore, a judge may reconsider a pretrial motion for dismissal after jeopardy attaches, *e.g.*, Lee v. United States, 432 U.S 23 (1977), or the defendant may raise his motion again after the trial begins. *E.g.*, United States v. Scott, 437 U.S. 82 (1978).

[87] 420 U.S. 358 (1975).

would be required to undergo the expense, ordeal, and anxiety of a second prosecution.

Three years later, the Court overruled *Jenkins* in *United States v. Scott*.[88] The *Scott* Court concluded that the concerns expressed in *Jenkins*, while appropriate in other circumstances, do not apply to the situation "in which the defendant is responsible for the second prosecution" by seeking a dismissal of the charges against him. The latter case, the Court reasoned, "is scarcely a picture of an all–powerful state relentlessly pursuing a defendant who had either been found not guilty or who had at least insisted on having the issue of guilt submitted to the first trier of fact." As with mistrials, "the Double Jeopardy Clause, which guards against Government oppression, does not relieve a defendant from the consequences of his voluntary choice."

[2] Dismissal Over the Defendant's Objection

A judge rarely dismisses criminal charges against a defendant during a trial, except on the latter's motion or, at least, with his consent. However, suppose that a judge were to conclude that charges should be dismissed because of government misconduct, but the defendant objects because he wants his fate settled "once and for all" by the original trier of fact. Would principles of double jeopardy prohibit a prosecutorial appeal of a defense–opposed dismissal?

The Supreme Court has not resolved the issue. However, the reasoning of *Scott* does not apply in such a situation, as the defendant in such a case does not have primary control over his fate. At least one post–*Scott* lower court[89] has held that a dismissal under such circumstances bars further proceedings in the case, although it is possible that the Supreme Court might apply some variation on the "manifest necessity" standard used in mistrial cases in such a situation.

§ 203 Reprosecution After a Conviction

[A] General Rule

It is a "well–established part of our constitutional jurisprudence"[90] that, with one exception discussed in subsection [B], the double jeopardy clause does not bar reprosecution of a defendant who successfully appeals his conviction on the basis of prejudicial error in the prior proceeding.[91] Although the Supreme Court has offered various explanations for the rule,[92] the modern explanation is as follows:

---

[88] 437 U.S. 82, *reh'g denied*, 439 U.S. 883 (1978).

[89] United States v. Dahlstrum, 655 F.2d 971 (9th Cir.), *cert. denied* 455 U.S. 928 (1981).

[90] United States v. Tateo, 377 U.S. 463, 465 (1964).

[91] United States v. Ball, 163 U.S. 662 (1896). Of course, the government may not reprosecute a defendant for the same offense if he does not appeal his conviction or if his appeal is unsuccessful. It is only in this sense that it can generally be said that the Fifth Amendment protects against reprosecution after a conviction.

[92] For example, the Court has stated that the defendant "waives" his double jeopardy rights by appealing his conviction. *See* Trono v. United States, 199 U.S. 521 (1905). Because it is unfair to treat the defendant's appeal as voluntary if it is taken in response to government–caused prejudicial error, this argument is rarely advanced any longer. It has

Corresponding to the right of an accused to be given a fair trial is the societal interest in punishing one whose guilt is clear after he has obtained such a trial. It would be a high price indeed for society to pay were every accused granted immunity from punishment because of any defect sufficient to constitute reversible error in the proceedings leading to conviction.[93]

This explanation loses much of it force, however, if the basis for the appeal is that the prosecutor intentionally sought to provoke a mistrial motion by the defendant, which was wrongly denied by the judge. For example, assume that the prosecutor is aware that the trial is going poorly for the government, so he purposely infects the trial with prejudicial information, in order to goad *D* into requesting a mistrial. If *D* makes such a motion, and it is granted, reprosecution is barred under the principles of *Oregon v. Kennedy.*[94]

However, suppose that the judge denies the mistrial motion, and allows the trial to proceed to a judgment of conviction with an ineffectual cautionary instruction to the jury to disregard the prejudicial information. If *D* appeals, and the appellate court rules that the mistrial motion should have been granted because of the prosecutorial misconduct, it would seem that the *Kennedy* mistrial doctrine should apply to bar reprosecution, even in the context of a conviction. To date, however, the Court has not resolved a case involving such facts.

[B] Exception to the Rule: The *Burks* Principle

Notwithstanding the general rule, the Supreme Court ruled in *Burks v. United States*[95] that the government is barred from reprosecuting a previously–convicted defendant, if an appellate court reverses the conviction on the sole ground that the evidence presented at the trial was insufficient to sustain the guilty verdict. The *Burks* rule also applies if the trial judge grants a new trial on the basis of insufficiency of the evidence.[96]

The reasoning behind the *Burks* rule is that in the circumstances in which it pertains, the reversal of the conviction, or the granting of the motion for a new trial, "is in effect a determination that the government's case against the defendant was so lacking that the trial court should have entered a judgment of acquittal, rather than submitting the case to the jury."[97] Therefore, although convicted, the defendant's case is subsumed within the acquittal principles of the double jeopardy clause.

The *Burks* exception does not apply "beyond the procedural setting in which it arose."[98] Therefore, reprosecution is not barred if the appellate court or trial judge reverses the conviction on the basis of the weight, rather than the sufficiency, of the evidence.[99] That is, if a court concludes that sufficient evidence was

---

also been argued that the jeopardy of the first trial continues through the appeal and second trial (and any subsequent convictions, reversals, and trials). Kepner v. United States, 195 U.S. 100, 134–37 (1904) (Holmes, J., dissenting).

[93] United States v. Tateo, 377 U.S. at 466.
[94] 456 U.S. 667 (1982). *See* § 200[C][2] *infra.*
[95] 437 U.S. 1 (1978).
[96] Hudson v. Louisiana, 450 U.S. 40 (1981).
[97] Lockhart v. Nelson, 488 U.S. 33, 39 (1988).
[98] Richardson v. United States, 468 U.S. 317, 323 (1984).
[99] Tibbs v. Florida, 457 U.S. 31 (1982).

introduced at trial to justify a conviction, reprosecution is allowed even though the court, serving as a "thirteenth juror" (as is permitted in some states) would have acquitted the defendant.

Nor does the *Burks* rule apply after a mistrial is granted. For example, in *Richardson v. United States*[100] a mistrial was granted due to a hung jury. The trial court subsequently denied *D*'s motion for a judgment of acquittal based on insufficiency of the evidence. The Supreme Court held that *D* was not entitled to appeal the denial of the latter motion, stating that *Burks* was not intended to overturn the Court's long history of mistrial jurisprudence, which has "its own sources and logic."

The Court also considered *Burks* inapplicable in *Lockhart v. Nelson*.[101] In *Lockhart*, an appellate court overturned *D*'s conviction on the ground that evidence was erroneously and prejudicially introduced against him at trial. It further held that in the absence of that evidence there were insufficient grounds to convict *D*; therefore, applying *Burks*, it barred reprosecution.

The Supreme Court reversed the lower court's double jeopardy ruling. Distinguishing *Burks*, which involved a conviction overturned *solely* on the basis of evidentiary insufficiency, the Court held that reprosecution is permitted after a successful appeal by the defendant as long as "the evidence offered by the State and admitted by the trial court — whether erroneously or not — would have been sufficient to sustain a guilty verdict."

The Court concluded that its holding constituted a proper accommodation of the competing interests, in that it "recreates the situation that would have been obtained if the trial court had [properly] excluded the evidence." Under such circumstances, the defendant is provided an opportunity to obtain a new trial, and the government is given the chance to present other evidence that might have justified the guilty verdict, but which was held back because it appeared to be unnecessary in light of the trial court's erroneous evidentiary rulings.

The Court hinted in *Lockhart* at another area for litigation regarding the scope of the *Burks* rule: "[W]hether the rule that retrial is prohibited by an *appellate* court for evidentiary insufficiency . . . is applicable when the determination . . . is made instead by a federal habeas corpus court in a collateral attack on a state conviction. . . ." The Court assumed, without deciding, an affirmative answer to this question.

[C] Special Problem: Convictions With Implied Acquittals

[1] Verdict Acquittal

A criminal conviction can simultaneously result in an implied acquittal of a greater offense. For example, if *D* is charged with first–degree murder and the jury convicts him of second–degree murder, the conviction of the latter offense serves as a implied acquittal of the greater charge.[102] In such circumstances, if *D* successfully appeals from his second–degree murder conviction, the reprosecution–after–conviction rules apply to the *second*–degree murder charge, *i.e.*, *D* may

---

[100] 468 U.S. 317 (1984).
[101] 488 U.S. 33 (1988).
[102] Green v. United States, 355 U.S. 184 (1957).

be reprosecuted for that offense, but the reprosecution–after–acquittal ban applies to the *first*–degree charge, of which he was implicitly acquitted.

If *D* is nonetheless improperly retried and again convicted of the greater offense (first–degree murder), the appropriate remedy is to reduce the conviction to "a lesser included offense which is not jeopardy barred [*e.g.*, second–degree murder], [unless] . . . the defendant [is able] to demonstrate a reasonable probability that he would not have been convicted of the nonjeopardy–barred offense absent the presence of the jeopardy–barred offense."[103]

[2] Sentence "Acquittal"

Ordinarily, the concept of "implied acquittal" has no application to resentencing after a defendant is reprosecuted following a successful appeal of a conviction. The Supreme Court held in *North Carolina v. Pearce*,[104] therefore, that the double jeopardy clause is not violated if a judge imposes a more severe sentence after a second trial.[105]

For example, under *Pearce*, if a judge imposes a five–year prison sentence on *D* at his first trial, although the maximum punishment for the crime is 20 years, this decision cannot be treated as if it were an "implied acquittal" of 15 years. Double jeopardy is not violated, therefore, if the judge imposes a greater punishment, up to the maximum allowed under the law, after any subsequent reprosecution and conviction.

However, a different rule applies in the capital sentencing context. A typical capital–sentencing proceeding is conducted much like a trial: after a defendant is convicted of a capital offense, a separate hearing is held at which the prosecutor must prove to the trier of fact beyond a reasonable doubt that aggravating factual circumstances exist, and that they outweigh whatever mitigating circumstances the defendant may prove at the hearing. The trier of fact, usually a jury, then deliberates on whether to impose (or recommend) the penalty of death or life imprisonment.

The Supreme Court held in *Bullington v. Missouri*[106] that a determination at such a trial–like proceeding that the convicted defendant should be sentenced to life imprisonment is comparable to an acquittal of the "verdict" of death: it has "the hallmarks of the trial on guilt or innocence." Therefore, if the defendant succeeds in overturning his murder conviction for any reason, the state may not seek the death penalty on reprosecution of the capital offense.

A separate question relates to whether a prosecutor may, in the non-capital context, appeal a sentence it believes is too lenient. This issue is considered next.

---

[103] Morris v. Mathews, 475 U.S. 237, 246–47 (1986).

[104] 395 U.S. 711 (1969).

[105] The more severe sentence may raise due process concerns. *See* § 198 *supra*.

[106] 451 U.S. 430 (1981).

§ 204 Government Appeals of Criminal Sentences[107]

The federal government has no constitutional right of appeal in a criminal case, absent explicit statutory authority.[108] Although government appeals of certain dismissals have been permitted for a long time, broad authority did not exist until 1971, when Congress (as many states now do) authorized government appeals in criminal cases except "where the double jeopardy clause of the United States Constitution prohibits further prosecution."[109]

The federal government also has statutory authority in specified types of criminal cases to appeal a sentence imposed by the trial judge that it believes is too lenient.[110] Under this statute, the appellate court may impose a more severe sentence (thus, requiring no reprosecution), or remand the case to the trial court for resentencing (which, again, requires no retrial) if it determines that the sentencing court's findings were "clearly erroneous" or that it abused its discretion in imposing sentence.

The Supreme Court upheld the latter sentencing statute in *United States v. DiFrancesco.*[111] The Court stated that "a sentence does not have the qualities of constitutional finality that attend an acquittal." It also reasoned that the government's right to appeal the sentence does not involve the sort of government oppression that the double jeopardy clause bars.

§ 205 Multiple Prosecutions of the "Same Offense"[112]

[A] Explanation of the Issue

A single act may constitute a violation of two or more distinct statutory provisions. For example, if *D* assaults *V* with a deadly weapon, he simultaneously commits the crimes of "assault with a deadly weapon" and "assault." Similarly, when *D* burglarizes *V*'s home, he also commits the crime of trespass.

The Supreme Court observed in *Brown v. Ohio*[113] that "[i]t has long been understood that separate statutory crimes need not be identical . . . in order to be the same within the meaning of the constitutional prohibition." In other words, the fact that an act or series of acts is prohibited under two or more distinct provisions of a criminal code does not in itself mean that the conduct constitutes "separate offenses" for Fifth Amendment purposes.

---

[107] *See generally* Westen, n. 1 *supra.*
[108] United States v. Scott, 437 U.S. at 84–85.
[109] 18 U.S.C. § 3731.
[110] 18 U.S.C. § 3576.
[111] 449 U.S. 117 (1980).
[112] *See generally* Thomas, *The Prohibition of Successive Prosecutions for the Same Offense: In Search of a Definition,* 71 Iowa L. Rev. 323 (1986); Westen & Drubel, n. 1 *supra,* at 111–22. For purposes of clarity, in this and the next chapter section, the text uses the American spelling of "offense," although the English spelling ("offence") is used in the original version of the Fifth Amendment.
[113] 432 U.S. 161 (1977).

This section considers the meaning under the Fifth Amendment of the term "same offense." The issue is critical: the government may subject a defendant to successive prosecutions of separate offenses, even if the crimes were committed in a single criminal transaction;[114] but, subject to limited exceptions discussed in subsection [D], it is forbidden to put a defendant through the expense, anxiety, and ordeal of separate prosecutions of the "same offense."[115]

[B] "Same Offense": The *Blockburger* Test

In *Blockburger v. United States*[116] the Supreme Court stated that the test for determining whether two distinct statutory provisions constitute two offenses or only one for double jeopardy purposes "is whether each provision requires proof of an additional fact which the other does not."

For example, if Crime 1 requires proof of elements A, B, and C, and Crime 2 requires proof of elements A, B, and D, the two crimes are separate offenses, because each statute requires proof of a fact that the other does not (elements C and D, respectively).

However, if both offenses have identical elements — they both consist of statutory elements A, B, and C — they are the "same offense" under *Blockburger*. Or, if Crime 2 in the example above requires proof only of elements A and B, then the offenses are not distinguishable, because Crime 2 does not require proof of an additional fact, *i.e.*, when Crime 1 is proved, Crime 2 is necessarily proved.

As the Supreme Court explained in *Grady v. Corbin*,[117] "[i]f application of th[e *Blockburger*] test reveals the offenses have identical statutory elements or that one is a lesser included offense of the other, then the inquiry must cease, and the subsequent prosecution is barred." Furthermore, the sequence of the successive prosecutions is constitutionally immaterial: conviction of either offense bars subsequent prosecution of the other, absent a relevant exception to the rule.

For example, in *Brown v. Ohio*[118] D pleaded guilty to the offense of joyriding. After completion of his sentence for the offense, he was prosecuted for auto theft, based on the same conduct. Under state law, joyriding consisted of taking or operating a vehicle without the owner's consent; auto theft consisted of the same acts, but with the intent to steal the car. Under *Blockburger*, therefore, the two crimes in *Brown* were the "same offense": joyriding was a lesser–included offense of the other. Therefore, the government was forbidden to bring the second

---

[114] For example, if *D* kidnaps, robs, and rapes *V* in a single criminal transaction, the government may (as a matter of constitutional law) bring separate prosecutions for each charge. Various members of the Court have argued that the government should not be permitted to bring successive prosecutions in such circumstances. *E.g.*, Ashe v. Swenson, 397 U.S. 436, 448–460 (1970) (Brennan, Douglas, and Marshall, JJ. concurring). However, the Court has "steadfastly refused to adopt the 'single transaction' view of the Double Jeopardy Clause." Garrett v. United States, 471 U.S. 773, 790 (1985).

[115] The issue of multiple *punishment*, as distinguished from multiple *prosecutions* of the "same offense," is considered in § 206 *infra*.

[116] 284 U.S. 299 (1932).

[117] 110 S.Ct. 2084, 2090 (1990).

[118] 432 U.S. 161 (1977).

prosecution. The same result would apply if the order of the prosecutions were reversed.

[C] "Same Offense": Beyond *Blockburger*

[1] *Harris v. Oklahoma*

As discussed immediately above, under *Blockburger*, two offenses are the same for double jeopardy purposes if they have identical statutory elements or if one crime is a lesser–included offense of the other.

Consider, however, the circumstances in *Harris v. Oklahoma*.[119] *D* killed *V* during the commission of a robbery, for which he was convicted of felony–murder. Subsequently, he was prosecuted for the robbery that resulted in the death. In a brief *per curiam* opinion, the Court unanimously held that the robbery prosecution was barred by the double jeopardy clause.

Under a strict application of the *Blockburger* test, however, the two crimes — felony–murder and robbery — were not the "same offense." The felony–murder statute under which *D* was prosecuted, like most of its kind, prohibited the killing of a human being during the attempted commission of any one of various enumerated felonies, including (but not limited to) robbery.

Put slightly differently, the crime of "felony–murder" consists of elements A (a death), B1, B2, or B3 (the attempted commission of an enumerated felony), and C (a causal connection between A and B1 or B2 or B3). As a statutory matter, therefore, under *Blockburger*, the crimes of "felony–murder" and "robbery" each require "proof of an additional fact which the other does not": felony–murder requires proof of a killing (which robbery does not); robbery requires proof of the forcible taking of another's person property (which felony–murder need not, in view of the fact that other felonies suffice).

Although the Court's reasoning in *Harris* was not laid out in any specificity, it is evident that the Court went beyond an analysis of the statutory elements of the two crimes. Instead, it looked at the facts of the actual case: because the felony–murder committed in this case involved a robbery, the two crimes were the "same offense" for purposes of the *Brown v. Ohio* no–multiple–prosecution rule.

[2] *Grady v. Corbin*

The precise scope of the *Harris* holding — and thus the extent to which the Court was willing to go beyond *Blockburger* in its definition of the "same offense" — remained uncertain until 1990, when the Court announced its decision in *Grady v. Corbin*.[120]

In *Corbin*, in an opinion authored by now-retired Justice Brennan, the Court held, 5–4, that even if two criminal statutes do not constitute the "same offense" under *Blockburger*, "the Double Jeopardy Clause bars a subsequent prosecution if, to establish an essential element of an offense charged in that prosecution, the government will prove conduct that constitutes an offense for which the defendant has already been prosecuted."

---

[119] 433 U.S. 682 (1977).
[120] 110 S.Ct. 2084 (1990).

The facts in *Corbin* were these: *D* drove his automobile across a double yellow line, striking two oncoming vehicles. As a result, *D* received two traffic tickets, one of which charged him with the misdemeanor offense of driving while intoxicated, and the second of which charged him with failing to keep right of the median.

Hours after the accident, a driver of one of the cars struck by *D*'s vehicle died from injuries stemming from the incident. However, the prosecutor involved in the homicide investigation failed to inform the judge hearing the traffic offenses or the prosecutor covering that court of the fatality. Three weeks after the accident, *D* pleaded guilty to the traffic offenses.

Subsequently, *D* was indicted for various felonies arising from the traffic accident, including the offense of reckless manslaughter. In a bill of particulars,[121] the prosecutor indicated three acts that he would rely on to prove that the homicide was reckless: (1) that *D* drove his vehicle in an intoxicated condition; (2) that *D* did not keep his vehicle to the right of the median; and (3) that *D* drove too fast during a heavy rain.

The reckless manslaughter prosecution was not barred under the *Blockburger* test. Under a statutory analysis of the offenses in question — "reckless manslaughter," on the one hand, and "driving while intoxicated" and "failing to keep to the right," on the other hand — *D* committed separate offenses. That is, manslaughter requires proof of a fact — a killing — that is not a statutory element of either driving offense. In turn, those offenses involve conduct — intoxication and failure to stay to the right, respectively — that are not statutory elements of manslaughter.

Nonetheless, the majority held that the second prosecution was barred by the double jeopardy clause because, based on the bill of particulars filed by the prosecutor, it was evident that the state would seek to prove reckless manslaughter on the basis of the conduct — driving while intoxicated, and crossing the center line — for which the defendant had already been prosecuted. The second prosecution would not have been barred if the bill of particulars had revealed that, to prove recklessness, the prosecutor intended to rely solely on *D*'s alleged conduct of driving too fast.

Justice Scalia, with whom Chief Justice Rehnquist and Justice Kennedy joined, dissented in *Corbin*.[122] He stated that the majority opinion failed to take into account the text of the double jeopardy clause, which protects individuals from being twice put in jeopardy for the "same offence," but not for the "same conduct."

Furthermore, by its language, the Fifth Amendment protects a person from being "twice put in jeopardy," the implication of which is that the double jeopardy issue should be determined before the second trial begins. Yet, as Justice Scalia pointed out, a prosecutor cannot be compelled in some states to file a bill of particulars; therefore, a court will often be unable to ascertain prior to the second

---

[121] In the context of a criminal prosecution, a "bill of particulars" is a written specification of the facts that the prosecutor intends to prove to support the charges set out in the indictment. Under federal rules and in various states, a trial court may order the government to file a bill of particulars after an indictment is issued. FRCP 7(f).

[122] Justice O'Connor filed a separate dissent in which she stated that she agreed with much of Justice Scalia's dissent.

trial whether the Court's "proof–of–the–same–conduct" test will be satisfied. This problem does not arise under *Blockburger*, which focuses solely on the statutory elements of the offenses.

[D] Exceptions to the No-Successive-Prosecution Rule

Even if two statutory provisions constitute the "same offense" under *Blockburger* or *Corbin*, multiple prosecutions are not barred in all circumstances.

First, in *Brown v. Ohio*,[123] the Court suggested that "[a]n exception may exist where the State is unable to proceed on the more serious charge at the outset because the additional facts necessary to sustain that charge have not occurred or have not been discovered despite the exercise of due diligence." For example, if *D* were prosecuted and convicted of attempted murder of *V*, after which *V* dies as the result of the wounds inflicted upon him by *D*, a murder prosecution would not be barred.[124]

Second, the Court stated in *Brown* that the no–multiple–prosecution rule might not apply "when a defendant is retried on the same charge after a mistrial, . . . dismissal . . . , or after a conviction is reversed on appeal."

Indeed, the Court held in *Montana v. Hall*[125] that the rule in *Brown* does not apply if the first prosecution ends in the reversal of a conviction. In *Hall*, *D*'s incest conviction was reversed on the ground that the specific sexual acts charged against him did not constitute incest within the meaning of the statute. Consequently, the state charged *D* with sexual assault, an offense that the state court determined was the same as incest under the *Blockburger* test.

The Supreme Court allowed the second prosecution, notwithstanding *Brown*. It distinguished the latter case on the ground that the defendant in *Brown* did not successfully overturn the first conviction, but instead served the sentence assessed as punishment at the first trial. In contrast, in *Hall*, *D* successfully sought to invalidate the first conviction; therefore, the Court believed it was appropriate to apply the ordinary rule that reprosecution after a conviction is overturned is permissible.

Third, the double jeopardy clause is not violated when the defendant requests separate trials on the greater and the lesser offenses, or "in connection with his opposition to trial together, fails to raise the issue that one offense might be a lesser included offense of the other."[126]

---

[123] 432 U.S. 161 (1977).

[124] This exception did not apply in *Corbin* because the death from the accident occurred *before D* pleaded guilty to the traffic offenses, a fact of which a prosecutor was aware.

[125] 481 U.S. 400 (1987).

[126] Jeffers v. United States, 432 U.S. 137, 152, *reh'g denied*, 434 U.S. 880 (1977).

§ 206 Multiple Punishment for the "Same Offense"[127]

[A] Excessive Punishment for a Single Crime

In *Ex parte Lange*,[128] D was convicted of an offense punishable by a fine of $200 *or* a one–year prison term. However, the judge imposed a fine of $200 *and* sentenced D to one year in prison. D paid the fine and spent five days in prison before the trial court vacated the earlier judgment and re–sentenced D to one year in prison, commencing from the date of the second judgment. The fine, however, could not be returned because it had passed into the Treasury. Effectively, therefore, D suffered punishment of $200, and one year and five days in prison.

The Supreme Court held that D's punishment violated the Fifth Amendment double–jeopardy–clause prohibition on multiple punishment. Although the case could be interpreted in various ways, *Lange* now "stands for the uncontested proposition that the Double Jeopardy Clause prohibits punishment in excess of that authorized by the legislature."[129] D's punishment was excessive on two accounts: he was fined and imprisoned, which the statute did not permit; and he was subjected to imprisonment greater than that permitted under the law.

The holding in *Lange*, in particular the judge's failure to credit D's five days already served on the first judgment, was the basis for the Court's holding in *North Carolina v. Pearce*,[130] which explicitly held that the double jeopardy clause is violated "when punishment already exacted for an offense is not fully 'credited' in imposing sentence for a new conviction for the same offense."

In *Pearce*, D successfully appealed his first conviction; when he was retried and again convicted, the trial judge did not credit him for the time served by D while appealing the first conviction. This failure to give credit constituted a violation of the double jeopardy clause.

The holding in *Pearce* arguably goes further than was required under the Fifth Amendment. Credit for time served clearly should have been required if D had received the maximum punishment for his offense upon the second conviction: in such circumstances, without credit, D would have served a sentence in excess of that authorized by the legislature, in violation of *Lange*.

But, *Pearce* went further by requiring credit in all cases. For example, suppose that D were sentenced after the second conviction to five years in prison, for an offense punishable by imprisonment up to ten years. Suppose further that D received no credit for one year served before the first conviction was overturned. The effect of this no–credit sentence would be that D would serve six years in prison, which is still within the maximum punishment allowed by the legislature. As a matter of double jeopardy principles, there ought to be no difference between sentencing D the second time to six years in prison with one year of credit for time already served, or to sentence him (as hypothesized) to five years with no credit.

---

[127] *See generally* Thomas, *A Unified Theory of Multiple Punishment*, 47 U. Pitt. L. Rev. 1 (1985); Thomas, *Multiple Punishments for the Same Offense: The Analysis After Missouri v. Hunter*, 62 Wash. U.L.Q. 79 (1984).

[128] 85 U.S. (18 Wall.) 163 (1874).

[129] Jones v. Thomas, 109 S.Ct. 2522, 2526, *reh'g denied*, 110 S.Ct. 12 (1989).

[130] 395 U.S. 711 (1969).

Nonetheless, under *Pearce*, if the judge wants *D* to serve a total of six years, he must follow the former approach.

[B] Multiple Punishment for Different Crimes

As discussed above,[131] a single act may constitute a violation of two or more statutory provisions. Furthermore, under the traditional *Blockburger* test,[132] separate crimes constitute the "same offense" for double jeopardy purposes if they contain identical statutory elements, or if one offense is a lesser–included offense of the other.

After earlier intimations to the contrary, the Supreme Court ruled in *Missouri v. Hunter*[133] that imposition of cumulative punishments for two crimes that constitute the "same offense" under the *Blockburger* test is not always a violation of the double jeopardy clause.

For example, in *Hunter*, *D* was prosecuted in a single trial for armed robbery and "armed criminal action." The latter crime, which was treated as a lesser–included offense of robbery under the *Blockburger* test, expressly provided that punishment imposed for it "shall be in addition to any punishment provided by law for the crime committed . . . with . . . a dangerous or deadly weapon."

The Court in *Hunter* held that punishment for multiple crimes, although a "single offense" under *Blockburger*, is not barred "[w]here . . . a legislature specifically authorizes cumulative punishment under two statutes." According to the Court, in such circumstances, "a court's task of statutory construction is at an end and the prosecutor may seek and the trial court or jury may impose cumulative punishment. . . ."

Thus, although the prosecutor is generally required to *prosecute* a defendant for two "same offense" crimes in a single prosecution, *punishment* for both crimes after a *single* trial is not barred if the legislature intended to permit it. Essentially, the *Blockburger* "same offense" test creates only a rebuttable presumption against multiple punishment for "same offense" crimes.

§ 207 Collateral Estoppel

[A] Nature of the Doctrine

The Supreme Court declared in *Ashe v. Swenson*[134] that the doctrine of "collateral estoppel" is embodied in the guarantee against double jeopardy. As the Court explained the concept, collateral estoppel "means simply that when an issue of ultimate fact has once been determined by a valid and final judgment, that issue cannot again be litigated between the same parties in any future lawsuit."

The facts in *Ashe* demonstrate how the doctrine is applied. In the case, six poker players were robbed at the home of one of the victims by three or four armed men.

---

[131] *See* § 205[A] *supra.*
[132] Blockburger v. United States, 284 U.S. 299 (1932).
[133] 459 U.S. 359 (1983).
[134] 397 U.S. 436 (1970).

D and three other men were charged with six counts of armed robbery, one count for each victim at the poker game.

The prosecutor could have joined all six robbery counts in a single prosecution.[135] Instead he chose to prosecute *D* for each robbery seriatim. At the first trial for robbery of one victim, *D*'s sole basis for acquittal was that he was not at the scene of the crime, *i.e.*, that he was misidentified as one of the robbers. The jury acquitted *D*.

When the prosecutor sought to bring *D* to trial again for the robbery of another poker player, *D* sought to bar the second prosecution. Because each robbery constituted a separate offense, the prosecutor's multiple prosecution strategy did not offend ordinary double jeopardy principles.[136] Nonetheless, the Court held that the doctrine of collateral estoppel barred further criminal proceedings against *D*.

As the Court explained in *Ashe*, in order to apply the doctrine of collateral estoppel, a court must examine all of the relevant matters in the case in order to determine "whether a rational jury could have grounded its verdict upon an issue other than that which the defendant seeks to foreclose from consideration."

In this case, a realistic interpretation of the facts could "lead to but one conclusion," namely that the jury did not accept the prosecutor's claim that *D* was one of those in the house. Therefore, as that issue could no longer be relitigated, there was no basis for prosecuting *D* for the remaining robberies.[137]

[B] Limits on Application of the Doctrine

The collateral estoppel doctrine is of limited practical value to criminal defendants. First, it can be used only if a rational jury could not have grounded its verdict on any basis other than the claim that the defendant seeks to foreclose from further consideration. Usually, however, criminal defendants raise multiple exculpatory claims at trial: they attempt to instill a reasonable doubt in the jurors' minds regarding one or more elements of the crime, and they raise defenses. In such circumstances, the jury's general verdict of acquittal is too ambiguous to justify use of the collateral estoppel doctrine. If a defendant wishes to take advantage of the *Ashe* rule, therefore, he must place "all of his eggs in one basket," rarely a safe strategy.

Second, the doctrine applies only if the issue in question has been adjudicated to a valid and final judgment. It does not apply if the first prosecution is concluded

---

[135] Under federal rules and in most states, two or more offenses "based on the same act or transaction" may be charged in the same indictment and, therefore, prosecuted in a single trial. FRCP 8(a). If such joinder would be prejudicial to the interests of either party, the court may sever the charges, subject to double jeopardy principles. FRCP 14.

[136] The double jeopardy clause does not require that multiple offenses stemming from the same incident be prosecuted in a single trial. *See* n. 114 *supra* and accompanying text.

[137] The prosecutor is not permitted to take advantage of the collateral estoppel doctrine in criminal cases. For example, in *Ashe*, if *D* had been convicted rather than acquitted at the first trial — if the jury had been convinced beyond a reasonable doubt that *D* had been one of the robbers — the prosecutor could not bar relitigation of the identification issue at subsequent trials. *See* Simpson v. Florida, 403 U.S. 384 (1971).

by a guilty plea, because in such circumstances there is no "adjudication on the merits after full trial."[138]

Third, the doctrine is inapplicable in a proceeding in which a lower standard of proof is permitted than at a criminal trial. For example, even if *D* is acquitted of an offense, he may not invoke collateral estoppel to bar a forfeiture proceeding in which the government may prove by a preponderance of the evidence that *D* committed the crime for which he was earlier acquitted.[139]

Similarly, consider the facts in *Dowling v. United States*.[140] In *Dowling*, a man wearing a ski mask burglarized *V*'s home. During the crime, *V* unmasked the intruder, whom she identified at trial as *D*. Despite this testimony, *D* was acquitted.

Subsequently, *D* was prosecuted for an unrelated bank robbery, at which the perpetrator also wore a ski mask. An eyewitness to that crime observed the culprit pull off the mask after he departed the bank. The witness identified *D* as the robber. At the second trial, in order to buttress this identification claim, the government sought to introduce testimony from *V* regarding the earlier burglary of which *D* had been acquitted.

The Supreme Court held that the doctrine of collateral estoppel, even if it were otherwise applicable to the case, did not bar introduction of the evidence that tended to prove that *D* committed the prior crime. The acquittal at the first trial proved that the jury had a reasonable doubt regarding *D*'s guilt for that offense; under the applicable evidentiary code the "prior crime" evidence was admissible at the second trial if a jury "could reasonably conclude" that *D* committed the previous offense, a lesser, civil burden of proof.

---

[138] Ohio v. Johnson, 467 U.S. 493, 500 n.9, *reh'g denied*, 468 U.S. 1224 (1984).
[139] United States v. One Assortment of 89 Firearms, 465 U.S. 354 (1984).
[140] 110 S.Ct. 668 (1990).

TABLE OF CASES

[References are to Sections.]

A

Abbate v. United States . . . 199[B]
Acevedo; People v. . . . . . 79[C][4]
Adams v. Texas . . . . 3[C][8]
Adams v. United States ex. rel.
  McCann . . . . 178[B][1]
Adams v. Williams . . . . 95[B][3];
  98[B][1]
Adamson v. California . . 9[A], [B];
  10[B]–[D]
Aguilar v. Texas . . . 45[A]; 46; 51
Ake v. Oklahoma . . . . . 177[A][2]
Alabama v. Smith . . . . 198[C][1],
  [2][a]
Alabama v. White . . . . . 95[B][3]
Albernaz v. United States . . 199[C]
Albertson v. Subversive Activities
  Control Board . . . . . . 160[B]
Alderman v. United States . . . 109;
  110; 112
Allen v. Illinois . . . . . 161; 163[B]
Almeida Sanchez v. United States . .
  106[B]
Anders v. California . . . 177[B][2]
Andresen v. Maryland 27;
  42[E][2]; 53[C];
  163[C][2]
Appeal of (see name of party)
Application of (see name of applicant)
Argersinger v. Hamlin . . . 3[C][8];
  176[B][4][a]
Arizona v. Fulminante . . . . 13[C];
  130
Arizona v. Hicks . . . 39[A]; 67[D];
  80; 81[C]; 82
Arizona v. Roberson . . 145[D][2][a]
Arizona v. Washington . . . .
  200[B][2][d]
Arkansas v. Sanders . . . . 49[B][3];
  79[B][C][2]
Ash; United States v. 167
Ashcraft v. Tennessee . . 128[B][1],
  [C], [D]

Ashe v. Swenson . . 199[D]; 205[A];
  207[A]

B

Bagley; United States v. . . . . 75[B]
Baldasar v. Illinois . . . 176[B][4][c]
Ball v. United States . . . . 201[A];
  203[A]
Ballew v. Georgia . . . . . . 3[C][8]
Baltimore City Department of Social
  Services v. Bouknight . . . 160[B];
  163[C][2]
Bandy v. United States 186
Bank of Nova Scotia v. United States
  . . . . 13[A]; 14
Barnard v. State . . . . 33[C]
Barron v. Baltimore 8
Bartkus v. Illinois . . . . . . 199[B]
Batson v. Kentucky . . . . . 3[C][8]
Beck v. Ohio . . . . 42[B]
Beckwith v. United States . . . . . .
  142[B][1]
Bell v. Clapp . . . . 54[B]
Bell v. Wolfish . . . . 69[A]; 185[A],
  [B]; 188[C][1]
Bellis v. United States . . . . 160[A]
Belton; People v. 72
Benchimol; United States v. . . 194
Benton v. Maryland . . . . . . 9[B];
  199[A][1]
Berger v. New York . . 32[A]; 39[A]
Berger v. United States . . 178[A][2]
Berkemer v. McCarty . . 55; 67[C],
  [D]; 69[A]; 71[A]; 73;
  74; 142[A], [B][3], [4];
  146[B]
Betts v. Brady . . . . . 176[B][2][b]
Biswell; United States v. 104
Bivens v. Six Unknown Named Agents
  . . . . 120[C][2][b], [D]
Blackburn v. Alabama . . 131; 132;
  133[A]
Blackledge v. Perry . . . . . 197[B];
  198[B][2], [C][1], [2][b]

[References are to Sections.]

Blanton v. City of North Las Vegas . . . . 3[C][8]
Blockburger v. United States . . . . . 205[B], [C]; 206[B]
Boland; State v. 37
Bordenkircher v. Hayes . . . . 198[C][2][b]
Boyd v. United States . . 17; 26; 29; 33[B]
Boykin v. Alabama . . . . . 195[A], [C][3], [4]
Brady v. United States . . . 191[A]; 192[B][1]; 195[B], [C][4]
Bram v. United States 126
Breed v. Jones . . . . 199[A][3]
Breithaupt v Abram . . . . . 117[C]
Brewer v. Williams . . . . . . 12[A]; 143[B], [C][1]; 149[E]; 150; 151; 152[A]; 153[A], [B]; 155[E]
Brignoni–Ponce; United States v. . . 106[B]
Brinegar v. United States . . . . 41; 42[A]; 43; 44[A], [B]
Broce; United States v. . . . 197[B]
Brock v. North Carolina . . . . 200[B][2][a]
Brooks v. Tennessee 180
Brower v. Inyo County . . . . . 22; 40[A], [C]
Brown v. Illinois . . . . . 122[A][3]; 125[E][1], [2][c][d]
Brown v. Mississippi . . . . 117[C]; 126; 129[B]; 131
Brown v. Ohio . . . . . 205[A], [B], [C][1], [D]
Brown v. Texas . . . . . 40[B]; 102
Brown v. United States . . 113; 114
Brown v. Walker . . . . 163[B]
Bryan v. State . . . . . 145[C][2][b]
Buie v. State 100
Bullington v. Missouri . . 203[C][2]
Bumper v. North Carolina . . 89[A], [B]
Burch v. Louisiana . . . . . . 3[C][8]
Burdeau v. McDowell 20
Burger v. Kemp . . . . 181[B][2][b]; 182[A]

Burks v. United States . . . 199[C]; 203[B]
Burns v. Ohio . . . . . . 177[A][2]
Butler v. McKellar . . . 11[D][2][b]

C

Cady v. Dombrowski . . . 78; 84[B]
Calandra; United States v. . . . 119; 120; 121[A], [B][1]
California v. Beheler . . . . . 142[A]
California v. Byers . . . . . . 160[B]
California v. Carney . . . . 75[B]; 78
California v. Ciraolo . . . 35[A], [B]
California v. Greenwood 37
California v. Hodari D . . . . 40[C]
California v. Minjares 118
California v. Prysock 144
Camara v. Municipal Court . . . 20; 47; 48[A]; 49[B][2]; 93
Camara v. Superior Court . . . 104
Campbell; State v. . . . . . 30[D][3]; 31[B]; 34[B]
Canton, Ohio, City of v. Harris . . . 120[D]
Caplin & Drysdale, Chartered v. United States . . . . . . 179[B][1]
Cardwell v. Lewis . . . . . 75[C]; 78
Carroll v. United States . . . 42[A]; 75[B]; 76; 77; 78
Carter v. Kentucky . . . . . . 3[C][8]
Ceccolini; United States v. . . . . . . 125[E][2][e]
Chadwick; United States v. . . . 27; 69[A], [B][1]; 79[C][4]; 116[D]
Chaffin v. Stynchcombe . . . . 198[C][2][a]
Chambers v. Maroney . . 13[B]; 27; 75[C]; 77; 78; 79[C][2]
Chapman v. California . . . . 13[B], [C]; 16
Chapman v. United States 16
Charles v. United States . . . 69[A]
Chimel v. California . . . . . . 25; 49[B][1]; 66; 67[A]; 69[B][1]; 70; 72 [B]; 73
City of (see name of city)
Clinton v. Virginia 26

[References are to Sections.]

Coker v. Georgia . . . . 11[D][2][a]

Coleman v. Alabama . . . . 3[C][4]

Colonnade Catering Corp. v. United States 104

Colorado v. Bannister . . . . . 75[B]

Colorado v. Bertine . . . . . . 84[B]; 85[A][1], [3], [C]; 86[A]

Colorado v. Connelly . . . 131; 132; 133[A]; 145[A], [C][1], [3]

Colten v. Kentucky . . 198[C][2][a]

Commonwealth v. (see name of defendant)

Connally v. Georgia 51

Connecticut v. Barrett . . . . 145[D][2][c]

Coolidge v. New Hampshire . . . . . 49[B][2]; 51; 75[A]–[C]; 80; 81[C]; 83

Coolidge; United States v. . . . . . . 200[B][2][b]

Cooper; United States v. . . . . 142[B][3]

Cortez; United States v. . . 95[B][1]

Costello v. United States . . 3[C][5]

Couch v. United States 134

Crews; United States v. . . . . 57[B]; 125[C][1]

Crist v. Bretz . . 199[A][2], [C], [D]

Cronic; United States v. 7

Culombe v. Connecticut . . . 89[A]; 133[A]

Cupp v. Murphy 55; 64

D

Dahlstrum; United States v. . . . . . 202[B][2]

Dantzler; People v. . . . . 122[A][3]

Davis v. Mississippi . . . . . 97[C]

DeCoster; United States v. . . . . . . 181[B][1]

Defore; People v. . . . . 120[C][2][b]

Delaware v. Prouse 102

Delaware v. Van Arsdall . . . 13[B]

Desist v. United States . . . . 11[C], [D][1]; 120[C][2][b]

Dew v. United States . . . . 153[C][2][b]

Di Re; United States v. . . . . 79[A]

DiFrancesco; United States v. . . . . 201[A]; 204

Dinitz; United States v. . . . 12[B]; 200[C][1]

Dionisio; United States v. . . . . . . 163[A][2][b]

Dixson; State v. . . . . 33[C]

Doe; United States v. . . . . 160[A]; 163[A][1], [2][b], [C][2]

Donovan v. Dewey 104

Douglas v. California . . . 177[B][1]

Dow Chemical Co. v. United States . . . . 35[A]

Dowling v. United States . . 207[B]

Doyle v. Ohio . . . . 147[B]

Draper v. United States . . 45[B][2]; 56

Dreyer v. Illinois . . . . 200[B][2][a]

Duckworth v. Eagan 144

Dunaway v. New York . . . . 40[A]; 41; 48[A]; 55; 57[A]; 96[A][B]; 125[E][2][c]

Duncan v. Louisiana . . . . . . 9[D]; 176[B][4][a]

Dunn; United States v. . . 33[A][B]

E

Edwards v. Arizona . . . . . 143[A]; 145[D][2][a]; 146[B]; 153[C][1]; 155[D]; 156

Edwards; United States v. . . . . 27; 68[C][2]; 69[A]; 87

Elkins v. United States . . . . . 118; 120[B]

Entick v. Carrington 29

Escobedo v. Illinois . . . 7; 128[C]; 137; 138; 142[B][1]; 148; 149

Espinosa–Gamez; State v. . . 46[A]

Estepa; United States v. 14

Evitts v. Lucey . . 177[B][2]; 181[A]

Ex parte (see name of applicant)

F

Faretta v. California . . . . . 178[A]; 182[D]

[References are to Sections.]

Ferguson v. Georgia 180
Figueroa; United States v. . . 46[A]
Fikes v. Alabama . . . . 133[B]
Fingerprinting of M.B., In re . . . . .
97[C]
Fisher v. State 131
Fisher v. United States . . . .
163[C][1], [2]
Fletcher v. Weir . . . . 147[B]
Florida v. Meyers . . . . 5[C]
Florida v. Riley . . . . . 30[A], [C];
35[A]–[C]
Florida v. Royer . . . . 40[B]; 42[B];
95[B][2]; 96[A], [B];
97[B]
Florida v. Wells . . . . 85[A][1], [3];
86[A]
Fong Foo v. United States . . . . . .
201[A]
Forte v. State 148
Frank; United States v. . . . . 85[B]
Franks v. Delaware . . 52; 122[A][3]
Frazier v. Cupp . . . . 133[B]
Frisbie v. Collins . . . . 57[B]; 68[B]

G

Garner v. United States 162
Garrett v. United States . . . 205[A]
Garrity v. New Jersey . . 163[C][1]
Geders v. United States . . . 13[C];
180
Gerstein v. Pugh . . . 3[C][2]; 57[B];
58
Gideon v. Wainwright . . . 3[C][8];
11[D][2][a]; 13[C]; 119;
127[C][1]; 148; 175;
176[A], [B][1], [3]
Gilbert v. California . . . .
163[A][2][b]; 165
Giordenello v. United States . . . . .
121[B][1]
Gomez v. United States . . . . 13[C]
Gonzalez; United States v. . . 46[A]
Gooding v. United States . . . 54[A]
Goodwin; United States v. . . . . . .
198[C][1]
Gouled v. United States . . 42[E][1];
89[C]

Gouveia; United States v. . . . 151
Grady v. Corbin . . . 205[B], [C][2]
Graham v. Connor . . . . . . 61[B]
Grau v. United States . . . . . 44[A]
Green v. United States . . . 199[D];
201[B]; 203[C][1]
Griffin v. California . . . . . 3[C][8]
Griffin v. Illinois . . 5[C]; 177[A][2]
Griffin v. Wisconsin . . . . 49[B][3];
103
Griffith v. Kentucky . . . . 11[D][1]
Griswold v. Connecticut . . . 10[C]
Groban, In re . . . . 3[C][5]
Grunewald; United States v. . . . . .
159[B][1]

H

Hale v. Henkel . . . . 39[A]; 160[A]
Halling State v. . . . . 198[A], [C][1]
Halper; United States v. . . . .
199[A][3]
Hamilton v. Alabama 148
Hammand; United States v. . . . 14
Hampton v. United States . . . . . .
174[B]
Harris v. New York . . . . . 147[A]
Harris v. Oklahoma . . . . 205[C][1]
Harris; United States v. . . . 45[C];
70
Harrison v. United States . . 135[B]
Hasting; United States v. . . 13[A],
[B]; 14
Havens; United States v. . . . .
121[B][2][b]
Hawkins v. State 22
Hayes v. Florida . . . . 40[A]; 97[C]
Heath v. Alabama . . . . . . 199[B]
Heike v. United States . . . . 163[B]
Helvering v. Mitchell . . . 199[A][3]
Hempele; State v. 37
Henderson v. Morgan . . . 195[C][2]
Henry v. United States . . . . 40[A];
149[E]; 150;
152[B][2][a], [C]
Hensley; United States v. . . 40[A];
95[B][4]; 97[A], [B]
Herring v. New York 180

[References are to Sections.]

Hester v. United States . . . 22; 26;
32[A]; 33[A]
Hill v. California . . . . 68[B]
Hill v. Lockhart . . . . . . 195[C][4]
Hoffa v. United States . . . . 32[B];
133[B]; 155[E]
Hoffman v. United States . . 163[B]
Holland v. Illinois . . . . . . 3[C][8]
Holloway v. Arkansas . . . . 13[C];
182[B]
Holt v. United States . . . .
163[A][2][c]
Hopt v. Utah . . . . . . 126; 129[A]
Horton v. California . . . 53[C]; 74;
80; 81[A], [B]; 83
Hovey; People v. . . . . 86[C]
Howard; United States v. 14
Hudson v. Louisiana . . . . . 203[B]
Hudson v. Palmer 107
Hurtado v. California . . 9[B]; 10[F]

I

Illinois v. Allen . . 12[B]; 178[A][2]
Illinois v. Andreas . . . . 30[C]
Illinois v. Gates . . . . 43[A]; 44[B];
46[A]; 95[B][1];
122[A][3]
Illinois v. Lafayette . . 84[B]; 85[C];
87
Illinois v. Perkins . . . . . . 133[B];
142[B][3]; 146
Illinois v. Rodriguez . . . . 2; 12[A];
43[A]; 49[B][3]; 88; 91
Illinois v. Somerville . . . . 199[D];
200[B][2][c]
In re (see name of party)
I.N.S. v. Delgado . . . . 40[A], [B];
95[A]
I.N.S. v. Lopez-Mendoza . . 121[A]
Irvine v. California . . . . . . 117[C]

J

Jackson; United States v. . . . 195[B]
Jacobsen; United States v. 20;
36[B]; 39[A]
Jacumin; State v. . . . . . . 46[C][1]
James v. Illinois . . . . 121[B][2][b]

Janis; United States v. 118;
121[A]; 134
Jeffers; United States v. . . 49[B][1];
111; 113; 114; 116[D];
205[D]
Jenkins v. Anderson . . . . . 147[B]
Jenkins; United States v. . . . . . .
202[B][1]
Johns; United States v. . . . . 75[C];
79[B], [C][3]
Johnson v. Louisiana . . . . 3[C][8]
Johnson v. New Jersey 138;
147[C][2]
Johnson v. United States . . 3[C][2];
11[D][1]; 42[B];
49[B][1]; 50; 163[C][2]
Johnson v. Zerbst . . 12[A], [B]; 90;
139[B][3][a]; 153[A];
176[B][1]
Jones v. Barnes . . . . 3[C][9]
Jones v. Thomas . . 199[C]; 206[A]
Jones v. United States 21; 43;
49[B][1], [3]; 109; 111;
113; 114; 115 116[B]
Jorn; United States v. . . . . 199[D];
200[B][2][b], [c]; 202[A]

K

Karo; United States v. . . . . 34[B];
39[B]
Katz v. United States . . 17; 24; 25;
29; 30[A], [C], [D][1],
[3]; 31[A]; 32[A], [B];
33[A]; 34[A]; 35[C]; 37;
49[B][1], [3]; 93; 114;
115; 116[D]
Kennedy v. Mendoza–Martinez . . .
188[C][1]
Kepner v. United States . . . 203[A]
Ker v. California . . . . 54[B]
Kimmelman v. Morrison . . . . . .
181[B][2][b], [3][b]
The King v. Warickshall . . 129[A]
Kirby v. Illinois 138; 151;
166[B][2]
Knotts; United States v. . . . 34[B]
Kotteakos v. United States . . 13[A]

[References are to Sections.]

Kuhlmann v. Wilson . . . 152[C][2]

L

La Buy v. Howes Leather Co. . . 14
Lange, Ex parte . . . . . . 199[A][3];
206[A]
Lanza v. United States 29;
199[B]
Leach; State v. 91
Lee v. United States . . . 29; 202[A]
Lefkowitz v. Turley 157; 161
Lego v. Twomey 130
Lemmon; State v. . . . . . . 40[C]
Leon; United States v. 51;
120[B], [C][1], [2][a];
121[B][2][a];
122[A][1]–[3]; 123;
124[A], [B]
Lewis v. United States . . . . 32[B]
Leyra v. Denno . . . . 133[B]
Lilienthal; People v. . . . . . . 31[B]
Linkletter v. Walker . . . 11[A], [C],
[D]; 120[B]
Lisenba v. California 131
Lockhart v. Nelson . . . . . . 203[B]
Lo-Ji Sales, Inc. v. New York . . 51;
122[A][3]
Lopez v. United States 29
Los Angeles, City of v. Lyons . . . .
120[D]
Lovato v. New Mexico . . . .
200[B][2][a]
Love; United States v. . . . . 46[A]
Lynumn v. Illinois . . . . . . 133[B]

M

Mabry v. Johnson 194
Mackey v. United States . . . . . .
11[D][1], [2][a]
Maine v. Moulton . . . . 74; 149[E];
152[B][2][b]; 153[C], [1],
[2][b]; 155[B]
Malcolm v. State . . . . 46[A]
Mallory v. United States . . . 43[A];
45[C]; 50; 129[C]
Malloy v. Hogan . . . . . [127[B][1];
129[B][1]; 137; 157

Mandujano; United States v. . . . . .
3[C][5]; 162
Manson v. Brathwaite 168
Mapp v. Ohio . . . 9[D]; 11[A], [B];
16; 19; 117[B], [D]; 118;
119; 120[A]; Ch. 21
Marion; United States v. 151
Marron v. United States . . . 53[C]
Marsala; State v. . . . . . . 124[A]
Marshall v. Barlow's Inc. 104
Marshall v. Lonberger . . 195[C][2]
Martin Linen Supply; United States v.
. . . . 201[A]
Martinez-Fuerte; United States v. . .
102; 106[B]
Maryland v. Buie . . . 54[C][2]; 59;
65; 67[A], [C]; 69[C];
70; 99; 100
Maryland v. Garrison . . . . 53[B]
Massachusetts v. Sheppard . . . . .
122[A][1]
Massiah v. United States 137;
149[A]; 150; 152; 154;
155
Mathis v. United States . . . . . .
142[B][3]
Matlock; United States v. . . 91; 92
Matthews v. Correa . . . . . 42[E][2]
McCarthy v. United States . . . . . .
195[A], [C][1]; 196[A]
McCoy v. Court of Appeals of
Wisconsin, Dist. 1 . . . 177[B][2]
McCray v. Illinois . . . 44[A]; 45[C]
McDonald v. United States . . . . .
49[B][1]; 70; 112
McKane v. Durtson . . . . . 3[C][9]
McKaskle v. Wiggins . . . . 13[C];
178[B][4]–[6]
McMann v. Richardson . . 181[A],
[B][1]; 191[A]; 195[C][4];
197[A]
McNabb v. United States 14;
129[C]
Melilli; Commonwealth v. . . 34[A]
Mendenhall; United States v. . . . .
40[A], [B]
Menna v. New York . . . . . 197[B]

[References are to Sections.]

Michigan v. Chesternut . . . 40[A], [C]
Michigan v. Clifford 105
Michigan v. Harvey . . 145[D][2][a]; 153[C][1]; 155[D]; 156
Michigan v. Jackson . . . 153[C][1]; 155[D]; 156
Michigan v. Long . . . . . 96[C]; 99
Michigan v. Mosley . . . . 145[D][1]
Michigan v. Summers . . . . . 54[D]
Michigan v. Thomas 78
Michigan v. Tucker . . . . 136; 147[C][2]
Michigan v. Tyler 105
Michigan Dept. of State Police v. Sitz . . . . 48[A]; 102
Miller v. Fenton . . . . 131; 133[A]
Miller; United States v. . . . . 34[A]
Milton v. Wainwright . . . . . 13[B]
Mincey v. Arizona . . . . 65; 135[A]
Minnesota v. Olson . . . 54[B]; 59; 60[B][2], [C]; 65; 116[B], [C][2], [D]
Minnick v. Mississippi . . . 128[C]; 145[D][2][a]
Miranda v. Arizona . . . 4[B]; 5; 15; 73; 125[B]; 127[B][2], [C][2]; 129[C]; 131; Ch. 24; 149[A]; 156
Missouri v. Hunter . . . . . 206 [B]
Mitchell; People v. . . . . . . 46[A]
Monell v. Department of Social Serv. . . . . 120[D]
Monia; United States v. 162
Monsanto; United States v. . . . . . 179[B][1]
Montalvo-Murillo; United States v. . . . . 13[A]; 188[A]
Montana v. Hall . . . . 205[D]
Montoya de Hernandez; United States v. . . . . 48[A]; 63; 106[A]
Moody v. United States 14
Moore v. Illinois . . . 13[B]; 166[C]
Moore v. Michigan . . . . . . 195[A]
Moran v. Burbine . . . . 12[A]; 145[C][1], [2][a], [b]; 148; 175
Morris v. Mathews . . . . 203[C][1]

Morris v. Slappy . . . . 179[A]
Mullen v. United States 14
Murphy v. Waterfront Commission . . 159[A], [B][1][2], [3], [4]
Murray v. Giarratano . . . . 177[C]
Murray v. United States . . . . . . 125[C][3]

N

N.A.A.C.P. v. Button 109
Nathanson v. United States . . . . . 44[B]
National Treasury Employees Union v. Von Raab . . . 49[B][3]; 108[A]
Neil v. Biggers 168
New Jersey v. Portash . . . 135[A]; 164
New Jersey v. T.L.O. 20; 23; 103; 107
New York v. Belton . . 69[B][2]; 72; 73; 79[A]
New York v. Burger 104
New York v. Class . . 39[A]; 75[A]
New York v. Harris . . . . . . 57[B]; 125[C][4]
New York v. P.J. Video, Inc. . . . . 48[A]
New York v. Quarles . . . . 146[A]
Nix v. Whiteside 183
Nix v. Williams . . . . . 125[C][1]; 155[E]
North Carolina v. Alford . . 195[A], [D]
North Carolina v. Butler . . 145[B]
North Carolina v. Pearce . . . . . . 198[B][1]; 203[C][2]; 296[A]

O

Ohio v. Johnson . . . . 207[B]
Oliver v. United States . . . 24; 26; 27; 28; 33[A]; 88
Olmstead v. United States 24; 25; 29
On Lee v. United States 29

[References are to Sections.]

One 1958 Plymouth Sedan v. Pennsylvania . . . . 121[A]

One Assortment of 89 Firearms; United States v. . . . . . . 207[B]

Opperman; State v. . . . . . . 84[A]

Oregon v. Bradshaw . . . . 145[D][2][a], [d]

Oregon v. Elstad . . . 15; 145[C][1], [2][a]

Oregon v. Kennedy . . . . 200[C][2]; 203[A]

Oregon v. Mathiason . . . . 142[A], [B][2]

Orozco v. Texas . . . 141; 142[B][2]

Ortiz; United States v. . . . . 106[B]

P

Palko v. Connecticut . . . . . . 9[B]; 159[A]; 199[A][1]

Parker v. North Carolina . . 191[A]

Patterson v. Illinois . . . 153[C][1], [2][a], [D][2]

Paulino v. United States . . . 116[E]

Payne v. Arkansas . . . . 13[C]; 130

Payner; United States v. . . 14; 110

Payton v. New York . . . . . . 17; 49[B][2]; 59; 60; 116[B]; 125[C][4]

Pearse v. Pearse 6

Pennsylvania v. Finley . . 177[B][2], [C]

Pennsylvania v. Mimms . . . 96[B]; 98[A]

Pennsylvania v. Muniz . . . 143[B], [C][3]; 146[C]; 159[B][2]; 163[A][1], [2][c], [3]

Penry v. Lynaugh . . . . 11[D][2][a]

Penson v. Ohio . . . . . . 177[B][2]

People v. (see name of defendant)

Perez; United States v. . . 200[B][1]

Perry v. Leeke 180

Phelps; State v. . . 133[B]; 163[C][1]

Place; United States v. . . . . 36[A], [B]; 39[A]; 96[A]; 101

Poe v. Ullman . . . . 9[C]

Powell v. Alabama . . . 176[B][2][a]

Prado; Commonwealth v. . . 3[C][4]

Preston v. United States . . 68[C][1]

Q

Quinn v. United States . . 159[B][4]

R

Rabinowitz; United States v. . . . . . 49[B][1], [2]; 70

Rakas v. Illinois . . . 111; 113; 114; 115; 116

Ramsey; United States v. . . 106[A]

Rawlings v. Kentucky . . . . . 115; 116[A][D]

Reid v. Georgia . . . . . . 95[B][2]

Rhode Island v. Innis . . . . 143[A]; 146[B]; 156

Richardson v. United States . . . . . 203[B]

Rizzo v. Goode . . . . 120[D]

Robbins v. California . . . 49[B][2]; 73; 79[B], [C][3]

Robinson; United States v. . . . 55; 67[C], [D]; 71[A]; 73; 74

Robison v. Miner & Haug . . . . . . 49[B][1]

Rochin v. California . . . 9[A], [B]; 117[C]; 174[A]

Rogers v. Richmond 7; 131

Romano; People v. 22

Ross v. Moffitt . . . . 177[C]

Ross; United States v. . . . 49[B][2]; 53[B]; 78; 79[B], [C][3], [4]; 79[C]; 116[D][4]

Rummel v. Estelle 8

Rushen v. Spain . . . . 13[B]

Russell; United States v. . . 171[A]; 172; 173; 174[A];

S

Saffle v. Parks . . . . . . 11[D][2][b]

Sagansky v. United States . . . . . . 171[C][1]

Salerno; United States v. . . 185[A]; 188[C][1]

Salvucci; United States v. . . . 109; 113; 114; 115; 116[B]

[References are to Sections.]

Sanabria v. United States . . 201[A]

Sanchez; United States v. . . . . 79[C][4]

Sanford; United States v. . . 201[A]

Santana; United States v. . . 60[A], [B][1]

Santobello v. New York . . . . 192[B][1]; 194

Sawyer v. Smith . . 11[D][2][a], [b]

Schmerber v. California . . . . . 25; 48[A]; 63; 69[A]; 108[B]; 117[C]; 163[A]; 169[B]

Schneckloth v. Bustamonte . . . . . . 12[B]; 73; 89[A]; 90; 133[A]

Scott v. Illinois . . 176[A], [B][4][b]

Scott v. United States . . . . . . 74; 199[D]; 200[A]; 201, [A]; 202[A], [B][1]; 204

See v. City of Seattle 26; 104

Segura v. United States . . 39[A]; 65

Serfass v. United States . . . . 199[A][2]

Shadwick v. City of Tampa . . . 51

Shamblin; State v. . . . . . 85[A][2]

Shapiro v. United States. . . 160[B]

Sharpe; United States v. . . . 96[A], [C]

Shelton v. United States . . . 195[B]

Sherman v. United States . . . . . : 171[A]; 172; 173

Sibron v. New York . . . . 98[B][1]

Silverman v. United States . . . 24; 29

Silverthorne Lumber Co. v. United States . . . . . 117[A]; 125[C][1]

Simmons v. United States . . . 113; 168; 200[B][2][a]

Skinner v. Railway Labor Executives' Ass'n . . . 20; 36[B]; 41; 49[B][1], [3]; 103; 108; 108[A]

Smalis v. Pennsylvania . . . 201[A]

Smith v. Illinois . . . . 145[D][2][b]

Smith v. Maryland . . 30[C], [D][2], [3]; 34[A]; 37

Snyder v. Massachusetts . . . . 9[B]

Sokolow; United States v. . . 95[A]; 96[C]

Sorrells v. United States . . 171[A]; 172

South Dakota v. Neville . . . . . . 163[C][1]

South Dakota v. Opperman . . . . 84[A]; 85[A][2], [3], [C]; 86[B]

Spano v. New York . . 129[B]; 130; 131; 133[B]

Spencer; State v. 148

Spinelli v. United States . . . 44[B], [C]; 45[A], [B][2], [D]

Sporleder; People v. . . . . . . 34[A]

St. Amant v. Thompson 51

St. Paul, City of v. Vaughn . . . 22

Stack v. Boyle . . . . . . 185[A], [B]

Stanford v. Texas . . . . 53[C]

Stanley v. Georgia . . . . 11[D][2][a]

State v. (see name of defendant)

Steagald v. United States . . . 60[C]; 74

Steele v. United States . . . . 53[B]

Stone v. Powell . . . . 118; 120[C][2][a], [b]; 121[B][1];

Stoner v. California . . . 26; 88; 91; 92

Stovall v. Denno . . . . . 11[C]; 168

Strickland v. Washington . . . . . . 176[B][5]; 180; 181[A]

Sullo; Commonwealth v. . . . . 85[A][2]; 86[C]

Swain v. Alabama . . . . . . 3[C][8]

Szott; United States v. . . . . 187[C]

T

Tague v. Louisiana . . . . . . 145[B]

Tateo; United States v. . . . 203[A]

Taylor v. Alabama . . . 125[E][2][c]

Taylor v. Louisiana . . . . . 3[C][8]

Taylor v. United States 26

Teague v. Lane . . . . 3[C][10]; 11[D][2][a], [b]

Tennessee v. Garner . . . . . 40[A]; 61[A]

Terry v. Ohio . . . . 25; 40[A], [B]; 48[A]; 49[B][2]; 54[C][1]; 68[A]; 70; Ch. 18

[References are to Sections.]

Texas v. Brown . . . . 39[A]; 43[A]; 79[B]; 80

Texas v. McCullough . . 198[C][1], [2][a]

Texas v. White . . . . 75[C]

Thigpen v. Roberts . . 198[C][2][b]

Thomas; People v. . . . . 44[A]

Thomas; United States v. 14

Thompson; State v. . . . . . . 34[A]

Thompson v. United States . . . . 200[B][2][a]

Thurman; People v. . . . . 54[C][2]

Tibbs v. Florida . . . . 203[B]

Tollett v. Henderson . . 197[A], [B]

Torres; People v. 99

Townsend v. Sain 132

Triggs; People v. . . . . 31[B]

Trono v. United States . . . 203[A]

Tumey v. Ohio . . . . 13[C]

Twining v. New Jersey . . . . 129[B]

U

Ullmann v. United States . . . . . . 159[A]; 163[B]

United States v. (see name of defendant)

United States District Court; United States v. 17; 65

V

Van Leeuwen; United States v. . . . 101

Van Pelt; People v. . . . 198[C][2][a]

Vasey; United States v. . . 69[B][1]

Ventresca; United States v. . . 42[D]

Verdugo–Urquidez; United States v. 21

W

Wade v. Hunter . . . . . . 199[D]

Wade; United States v. . . . . . 148; 163[A][2][b], [c]; 165; 166[B][1]

Wainwright v. Greenfield . . 147[B]

Walder v. United States . . . . . . 121[B][2][b]

Ward; United States v. 161

Warden v. Hayden . . . . . . 17; 27; 42[E][2]; 60[B][1]; 65; 67[D]

Washington v. Chrisman . . . . . . 69[B][1]; 81[B]

Watson; United States v. . . 58; 90

Weatherford v. Bursey . . . . 149[E]

Weeks v. United States . . . . . 19; 117[A]; 118; 119

Welch v. State . . . . 33[C]

Welsh v. Wisconsin . . 59; 60[B][1], [2]; 65

Wheat v. United States . . . . . . 178[A][2]; 179[A]; 182[D]

White; United States v. . . . . 30[D][1]–[3]; 32[B], [C]; 160[A]

Whiteley v. Warden . . 51; 95[B][4]

Wilkins v. Erickson . . . . 195[C][3]

Williams v. Florida . . . 3[C][8]; 7; 9[D]

Wilson v. United States . . 160[A], [B]; 163[C][2]; 201[A]; 202[A]

Winship, In re 1

Winston v. Lee . . 48[A]; 63; 69[A]; 108[B]

Wolf v. Colorado . . . . 9[D]; 11[A], [B]; 16; 117[B]; 120[A]

Wong Sun v. United States . . 112; 125[E][1]; 147[C][2]; 155[E]

Wood v. Georgia . . . . 3[C][5]

Wright; United States v. . . . . 181[B][1]

Y

Ybarra v. Illinois . . . 54[C][1]; 100

Z

Ziang Sun Wan v. United States . . . 130

Zurcher v. Stanford Daily . . . . . . 42[E][2]; 48[A]

FEDERAL RULES OF CRIMINAL PROCEDURE

[References are to sections]

3 . . . . § 3[C][1]
5(a) . . . . . . §§ 3[C][3], 14, 129[C], 169[A], 184
5(c) . . . . §§ 3[C][4], 178[B][1]
5.1(a) . . . . . . §§ 3[C][4], 121[B][1]
6(d) . . . . § 3[C][5]
7(f) . . . . § 205[C][2]
8 . . . . § 3[C][7]
8(a) . . . . § 207[A]
10 . . . . § 189
11 . . . . § 191[C]
11(a)(1) . . . . § 189
11(a)(2) . . . . §§ 189, 197[C]
11(b) . . . . § 189
11(c) . . . . § 196[B]
11(d) . . . . § 196[A]
11(e)(1) . . . . § 193
11(e)(4) . . . . § 191[C]
11(f) . . . . § 196[C]
11(h) . . . . § 196[A]
12(b) . . . . § 202[A]
12(b)(2) . . . . § 202[A]
12(b)(3) . . . . § 130
12(f) . . . . §§ 12[B], 130
14 . . . . §§ 3[C][7], 207[A]
16 . . . . § 3[C][7]
18 . . . . § 3[C][7]
20(a) . . . . § 3[C][7]
23(a) . . . . § 3[C][8]
24(b) . . . . § 3[C][8]
29(c) . . . . § 201[A]
31(a) . . . . § 3[C][8]
41(b) . . . . §§ 42[E][2], 53[C]
41(c)(1) . . . . § 54[A]
41(c)(2)(A) . . . . § 50
41(e) . . . . § 109
44(a) . . . . § 184
48 . . . . § 3[C][7]
52(a) . . . . §§ 13[A], 14

FEDERAL STATUTES

[References are to sections]

18 U.S.C. §§

111 . . . . § 199[B]
242 . . . . § 120[D]
2510-2521 . . . . §§ 2, 32[A]
3109 . . . . § 54[B]
3141-3150 . . . §§ 2, 187[C], 188[A]
3142(f) . . . . § 121[B][1]
3501 . . . . . . §§ 129[C], 136, 141
3501(c) . . . . § 14
3576 . . . . § 204
3731 . . . . § 204
6002 . . . . § 162

18 U.S.C. App. §

6B1.1 . . . . § 191[C]

6B1.2 . . . . § 191[C]

21 U.S.C. §§

831 . . . . § 179[B]

28 U.S.C. §§

391 . . . . § 13[A]
1651 . . . . § 14
1865 . . . . § 2
2241-2244 . . . . § 3[C][10]
2254-2255 . . . . § 3[C][10]
2680(h) . . . . § 120[D]

42 U.S.C. §§

1983 . . . . §§ 61[A], 120[D]

INDEX

[References are to sections]

A

ADMINISTRATIVE SEARCHES (See also INVENTORY SEARCHES, SPE-CIAL NEED SEARCHES)
Probable cause . . . . . § 47
Warrant requirement . . . . . § 104

APPEALS
Generally . . . . . § 3[C][9]

ARRAIGNMENT
Generally . . . . . § 3[C][6]

ARRESTS (See also "SEIZURE")
Common law rules . . . . . § 56
Constitutional law
    In home . . . . . §§ 59, 60
    In public places . . . . . §§ 58, 60[A]
    Overview of . . . . . § 57
Deadly force, use in . . . . . § 61[A]
Distinguished from other "seizures" . . . . . §§ 55, 96
Nature of . . . . . § 55
Non-deadly force, use in . . . . . § 61[B]
Statutory rules . . . . . § 56

AUTOMOBILE SEARCHES
Border . . . . . § 106
Containers in . . . . . § 79
Rationale of warrant exception . . . . . §§ 76-78
Warrant exception, generally . . . . . § 75

B

BAIL (See PRETRIAL RELEASE)

BEEPERS (See ELECTRONIC SURVEILLANCE)

C

CAR SEARCHES (See AUTOMOBILE SEARCHES)

COERCED CONFESSIONS (See INTERROGATIONS)

COLLATERAL ESTOPPEL (See DOUBLE JEOPARDY CLAUSE)

COMPLAINT
Issuance of . . . . . § 3[C][1]

[References are to sections]

CONFESSIONS (See INTERROGATIONS)

CONSENT TO SEARCH
Apparent-authority doctrine . . . . . §92
Generally . . . . . § 88
Third-party consent . . . . . § 91
Voluntariness, requirement of
    Claim of police authority . . . . . § 89[B]
    Deception . . . . . § 89[C]
    Generally . . . . . § 89[A]
    Knowledge of the right to refuse . . . . . § 90

CONTAINERS, SEARCHES OF
During arrest inventory . . . . . § 87
During automobile inventory . . . . . § 86[A]
During automobile search . . . . . § 79
Garbage bags . . . . . § 37
Incident to a lawful arrest . . . . . §§ 69[B][2], 72

CONVERSATIONS
"False friends" . . . . . § 32[B]
Protected by Fourth Amendment . . . . . § 25
"Seizure" of . . . . . § 39[A]
Wiretapping of . . . . . §§ 29, 30, 32[A]

COUNSEL, RIGHT TO (See also INTERROGATIONS, *MIRANDA*)
Appeals . . . . . § 177
Arraignment . . . . . § 3[C][6]
Generally . . . . . § 148
Gerstein hearing . . . . . § 3[C][2]
Grand jury . . . . . § 3[C][5]
Importance of . . . . . § 175
Lineups . . . . . § 166
Preliminary hearing . . . . . § 3[C][4]
Trial
    Attorney of choice . . . . . § 179
    Generally, §§ 3[C][8], 176[B]
    Ineffective assistance at . . . . . §§ 181-183
    Interference with . . . . . § 180
    Right of self-representation . . . . . § 178

CRIMINAL PROCEDURE
Controversies of
    Adversarial versus Inquisitorial . . . . . § 7
    Due process versus Crime Control . . . . . § 5
    Truth, importance of . . . . . § 6
Criminal law contrasted to . . . . . § 1
Sources of law . . . . . § 2
Stages of . . . . . § 3

[References are to sections]

CURTILAGE (See OPEN FIELDS, "PERSONS, HOUSES, PAPERS, EFFECTS")

D

DOUBLE JEOPARDY CLAUSE
Acquittal, reprosecution after
    General rule . . . . . § 201[A]
    Implied-acquittal rule . . . . . § 203[C]
    Rationale of the rule . . . . . § 201[B]
Collateral estoppel . . . . . § 207
Conviction, reprosecution after
    Exceptions to general rule . . . . . § 203[B]
    General rule . . . . . § 203[A]
    Implied-acquittals with . . . . . § 203[C]
Dismissal, reprosecution after
    General rules . . . . . § 202[B]
    Nature of . . . . . § 202[A]
General principles of . . . . . § 199
Mistrial, reprosecution after
    Generally . . . . . § 200[A]
    Over defendant's objection . . . . . § 200[B]
    With defendant's consent . . . . . § 200[C]
"Same offense"
    Definition of . . . . . § 205[B]-[C]
    Multiple prosecution of, §§ 205[A], 205[D]
    Multiple punishment of . . . . . § 206
Sentences
    "Acquittal," in death penalty cases . . . . . § 203[C][2]
    Government appeals of . . . . . § 204

DRUG TESTING
Generally . . . . . § 108

E

ELECTRONIC SURVEILLANCE
"Beepers"
    Installation of . . . . . § 39[B]
    Use of . . . . . § 34[B]
Conversations
    Current law . . . . . §§ 30, 32[A], 32[C]
    Old law . . . . . § 29

ENTRAPMENT
Debate regarding . . . . . § 173
Due process and . . . . . § 174
Generally . . . . . § 170
Objective test of . . . . . § 172
Subjective test of . . . . . § 171

[References are to sections]

EXCLUSIONARY RULE (See also FRUIT OF THE POISONOUS TREE DOCTRINE)
Coerced confessions, § 135
Counsel, violations of right to
    Eyewitness-identification . . . . . § 166[A]
    Interrogation cases . . . . . § 155
Fourth Amendment
    Constitutional nature of . . . . . § 199
    Debate regarding . . . . . § 120
    Development of . . . . . § 117
    Generally . . . . . § 19
    Good-faith (*Leon*) exception to . . . . . §§ 122-124
    Limits on, generally . . . . . § 121
    Rationale of . . . . . § 118
Miranda violations . . . . . § 147
Self-incrimination, generally . . . . . § 164

EXIGENT CIRCUMSTANCES
Arrest-warrant exception . . . . . § 60[B]
Search-warrant exception . . . . . §§ 62-65

EYEWITNESS IDENTIFICATION PROCEDURES
Counsel, right to
    Corporeal procedures . . . . . § 166
    Non-corporeal procedures, § 167
Due Process Clause . . . . . § 168
Fourth Amendment issues of . . . . . § 169[A]
Self-incrimination, issues of . . . . . §§ 163[A], 169[B]
Unreliability of . . . . . § 165

F

FIRE-SCENE SEARCHES (See SPECIAL-NEED SEARCHES)

FOURTH AMENDMENT, GENERALLY
Abandonment of property . . . . . § 22
Controversies regarding
    Bright-line rules versus case-by-case adjudication of . . . . . § 73
    Pretextual conduct . . . . . § 74
    Warrant clause, role of . . . . . § 49
Extraterritorial searches . . . . . § 21
Historical purposes of . . . . . §§ 17, 29
Private searches . . . . . § 20
Study checklist of . . . . . § 23
Text of . . . . . § 16

FRUIT OF THE POISONOUS TREE DOCTRINE
Coerced confessions . . . . . § 135[B]
Counsel, right to
    Eyewitness-identification procedures . . . . . § 166[A]

[References are to sections]

FRUIT OF THE POISONOUS TREE DOCTRINE—Cont.
Counsel, right to—Cont.
    Interrogation cases . . . . . § 155[E]
Fourth Amendment
    Attenuation (*Wong Sun*) rule . . . . . § 125[E]
    Comparison to *Miranda* "tree" . . . . . § 125[B]
    Generally . . . . . § 125[A]
    Independent-source doctrine . . . . . § 125[C]
    Inevitable-discovery rule . . . . . § 125[D]
Miranda . . . . . § 147[C]

G

GERSTEIN V. PUGH HEARING
Generally . . . . . § 3[C][2]

GRAND JURY
Applicability of Grand Jury Clause to states . . . . . § 10[F]
Generally . . . . . § 3[C][5]

GUILTY PLEAS
Effect of, on antecedent claims . . . . . § 197
Plea bargaining
    Broken deals . . . . . § 194
    Debate regarding . . . . . § 192
    Generally . . . . . § 191
    Judicial participation in . . . . . § 193
    Validity of . . . . . § 195
Policy issues . . . . . § 190
Procedures for obtaining . . . . . § 196
Prosecutorial vindictiveness in obtaining . . . . . § 198

H

HABEAS CORPUS
Generally . . . . . § 3[C][10]
Retroactivity law, and . . . . . § 11[D][2]

HARMLESS ERROR
Constitutional errors . . . . . § 13[B]-[C]
Non-constitutional errors . . . . . § 13[A]

I

INCORPORATION DEBATE
Fundamental-rights theory . . . . . §9
Neo-incorporationism . . . . . § 10
Total-incorporationism . . . . . §8

INDICTMENT
Defined . . . . . § 3[C][5]

[References are to sections]

INFORMATION
Defined . . . . . § 3[C][4]

INTERROGATIONS (See also *MIRANDA*)
Counsel, right to during
    Comparison to *Miranda* . . . . . §156
    "Deliberate elicitation" . . . . . § 152
    Escobedo right . . . . . § 138
    Exclusionary rule . . . . . § 155
    Generally . . . . . §§ 127[C], 150
    Massiah right . . . . . § 149
    Role of . . . . . § 149[E]
    Standing to raise . . . . . § 154
    Waiver of . . . . . § 153
Historical overview of . . . . . § 126
McNabb-Mallory rule . . . . . §§ 14, 129[C]
Policy controversies, generally . . . . . § 128
"Voluntariness" requirement
    Exclusionary rule . . . . . § 135[A]
    General rule . . . . . §§ 130, 133
    Historical development of . . . . . § 129
    Rationale of . . . . . § 131
    Standing to assert claim . . . . . § 134
    State action requirement . . . . . § 132

I

INVENTORY SEARCHES
Arrest inventories . . . . . § 87
Automobile inventories . . . . . §§ 84-86

J

JURIES
Generally . . . . . § 3[C][8]
Jury-nullification doctrine . . . . . § 201[B]

L

LINEUPS (See EYEWITNESS IDENTIFICATION PROCEDURES)

M

***MCNABB-MALLORY RULE* (See INTERROGATIONS)**

MERE-EVIDENCE RULE
Generally . . . . . § 42[E]

MIRANDA V. ARIZONA
Case summarized . . . . . § 139
Constitutional nature of the rule . . . . . § 141
"Custody" . . . . . § 142

[References are to sections]

MIRANDA V. ARIZONA—Cont.
Debate regarding . . . . . § 140
Escobedo, as lead in to . . . . . § 138
Exceptions to . . . . . § 146
Exclusionary rule of . . . . . § 147
"Interrogation" . . . . . § 143
Legal context of . . . . . § 137
Overview . . . . . § 136
Waiver of . . . . . § 145
Warnings, nature of . . . . . § 144

O

OPEN FIELDS
"Curtilage" distinguished from . . . . §§ 26, 33[B]
"Effect" distinguished from . . . . . § 27
"House" distinguished from . . . . . § 26
"Search" distinguished from . . . . . § 33

P

"PERSONS, HOUSES, PAPERS, EFFECTS"
Curtilage . . . . . §§ 26, 33[B]
"Effects" . . . . . § 27
Generally . . . . . § 24
"Houses" . . . . . §26
Open fields . . . . . §§ 26, 27
"Papers" . . . . . § 27
"Persons" . . . . . § 25

PLAIN-VIEW DOCTRINE
Elements of, explained . . . . . §§ 81-82
Generally . . . . . § 80
Inadvertence, debate regarding . . . . . § 83

PLEA BARGAINING (See GUILTY PLEAS)

PRELIMINARY HEARING
Generally . . . . . § 3[C][4]

PRETRIAL RELEASE
Federal law . . . . . § 187
Interests at stake . . . . . § 185
Preventive Detention . . . . . § 188
Procedural context . . . . . § 184

PREVENTIVE DETENTION (See PRETRIAL RELEASE)

PROBABLE CAUSE
Aguilar test of . . . . . § 45
Camara principle of . . . . . § 47
Constitutional role of . . . . . § 41

[References are to sections]

PROBABLE CAUSE—Cont.
Determining, generally . . . . . § 44
Gates test of . . . . . § 46
General principles of . . . . . § 42
How probable . . . . . §§ 43, 48
Sliding-scale debate regarding . . . . . § 48

PROPHYLACTIC RULES
Generally . . . . . § 15

PROTECTIVE SWEEPS
Generally . . . . . § 100
Incident to an arrest . . . . . § 69[C]

R

REASONABLE SUSPICION (See also *TERRY V. OHIO PRINCIPLES*)
Probable cause, compared to . . . . . § 95
Types of information allowed
    Drug-courier profiles . . . . . § 95[B][2]
    Hearsay information . . . . . § 95[B][3]
    Personal observations . . . . . § 95[B][1]
When not required, §§ 102, 106

RETROACTIVITY
Common law of . . . . . § 11[B]
Current constitutional law of . . . . . § 11[D]
Linkletter doctrine . . . . . § 11[C]
"New rule" defined . . . . . § 11[D][2][b]

ROADBLOCKS
Border . . . . . § 106
"Seizure" by . . . . . § 40[C]
Sobriety checkpoints . . . . . § 102

S

**"SEARCH" (See also, SEARCH WARRANTS, *TERRY V. OHIO*
PRINCIPLES)**
Aerial surveillance . . . . . § 35[A]
Constitutional significance of . . . . . § 28
Contraband, testing for . . . . . § 36
Conversations . . . . . § 32
Dog sniffs . . . . . § 36[A]
Electronic tracking devices . . . . . § 34[B]
Garbage bags . . . . . § 37
Katz, explained and critiqued . . . . . § 30
Open fields . . . . . § 33
Pen registers . . . . . § 34[A]
Pre-*Katz* analysis of . . . . . § 29

[References are to sections]

SEARCH INCIDENT TO LAWFUL ARREST
Belton analyzed . . . . . § 72
Chimel analyzed . . . . . § 70
Probable-cause requirement, exception to . . . . . § 67[C]-[D]
Robinson analyzed . . . . . § 71
Warrant exception, in general . . . . . §§ 67-69

SEARCH WARRANTS
Application process . . . . . § 50
"Neutral and detached magistrate" . . . . . § 51
"Oath or affirmation" . . . . . § 52
Mode of entry, in execution of . . . . . § 54[B]
Particularity requirement . . . . . § 53
Search of persons, while executing . . . . . § 54[C]
Seizure of persons, while executing . . . . . § 54[D]
Time of execution of . . . . . § 54[A]
Warrant clause, constitutional role of . . . . . § 49

"SEIZURE" (See also ARRESTS, *TERRY V. OHIO* PRINCIPLES)
Articles, subject to . . . . . § 42[E]
Constitutional significance of . . . . . § 38
Definition of
     Persons "seized" . . . . . § 40[A]
     Property "seized" . . . . . § 39[A]
Electronic devices, installed . . . . . § 39[B]
Pursuit, as means of . . . . . § 40[C]
Questioning, as means of . . . . . § 40[B]

SELF-INCRIMINATION, PRIVILEGE OF (See also INTERROGATIONS, *MIRANDA*)
Collective-entity doctrine . . . . . § 160[A]
Debate regarding . . . . . § 159
Elements of . . . . . § 163
Exclusionary rule, violation of . . . . . § 164
Generally . . . . . § 157
History of . . . . . § 158
Immunity orders . . . . . § 162
Lineups . . . . . §§ 163[A], 169[B]
Procedures, in asserting . . . . . § 162
Proceedings, assertable at . . . . . § 161
Purpose of . . . . . § 159
Required-records doctrine . . . . . § 160[B]
"Testimonial or communicative" requirement . . . . . § 163[A]

SOBRIETY CHECKPOINTS
Generally . . . . . § 102

SPECIAL-NEED SEARCHES
Administrative-code inspections . . . . . § 104
Border searches . . . . . § 106

[References are to sections]

SPECIAL-NEED SEARCHES—Cont.
Drug testing of public employees . . . . . § 108
Fire-scene inspections . . . . . § 105
Generally . . . . . § 103
Public-school searches . . . . . § 107

STANDING
Coerced confessions . . . . . § 134
Counsel, right to . . . . . § 154
Fourth Amendment
    Automatic . . . . . § 113
    Derivative . . . . . § 112
    Generally . . . . . §§ 18, 109
    Pre-*Rakas* law of . . . . . § 114
    Rakas . . . . . § 115
    Rakas, implications of . . . . . § 116
    Rationale of requirement . . . . . § 110
    Target . . . . . § 111

STATE ACTION
Due process clause . . . . . § 132
Fourth Amendment . . . . . § 20
Miranda . . . . . § 145[C][1]

STATE CONSTITUTIONAL LAW
Generally . . . . . § 2

SUPERVISORY POWER
Generally . . . . . § 14

SUPREME COURT, PERSONNEL
Generally . . . . . § 4[E]

T

***TERRY V. OHIO* PRINCIPLES (See also REASONABLE SUSPICION)**
Arrest, distinguished from . . . . . § 96
Property, *Terry*-level seizure of . . . . . § 101
Protective sweeps . . . . . § 100
Significance of *Terry* . . . . . § 93
Terry summarized . . . . . § 94
Terry-stop, grounds for . . . . . § 97
Weapons-search
    Automobile . . . . . § 99
    Person . . . . . § 98

V

VINDICTIVENESS
Generally . . . . . § 198

[References are to sections]

W

WAIVER
Generally . . . . . § 12

WIRETAPPING (See ELECTRONIC SURVEILLANCE)

INDEX [J–W]

[References are to sections]

W

WAIVER
Generally .... § 17

WIRETAPPING. See ELECTRONIC SURVEILLANCE.